TO BEGIN THE WORLD OVER AGAIN

TO BEGIN THE WORLD OVER AGAIN

How the American Revolution Devastated the Globe

MATTHEW LOCKWOOD

YALE UNIVERSITY PRESS
NEW HAVEN AND LONDON

Published with assistance from the Annie Burr Lewis Fund.

For information about this and other Yale University Press publications, please contact:
U.S. Office: sales.press@yale.edu   yalebooks.com
Europe Office: sales@yaleup.co.uk   yalebooks.co.uk

Set in Fournier MT by IDSUK (DataConnection) Ltd
Printed in Great Britain by TJ International Ltd, Padstow, Cornwall

Library of Congress Control Number: 2019941057

ISBN 978-0-300-23225-7

A catalogue record for this book is available from the British Library.

10 9 8 7 6 5 4 3 2 1

For Lucy

CONTENTS

ILLUSTRATIONS

11. *Portrait of Woollarawarre Bennelong*, George Charles Jenner and William Waterhouse (pre-1806). State Library of New South Wales.

12. *View from the Western Side of Sydney Cove Looking to Bennelong Point*, Adolph Jean-Baptiste Bayot (1841). The Picture Art Collection / Alamy Stock Photo.

13. *The Death of Major Pierson*, John Singleton Copley (1783). Tate Britain. Lebrecht Music & Arts / Alamy Stock Photo.

14. *A View of Freetown on the Sierra Leone River*, Thomas Masterman Winterbottom (1803). The Picture Art Collection / Alamy Stock Photo.

15. *The European Factories, Canton*, William Daniell (1806). Yale Center for British Art, Paul Mellon Collection.

16. *British Ambassador, George, 1st Earl Macartney, Pays Homage with Bent Knee Before the Qianlong Emperor of China* (1797). Everett Collection Historical / Alamy Stock Photo.

ACKNOWLEDGMENTS

I wrote my first "book," a hand-illustrated history of Sparta, for a school assignment when I was ten. With the confident solipsism of youth, I ignored the help I had received from my teacher and my parents and dedicated the book "to myself, because I wrote it." Thankfully, experience brings a degree of humility. Over the years I have learned that writing and publishing a book would be impossible without the contributions of scores of people, from friends and family to colleagues, archivists, agents, editors, reviewers, designers, and publicists. I have thus acquired more debts in writing this book than my ten-year-old self could have ever imagined.

The book was begun in New Haven, where I was a fellow at the Yale Center for the Study of Representative Institutions, and has followed my academic wanderings to the University of Warwick and my present home at the University of Alabama. This book would not have been possible without the institutional support offered by these universities or the rich intellectual environments created and fostered by my colleagues at Yale, Warwick, and Alabama. Special thanks to Keith Wrightson, Steven Smith, Dan Branch, Peter Marshall, Mark Knights, Mark Philip, and Josh Rothman for making each institution an intellectual home.

The book only really took on its present form after a series of sparkling conversations with Bill Hamilton, my agent at A.M. Heath. Bill rescued the kernel of a good idea from the slagheap and helped polish it until it was fit for consumption. His steady hand, deep knowledge, and probing questions have shaped and reshaped this book from its inception. In many ways, this book was forged in Bill's Socratic crucible.

Julian Loose, my editor at Yale University Press, believed in this book from the start and has expertly guided its construction. His keen judgment, unfailing acuity, and unflagging energy have worked wonders beyond measure. Marika Lysandrou, Rachael Lonsdale, Percie Edgeler, and the anonymous readers at YUP have all helped to transform a chaotic manuscript into a sharper intellectual endeavor and a wonderful physical product. That they have made the oft-frustrating publishing process smooth and enjoyable is a testament to their skill.

My friends and family have spent the last few years suffering through my latest obsession. This book would look very different without the input and support of Keith Wrightson, Richard Huzzey, Justin duRivage, Amanda Behm, Sarah Miller, Jamie Miller, Megan Cherry, Charles Walton, Steve Hindle, Lawrence Cappello, Margaret Peacock, Erik Peterson, John Beeler, my brothers Jack, Kaleb, John, Joey, and Josh, my delightful in-laws Caitlin, Emma, Eric, Donald, and Wendy, and my parents, Jack and Nancy.

As ever, Lucy Kaufman deserves my perpetual and eternal gratitude. An intellectual whirlwind with the patience of a saint, Lucy read and edited the entire manuscript, line by line, word by word, more than once, expertly hacking away at its initial monstrosity until a book at last emerged. She did not simply listen to my incessant droning, but constantly, brilliantly, engaged with my ideas and my writing. Her insight, vision, and forbearance are of truly Herculean proportions. This book, and I myself, would be nothing without her. This book, and all past and future books, is for her.

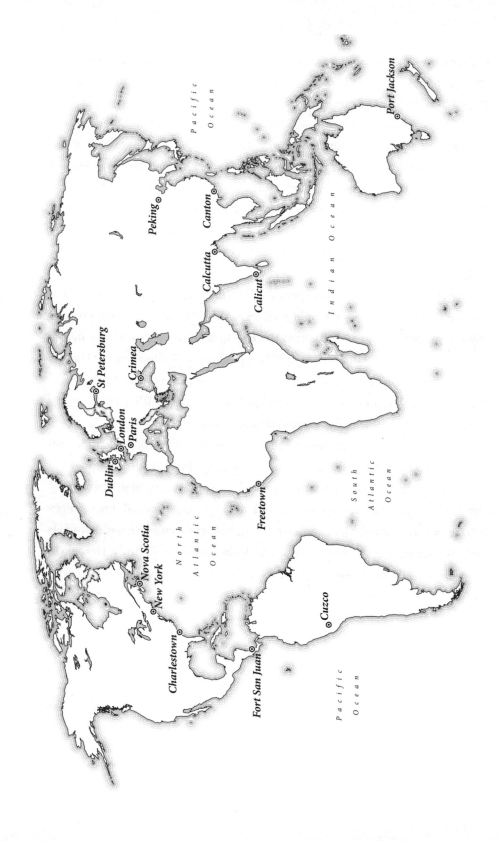

Port Jackson

*Pacific
Ocean*

Peking Canton
Calcutta
Calicut

Indian Ocean

St Petersburg
Crimea
London
Paris
Dublin

*South
Atlantic
Ocean*

Freetown

Nova Scotia
New York
Charlestown

*North
Atlantic
Ocean*

Fort San Juan
Cuzco

*Pacific
Ocean*

INTRODUCTION
THE WORLD THE AMERICAN
REVOLUTION MADE

We have it in our power to begin the world over again.

—Thomas Paine, *Common Sense*

Revolutions have never lightened the burden of tyranny; they have only shifted it to another shoulder.

—George Bernard Shaw, *Man and Superman*

In 1779, after a month-long journey across Europe, through the Mediterranean Sea, across the Sinai Desert, and down the Red Sea, after weeks on a crowded ship in the storm-tossed Indian Ocean, Eliza Fay arrived on the sun-kissed shore of Malabar in south India. The tropical tranquility that greeted Eliza and her husband Anthony after their trying ordeal was, however, a mirage. With war spreading from the Atlantic to the subcontinent, the British embassy had fled, leaving Eliza and Anthony at the mercy of William Ayers, an English convict and one-time soldier now employed by the ferociously anti-British Sultan of Mysore. As Ayers escorted the pair to prison, Eliza Fay must have wondered just how she had come to such a pass. In the years to come, tens of thousands of captives and refugees—Muslims, Hindus, and Indian Christians as well as countless British, French, and Indian soldiers—would ask themselves similar questions. The answer lay not in Malabar, but in an unexpected source: the American Revolution.

1

On May 18, 1781, Micaela Bastidas stood in the square in Cuzco in a pool of her own sons' blood defiantly awaiting her fate. Her rebellion against the Spanish Empire had failed and so now, as her husband Tupac Amaru II, co-leader of the uprising, looked on in horror, it was her turn to face the executioner. At least she would be spared the awful sight of what the Spanish had planned for her husband. After her death he would be pulled apart by horses, then quartered and beheaded, his limbs sent across Peru as symbols of Spanish vengeance. With her death, and the death of her husband, an indigenous rebellion would end, but a spark had been lit and a pair of martyrs had been born. Their fates too were rooted in the struggle for American independence.

In 1810, Britain's first Indian restaurant, the Hindoostane Coffee House, opened its doors in George Street in London. Entering the establishment, patrons might well have thought themselves transported to the Orient itself. Reclining on bamboo-cane sofas, guests gazed upon walls covered with rich paintings of Indian landscapes and scenes of Indian life. As the aroma of curries and seasoned rice wafted in from the kitchen, the scent of Indian herbs and spices mixing with the fragrant tobacco of the ornate hookahs lining the floor of the smoking room, 'India gentlemen', Britons who had lived and worked in India, must have harkened back to their previous lives half a world away.

With Britain's ever-expanding empire and its growing involvement in the affairs of the subcontinent, it was perhaps no surprise that such an establishment might grace the crowded streets of the imperial capital. Its proprietor, however, was no British nabob newly returned from plundering the crumbling empires of the east, no British soldier hoping to recreate the sights, smells, and tastes of his formative years, no British merchant hoping to expand his interests from shipping spices to cooking with them. Instead, as an advertisement in *The Times* made clear, the restaurant was owned and operated by Dean Mahomet, a Muslim Bengali soldier from Patna and his Irish Protestant wife. The more literary among the advertisement's readers may well have recognized the proprietor's name. Nearly two decades earlier, the very same Dean Mahomet had been involved in another first, becoming the first Indian to publish in English when his *Travels* were released in 1793. How did Mahomet come to find himself opening England's first curry house, publishing the first English-language book

2

by an Indian, and marrying the daughter of an Irish Protestant? Once more the War for American Independence had intervened.[1]

Nearly two centuries later, on a cold January day in 1988, two men stood in solemn ceremony over a grave in the churchyard of St. John's church in Eltham in south-east London. One of the men standing before the headstone was the parish priest, whose predecessor had conducted the burial service nearly two hundred years before. The other had come much further to stand in the winter chill contemplating events now centuries old. His name was Burnum Burnum, an athlete, actor, and activist of Wurundjeri people, and he had made the pilgrimage from his native Australia to retrieve a body and right an injustice. A few days earlier, to mark the bicentennial of Britain's first colonization of Australia, he had planted a flag on the white cliffs of Dover and issued a proclamation full of biting, tragic humor. In mocking parallel of British actions in 1788, Burnum Burnum announced that he was claiming Britain on behalf of Aboriginal people and that though Britons would henceforth see Aboriginal figures on their money and stamps "to signify our sovereignty over this Domain," he could promise that "we do not intend to souvenir, pickle, and preserve the heads of 2,000 of your people or to publically display the skeletal remains of Your Royal Highness" as the British themselves had done.[2]

But now, as he stood before the resting place of a fellow native Australian, his righteous humor was gone, replaced by sadness tinged with indignation. On the simple headstone were inscribed the barest of facts about the young man it memorialized: "In memory of Yemmerawanyea a Native of New South Wales who died the 18th of May 1794 in the 19th year of his age." Newspapers at the time gave little more detail. The *Morning Post* reported that "one of the two natives of Botany Bay, who came over with Governor Phillip, is dead: his companion pines much for his loss." It was Burnum Burnum and many of his countrymen's hope that two hundred years after the British first began their penal colony at Botany Bay, the body of Yemmerrawannie might at last be returned to his native shores. But there would be no symbolic homecoming for Yemmerrawannie, no peaceful rest, no symbolic righting of colonial wrongs, for unbeknownst to priest and activist alike, by 1988 there were no bones beneath the headstone in Eltham churchyard. Yemmerrawannie's body had been lost. How had this young man of the Eora people come to be buried in a churchyard in suburban London, a symbol of Britain's imperial sins? Here too, the roots of this modern tragedy lay not just in the Pacific, or even in London, but in the aftershocks of the American Revolution.[3]

The American Revolution is blessed with some of the most dramatic, most soul-searing stories and images in all of history: Paul Revere riding through the night-black streets of Massachusetts to warn his fellow Americans that the British were coming to seize their arms; The Sons of Liberty creeping aboard a British ship disguised as Native Americans to cast its cargo of over-taxed tea into Boston Harbor; George Washington and his ragged band of Continental soldiers freezing, but surviving, at Valley Forge; General Cornwallis and his defeated British army playing "The World Turned Upside Down" as they surrendered to Washington's victorious army at Yorktown. These tales of daring deeds and noble sacrifice have a tendency to crowd the mind, overshadowing other less well-known stories and images of the Revolutionary War beyond America's shores.

Most previous accounts of the American Revolution have by and large restricted their attention to the thirteen colonies that declared independence from Great Britain in 1776. In so doing they have limited their focus to the stone that caused the splash rather than the waves and ripples that radiated out from its epicenter, the quick, sharp, shock rather than the enduring reverberations. This stubbornly national focus has largely obscured the wider ramifications of America's struggle for independence. Stories like those of Micaela Bastidas, Dean Mahomet, and Yemmerrawannie provide a unique window onto a world at war and the new world that war created. These stories are no less important to the story of the American Revolution, no less a part of its history, but they are largely forgotten, disconnected from the more stirring, glorious, triumphant tales of Washington and Jefferson, Bunker Hill and Yorktown.

As compelling as these heroic stories are, limiting our focus to the familiar, even comforting, tales of the American Revolution not only skews our understanding of what was in fact a global crisis, but also molds our understanding of America's national history in dangerous ways. The idea of American exceptionalism, of the United States as a uniquely moral and chosen nation, in many ways began with the revolution itself and has been forged and strengthened by the telling and retelling of the familiar stories of that mythic birth. The portrayal of the American Revolution as a noble movement that created an incomparably just, enlightened society has long been the cornerstone of such ideas. But while the popular belief in America's unique status has at times provided a welcome sense of unity, it has had pernicious effects as well. In an increasingly globalized world, a stubborn adherence to the idea of American exceptionalism has helped create a narrow, jingoistic worldview and a selfish pursuit of American interests above all else. In order to undermine such a solipsistic isolationism in foreign affairs we must complicate and challenge the lazy idea of America's exceptionalism, and to do this we must complicate the story of its foundational moment.

In recent years historians like Gary Nash, Carol Berkin, Holger Hoock, and Alan Taylor have begun to undermine the simplistic narrative of the American Revolution, highlighting forgotten stories of women, Native Americans, and African Americans, and exposing the contradictions and hypocrisies of our founding. Though such accounts provide an important corrective, they do not entirely upend the myths of America's conception. They still allow us to believe that though the founding fathers were flawed and imperfect in many ways, and though the blessings of the revolution were not shared equally among the inhabitants of North America, the goals and ideals of the revolution remain an example of America at its best, as it sought to be. Indeed, even those accounts that aim to explain the wider, international story of the American Revolution have largely failed to adequately complicate the story of American exceptionalism.[4]

From Justin du Rivage and Nick Bunker we have learned that the American Revolution had global, imperial causes, that the outbreak of war in North America had as much to do with developments in Europe and Asia as it did with events in the American colonies. C.A. Bayly, P.J. Marshall, and Maya Jasanoff have similarly expanded our understanding of the consequences of the war for the British Empire. Despite these pathbreaking contributions, however, most accounts of the revolution's international impact have still dealt solely with its place in the wider Age of Revolutions. Important works by R.R. Palmer, Lester Langley, Janet Polasky, and Jonathan Israel have certainly broadened our horizons and helped to situate the American Revolution within a shared Atlantic context, but by focusing exclusively on the ideological facets of the American struggle for independence and that struggle's role in shaping similar revolutions in France, Poland, Haiti, and South America, such histories have not only neglected much of the world, but have often reinforced and reified the belief in America's unique legacy as the first swelling of a global democratic wave.[5]

While such works are admirable and often invaluable, unraveling the ideological threads of the American Revolution does not alone reveal the entire picture. Many of its most important legacies had little to do with ideology, with the words and writings of the sainted founders or the government they created. Examining the revolution from a truly global perspective, both geographically and thematically, forcefully reveals the often tragic interconnectedness of the world, compelling us to contemplate ourselves in an entangled world rather than as an isolated, exceptional chosen people. Removing the blinkers of a narrowly national political point of view opens new horizons of understanding, allowing us to realize the most urgent lesson taught by America's founding moment: American actions have, and have always had, unforeseen, unimagined global consequences. Only when we examine the global impact of the American Revolution through a wide range of both political and personal perspectives can we discover a unique and long overlooked window into the thousands of men, women, and children, individuals of all social, economic, religious, and ethnic backgrounds, who had their worlds turned upside down by global war. Their stories, their struggles and successes, their lives and their deaths are the very lifeblood of the full story of the American Revolution. When we decenter the story of the War for American Independence and take a wider view, our understanding of the revolution and its place in world history is fundamentally transformed.

It becomes clear that though the war began in Massachusetts, it did not end with the surrender of a sword at Yorktown or the scratch of a pen in Paris. Instead, a local protest over taxes in a remote corner of North America would end on the streets of Dublin, the mountains of Peru, the beaches of Australia, and the jungles of India. In the increasingly interconnected world of the eighteenth century, an American spark would ignite an unexpected flame that would consume the globe, leaving in its wake a new world and an altered balance of power. The birth of a new nation in the west would sow the seeds of collapse for millennia-old civilizations in India, Australia, Africa, China, and the Middle

East, and help speed the rise of the great powers of the nineteenth and twentieth centuries: America, Russia, and Great Britain. The American Revolution was a war within, between, and over empires, and when the smoke cleared, new empires would emerge and old empires would be forced to fundamentally change or face a steep decline.

The shots fired at Lexington and Concord in April 1775 echoed across the globe from the Atlantic coast to the English Channel, from Central America and the Caribbean to Africa, India, and Australia, heralding a new world that none could have predicted and few could have imagined. Advocates of revolution in America and in Europe had hoped that the uprising in the colonies would create a global movement, a revolution without borders. But if revolutionary fervor did indeed become international, the true consequences of the revolution without borders, its remaking of institutions and reshaping of lives across the world, were not what anyone expected. A revolution in favor of liberty in one corner of the map initiated a reactionary revolution in the wider world, inflicting new suffering and new restraints on people for whom freedom and independence were not available. In the empires of France, Spain, and Britain, the hard lessons learned from the American Revolution were rigorously applied, inaugurating an authoritarian counter-revolution that stabilized and expanded Britain's empire while fatally weakening France and Spain. The Age of Revolutions was not simply the child of the enlightened ideals of the American Revolution, but also of the fear, financial crisis, and authoritarian reaction brought by the American War.

Perhaps the most miraculous thing about the American War when viewed holistically is not that America won, but that, given the global scope of the conflict; the numerous powers arrayed against it in America, Europe, and Asia; the rioting, unrest, and threats of invasion at home and in the empire, Britain and its empire were not destroyed entirely. Not only did Britain avoid utter ruin, more than any of its rivals it emerged from the war well positioned to pursue global imperial supremacy. Far from teetering on the brink, the post-war British Empire, and commitment to it, was strengthened by the refashioning that the American crisis necessitated. The American Revolution thus did not delay Britain's imperial rise but was instead crucial to it. The expansion of Britain in the nineteenth century was in fact predicated upon Britain's loss in the American Revolution. The war forced Britain to think about its empire in new, more centralized, hierarchical, authoritarian ways, allowing Britain to tighten its grasp both at home and in its far-flung possessions. Britain's survival of the French Revolution and the wars it spawned owed much to the counter-revolutionary measures it had already undertaken in the years between 1776 and 1789. At the same time, the loss of the American colonies transformed British conceptions of empire. The American War gave Britons scope to reimagine their empire—once viewed by many corrupt, indecent, and unethical—as a noble harbinger of national honor, morality, and civilization. The imperial confidence that fueled Britain's global expansion in the nineteenth century would not have been possible without the experience of the American War.[6]

While the British Empire was internally stabilized, the American War destabilized Britain's primary rivals in Europe, Asia, and the Americas. France's pyrrhic victory bankrupted the nation and put it on the path to revolution. Spain's triumph came at the cost of dissension and division within its American possessions, sowing the seeds of insurrection and blunting its attempts to revive its empire. During and after the war, Austria, Russia, and the Ottoman Empire became too focused on eastern Europe to disrupt Britain's expansion in Asia. In India too, once vibrant, expansionist powers like Mysore and the Maratha Empire were fatally undermined by the American Revolution, missing their last best chance to prevent British domination. Defeat in the American War thus paradoxically strengthened the British government in Britain, Ireland, and India, expanded the empire in Asia, Africa, and the Pacific, and everywhere undermined their chief rivals for global imperial hegemony.

If measured by the goals of 1775, when Britain still hoped to retain its North American colonies, Britain's eventual defeat may well have seemed a failure. But in hindsight, from the perspective of Britain's nineteenth-century rise to world dominance, the war was a smashing success, a confirmation of British preeminence in the face of its most challenging threat. Britain had been buffeted on all fronts, by the combined power of all its major rivals in Europe, the Americas, and Asia, and yet, while it lost some troublesome possessions in the Atlantic, it had fended off the challenge, secured its supremacy of the oceans, solidified its grasp in the Caribbean, expanded its interests in India, Asia, Africa, and the Pacific, and dealt a serious, in some cases fatal, blow to its rivals. The

American Revolution, for all its importance for the United States, was also, perhaps as importantly, a British victory and a world disaster.

Though very much the story of how Britain won the American Revolution, *To Begin the World Over Again* is not simply a triumphalist narrative of British victory against the odds, not a story of plucky British daring to place alongside tales of the Spanish Armada or the Battle for Britain. Instead, in a world of empires and imperialism, Britain's gains in the American War came with dire consequences for people in Britain and around the globe. Hidden in the shadows of the more familiar stories of military clashes and imperial contestation, countless lives and institutions were fundamentally altered in ways that reverberate to the present day. For the vast majority of Earth's inhabitants, who did not give a damn about a civil war in British North America or the ideas and ideals that inspired it, the American Revolution was a disaster: not the birth of a new world, but the death of the old and familiar. For indigenous peoples in South America, India, Australia, Africa, and the Crimea, it marked the beginning of a steep decline. For the old empires of Spain, China, the Ottomans, and the Dutch, it spelt the curtain call from the grandest stage of world powers. For India and Ireland, it was the last real shot for independence on their own terms until the middle of the twentieth century. For France it would usher in an age of chaos and blood. Ironically, only in America, Britain, and Russia were the results remotely positive.

The American Revolution thus certainly remade the world, but not simply through its ideals. In most accounts of the American Revolution, battlefields and debate halls, noble generals and enlightened politicians crowd the scene, providing a veneer of haloed respectability to what was in reality a nasty, bloody, confused and chaotic era. However, in the shadows of these well-worn settings and familiar figures, ordinary people had their worlds turned upside down. The violence of this imperial civil war—which stretched from kings and congressmen to paupers and felons, from Boston and Philadelphia to London, Calcutta, and Botany Bay—was one of the defining features and most important legacies of the global American Revolution. *To Begin the World Over Again* tells these forgotten personal stories for the first time, demonstrating how the individual and the institutional, the local and the global, were irrevocably intertwined. The geopolitical and economic aftermath of the American Revolution is well known, if passionately argued over and deeply contentious. The wartime experience of the wealthy, the well-educated and well-heeled is often discussed and easily illustrated in the countless diaries, books, newspapers, and letters that proliferated in the final decades of the eighteenth century. The voices of the poor, the struggles and triumphs of the common man and woman are, as always, nearly silent. But they can be heard, if faintly, through a close and careful reading of the archives. Here, hundreds of heart-rending accounts reveal the sheer scale of the consequences of war across the world. The imperial American Revolution altered forever the lives of everyday people, ravaging communities and sending thousands of individuals to new homes in distant lands, to opportunity, to ruin, to prison, and to the gallows. While one set of people struggled to free themselves from the bonds of empire, men and women like Micaela Bastidas, Dean Mahomet, and Yemmerrawannie found themselves bound, incarcerated, and exiled, struggling to survive in the world the revolution created. These are their stories.

1

⇥ ⇤

THE REVOLUTION
COMES TO BRITAIN

On Tuesday, June 6, 1780, Ignatius Sancho, former slave, abolitionist, cele-brated man of letters, and the first African to cast a ballot in an English election, looked out the window of his grocer's shop in Charles Street in Mayfair onto a scene of menace and mayhem. Sancho's life had begun in tragic circumstances, born on a slave ship en route to the Spanish colony of New Granada, where his mother would succumb to the harsh rigors of plantation life and his father would kill himself in despair. He arrived in England in 1731 still a child, still enslaved, where his quick intelligence caught the attention of the Duke of Montagu, whose family became his employers, supporters, and patrons for the rest of his life. Through the Montagus, Sancho met and charmed literary London, becoming friend and correspondent to Laurence Sterne, Thomas Gainsborough, and David Garrick among others. Though he lived in England nearly all his life and rose to become a property-holder and public figure, Sancho never felt entirely at ease in England. As an African adrift in a sea of white faces he felt himself to be "only a lodger" in England, "and hardly that."[1]

And yet, he loved his adopted home and cherished its freedoms, grateful for the "many blessings" he enjoyed. He could be a harsh critic of Britain, especially its role in the slave trade, but when trouble with the American colonies began to brew, he instinctively sided with king and country against the rebels. At first the conflict had seemed remote, but now, in 1780, the war seemed to be bursting forth on the streets outside his own hard-won door. As he wrote to a friend, "about a thousand mad men, armed with clubs, bludgeons, and crow[bar]s" swarmed past his door on that sweltering summer evening. Led by a sailor newly returned to shore from the fight against America and its allies, the mob was, they said "off for Newgate, to liberate . . . their honest comrades." When they arrived before the newly finished prison, a hated symbol of a new system of British justice, the crowd roared into furious action, tearing into the prison, releasing its 117 inmates—thieves, robbers, rapists, and murderers alike— smashing windows and doors, destroying the chapel and the keeper's house before setting the hulking edifice aflame. By morning the new prison had been nearly razed to the ground.[2]

But the outburst of rage that summer night did not cease with the burning of Newgate Prison, and other symbols of the criminal justice system quickly fell to the combustible anger of the mob. "The Fleet Prison, the Marshalsea, King's Bench, both Compters, Clerkenwell, and Tothill Fields, with Newgate are all flung open; Newgate partly burned, and 300 felons from thence only let loose upon the world," a horrified Ignatius Sancho recorded. In all some 1,600 inmates, seen by many rioters as victims of an overly repressive system rather than as threats to order, were broken free from London prisons. As one rioter sentenced to die for his role in the tumult later confessed, the crowd hoped to see that "there should not be a prison standing . . . in London." The private homes of prominent judicial officials were also targeted for destruction. Justice William Hyde's house was pillaged and its contents spilled on the street and burnt; Justice David Wilmot's house was leveled; and the home of Sir John Fielding, driving force behind the new policing of the capital and brother of the writer Henry Fielding, was set alight as well. Even the residence of Lord Chief Justice Mansfield in fashionable Bloomsbury Square "suffered martyrdom" and had its railings ripped away, its windows shattered, and its paintings, furniture, and 200 notebooks cast into a bonfire, all while Lord Mansfield and his wife fled for their lives out the back door. Six rioters were killed at Lord Mansfield's, including a condemned man freed from Newgate earlier that day who, Sancho bitterly commented, "found death a few hours sooner than if he had not been released." Looking out that night at the artificial glow, it seemed to the diarist Fanny Burney as if all of judicial London was engulfed in flame. "Our square was light as day by the bonfire from the contents of Justice Hyde's house . . . on the other side we saw flames ascending from Newgate, a fire in Covent Garden which proved to be Justice Fielding's house, and another in Bloomsbury Square which was at Lord Mansfield's," all sure signs of the popular anger with the changing justice system inaugurated by the American Revolution.[3]

These riots, the worst in English history, were at least nominally precipitated by anti-Catholic feeling and a reaction to the Catholic Relief Act of 1778. But the vast destruction visited upon these prisons and the homes of London's jurid-ical elite were not merely casualties of religious bigotry, but also of the American Revolution itself. What Ignatius Sancho and Fanny Burney chronicled was a violent reaction to a new British order, one that turned old notions of justice and punishment on its head—and one forged deliberately in the light of the American Revolution and the crisis of crime, disorder, and fear it generated. The descent into madness Ignatius Sancho charted in the summer of 1780 was the culmination of pressures that had been building for years. The war that had begun five years earlier in 1775 had since spread beyond Britain's American colonies, sucking France, Spain, and the Dutch Republic into a global maelstrom that threatened to engulf the world. What had been an imperial civil war had become an imperial world war as well, ensuring that the fighting did not remain limited to the distant shores of the western Atlantic. As the theater of war rapidly expanded, and Britain moved from the sidelines to the frontline, Britons were transformed from comfortably detached observers safely ensconced in their island fastness to active participants in the traumas of the times.

Threats now appeared disconcertingly close to home—foreign invasions, revolutionary sympathizers, and emboldened criminals seemed to materialize everywhere at once. Britain, once arrogantly sure that an easy victory over America was foreordained, now became suffused with fear, paranoia, and panic. The mood of the country changed. Attitudes toward dissent and disloyalty, crime and disorder hardened, precipitating the worst popular violence in London's history. The riots, in turn, only served to confirm and reinforce Britons' worst fears about the vulnerabilities of the nation and the dangers posed by a revolutionary age. As Londoners sifted through the charred rubble of a war-torn city, the country embarked on a mental and institutional refash-ioning, a counter-revolutionary reimagining that would reshape domestic policy and help keep the tide of crime, disorder, and revolution at bay in the turbulent years to come.

The first sign that the American War was no ordinary conflict, that Britain was not immune to the dangers of a revolution an ocean away, could be seen on the streets of the capital, where crime and disorder appeared to be growing at an alarming rate in the years after 1775. This in itself was unusual. For most of English history crime rates had fallen during times of war as those individuals most likely to fall into criminality—poor young men—were drafted into the military and sent abroad to fight. Contrary to established historical patterns, however, crime rates began to rise dramatically during the American Revolution, with prosecutions increasing by as much as 50 per cent in London between 1779 and 1782 and only grew in the years following the end of the war in America. This surge in crime was in part a result of the enormous pressures placed upon the British people by a truly global conflict. Eighteenth-century crime rates were largely driven by men, but the war witnessed a highly unusual phenomenon: men and women were equally affected by the growth in crime. The war placed a great deal of strain on the wives left behind by soldiers and sailors, and it is no surprise that growing numbers turned to crime as a way to survive. Mary MacDaniel explained her own sad descent into crime; "we happened to get a little drop of liquor in our heads, it is natural, Sir. My husband and son were killed in America." With her husband and son dead an ocean away, MacDaniel had turned first to the menial labor often undertaken by poor women with few options, working as a cleaner or servant in the homes of her better-off neighbors. "I go out a charing very hard for my bread," she told the court, but in the absence of a reliable income and with the difficulty of securing one when alcohol has become a daily necessity, MacDaniel turned to theft, robbing newly enriched soldiers who, unlike her husband, had returned from the war. She was not alone in her desperate turn to crime.[4]

Of all the criminal activities that grew and thrived during the desperate years of war, none caused more disorder, more concern and fear for the British government than smuggling. Britain's coasts became hives of disorder as many desperate and enterprising Britons seized the opportunity presented by the war to join a booming smuggling trade. Americans may have bristled at the imposition of duties on luxury goods such as the ubiquitous tea, but such taxes were in line with similar duties on tea, tobacco, and spirits paid by the inhabitants of Britain. These taxes were a crucial component of the growing fiscal-military state, raised in times of war as a key component in funding the almost constant conflicts of the eighteenth century.[5]

The monopoly on the importation of tea granted to the East India Company (EIC) only made the problem worse. The EIC used its privileged position to control the volume of sales and to increase prices, artificially inflating the cost of tea relative to the prices found in other European countries. While tea could be had for 6 pence per pound in Amsterdam, in London it cost 5 shillings or more, with 4 shillings and 9 pence of the British price a direct result of the customs duty. With the difference between prices so great and the distance between Britain and the Netherlands so small, illicit trading was bound to explode alongside the legal trade that had been moving between the Low Countries and the British Isles for centuries.[6]

Deep resentment of consumption taxes was a transatlantic phenomenon, and smuggling in Britain and America had flourished for as long as tariffs had existed. The Seven Years' War, and the American Revolution it helped to spawn, however, witnessed both an explosion of anger over consumption duties and a surge in smuggling. With taxes on such luxury goods as tea and spirits high, those who dared to skirt the customs house stood to make a fortune. This increased financial incentive led to a wave of smuggling throughout the British Isles in the years of the American Revolution.

So rampant was the contraband trade that by 1783 it was estimated that at least 120 large ships and 200 smaller vessels along with 20,000 people were employed in smuggling full time. When one considers that the population of Britain was roughly 8 million people in the late eighteenth century, the sheer scale of illicit trade comes into focus. While a large and growing segment of the population benefited from smuggling, either directly through the profits of the trade in contraband, or indirectly through the greater availability of cheap tea, tobacco, spirits, and silks, the British government was losing a fortune in lost revenues at a time when it could ill afford to do so. In 1783 a report issued by the Board of Customs estimated that a staggering 21.1 million pounds of tea were being smuggled into Britain every year at a monumental cost to government finances. It was estimated that £1 million of revenue was lost to the illicit trade conducted through the Channel Islands alone.[7]

The increased tariffs of the 1760s and 1770s were not the only spur to this astonishing growth in black market activities. As the army and navy's need for men grew with the outbreak of war in America, the manpower of the customs service was rapidly drained to fill the gaps in Britain's armed forces. With fewer men and fewer ships to patrol the coasts, smugglers were left with a relatively free hand. In Sussex, at Cuckmere Haven in 1783, the smugglers had more to fear from the tempestuous autumn seas than the customs service. It was reported that

> between two and three hundred smugglers on horseback came to Cookmere [sic] and received various kinds of goods from the boats, 'till at last the whole number were laden, when, in defiance of the King's officers, they went their way in great triumph. About a week before this, upwards of three hundred attended at the same place; and though the sea ran mountains high, the daring men in the cutters made good the landing.[8]

The rewards of smuggling were such that whole communities were often involved, or at least complicit, in the black market. While many took an active role in landing, hiding, or transporting contraband goods, others were simply guilty of providing a market for duty-free merchandise or looking the other way, studiously ignoring the illegal activity in their midst. By the late eighteenth century, the British had become a nation of tea drinkers, with much of the population consuming the aromatic brew twice a day or more. Much of this tea, however, was contraband. A government estimate surmised that two-thirds of the tea consumed in the British Isles had not passed through customs, and was thus illegal. The consumption of illicit tea, brandy, and tobacco, and dealing with smugglers, however, had become an everyday fact of living in the eighteenth century.[9]

Even if local populations and many local officials felt sympathy, or at least ambivalence, regarding smuggling, the government could not afford to take such a lenient tack. In the best of times smuggling undermined the revenue of the state, but in the midst of war with America, France, Spain, the Netherlands, the Marathas, and Mysore, the funds derived from tariffs were a crucial part of

Britain's very survival. In such times, when every shilling was needed to pay for troops, ships and armaments, smuggling could not be tolerated. With both smugglers and the government highly motivated by the heightened stakes of wartime profits and revenue needs, violence was inevitable.

Armed confrontations between smugglers and customs officers multiplied after the onset of the American Revolution, taking on a bloody aspect that reflected the tensions of the era. With France, Spain, and the Netherlands joining the war in 1778, the encounters only intensified. The Orford militia was forced into a firefight with a local band of smugglers in July of 1778, when they attempted to land a cargo of uncustomed goods on the Suffolk coast. The militiamen had received the full force of the smuggler's cutter's broadside when they attempted to challenge them on the beach, and it was only the arrival of the army that prevented a victory for the smugglers. Five years later bloodshed returned to the beaches of Suffolk when seventy smugglers, their faces "blacked" to avoid detection, clashed with a combined force of customs agents and dragoons at Southwold beach. When the smoke cleared, one smuggler lay dead on the sandy Suffolk shore.[10]

The east coast of England was not alone in seeing the grim consequences of the contraband trade. In July 1784 William Allen, captain of the Royal Navy sloop HMS *Orestes*, received information that smugglers were attempting to land a cargo of contraband brandy and tea on Mudeford beach just outside the harbor at Christchurch, Dorset. When the *Orestes*, accompanied by a pair of revenue vessels, rounded the point and Mudeford beach hove into view they espied two luggers newly arrived from the Channel Islands laden with illicit goods. The beach swarmed with activity as 300 smugglers and sympathetic locals hurried to unload the roughly 120,000 gallons of brandy and 25 tons of tea from the smugglers' ships and move them inland on 50 carts drawn by upwards of 300 horses. Captain Allen knew how desperately the war-ravaged fleet could use the revenue such a large quantity of goods should supply, and so he was in no mood to let the smugglers make their landing unchallenged. Allen ordered his men to lower six boats packed with armed sailors and commanded them to row to the beach and seize the luggers and their contraband.

The arrival of the revenue service did not go unnoticed by those onshore, however, and John Streeter, a notorious local smuggler, quickly rode to the

Haven House, a nearby pub, to recruit more men to transport the tea and brandy and resist the representatives of the law. While some helped move the goods inshore to designated hiding places, others dug in on the beach and readied themselves for a fight. They did not have long to wait. As Captain Allen and his men neared the luggers he demanded that the smugglers surrender, a demand met by a volley of shot from the brazen criminals. The sailors returned fire and eventually pushed the smugglers from the shore before following them to Haven House where a firefight erupted that lasted for more than three hours.

In the end, the costs of the battle were high. Captain Allen was struck down early in the fighting and died of his wounds a short time later. Christchurch Priory was damaged by an errant shot from the *Orestes'* guns, which had attempted to reduce the Haven House to rubble. The luggers had been seized, but the smugglers and their prize had escaped, with only one man arrested and charged for the murder of Captain Allen. George Coombes was convicted and hanged for his role in the fight, and his corpse hung in chains at Haven House Point as a message to other smugglers. The community, however, was hardly cowed by the hanging and cut down Coombes' body for proper burial. For government and smuggler alike, the financial stakes of customs duties were great enough to fight for, even enough to die for.[11]

By 1783 it was becoming clear that something had to be done. Smuggling was rampant, revenue was desperately needed, and the current state of affairs was having little impact on contraband or revenue. When the Fox–North Coalition swept into power in April of 1783, and the Duke of Portland replaced Lord Shelburne as prime minister, the time to act had come. The famed orator, philosopher and Member of Parliament Edmund Burke was appointed Paymaster of the Forces and quickly looked for ways to balance the revenues. He called for the Board of Customs to produce a report on illicit trade, the results of which at last shocked the government into action. Before it could finish its custom reforms, the Fox–North Coalition, and Burke with it, was replaced by the new ministry of the 24-year-old William Pitt the Younger. Burke's East India Company Bill had been defeated, and with it the Coalition, but the much-needed customs reforms were continued by Pitt.

It had long been recognized by some in Britain that moderate customs duties might actually bring in more revenue than heavy duties simply by undercutting the incentives for avoiding the tariffs. In his 1776 economic opus *The Wealth of Nations*, Adam Smith argued that by creating a rational incentive for avoiding customs, high duties would invariably lead to reduced revenue, the opposite of its intent. Rather than blame the smuggler, who was merely behaving rationally in relation to the conditions of the market, Smith considered such a man to be one who, "though no doubt highly blameable for violating the laws of his country, is frequently incapable of violating those of natural justice, and would have been, in every respect, an excellent citizen had not the laws of his country made that a crime which nature never meant to be so." Poorly conceived customs laws made criminals where none should have existed. Thus, the solution to smuggling was not ever-higher duties or repression, but lower duties.[12]

The newly empowered Pitt took this suggestion to heart, and in 1784 began a massive overhaul of the customs. He reduced the tax on tea from 119 per cent to 12 per cent and the tax on brandy from over £90 a tun to just over £43 per tun. In addition, Pitt also streamlined the system of accounting and eliminated the practice of differential tariffs, all while using a firm hand with those who continued to ply the trade in smuggled goods. With the Hovering Act of 1784, Pitt gave the government the power to seize any and all ships under 60 tons found to be carrying tea, coffee, or wine within 3 miles of the coast. Similarly, any ship carrying spirits in barrels smaller than 60 gallons could be confiscated. In 1785, when a storm drove the smugglers' ships into the harbor at Deal, Pitt wasted no time in putting his new principles into action. He sent an army regiment to that notorious den of smugglers and had every ship in sight seized and burnt. With reduced customs duties came harsher treatment of those who continued to flout the law.[13]

The impact of Pitt's reforms was real and impressive. Prior to the reforms, 4.96 million pounds of tea went through customs as required by law. In 1785, only one year after the reduction in duties, 16.3 million pounds of tea, an almost fourfold increase, were customed. Pitt, and Smith before him, were vindicated. The reduction in duties both cut smuggling significantly and increased the revenue of the nation. The attitude of many in the country began to shift as well, with smugglers increasingly seen as a menace rather than an acceptable part of everyday economic life. Penalties for smugglers noticeably stiffened, with more men executed for what had previously been penalized with a fine. By

1785, the outburst of smuggling that had greeted the American Wars had largely been contained and the days of pitched battles between excise officers and smugglers were quickly becoming a relict of another age. The American War, and the crime wave it caused, however, forced Britain to fundamentally rethink its justice system. For just as crime and disorder were on the rise, the war cut off Britain's traditional safety valve.[14]

The burgeoning number of criminal trials was not a result of growing criminality alone. Fear of disorder was also a significant driver of prosecutions. During previous wars, the government responded to changed conditions by granting greater numbers of pardons, especially for non-violent offenses. During the American War, however, heightened concerns over internal disorder meant that such leniency was unconscionable. Thus, as the war intensified and concerns about crime and disorder increased, new measures were sought to combat this emergent scourge. One of the first results of these growing fears was a violent crackdown on criminals appearing in the courts of the capital. At the Old Bailey, capital sentences tripled in the war years and executions rose fourfold as the authorities began to reduce the number of pardons it allowed. Whippings and brandings—the traditional punishment for theft—also surged during these years, all part of a growing intolerance of criminality in an atmosphere riven with fear. The sheer number of those punished is astounding. Between 1780 and 1787, 500 individuals were hanged in London alone, a third as many executions as occurred over the previous 80 years combined.[15]

The end of the war only made things worse. War, especially a global war such as the American Revolutionary War, expanded the army and navy by leaps and bounds, offering the prospect of regular wages to a segment of society often living hand to mouth, day to day in an economy of makeshift, where temporary, seasonal work was the norm. But mass mobilization had dire societal consequences as well. Britain had long feared that a standing army would lead inevitably to the monarchical tyranny they saw across the Channel in France and so would not abide a professional army quartered in Britain in peacetime. If such tactics kept the nation safe from domestic tyranny, they also created the need to raise large numbers of troops quickly at the outbreak of war and the concomitant need to rapidly disperse soldiers at war's end. Mass mobilization might have been a boon for those unable to find steady employment elsewhere, but the subsequent mass dismissals put the country at risk from the predatory potential of well-armed, well-trained men without jobs or prospects. In times of war, and especially in the liminal moments between war and peace, the line between hero of empire and criminal villain was fine indeed. When safely abroad fighting for the crown in America or India or on the high seas protecting the homeland, soldiers and sailors were easy to portray as upholders of British interests, useful cogs in the war machine. Once home again, they instantly transformed into a potentially dangerous, criminally inclined excess population. War could provide a wonderful opportunity to use marginal elements of the population for strategic purposes, but brought with it the reality that trained killers, mostly poor and underpaid, would in time be let loose on British shores.

In the eighteenth century, international peace usually meant domestic disorder. Crime waves followed in the wake of every major war as tens of thousands of surplus soldiers and sailors found themselves suddenly, all at once, unemployed. The outbreak of war was seized by governments as a means of both pursuing strategic interests and ridding Britain of its marginal, excess population. Conscription for both army and navy tended to target the poor and unemployed, young men most likely to turn to crime. At every level of the judicial system—before trial, during trial, and after conviction—military service was used an alternative punishment, swelling the ranks rather than crowding the gallows.

Those who returned from the war, which was hardly guaranteed given the mortality rates of the eighteenth-century military, were left with no employment and often with their pay severely in arrears. They descended on London and the ports of the south in swarms, causing crime rates to skyrocket. In the 1780s, more than 130,000 men were demobilized, representing fully 2 per cent of the entire British population and 20 per cent of the adult male laboring poor. The country, racked by years of war, could in no way accommodate so many men so fast, and crime rose by 35 per cent or more in the years surrounding the end of the American conflict; it would remain alarmingly elevated until the commencement of war with revolutionary France in 1793. As one contemporary ruefully remarked, "the age that makes good soldiers mars good servants, cancelling their obedience and allowing them too much liberty."[16]

John Fitzpatrick, a gardener from Fulham, had first-hand experience of the potential danger of poor, demobbed soldiers. In March 1783, Fitzpatrick was traveling on the highway between London and Fulham. In those days Fulham was still a rural community, separated from London by fields and heath. The roads in and out of London were notoriously the hunting grounds of high-waymen, so Fitzpatrick must have already been on edge when two men appeared out of the "star-light night" and commanded, in the traditional language of British highwaymen, that the terrified gardener stand and "deliver." One of the men had a knife "putting him in fear," so Fitzpatrick complied, losing his watch and chain, some seals, a key, and two half-crowns to his nocturnal assailants. After the robbers had disappeared into the night, Fitzpatrick called the night watch, who captured one of the suspects. The second highwayman was appre-hended a few weeks later when Fitzpatrick recognized him in Litchfield Street.

At trial it quickly became clear how Fitzpatrick had been able to pick out the man who robbed him weeks after the event. It had been dark that night, with only the stars to light the robbers' faces, but John Rogers, who now stood charged with highway robbery, had only one hand. Rogers explained in court that, he had been pressed into the army "and sent to America in Lord Cornwallis's army, and had my hand shot away, which was cut off in six hours after." It would have been difficult for a poor, discharged soldier to make a living in the best of circumstances, but without a hand, crime must have seemed one of the only options left. In the end, the wound that marked his loyal service to the crown also marked him out for death. He was identified in court, found guilty, and sentenced to death.[17]

Soldiers, and especially wounded soldiers, appear with depressing regu-larity in the criminal records of the period. William Harris was charged with the theft of a watch in 1782, but was discharged after the court was told that "ever since the prisoner has been in gaol he has had all the appearance of insanity." "Then you will acquit him, to be sure, Gentlemen," the court responded. It seems likely that Harris had suffered a traumatic brain injury during the war. He informed the court, "I have been in America this eight years . . . I was wounded in the head with three buck shot in America with my Lord Cornwallis, in five different places; I came home last November; at the full of the moon I am distracted in my head."[18]

The massive growth of crime and convictions that had been spurred by the American War left British authorities with a serious dilemma. In the draconian days of the late eighteenth century, when the Black Act and the Bloody Code still worked their morbid ways, theft of anything valued at more than 1 shilling was a capital offense. Indeed, by the end of the century there were more than 200 separate offenses that carried the penalty of death.[19] And yet, while the triple tree and other gallows around Britain hardly lacked for occupants, the sensibilities of the time were hardly so bloody in practice as they appear on paper.

In the face of such a crime wave, the sheer number of capital offenses required some clever workarounds if whole swaths of the British population were to be spared the noose. Who, after all, would till the fields, wash the linen, and serve the tables if the full effects of the law were brought to bear in every instance? Thus, we encounter the all too frequent farce of the jury that found 10 shillings in coins to be worth only 5 shillings, sparing the life of a petty thief with their pious perjury. And yet as ridiculous as they sometimes were in practice, the laws could not simply be reformed and re-written. Law-makers argued that the terror and majesty of the law were necessary to punish hardened criminals and to provide a deterrent example for more impressionable youths. With harsh laws and merciful hearts at an impasse, a solution was needed that allowed terror and mercy, the twin functions of the British justice system, to work in tandem, showing righteous vengeance to the wicked without executing thousands for theft and other minor crimes.[20]

As was so often the case in the period, an answer to this thorny legal dilemma was found in Britain's colonial possessions. Since the early seventeenth century, British America had been a convenient outlet for the overabundant landless poor, with those tasked with improving the criminal justice system turning to this pleasantly distant dumping ground as a social safety valve for criminals deemed too hardened to remain in Britain but not dangerous enough to necessitate extermination. Such convicts would be transported to the Americas for a term of seven to fourteen years.

In many ways, the search for novel punishment solutions in Britain helped to remake the Atlantic world, forcibly shifting an estimated 50,000 individuals from the Old World to the New, thereby helping to relieve population pressures in Britain and providing much-needed labor to the colonies. Experiments with penal transportation began under the reign of James I, and bills were proposed to codify the process in the late seventeenth century, but the large-scale movement of convicts to the New World only really began in earnest after the passage of the Transportation Act in 1717. This innovative, seemingly humane punishment steadily grew in popularity over the course of the eighteenth century, peaking in 1765 when transportation represented an astonishing 73.1 per cent of all criminal sentences handed out in London. Even if some judges and politicians began to doubt the penal rigor of transportation to the increasingly prosperous American colonies, at the outbreak of war in 1775 transportation still represented well over half of all criminal sentences in London.[21]

Capitalism, as it is wont to do, quickly wormed its way into the transportation system, with contractors vying for the right to ship convicts across the Atlantic and recouping their expenses by selling the labor of the men and women they transported. Upon arrival in Maryland or Virginia, convicts were sold as indentured laborers to the labor-hungry planters of the Chesapeake Tidewater, augmenting the ever-growing supply of other unfree agricultural workers, African slaves and European indentured laborers. Conditions for convict workers varied but, as with all coerced labor, they could be dismal. Like slaves, convict laborers who fled from their masters were actively sought, captured and returned—newspapers of the era are filled with advertisements offering tempting rewards for the return of convict servants.

The American colonists had mixed feelings about criminal transportation. On the one hand, in many places convicts were a relatively cheap source of labor, a favorable alternative to African slavery. Roughly half of all transported convicts were sent to Maryland and Virginia where they were employed in the labor-intensive tobacco industry. George Washington himself purchased convicts to work his estate at Mount Vernon as late as 1774. The value of convict labor to many Chesapeake planters was real, and alongside the more familiar advertisements for fugitive slaves, newspapers of the time were rife with advertisements seeking the return of convict laborers. For instance, in November 1775, James Braddock of Talbot County, Maryland placed an ad in the *Maryland Gazette* offering a reward of up to £5 for the capture and return of two convicts.[22]

Transportation worked to the benefit of many in the Americas, but there was a dark side to the practice as well. Few Americans trusted convict laborers and sensational stories of their ingrained and unrepentant criminality abounded.

When Marylanders gathered to discuss the coming of a new political order and to consider a possible end to penal transportation in the 1770s, they would have remembered John Swift's brutal murder of the young children of John Hatherly, a prosperous tobacco planter in Elkridge, Maryland, only twenty years earlier. For many Americans, it seemed clear that Britain had sent the dregs of European society to their shores, and hard labor and a change of climate could do little to change such unredeemable refuse. There was no place for such scum in America's new enlightened empire of liberty.[23]

Beyond the practical dangers of accepting perhaps a thousand convicted felons each year, being on the receiving end of the transportation system had a perverse psychological, or at least public relations, impact. Americans bristled with incensed indignation at Samuel Johnson's cutting quip that the colonists were nothing but "a race of convicts, and ought to be thankful for anything we allow them short of hanging," and Benjamin Franklin called the practice of penal transportation, "an insult and contempt, the cruelest perhaps that ever one people offered another." Thomas Jefferson did his level best to sweep the whole sordid history of transportation under the rug. In the years after the revolution and the end of transportation he defensively claimed that:

> the Malefactors sent to America were not sufficient in number to merit enumeration as one class out of three which peopled America. It was at a late period of their history that the practice began. I have no book by me which enables me to point out the date of its commencement. But I do not think the whole number sent would amount to 2000 & being principally men eaten up with disease, they married seldom & propagated little. I do not suppose that themselves & their descendants are at present 4000, which is little more than one thousandth part of the whole inhabitants.[24]

In reality, large numbers of felons were still appearing on American shores right up until the outbreak of warfare in 1775. At first, transportation was merely disrupted by the war, with British blockades and the hostility of American ports toward British ships making it difficult for convict ships to land. Most believed this to simply be a temporary halt rather than the end of a system, and as late as May 1776 the British solicitor-general, Alexander Wedderburn, was convinced that once "tranquility was restored to America, the usual mode of transportation might be again adopted."[25] Colonists themselves were unsure of where their provisional governments stood on transportation. When a convict transport landed in Maryland in July 1775, it was met by four men deputed by the local Committee of Observation who scrutinized its logbook, found that it was transporting fourteen felons from Britain and immediately ordered it to turn around in accordance with the boycott on British goods. The captain asked permission to at least land the convicts, citing recent arrivals of convicts at Annapolis and Baltimore, who were just then being advertised for sale. The deputation conferred and came to the decision that the convicts could be landed at the captain's own risk, because, as they reasoned, "they could see nothing in the proceedings of the congress relative to convicts or servants."[26]

As it transpired, Wedderburn's optimism was gravely misplaced. For a people determined to create a new, more perfect society independent of Britain, the importation of criminals could hardly be tolerated. To many colonial minds criminal immigrants clogged the courts and slowed the civilizing of American society. In 1751, Benjamin Franklin decried British intransigence in colonial legislation on these matters, stating that "such Laws are against the Publick Utility, as they tend to prevent the Improvement and Well Peopling of the Colonies." Never short on wit, Franklin turned the logic of transportation as a method of rehabilitation on its head by suggesting that perhaps the British would agree to an exchange of American rattlesnakes for British convicts—perhaps both simply needed a change of climate to reform—concluding that at least "the Rattle-Snake gives Warning before he attempts his Mischief; which the Convict does not." In the 1770s, America's leaders once more realized that if their young nation was to be "well peopled" and free from undesirable elements that might breed crime, disobedience, and disorder, British convicts could not be welcomed on their shores, even as low-cost labor. Unwilling to meekly accept the importation of such undesirable cargo any longer, the nascent American states closed their ports to the transportation of convict laborers. And so, in April 1776, a lone convict ship landed in Virginia, the last in a long line of such vessels, disgorging from its hold, for the final time on American shores, the wretched residue of Britain's courts.[27]

By closing the primary outlet for Britain's criminal underclass, the revolution forced innovations in empire building, colonial settlement, and judicial philosophy. American critics of criminal transportation could not have imagined that the closing of their ports to British convicts would fundamentally alter the history of the world, not just in Britain and America but in Asia and Oceania as well. Within a few years, the search for new dumping grounds for British felons would help lead to the growth of the penitentiary, the conquest of India, and the settlement of Australia.

The safety valve of colonial exile had been closed by the war, and although harsher and harsher punishment became the norm, nobody could realistically condone executing thousands of desperate souls for petty theft and other minor crimes. But these thousands of convicts could not be freely pardoned, nor their disorderly behavior blithely excused. There were rational, utilitarian considerations to take into account as well. Transportation had been introduced not only as a method of tempering the harshness of English law, but also as a means of best utilizing population resources at a time of growing international competition. The English had long gazed across the Channel with nervous envy at the numerical advantages of France. With concerns over the expense of foreign trade and colonization firmly fixed in their minds, wasting precious manpower by executing criminals became increasingly unconscionable, or at least poor imperial strategy.

Charles Davenant, the political economist who introduced the idea of the centrality of "balance of trade" for national health, had also claimed:

> The Bodies of Men are without a doubt the most valuable Treasure of a Country . . . the People being the first Matter of Power and Wealth, by whose Labour and Industry a Nation must be Gainers in the Balance, their Increase and Decrease must be carefully observ'd by any Government that designs to thrive; that is, their Increase must be promoted by good Conduct and wholesome Laws, and if they have been Decreas'd by War or any other Accident, the Breach is to be made up as soon as possible, for it is a Maim in the Body Politick affecting all its Parts.[28]

Those countries that could best utilize even their marginal populations, the poor and criminal alike, would have an advantage in an increasingly global contest. Transportation had seemed to solve this problem nicely, turning potential corpses into settlers and cheap plantation labor. The closure of American ports to convicts, however, created the need for a new penal solution that gave proper consideration to the needs of retribution, deterrence and national utility.

With few other options at hand, the authorities took a radical new step in British judicial history, imprisonment as punishment. Imprisonment had, of course, been used for centuries, but until the crisis of the late eighteenth century had usually been reserved for debtors and those awaiting trial. During the American Revolution, however, the British turned to incarceration with gusto. By the end of the war, as many as 30,000 individuals were being imprisoned each year in London alone, representing nearly 3 per cent of the entire population. This figure is all the more astounding when one considers that England's current incarceration rate is 0.001 per cent of the population, and that even the United States, which has one of the largest prison populations in the world, only imprisons about 0.9 per cent of its population.[29]

The birth of a carceral culture in Britain had a long period of gestation. In the face of rapid population growth at a time of economic stagnation, Tudor London converted a former royal palace at Bridewell into an institution designed to house vagrants found within the city, where inmates were to be put to work as a means of correcting their idle and criminal habits. The idea of incarcerating and disciplining the transient poor spread across the country and "workhouses" began to crop up in many English cities and towns. Over the next two hundred years, the idea of reforming criminals, or the poor population from which they were invariably thought to come, through forced labor would become a regular feature of political debate. In 1576, Parliament pressed every English county to set up a workhouse and fifty years later James I created a commission with the power to convert sentences of transportation to "toyle in some such heavie and painful manuall works and labors here at home and be kept in chaines in houses of correction." In 1652, a commission directed by Sir Matthew Hale tasked with investigating possible law reforms, proposed a broad system of incarceration, but its recommendations were rejected when Oliver Cromwell dismissed the Barebones Parliament that had established the commission. A similar commission under the direction of the novelist and magistrate Henry Fielding likewise had its recommendation that some felons should be sentenced to work in the royal dockyards rejected when it failed to pass in the House of Lords in 1751.[30]

The sad state of existing prisons and jails had long been public knowledge, and throughout the eighteenth century attempts were made to reform the system and improve conditions. As early as 1729, James Oglethorpe, the eventual founder of the colony of Georgia, had been tasked with leading a parliamentary inquiry into the wretched state of the country's jails and prisons. By the second half of the eighteenth century, these reformers began to turn to calls to replace capital sentences and other forms of physical punishment with imprisonment. Perhaps the most influential voice in the rising chorus of penal reformers belonged to the Italian theorist Cesare Beccaria. In his highly influential 1764 treatise, *On Crimes and Punishments*, Beccaria advocated for a rationalization of criminal justice that would bring European legal systems in line with Enlightenment principles of order, consistency, and utility. To this end, Beccaria argued that punishment should be designed to serve the greatest public good. Capital punishment, which focused on retribution, was by this metric of less value to society than incarceration, which allowed for both deterrence and the possibility of rehabilitation.[31]

Beccaria's reformist agenda, and perhaps especially his advocacy of imprisonment over execution, would influence the thinking of countless luminaries of the era, including Jeremy Bentham, Thomas Jefferson, and John Adams, but in Britain his Enlightenment principles would become suffused with evangelical Protestantism in a manner that had long-lasting consequences for the history of penal reform. For men such as John Howard, one of Britain's foremost philanthropists and prison reformers, if incarceration was to lead to rehabilitation, the removal of the negative influences of prison sociability and the institution of enforced silence and personal reflection were pre-requisites. Howard came by his reformist views by experience. In 1755, while en route to Portugal, Howard had been captured by the French and imprisoned at Brest. Thus, when in 1773 he was appointed Sherriff of Bedfordshire, he quickly became alarmed at the dreadful state of the county's prisons. Over the next four years Howard toured prisons throughout Britain and Europe, with his fact-finding mission culminating in his 1777 work, *The State of the Prisons in England and Wales*. Howard's opus not only detailed the poor conditions of most prisons and the ill-health of the prisoners housed within, but also put forward a much-needed reform agenda. Among a host of suggestions, Howard advocated for single-cell housing of prisoners as a means of preventing the spread of disease, ensuring order and forcing reflection on sin and misdeeds. Howard's ideas were well received, earning the support of other reformers such as the philanthropist Jonas Hanway, who argued for the use of imprisonment as a method for reforming the idle and criminal poor. Spurring the government to take concrete action, however, was nigh on impossible in ordinary times. Only in a time of crisis would the government be forced to act. The American Revolution provided just such a crisis.[32]

The effort to create a penal system based on incarceration, religious indoctrination, and labor discipline were given the boast they sorely needed with the outbreak of war and the disruption of criminal transportation to the colonies. Unfortunately for the reformers, however, the existing prisons were in no shape either to house more prisoners, or to offer the type of rehabilitation that men like Hanway and Howard advocated. The overcrowded, outdated prisons exemplified by London's notorious Newgate were rife with disease. Regular outbreaks of "gaol fever," later identified as typhus, decimated the ranks of prisoners and threatened the health of those living or working near prisons. John Howard estimated that as many as a quarter of all prisoners died from illness, most before even reaching trial. It was proverbial that more suspected criminals would succumb to the doleful conditions of the prisons than would meet their end through court-mandated executions. Imprisonment was tantamount to a death sentence, hardly an amenable circumstance for those who wished to enforce discipline and instill a work ethic.[33]

Measures were made to address these shortcomings—the Goal Act was passed in 1774 and prisons like New Prison in Clerkenwell were renovated in an attempt to stave off disease—but the available prisons still lacked necessary space and some of the features required to make criminals into workers. When William Smith visited London's prisons in 1776, he noticed an interesting aspect of prison culture that may seem cheering to modern eyes, but was deemed counterproductive for eighteenth-century penal reformers. Most prisons of the day were open plan, with prisoners moving with relative freedom throughout the space and freely mixing with fellow prisoners and visiting friends and family. Smith noticed that this ease of movement allowed for the fostering of relationships of mutual support and camaraderie among the population, which he considered a dangerous block to rehabilitation. According to Smith, prisoners shared food, socialized, "and by such means they form into companies, and become more formidable to society."[34]

For men such as William Smith and John Howard, this artificial community defeated the purpose of the new reformative justice. In their view, prisoners needed to be separated in solitary confinement so that they could reflect on their sinful ways and so as to prevent their corruption by other prisoners. If the idle and criminal poor were to be made to work, their communities of solidarity needed to be removed and destroyed, replaced by a Christian ethic of discipline and productivity. Smith argued that "under no pretence whatever should any two or more felons be suffered to associate, even for one minute." In the words of a committee reporting on the state of one London prison, the mixing of prisoners led to the "contamination of manners and morals," something that needed to be avoided at all costs if discipline was to be instilled and rehabilitation made possible.[35]

The existing prisons were ill equipped for such a task, and new, purpose-built structures were needed if the penal reform forced by the American crisis was to become a reality. But the "Panopticons" of the reformers' imaginations would take time and money to build and, as the war dragged on, stop-gap solutions were needed. The same year that William Smith visited the prisons of London, in the face of growing fear of the war-induced wave of crime and disorder, Parliament passed the so-called "Convict" or "Hulks" Act of 1776. As a temporary expedient, the act allowed convicted felons to be given alternative forms of punishment. Male prisoners were to put to work dredging the Thames and widening its banks to make it better suited to the increased volume of shipping and larger ships of the late eighteenth century. The infrastructure needed to run such a program was non-existent, so the authorities turned to a tried and true policy. A contract for the work was given to Duncan Campbell, himself a veteran of the transportation industry having previously been hired by the government to ship felons to America before the war. Campbell was not provided with housing for his convict laborers, so he converted two disused ships, the *Censor* and the *Justicia*, into floating prisons usefully docked in the

Thames. In just two years, the hulks were housing 370 men between them, with numbers rising to more than 500 by 1779.

That the "Hulks" Act was passed in the same year as the American colonies' Declaration of Independence was no mere coincidence. The influential *London Magazine* recognized as much in its discussion of the act, informing its readers that "the unhappy rupture with America, forced the legislature to attend to this amendment" to England's Penal Laws. The war was forcing people to look for new solutions to the problem of criminals, with deterrence *and* utility always at the forefront of the debates. The "Hulks" Act used imprisonment and Spartan conditions as a means of deterrence, and hard labor for the national good as a method of rehabilitation. The convicts were to be fed on simple fare, drinking only water, and sent daily to work constructing embankments and dredging ballast to improve the Thames' capacity to receive the thousands of ships, which, like so many sinews, linked the capital with the colonies and trading centers of America and Asia. This project certainly provided a useful return for the country, but there were other suggestions for how convicts could be made to work for British interests. One proposal suggested that in a time of war, convicts "might be so much better employed on board Men of War."[36]

The conditions on the hulks were no improvement on the prisons. A female correspondent to the *Westminster Magazine* reported her impressions of "the unhappy wretches, whose liberty is forfeit of their violations and outrages of the Laws of Society," after an exploratory trip to the hulks docked at Woolwich. After hiring a barge to row out to the three hulks—one a former man-of-war and two decommissioned East Indiamen—she relayed a vivid scene of grinding work and suffering that contrasted sharply with a day that was "lovely beyond description." "The Deck was crowded with felons, the clanking of chains struck horrible on the ear," the correspondent wrote.

> Several were well dressed, but the greater part bore marks of their poverty on their backs; and the cloaths suspended by cords in the air to dry, communicated every possible idea of wretchedness. Their meal over (during which they had fed on hard meats) they slowly descended in pairs from the Hulks, and had all the appearance of what their crimes had rendered them—the

out-casts of Society—the living testimonials of Guilt—the reproach and dread of the Community.

When they later returned from their work improving the Thames the change in their demeanor was palpable.

> Labor had deprived their features of risibility, and, as it were, unstrung their nerves: they drooped—they hung their heads—they re-ascended the Hulks in apparent disconsolateness; and it is presumable moistened their coarse and mortifying fare with their tears—the tears of despair, if not contrition—of regret for past enjoyments, if not piercing sense of their present sufferings—of unavailing anguish; for the broken Law will have its atonement, and gripes with iron paw all the unwary and the wicked that are thrown within its power. This is the fact. Working on the Thames is not a sport: the Convicts know little of indulgence—they are hard ruled, hard fed, hard lodged, and drag on an existence from which the gallows would be a deliverance.[37]

The unnamed correspondent's impressions of the horrors of the hulks were not misplaced. In the first two years of the hulks' existence, well over 200 of the convicts perished, most from illness and disease brought on by the cramped conditions, poor ventilation and sub-standard nutrition. The prisoners were not idle in the face of such dire conditions, and there were mass escape attempts in 1777 and a mutiny in 1778. By 1780 perhaps forty convicts had escaped the hulks, although most were eventually recaptured. Their violent protests over the conditions on the ships did lead to some improvements—including a better diet and medical care. However, despite complaints from the convicts them-selves and widespread outcry from the public at large, the hulks were there to stay, becoming a familiar feature of British life in the late eighteenth and nine-teenth centuries, long after the American crisis had passed.[38]

But there were other problems with the hulks beyond their squalid conditions. For many, one of the crucial aspects of a new penal regime of incar-ceration and hard labor was the concomitant removal of convicts from the dangerous effects of their social environment—criminal behavior could only be prevented by breaking bad habits and instilling good ones. One could not simply "compel people to be virtuous"; they had to be brought to virtue by removing negative influences and allowing for reflection on sin. One of the foremost proponents of solitary confinement, the reformer Jonas Hanway, argued that "solitude is the most humane and effectual means of bringing malefactors . . . to a right sense of their condition." Jeremy Bentham agreed, although he was dismissive of the religious undergirding of Hanway's argument. In his design for the Panopticon, a prison built along rational, utilitarian principles, Bentham contended that the prisoners should be housed in solitary cells and put to work alone rather than in groups. Others felt that solitary confinement at night and group labor during the day would be just as effective, but the general principle remained: work and isolation would reform minds, disciplining the marginal population for the ends of state and society.[39]

Less rational observers also agreed that the lack of isolation aboard the hulks was undermining any potential success. In 1782, a London grand jury received numerous complaints about the hulks, arguing that newly released convicts quickly returned to crime, sowing fear and disorder among the good citizens of the capital. The grand jury concluded that the dangers were so great that it had become necessary to "make application to his Majesty's Ministers, the Secretaries of State, to procure fresh alteration in the mode of punishment for convicts . . . to provide some effectual remedy against the dangers to be apprehended from the immediate dismission of such, whose time of servitude is completed, by press or entitlement, or any other manner which may be deemed efficient." The hulks, the jurors continued, could not serve the needs of community or country while "the place intended for purgatory to cleanse from past offences [i.e. the hulks], proves virtually a seminary, whose every species of villainy and corruption is systematically taught and imbibed by too successful proficients, shortly to be let loose on the public, ripe for execution of those diabolical designs they have formed in these horrid schools of infamy and destruction." The hulks made convicts work for king and country, but did little to reform them. If the new penal regime was to work, both bodies and minds would need disciplining, something that could only be achieved by separating criminals from society and each other.[40]

In the context of the war with America and the end of Atlantic penal transportation, the only option to achieve these twin ends was to create a new system of penitentiaries. In 1779, an act was passed by Parliament that mandated the construction of a series of "Penitentiary Houses" designed to house convicts with the goal of "not only deterring others from the Commission of the like Crimes, but also of reforming the Individuals, and inuring them to Habits of Industry." Drafted by the prison reformers William Eden and John Howard in conjunction with the eminent jurist Sir William Blackstone, the Penitentiary Act of 1779 proposed a regime of hard labor by day and solitary confinement at night that would become the standard of penal philosophy for the next hundred years and more.[41] The construction of the penitentiaries themselves took time, especially given the costs involved and the other demands on Britain's coffers, but incarceration, hard labor, and isolation would quickly become the new normal in British judicial practice.

Although many decried the foul and fetid conditions of the hulks, the initial experiment was repeatedly renewed and extended, ultimately lasting for upwards of eighty years, housing convicts and prisoners of war during of the wars with revolutionary and Napoleonic France and beyond. The prison hulk would become a regular feature of British ports throughout the empire in the nineteenth century. From London and Portsmouth to Cork, Bermuda, Hobart and Sydney, the hulk blighted the empire for decades to come. Its roots lay squarely in the years of the American Revolution. When the more imposing walls of Milbank Prison, the first modern penitentiary, rose a short distance up the Thames, ushering in a new era of criminal justice, it too could trace its roots back to the American Revolution. By cutting off traditional outlets for British convicts while also creating a crisis of criminality and fear, the American War fundamentally reshaped the British justice system, with enduring consequences for penal systems around the globe.

The impact of the shift to incarceration as the primary method of criminal punishment is hard to overestimate. Over the centuries following the war, what began as a liberal, progressive movement for penal reform morphed into a system every bit as repressive, violent, and inhumane as the judicial regimes that preceded it. Indeed, many of the primary problems with our current penal systems can be traced directly to the reforms initiated in the eighteenth century. Currently nearly 90,000 people in the UK and more than 2,000,000 in the United States are incarcerated. This mass incarceration is a direct reflection of the

Beccarian judicial philosophy that contended that certainty of punishment was a more effective deterrent than harsh punishment applied irregularly. One of the overlooked consequences of the judicial reform forced by the American Revolution is that by replacing execution with prison and transportation, juries felt more comfortable imposing the full rigor of the law. As a result, whereas most convicts, even those found guilty of capital crimes, had previously escaped with a fine or flogging, a far greater proportion were now being sentenced to significant periods of exile, imprisonment, and hard labor. Thus, for most people, the legal reforms of the eighteenth century meant harsher punishment rather than more lenient ones. Jurors who had been reluctant to impose the death penalty now willingly sentenced a greater and greater proportion of the population to the new modes of punishment. Our current levels of incarceration began with these reforms.

The rise of the prison had other long-term consequences as well. First, the introduction of imprisonment as a criminal sanction rather than merely a method of ensuring appearance at court fundamentally altered the nature of pre-trial procedure. Then, as now, incarceration was expensive and space, if anything, more limited. When the potential costs of incarceration were all pre-trial, judicial systems were more likely to press for speedy trials and allow for bail as often as possible. When the potential costs of incarceration are likely to continue post-trial, there is less financial incentive to avoid delays or to allow bail. The results have been catastrophic for modern defendants, who now face long spells in prison before trial, while bail is used as a cudgel to force plea deals.

Only recently have people begun to become aware of the final drastic effect of the eighteenth-century penal reform movement. The evangelicals and Utilitarians who advocated for solitary confinement hoped that separating criminals from their corrupting environment and allowing them time and space to reflect on sin, punishment, and the consequences of a life gone wrong would help discipline their minds for productive work. Their modern descendants have similarly used solitary confinement as a tool of control: a means of breaking down supposedly hardened criminals and thereby creating well-ordered penitentiaries. Whatever its success as a method of control within the prison, the ubiquitous use of solitary confinement on modern inmates has had an alarming impact on their mental and physical health. Far from reforming them for society, solitary confinement has ensured that many prisoners will never be able to function properly again.

The great ills of modern criminal justice—solitary confinement, delayed dockets, unequal bail, and mass incarceration—were all present at the birth of the penal reforms of the eighteenth century. These reforms had long been firing the minds of philosophers and philanthropists, and the American Revolution granted them the state backing they had long been denied. In Britain and America, governments in search of novel solutions to the problems of marginal populations, imperial competition, and rampant fear of disorder, embraced incarceration as a means of controlling their people and maintaining order while still utilizing their precious resources for the ends of state. We are still living in the penal world the American Revolution birthed.

2

→→ ←←

TREASON, TERROR,
AND REACTION

Although the riots that rocked London in June 1780 coalesced into an attack on the hated new system of justice, they had not started that way. It had all begun rather peacefully on June 2 when as many as 50,000 men and women gathered in the open ground at St. George's Field, a mile south of Westminster. As the scene of the massacre of protesters back in 1768, it was a site pregnant with meaning for London radicals, but this time the crowd had come not to support the radical firebrand John Wilkes but instead in support of Lord George Gordon and his Protestant Association. Once assembled, the plan was for an orderly march to Parliament, where Gordon and his supporters would present a petition for the repeal of the Catholic Relief Act. Passed two years earlier in 1778, the Catholic Relief Act was designed to aid British military recruitment at a time of great need by removing the stipulation that soldiers take oaths to the crown, including a condemnation of the Catholic Church. With this require-ment suspended, it was hoped that British Catholics would enlist, helping buoy the numbers of a British army critically overstretched by the ever-expanding American War.

Since Pope Pius V had threatened Queen Elizabeth with the prospect of assassination in 1570, and Catholic plotters conspired to blow up Parliament in 1605, anti-Catholic paranoia had played a prominent role in the British imagi-nation, bringing with it periodic fears of Catholic conspiracies, and real legal restrictions on the economic and political lives of British Catholics. By 1780, this long tradition of anti-Catholic feeling had combined with a series of worrisome international developments to create a potent brew of anti-Catholicism. In February 1778, four months after the British disaster at Saratoga convinced the world that the rebellious American colonies might well win the war, France officially joined the fray on the American side. In June 1779 Spain, like France still smarting from the loss of territory in earlier imperial wars, and sensing a prime opportunity in Britain's moment of weakness, threw its hat into the ring and declared war on Britain.

Even before the entrance into the war of Britain's Catholic enemies, fears grew that the war would not remain confined to American shores forever. The entrance of France and Spain into the conflict, however, drew forth from the collective memory of Britain historic fears of invasion and armada. Despite Britain being an island fastness, its history was shot through with foreign invasions: the Romans in 55 and 43 BC; the Angles and Saxons in sixth and seventh centuries; the Viking scourge in the eighth century; the Normans in 1066. Even the Glorious Revolution of 1688, the foundational moment for Patriots on both sides of the Atlantic, was in many ways a foreign invasion. More recently, France and Spain had been at the center of Britain's nightmares of invasion. The Spanish had tried their hand at invasion before in 1588, only to have their infamous armada blown away by a fortuitous Protestant wind. The French had repeatedly allied with the Scots (the so-called "auld alliance") against the English, supporting the Jacobite rebellions of 1715 and 1745, and had even plotted an amphibious assault on Britain in 1759 during the Seven Years' War.

With such grim historical precedents lodged firmly in their minds, it is little wonder that the British greeted the entrance of France and Spain into the war with alarm at the prospect of a new invasion. The effects were felt almost immediately. In April 1778, the daring raids of the American privateer John Paul Jones commenced with an assault on Whitehaven on the north-west coast of England, sending shockwaves through a still-complacent British public. While at the opera in May 1778, Lord North received a desperate message reporting that the French had landed in Sussex and that the inhabitants had refused to join the militia billeted to oppose the landing. It was a false alarm—the French were merely sailing down the Channel in search of the British fleet—but the panic did not subside. The movements of the French fleet were closely watched by the British public for signs of a pending invasion. In July 1778, notices describing the activities of the French fleet posted at Lloyd's Coffee House in London (the precursor to the insurance giant Lloyd's of London) caused stocks to fall as fears of invasion mounted. So great was the terror of France "laying waste and burning houses on our long line of defence-less coasts" that some, like Mr. Coke, a Member of Parliament for Norfolk who possessed land on the vulnerable coasts, demanded that Parliament disavow General Henry Clinton's "Manifesto and Proclamation to the Members of Congress." In a last desperate attempt to negotiate peace, in May 1778 Clinton had offered an amnesty to any and all American rebels willing to come to terms with Britain. In offering the amnesty, however, Clinton had also warned that the colonies' recent alliance with France had changed the nature of the war. By "mortgaging her self and her resources to our enemies," he declared, the Americans could expect no mercy if they continued a war that now seemed designed to ruin Britain and benefit France. For men like Mr. Coke, terrified at the prospect of French invasion, Clinton's proclamation was dangerously provocative.[1] The administration attempted to assuage such concerns by claiming that the English had "resisted Danish invasion, Norman usurpation, and Scottish inroads," and that the people of England were more than up to the task of opposing the French should they indeed arrive on English soil. "Even the ladies would cast away their feathers, and show how they despised Frenchmen," Lord Shelburne claimed to the derision of many.[2]

English concerns quickly proved to be more than justified. Shortly after Spain's declaration of war, plans were developed for a joint Franco-Spanish invasion of Britain. The poor performance of the British fleet at the Battle of Ushant in 1778 had convinced the French of the weakness of Britain's hold on the English Channel. With Britain's fleet stretched thin across the Atlantic, the time seemed ripe for an attack on vulnerable British shores. In July 1779, a French fleet of thirty ships under Admiral d'Orvillers and a Spanish fleet of thirty-six ships under Don Luis de Córdova began to assemble near the Sisarga Islands off the north-west coast of Spain. At the same time, an invasion force of 40,000 troops and 400 transport ships began to gather on the Breton coast. The plan was for the combined fleet to decimate the British Channel fleet, esti-mated at only forty ships, allowing the transports to land the invasion force on the Isle of Wight to establish a beachhead before moving on to the capture of the vital naval base at Portsmouth.

Though already weakened by disease and delayed by unfavorable winds, the armada began to lurch into action at the end of July 1779. A diversionary squadron of French ships bearing American colors and led by the already notorious John Paul Jones was sent toward Ireland, long feared to be Britain's vulnerable underbelly. By August 14 coastal Britons began to spot the armada, spreading alarm throughout the country. Once more, however, the winds seemed to be on Britain's side. On July 18 a gale swept the Franco-Spanish fleet out of the Channel and into the Atlantic. The setback allowed the British fleet time to slip past the armada and into Portsmouth, strengthening its defenses. In the Franco-Spanish fleet, disagreements and confusion over the designated landing point, combined with still-rampant disease, the lateness of the season, and the newly entrenched British fleet convinced the leadership to abandon the invasion and disperse.

For France and Spain the aborted armada was a disaster they could ill afford. It was ruinously expensive and diverted resources from other theaters of the war, compromising France's drive against Britain in the West and East Indies and undermining Spain's preeminent war aim, the recovery of Gibraltar. For the British, despite yet another miraculous meteorological deliverance, what had been a distant conflict now seemed to many to have arrived with all its horrors on their own shores. The mood of the time is viscerally captured by Ignatius Sancho. In August 1779, with the Franco-Spanish fleet sailing menacingly toward Britain, he recorded:

> I awake to fears of invasion, to noise, faction, drums, soldiers, and care: the whole town has now but two employments, the learning of French, and the exercise of arms . . . What's to become of us? We are ruined and sold, is the exclamation of every mouth, the monied man trembles for his funds, the landowner for his acres, the married men for their families, old maids and old fusty bachelors for themselves.

At this crucial juncture, when Catholic powers threatened to invade Britain itself, it is hardly surprising that many agreed wholeheartedly with the bigoted sentiment of *An Appeal from the Protestant Association to the People of Great Britain*, that "Popery has long been chained in Britain: the consequences of unchaining it will be dreadful to posterity . . . to tolerate Popery, is to encourage what by Toleration itself we mean to destroy, a spirit of persecution and bigotry of the most notorious kind."[3]

With the prospect of Catholic invasion plaguing the minds of Britons there was thus every reason to fear that this gathering in St. George's Field might well turn violent. As one witness caustically quipped, "What! Summon 40,000 fanatics to meet together, and expect them to be orderly! What is it but to invite hungry wretches to a banquet, and at the same time to enjoin them not to eat?" The country, and London in particular, had long been divided over the American War. When the war began in 1775, perhaps one in three members of the voting public opposed the government's bellicose American policy, and though support for America decreased as the war dragged on and France, Spain, and the Netherlands entered the fray, dissatisfaction with the government's management of the war only increased. London itself was a hotbed of pro-American, anti-government opposition. In this divisive and divided context, violence had already broken out at several junctures.[4]

If the violent disturbances and "desperate conspiracies" of the day had been confined to the distant shores of North America, residents of London might have slept easily enough, concerned but not afraid. As it transpired, however, one of the sparks that had helped to ignite the fire of independence in America was a British journalist, politician, and sometime mayor of London, John Wilkes. Instantly recognizable by his cross-eyed visage, rakish attire, and outrageous manners, Wilkes was in politics an opposition Whig, a vocal enemy of the ministries of George III, and a tireless advocate for greater popular representation in government.

What made Wilkes particularly worrisome for the ministry was that he had the support of the London mob. Riot had long been an accepted if oft-bemoaned tactic of British popular politics, with crowds using violence or its threat to voice its displeasure or show its support for a politician or political cause. Property and other symbols were generally the prime targets, and a favored tactic was to demand householders put lights in their windows in support of a particular person or cause. Those who refused to join would have their windows smashed in protest. Many a politician sought to harness the power of the mob for their own ends — election riots were common throughout the eighteenth century—but few with the sustained success of Wilkes. Wilkes intentionally and expertly cultivated the support of London crowds, seeing in them a wellspring of power. In 1763 a crowd chanting "Wilkes and Liberty" had attacked officials tasked with ceremonially burning his libelous issue no. 45 of *The North Briton*. In 1768, when Wilkes was elected as Member of Parliament for Middlesex, a celebratory riot targeted his political opponents. Cries of "Wilkes and Liberty" rang out once more when he was arrested and prevented from taking his seat in Parliament, ultimately leading to the mob's suppression by government troops that left at least six people dead in what would come to be branded the St. George's Field Massacre.[5]

By 1776 the "Wilkes and Liberty Riots" had largely tailed off. The threat of the mob, however, very much remained. Wilkes was no mere rabble-rouser. His radical Whig politics and his advocacy for American liberties made him a hugely popular and influential figure in Britain and America. Many Americans viewed his battles with the government of George III as evidence of the fundamentally corrupt nature of British politics and the need for greater rights of representation. The chant of "Wilkes and Liberty" echoed on both sides of the Atlantic in the years leading up to revolution, and many public demonstrations of fellow feeling were made. In 1768, as a gesture of support, Maryland voted to send a symbolic forty-five hogsheads of tobacco to the embattled Wilkes in celebration of issue no. 45. The Sons of Liberty of Boston sent a letter signed by luminaries such as Samuel Adams, John Hancock, Josiah Quincy, and John Adams that encapsulated American opinions of Wilkes in these years. "May you convince Great Britain and Ireland in Europe, the British Colonies, islands and plantations in America," the letter began, "that you are one of those incorruptibly honest men reserved by heaven to bless and perhaps save a tottering Empire." A few years later, at a celebratory dinner Connecticut militia officers drank a toast to "the Lord Mayor [Wilkes] and the worthy citizens of London." In the eyes of the government, such a toast may well have been to "Wilkes and his Mob."[6]

In June 1776, with America on the point of declaring its independence, Ignatius Sancho reported that all of London was abuzz with talk of Wilkes. But

Wilkes was not the only influential figure to speak out against Britain's policy in America. In 1776, the nonconformist philosopher Richard Price's pamphlet lambasting the government's American policy, and especially the Declaratory Act that stipulated Parliament's right to legislate for the colonies, sold tens of thousands of copies and garnered him the friendship of Benjamin Franklin, the freedom of the City of London, and an offer to advise America on its financial structure. In 1777, John Horne Tooke, another member of England's radical opposition inspired by John Wilkes, was imprisoned for a year for his role in a public petition seeking donations for the families of Americans "murdered by the king's troops at Lexington and Concord." Both men won popular acclaim and the support of London crowds for their daring critiques of the administration. In the febrile, divisive atmosphere of the 1770s, the existence in England of vocal supporters of the American cause with real political power and backed by the threat of popular political violence was enough to put the government on high alert. America had many friends in England and none of them could be trusted.[7]

During the previous wars of the eighteenth century Britons had been comforted and unified by common political ideals, religious antagonisms, and commercial interest, but the American War, a civil war against fellow Protestants, British subjects no less, provided few of the usual inducements to loyalty. Instead of rallying around the ministry, the monarchy, and the empire as before, in 1775 Britons were deeply divided over the emerging conflict with the American colonies. From across Britain officially encouraged and loudly trumpeted statements of loyalty poured in from towns and corporate bodies that supported the war. At the same time, however, peace petitions proliferated calling for conciliation, appeasement, and peace.

Ignatius Sancho found himself equally ambivalent. On the one hand as a loyal British subject, indeed a property owner, he greeted the birth of Princess Sophia in November of 1777 with toasts to "the defeat of Washintub's army," "thirteen counties return[ed] to their allegiance," and the hope that "this cursed carnage of the human species may end, commerce revive, sweet social peace be extended throughout the globe and the British empire strongly knit in never-ending bands of sacred friendship and brotherly love!" On the other hand, he could also be moved to strike a less triumphant more admonitory note. "War in all its horrid arrangements," he wrote to a friend, is "the bitterest curse that can fall upon a people; and this American one, as one of the very worst, of worst things," was divine judgment brought upon Britain by its "stoneblind" rulers. Like many Britons, Sancho's business had been hit hard by the dislocations of the war, and while he was no friend of the American rebels, he was deeply frustrated by his own government's conduct of the war. "How can you expect business in these hard times?" he complained. Trade could only flourish and prosperity return if both sides regained their senses, when "things shall take a better turn in America, when the conviction of their madness shall make them court peace, and the same conviction of our cruelty and injustice induce use to settle all points in equity." For many Britons there was plenty of blame to go around.[8]

The Declaration of Independence—viewed by many Britons as secession rather than national self-determination, a violent sundering of the familiar British world—the defeat at Saratoga in 1777, and the entry of Catholic France into the war in 1778 began to shift public perception. As losses mounted and enemies multiplied the war began to seem more hopeless, the British more isolated, but in that hopeless isolation, and the fears it engendered, were the seeds of British unity. As recently as April 1777, the well-connected Whig Horace Walpole, son of Britain's first prime minister and sharp critic of the present one, had written to his friend Horace Mann of the "inveteracy" and "unnatural enmity" that had been "sown" between Britain and her American brethren by a government that "have preferred the empty name of sovereignty to that of alliance, and forced subsidies to the golden ocean of commerce!" The declaration of war with France, however, blunted even Walpole's waspish wit and transformed him into a reluctant champion of his country. "War proclaim!" he informed William Mason in July 1778, "and I am near sixty-one. Shall I ever live to see peace again? and what peace!" "I condem my countrymen," he continued, "but I cannot, would not divest myself of my love to my country . . . I cannot blame the French whom we have tempted to ruin us: yet to be ruined by France!—there the Englishman in me feels again . . . I wish for nothing but victory and then peace." "Two years ago I meditated leaving England if it was enslaved." Walpole concluded, "I have no such thought now. I will steal into its bosom whem my hour comes, and love it to the last."[9]

Ignatius Sancho might likewise dejectedly write of "a detestable Brothers war, where the right hand is hacking and hewing the left, whilst Angels weep at our madness and the Devils rejoice at the ruinous prospect," of newspaper coverage full of "mistakes, blood, taxes, misery, murder, the obstinacy of a few and the madness and villainy of a many," but he also publicly called for British landowners to donate their plate to help fund the war against France. In such times, the proximity and omnipresence of threats to Britain itself convinced many that whatever the merits of the war, or the failings of the ministry, the world had become too dangerous to tolerate open dissent and division. Henceforth, radical opponents of the American War came to be seen not just as critics of British imperial policy, but as traitors. Proof of their potential treachery was not long in coming.[10]

In 1775, before America had even declared its independence, Stephen Sayre, an American merchant, adventurer, and friend of Wilkes, was accused of plotting to kidnap King George III. Most observers on both sides of the Atlantic agreed the plot was absurd, and many took Sayre's arrest as evidence of British tyranny, but the authorities took the accusation seriously and many in the public began to worry about the implications of the American troubles for Britain. However, as shocking and daring as they seem in retrospect, the tactics allegedly proposed by Sayre and his fellow conspirators were, if anything, highly traditional. Seizing the body of the monarch as a means of forcing political change was a common enough ploy throughout English history. Even the assassination of political figures was not unexpected. The tensions of imperial civil war, however, led to the rise of a wholly new form of violent political action, a form of action that would come to shape international conflict in the modern world. One man chose as his target not the heart of government, but the birthing ground of the British war machine, harnessing the primordial power of fire to undermine the war effort and terrorize the nation.[11]

As the war in America intensified waves of loyalists and other refugees arrived in Britain fleeing the violence and chaos of the colonies. Among the floodtide of men, women, and children pouring into British ports, few had anything on their minds other than escape and survival. Some, however, dove into the tumultuous world of political advocacy and intrigue. Others sought to help the war effort in other small ways, printing propaganda, raising funds, and passing on information. Few among them, however, arrived on British shores with plans as radical as John Aitken. Aitken was a Scotsman by birth, born to a blacksmith in Edinburgh in 1752, the eighth of twelve children. Although he received a decent education at George Heriot's Hospital, his apprenticeship to a painter—the source of his later nom de guerre—did not stick and when his indenture was up he cycled through a series of menial occupations before deciding that crime was perhaps the profession best suited to his restless personality. In his memoir-cum-confession, Aitken admitted to a litany of criminal acts committed in the course of his wanderings throughout Britain, ranging from the mundane (shoplifting and burglary) to the daring and the reprehensible (highway robbery and rape).[12] While he remained at large, the would-be painter's proclivity for crime did not go unnoticed, and, worried that the authorities were closing in, Aitken signed indentures in exchange for passage to America, arriving in Virginia in 1773.

The long arm of the law was not the only thing that drove the young Scotsman to the New World, and in words that deftly capture his insouciant brand of restless romanticism, he later claimed to have been led to America by "curiosity," "as an adventurer, to seek his fortune."[13] The wanderlust and inability to stick to a calling that led Aitken from Edinburgh to London to Jamestown did not let up on the western shores of the Atlantic, and he quickly skipped out on his indenture and roamed the colonial countryside from Virginia to North Carolina, Pennsylvania, New York, New Jersey and Massachusetts. The newly arrived immigrant did not, perhaps unsurprisingly, pick up a profession in his ramblings, but as he traveled up and down the colonies he began to absorb the political teachings so prevalent in America in the 1770s. Aitken had always been a young man in search of something, a sense of purpose, a calling, a place in the world that would garner him notice and respect. Whatever he was looking for in his years of wandering, whatever drove him from his home in Scotland to the shores of the Chesapeake, he had found what he sought in the radical political message of the nascent independence movement.[14]

For a restless young journeyman with few prospects, the atmosphere of revolutionary America must have been intoxicating, full of possibility, stirring rhetoric, and bold action. Aitken was quickly entranced by what he heard and what he read. Aitken was almost certainly exposed to the works of Thomas Paine and other polemicists of the day, but of all the political tracts published in the 1770s, Aitken chose as his unlikely call to arms Richard Price's *Observations on the Nature of Civil Liberty, the Principles of Government and the Justice and Policy of the War with America*. Price, a Welsh Unitarian minister, was one of the most influential moral philosophers of the eighteenth century, admired by many on the political left and visited by a who's who of illustrious Patriots, including Benjamin Franklin, Thomas Jefferson, Thomas Paine, and John Adams. His *Observations* were widely read in both Britain and America, where his forceful defense of American self-determination in response to British intransigence was well received by those with radical republican sympathies. Price did not in any way encourage violence, but his justification of rebellion as self-defense clearly appealed to the aimless Aitken and helped cement the political positions he had acquired in America.[15]

Armed and inspired by the rhetoric of liberty and revolution, in March 1775 John Aitken joined the waves of refugees departing America for exile in Britain. But while he shared quarters, meals, and long, cramped hours with the refugees, the young Scotsman did not share their melancholy resignation at quitting the turbulent colonies for the metropole. Instead of feeling a mixture of defeat and relief, Aitken was alive with a heady and dangerous ambition, determined to strike a blow for American liberties, a blow that would cripple the British navy and bring him the notoriety he had long desired. As he later confessed, he had devised a plan to target British shipyards as soon as the troubles in America began, and he set out for England with the thought of burning down the ships of the Royal Navy "continually running in his mind," and committed to viewing and inspecting the dockyards and shipping of Britain to see how they might best be attacked.[16]

Aitken did not have to go far to begin his surveillance of British naval yards. Upon arriving in London in October 1775 he quickly enlisted in the 32nd regiment at Gravesend, which, with the newly recruited Scot in tow, marched off to Chatham the next day. Chatham was home to a royal dockyard stretching for more than a mile along the River Medway near the coast of Kent on the North Sea. A center of British shipbuilding since the sixteenth century, though superseded by Portsmouth and Plymouth in the eighteenth century, Chatham still remained a vital shipyard and a potent symbol of British naval power. It was also famous in English memories as the site of one of its greatest military humiliations, the burning of the English fleet by the Dutch admiral Michiel de Ruyter during the Second Anglo-Dutch War in 1667. This connection with previous military defeat and with the burning of ships may well have been the reason Aitken was originally drawn to Chatham upon his return from America.

The army, however, was not the place for a restless would-be terrorist, and Aitken deserted a short time after arriving in Chatham. Perhaps he had completed his inspection of the vulnerabilities of the Chatham naval yard, or perhaps the security at Chatham was too robust, but whatever the reason, Aitken shifted his attention to another vital naval station, Portsmouth, on the south coast. By 1776, Portsmouth had replaced Chatham at the heart of British naval power and thus perhaps a more appropriate target for one seeking to strike a blow against the British war machine. As at Chatham, Aitken surveyed the docks and shipyards and their associated buildings, taking note of security measures and contemplating the best way to start fires undetected.

Having completed his sketches of the various naval yards and plans for his incendiary attack, Aitken set out for France. He had planned to return to America, hoping to show his plans to the Continental Congress. In the end, however, the journey was too dangerous and too costly in a time of war, and thus Aitken turned his sights on the nearest representative of the fledgling American government, the congressional representative in Paris. After a harrowing journey in a small packet ship across the Channel, constantly in fear of discovery by the many soldiers and spies infesting the English coast, Aitken landed in France in mid-October 1776 and quickly made his way to the capital.

In Paris, Aitken made a beeline for the home of Silas Deane, the newly minted American ambassador to France. France had already become interested in America and its conflict with Britain when the fighting broke out in Massachusetts in 1775. In the eighteenth century America had come to represent a natural paradise free from the vices that riddled the old world, a land of simplicity, honesty, and liberty, a Rousseau-ian paradise, and a potent antidote to the vapid artificiality of a decaying France. In a culture already suffused with shared ideals of liberty and freedom, the American struggle for independence from European despotism was greeted in France with interest and sympathy. Paris buzzed with talk of America, and American pamphlets like Thomas Paine's *Common Sense* became bestsellers. The leading figures of the revolution became national heroes. Washington and Franklin in particular were enormously popular, model men, the flesh and blood personification of the ideals of the age: Washington, the stoic, modest citizen-soldier, a throwback to the virtues of the classical world, and Franklin the citizen philosopher, the embodiment of simple truths and homespun wisdom, the Enlightenment come to life. The cause and its heroes struck a chord in France, providing a stark contrast to the hedonism of the French court in a country increasingly disgusted by it.

That such a vibrant new nation should be locked in combat with France's perennial nemesis only made the whole affair more appealing. For, above all, to the French the American fight for independence represented a long-wished-for opportunity to restore the wealth, power, and prestige lost during the Seven Years' War. That war had seen Britain in the ascendant and France humbled and humiliated across the globe from North America to India. In its wake, the French empire lay nearly in ruins, with its East India Company barely able to make a profit, while British might and British trade expanded by leaps and bounds. For this national shame, France had to take vengeance, and Britain, "the modern Carthage" to France's Rome, brought low. Looking back at his own motivations for joining the war, the Comte de Ségur remembered that "we were tired of the longueur of peace that had lasted tens [of] years, and each of us burned with a desire to repair the affronts of the last wars, to fight the English and to fly to repair the American cause."[17]

Preparations for a future war with Britain had begun almost before the guns had cooled in 1763. In the years after the war, France's powerful foreign minister, the Duc de Choiseul, began to rebuild the French navy, sure that naval power was the key to success against the British going forward. In 1768 he went so far as to send the German mercenary captain, Baron de Kalb, to America to weigh the prospects of an eventual American rebellion. Within France, others, like the Comte de Vergennes, were convinced that the removal of the French threat to Britain's American colonies after the Seven Years' War would eventually sow the seeds of civil war, giving the colonies the security needed to strike "off their chains." By 1776 Vergennes, now France's increasingly influential foreign minister, was sure that the conflict in North America presented France with a golden opportunity. In 1775, he sent Julien Alexandre Achard de Bonvouloir to America as a secret agent, tasked with making contact with influential American rebels and assessing the prospects of a colonial victory. In Philadelphia de Bonvouloir conferred with the renowned Benjamin Franklin about the possibility of a Franco-American alliance against their common enemy. No formal agreement was reached, but with sources everywhere alerting him to the potential offered by the emerging conflict, Vergennes urged Louis XVI to intervene in North America, arguing that at last, "providence had marked out this moment for the humiliation of England."[18]

Not everyone was as convinced as Vergennes. The queen, Marie-Antoinette, was said to oppose intervention, as did conservatives more generally, fearing that aiding a republican rebellion against a legitimate monarch, even a British one, set a dangerous precedent. Others, like the former finance minister Turgot, warned with remarkable foresight that the costs of another imperial war would be too much to bear. "The first gunshot," he predicted, "will drive the state to bankruptcy," beggaring France without necessarily weakening Britain. In America too, the prospect of a French alliance seemed difficult to stomach. Catholic France had long been the *bête noire* of the firmly Protestant colonies, a source of conflict and anxiety throughout the eighteenth century. The colonies desperately needed outside aid if they were to defeat the most powerful empire on earth, but the idea still rankled many.[19]

With such concerted opposition on both sides of the Atlantic, France moved slowly at first. From 1776, France, directed by the spiderlike Vergennes, negotiated a system of clandestine aid with Silas Deane, and later with his replacement Benjamin Franklin. America desperately needed supplies, arms, and expertise from France. This represented a considerable French investment in a cause with uncertain prospects for success, but Deane was able to offer one thing that the French greatly coveted: access to American markets previously closed to them by Britain's Navigation Acts. If victorious, Deane suggested, a "great part of our commerce will naturally fall to the share of France." Sure that replacing the British as the prime beneficiary of the ever-expanding American market would more than make up for the costs incurred by aiding the colonies, neatly negating Turgot's grim prediction, in July 1776 Vergennes agreed to funnel much-needed money and supplies to the rebels through a company set up by the playwright Pierre Beaumarchais.[20]

It was not just French guns, clothing, and money that secretly flowed across the Atlantic after 1776. The romantic fight for liberty had captured the imagination of many young men, and the prospects of glory, position, and reward led a host of Europeans to offer their services to the United States even as their own countries remained officially neutral. Led by the Comte de Broglie and the Bavarian soldier of fortune Johannes de Kalb, Silas Deane was soon swamped by French and German officers jockeying for positions in the American army. "Had I ten ships here," Deane informed Congress, "I could fill them all with passengers for America." So great did the press of officers become that Deane noted that he felt "nigh harassed to death" by offers to join the Continental Army. Overwhelmed by applications he might well have been, but Deane had enough foresight to see that European officers would provide badly needed expertise and legitimacy to the American war effort. And so he did not hesitate to grant lofty commissions to scores of French officers.[21]

Silas Deane's role in securing foreign mercenaries to fight in America was an open secret, so it is no surprise that Aitken, intent on becoming an American mercenary as well, would seek him out. Although Deane's lodgings at the Hotel d'Antraigues were regularly swarming with foreign fortune-hunters seeking to gain a commission in the American army (in the course of his time in Paris Deane would recruit such luminaries as the Marquis de Lafayette, Thomas Conway, Casimir Pulaski, and Baron von Steuben to the American cause), Aitken eventually managed to secure two meetings with the American agent. At the first meeting Aitken, who Deane thought had the "sparkling and wild" eyes of a "zealot or a madman," claimed that "though I may appear to your honor a very weak and insignificant creature, yet if you will give me another audience I will show you from the intelligence I can give you that I can strike a blow, ay, such a blow as will need no repetition." He would give no firm details other than that he had visited all the "principal ports" of England. At the second meeting, Aitken laid out his plan to set fire to the naval yards and shipping at Portsmouth, Plymouth and Bristol. Although he had a detailed plan of attack, Deane was skeptical, sure that Aitken would be caught immediately. Ever bold, Aitken claimed he had devised an incendiary device, a sort of lighter that would allow him enough time to escape a naval yard before the blaze was noticed. In a move that finally clinched Deane's support, Aitken even showed reluctant ambassador blueprints of the device, a device that was small enough to be easily concealed, but would, in the words of one historian, "smolder for hours before bursting into flames." With Deane's consent, a small sum of money and the promise of a future reward if successful, Aitken returned to England, determined to finally set his plan in motion.[22]

Back in England in November 1776, Aitken chose his first target, the naval docks of Portsmouth. Aitken had devised a simple but ingenious plan. First, he had an apprentice brazier make several of the incendiary devices he had described to Deane in Paris—approaching a master brazier might have aroused suspicions as to the purpose of the device. Second, he placed the devices in a hemp-drying house and a rope-making house in the dockyard and lit a third fire in his lodging house. The lodging house fire was intended to serve as a diversion. Aitken hoped that lighting this fire first, while the devices in the hemp house and rope house were still smoldering, would draw the fire-fighting services away from the dockyard. If all worked as planned, by the time the fires in the dockyard were noticed, it would be too late to move the fire-fighting equipment quickly enough to battle the flames effectively. The plan worked to some degree (though the hemp and rope house fires failed to spread to the ships as he had hoped), and with the fires glowing in the distance, Aitken fled in haste to London, hurried on by the certain belief that the authorities were in hot pursuit.[23]

Even in the buzzing hive of London with its throngs and multitudes, Aitken was sure he was only one step ahead of the law. He needed a place of refuge. In Paris, Silas Deane had given the ambitious arsonist the name of an American contact in Westminster, and, hoping to receive the promised aid from a fellow Patriot, Aitken made a beeline for the house of Edward Bancroft. Little did he know, as few did, Edward Bancroft was in fact a double agent. Bancroft had been born in Massachusetts and raised in Connecticut, where he was educated by Silas Deane before embarking on a career as a plantation doctor in Dutch Guiana. While in South America, Bancroft's moonlighting as a naturalist—he wrote an influential early account of the electric eel—brought him to the attention of Benjamin Franklin. Bancroft had relocated to London in 1769 and since

1776 had, at Franklin and Deane's behest, agreed to act as a spy for the Americans. What Deane did not know was that Bancroft was in fact supplying information to the British authorities, relaying accounts of Deane's activities in Paris and even helping to scupper American attempts to buy ships from Europe.[24]

For Bancroft, the arrival at his door of an agent in service to America was a highly dangerous and vexing turn of events. He could not very well hide a wanted man in his own home without drawing the suspicions of his British contacts. Nor could he completely ignore a man sent by the American representative in Paris without potentially alerting his supposed allies to his double-dealing. At first, Bancroft refused to hide Aitken, but when the Scot cryptically replied that he "would soon see or hear, by the papers, of an extraordinary accident," Bancroft agreed to meet him again the following day. The arsonist and the double agent met for a second time at a coffee-house where Aitken pledged to the American that "he would do all the prejudice he could to this kingdom." Bancroft, who had turned to spying for the British because of his dislike of the independence movement, was not a sympathetic audience for the ravings of an unstable radical. He told Aitken that "he could not be of an opinion with him in that respect, for that he got his bread in that kingdom [Britain] and therefore would not be concerned with him." Fearing that Bancroft would give him up, Aitken begged him not to inform the authorities. Although Aitken did not know it, Bancroft was playing both sides and was thus in no position to expose him and merely sent the Scotsman on his way.[25]

With little assistance forthcoming in the capital, and much left to burn, Aitken left London, making his way through High Wycombe, Oxford, and Abingdon, funding his journey by means of a series of burglaries, break-ins, and petty thefts, before turning south-west toward Plymouth and another of the great naval dockyards. In Plymouth—and later at Woolwich—Aitken made several attempts on the shipyards, but security was too tight and he never got further than the top of the wall surrounding the station. His lack of success, combined with fears that he would not go unnoticed for long, drove Aitken from Plymouth to yet another vital port, Bristol, on the River Avon near its entrance into the Irish Sea. After yet another series of abortive attempts, Aitken succeeded in setting a dockside warehouse on fire, once more employing his home-made incendiary device. Bristol was heavily involved in trade with America and, in an ironic twist, some of the damaged property belonged to an American merchant.

The nation was now on edge. Fires had been set deliberately in multiple cities and rumors of an American conspiracy were spreading rapidly with each new fire immediately seen as part of the plot, whatever its true cause. With the country panicked and no leads forthcoming, the Admiralty turned to the venerable Sir John Fielding, England's foremost expert on criminal investigation and its most famous magistrate. He suggested a two-pronged strategy: the offer of a £1,000 reward for the anonymous incendiarist's capture and the printing of descriptions of the suspect in consecutive issues of a wide range of newspapers, including Fielding's *Hue and Cry*. For all its apparent simplicity, Fielding's plan worked and Aitken was quickly apprehended in Hampshire by a man whose shop Aitken had attempted to rob and another local who recognized his image from the newspapers.[26]

In a letter to the *Waterford Chronicle* in Ireland, one witness dolefully described the execution of John Aitken at Portsmouth on March 10, 1777: "This morning John the Painter brought here from Winchester, attended by the under-sheriff, and hung near the dock gates on a gibbet sixty-five feet high, amidst an amazing concourse of people." Before he reached the unusually tall gibbet—in fact the mizzenmast of a naval ship refitted for the purpose—and the waiting crowd of over 20,000 spectators, Aitken had been "conducted from the gaol in this town in a cart, through the Quat-gate to the common; after which they proceeded round the rope house where the fire happened, that he might himself be witness to the devastation he had occasioned." Most reports mentioned that he was calm, resolute, and even humorous on his way to the gallows—just as Guy Fawkes, England's great traitorous boogeyman, had been when facing execution after his attempt to blow up Parliament almost two hundred years earlier one paper suggested. As was customary, at the gallows he made a speech to the assembled crowd. Some reports had it that he admitted his guilt and the justness of his execution. Others suggested he was only sorry he had not been able to fulfill his plans—"I intended to give a stab in the side, but it has only been a slight scratch in the hand." One account even reported that he had disavowed the American cause, "wishing success to his majesty's arms, against a set of rascals and villainous rebels now in America." Whatever he said to the crowd, he faced his execution with dignity. Immediately after his death, his body was moved to another gibbet set up on the beach at the entrance to Portsmouth harbor, a message to all who entered of the fate of arsonists and traitors.[27]

The reaction in Britain to this new and terrible form of warfare was a mixture of shock, apprehension, and vitriolic condemnation. For many, the actions of John the Painter were the logical culmination of American revolutionary principles. The conflict had begun with bloody rhetoric, violence, riot, and rebellion, and such grisly words and deeds had led ineluctably to the terrorism of Portsmouth and Bristol. Since Aitken had admitted to reading and taking inspiration from Richard Price's *Observations on the Nature of Civil Liberty*, much spleen was vented in his direction. In a letter to the *Public Advertiser* one commentator castigated Price and others of his ilk for riling up the masses and stoking the fires of rebellion.

> I must not desist from laying before you and the People who you would seduce to Rebellion one declaratory Instance of the nefarious Consequences of your Tenants; an Instance avowedly founded on your Principles, and which *more* than threatened the most deplorable of all Calamities, a general conflagration. John the Painter, by Nature a *villain*, and by Religion a *Presbyterian*, was perfectly prepared to receive *your* Doctrines of Liberty . . . These Doctrines falling on his Head, like sparks of Fire on Gunpowder, gave full Explosion to his Iniquities, and inflamed his soul to prove that he was truly your disciple. Conscious that he was able to *act*, convinced the *Freedom* consisted of the Power of *self-determination* and *self-government*, he resolved to be free, and *stand* or *fall* by your Principles, and forthwith set fire to Portsmouth and to Bristol.[28]

For the author, as for many in Britain and America who opposed or feared the revolution, the problem was not that Price or Paine or other writers specifically encouraged violence. The problem was that such writings encouraged people, especially the common people who they thought had little understanding of political philosophy, to believe that they had the power, the freedom, or the liberty to act as they wished, to take matters into their own hands for their own ends. Such political principles presaged danger, the opening of a Pandora's box of mob rule and political chaos. Price may not have advocated arson, but by encouraging people to seize their liberties and freedoms and by advocating self-government, he might as well have put the torch in Aitken's hands. Such rhetoric was bound to set the mob ablaze.

While some castigated the American rebels and their British supporters, others found distinctly familiar sources of fear, pointing the finger at France. It was known that Aitken had traveled to France to receive his instructions, and several newspapers published details of his French passport, which had also been presented as evidence at his trial. Though the passport was perfectly normal, the insinuation was made by several papers that while France was officially neutral, secret aid was being given to the American cause by supporting and encouraging men such as John the Painter. Fears of French involvement in the war had been present from the earliest days, and such fears would only increase as the years progressed.[29]

Whether the ultimate source of anxiety lay in America, France, or Britain, all agreed that the actions of John the Painter set a worrying precedent. Newspapers all over Britain and Ireland nervously reported Aitken's boast that had he evaded capture, "the consequence must have been fatal to the kingdom." If any were foolish enough to breathe a sigh of relief at the arsonist's capture, however, they were quickly disabused of their feelings of security by Aitken's advice that the authorities should be "particularly cautious who was admitted into any of the Docks, as he had reason to think other attempts would be made." In reality, Aitken had no reason other than his own fevered imagination to believe other attacks were imminent, but his words of warning certainly had an effect on the mindset of Britons thereafter. As long as the radical, incendiary principles of the American rebels and British provocateurs like Richard Price and Thomas Paine were allowed to circulate, they argued, other arsonists would surely follow. "But what avails it," one vocal critic cried:

that one Villain has been executed, when the *Man* [Price] and his principles, by which the Villain was seduced and justified, are still in full Powers to spread their Corruptions through the world? Will not the same motives instigate other *Johns* and *other* villains to perpetrate the like detestable acts of Conflagration? . . . One savage beast is put to death, but the parental origin from which he sprung is still surviving to engender others equally destructive.

In British eyes, John the Painter was perhaps the first of many radical terrorists still to come.[30]

Despite the different historical context, the clothes, the language, and the characters, the career of John Aitken has all the hallmarks of a modern terrorist. As a youth he was restless and purposeless, having difficulty finding a place or a profession in his local world. This restiveness in turn led to an escalating criminal career, moving from petty crime to serious felonies. Like many twenty-first-century terrorists who travel abroad and return home radicalized, Aitken was radicalized overseas, latching on to a radical rhetoric in the excitement and chaos of a civil war. He then returned home bent on proving his commitment to his new cause by attacking some of the most visible symbols of British power, the navy. Although he believed his actions to be sanctioned and directed by leaders of his movement, like modern terrorists Aitken largely acted on his own initiative with little central direction or even approval from the leaders of the movement of which he felt part. Finally, although he acted in the name of a specific cause, Aitken's actions were also, in large measure, an attempt by a purposeless young man to gain the notice and respect of the world that had long ignored him.[31]

While Aitken's attacks on the dockyards of Portsmouth and Bristol had a negligible practical effect on the British war effort, they did have a psychological impact familiar in cases of modern terrorism. Fears of similar attacks were rampant in the wake of Aitken's capture. The outrage and shock was palpable, as was the fear that once such an act was publicly known, imitators would not be far behind. "Firing of Dock-yards is such a Crime so uncommonly atrocious and so much of a public Calamity and which every Power in Europe may be object of," one newspaper cried, "if once the Success of it be tried" the perpetrators should be treated as "offenders against the Law of Honour and the Law of Nations." By 1777 steps were being taken to prevent what seemed like the inevitable future attempts at deliberate arson in the name of rebellion.

Edmund Burke, no enemy of the American cause, proposed a bill in Parliament to "secure the nation's ports, docks, dockyards and shipping from fire" and to institute more severe punishment upon those who might "attempt to set the same on fire." Though the war would continue much the same as before, the home front would never be the same again. Terrorism had made its first mark on British soil.[32]

At the same time that Aitken was burning his way through Britain's dockyards, British authorities began to crack down on sedition throughout the empire. In 1776 Ebenezer Platt, a 24-year-old Patriot from Georgia, was arrested at Savannah and charged with diverting a shipment of arms and ammunition intended for pro-British forces to the Continental Army. Charged with treason, Platt was transferred to Jamaica for trial only to be acquitted. Instead of releasing Platt after his acquittal, the authorities sent him to England still in chains. In England supporters of Platt—who would come to include such luminaries as Benjamin West, Benjamin Franklin, and William Jones—managed to secure a writ of habeas corpus, legally requiring the government to either try Platt or release him.

Platt presented a dilemma for the British authorities. Under normal circumstances, no one could be tried in Britain for an offense committed in another dominion, nor could anyone be tried a second time on charges of which he had already been acquitted. But these were not normal circumstances. In the context of the American War, setting Platt free would set a dangerous precedent. If the government released Platt and admitted that he could not be held indefinitely without trial, they could not continue to hold the hundreds of captured American sailors imprisoned in British hulks. Rather than hold these sailors as prisoners of war, which would tacitly confirm the colonies' claims of independence, the American captives were held as criminals—traitors and pirates—who thus should have been eligible for habeas corpus. So instead of either trying or freeing Platt, in February of 1777, Lord North introduced a bill to suspend habeas corpus. Suspending habeas corpus would allow the American prisoners to be held indefinitely without trial while not admitting their status as prisoners in a war between independent sovereign powers.[33]

In its original context, the 1777 suspension act was targeted at suspected traitors and rebels in North America or on the high seas rather than those in Britain, but even this narrow suspension of habeas corpus raised the hackles of Britons already alarmed by growing ministerial power. The opposition Whig leader Charles James Fox, eloquent to a fault, charged that the act "strides not only to destroy the liberty of America, but this country likewise." John Wilkes feared the suspension would "arm the ministers with an unconstitutional power," while Granville Sharp, reformer, evangelical, and future abolitionist, thought the act proof of "the haughty omnipotence of Parliament, the Pope of England!" As ever, the cries of the reformers went unheeded, but they were right to worry. The 1776 Habeas Corpus Act ushered in a number of consequential innovations. Habeas corpus had been suspended before in times of acute crisis, but only for a limited period (usually no more than five months) specifically stipulated in the legislation. After 1777, suspensions could be and were extended indefinitely. Indeed, as the American crisis deepened and new threats appeared closer to home, the suspension of habeas corpus, "the Great Writ of Liberty," would be renewed again and again until 1783. Platt's case had been a rallying point for opposition to the government and its heavy-handed trampling of British liberties. But the reformers' ultimate failure to prevent the suspension of habeas corpus was a sign that the mood in Britain was shifting away from the radicals and toward a more conservative outlook that welcomed authoritarian measures in the name of national defense and public safety.[34]

In the years after Aitken's execution and Platt's sedition, troubling disturbances continued to rock Britain, pushing more and more moderates toward the support of authoritarian measures. In 1779, further riots broke out in London after the acquittal of Admiral Keppel at a court-martial for treason. An opposition Whig and opponent of the war with America, Keppel was a vocal critic of Britain's naval deficiencies and only agreed to undertake active service in the navy with the entrance of France into the war in 1778. He quickly saw action at the Battle of Ushant off the coast of France in 1778. The battle was inconclusive but perceived to be a British failure by many, leading to back-biting, recrimination, and accusations of treason between Keppel and his second-in-command Sir Hugh Palliser. Keppel believed that as he was an opponent of the current government, Lord Sandwich, the first Lord of the Admiralty, and Palliser, a member of the Admiralty Board, wished to see him fail and were actively conspiring to undermine his command. When Keppel was brought before a court-martial and accused of treason, many in London viewed the affair as a politically motivated prosecution designed to attack a member of the opposition. The trial thus became a patriotic *cause célèbre*, and Keppel's eventual acquittal was greeted with riots targeting Lord Sandwich and members of the government.

When the news of the acquittal broke on February 11, 1779, Palliser fled Portsmouth at five in the morning to take refuge in the Admiralty. In London, windows were illuminated in a time-honored show of support, guns were fired, and firecrackers set off. A house in Pall Mall formerly belonging to Palliser was looted and its windows smashed, as were the windows of Lord Mulgrave, Captain Hood, Lord Germaine, and Lord Lilburne. A panicked Lord Sandwich was forced to escape through his garden, "exceedingly terrified," with his mistress. On February 20, a reluctant Admiral Keppel was granted the freedom of the City of London, his carriage pulled through the streets to a dinner in his honor at a London tavern. Windows were once more illuminated in Keppel's honor and those who failed to show their support had their windows smashed, including members of the opposition such as Charles James Fox. Three rioters were arrested, but so great were the fears of further disorder that none were actually convicted.[35]

Scotland was beset by turmoil and tumult as well. Many in Scotland had opposed the war with America based on commercial interests, especially the great tobacco merchants of Glasgow who relied on American supplies of the commodity. By the 1760s, Scotland had a stranglehold on the American tobacco trade, controlling as much as 98 per cent of American exports and importing as many as 47 million pounds per annum, one-third of total Scottish imports. With such deep commercial ties, Scotland and America were closely bound, and these ties only increased with significant Scottish immigration to America in the eighteenth century. With these immigrants came the ideas of the Scottish Enlightenment, the ideas of David Hume, Adam Smith, Lord Kames, and William Robertson. The work of these Scottish thinkers was transmitted by influential Scottish immigrants such as John Witherspoon, President of the College of New Jersey, and William Smith of the College of Philadelphia, and in turn provided much of the intellectual framework for the colonies' fight for independence.[36]

In September 1778, a Scottish regiment mutinied in Edinburgh after rumors spread that they were to be sent to the developing theater of war in India. The riots saw "400 banditti keep 50,000 people in awe and alarm" and convinced many that it was impossible to conduct a war on so many fronts and keep the home front safe and secure. But the real trouble came in 1779 when major riots broke out in Edinburgh and Glasgow in response to an attempt to push the Catholic Relief Act upon the Scots. In January, opposition to the extension of the Relief Act began to gather steam among Scottish Presbyterians, with the Scottish Kirk coming out publicly against the bill at the end of the month. Instigated by the Church, mobs rose in Glasgow and Edinburgh. In Edinburgh, rioters destroyed two Catholic "mass-houses" and accosted two Catholic lords. The university was also attacked, as the historian and principal of the university, Dr. Robertson, was regarded as one of the most vocal proponents of Catholic Relief. The riot was only quelled when the bill was withdrawn and Lord Weymouth, one of Scotland's secretaries of state, agreed to pen a letter to the Scottish clergy promising that the administration had no plans to relax restrictions against Catholics in Scotland. Pushed through in an attempt to appease Irish Catholics and secure Catholic troops, after France's entry into the war in 1778, Catholic Relief became an object of fear for many in Britain.[37]

Lord Gordon had led the Scottish opposition to the act, and his success in defeating it in north of the Tweed gave him supreme confidence that he could defeat the act in England as well. He knew that his Protestant Association had backers in London, not only among the tradesmen and working class, but also among the City government itself. The City Corporation was, for both political and economic reasons, largely opposed to the American War, and could be expected to resist the drastic measures undertaken by the government to re-stock the army by relaxing restrictions on Catholics. And so just before noon on June 2, 1780, Gordon and the Protestant Association began to march from St. George's Field to Parliament, flags flying, banners shimmering in the summer heat, sure that they would succeed in repealing the hated act and save Britain from Catholic traitors and French invaders.

Despite the reasonable fears of many observers, the crowd that gathered that day was hardly a disorderly rabble. It was reported that the initial crowd largely consisted of honest, respectable tradesmen, dressed for the occasion in their

Sunday best and topped with blue cockades, a symbol of anti-government solidarity. One of the four columns of marchers was even led by a Scottish Highlander in full tartan, a broadsword clasped in his hand and accompanied on either side by pipers. It all had the feel of a parade, a triumphant march to present the grievances of the people to their elected representatives. When they reached Parliament however, the mood of the assemblage quickly turned angry.[38]

As the crowd milled in Parliament Square, Members of Parliament began to arrive. Members of the opposition, opponents of the American War, and critics of Catholic Relief were cheered and escorted into the building, while members of the government and supporters of Catholic Relief were jeered and jostled, their coaches attacked, windows smashed, and their wigs torn from their heads. Inside Parliament the situation was no less fraught. As the politicians attempted to conduct business, the crowd broke into the lobby and began shouting at the MPs. Lord Gordon charged onto the debating floor to deposit the massive petition, signed by some 44,000 citizens, before climbing into the gallery to address the protesters. As one observer complained, the crowd was attempting to use intimidation to "exercise the most arbitrary and dictatorial power over both Lords and Commons." The House of Commons, somehow, held its nerve and voted nearly unanimously to adjourn debate on the Relief Act until the following Tuesday.[39]

News of the petition's initial failure was greeted with disbelieving anger by the crowd assembled outside. But anger had not yet been transformed into action, and when troops were called in to clear the squares and streets around Parliament, they were allowed to perform their task with minimal interference and no violence. It seemed that the worst was over, the threat had passed. As night fell, however, some among the petitioners, still stinging from their defeat and incredulous that their representatives were not taking seriously the Catholic threat, began to target prominent Catholic homes and establishments throughout the city. The Catholic chapel of the Sardinian embassy in Lincoln's Inn Fields was the first to feel the rage of the mob. Rioters forced their way inside, set the building alight and made a bonfire of its contents in the street. The chapel of the Bavarian ambassador was next, its possessions looted and burnt. For the next three days, rioters continued to attack Catholic properties, suspected Catholic sympathizers, and supporters of the Catholic Relief Act. Areas of high Irish settlement around Moorfields were particularly targeted for violence.

A Catholic silk merchant whose house was ransacked even saw his prized pet canaries, "Popish birds" in the minds of the mob, added to the flames.

The scale of the riots was unprecedented in English history, and yet the London authorities, sympathetic to many of the rioters' aims and fearful of becoming targets themselves, refused to act. In desperation, many in London donned blue cockades and chalked "no Popery" on their homes and carriages in the hopes of placating the crowds. "We were in hourly expectations of receiving a Visit from the Rioters as they threatened one to our opposite Neighbour L[ord] Stormount," Elizabeth Lee wrote to her son:

> [B]ut I thank God they were prevented putting their wicked intentions into execution by having a strong Guard close to the House so they did not attempt entering the street however it was impossible not to feel very anxious . . . We passed the Day and night at L[ady] Mar[garet's] in Cavendish Square . . . I did not spend a very comfortable night as you may imagine, for with so desperate a Mob who had been guilty of such atrocious crimes in destroying so many people's property by Fire and letting loose so many Fellons from Prison it was impossible at such a time not to feel very unhappy for one's fellow Creatures and also to dread the worst.[40]

Horrified at how far things had gone, Lord Gordon and the Protestant Association condemned the violence, but to no effect. For four days, as war raged across the globe, the mob reigned in the capital of the British Empire.

On Tuesday June 6 there was hope on all sides that the violence and chaos were at an end. But when Parliament met as scheduled to debate the petition for the repeal of the Catholic Relief Act, they refused to be moved by the baying of the mob, once more refusing to debate the issue. London exploded. Crowds "with lighted firebrands in their hands, like so many furies" renewed their attacks on Catholic properties. A Catholic-owned distillery was consumed in flames, causing a scene seemingly straight from hell. Rivers of fire, gallons of burning gin ran down the streets, and thirsty men scorched to death consuming the fiery spirits. The conflagration raged so furiously bright that it lit up the night sky. The eighteenth century was a darker world than our own, with nights as yet unspoiled by the perma-glow of modern electric lights. A city on fire in such shadow-shrouded times must have seemed to have set the night aflame, bathing the world for miles around in a primordial, malevolent light. William Lee, studying at Harrow while his parents remained besieged in the city, could see the eerie glow of the fires 12 miles away.[41]

By Wednesday, June 7—"Black Wednesday" as it was later called—the riots had reached their apex as the target of the mob's rage began to widen. From Catholic establishments, the crowd now began to target symbols of justice and authority. London's hated prisons were smashed and burnt, forced collections made for the support of freed inmates, and the homes of London's justices ransacked. "In the midst of the most cruel and ridiculous confusion, I am now set down to give you a very imperfect sketch of the maddest people, that the maddest times were ever plagued with," Ignatius Sancho wrote a friend:

There is at this present moment at least a hundred thousand poor, miserable, ragged rabbled . . . all parading the streets, the bridge, the park, ready for any and every mischief. Gracious God! What's the matter now? I was obliged to leave off, shouts of the mob, the horrid clashing of swords, and the clutter of a multitude in swiftest motion drew me to the door . . . This, this is liberty! genuine British liberty! This instant about two thousand liberty boys are swearing and swaggering by with large sticks, thus armed in hopes of meeting with the Irish chairmen and labourers . . . Thank heaven, it rains; may it increase so as to send these deluded wretches safe to their homes, their families, and wives![42]

Symbols of the abuses of the war effort came under attack as well. Crimping Houses, the jails designed to hold sailors captured and impressed into service on Britain's naval fleet, were smashed open. The property of an army clothier was attacked. Among the prisoners sprung from Newgate were a Pennsylvania apprentice who had fled "the trouble in America," a deserter from the army, and a woman convicted of murdering a constable who had tried to press her husband. Given that many of the most active rioters were sailors themselves, these targets are hardly surprising, but the war had affected many of the poor in London, making anger at the war and its social and economic consequences an important part of the mob's mentality.[43]

The Bank of England was next in the rioters' sights, but these attacks on judicial and royal authority had now gone too far in the eyes of the state. If London's governors would not act, the crown would. On the night of June 7, the king ordered thousands of troops into his capital, effectively placing the city under martial law. In contravention of both tradition and legal precedent, the troops were ordered to fire on the rioters on sight, without first reading the Riot Act. At the Bank of England, two prominent supporters of radical London turned their backs on the crowds and joined the cause of repression. Lord Gordon attempted to quiet the mob, appealing for peace. When he was instead shouted down, he threw his support behind the forces of law and order. John Wilkes, a hero of the London mob and central figure among London radicals, had had enough as well, and in his role as a London magistrate joined the defense of the Bank of England. As such vital institutions came under attack, men like Wilkes were forced to pick a side. Wilkes' influence was as much based on the financial muscle and mercantile wealth of the City of London as it was on his popular appeal. As long as mob and merchant were united in their opposition to the American War and the ministry responsible for it, Wilkes and other radicals could please both sides. When the interests of the City and those of the mob diverged, however, choices had to be made. The Gordon Riots, and especially the attack on the Bank of England, both source and symbol of Britain's commercial fortunes, thus represented a watershed for British radicals. Political opposition was quickly becoming associated with chaos, and violence. Henceforth reformers and radicals would have to choose between opposition to the war and opposition to the dangerous disorder it created.[44]

From the night of June 7 until the evening of June 8 London witnessed a new form of indiscriminate violence as soldiers suppressed the riots and crushed and dispersed the mob. "Fired 6 or 7 times on the rioters at the end of the Bank," an entry in John Wilkes' diary reads, "Killed two rioters directly opposite to the great gate of the Bank; several others in Pig street and Cheap-side." As many as 700 men and women were killed over the course of the day: official estimates of 300 dead were much lower, but eyewitnesses like Nathaniel Wraxall testified that many of the deceased were cast into the Thames or burnt in the fires, artificially, and intentionally, depressing the casualty figures. These days of rage had been without equal in English history, and by June 8 the reign of King Mob was at an end, drowned in an effusion of blood.[45]

By June 9 Ignatius Sancho's melancholy tone began to give way to a faint glimmer of hope. "Happily for us, the tumult begins to subside," he wrote. "There is about fifty prisoners taken, and not a blue cockade to be seen: the streets once more wear the face of peace." With the riots suppressed, the mopping up had begun. Dozens, perhaps hundreds of arrests were made, creating a new issue given the lack of prisons to house them. Among the captured was Lord Gordon, arrested on the morning of June 9 and driven through the city in an old hackney coach to the Tower of London, escorted along the way by a regiment of militia and a troop of light horse. Wagers were made that he would be hanged within eight days.[46]

Though the riots appeared to be at an end, the authorities were not taking any chances. The violence had been on an unimaginable scale, and there was the sense that order still very much hung in the balance. That such "dreadful and shocking enormities" could have been committed "in the very heart of the metropolis" was an alarming, destabilizing proposition, and caused Britons to seek out explanations for what could have caused such frightful "scenes of desolation." There were rumors, some spread by figures connected with the administration itself, that a foreign hand, perhaps French or American agents it was whispered, had been behind the riots, part of a plot to destabilize, distract, and destroy the British war effort. Other tales spread that the opposition party had done the plotting and inciting. Lord Gordon, the driving force precipitating the riots, had himself long been a violent critic of the government and an ardent supporter of the American rebels. In 1776 Gordon had been one of the vocal minority who condemned "the folly and injustice of the Government in endeavouring to dragoon the Americans into unconditional surrender." That same year he urged a friend to rename a ship he owned in honor of the American Patriots, arguing, "I think in compliment to the worthy patriots of our injured colonies . . . you ought to call your cutter the *Congress*." Lord Gordon's status as a well-known radical and opponent of the war ensured that many interpreted the riots through a political lens of loyalty and disloyalty, with opposition increasingly viewed with suspicion. As far away as Russia, the British ambassador James Harris heard that "American treachery and English treason . . . are at the bottom of it."[47]

Others, already unnerved by the rising tide of crime in the capital, held London's criminals, and the indulgent justice system that had thus far failed to keep them in check, responsible. The coachman who showed William Hickey the charred ruins of the riots' aftermath claimed, like many, that initially the crowds had mostly consisted of women and children, hardly a threat, until the weak response of the over-lenient authorities encouraged London's criminal class—"pickpockets, house-breakers, and thieves of every description"—to join the fray. That common criminals might make common cause with foreign spies and domestic radicals was enough to shock most Britons into acceptance of a draconian reaction.[48]

London was transformed into an occupied city, with armed camps springing up in any spot of open ground, in Hyde Park, St. James's Park, St. George's Field, in the garden of the British Museum, and in the West End. William Hickey described the ominous new cast of a "city and suburbs . . . filled with the military," with "regular guards continuing to be mounted daily at the Bank, St. Paul's, the Old Bailey, and several other public buildings." On June 13, news spread that the specter of the mob had now arisen at York, where rioters released 3,000 French prisoners of war to rampage through the heart of England. The reports proved false, but the whole of England was mired in the "suspicious turbulence of the times." On June 16, the government began an effort to disarm the populace as the fear of foreign invasion transformed into terror of internal insurrection. For many, England was beginning "to exhibit the features of French Government," with martial law and the order to give up arms. But for others the nature of the riots proved that such authoritarian measures were a necessary evil. The combination of foreign war, internal unrest, and rampant criminality ensured that the swirl of rumors and conspiracy theories that followed in the tumult's wake pointed the blame at a potent mixture of foreign enemies, radical traitors, and wanton criminals, creating a new association between the three and coloring how political dissent and criminal justice were viewed. In such times, with such enemies, a strong hand was required. The summer "had brought with it sick times," Sancho lamented, sickness now "triumphed through every part of the constitution: the state is sick, the church (God preserve it!) is sick, the law, navy, army all sick, the people at large are sick with taxes, the Ministry with Opposition, and the Opposition with disappointment."[49]

For an unlucky few, the cure for the sickness was worse than the disease. In July, twenty-five men and women were executed at gallows across London for their role in the riots. Most were poor and many had connections to the conflict with America. Henry Maskall, a prominent radical and opponent of the government's American policy, was charged with inciting the attack on Lord Mansfield's house in Bloomsbury, though he was lucky enough, or connected enough, to escape the rope. William Brown, one of the many sailors who took an active part in the riots, had been on the *Serapis* when it clashed with John Paul Jones's *Bonhomme Richard* off Flamborough Head in Yorkshire in September 1779. It was a bloody affair with high casualties on both sides, but Brown's ship had been defeated, and he himself among the 500 prisoners Jones transported to France. He managed to make his way back to London, poor and still suffering from wounds received in the battle, just in time to take part in the riots that cost him his life. Three of the other victims of the hangman's noose were members of London's growing African community, former slaves who had escaped to London only to find that with their freedom came poverty. John Glover, a "quiet, sober, honest" servant in Westminster and Benjamin Bowsey, a well-dressed servant with a commanding presence, were condemned for taking leading roles in the attack on Newgate Prison and the keeper's house. Charlotte Gardiner was hanged for being the instigator of an assault on the home of an Irish publican near Tower Hill—she was heard to call for more for the fire and to cheer on the mob with shouts of, "Huzza, well done my boys—knock it down, down with it." The riots, in their causes, targets, leaders, and victims were shot through with American affairs.[50]

While the men and women he helped rile up swung from the gallows, Lord Gordon languished in the Tower charged with treason. In his defense, he pointed to the fact that he had tried to calm the mob when it turned violent and had joined the forces of law and order after the assault on the Bank of England. He claimed he would have turned against the mob sooner but had hoped that by remaining at its head he might prevent the rise of "some Wat Tyler [the infamous leader of the great Peasants' Revolt in 1381] who would not have the patience to commune with the Government, and might very possibly chuse to embroil the whole nation in civil war." Many, like the ever-perceptive Horace Walpole, thought Gordon a madman, but whether because they believed his excuses, feared his martyrdom, or valued his important family ties, Lord Gordon was acquitted in 1781.[51]

Ignatius Sancho did not live to see Lord Gordon tried or peace return. When he died in December 1780, London was still reeling from the Gordon Riots. As he lay on his deathbed, it must have seemed as if the whole world was crumbling around him, as if the collective madness of the age had doomed Britain's once promising future. He departed a world in the midst of crisis, his adopted home seemingly on the brink of ruin, and yet, despite a world turned upside down, Ignatius Sancho left his mark. Born in the middle of the Atlantic on a slave ship bearing him into a life of bondage, he died respected, beloved, and much mourned. He was one of the first public figures of African descent, one of the first former slaves whose name was widely known and whose life was widely celebrated. In a fitting tribute to his trailblazing influence, his obituary would mark the first time the British press had bestowed such an honor on a person of African descent.

On a sweltering July morning in 1781, almost a year exactly after the Gordon Riots had engulfed London, 80,000 British men, women, and children gathered in yet another collective exorcism of fear. The war with the American colonies was going from bad to worse. In the preceding years they had seen British radicals riot in the streets of London, shivered as a home-grown terrorist menaced Britain's shipyards, quaked at the very real prospect of a new armada, and watched in horror as London burnt before their eyes. Now, less than a year after the worst riots in English history, Britons received a new and chilling confirmation that the runaway paranoia of 1780 had not been entirely unwarranted. French agents could well be hiding around the next corner, listening and reporting, perhaps even preparing the way for that most awful prospect, invasion. With the specter of the French menace plaguing their dreams, tens of thousands of people streamed out of the city that summer day to see the execution of the man who had come to symbolize their terror.

As the teeming assembly looked on, a lone man tied fast in a cart was dragged through the streets of London from the court at the Old Bailey to the ancient place of execution at Tyburn. After braving the cheers and jeers of the London mob, lining the route on foot and in purpose-made stands, the man was drawn to the gallows, the notorious triple tree of Tyburn, and a noose placed around his neck. An opportunity was given for the condemned to fulfill his didactic role, to give his confession, make his peace with God and so die a good death; then with speeches finished, the cart was pulled away and the poor wretch left swinging by his neck. In ordinary executions this would have been the end of the matter, but this was no ordinary execution, and before the man succumbed, he was cut down. While still alive, the bowels of the man were cut from his body and burnt in front of his half-conscious eyes. It was a terrible end, but one thought fitting for a man who had come to symbolize the fears of a nation. This potent symbol of British paranoia and French duplicity was François Henri de la Motte, a French spy. As the prosecution had argued, "a more vigilant, a more industrious, or a more able spy, was never placed in any country. The intelligence he procured will astonish you."[52]

In the early months of 1780, in the port town of Folkstone on the Kent coast, Stephen Ratcliffe was approached by a man named Isaac Roger, who proposed a business arrangement between the Kentish captain and his own unnamed master. Ratcliffe owned and operated a cutter, one of many small sailing vessels that plied the waters of the English Channel and the coastal trade within Britain. Roger asked the captain if he would take regular shipments of papers from Kent to the French city of Boulogne, just across the Channel from Kent. Carrying packets and letters across the Channel or along the coast was common practice for ship-owners such as Ratcliffe, an easy way to add a little profit to the usual shipments of wine and brandy; besides, Roger was offering the large sum of £20 for every parcel he transported with bonuses for speedy deliveries. Ratcliffe agreed to the arrangement and began to take regular packets of papers to the commissary of marines in Boulogne.[53]

Although he had initially jumped at the offer, posing few if any questions about the nature of the papers he was carrying, Ratcliffe's suspicions were eventually aroused in June 1780. Reflecting on Roger's repeated calls for secrecy about the shipments, Ratcliffe unburdened himself to his friend Joseph Stewart, a merchant from nearby Sandwich. Stewart immediately saw the possible danger inherent in secretly transporting unknown documents from a shadowy figure in England to a naval official in France. On Stewart's advice, the two men resolved to deliver the next packet to Lord Hillsborough, one of the secretaries of state. When Stewart eventually brought the papers to Hillsborough's office, the seriousness of the matter became quickly apparent, for the packet contained a letter addressed to Monsieur Antoine de Sartine, Comte d'Alby, Secretary of State for the Navy, outlining the state of affairs in India and providing minute details of "the India ships preparing to sail; and of the troops that are going there, and of the ships expected home, and a great deal of information respecting the India possessions" as well as the locations, ships and manpower of the British fleets under Admiral Rodney and Admiral Geary.[54]

This was shocking enough, but there was more to come. The packet contained a second letter that provided a detailed list of all known ships in the British navy. As the author wrote, "I have the honour to send you herewith a very exact state of the naval forces, armed and to be armed this year . . . A list of the naval forces, armed or to be armed; their stations, destination, and crews." The level of detail provided was astounding. Ships were listed according to their naval station, with information regarding each ship's number of men and guns, commander, whether it was in port or out, its destination and its last reported location in longitude and latitude. For instance, a naval detachment under Admiral Geary was described as being:

> on the 26th of July, off the bay of Ushant; longitude, E, of London, 11 deg. 12 min. lat. 49 deg. Wind, E.N.E., changeable . . . Total 26 ships of the line, nine frigates, five cutters, and three fire-ships . . . the utmost endeavours are used to reinforce the fleet under the command of Admiral Geary; that they had dispatched the Valiant of 74 guns, and the Biensaisant of 64 guns. The Fortitude of 64 guns, the Prince William 64, the Monarque 70, the Princess 70, and the Gibraltar 80; these five ships are setting out, one by one, and will be sent out, as they are in order, to join Admiral Geary.[55]

It must have quickly dawned upon those gathered in Lord Hillsborough's office that a major French intelligence network had just been unearthed. They also must have realized with a creeping sense of dread that this cache of intercepted intelligence stunk of treason, for among the lists of ships and the number of troops to be sent to India and New York, the packet contained a verbatim copy of a letter from Admiral Geary to the authorities in England detailing the status of his fleet. Put together, the number and specificity of the details on the British war effort, combined with the copy of the admiral's letter, suggested that the information could not possibly have been gleaned by one man nor without the help of well-placed British citizens.

Although the British authorities now had evidence of a traitorous plot in their midst, they had no idea who had written the letters or supplied the information. So as not to spook the potential conspirators, the intercepted letters were copied and returned to Ratcliffe with instructions to keep delivering the packets as had been originally agreed. Each subsequent parcel of papers was thereafter brought to the post office, where the contents were copied by government officials before the originals were delivered back to Ratcliffe. After copying several further letters, it was determined that the time had come to spring a trap. Ratcliffe was instructed to invent an argument with Roger over his payment, and in his manufactured anger demand to see the go-between's employer. The ploy worked, and the unsuspecting servant led Ratcliffe to his master, François Henri de la Motte. On January 4, 1781 the trap was finally sprung and de la Motte was arrested at his home in Bond Street.

While de la Motte was clapped in irons in London, off the coast of Africa, his daring espionage was bearing fruit. When the Dutch entered the war in 1780, and their colonies became fair game, Britain began to turn its greedy gaze toward the Dutch Republic's prize possession on the southern tip of Africa. By the eighteenth century, the Cape Colony, established by the Dutch in 1652, had become a key stopping place and resupply station for European ships sailing for India, China, and Southeast Asia. As its importance grew, so too did its strategic value, attracting the attention of the British. With the Cape now a legitimate target, in March 1781, an expedition was sent under Commodore George Johnstone to seize the colony. Johnstone, however, had no idea that as his fleet of forty-six ships sailed from Spithead that spring, the French were preparing a fleet of their own to intercept the expedition. Among the mountains of paperwork de la Motte had passed to the French were details of Johnstone's mission to the Cape.

In April 1781, Johnstone's fleet, still unaware of the danger, paused at Porto Praya in the Cape Verde Islands to take on fresh water. On April 16, the French, under Admiral de Suffren, overtook the unprepared British fleet and battle was joined. In his ignorance, Johnstone had left much of the fleet exposed, but just managed to drive off the French. De Suffren had failed to destroy the expedition, but the damage he had caused to Johnstone's ships ensured that the French forces were not pursued. Johnstone was still convinced that the French were clueless about the expedition's target, and assumed de Suffren would head to Brazil or the West Indies to make his repairs. However, when Johnstone's fleet at last arrived at the Cape, he found de Suffren, alerted by de la Motte's information, already in place. With the Cape Colony reinforced, Johnstone had no choice but to abandon the mission and return to England in defeat.

At trial, further sordid details of the traitorous conspiracy were revealed. Among the papers found in the raid on the house of Henri de la Motte were letters from a Mr. Lutterloh, a resident of Wickham near Portsmouth, one of the chief ports and naval bases of the British Empire. Lutterloh was quickly arrested, and under questioning by Lord Hillsborough he acknowledged that most of the information de la Motte had sent to France had been first supplied by him. Lutterloh had been in French employ since 1778, the year war was first declared between the two nations. Although his motivations were unclear, Lutterloh had been paid the princely sum of £50 per month to pass information regarding the British military to the French. Lutterloh himself had gained privileged access to such information by using the funds paid to him to corrupt a clerk in a government office in Portsmouth. David Tyrie, the duplicitous clerk, thus found himself the subject of a special session of the Winchester Assize where the full nature of his crimes was laid out for all to see.

The case had been a sensational one, followed closely by readers in London and around the country. The uncovering of a grand French conspiracy in their very midst must have confirmed the long-held fears of many in such inauspicious times, and so it is no surprise that the execution of Henri de la Motte was well attended. Criminal executions had long taken on the aspect of carnival, with hundreds or even thousands jostling together at Tyburn on the outskirts of London to watch the macabre theater of vengeance and justice. The execution of de la Motte was, however, unique. Whereas most hangings were of groups, de la Motte was executed alone. Seven men had swung from Tyburn's triple tree on the previous day, but the Frenchman was fated to swing alone. And while Tyburn crowds, especially in celebrity cases, often contained a strong contingent sympathetic to the condemned—glamorous highwaymen such as Jack Sheppard and Dick Turpin could expect to be cheered, toasted, and offered drinks on their parade to the gallows—there were few if any among the crowd on July 27 who had any sympathy for the French spy.[56]

The execution of de la Motte's British co-conspirator was similarly spectacular. Thirteen months later on the Southsea Common at Portsmouth it was David Tyrie's turn to face the angry crowds, justice, and the noose. As many as 100,000 people gathered on the common to watch the spectacle of a traitor's death, and if they hoped to see a potent mixture of equanimity and gore they would not have been disappointed. In the parlance of the times, David Tyrie's was a good, if gruesome, death, and the young naval clerk faced his fate with admirable sangfroid. As one witness later related:

> He conducted himself from the prison here to the place of execution, and during the whole of the preparation for his miserable dissolution, with the most singular composure and magnanimity . . . When arrived at the place of execution, no halter was provided, upon which he smiled, and expressed astonishment at the inattention and neglect of his executioners; and indeed the business would have been retarded for some time, had not a rope and pulley been procured out of a lugger that lay under shore, during which time he read several passages in a bible he carried in his hand . . . After hanging exactly twenty-two minutes, he was lowered upon the sledge, and the sentence literally put in execution. His head was severed from his body, his heart taken out and burnt, his privities cut off, and his body quartered. He was then put into a coffin, and buried among the pebbles by the sea-side; but no sooner had the officers retired, but the sailors dug up the coffin, took out the body, and cut it in a thousand pieces, every one carrying away a piece of his body to shew their messmates on board. A more dreadful, affecting execution was perhaps never seen.[57]

It was the last time such a shocking and brutal punishment would ever be seen in England. For several years after his execution, curious visitors in Portsmouth could see exhibited at Gosport Prison the head of David Tyrie. In the scrum that followed the burial, the master of Gosport Prison had secured the greatest prize of all, the traitor's head, which he preserved in spirits to show curious tourists of the macabre. The punishment meted out to David Tyrie and François Henri de la Motte, and the extended physical presence of their mutilated remains was very much an intentional message to Britons and their enemies alike. The whole world was at war. Treason would not be tolerated.[58]

Britain had thrown off kings before when they trampled too heavily on their rights and privileges, but despite significant sympathy for the American cause, an influential cadre of committed reformers, and deep disillusionment with the ruling regime, Britons never seriously contemplated joining their transatlantic cousins in revolt. Fear of the disorder and violence represented by the mob convinced most Britons that radicalism and revolt would bring with them only chaos and anarchy, and in Britain the American Revolution created and amplified disorder like no event before it. For while American colonists picked up their guns and began a revolution, Britons confronted crime, invasion, terrorism, treason, and popular violence on an unprecedented scale, creating an environment so fraught with fear that the idea of revolution, even of reform, was largely abandoned for the safety and security of a more authoritarian government.

The eighteenth century was already an era of growing concern about crime and disorder before the American crisis intervened. Urbanization, geographic mobility, and commercial growth all conspired to loosen traditional social bonds to a worrying degree. The fears caused by the constant moving and mixing of the age were only exacerbated by the explosion of newspapers across the country, bringing sensationally maudlin tales of crime and criminals into the public view as never before. Once a local concern, crime now became a national issue, at the forefront of public debate. During times of crisis, when war or famine or depression threatened further destabilization, concern became particularly acute, sometimes even verging on moral panic. In the midst of economic disruption and fears of demobilized soldiers and sailors, such moments could also lead to calls for new laws and regulations to alleviate the dread of crime run rampant.

A time of almost unprecedented disorder—a time when smuggling was rampant, when theft was common, when potential traitors and terrorists lurked behind every corner, and much of London reduced to a smoldering ruin—the intensity of the American crisis provoked an intense moral panic in the early

1780s. Across the country newspapers brimmed with accounts of "cruel murders and robberies," of pitched battles between smugglers and customs officials on Britain's beaches, and of former soldiers and sailors turned "desperadoes" haunting the streets and highways. Such stories fed into popular fears and reinforced the feeling of a nation under siege. In his speech to Parliament in December 1782, the king joined the panicked chorus, urging "a strict and severe execution of the laws" to combat "the great excess, to which the crimes of theft and robbery have arisen, in many instances accompanied with personal violence." In an increasingly national news market, such stories and speeches, even if they did not accurately reflect local conditions, induced fear throughout the country.[59]

On the surface, there was nothing unusual about this moral panic, as times of national emergency often brought heightened fears of crime. However, the nature of the American crisis meant that the panic that followed had consequences altogether more significant than had been the case for more than a century. Because the crisis caused by the American War combined traditional fears of rampant criminality with concerns over radical political ideology, the panic of the 1780s helped to transform attitudes toward criminality and fundamentally alter conceptions of justice. Rather than considering crime to be a function of poverty or immorality, many came to believe that crime was the result of unseemly ambition and insubordination among the common people. Just as they shivered at recent displays of popular political action—such as Wilkes and Liberty, the Gordon Riots, and, as we will see, the Irish Volunteer movement and the Association movement—they now saw theft, robbery, and murder as part of the same degradation of a common people infected with dangerous new ideas that told them that both political and economic power was theirs for the taking. The *Newcastle Journal* made the connection between revolution and crime explicit:

Riots and mutinies rather increase than subside! The reflux of the war seems to be more dangerous than the war itself. The soldiers and sailors, seeing or hearing of their superiors quarrelling, follow their example, and the State malady becomes contagious! Those Members of the State, who, in order to thrust themselves into power, strongly inculcated on the people the doctrine of self-government, now feel its effects, and see the evil of stirring up the multitude to affect a greater degree of power . . . May the great hand of Divine Providence interpose to save us from our numerous enemies, and our own vices and folly! Or we are undone.[60]

After the war, commentators began to speak of crime as a "contagion," and of criminals as part of a degenerate "criminal class." According to Patrick Colquhoun, a Scottish merchant, opponent of the American Revolution, and advocate of policing reforms, Britain was now in a "state of criminal warfare," with criminals as "enemies of the state." Years of riots, invasion scares, treasonous plots, and radical ideology had transformed crime from a local domestic concern into a national political issue that threatened the peace, prosperity, and stability of Britain itself. War and radical politics had turned the common criminal into a traitor. New fears, new conceptions of crime and criminality required new approaches to law and order that reflected the newly politicized nature of the problem. In the 1780s and 1790s, a variety of proposals were advanced all designed to take law, justice, and punishment out of the hands of a people who could no longer be trusted.

As we have seen, the period surrounding the American War saw the advent of a new carceral regime. The more uniform, more rigorous punishment represented by prisons reflected the shifting view of criminality of the post-war period, but it also began to strip away the role of the public. Prisons were intentionally anti-discretionary, replacing human considerations of mercy and terror with government-mandated standardization. This may have seemed more logical to enlightened reformers, but it was also a means of taking more judicial decision-making out of the hands of a now suspect people. Prisons also removed other aspects of popular participation in criminal justice by replacing public corporal punishments with private, state-controlled incarceration. In a similar institutionalization of punishment, after 1783 the execution of condemned criminals was moved from its traditional site at Tyburn to outside Newgate Prison. After the dreadful riots of the war years, the authorities no longer trusted the crowds that had habitually gathered at Tyburn to witness executions. Step by step, Britain's public, participatory justice system was being dismantled in the name of centralization and state control.

Fears of disorder and disloyalty, and new conceptions of crime and criminality also led to radical shifts in views of policing. Historically, British criminal justice had relied on locally elected or selected part-time amateurs to enforce the law. Though there had been some small-scale innovations in formal policing, for most of the eighteenth century Britons had looked at French innovations in government-controlled professional policing with deep skepticism. A police force, many believed, would be detrimental to British liberty and to traditions of local self-government, the tool of tyrannical state power. Few had forgotten how Oliver Cromwell had used his New Model Army as an "evangelical constabulary" to suppress dissent and shut down popular pastimes and public gatherings. Neither had Britons ignored the part the French police played in propping up the despotic power of their monarchs. A professional police force had thus long been anathema in Britain. The American crisis, however, led more and more Britons to embrace the idea of professional policing as a positive means of protecting property and keeping the disorderly mob in line. In the wake of the Gordon Riots, Horace Walpole had sensed the change in mood, fearing that Lord Gordon and his riots would be "the source of our being ruled by an army." The army would prove a temporary expedient for quelling London's wartime turmoil, but Walpole was right that the post-war world would witness a raft of legislation giving greater policing powers to the state.[61]

The office of Home Secretary was created in 1782 to ensure domestic order and direct efforts to control crime and popular agitation. In 1783, the City of London ordered salaried city marshals and constables to make regular patrols in large numbers to ensure order. In 1785, Solicitor-General Sir Archibald Macdonald introduced the London Police Bill, which sought to establish police districts in Greater London, with oversight of the new system placed firmly in the hands of a centrally appointed commission answering to the Home Office. Not only would this bill concentrate policing power in the hands of the state, it also sought to expand preventative policing by authorizing officers to conduct searches, surveil suspects, and arrest and summarily convict suspected vagrants. The 1785 bill failed in the face of opposition from the City of London, but many of its provisions would be revived in future legislation in 1787, 1792, and 1798 that set the stage for the formation of modern, professional policing in

Britain. Coming as it did on the heels of a period of profound crisis and disorder, most welcomed this authoritarian, centralizing turn. Others, like the Whig champion Charles James Fox, were less pleased, fearing "a new principle which overturned the tradition of magisterial detachment and threatened perverting the law to oppression." Despite Fox's fears, however, the American War would prove a watershed moment in which widespread opposition to professional policing was replaced for the first time with broad acceptance.[62]

Fox had been one of the most vociferous opponents of the Habeas Corpus Act of 1777, but here too the precedent of expanded ministerial power had been set. The suspension of habeas corpus lapsed in 1783, but the emergency measures of wartime legislation would form the basis for future government attempts to quash internal dissent. When the threat of British radicalism reared its head under the looming cloud of the French Revolution in the 1790s, the government would look back to the tactics of the American War to stifle unrest. In 1793, acts targeting foreigners and requiring friendly societies to officially register were passed. In 1794–5 and 1798–1801, habeas corpus was once more suspended, and in 1795 rights of free speech, the press, and assembly were all heavily restricted. These measures were certainly a reaction to the perceived dangers of the French Revolution and its fellow-travelers in Britain, but they were also in many ways a result of the experiments made and the lessons learnt during the American crisis. The rebellion of Britain's American subjects, the terror caused by John the Painter, Henri de la Motte, and the Gordon Riots, the fears of crime run rampant, all convinced many Britons that the further concentration of power in the hands of the government was necessary. The war for American liberty fundamentally shifted the mood in Britain to one in favor of greater government control. The people had proved they could not be trusted.

The years 1797 and 1798 were *anni mirabiles* for William Wordsworth and Samuel Taylor Coleridge. They had removed themselves from the breakneck pace of a Britain in the full swing of the Industrial Revolution, renting idyllic retreats in the Quantock Hills of Somerset and reaping the artistic benefits of rural seclusion. It was here, in these years, that Wordsworth and Coleridge would write some of their best-loved works, the joint effort *Lyrical Ballads* and Coleridge's opium-inspired *Kubla Khan*. But if they thought that full immersion in the glories of their personal poetic Xanadu would spare them from the tribulations of the times they were sorely deluded. For even in this West Country idyll, eyes were watching and agents reporting the poets' every action and every visitor. This was the reality in the world first spawned by the American Revolution.

By 1797 the war with France that had begun in 1778 had been grinding on for over two decades, with a hiatus between the Treaty of Paris in 1783 and the renewal of hostilities in 1793. Radicals in France had overthrown the monarchy in 1789 ushering in an age of terror and revolution on the continent. In a Britain terrified at the prospects of invasion from without and radical revolution within, perceived enemies of the state continued to abound. Innocuous-sounding groups like the Society for Constitutional Information and the London Corresponding Society, which advocated constitutional and parliamentary reform, were viewed by the government as sparks that might light the fires of revolt and were thus closely monitored. In 1792, 1793, and 1794 suspected radicals such as John Thelwall and John Horne Tooke were tried for treason. Thomas Paine, whose *Common Sense*, one of the most important rallying cries of revolution in America, had escaped official prosecution, was now indicted *in absentia* for treason alongside the British publishers of his *Rights of Man*. In a desperate attempt to forestall the radicalization of the nation, Prime Minister William Pitt the Younger passed measures in 1795 that reinforced the treason laws and limited public meetings to no more than fifty people.

Inspired by radical politics, Coleridge had been corresponding with John Thelwall since 1796, and the redoubtable reformer had visited both poets at their Somerset retreat. In the paranoid atmosphere of the times, such connections were enough to draw the gaze of the government, and spies were placed to watch the activities of the budding Romantics. Though Coleridge and Wordsworth escaped official censure, the heightened fear of internal radicalism and revolutionary France would ensure that treason and terror plagued the dreams of governments and individuals until the final fall of Napoleon in 1815. These forty years of paranoia began with imperial civil war in 1775 and exploded with new force in the years after France joined the war in 1778. In the aftermath of the American Revolution radicalism and reform increasingly became associated with treason, terror, and violence, and as more and more of the British populace turned their backs on reform, new, more authoritarian policies were put in place to prevent the country from following America into the abyss. The lessons learned from the disorder of the American War thus ensured Britain avoided the revolutionary tide that swept across continental Europe in the 1780s and 1790s, but it did so at a cost. Countless men and women, from French spies, to American students to English poets had their lives fundamentally altered by these years of treason, terror, and paranoia.

3

➵ ➵

REVOLUTION, REACTION, AND SECTARIANISM IN IRELAND

The Gordon Riots, and the fears that helped produce them, were born of international events, and their impact would likewise stretch far beyond the bounds of London. Ignatius Sancho worried that the riots meant that "America seems to be quite lost or forgot amongst us; the fleet is but a secondary affair." But if Britain was distracted by its own catastrophic self-immolation, the eerie glow of the burning metropolis cast a far different light on American soil. The rest of the world was certainly watching. George Washington welcomed the news of England's "disturbances," seeing in them the possibility of a strategic advantage in his contest with Britain. The riots, he confided to a friend, presented dramatic evidence that America's "hour of deliverance was not far distant." Alexander Hamilton agreed with his mentor's assessment, writing to his fiancée Elizabeth Schuyler that "the affairs of England are in so bad a plight that . . . it will seem impossible for her to proceed in the war."[1] Britain seemed to be consuming itself, forced to marshal money and manpower to restrain its own subjects, resources that were sorely needed in North America. Perhaps the Gordon Riots would be the final straw that broke the empire's back. Americans, however, were not the only ones to see the prospect of independence in the Gordon Riots.

Though it was London that nearly consumed itself in an orgy of riot, fires, and repression, the original source of the problem, the root cause of the fear, the terror, and the rage, lay across the sea, in America, and in Ireland. Given the anxieties of wartime Britain, what possessed the government to attempt so desperate, so controversial a gambit as Catholic Relief at the height of a period of crisis? As Ignatius Sancho lamented from his vantage point in London, "the present time is rather *comique*. Ireland is almost in as true a state of rebellion as America. Admirals quarrelling in the West-Indies—and at home admirals who do not chuse to fight. The British empire mouldering away in the west— annihilated in the north—Gibraltar going—and England fast asleep." In the midst of this unhappy, this disordered, this "dark and critical time," the Irish had taken up arms. For Britain, the war brought danger, but for the Irish, it brought leverage and opportunity.[2]

That London's vengeful crowds attacked Irish immigrants came as no surprise. The Irish had long been vilified, even dehumanized, as barbaric, unciv- ilized, and untrustworthy, a morally compromised criminal element, a festering sore in London's slums. This attitude had become more prevalent in the eight- eenth century as Irish immigrants poured into London in ever greater numbers. At the root of much of this bigotry was English fear and hatred of Irish Catholicism. Sure that the Irish would choose religion over political allegiance, many Britons feared that the Irish, at home and in England, would welcome or even aid an invasion by Catholic France and Spain. In 1780 the London mob, reflecting popular prejudices, thus lashed out at Irish immigrants as Catholic fifth columnists ready to betray Protestant England from within.

In Ireland itself, however, there was genuine concern about the dangers posed by American privateer raids and a Franco-Spanish invasion, especially among the minority Protestant Ascendancy that dominated Irish politics. Contrary to its legal obligations, Britain, in constant need of soldiers for its American war, had drained Ireland of its fighting men. Ireland was thus left vulnerable to foreign attack. In response to this British neglect, Protestants around the country banded together in militia units to protect their island from foreign invasion. The Volunteer movement, as the militia companies came to be known, soon spread across Ireland, with as many as 60,000 under arms.

But though the Volunteers had originally organized for the defense of their homes from foreign threat, their resolutions rapidly began to take on a more political, more radical tone. From repelling French invasion, the Volunteers began to talk of a new target, a new aim. They composed new resolutions that pledged the Volunteers to free Ireland "forever from English domination," with every man swearing, "as he kissed the blade of his sword, that he would adhere to these resolutions to the last drop of his blood, which he would by no means spare, till we had finally achieved the independence of our country." For Ireland, the American Revolution would provide a clear, if fleeting, opportunity for independence.[3]

Britain's war with America found little support among the Irish. Since the early days of colonization, Ireland had maintained close links with America. In an ideal position to engage in the colonial trade, Ireland rapidly became an integral part of the transatlantic economy, exporting cheap linens, butter, pork, and salted beef to the West Indies and North America in ever-growing amounts. With the burgeoning trade to the colonies came Irish immigrants—as many as 70,000 Scots-Irish from Ulster alone in the century before the revolution—in search of cheap land, often in the backcountry of the colonies. When war broke out with Britain, Irish immigrants were frequently found at the forefront of the revolution. Irishmen like Thomas Conway and Arthur Dillon helped lead the colonial war effort, and Irish settlers, especially the Ulstermen scratching out a living on the American frontier, overwhelmingly took up arms in support of their adopted nation.

Many back in Ireland were sympathetic to the colonial cause as well. Early in 1776, at a performance of John Gay's *The Beggar's Opera* in Dublin, the spectators rioted when "Americans were styled rebels" in the play's epilogue. The critique of British imperial policy and the movement to reform the relationship between metropole and colony that coalesced into revolution in America was not unique to the New World. Instead, it was merely one strand of a broader movement for imperial reform that included vocal advocates in Ireland and Britain as well. For many Irishmen, the connection between their own struggles for greater legislative independence and free trade and those of the rebellious colonies were clear enough. Ireland had been at least nominally an English imperial possession since the Normans invaded in 1171, a kingdom of the English monarch governed by a Lord Lieutenant appointed by the English crown. Under the Tudors, Poyning's Law, reconfirmed under the Declaratory Act of George I in 1719, made Ireland's Parliament subordinate to the Parliament of England. Ireland's representatives could only propose legislation, which could be vetoed in Westminster. Fearful that Irish competition might undermine and outstrip England's colonial trade, restrictions were placed on Irish trade beginning in the 1650s, forbidding direct trade between Ireland and the Americas and mandating that Irish trade must be conducted in English ships and flow through English ports. Thus, in many ways, Ireland's political and economic position on the eve of the revolution was very similar to that of the American colonies, her Parliament subject to English oversight and her trade restricted.[4]

On both sides of the Atlantic, people were quick to realize the similarities between Ireland's and America's roles in the British Empire, and the implications of the American Revolution for Ireland. Indeed, as early as the Stamp Act crisis in the 1760s, American reformers had taken steps to ensure Irish support by exempting Irish goods from the colonial boycott of British commerce. When the confrontation between Britain and the colonies turned violent in 1775, it was clear to many that the constitutional issues at stake would affect Ireland, that a British victory would confirm Britain's right to levy taxes on its imperial possessions without their consent, and that an American defeat might well spend the end of any hope for legislative independence in Ireland.

From the beginning of the conflict, Irish newspapers were filled with discussions of the emerging war, and the Irish press churned out hundreds of pamphlets shouting support for America and opposition to British policies. When Parliament opened in Ireland in October of 1775, the war with America had divided its members. In the address to the Lord Lieutenant, the revolution was called a rebellion in keeping with official British policy. Others in Parliament, however, sought to make clear that though they disagreed with the method of American resistance, they saw the justness of the underlying grievances and opposed Britain's military policy. Reformers in Parliament advocated conciliation and debated whether or not Irish troops should be sent to fight for Britain in America. Denis Daly condemned the war, warning that it would surely lead to greater taxation in Ireland, taxation that would be enforced by the sword if necessary. John Ponsonby concurred, adding that if Ireland helped Britain suppress American opposition to taxation, "she furnished an argument against herself." Walter Hussey Burgh likewise urged Ireland to reject giving Irish aid for Britain's war, declaring, "I foresee the consequences of this war. If the Ministers are victorious, it will only be establishing a right to harvest, after they have burned the grain—it will be establishing a right to the stream, after they have cut off the fountain." Jonah Barrington spoke for many when he worried that: "The subjugation of America might confirm the dependence of Ireland," and that Ireland could only hope to "obtain her own constitutional rights . . . by the complete success and triumph of her [Britain's] colony." The critics were quickly proved right in their fears for Ireland. In an attempt to starve the colonies of provisions and ensure the stable supply of their own forces, the government imposed an embargo on the export of Irish provisions to the colonies, souring the public mood even further.[5]

For the moment, however, not even the most vociferous Irish critics of British imperial policy contemplated joining forces with America against Britain. For starters, even the burgeoning trade with America could not compete with the central importance of Ireland's direct trade with Britain, a trade few wished to see disrupted. Ireland was also internally divided between the ruling Protestant Ascendancy, a growing minority of dissenting Presbyterians, centered in Ulster, and a disenfranchised Catholic majority. Despite the widely held belief that the imperial position, the grievances, and the fate of Ireland and the American colonies were closely tied and widely similar, few among the Irish political class considered themselves to be colonists or Ireland to be an English colony.

Instead of adopting an oppositional anti-English mindset, the Protestant Ascendancy viewed themselves as Englishmen, descendants of those Englishmen who had fought against the forces of Catholic despotism in the seventeenth century and the rightful inheritors of the rights and liberties that their forebears had won with their loyal sacrifice. As such, loyalty to the crown was central to their identity as Protestant Englishmen in an Irish Catholic country. Efforts at reform were thus initially couched in the language of "English liberties" and directed against the administration rather than against the crown of Britain itself. While America sought separation from Great Britain, Ireland sought only to "obtain just participation of her constitution." Irishmen remained among the most vocal critics of Britain's American policy and continued to press for reforms similar to those pursued by their American cousins, but they did so, at least initially, from within a framework of loyalism.[6]

When France declared war on Britain in 1778, it was not just Englishmen who began to quake at the prospect of French invasion. Ireland had long been seen as the Catholic back door into Britain. As recently as 1760, during the Seven Years' War, the French had attempted an invasion of Ireland at Carrickfergus in Northern Ireland as a prelude to a larger invasion of England, and there was every reason to believe they would try it again. It was, after all, hardly surprising that France would see welcome allies among the Catholic-majority Ireland. Since England's adoption of Protestantism in the sixteenth century, Irish Catholics had been restricted by a series of Penal Laws, laws that prevented them from holding property, serving in office, possessing weapons, or voting in elections. The disenfranchised Catholic majority had frequently resorted to insurrection in the past, and though there had not been a major Catholic rising in nearly a century, many in Ireland, Britain, and France still considered English rule as balanced precariously on a ledge of sectarian division. For the Protestant Ascendancy in particular, French invasion held more concrete and substantial terrors. As a precarious ruling class, and one knowledgeable regarding Ireland's long and turbulent history of insurrection, there was every reason to think that a French invasion might well lead to a Catholic rebellion and the destruction of their rather fragile position. Britain had sought to secure Catholic manpower and Catholic loyalty by passing the Catholic Relief Bill in 1778, yet many Irish Protestants remained decidedly nervous about their position in the event of a French invasion.

To guard against just such an eventuality, the British had promised to maintain a force of 12,000 troops in Ireland for internal defense at all times, a figure increased to 15,000 in 1771. But these were not ordinary times, and by the time France entered war and made the threat to Ireland's shores a potent reality, the latter's defense force had been fatally depleted, siphoned off to fight in the American quagmire and the dizzying array of battlefronts around the globe. In 1775, 4,000 Irish soldiers—"armed negotiators" as Henry Flood, who opposed the move in Parliament, termed them—were sent to America with more Irish troops to follow. It was an unpopular policy, both because many Irishmen were sympathetic to the American cause and because they feared for the safety of their own island.[7]

At the outset, however, some Irishmen had been eager enough to join. Even a scion of one of Ireland's first families of resistance to English rule enthusiastically joined the fray. Edward Fitzgerald, brother of the Duke of Leinster and descendant of the rebellious earls of Kildare, only 12 years old when the first Irish troops were sent across the Atlantic, secured a commission in the army as soon as he was old enough. He balked at the delays in shipping out, prayed that he would be sent to fight the colonials rather than to the defense of Gibraltar, and even turned down a comfortable commission for fear that it might mean missing out on the action in America. He was thrilled when he was sent to Charleston to aid in the defense of the city from the resurgent Patriots in the south. Young, energetic, and eager to prove himself, Fitzgerald represented a different strand of Irish opinion. He was more concerned with his own prospects for glory and advancement than the ideological principles that undergirded the war.[8]

Back in Ireland, however, Britain's desperate, unquenchable need for troops left the island undefended, vulnerable, and terrified. Pleas were made to the British authorities to fulfill their promise to maintain Ireland's defenses, Militia bills were proposed in Parliament, and offers were made by wealthy elites to raise regiments of militia. There were no soldiers to spare, however, and no money to fund the recruitment or arming of militia. When these pleas fell on deaf ears, leaving the country exposed and defenseless, the Irish resolved to take up their own defense. "Ireland," Jonah Barrington lamented, "without money, militia, or standing army . . . almost abandoned by England, had to depend solely on the spirit and resources of her own natives."[9]

It began in Ulster, a stronghold of Protestantism and dissent currently in the throes of a catastrophic recession caused by the war's disruption of its vital linen trade. As early as 1778, when John Paul Jones's raid on British ships at Carrickfergus first brought the war to Ireland, Ulster had been calling out for protection. A year later, in May 1779, reports of an imminent French invasion of Northern Ireland engendered widespread panic. The authorities of Belfast and Carrickfergus sent word of the rumored invasion to the Lord Lieutenant, the Earl of Buckinghamshire, at Dublin Castle, imploring him to send troops to their aid. Buckinghamshire was sympathetic, but could only spare about sixty soldiers for the defense of Ulster, and so, as the alarmed Lord Lieutenant wrote to his superiors in London, the people of Belfast and Carrickfergus began to arm themselves, "and, by degrees, formed themselves into two or three companies" to repel the invaders. From these initial outbreaks, these popular militias or

"Volunteers" began to crop up around the country. "The spirit" of the Volunteers "quickly diffused itself into different parts of the kingdom, and the number became considerable," Buckinghamshire reported until perhaps as many as 60,000 Irishmen were under arms. The Volunteer corps consisted of middle-class Protestants organized into local units led by Protestant elites. Catholics, forbidden to hold arms and distrusted by both government and their Protestant neighbors, were not generally allowed to join the Volunteers but showed their support for the movement, and opposition to French incursion, by sending aid and messages of support to the Volunteers.[10]

The authorities in Dublin could do little but offer rather disingenuous thanks and gently discourage the trend where they could. The Earl of Buckinghamshire did not dare antagonize the Volunteers. Moreover, he knew full well that seizing so many arms would be almost impossible in a country in which the arm of the law was weak at the best of times and where the right of Protestants to bear arms had been enshrined in law since the seventeenth century. Furthermore, the Lord Lieutenant argued, it would be churlish to refuse Irish Protestants the right to arm themselves at the very moment when new freedoms had been granted to Catholics, "a denomination of men, whom they so long had deemed their inveterate enemies." Besides, Ireland was in a vulnerable position. In case of an invasion, these men would be needed to defend the coast and protect the rest of the country from the prospect of Catholic insurrection. In such an unenviable position, the Irish authorities outwardly tolerated and even praised the Volunteers, going so far as to heed requests to send arms and supplies to some of the units.[11]

Like many Irishmen of his day, 19-year-old Jonah Barrington was swept away by the spirit of the times. Born in 1760 at his father's country seat of Knapton in Queen's County, Barrington was a member of the minority Protestant gentry, the so-called "Ascendancy," that ruled over Ireland's Catholic majority. Like Barrington's family, the Ascendancy were descendants of English settlers who had arrived in the sixteenth and seventeenth centuries, had sided with Britain during the crisis of the Glorious Revolution, and viewed themselves first and foremost as Protestant Englishmen, the hereditary gover-nors of Britain's empire in Ireland. With such loyalist bona fides, when Britain and Ireland were threatened with foreign invasion in 1779, Barrington was seized by the contagious desire to defend his homeland from the attack that everyone was sure would come.

"Military ardour," Barrington remembered, had seized the whole country. Across Ireland men were banding together into Volunteer companies to repel the expected invasion. As a member of the local Protestant gentry, Barrington's father and brother raised and commanded their own Volunteer corps, and Jonah, though still very young, joined one of his family's companies. "I found myself a military martinet and a red-hot patriot," he later recalled, and, as a "university man," took a central role in drawing up the orders and resolutions of the region's Volunteer units.[12]

It did not take long for Irish reformers to realize the potential of a nation in arms. Since at least 1720, Irish Protestant supporters of the British Whig Party, and especially the Patriot faction of the Whig Party, had begun to coalesce into an opposition movement advocating for reform of Ireland's political and economic systems. Called the "Irish Patriot Party," this group advocated for the independence of Ireland's Parliament, greater control over Irish economic policy, and the elimination of other British abuses of Ireland's government. Over the eighteenth century, they pushed for autonomy from Britain, relaxation of the Penal Laws against Catholics, the independence of Ireland's justice system, and the repeal of the laws that made Ireland's Parliament subordinate to Britain's. Previous attempts at reform had mostly failed, but by the 1770s, inspired by British reformers and American revolutionaries, the Irish Patriot Party, led by Henry Flood in the House of Commons, and Lord Charlemont in the House of Lords, were ready to seize any opportunity presented by Britain's imperial crisis to demand reform. The Volunteer movement presented exactly the opportunity the Irish Patriots were looking for.

The Volunteers had done much to unify the country, to create a new sense of Irishness, and provide the momentum and zeal necessary to pressure the government. In an era when government and people were seen to be connected by a series of mutual obligations, Britain, by failing in its obligation to protect and aid Ireland, had forfeited its rights over Ireland, removing Ireland's reciprocal obligation of obedience. And so, when Parliament opened in 1779, Henry Grattan, a reform-minded lawyer of little note, but blessed with great powers of rhetoric and awe-inspiring oratory, addressed the chamber, offering an amendment to the government's opening address. In "fiery, yet deliberative language," Grattan beseeched the king to take note of the distressed condition of his Irish kingdom, arguing that "the constant drain to supply absentees, and the unfortunate prohibition of our trade, have caused such a calamity, that the natural support of our country has decayed, and our manufacturers are dying for want; famine stalks hand in hand with hopeless wretchedness; and the only means left to support . . . this miserable part of your Majesty's dominions, is to open a free export trade."[13]

While Grattan called for free trade within Parliament, outside the public began to press for reform as well. Petitions were sent to the administration at Dublin Castle detailing the suffering of Irish commerce and the Irish people. Buckinghamshire received a deputation of representatives of the linen industry who informed him of the economic destruction of their crucial industry, describing warehouses full of unsold linens. A government inquiry found that Ireland's merchant community, especially those at Dublin and Limerick, had been devastated by the war and the embargo, with "numbers of them ruined." In Parliament Grattan castigated the government, arguing that the taxes imposed on Ireland to fund Britain's war, combined with the restrictions placed on Ireland's linen and provisions trades, had caused the immiseration of thousands. It was claimed that "ten thousand of them were thrown out of employment," and that "the streets of Dublin were paraded by numerous bodies of starving manufacturers, who displayed a black fleece as a token of their distress and despair."[14]

Supporters of the ministry objected to Grattan's amendment, but the young reformer convinced many of the justness of his resolution. Henry Flood, long among the most vocal and influential advocates of reform, voiced his firm support as did other members of the opposition. However, the tide truly changed when Walter Hussey Burgh, Prime Sergeant and thus a prominent member of the ministry, rose and exclaimed that he could not support any measure that "fraudulently concealed from the King the right of his people." With Burgh and other members of the government refusing to oppose Grattan's amendment, the measure passed. Though the amendment had no actual teeth in it, its effects were immediate and striking. The Volunteers saw the measure as a vote of support for their movement and considered Parliament's adoption of their grievances to be a visible sign of the effective power of the Volunteer Movement to drive real political change. In Dublin, Jonah Barrington, who had been present for Grattan's momentous speech, looked on while the local Volunteers lined the streets leading to Dublin Castle and provided military honor guards for members of the opposition, a memory, he related, that could "never be effaced." Around the country, people encouraged by Parliament's perceived support, rushed to join the Volunteers, swelling their ranks.[15]

Across the Irish Sea in England, notice was taken of both the Volunteers and Grattan's speech. Irish peers like Lord Shelburne attempted to introduce the issue of Ireland's grievances in Britain's Parliament but were defeated in their effort to resolve the growing crisis. With the failure of Britain to alleviate the suffering of the Irish, it became increasingly evident that Irish problems would require Irish solutions. Mirroring the efforts and tactics of their American cousins during their quarrels with Britain, the Irish, led once more by the Volunteers, resolved to boycott British goods and trade with Britain until the trade restrictions on Irish exports to America were lifted. Volunteer groups, town corporations, and individuals pledged, in the words of "the Freemen and Freeholders of the City of Dublin" at a public meeting, "That we will not, from the date hereof, until the *grievances of this country* shall be *removed*, directly or indirectly import or *consume* ANY of the manufactures of Great Britain; nor will we deal with any merchant, or shopkeeper, who shall import such manufactures." The protest spread rapidly around the country, enforced, as it was in America, by "popular retribution," violence and intimidation cowing any who contravened the ban or wavered in their support for the cause.[16]

With growing numbers and expanding political power, the Volunteer Movement began to adopt measures to formalize their organization, improve their collective direction, and encourage unity of action. Leaders were selected to coordinate their activities, starting with the Volunteers of Dublin who coalesced under the command of the Duke of Leinster, Ireland's preeminent nobleman and, as a member of the Fitzgerald family, a man with impeccable credentials to lead opposition to British tyranny. As aides-de-camp, Leinster chose prominent parliamentary reformers such as Henry Grattan, Barry Yelverton, and Hussey Burgh. In Ulster, the Volunteers selected another prominent nobleman and moderate reformer, the Earl of Charlemont, who helped lead the effort to secure redress in Ireland's Parliament. With these innovations, the Volunteers were transformed from an ad hoc body of militia into something approaching a formal Irish army, though one commanded by Irishmen rather than Britons.

With a more unified organizational structure came more concerted action, and the Volunteers now began more radical and more vocal demands for reform. Placards calling for "Free Trade" appeared throughout the county. In Dublin, the Volunteer artillery, commanded by James Napper Tandy, affixed a dire warning to the mouths of their cannons, parading guns labeled "Free Trade or speedy Revolution" on the very doorstep of Dublin Castle. The regular army, stationed in Dublin to cow the Irish, conspicuously avoided offending or provoking the Volunteers, well aware of their greater numbers and the fact that a large proportion of the regular army and navy were themselves Irish. Faced with such concerted opposition and the very real threat of a second revolution in the British Empire, concessions were granted and Ireland's trade restrictions were lifted.[17]

Many in Ireland feared that the concessions to Irish trade—granted at a moment of extreme distress, of imperial crisis—would be repealed as soon as the American War was over and Britain could once more focus on Ireland. With this concern in mind, reformers and Volunteers began to agitate for legislative independence, arguing that a sovereign Irish Parliament and the right of Ireland to create her own laws were the only safeguards against future British treachery. The success of the drive for free trade, the ability to force reform at the barrel of the gun, encouraged many to adopt a new aim, an independent Irish Parliament. Once more, the Volunteers were central to this agitation.

On February 15, 1782, delegates from the Volunteer associations of Ulster gathered at Dungannon to discuss further action, aims, and tactics. That morning 200 "steady, silent, and determined" delegates, fully armed and clothed in the uniforms of their regiments, marched two by two into the church of Dungannon for a solemn meeting. After several hours of discussion and debate, the delegates emerged with a resolution that framed the "rights and grievances" of the Irish nation. They had first resolved that the existence of armed paramilitary groups did not mean rebellion or the forfeiture of any civil rights. Second, and most importantly, they resolved that "a claim of *any* body of men, other than the King, Lords, and Commons of Ireland, to make laws that bind *this* kingdom, is *unconstitutional, illegal, and a grievance*." The delegates also resolved that Poyning's Law was unconstitutional, as were the restriction of Irish trade and the dependence of Ireland's judiciary. After voting support for the relaxation of the Penal Laws against Catholics and pledging to support reformers and reform efforts in Parliament, the delegates agreed to create a governing committee for Ulster and to send representatives to Dublin for a general convention of Volunteers.[18]

The Dungannon convention was a turning point in Irish history, its resolutions in many ways Ireland's first Declaration of Independence. Other Volunteer groups quickly voted to adopt the Dungannon resolutions. The Dublin Volunteers, the most active and influential association outside Ulster, agreed to accept the resolutions within a matter of weeks. Barrington, whose father and brothers commanded four Volunteer regiments between them, was dragooned to compose resolutions for their regiments as well as an agreement to adopt the resolutions of Dungannon. This was Barrington's "first essay," but also, for the rest of his life, proof that he had been on the right side of history, firm in his support for constitutional independence. It was a transformative moment for both Barrington and the nation, a moment of popular ferment and radicalization. As one Leinster Volunteer put it, "Kings are, we now perceive but human institutions, Parliaments are but human institutions, Ministers are but human institutions, but Liberty is a right Divine, it is the earliest gift from heaven, the charter of our birth-right, which human institutions can never cancel, without tearing down the first and best decree of the Omnipotent Creator."[19]

With the adoption of the Dungannon resolutions, as Jonah Barrington remembered, "the proceedings of the people without doors, now began to have their due weight on their representatives within," and many within Parliament adopted the Volunteers' resolutions and renewed their push for legislative independence. Their strategy was simple but effective. Remembering well their English history and the tactics of Parliament in its great seventeenth-century disputes with the king, reformers in Ireland's Parliament resolved to use their control of the country's purse strings to force further reform. As such, they refused to vote on a Money Bill to fund the government for more than six months until their grievances were addressed.

With the nation in arms, and the financial tap closed to a trickle, the administration once more began to listen to the rising chorus of Irish complaint. On April 14, 1782, the Duke of Portland arrived in Dublin as the new Lord Lieutenant of Ireland. The removal of the more intransigent Earl of Carlisle from office was a clear sign that the British ministry was wavering in their opposition to reform, hoping to appease Irish complaints by a change in government. The prospect of victory became even clearer when, in his opening address to Ireland's Parliament, Portland declared that the "mistrust and jealousies" that had arisen in Ireland were in need of "immediate consideration" so that a "*final* adjustment" of the relationship between Ireland and Britain could be made. No one, however, was quite sure what "final adjustments" the British government had in mind. Some feared a union between Ireland and Britain similar to the 1707 union between Scotland and England, would follow, allowing for Irish representatives in Britain's Parliament, but at the same time eliminating Ireland's own Parliament.

The reformers refused to wait passively to see what Portland had in store. On April 16, 1782, "a multitude of people" crowded the streets outside Parliament in Dublin. Inside, the Members of Parliament waited in breathless anticipation for the entrance of Henry Grattan, the great champion of reform. He entered accompanied by a cadre of reformers, and, for the second time in three years, rose to address the chamber. There, he proposed a Declaration of Rights that outlined a new relationship between Ireland and Britain. In Grattan's conception of this altered British empire, Ireland and Britain would share a monarch and a constitution, but Ireland would become an independent nation with an unquestioned right to legislate for herself, a nation with an independent Parliament, an independent judiciary, and an independent army. It was not, he argued, a question of Britain granting Ireland the privilege of independence, but Ireland's natural right. "The question," Grattan declaimed, "is not whether Ireland has a right to be free, but whether Great Britain has a right to enslave her. When the latter country asks what right have the Irish to make laws for themselves? Ireland will not answer, but demands, what right has England to make laws for Ireland—from nature she has none—nature has not given any one nation a right over another." Britain, Grattan reasoned, had already conceded the point. In 1778, reeling from the defeat at Saratoga and the French entrance into the war, Britain had sent a peace commission, led by Ireland's erstwhile Lord Lieutenant the Earl of Carlisle, to negotiate a peace with America. The terms they offered the rebellious colonies, including legislative independence, were well known in Ireland, and many there firmly believed that if Britain was willing to offer such concessions to people they had so vigorously castigated for rebellion, similar terms should be offered to loyal Ireland. That Ireland was engaging in what amounted to armed blackmail did not stop reformers and Volunteers from making the connection between loyalty and independence at the same time as they used the threat of rebellion to push their agenda.[20]

Grattan's motion was passed, with even the ministry's representatives in Parliament agreeing that the reformers' demands needed to be addressed. Outside Parliament, the Volunteers continued to agitate, keeping up the pressure on the administration. Around the country Volunteer associations voted to adopt the positions Grattan had outlined and to support the cause of independence with their "lives and fortunes." While the ministry considered its options, "the Irish nation was not idle." According to Barrington, "No relaxation was permitted in the warlike preparations" of the Volunteers. They continued to hold reviews, to parade through Dublin, and to conduct military exercises in Phoenix Park. When Parliament reassembled in May, the Volunteers of Dublin again turned out in great numbers, at once a show of force and a warning. In an intimidating strategic display, Volunteer artillery under James Napper Tandy took up positions on the quays of the city, as well as all of the bridges connecting the army barracks to Dublin Castle. Units of infantry and cavalry were stationed throughout the city, lining the route to Parliament. They were, Barrington reported, awaiting the reply of the British government to the Declaration of Rights, and were fully prepared to either "return to their homes for peaceful enjoyment of their rights or instantly to take the field."[21]

In another time such provocative insubordination might have been met with violence and repression, but by this point Britain was in no position to act. With her armies stretched thin and in retreat, with her finances drained by war without end, with opposition to the American War growing daily at home and abroad, it was the perfect time for Ireland to secure its independence. Henry Grattan made Britain's precarious position forcefully clear and urged Ireland to seize this unprecedented opportunity to claw back its liberty and independence. "England now smarts under the lesson of the American war," Grattan thundered:

> The doctrine of imperial legislature she feels to be pernicious—the revenues and monopolies annexed to it, she found untenable. Her enemies are a host pouring upon her from all quarters of the earth—her armies are dispersed—the sea is not hers—she has no minister, no ally, no admiral, none in whom she long confides, and no general whom she has not disgraced. The balance of her fate is in the hands of Ireland. You are not only her last connexion—you are the only nation of Europe, that is not her enemy . . . Nothing can prevent your being free, except yourselves: it is not in the disposition of England, it is not in the interest of England, it is not in her force. What! can 8,000,000 Englishmen opposed to 20,000,000 of French, 7,000,000 of Spanish, to 3,000,000 of American's reject the alliance of 3,000,000 of Ireland? Can 8,000,000 of British men thus outnumbered by foes, take upon their soldiers the expense of an expedition to enslave Ireland? Will Great Britain, a wise and magnanimous country, thus tutored by experience and wasted by war, the French riding her channel, send an army to Ireland to levy no tax, to enforce no law, to answer no end whatever, except to spoliate the characters of Ireland and enforce a barren oppression?

Given this state of affairs, all that was left was for Ireland to seize its destiny. "I wish for nothing," Grattan concluded:

> but to breathe in this our island, in common with my fellow subjects, the air of liberty. I have no ambition, unless it be to break your chain, and contemplate your glory. I never will be satisfied, so long as the meanest cottager in Ireland has a link of the British chain clanking to his rags: he may be naked, he shall not be in irons; and I do see at hand; the spirit is gone forth . . . and though great men should fall off, yet the cause shall live; and though he who after this should die, yet immortal fire shall outlast the humble organ who conveys it; and the breath of liberty, like the word of the holy man, will not die with the prophet, but survive him.[22]

In London, the British administration was no less clear about its position. Britain was beset by war with America and France, and by 1779 a movement for reform was building in Britain that threatened to bring down the ministry from within. Dissenters and radicals in London had been advocating for political reform since the days of Wilkes, but now the provinces were beginning to groan as well. The embargos and other disruptions of trade caused by the war had pushed Britain into a recession: unemployment soared and prices skyrocketed, while land values, wages, and stock prices plummeted. High taxes levied to pay for the war only made the economic squeeze worse. As in Ireland and America, government corruption, unscrupulous contractors, and a lack of adequate representation were held responsible for the worsening economic conditions and a disastrously mismanaged war.

In Yorkshire, in December 1779, Christopher Wyvill, a clergyman and country gentleman, convened a large public meeting to debate the structural deficiencies of Britain's government, refocusing criticism from Lord North's ministry to the more general problems with the state as it existed. Like his Irish and American counterparts, Wyvill believed that the English constitution had been degraded since the days of the Glorious Revolution. The political system had become "deranged," and the only solution was for the people of Britain to take matters into their own hands to reform the government. "When dangerous disputes have arisen between the Executive Power and the Parliament," Wyvill declared, "the People are the UMPIRE to whose judgment alone they can be referred, and by whose decision they can be happily adjusted." It was up to the people, or at least England's provincial landowners, to step in to fix what ailed the country.[23]

The result of Wyvill's Yorkshire meeting was a petition calling for an end to the inefficiencies and corruptions of the current system. From Yorkshire, the movement spread rapidly. As many as forty county Associations were formed across England and Scotland, creating a national network. The new movement united the interests of the county gentry with those of the provincial cities to form a broad-based coalition that petitioned for the end of rotten boroughs, the extension of the franchise, a secret ballot, and the rooting out of corruption, placemen, and other government abuses that placed too much power in the hands of the crown. In the shadow of the American Revolution, the mood of the country had shifted, with opposition to the ministry and king growing.[24]

The Association movement was a dangerous development for Lord North's administration. They represented England's county gentry, the backbone of the English electorate and the core constituency for both the ministry and the war. Their opposition threatened to turn the tide against the government at a crucial juncture. They also espoused ideas and used language that seemed awfully close to that of the American rebels and the Irish Patriots. And this was not coincidental. Not only were the Associators influenced by the same strands of Enlightenment thought as the reformers in London, America, and Ireland, but they also consciously adopted the rhetoric and tactics of these other groups. Many argued that America was better governed, its government more popular and less expensive than Britain's, and sought to emulate it through internal reform rather than resorting to revolution. The example of Ireland was also instructive. Even before the first meeting was held, Wyvill and others looked to the Volunteer movement for inspiration. From the first, Wyvill hoped to create a nationwide alliance of county Associations with a national convention to pressure the government. The Irish, the Associators realized, faced the same problems of corruption and recession as England, but the Irish had scorned "the humility of supplication" and instead had "taken up arms to defend herself," leading to success "ten times more" than had been achieved in England. "The account given by the Volunteers," Wyvill noted, "exhibits abuses exactly similar to those which deform the Parliament of Britain; and, if not corrected by National Interposition in each country, appear but too likely to increase; till they become the destruction of every valuable end for which parliaments were originally ordained." With this precedent in mind, there was from the beginning a veiled threat of violence around the Associations. The initial Yorkshire meeting was explicitly timed to coincide with a muster of Yorkshire's militia, commanded by the very same men who now gathered to debate reform.[25]

By 1780, the county Associations began to take on a more menacing aspect. They formed a "congress" or national convention of representatives from every Association, swore not to pay any taxes until their grievances were addressed, and sent a mountain of petitions to Parliament. They now voted themselves the right to debate and decide on issues pending in Parliament, demanded regular parliaments, the addition of 100 new Members of Parliament, and an end to the "civil war" with America. They also began to arm, with the Devonshire

Association first voting to create a fund to purchase weapons in January and others, including Yorkshire, quickly following suit. The Yorkshire Association threatened "redress" if their concerns continued to be ignored, and some among the movement began to argue that if Parliament would not act, the delegates of the counties should seize control. Some moderate reforms, many championed by Edmund Burke, began to wend their way through Parliament in an attempt to appease the Associations. But their great success came in April 1780 when they secured a parliamentary resolution, stating that "the influence of the crown has increased, is increasing, and ought to be diminished." The resolution represented not just a condemnation of royal power, but also a change in the mood of the country and a shift in the balance of power between the North ministry and the opposition.

The government was horrified. It seemed to many as if the Volunteer movement had been transported from Ireland to England. Indeed, Wyvill and the Associations were in direct contact with the Ulster Volunteers, exchanging advice and tactics for "destroying, restraining, or counter-acting this Hydra of corruption." Horace Walpole, no friend of the ministry himself, thought the movement was a "mutiny" of county gentlemen—men who supported the war when they thought it was in their interests, but now turned against the administration when they felt their pockets pinched. When the crown asked for his advice on the matter, he warned that it was a disastrous moment to "experiment" with government:

when we are at war with America, France, and Spain, and when we are in danger of seeing Ireland separate itself from this country. Alas! it is unhappy that by the enormities of the Court, and the incapacity of our present *Governors*, the nation should be forced to enter into such discussions, the very attention to which doubles our danger; for when the Opposition think of nothing but vanquishing the Court, and the Court can think of nothing but defending itself at home, no plans can be formed abroad, nor does either side think of attacking or defending the country from France.

The specter of civil war now invaded the minds of Englishmen, distracting focus from the struggle in America and ensuring that Irish demands were seen in a new, more conciliatory light. France threatened to invade, America seemed all but lost, and even Englishmen were up in arms in a state of near revolt. There was little the British ministry could do in the face of Irish threats but acquiesce. "Reform alone," many now concluded, "might prevent a civil war."[26]

And so it was that on May 27, 1782, Lord Lieutenant Portland informed Ireland's Parliament that their demand for legislative independence had been met. New Catholic Relief bills were also passed, allowing Irish Catholics to purchase land and Catholic landowners to vote. So great was the perceived need to placate Ireland that, in the face of strong British opposition led by Lord Gordon's Protestant Association, Parliament had even refused to repeal the Catholic Relief Act of 1778, touching off the spectacular violence of the Gordon Riots, but helping to prevent insurrection in Ireland. It was, or so many believed, the birth of the Irish nation, a birth of Irish independence that, once granted, could never be relinquished. It was a moment of joyous celebration, but the festive atmosphere and the Irish nation would both prove to be short-lived.

The Irish Ascendancy's quest for reform had grave, unintended consequences for the future of Ireland. The seeds of faction and union were sown in the very nature of Ireland's independence. The reformers and the Volunteers had initiated a sea-change in Irish conceptions of themselves and their country. Identity based on sectarian division began to be replaced by a more collective national identity and the development of the rhetoric of an Irish nation opposed to English imperial tyranny. As Jonah Barrington, himself swept up in the spirit of the time, remembered, starting in 1779 Ireland's:

> determination to claim her constitution from the British Government became unequivocal, and she began to assume the attitude and language of a nation "*entitled to independence*." The sound of arms and the voice of freedom echoed from every quarter of the Island—distinctions were forgotten, or disregarded—every rank, every religion, alike caught the general feeling . . . she gradually arose from torpor and obscurity—her native spirit drew aside the curtain . . . and exhibited and armed and animated people claiming their natural rights.

It was, for Barrington and many others, the very moment of Ireland's birth as a nation.[27]

And it was an increasingly politically aware nation as well. The Volunteer Movement was the key to this growing awareness and widening political participation. Originally, most had joined the Volunteers out of genuine fear of invasion or as a result of personal connections and loyalties to their local leaders or landlords. They had been raised for the defense of their homes by their traditional leaders and their motives had been self-interested. Once gathered, however, the mindset of the rank and file began to be transformed. In Barrington's experience, "the blending of ranks, and more intimate connexion of the people . . . quickly effected an extensive and marked revolution in the minds and manners of the entire nation." The experience of the Volunteer Movement:

> opened the road to better information. Thus, he [the Volunteer] soon learned that the Irish people were deprived of political rights, and his country had endured political injuries: his ideas became enlarged, and quickly embraced more numerous and prouder objects; he began for the first time, to know his own importance to the state; and as knowledge advanced, the principles of constitutional independence better understood.

Thus equipped, the Irish nation, "familiarized with arms and more intimated with his superiors . . . every day felt the love of liberty increase." The Volunteers thus provided a political education and helped spark a new adherence to political action and Irish independence.[28]

This shift in mentality helped drive the successful reforms of 1779 and 1782, but they also created a new national and imperial status quo that was not indefinitely viable. Like Britain's American colonists at the beginning of the American War, the Irish Ascendancy, who formed the core of the reform movement, did not consider themselves to be inhabitants of a British colony or victims of British colonialism or imperialism: they viewed themselves as Englishmen who shared in the bounty and governance of the British Empire. As such, their initial protests were framed as efforts to reclaim and reassert these rights. But the repeated failure of their efforts and the intransigence of the

British and Irish administrations caused a consequential shift in rhetoric. They continued to appeal to their rights under the English Bill of Rights but they also began to appeal to a conception of a unified Ireland in opposition to Britain and the British Empire. This was a crucial moment for the future of Irish politics, the creation of an oppositional Irish national identity. Just as the revolution mentally transformed British colonists from Englishmen to Americans, the war helped create a new sense of Irishness as a distinct and separate identity.

There was little time to celebrate the successes of 1782. Almost immediately there were debates and divides over questions still left unanswered. Front and center was the question of Ireland's future relationship with Britain. Henry Flood and others feared that Britain's grudging acceptance of Irish commercial, legislative, and judicial independence was a temporary expedient. Once the war was over and the danger passed, Britain, they warned, was sure to attempt to claw back control over Ireland. In Parliament, Flood focused his efforts on securing a demand that Britain pass new legislation guaranteeing Ireland's newly won independence from Britain. Britain had repealed the act that granted its Parliament supremacy over Ireland, but it had not formally abjured the underlying principle. Flood thus wanted a positive act renouncing the very idea of Britain's right to rule Ireland.

Flood and his allies were correct to worry about Britain's commitment to Irish independence, but in 1782 the prospect of Britain regaining its supremacy over Ireland seemed distant, even foolish. Grattan dismissed Flood's concerns, ridiculing the very idea that Ireland's independence, her natural, inalienable rights required the acquiescence, let alone the protection, of foreign, English laws. "If the security that the honourable gentleman desires be a British statute," Grattan thundered, "I reject it: I would reject Magna Charta under a British statute. We have not come to England for a charter, but with a charter; and we have asked her to cancel all her declarations made in opposition to it. This is the true idea of the situation of Ireland: no man will be content with less than a free constitution; and I trust no man will be frantic enough to hazard that, in attempting to gain more." He continued:

> We are, he [Flood] had said, independent of the Parliament of England by
> the ancient charters of Ireland; and then he calls on that Parliament to give

Ireland liberty: he first proposes to measure a transaction common to both nations, by the municipal law which is peculiar to each, and thus subjects his country to the comment of Westminster Hall: he calls for legal security by operation of statute, and subjects his liberty to the Parliament of England: he proceeds insensibly on the principle of an ancient hereditary supremacy in the British nation; and he proceeds on the idea of an inferior country, who cannot measure a joint transaction by rules which obtain between equal nations.

See America: the establishment of American independence is, in the opinion of some of the judges of England, illegal. According to the municipal laws of England, no English statute has expressly recognized her independence; the statute that should have enabled the King to do so is not expressed. According to this, America has no legal security, no explicit emancipation. Does America complain? Does she expostulate, that "her liberty is equivocal, placed on construction and the fleeting base of interpretation?" Does she put questions to the twelve judges of England to learn the privileges of the thirteen states of America? No! America is too high for such expostulation; America is not only free, but she thinks like a free country; and having given herself liberty, does not ask for legal security under the laws of any other nation.[29]

Grattan was an indefatigable champion of an independent Irish nation, but he was still careful to stress the importance of Ireland's connections to George III and Britain. For men like Grattan, alienating Britain by demanding further, and in his view unnecessary, concessions risked destroying hopes for a reconceived British Empire. Grattan and his supporters envisioned independent Ireland as an equal partner in a new imperial confederation, bound together by a common king and shared economic and military interests. To cement this new Empire of Great Britain and Ireland, Ireland's Parliament, led by Grattan, went to great lengths to assure the king of their continued loyalty. In their "Humble Address" to George III, they stressed their "unfeigned attachment to his royal person and government" and promised that Britain could "rely on our affection." "We remember," the address continued:

and do repeat our determination to stand and fall with the British Nation . . . Common interest, perpetual connection, the recent conduct of Great Britain, a native affection to the British name and nation, together with the constitution which we have recovered, and the high reputation which we possess, must ever decide the wishes as well as the interest of Ireland, to perpetuate the harmony, stability, and glory of the empire. Accordingly, we assure His Majesty, that we learn, with singular satisfaction, the account of his brilliant successes in the East and West Indies, gratified at one and the same instant in our dearest wishes, — the freedom of Ireland and glory of Great Britain.[30]

Lest the Irish Parliament's commitment to Britain be seen as a matter of mere words, Ireland also pledged 20,000 sailors and £100,000 for "the common defence of the empire" and urged its Members of Parliament to raise men for the war effort, "manifesting their zeal for the common cause of Great Britain and Ireland."[31]

That such demonstrations of loyalty could come so closely on the heels of cries for freedom and condemnations of British barbarity may appear strange, but for most members of the Protestant Ascendancy 1782 was the end of the Irish Revolution, not the beginning, a time to consolidate their gains rather than continue the work of reform. For many Catholics, Dissenters, and radicals, however, the intoxicating but incomplete success of 1782 seemed a mere prelude to full equality or a true democratic revolution. Catholics and some Protestants called for a complete repeal of the Penal Laws that kept Ireland's Catholic majority from owning land, holding office, or worshipping freely. Grattan and other Patriots backed Catholic emancipation in Parliament, arguing that Ireland's Catholics had proved their mettle during the crisis of 1778–9. They had earned the right to be emancipated.

[T]heir conduct . . . should fully convince us of their true attachment to their country. When this country had resolved no longer to crouch beneath the burden of oppression that England had laid upon her, when she armed in defence of her rights, and a high-spirited people demanded a free trade, did the Roman Catholics desert their countrymen? No; they were found among the foremost. When it was afterwards thought necessary to assert a free constitution, the Roman Catholics displayed their public virtue; they did not endeavour to take advantage of your situation; they did not endeavour to make terms for themselves, but they entered frankly and heartily into the cause of their country, judging by their own virtue that they might depend upon your generosity for their reward . . . In 1779 when the fleets of Bourbon hovered on our coasts, and the Irish nation roused herself to arms, did the Roman Catholics stand aloof? or did they, as might be expected from their oppressed situation, offer assistance to the enemy? No; they poured in subscriptions for the service of their country, or they pressed into the ranks of her glorious volunteers.[32]

Beyond gratitude, there were other reasons to grant Catholic Relief. For Grattan, the creation of a unified Irish nation was one of the greater goals of the revolution. If Ireland was to remain independent, if Ireland was to reach its true potential, all Irishmen, Catholics and Protestants alike, must embrace a sense of common identity and common causes. The question was not simply about property rights or freedom of worship, but:

whether we shall be *a Protestant settlement or an Irish nation?* whether we shall throw open the gates of the temple of liberty to all our countrymen, or whether we shall confine them in bondage by penal laws? So long as the penal code remains, we never can be a great nation. The penal code is the shell in which the Protestant power has been hatched, and now it has become a bird it must burst the shell or perish in it.[33]

Many among the Ascendancy disagreed with Grattan and his allies. Though Catholics had enthusiastically supported the Volunteer Movement, donating money and in some cases even joining Volunteer units, the Volunteers as a whole were deeply divided on the Catholic question. The majority of Volunteers, especially among the leadership, felt there was more to be gained from Catholic support than there was to fear from the relaxation of the Penal Laws. Volunteer support contributed considerably to the passage of Catholic Relief Acts in 1778 and 1782, which in turn helped to secure Catholic support for the Volunteers and the British war effort. By 1779 Catholics were joining Volunteer companies in significant numbers in some areas and holding fasts throughout the country as a sign of solidarity. But distrust remained. Even after the passage of two Catholic Relief Acts, the Catholic hierarchy remained wary of the Volunteers, and for many Protestants the feeling was mutual. At the Dungannon Volunteer Convention in 1782 the representatives voted to fully support Catholic Relief, but at the same time its members still resolved that some restrictions on Catholics should remain in place for the safety and security of the country. This ambiguous position was common. That the Penal Laws should be relaxed was largely accepted, but that Catholics should be granted full equality was, for a significant number of Protestants including Volunteers, a step too far.[34]

When the issue was proposed in Parliament in 1782, some of the most prominent leaders of the Patriot Party likewise questioned the wisdom of giving full rights to the Catholic majority. In debates on Catholic Relief, many of the most influential members of the Patriot Party were keen to put the brakes on what they now considered runaway reform. Henry Flood, leading light of the Patriot Party, made clear the proper limits of reform. Flood spoke vociferously against full emancipation for Ireland's Catholics, arguing that while he was in favor of religious toleration, it was necessary to prevent Catholics from gaining "any influence in elections." Full emancipation, he contended, "goes beyond toleration; it gives them a *power*, and tends to make a change in the state." The Penal Laws, he continued, were not persecution of Catholics "but political necessity"; tyranny and persecution would naturally follow in the wake of Catholic suffrage, a lesson that should have been learned in 1688. The consequence of granting Catholics full equality with Protestants was thus the death of "a protestant constitution." "We wish to extend toleration to Roman Catholics," Flood concluded, but "we do not wish to shake the government."[35]

Even Grattan granted that the "prejudices" of the Protestant population must be taken into account when weighing how much to grant Ireland's Catholics. In the end, perhaps his most persuasive argument in favor of granting Catholic Relief was to illustrate that granting Catholics greater property rights and greater religious freedom gave them "no new power in the state." Though he spoke passionately of Catholic sacrifice and eloquently in favor of granting toleration, Grattan conceded that granting Catholics full political equality was both unrealistic and potentially dangerous. Indeed, one of the greatest compliments he offered Ireland's Catholics was that their recent actions showed that either they were willing to "depart" from their creed "or . . . do not carry its principles into life." If Ireland's Catholics only deserved toleration because they had ignored the principles of their faith, there was little reason to suppose they did not remain a possible threat in the minds of the country's ruling Protestant minority.[36]

In 1782 Parliament passed a compromise Catholic Relief Bill that granted Catholics full property rights and freedom of worship but did not give Ireland's majority full political equality. Catholics and their supporters in the Patriot Party were disappointed, but there remained hope that the 1782 Relief Act was the first step in an incremental reform process. In reality, however, many Protestants opposed further emancipation. The outbreak of sectarian violence in the 1780s seemed only to confirm Protestant prejudices. For Ireland's Protestants, conditioned to live in perpetual terror of a rebellious Catholic population, the eruption of clashes between Catholics and Protestants proved that Grattan's hope that toleration would ensure unity and loyalty was wishful thinking.

Catholics were not the only Irishmen to press for further reform in the years after 1782. Radical Patriots and Dissenters, especially in Dublin and Belfast, hoped that the legislative independence secured by the Volunteers would lead to parliamentary reform. Though now free from British supremacy, Ireland's political system remained deeply undemocratic. Entrenched undertakers and officeholders controlled many parliamentary seats and judicial posts, and representation in Parliament was unequally distributed across the country. With dissatisfaction with the current system widespread, there was belief in many quarters that further reform was necessary. As a later commentator put it, "what had been conceded by the British legislature . . . did not suffice for the rising spirit of the Irish nation," and within a year of their revolutionary success in 1782, renewed pressure was building to complete the work of reform. Radical elements among the Volunteers were in the vanguard.

In 1783, they sent reform proposals to Lord Charlemont, their overall commander and leader of the Patriot Party in the House of Lords. Charlemont's support for their proposals was only lukewarm, but nonetheless, later in the year delegates from the country's Volunteer units once more gathered together at Dungannon, and then in November in Dublin in a National Convention, where they attempt to develop a clear platform and direct further reform of Ireland's government. With the support and guidance of Henry Flood— though no friend of Catholic emancipation, he remained an advocate of further parliamentary reform—the National Convention met for nearly three weeks before eventually agreeing on a series of demands to be submitted to Parliament. Their complaints and demands closely resembled those of reformers in Britain: regular parliaments as a means of limiting the power of any one ministry; the elimination of rotten boroughs and the addition of more urban seats to more adequately address the proportionate representation of an increasingly urban society; a crackdown on placemen who allowed elites to capture electoral power; and the restriction of absentees, often English aristocrats rewarded with Irish titles and lands, and paid annuities out of Irish coffers.[37]

Once agreed upon, the platform of the National Convention was presented by Henry Flood as a bill in Parliament where it received the support of Grattan and other influential Patriots. The situation, however, had changed. The American Revolution had ended with the Peace of Paris in 1783. The end of the immediate wartime crisis meant there was less pressure to accommodate the demands of reformers. At the same time, the disorder of the war years ensured that most viewed reform suspiciously, as likely to lead to a renewal of the chaos of the war. As would happen around the world in the wake of this great war for and against empire, the initial victory of the forces of democracy was quickly undercut by a conservative reaction. Grattan's Parliament represented property rather than people, the establishment rather than the powerless, and even among the Volunteers there were concerns about the dangerous radicalism growing in the ranks and among Ireland's Catholics and Dissenters.

Some among the Ascendancy feared that the armed threat of the Volunteers might usurp the sovereignty of Parliament, the proper representatives of the people, and become the real power in the state like "the pretorian legions of Rome." To acquiesce to their demands now, just when the first independent Parliament was meeting for the first time, would set a dangerous precedent. Many, even among the Irish Patriot Party, had joined the government or accepted offices and had no desire to see their positions threatened or the new status quo undermined. The government of Britain had also changed, with the despised and defeated Lord North swept out and more amenable ministers rising in his place. Irish Patriots now found themselves looking across the Irish Sea at political allies, not enemies. With the encouragement of a new British administration, they now opposed further reforms that would separate the country from Britain more fully and finally. The Irish Patriot Party was also beginning to fracture internally over the question of Catholic suffrage, the viability of a standing army, economic cost-cutting, and the nature of Ireland's future relationship with Britain. Most dramatically, Flood and Grattan, the two most prominent champions of 1782, fell out, leading to violently vituperative exchanges in the Irish House of Commons and an aborted duel.[38]

Crucially, in 1783 the Volunteers also lacked a key component of their success in 1782, the support of Ireland's Catholics. In 1782 a unified Irish nation had been able to force Britain to acquiesce to their demands for legislative independence. Convinced that an independent legislature would grant emancipation, Irish Catholics had been eager to support this movement. But the Relief of the Poor Act 1782 was a disappointment and Catholics remained largely shut out of the political nation. As such, they had little reason to care whether political representation was more evenly spread among the Protestant minority, and little reason to trust that a Protestant Parliament would ever grant full political equality to their Catholic neighbors. Instead of throwing their weight behind Flood and the Volunteers, in 1783 Ireland's Catholics remained largely aloof, helping to undermine efforts for further reform.

In the end, Flood was not even allowed to present his bill. The Ascendancy controlled the levers of power and they now closed ranks to protect their positions and ensure that reform would go no further. Barry Yelverton, the attorney-general, condemned the bill, charging that it had originated "in an armed assembly," and was therefore "inconsistent with the freedom of debate" of a sovereign Parliament. That some of the same men who now opposed even hearing a bill backed by the Volunteers were among those who had praised the actions of the Volunteers in securing legislative independence just one year ago was an irony scarcely to be believed. Flood castigated his opponents as men who would willfully "conjure up a military phantom . . . to affright yourselves."

But opposition to the bill was steadfast. The Ascendancy had secured power for itself and now only desired to consolidate and maintain that power. A year earlier, in a letter to Henry Flood, Lord Charlemont had complained that stability rather than further reform was what Ireland needed most. "I wish to heaven that gentlemen would . . . let the country alone; suffer things to remain as they are, and not hazard the ruin of that growing coalescence, which . . . was beginning to take place between men of all persuasions." Ireland had already seen all of the political change that the Ascendancy wished to see. Reform would go no further.[39]

This oppositional, nationalist rhetoric had helped unite the country behind the Volunteers and the Irish Patriot Party of Grattan, Flood, and Charlemont, and thus helped Ireland secure free trade and legislative independence, but it also inspired Catholics and Dissenters, long shut out of the corridors of power, to imagine a more equal Ireland. Ireland's entrenched political class, however, even members of the Volunteers and the Irish Patriot Party, were largely composed of members of the Protestant Ascendancy, men who sought Ireland's independence in large measure as a means of asserting their own power and securing their own monopoly over the benefits of Ireland's place in the British Empire. This was not, as some have suggested, a democratic revolution, nor a struggle for the broader political rights of the Irish people. It was instead a revolt against British imperial policy over the proper division of the economic and political spoils of empire clothed in the rhetorical robes of nationalism, democracy, and independence. It sought not the democratic rights of Ireland, but to replace metropolitan control with local control, to replace London with Dublin, and to exchange one group of ruling Protestant elites with another. As such, the Patriot Party was generally uninterested in either sharing the bounty of independence with their Catholic and Nonconformist neighbors or further severing their relationship with Britain and her empire.

The failures of reform in 1782 and 1783 proved to be a watershed. Grattan's vision of a unified Irish nation began to disintegrate. The failure of further reform spelt the end of the Volunteers as a powerful, national movement. Despite their armed threats, they accepted their defeat peacefully, refusing to go beyond intimidation in their quest for greater political equality. In part, this decision to abjure violence was a result of its membership. The Volunteers, outside of Ulster, were largely members of the Protestant Ascendancy, and thus many were already skeptical of the more radical elements within the organization, and few wished to risk civil war in the pursuit of greater rights for Catholics and Dissenters. But the failure to back up their threats was also the result of changing international circumstances. By 1783, the American War was over, the British crisis passed, and a militia of regular troops once more stationed in Ireland. The moment for armed reform was gone, the *raison d'être* of the Volunteers no more, and with no power to push reform and no invasion threat to oppose, the Volunteers began to disintegrate.

The Ascendancy, wary of sectarian unrest and calls for further reform, began to crack down on dissent. Instead of completing the revolution begun in 1782, they now sought to freeze reform where it stood and protect the Ascendancy's landed interests. With legislative independence, Ireland's courts, previously lax in their dealings with libel, began cracking down on perceived critics of the Ascendancy and its government. In 1786 a bill proposing the creation of a new police force in Dublin was introduced. Its primary purpose was not to combat crime but, in the words of Attorney-General Fitzgibbon, to curb the "frequency of those tumultuous assemblies called aggregate meetings . . . restrain licentiousness, and to teach those citizens a due deference for the laws of their country." The political establishment was increasingly concerned about social and political unrest and moved to increase the power of the executive as a result. The new magistrates would be appointed by the Lord-Lieutenant— making them crown appointments—and the new constables granted the power to "break into any house under warrant of information" alone. As sensitive to the despotic dangers of a government-controlled constabulary as their English counterparts, Grattan and others opposed the bill, arguing that the new police would be a standing army by another name. Such a force, Grattan warned, was simply "an army in the state," a "mercenary army," a "ministerial army," "assassins of liberty feeding on the vitals of the constitution." The administration already "approaches too near an arbitrary government to have an armed rabble under the influence of the crown." Few heeded Grattan's words; the bill passed by a majority of four to one.[40]

A year later, Parliament went a step further and proposed a new bill "to prevent tumultuous risings and assemblies; and for the more effectual punishment of persons guilty of outrage, riot, and illegal combinations, and the administering and taking of unlawful oaths." Modeled on the English Riot Act, the 1787 bill was designed to give the government greater power to suppress the very activities that had secured the success of the 1782 revolution. The new law would make disorderly or unlawful gatherings illegal and make it a felony to "write, print, publish, send, or carry any message, letter or notice tending to excite insurrection." In the face of growing Catholic unrest in the south and west, the bill also proposed that any Catholic meetinghouse that held an illegal assembly should be pulled down. As usual, Grattan's faction opposed the measure as an increase in arbitrary government, but by 1787 even Grattan had to concede that the country had a "cast of lawlessness" and that "shabby mutiny and abortive rebellion" required strong measures. Thus even the most radical Members of Parliament now sought merely to temper the worst excesses of the bill. They succeeded in having the clause about the destruction of Catholic meetinghouses removed, but the bill passed with overwhelming support. Major Doyle, one of the bill's few opponents, responded to its passage with a lament and a prescient warning. "Who could have thought that within five years from the glorious Revolution of 1782, toleration would stand in need of advocates . . . I will say, that by toleration alone Ireland can continue free and independent; by being united you recovered your constitution. Suffer yourselves to be disunited and you will recover your chains." Time would prove Doyle right.[41]

When it became clear that many of the heroes of 1782 were not interested in expanding the political nation beyond the bounds of the Protestant Ascendancy, old divisions within Irish society were once more driven to the surface. Betrayed by the revolution they had done so much to create, disaffected Patriots, Catholics, and Dissenters began to move in more radical directions. Catholics still striving for full emancipation and Patriots and Dissenters still pushing for political reform began to coalesce into a new movement and plot a new revolution. Centered on the Dissenters in the north, and a small contingent of urban radicals in Dublin and Belfast, new, more radical groups of agitators began to emerge: armed, revolutionary groups modeled on the Irish Patriot Party and the Volunteers but committed to achieving further reform by any means necessary. Foremost among these new radical groups was the Society of United Irishmen, formed by a core of disappointed radicals inspired by the American Revolution, the Volunteer Movement, and the reform movement of 1782.

The years after reform's final defeat in 1784 had seen the growth of a variety of Whig clubs in Dublin and Belfast, but a more concerted movement was born when Belfast Volunteers, inspired by the French Revolution and Thomas Paine's outstandingly popular *The Rights of Man*, coalesced into the United Irishmen at a celebration marking the anniversary of the fall of the Bastille in Belfast in 1791. Led by an Anglican barrister named Theobald Wolfe Tone, the United Irishmen were committed to an end to British interference in Irish affairs, full parliamentary reform along the lines of Flood's 1783 bill, and a democratic union of Catholics, Anglicans, and Dissenters. Initially, the United Irishmen were limited to a small group of Protestant radicals in Dublin and Belfast, but the precedent for a democratic, nationalist armed resistance had been set during the years of the American War. In the 1790s this precedent would transform into a revolutionary movement that would shake Ireland to its core. In their opposition to Britain, the Patriots and Volunteers had set the stage for religious factional violence, rebellion, or reconquest by Britain. In the end they got all three.

Neither was everyone in Ireland satisfied with the religious reforms secured in 1779 and 1782. Despite the universalist, nationalist rhetoric of Volunteers like Barrington and Patriots like Grattan, there were still deep divisions in Irish society, divisions that were only exacerbated by the reform movement. The reformers and the Volunteers had provided a collective rhetoric and a tempting example of the power of a nation under arms to force political change, and they had helped to create a nascent sense of Irish nationalism in opposition to imperial Britain but they had not created a settled or accepted definition of just who constituted the Irish nation. Among Irish Catholics even ancillary participation in the reform and Volunteer movements secured practical gains through the Catholic Relief Acts, but also provided scope and precedent for political action, for their own redefinition of the Irish nation as one in which Catholics would play an important and growing role. As such, when some of the Penal Laws were rolled back, land-starved and land-hungry Catholics quickly flooded what had previously been a relatively restricted property market. Rural Protestants, especially in areas of more evenly mixed settlement like Ulster, were alarmed by this new Catholic competition, for land was not only the source of economic power, but political authority as well. The confessional competition was only intensified by a period of economic stagnation and steep rises in rental prices that racked Ireland in the late eighteenth century. Economically vulnerable, horrified by the new world Catholic Relief presaged, and terrified by the threat of foreign Catholic invasion, rampant rumors of Catholic priests gushing into Ireland, and the recent example of mass, armed political agitation, Protestants in Ulster began to gather together to combat what they saw as the growing threat of Catholic independence.

The trouble began in Armagh, where Catholics and Protestants lived in relatively equal numbers. Fearful of growing Catholic power and angered by the Catholic economic competition initiated by the reform movement, in 1784 a group of Protestant partisans from Portnorris banded together in a gang called the Nappach Fleet to harass local Catholics. The Portnorris Volunteers were rumored to have allowed Catholics to join their ranks, an alarming prospect for local Protestants conditioned to fear the idea of armed Catholics in their neighborhood. As commander of the Volunteers, Lord Charlemont had opposed the decision to allow Catholics into the Portnorris association, a fact that the Nappach Fleet gang interpreted as a justification for seizing Catholic arms. With this rationalization the Nappach Fleet began raiding Catholic houses in search of weapons. Armagh's Catholics, however, were not willing to take this new persecution lying down. For the defense of their homes and communities, Catholics began to form their own gangs, starting with the Bunker's Hill Defenders in Portnorris. The creation of opposing armed factions led inevitably to conflict and violence, first sporadic brawls, raids, and cattle maiming, but eventually confrontations more closely resembling pitched battles.[42]

By 1785, the Nappach Fleet had expanded greatly, rebranding itself the Peep O'Day Boys for their penchant for raiding Catholic homes at dawn. The targets of their raids had shifted and broadened as well. Where once they justified their attacks by focusing on the confiscation of illegal arms, now they widened their violence to include attacks on religious symbols and buildings, and on the economic livelihood of Catholics. Chapels were razed, houses looted, crops burnt, and looms destroyed as the logic of Protestant violence shifted from self-preservation to economic competition. It was no longer enough to prevent a Catholic rising, now the Peep O'Day Boys and their allies wished to eliminate Catholic economic competition and drive Catholics out of the county.

These Protestant paramilitary attacks alarmed the authorities in Dublin, but local law enforcement, judges and juries were, as Protestants, often more sympathetic toward the Peep O'Day Boys than to their victims. As a result, few of the partisans were arrested, let alone convicted, forcing Armagh's Catholics to rely on their own for protection. At Grangemore, local Catholics organized their own armed faction, named the Irish Defenders, and began to patrol Catholic territories and raid Protestant houses for guns. Over the years after 1785, they transformed from a series of autonomous defense groups to a unified secret organization of cells or lodges spread across Ulster. The result was that by 1786, clear Protestant and Catholic paramilitary factions had emerged and spread, increasing the frequency and intensity of violence.

It was the most intense sectarian violence Ireland had seen in generations. The failure of the local authorities to contain the strife meant that alternative peace-keepers were needed. With few resources at their command, the authorities in Dublin turned to the Volunteers. Though they had petered out in most of Ireland, in Ulster, the Volunteers retained their numbers and influence. As such, they were now sent into Armagh to restore order. The Volunteers, however, were hardly the neutral peace-keepers Armagh needed. Still made up of Protestants, many Volunteers openly supported the actions of Armagh's Protestants. Some had even gone so far as to join the Peep O'Day Boys, and many Peep O'Day Boys scrabbled to join the Volunteers. Unsurprisingly, instead of keeping order, the Volunteers only exacerbated the problems. The arrival of the Volunteers signaled a new phase of more open, concerted violence between Protestants and Catholics. At Tillysaran in 1788, the Benburb Volunteers intentionally antagonized Catholics by disrupting their worship with marching and anti-Catholic songs. When the outraged Catholics attempted to prevent a second march through their village, the Volunteers opened fire, leading to a cycle of retaliation and reprisal. At Forkhill in 1791, Catholics cut out the tongue of a Protestant schoolmaster, cut off his teenage son's calf, and removed several of his wife's fingers.

The escalation of raid and riot eventually led to open battle between Catholic and Protestant. In September of 1795, at a crossroads known as the

Diamond near Loughgall, several hundred armed Peep O'Day Boys faced off against perhaps three hundred Defenders. In the battle that followed the Peep O'Day Boys struck a crushing blow. Well armed and well defended on a hilltop, they managed to kill thirty or forty Defenders with no casualties of their own. After they drove their enemies from the field, they repaired to a local tavern to celebrate their victory, where they once more changed their name and solemnly formed the Orange Order to defend "the King and his heirs so long as he or they support the Protestant Ascendancy." Fittingly, members of the Volunteers helped form the core of the new order. By 1795 the sectarian divisions, the Orange Order, and the Irish Defenders that would trouble Northern Ireland for the next two hundred years had been set. The American War had brought about the introduction and legitimation of the paramilitary faction's central place in Ireland's politics; it had given national identity and political aspiration to downtrodden Catholics and emergent Dissenters; it had created the context and conditions in which old authorities were challenged and old animosities intensified; it gave birth to the Irish nation, but also sowed the seeds of its division and destruction.

Protestant factions in Armagh followed up their victory at the Battle of the Diamond with a concerted effort to drive Catholics out of the county for good. William Blacker, a gentry member of the new Orange Order, reported that "a determination was expressed of driving from this quarter of the country the entire of its Roman Catholic population . . . A written notice was thrown into or posted upon the door of a house warning the inmates, in the words of Oliver Cromwell, to betake themselves to Hell or Connaught." Over the next year, as many as 7,000 Catholic refugees fled their homes for more hospitable areas, many eventually making their way to America. The Protestants had succeeded in driving their enemies out of Armagh, but as they would soon discover, they had unknowingly driven them into the hands of the United Irishmen.[43]

Since their founding in 1791, the United Irishmen had been stymied by lack of numbers. Their core of Dissenters and urban radicals was committed but small and relatively insignificant. They had attempted to revive a military system on the model of the Volunteers, but recruiting proved difficult and largely limited to Ulster and Dublin. After the Battle of the Diamond and the flight of Catholics from Armagh, however, the United Irishmen began to see the potential benefits of an alliance with the Defenders. Catholics, disgusted by the failure of the authorities to come to their aid and protection, began to contemplate an alliance with the United Irishmen as well. United Irish leaders like James Hope began actively to recruit Defenders, transforming secret cells of Defenders into secret cells of United Irishmen. And so, as Armagh was drained of its Catholics, the ranks of the United Irishmen began to swell.

The growth of the United Irishmen's membership led to a growth of ambition. Opposition to Grattan's Parliament, to increasing British encroachment on Ireland's sovereignty, and to war with France all grew in the early 1790s. But as the United Irishmen became more numerous and more vocal, the authorities became increasingly alarmed. When Britain went to war with revolutionary France in 1793, the United Irishmen were outlawed. For the authorities, the looming threat of the ideas and tactics of the French Revolution spreading to the British Isles, where they found fertile soil among disillusioned Irish reformers, necessitated a firm hand. As the United Irishmen transformed into a revolutionary organization with strong links to France, prominent members such as William Drennan and William Jackson, an exiled Irish priest sent back home to assess the possibility for French invasion supported by an Irish revolt, were arrested and charged with treason. The leadership of United Irishmen, including its general secretary Theobald Wolfe Tone, who had aided and encouraged Jackson, fled to America or France. Driven underground or into exile, the United Irishmen became more radical, dividing into cells of twelve men each. From 1796, vague plans of rebelling with French aid began to evolve into more concrete and concerted plans for insurrection. In that year, Theobald Wolfe Tone began secret negotiations with the French government in Paris.

At the same time, Lord Edward Fitzgerald traveled to Hamburg to begin negotiations with representatives of France. Since his days in America, the eager British soldier had been transformed into an ardent revolutionary. Perhaps his experience in the war against America had started him on this journey to radicalization, or his rescue when wounded by a former slave who became his lifelong companion, or his days after the war in Nova Scotia, where he experienced the freedoms of an equal society among Irish immigrants, or during his trip through the great lakes, down the Mississippi to New Orleans, where he met Joseph Brant, the famous Mohawk loyalist commander. Whatever the cause,

Fitzgerald had entered Ireland's Parliament as a member of the opposition and became a trenchant critic of British and Irish Ascendancy policy. When the French Revolution burst forth in 1789, Fitzgerald leapt at the opportunity to see this epochal movement for himself. In 1792 he traveled to Paris, where he lodged with Thomas Paine and rubbed elbows with the foremost figures of the revolution. He was so swept away by the excitement of it all that at a banquet to celebrate French victories he joined in toasts to "the army of France: may the example of its citizen soldiers be followed by all enslaved countries till tyrants and tyranny be extinct" and renounced his aristocratic titles.[44]

Back in Ireland and dismissed from the army in 1793, Fitzgerald received a visit from Eleazar Oswald, an American veteran of the revolution now returning the favor by fighting for France in her revolution. Oswald had been sent by the French authorities to establish the possibility of a concerted French invasion and United Irish Rising. Three years later, in 1796, Fitzgerald officially joined the United Irishmen, adding his illustrious name and pedigree to the cause of revolution and equality. His prominence, resources, and connections made him a natural leader, and a natural candidate to engage in negotiations with the French. The result of Fitzgerald's and Tone's negotiations was a treaty of alliance between France and the Society of United Irishmen. France would invade Ireland with the support of an Irish revolt, provided that "the French would come as allies only, and consent to act under the direction of the new [Irish] government, as Rochambeau did in America."[45]

An invasion was launched in 1796, but bad weather prevented the French general Hoche from landing his 15,000 men. The abortive invasion further alarmed the British authorities, and martial law was declared. By 1798, the United Irishmen had hundreds of thousands of members across Ireland, but they were increasingly besieged by government crackdowns on their activities and membership. No longer certain that the French would hold up their end of the bargain, it was decided that the United Irishmen would rise with or without French support on May 23, 1798. Before they could act, however, they learned that the British had infiltrated the United Irishmen and knew of the planned revolt. Fitzgerald and the other United Irish leaders went into hiding, but Fitzgerald's position was given away by visits from his wife. Fitzgerald resisted arrest, leaping from his bed to kill one of his attackers and wound another, but he was eventually shot in the arm and subdued. While he lay in prison, a loyalist friend of Fitzgerald's from his days as a soldier in America paid him a visit. He was shocked at this turn of events, how Fitzgerald had been transformed from wounded British soldier to wounded Irish rebel. Fitzgerald replied, "I was wounded then in a very different cause; that was in fighting *against* liberty—this, in fighting *for* it."[46]

While Fitzgerald slowly succumbed to his wounds in prison, fighting raged outside on the streets of Dublin. Despite the arrest, the United Irishmen had risen as planned. They were sure that the people of Ireland would rise with them to throw off their chains of British oppression, but in this they were disappointed. Few joined the rebellion, and even some among the United Irishmen decided that the better part of valor was discretion. Alarmed by the prospect of Ireland joining France in revolution, in June 1798, the villain of Yorktown Lord Cornwallis, fresh from a successful stint as Governor-General of India, was appointed Lord Lieutenant and commander of royal forces in Ireland. With reinforcements from Britain he set about mopping up the scattered Irish rebellions. In August, 1,000 French troops finally landed in County Mayo to aid the rebels, but it was too little too late. By the time Theobald Wolfe Tone arrived with 3,000 more French troops in October, the British had the upper hand. The fleet was intercepted by the British navy while still off the coast, and Tone captured and imprisoned. The defiant leader of the United Irishmen cut his own throat in prison to cheat the British of a traitor's execution. Sporadic guerrilla warfare and further risings would continue for several years, but none would pose a real threat to British control.

That same year, shortly after Wexford, the stronghold of the rebellion and scene of the most intense violence on all sides, had been recaptured, Jonah Barrington rode out from Dublin to survey the devastation. He had been to Wexford before, in fact quite recently, and as he made his way through the hills and valleys, his stomach tightened as he contemplated the fate of his many friends caught up in the insurrection. In April, a mere month before the desperate United Irishmen rose, Barrington had dined at the home of Bagenal Harvey in Wexford. The atmosphere of the dinner party had been a mixture of light-hearted jocularity and somber premonition. Most of the guests, including their host, were deeply involved in radical politics, many already secretly members of the United Irishmen—a fact that became increasingly clear as the night progressed. Barrington knew these men well, and had guessed at their political sympathies, but he was shocked at the frankness with which they now discussed the possibility of armed rebellion, its potential for success, and the new government that would follow. As they talked, it dawned on Barrington that this was no mere speculation but discussion of an actual plan, and a plan that was near to fruition. Unwittingly, Barrington had found himself "in the midst of unavowed conspirators. I perceived that the explosion was much nearer than the government expected; and I was startled at the decided manner in which my host and his friends spoke."[47]

Alarmed and deeply uncomfortable, Barrington, true to form, turned to humor, laughing at the prospect of rebellion and ridiculing its chance for success. Barrington was no friend of the British, and he had joined the Volunteers and backed the Irish Patriot Party of Henry Grattan. But he was no revolutionary either. Instead Barrington was a perfect embodiment of the moderate interests of the Protestant Ascendancy. He turned to his fellow guest Captain Keogh, one of the hottest for revolution, and joked that if a revolution were indeed to happen, he and Keogh would obviously be on opposite sides. Given their divergent views, Barrington jested, "one or the other of us must necessarily be hanged at or before its termination—I upon a lamp-iron in Dublin, or you on the bridge of Wexford." So Barrington proposed a deal, "if we beat you . . . I'll do all I can to save your neck; and if your folks beat us, you'll save me from the honour of the lamp-iron." The mock bargain broke the tension, and the guests left Harvey's house as friends. But Barrington's loyalties lay with the Ascendancy, and, without naming names, he quickly informed the government in Dublin of the heightened danger of insurrection. A month later almost all of Barrington's dinner companions would join the rebellion, Keogh and Harvey serving in important positions of the revolt's leadership.[48]

With this prescient scene now seared in his mind, Barrington traversed the area around Wexford, surveying the damage and inquiring into the fate of his former friends. The devastation was jaw-dropping,

Enniscorthy had been twice stormed, and was dilapidated and nearly burned. New Ross showed most melancholy relics of the obstinate and bloody battle . . . which had been fought in every street. The numerous pits crammed with dead bodies, on Vinegar Hill, it seemed on some spots actually elastic as we stood upon them; whilst the walls of an old windmill on its summit appeared stained and splashed with the blood and brains of the many victims who had been piked or shot against it by the rebels. The court-house of Enniscorthy, wherein our troops had burned alive above eighty of the wounded rebels; and the barn of Scullabogue, where the rebels had retaliated by burning alive above 120 Protestants—were terrific ruins! The town of Gorey was utterly destroyed, not a house being left perfect; and the bodies of the killed lying half-covered in sundry ditches . . .[49]

As he entered Wexford itself, Barrington began to despair. He had hoped to fulfill his bargain with Keogh and do what he could to save his friends, but as he approached the court-house his hopes were dashed. There on low spikes over the court-house door were the severed, blackened heads of his former companions: Bagenal Harvey, Mr. Colclough, and Captain Keogh. Keogh, as Barrington had predicted in jest, had been hanged from Wexford bridge the day before he arrived. He had been right, but he was too late. There was little he could do for his friends now except to plead with the general in charge of Wexford to allow the heads to be buried.[50]

The shock of the 1798 rebellion and the horrific brutality of its suppression convinced British authorities that neither the populace nor the Protestant Ascendancy could be trusted to govern Ireland effectively. The people had risen up at a renewed moment of international crisis. The Ascendancy had not only failed to prevent it, but, through its heavy-handed reaction, had ensured a lasting enmity between Ireland and her rulers. To a growing number, the solution to Ireland's ills was clear: union with Great Britain. A first attempt at union failed in 1799 after concerted opposition from Grattan, Barrington, and other members of the Irish Patriot Party, but when the measure was again pushed in 1800 support for the measure increased. Some were terrified by the events of 1798; others had been bribed with British peerages and other honors to vote for union. Cornwallis, who did much to push through union, was disgusted by the process of buying votes, but he held his nose and soldiered on all the same. "My occupation is now of the most unpleasant nature," he conceded, "negotiating and jobbing with the most corrupt people under heaven. I despise and hate myself every hour for engaging in such dirty work, and am supported only by the reflection that without an Union the British Empire must be dissolved." And so, in August 1800, the Irish House of Commons voted itself out of existence. Ireland would henceforth be governed by an expanded British Parliament. The United Kingdom was born; Irish independence was at an end.[51]

The American Revolution ultimately led to conservatism and retrenchment in Britain as well. Indeed, rather than encouraging radicalism and reform, the loss of America undermined dissent and strengthened loyalty. Instead of feeding a revolutionary fervor as in Ireland and France, in Britain the defeat and international isolation of the American War encouraged greater unity, an "us against the world mentality." Lord North's ministry was certainly vilified for its failures in conducting the war, but once it had been replaced, most Britons, and certainly most British elites, desired stability and order over a return to the divisive politics of the 1760s and 1770s. The lesson they took from the American Revolution was not that British rule had been overly strict and selfish, but that it had in fact been too weak. In the years after the war, Britain became more conservative and more authoritarian. The experience on the home front played its role in this shift as well. The very public instances of treason, terrorism, riot, and revolt in the British Isles had tainted radical opposition with the whiff of sedition, making it unpalatable to most Britons. With conservatism in the ascendancy there was little prospect that Britain would join France in revolution in the years after 1789. By 1789, popular British radicalism had largely been sidelined, choked out by the tumult and fear, the humiliation and repression of the years of the American War.[52]

4

⇥ ⇤

HORATIO NELSON AND THE IMPERIAL STRUGGLE IN SPANISH AMERICA

After a string of victories at the Battle of Cape St. Vincent, the Battle of the Nile, and the Battle of Copenhagen, instead of striding purposefully across the quarterdeck of a man-of-war as it safeguarded British shores, or basking in the glory of popular acclaim, on February 17, 1803, Horatio Nelson, hero of the British Empire, found himself in a crowded courtroom in London testifying on behalf of an Irish revolutionary charged with treason. Colonel Edward Despard and twelve others stood charged with plotting dockworkers, demobbed soldiers and sailors, and disaffected radicals and Irishmen, many of them members of the United Irishmen, to overthrow the government they thought to be a despotic "den of thieves." The conspirators had planned to fire on the carriage of the king as he traveled to the opening of Parliament before seizing the Tower, the Bank of England and Parliament itself, touching off a nationwide rebellion in conjunction with a similar rebellion planned by Robert Emmet in Ireland.

In his testimony Nelson informed the jury that during the American War he and the defendant had sailed "on the Spanish Main together; we slept many nights in our clothes upon the ground; we have measured the height of the enemies wall together." This intimate, harrowing, hazardous shared experience had forged a bond between the two men that transcended the intervening decades of separation and strife, ensuring that the comrade of Nelson's memory remained undiminished. "In all that period of time no man could have shewn more zealous attachment to his Sovereign and his Country, than Colonel

Despard did," Nelson continued, so that despite twenty-three years having passed since they last met, Nelson could say in all honesty that "if I had been asked my opinion of him, I should certainly have said, if he is alive he is certainly one of the brightest stars of the British Army."[1]

In 1779 both Horatio Nelson and Edward Despard had seemed poised for a steady rise through the ranks of the British military. Their lives and careers, however, had diverged sharply in the years since their service together during the American War. While Nelson had become one of "the most famous men in the world," a man "whose name distinguishes and adorns his country," the foremost hero of his age, Edward Despard had chosen to "associate himself with some of the worst traitors that exist." After more than a decade of service in Central America, Despard had returned to London in 1790 where he and his African American wife Catherine quickly threw themselves into the radical politics of abolitionism, the London Corresponding Society, and the United Irishmen. When the latter rebelled in 1798, Despard had been arrested on suspicion of conspiring with the rebels and held in Cold Bath Fields, the Tower of London, and Newgate, where he and his fellow prisoners were treated to meals funded by Lord Gordon, who had substituted for his anti-Catholicism a radical critique of prisons. "We have reason to cry aloud from our dungeons and prison-ships, in defense of our lives and liberties," Gordon had written, a sentiment echoed by Catherine Despard who took up the cause of prisoners' rights while her husband languished in prison. Like many others, Catherine Despard thought the new penal regime of confinement in "Separate Cells . . . Nearly dead with Cold & Hunger" monstrously cruel and inhumane. Despard's experience in prison confirmed his views of the British government and steeled his determination to strike a blow for liberty. But news of his plot to overthrow the government soon reached the authorities and he was re-arrested on November 16, 1802 on charges of high treason.[2]

The United Irish Rebellion had been defeated and 30,000 killed in its suppression. Thousands more transported to the Caribbean, Canada, and Britain's new penal colony in the South Pacific, but with the war with France still raging, with the memory of the Irish Rebellion still fresh, and after decades spent shivering at the prospect of foreign invasion and traitors in their midst, few in Britain had sympathy for Edward Despard. And yet, there was Horatio

Nelson testifying on his behalf all the same. Even Nelson's testimony, however, was not enough to save Despard, and he and his co-defendants were sentenced to death. Nelson did his best to intervene with the government to secure clemency or at least a pension for Catherine Despard, but to no avail. In February 1803, as Nelson prepared to sail for Toulon and the beginning of the campaign that would bring him to Trafalgar, his former comrade in the American War was hanged at Newgate Prison. It was, for sure, a strange circumstance fit for strange times, but just as the growth of Irish separatism and Irish republicanism could in part be traced back to one event, Nelson's relationship with Despard was a consequence of the American Revolution.

Horatio Nelson's naval career began much as it ended, laid low at the very moment when the victory he had spent so much of his sweat and blood to secure was being celebrated. But the circumstances of April 1780 were far removed from the triumphant felicity of October 1805. In 1805, at the moment of his apotheosis at the Battle of Trafalgar, Nelson had been surrounded, if the iconography of empire is to be believed, by a bevy of grief-stricken mourners including his surgeon William Beatty and his chaplain Alexander Scott. He breathed his last in his own ship, the renowned HMS *Victory*, while the fleet he had led so brilliantly achieved the most celebrated naval victory in British history. It was all suitably heroic, at least in the popular imagination, with Nelson only succumbing to his wounds once the decisive victory had been won, slipping away with suitably patriotic sentiments on his lips; "Thank God I have done my duty," according to Beatty, "God and my country," according to Scott. Trafalgar was Nelson's crowning glory, his death at the very hour of success completing his transformation from hero into legend, the death of an icon of the age and the birth of a deity in the pantheon of a resplendent British Empire.

In 1780 the scene was much the same in outline but very different in detail, more pathetic and mundane than tragic and heroic. It too was an age of imperial crisis and world war, an era of conflict and contestation around the globe that threatened to bring the British Empire to its knees. But in this moment of crisis, indeed at the very moment when the Spanish defenders of El Castillo de la Inmaculada Concepción in Nicaragua finally surrendered and Nelson's "jack" was at last fluttering over the fort, an emaciated Nelson, forced to abandon his men at the hour of victory, lay shivering in the bottom of an Indian canoe, sweating, emaciated, and disheveled, attended only by his former ship's purser as he writhed in agony. He had played a pivotal role in the expedition, commanding the military convoy from Jamaica to the mouth of the San Juan River, hauling boats, men, guns, and supplies 60 grueling miles upriver to the Spanish fort and helping to devise and direct the siege that followed. He had done well, well enough to earn the official praise of Colonel Polson, the commander of the expedition, but as he floated down the dense, jungle-clad banks of the San Juan River from his first real command, his first taste of real combat, stricken with malaria and dysentery, the defeated Nelson hardly seemed destined for a glittering career.

The scene that greeted Nelson at the mouth of river was no more auspicious. Rudimentary defenses had been built, and makeshift huts and hospitals constructed for the soldiers, but everywhere he looked he found sickness and disease. Men lay scattered and sweating in tents and shacks around the harbor, hoping in vain that the sea air would save them from the sweltering sun, the interminable rains, and the malignant air of the surrounding swamps. There were hardly enough men fit enough to hold a watch or bury the dead. Even the surgeons were too ill to minister to their languishing comrades. On the coast, far away from the pestilential swamps and jungles of the interior, the British expedition was equally stricken. Aboard the *Hinchinbroke*, the ship Nelson had left behind at the start of the expedition, four men had already perished. Over the next two weeks, 90 sailors would sicken and 15 more would succumb to disease. By the end of the year only 30 of the *Hinchinbroke's* original 200 would remain, the rest hastily buried in shallow graves on the sandy shore. Nelson's first victory would be a pyrrhic victory, the gains illusory, the consequences grim.[3]

From the coast Nelson was transported back to Jamaica, where he had been promised a new commission as captain of the frigate *Janus*. The command of such a ship had been the object of Nelson's ambition since he arrived in the Caribbean three years earlier, but in May 1780 he was in no fit state to take command. Instead he was placed in the care of Cubah Cornwallis. A former slave named for the man who freed her, Captain William Cornwallis, brother of the more famous General Charles Cornwallis and good friend of Nelson, in 1780, Cubah Cornwallis was a fixture of Jamaican society. She was so renowned for her medical skill and herbal remedies that both Cornwallis and Admiral Peter

Parker recommended her ministrations over the charnel house that was the British hospital. She would go on to run a successful hospital and hotel in Port Royal, and even treat Prince William Henry, the future William IV. His stories of her attentive care would inspire Queen Adelaide to send Cubah a gown in thanks for saving her husband's life. But for all her attention and skill, Nelson's condition did not improve, and so in September he was sent back to England aboard Captain Cornwallis's HMS *Lion* to recuperate. He would remain grateful to Cubah Cornwallis, praising her to all who would listen and asking friends and comrades heading for the West Indies to pass along his well wishes.[4]

In England, Nelson slowly regained his health, but he chafed at his forced inaction. He had always, would always, hate being on shore, removed from the current of events that swept across the globe. Active service meant excitement, glory, and the possibility of promotion—and besides, in 1781 it was clear that Britain could use every man it had in its global struggle. It had been a year of disasters for the British. In April, news reached Nelson that Commodore George Johnstone had been surprised and defeated at Porto Praya by the French fleet, alerted to the British position by the spy François Henri de la Motte. Johnstone, as yet unaware of de la Motte's treachery, had blamed the failure on one of his subordinates. He accused Captain Evelyn Sutton of dereliction of duty and placed him under arrest. At a later court-martial Sutton was acquitted of the charges, but like the dispute between Keppel and Palliser, the affair would drag on for years with suit and counter-suit until 1787. Nelson pitied Sutton, and thought Johnstone "a sad villain," but more importantly, the whole business was a disgrace to the navy, and proof of Britain's desperate need for able sailors and competent officers. It was a very public debacle. A satire was published lampooning Johnstone, mockingly rhyming that,

Port Praya's tar who cannot write,
swears he'll make all his Captains fight;
For *Frenchmen* cares not a button—
So he can lay the blame on Sutton.[5]

Nelson would have agreed with the need to take the fight to the French, for on the very same day in October 1781 that he reflected on "poor Captain

Sutton" and the defeat at Porto Praya, Nelson received news from North America that presaged an even greater disaster. In September, Real-Admiral Thomas Graves had been outmaneuvered by the French admiral the Comte de Grasse, who had at last ventured out from his secure confinement in Providence harbor and slipped passed Graves into the Chesapeake. "What sad news from America," Nelson confided in a letter to his friend and former Captain William Locker; "I much fear for Lord Cornwallis: if something was not immediately done, America is quite lost." Nelson's fears for his friend William's brother and for the British cause in America were quickly fulfilled. After escaping Graves' ships, the French fleet converged with the American forces of George Washington and the French army under Rochambeau at Yorktown, trapping Cornwallis's army and dealing a fatal blow to the British effort to subjugate her former colonies. By the time Nelson confided his fears to Locker, Cornwallis had already surrendered.[6]

In the popular portrayals of this signal American victory, pride of place has long been given to Washington's Continentals, Rochambeau's Frenchmen and the fleet of the Comte de Grasse. But another European power had played a vital role in this most stunning defeat. In the lead-up to the Yorktown campaign, the Franco-American army found itself short of supplies and in desperate need of funds. Charged with raising the needed funds, the Comte de Grasse turned to Francisco Saavedra de Sangronis, a Spanish official in Cuba, for aid. Realizing the import of this mission, Saavedra raised 100,000 pesos from the treasury of Santo Domingo and a further 500,000 from the citizens of Havana. With this money, the Franco-American army purchased the men, arms, and supplies necessary for the successful attack on Cornwallis at Yorktown. Thus, while American arms and French ships had won the fight, the victory had been purchased with Spanish money. As he sat helplessly in England awaiting a chance to take an active role once more, Horatio Nelson was among the few who knew full well the vital role Spain had played in America's struggle for independence. After all, he had begun his career in the southern theater of the American War, where Spanish and British empires battled for control of the Americas. He was unaware, however, that the very same Spaniard who had provided the crucial funds that helped secure Cornwallis's defeat only a year earlier had almost been within his grasp.

Horatio Nelson made his first appearance in the American War in 1777. He was only 18 when he arrived in the Caribbean in July of that year, but in an age when young men went to seas as young as 9, he already possessed significant and wide-ranging naval experience. Horace Nelson, as he was then called, was born at the rectory in Burnham Thorpe in Norfolk in September 1758, the sixth child of the Reverend Edmund Nelson and Catherine Suckling. His mother died when he was just 9 years old, but she left behind the vital contacts that would transform his life. Catherine had been well-connected, the grand-niece of Robert Walpole, Britain's first prime minister, and perhaps more importantly, the sister of Captain Maurice Suckling, a senior officer in the British navy. It was these family networks that first set Nelson on his path to fame and glory, turning a vicar's son into a sailor. In January 1771, Captain Suckling used his influence to secure his nephew a place on his own ship, HMS *Raisonable*, and a quick promotion to midshipman.

But in 1771 Britain was at peace and Suckling was stuck, assigned to tedious guard-duty at Nore, on the mouth of the Thames Estuary. Connections were important in the eighteenth-century British navy, but they would only take a person so far without talent, experience, and ability. If young Nelson was to gain the experience necessary to rise through the ranks, he would have to look elsewhere. With his nephew's future prospects in mind, Suckling looked to place Nelson on other ships on more active assignments. Restless, eager to impress, and impatient to take on the responsibilities of command, Nelson, guided by his uncle, leapt at every opportunity to gain experience and distinguish himself. In July 1771 he joined the crew of a West Indian merchant ship, the *Mary Ann*, twice sailing across the Atlantic on trading ventures that took him to Jamaica and Tobago.

Back in England in 1773, Nelson learned of an expedition led by Captain Constantine Phipps preparing to set out for the Arctic in search of the Northwest Passage, a hoped-for but illusory shortcut to India. Always adventurous, Nelson immediately volunteered to join the expedition, signing on as a midshipman aboard the *Carcass*, one of the two ships bound for the Arctic. He was joined on the mission by the naturalist Charles Irving and his assistant, the former slave and future abolitionist Olaudah Equiano. The ships sailed northwest to Svalbard, where Phipps became the first European to describe a polar bear in writing, before being driven back by the rapidly approaching sea ice. Ever the bane of wooden ships, the encroaching ice presented a grave risk to the expedition and its members. Nelson, as he would frequently do throughout his career, saw opportunity where others saw danger. When the *Carcass* became trapped in the grip of sea ice, he not only volunteered to help man the boats that were to be sent out to free the ships, but also "exerted myself" to gain the command of one of the twelve-man boats. Even this temporary, small-scale taste of independent command filled Nelson with pride and helped to kindle his innate desire for action and responsibility.[7]

The Arctic expedition was largely a failure, but for Nelson it had been an eye-opening exhilarating experience. For his next venture, he opted to join the HMS *Seahorse*, assigned to protect and escort British shipping in the East Indies. By the time Nelson and the *Seahorse* arrived in India, conflict was growing between the East India Company and some of the expansionist native states of the subcontinent. This was Nelson's first encounter with hostile waters, and in January 1775 he saw combat for the first time when the *Seahorse* skirmished with two ships belonging to the King of Mysore and future scourge of British India, Haidar Ali. As exciting and important as this experience was, in India a pattern began to emerge that would plague Nelson for the rest of his career. In 1776, he contracted malaria and was forced to return to Britain to convalesce. By the time he arrived home in England the conflict with the American colonies had deepened. As it became clear that the West Indies would become central to the contest, a now healthy Nelson was assigned to HMS *Lowestoffe* under Captain William Locker and in May 1777 set sail for the Caribbean.[8]

In 1777, before the European powers joined the fight, the action in the Caribbean was confined to protecting British commerce and chasing American merchants and privateers. Even so, Nelson and the *Lowestoffe* were quickly called into action. While navigating through the keys north of Hispaniola in treacherous waters and in heavy seas, the *Lowestoffe* encountered an American privateer. Drawing aside the American ship, Captain Locker ordered the first lieutenant to board the enemy vessel. The lieutenant refused, citing the tempestuous seas as reason to abandon the attempt. Enraged, Captain Locker cried out, "Have I no Officer in the Ship who can board the prize?" With his usual daring and desperate need to distinguish himself, Nelson thrust himself forward and boarded the prize, quipping to rest of the crew, "It is my turn now; and if I come back it's yours." It was Nelson's first experience of command in battle, his first taste of the American War, and, at least in his own self-aggrandizing mind, "an event . . . which presaged my character."[9]

Without a formal navy to speak of, the American colonies were forced to rely on such privateer vessels to disrupt British trade in the West Indies. By 1778, they were taking an active, aggressive role, raiding British merchant ships and even attacking British colonies. In April 1778, Nelson wrote to his uncle in frustration. Now aboard the HMS *Bristol*, the flagship of Admiral Peter Parker, commander of the British fleet in the Caribbean, Nelson was stuck in port at Port Royal, Jamaica itching to "give a good Account of some of the Yankeys". The American privateer *Rattlesnake* was then living up to its name, striking out to capture the *Lady Parker*, the tender of the *Bristol* and doing "a great deal of Mischief round the island." "The Rebels," Nelson raged, had sailed down the Mississippi to plunder the British plantations of Jamaica, capturing British slaves to sell to the Spanish in New Orleans. The small British island of Providence was captured by an American privateer working in concert with rebellious elements on the island. The island was recaptured, and the governing council flogged for surrendering so easily, but all the British ships in the harbor had been burnt.[10]

Unbeknownst to the British, American privateers were not the only threat lurking in the Caribbean. Since 1775, Spain had been using its colonies in the Caribbean and on the Gulf Coast to influence the war indirectly. In early 1776, sixteen men claiming to be traders arrived in New Orleans. Immediately after the long journey down the Ohio and Mississippi rivers, the leader of the party, George Gibson, sought out Oliver Pollock, a local merchant of Irish extraction who had developed close connections with the Spanish government of Louisiana. Pollock arranged for Gibson to meet with the Governor of Louisiana Luis de Unzaga y Mazaga, ostensibly to discuss commercial matters. In reality, however, the party of "merchants" had been sent from Fort Pitt bearing letters to the Spanish government from Charles Lee, second in command in the Continental Army and commander of American forces in the southern theater of the war with Britain. The letters, approved by civilian officials in Virginia, proposed an alliance between Spain and American forces in the south. In return for much-needed supplies of powder and other provisions, the Americans offered to aid Spanish forces against British encroachments on the Gulf Coast and to capture and hand over Pensacola to the Spanish, even going so far as to promise to launch a campaign against British Florida in the spring of 1777.

For Unzaga and the Spanish, this was a dangerous but attractive proposal. Since the loss of Florida in 1763 in the aftermath of the Seven Years' War, Spain had become increasingly concerned about British encroachments on the Gulf Coast. Possession of Florida placed British forces and British interests squarely in the middle of Spanish colonies in the northern Caribbean. From Florida, Britain could threaten Spanish trade from Louisiana and disrupt the formerly safe passage of Spanish treasure ships from New Spain to Europe. Florida was already proving to be a staging ground for the continual advance of British settlers and merchants along the Gulf Coast, into the interior and even to the Mississippi, threatening to displace Spanish commerce on the internal waterways of North America. Spain had gained Louisiana from the French in 1763, but even that consolation prize brought as many dangers as benefits. The population of Louisiana, and of New Orleans, its capital and largest city, was predominantly French or mixed race, with no natural loyalties to the new Spanish regime. Indeed, as recently as 1768, the previous governor, Alejandro O'Reilly, had been forced to put down a revolt with enough violence to earn the Irishman-turned-Spanish-soldier the sobriquet, "bloody O'Reilly." With Louisiana increasingly important to Spanish imperial interests, but with control still precarious, British intrusions in the area were most unwelcome. The previous war had also proved that British designs were not limited to the continent, and many in the Spanish government worried that British Florida would be used to launch an invasion of Havana, a repeat of the humiliating capture of that important colonial hub during the Seven Years' War.[11]

Unzaga responded that while he could not agree to a formal commercial alliance without permission from his superiors in Madrid, he would secretly begin shipping supplies of gunpowder from New Orleans upriver to Fort Pitt. In Madrid, Spanish authorities, led by José de Gálvez, Minister of Indies, agreed with Unzaga's assessment, with Gálvez informing the Council of Castile that Spain should "establish indirect and secret intelligence with the American colonies, inspiring them to vigorous resistance." In September of 1776, 9,000 pounds of gunpowder was transferred from the "king's stores" to Oliver

Pollock in return for a draft of $1,850, drawn from the Grand Council of Virginia. Pollock then loaded the powder in ninety-eight kegs in a riverboat for transport up the Mississippi and eventually to the battlefields of North America. To allay the suspicions of British spies plying their trade in New Orleans, Unzaga pretended to arrest Gibson while his men embarked on their supply mission. When he was released from his mock arrest, Gibson was provided with a ship, once more stuffed with Spanish supplies and sent to Philadelphia.[12]

Over the coming months, a sophisticated system of clandestine aid was developed in which Spanish money and supplies of powder were gathered in Havana and then funneled through New Orleans under the auspices of Oliver Pollock and the Spanish company Roderigue Hortalez operating out of Havana and the Gardoqui company operating out of Bilbao. The aid proved crucial to the survival of the American cause. In the early days of the war, American forces were constantly short of gunpowder, and it would take time for them to get their own production up to speed. Without timely Spanish intervention, much of the early momentum of the revolution might have been lost, especially on the frontier, where Spanish supplies likely saved Fort Pitt and George Rogers Clark's Ohio Valley campaign from defeat at the hands of the better supplied British.[13]

Perhaps most crucially, though now little recognized, Spain suspended its own monopoly on trade with its Caribbean colonies and gave official permission for American ships to trade freely in Havana. This proved to be a major boon for the beleaguered Americans. Since the war began, the American war effort had been undercut by a lack of cash and the very real prospect that inflation would render the new paper currency worthless. Without specie, America could not afford to purchase the arms and supplies necessary to combat the British nor to pay their soldiers regularly enough to prevent wholesale desertion. By allowing American merchants to trade with Cuba, Spain provided America's single greatest source of hard cash at a crucial juncture. Without this breach of Spanish protectionism, the United States might not have had the funds to hold out long enough for Britain's European enemies to intervene.

France and Spain had been chastened by their disastrous defeat in the Seven Years' War, but not cowed. Since 1768 they had agreed a "family pact" as Bourbon monarchies and enemies of Britain to renew the imperial struggle as soon as was practically possible. By the time the American colonies began to chafe openly at their imperial shackles, both countries had done much to address the fatal errors of the previous war and prepare for its renewal. It had become painfully clear that in a world of imperial competition, naval might would play a central role in any future contest between Europe's imperial powers. With this hard-learnt lesson in mind, both Spain and France had launched full-scale overhauls of their naval forces, employing cutting-edge construction, infrastructure, training, and tactics to create navies that more than matched the British navy. With its navy rebuilt and peace secured on its land borders by a treaty with Austria, by 1778 France was ready to take the fight to the British once more, though Spain would proceed more cautiously.

France's entrance into the war in 1778 fundamentally altered the conflict's center of gravity. Before 1778, the fighting had been almost entirely concentrated in North America, but now everyone realized that the key to the contest had changed. France and Britain both considered their Caribbean possessions to be the most valuable piece of their respective empires. The lucrative sugar islands—Barbados, Jamaica, Martinique, Guadeloupe—were the true lynchpins in their imperial systems, the wellspring of most of their wealth, and the source of their many conflicts. Britain was funding its war in large part through its Caribbean sugar wealth, both as a direct source of revenue and as a guarantee of future revenue that it used to secure larger and more favorable loans than its rivals. France too relied on its Caribbean possessions to fund its military endeavors. Both sides, therefore, realized that the battle over the Caribbean would be the most important theater of the emerging Franco-British War. Whoever succeeded in capturing or disrupting its opponent's Caribbean empire would likely win the war. As George III cautioned, "Our islands must be defended even at the risk of an invasion of this island [Britain], if we lose our sugar islands, it will be impossible to raise money to continue the war and then no peace can be obtained . . ."[14]

When the French fleet arrived in the Caribbean in 1778, Britain's forces were in a sorry state. Most of Britain's soldiers were still off fighting in North America, leaving some one thousand soldiers to defend more than a dozen possessions strung across the breadth of the Caribbean. With so few men to defend the islands and populations dominated by slaves, Britain's Caribbean empire was vulnerable to invasion from without and slave rebellion from within. Moreover, by the mid-eighteenth century Caribbean planters had converted almost all of their islands' land to sugar cultivation in pursuit of greater and greater wealth. The overwhelming focus on the sugar monoculture crowded out producers of foodstuffs, making Britain's Caribbean islands dependent on imports of food from the North American colonies, Ireland, and Britain. All of this meant that the Caribbean colonies were almost entirely dependent on Britain and its navy for food, for protection, and for trade, ensuring that few in the Caribbean seriously advocated joining their North American brethren in revolt.

But though they remained overwhelmingly loyal, British subjects in the Caribbean did not remain untouched by the war. Supplies from North America were entirely cut off, while Irish imports were reduced by British efforts to control Ireland's trade. Even shipments of food from Britain itself were reduced as voyages became more dangerous and more and more supplies were siphoned off to feed the hungry armies in the north. France's entrance into the war only exacerbated these problems, further disrupting British trade and ensuring that more and more supplies were consumed by the swarms of soldiers and sailors who arrived to fight the French. The effects were devastating. Prices for everyday staples such as flour skyrocketed, while the profits from the sugar trade plunged. As usual, it was the most vulnerable who were the hardest hit. Across the Caribbean famine hit and slaves starved as food became scarce. In British Antigua alone, nearly 8,000 slaves died between 1778 and 1781, casualties of a war that prioritized feeding sailors and soldiers over feeding civilians, let alone slaves.[15]

Though unquestionably better fed, the soldiers and sailors who contested the Caribbean suffered keenly as well. The Caribbean had long been a graveyard for European immigrants, with as many as one in three succumbing to the climate or disease in the first three years of residence. In the overcrowded barracks and ships of the war years, conditions were even worse, pestilence was rife, death frequent, and it was not uncommon for ships to be severely undermanned, with half their crews in the hospital or in the grave. As one sailor grimly reported, "we buried in six days about twenty seamen and seven marines . . . The 28th of this month the master, purser and surgeon was taken ill, and a few days after myself, gunner, surgeon's mate, and sixty more men were ill in severe fevers, during which time we had not men to work the ship." Even the usually energetic Nelson was not spared the frustrating enervation of illness and disease. In 1779, Captain Locker, Nelson's former commander, friend, and patron, fell ill, and eventually was forced to abandon the Caribbean permanently to convalesce in England. Within a year, Nelson would write to Locker of his own illness, and his growing fear that he too would be forced from the field of battle. "You must not be surprised to see me in England," he informed his former captain, "for if my health is not much better than it is at present, I shall certainly come home, as all the Doctors are against my staying so long in this country." The ravages of the Caribbean were not limited to humans. Like the men who manned them, British ships crumbled under the tropical conditions, eaten by worms, rotted by the climate, and smashed by storms. It was, Samuel Barrington, commander of the British fleet in the Leeward Islands, complained, the "most wretched sickly fleet, without stores, and in a most shattered condition."[16]

The French fleet that arrived under the Comte d'Estaing in 1778 was in much better condition, with more ships, more sailors, and more soldiers than the British could hope to muster. With such an advantage, France was determined to drive the British out of the Caribbean, starting with the Leeward and Windward Islands. Barbados—the wealthiest and most populous British possession outside of Jamaica—was the key to the entire chain. Its capture would be the pinnacle of French ambitions in the Caribbean. But knowing the British would expect an attack on Barbados, French forces under the Governor of Martinique, the Marquis de Bouillé, first attacked Dominica, a British possession located between the French islands of Martinique and Guadeloupe. Despite its precarious position and strategic importance, Dominica was unprepared and poorly defended, easy pickings for de Bouillé's forces who quickly overran the island and captured rich British vessels in the harbor.

The "commencement of the French war" spelt a sea-change for Nelson's fortunes as well. Since his arrival in the Caribbean the year before, Nelson had spent much of his time chasing American privateers, mostly fruitlessly and without effect. The arrival of the French and a proper enemy fleet, however, meant more danger, but also more opportunity for an ambitious young sailor. In July 1778 he was transferred from the *Lowestoffe* to the *Bristol*, the flagship of the newly arrived Admiral of the Fleet, Sir Peter Parker, and quickly rose through the ranks to become first lieutenant. In December of that same year, Parker gave Nelson his first independent command as commander of the brig *Badger*, assigned to protect British shipping on the Bay of Honduras and British settlements on the Mosquito Coast. Nelson would later reflect that Admiral Parker's "partiality for me" had put him on the path to rapid promotion, and years later he would write fondly of Parker, calling him "as good a man as ever lived" and promising to "drink his health."[17]

The year 1779 proved more favorable for Nelson than the British in the Antilles. His service on the coast of Central America was recognized with yet another promotion, this time to Post Captain of the 28-gun *Hinchinbrooke*. In August, while Nelson was in Jamaica waiting for his new ship to return to port, news arrived that d'Estaing's fleet of 26 ships of the line, 12 frigates and 22,000 soldiers had been spotted off the coast of Hispaniola. Pandemonium ensued as gossip and speculation spread that Jamaica, the centerpiece of Britain's Caribbean empire, was sure to be the intended target of this massive French fleet. The island was ill-prepared to repel such an overwhelming force. John Dalling, Jamaica's Royal Governor, declared martial law, raised the island's militia, repaired and constructed batteries and fortifications around Kingston, and sent plaintive letters to North America for aid. Still waiting for the *Hinchinbroke*, Nelson was given the command of Fort Charles, the seventeenth-century fort that commanded the entrance into Kingston harbor, and with it 500 soldiers. This was a heady responsibility for such a young officer, but even in "this critical state" Nelson immediately made an impression with his energy and confidence.[18]

Fort Charles's new commander, however, was not at all confident in the strength of Jamaica's defenses. For weeks, the British would wait in the sweltering heat of the Caribbean summer with the prospect of invasion "daily expected," tensions near to boiling, and faith in British might fading. In a letter to his former Captain William Locker, Nelson described Jamaica's defenses and left Locker to "judge what stand we shall make," adding his own prediction with grim humor, "you must not be surprised if you hear of my learning to speak French." But in the end, despite the fear, panic, and pessimism, the French invasion never materialized. A British ship reported that the French fleet had disappeared, heading north into the Atlantic. The threat, at least for the moment, had passed. Jamaica had trembled in terror, and two small islands had changed hands, but by the fall of 1779, the war in the Caribbean had reached a stalemate. It was at this moment that the Spanish decided at last to intervene, bringing yet another European empire into the contest over the Caribbean.[19]

Spain found itself in a delicate position at the outbreak of the American War. There was certainly much to be gained by a British defeat. Spain still smarted over the loss of Gibraltar to the British in 1704 during the War of Spanish Succession and the loss of Florida and Menorca during the Seven Years' War. Further still, since its victory in the previous war, Britain had become a tyrant on the seas, protecting its mercantile interests from any foreign incursion while undermining and invading the commerce of Spain. More recently, Britain and Spain had nearly come to blows over control of the Falkland Islands. Relations between the old rivals became even more tense in 1776 when British officials, already on edge because of the expanding crisis in America, insisted on being informed about a recent military build-up in Spain. Upon being informed that Algiers was the target of the military expedition, British officials wasted no time leaking the plans to the intended target, helping to ensure that the assault ended in disaster for Spain. There was little reason, therefore, for Spain to wish Britain success in its American quagmire.

On the other hand, as a few prescient Spanish ministers fully realized, a triumphant, independent United States could well pose an even greater risk to Spain's American possessions. Though an intractable problem on the seas, on land Britain's fear of the costs of imperial overstretch had done much to restrain the westward and southward expansionist impulses of her colonial subjects, blunting America's incipient sense of manifest destiny. Without this restraining hand, an independent United States, already poised to become a dominant power, would almost certainly set her sights on Spain's possessions in the Mississippi watershed, Louisiana and New Spain. It was thus with interests seemingly equally balanced and the senior ministers divided over which was the more pressing threat, that Spain had initially opted for a policy of official neutrality combined with informal, clandestine aid. The American War, Francisco Saavedra warned, could only serve to "disturb the spirits of our colonies with the example" of revolution, and "create a formidable enemy to the rear of our most opulent possessions."[20]

In 1779, Spain's clandestine aid to the American colonies was transformed into outright war. Initially, Spain's enlightened, reform-minded foreign minister the Conde de Floridablanca, had sought to continue Spain's position of official neutrality when he came into office in 1777. But France's declaration of war in 1778 changed everything. Spain and France had been close allies and joint opponents of British power since the War of Spanish Succession placed a Bourbon on the Spanish throne at the beginning of the century. Spanish and French interests had become as intertwined as their royal houses, and by the end of 1778, France and her representatives in Madrid were placing considerable pressure on Spain to join the anti-British crusade. The French foreign minister the Comte de Vergennes—the spider at the center of a continent-wide web of anti-British alliances and intrigues—promised Spain the return of Minorca, Gibraltar, and Florida, and perhaps even Jamaica, transforming the Caribbean back into a Spanish lake. In the end, King Carlos III was won over to the French cause with an appeal to ties of both kinship and revenge. Cornered by the French ambassador to Madrid, he was told, "Your Majesty is the Abraham of the House of Bourbon, and Heaven now offers you the decisive moment to avenge the great harm you have received from Great Britain; unite the great maritime forces you have provided and England will be humbled." On April 12, 1779 Spain and France secretly signed the Convention of Aranjuez, with the official declaration of war to follow in June. Still, Spain could not officially support a republican rebellion against a fellow monarch— a dangerous precedent—and so would never officially ally with the United States. Nevertheless, in 1779, the nature of the conflict was transformed, bringing new theaters and new objectives into play.[21]

Initially, Spain's primary focus lay in Europe. The terms of the Treaty of Aranjuez made Spanish priorities plain. Gibraltar, the tiny British possession on the southern coast of Spain, had been an affront to Spanish interests and Spanish honor since it was captured by the British seventy-five years earlier. It threatened Spanish trade and ensured Britain access to the Mediterranean, and so it became the first target of Spanish aggression in 1779. In June, a combined Franco-Spanish fleet blockaded the harbor, cutting off the British garrison from escape or resupply by sea. On land, the Spanish army dug trenches, threw up redoubts and batteries, and laid siege guns. By the winter of 1779, British forces were fully encircled and supplies began to dwindle. Food became scarce, fuel for fires dwindled, rations were cut and disease began to cut a swath through the ranks of the malnourished British defenders. It seemed to be only a matter of time before the British were forced to surrender, or wither away in their captivity. But just as the noose began to tighten around the British, Admiral George Rodney appeared in the Mediterranean. In January 1780, he had dealt a crushing blow to the Spanish navy, capturing a Spanish convoy and decisively defeating a Spanish fleet under Don Juan de Lángara at the Battle of Cape St. Vincent off the southern coast of Portugal. Rodney brought with him more than a thousand soldiers to supplement the flagging forces in Gibraltar, and enough supplies to withstand the siege for the foreseeable future. Rodney's heroic relief of Gibraltar was a godsend for the British, but for the Spanish it was a costly failure, and when combined with the aborted invasion of Britain in 1779, signaled a change in tactics and a re-evaluation of Spain's strategy and interests. The siege of Gibraltar would drag on for three more years, but after 1780, the focus of Spanish resources began to shift west.[22]

Across the Atlantic, the priority was to protect Spanish colonies and secure the transport of the New World treasure so central to Spain's imperial economy. In Louisiana, the new governor—Bernardo de Gálvez, son of General Matías de Gálvez, and nephew of José de Gálvez, Minister of Indies—was not content to wait. Gálvez was a direct man who bristled at the inaction and complacency he perceived among his compatriots in Havana. In 1779, Gálvez realized that with British forces still bogged down on the Atlantic seaboard and British positions on the Mississippi River and the Gulf Coast unprepared and undermanned, there was an opportunity to strike first and retake former Spanish possessions in Florida, driving Britain from the Mississippi and the Gulf Coast once and for all. This would secure Spanish possession of the Caribbean coast, helping to secure Spain's shipping from British depredations. It would also serve to strengthen Spain's position in the post-war world, a world in which America was likely to be Spain's primary foe in the battle for the continent's south and west. Capturing the coast and securing the Mississippi was thus also a means of forestalling American ambitions in the region in the now likely event of U.S. independence. There was no time to waste, and so without official permission Gálvez struck out from New Orleans on his own authority to take

Nanchac, Baton Rouge, and Natchez on the Mississippi before heading east across the Gulf Coast to drive the British from Mobile and Pensacola and make the Gulf a Spanish sea once more.[23]

With the French fleet occupied in the Atlantic and Bernardo de Gálvez blazing a swath of destruction across the Gulf Coast, by the end of 1779 an increasingly aggressive Spain had become Britain's most vigorous opponent in the Caribbean, the greatest threat to Britain's imperial interests, and thus the new target of British designs. In 1779, the Spanish widened their assault on Britain's empire with an attack on St. George's Key off the coast of Belize. In October, British forces under Captain John Luttrell and Captain William Dalrymple responded in kind, storming the fortress of San Fernando de Omoa on the Gulf of Honduras and capturing several ships that had taken shelter in the harbor. The British would be forced to abandon the post in short order. The conquest of Omoa may not have had lasting strategic significance, but the capture of several million Spanish dollars inspired many to see the potential benefits of further assaults on the Spanish empire, the first inkling that, in spite of the anxiety caused by the Spanish threat and the appearance of British vulnerability, the war with Spain might in fact tip the balance of imperial power in Britain's direction. In Jamaica, Governor John Dalling, a veteran of the Seven Years' War who had served under Amherst and the martyred General Wolfe, and in 1779 the most senior British official in the region, devised a cunning plan to distract the Spanish war effort, secure Britain's position in Central America, and sunder the Spanish Empire in two. Dalling's sedate, corpulent appearance belied a fiercely ambitious nature, and he now saw that the entrance of Spain into the war could provide rich pickings for those who dared to seize them. He was inspired by the bold actions of English privateer heroes of a previous era of Anglo-Spanish conflict, Sir Francis Drake who captured Spanish treasure ships and Sir Henry Morgan who sacked the Spanish city of Granada on Lake Nicaragua before settling into a more legitimate position as Jamaica's Lieutenant Governor. In consultation with Lord Germain, British Secretary of State for the Colonies, Dalling set about planning a military expedition designed to emulate those of his free-booting forebears.

The plan was certainly ambitious. Dalling proposed to send a large British force from Jamaica up to the mouth of the San Juan River in what is now

Nicaragua. The expedition would then sail up the river to Lake Nicaragua, where it would seize the Spanish settlements at Granada, Leon, and Realejo. Capturing this territory, it was hoped, would achieve a number of important ends. First, control of the Central American isthmus would sever the Spanish empire in two, dividing New Spain from South America. Second, access to Lake Nicaragua, only 12 miles from the Pacific, would provide Britain with access to the South Sea, allowing her to raid Spanish ships and settlements along the Pacific coast. Finally, a British incursion in this strategically important area would distract Spanish attention and resources from its bushwhacking campaign along the Gulf Coast.

The decision to invade Nicaragua was also influenced by the rumblings of discontent that had begun to reach British ears in 1779. There were murmurs of growing anger in Spanish America, of a Spanish Empire on the brink of revolt, rumors that centuries of Black Legends and Hispanophobia conditioned Britons to believe. But there was substance to these rumors. Spain had gained Louisiana from France at the end of the Seven Years' War, a small triumph in the wake of a dismal defeat. With possession of Louisiana, Spain added to its North American territories all lands between the Mississippi Valley and the valley of the Rio Grande. The contemplation of a vast continental empire in North America encouraged new efforts to expand and consolidate Spanish territory from the Mississippi to the Pacific. Conscious of Russian and British designs on the Pacific north-west, Spain sent an expedition under Juan Bautista de Anza from New Spain up the California coast to establish missions and strengthen Spanish claims to the region. A string of posts was created up the California coast to San Francisco, established in the fateful year of 1776.[24]

Further east, efforts to solidify Spanish claims in the south-west had put Spain on a collision course with another expanding imperial power, the Comanche. By the 1760s, the Comanche had transformed themselves from a small tribe of hunter-gatherers on the northern frontier of Spanish New Mexico into the dominant power in the region. Control of the horse market allowed the Comanche to construct a sprawling trade network that provided access to the guns the Spanish refused to sell them, independent sources of other European trade goods, and a mobile threat of violence that held all, the Spanish included, in check. By the 1770s, the Comanche Empire, not the Spanish, had emerged as the foremost political, economic, and military power in New Mexico, Texas, and the lower Mississippi Valley, better connected, better armed, and more feared than their European rivals.[25]

Alienated by Spanish efforts to secure its borders by allying with the Apache and stationing more troops in New Mexico, and lured by the intoxicating enticement of horses and slaves, the Comanche launched more than a hundred major raids on New Mexico in the decade between 1767 and 1777. In these lightning attacks hundreds of settlers were killed, or captured to be sold in a growing Comanche slave economy. Horses and mules, the source of Comanche power and wealth, were stolen in their thousands. Villages were burnt, livestock slaughtered, crops destroyed, and whole regions abandoned in the face of the onslaught. By the year America declared her independence from Great Britain, Spanish colonists lived "in such a state of terror that they sow their lands like transients and keep going and coming to the place where they can live in less fear." Alejandro O'Reilly did his best to fend off the attacks, but by 1779, vast swathes of Spain's North American empire had become desolate and devastated, its people having fled or living in thrall to new imperial masters.[26]

The outbreak of war with Britain only made matters worse for the beleaguered, overstretched Spanish. With their empire already on the brink of collapse, men and money were now siphoned away from the warzone of the northern borderlands of New Spain for redeployment elsewhere, leaving New Spain, New Mexico, and Louisiana "exposed to the sacrifice of inhumanity and fury of the enemies." An attempt was made to reach a peace agreement with the Comanche, but this too was scuppered in the name of the American War. To obtain and maintain peace, Spanish officials like de Anza in New Mexico—now charged with bringing the Comanche to heel—and Bernardo de Gálvez in Louisiana needed money to buy diplomatic gifts. But cost-cutting measures forced by the war with Britain ensured that such a vital and expected component of peace was sacrificed to interests elsewhere. The results were devastating. Comanche raids continued to grow in number and ferocity, peaking in 1780 and 1781, and leaving New Mexico and Texas desolate, captive territories. The population of Texas declined by 10 per cent by 1784, "at the moment not a foot of land is free of hostility. Its fruits of the field are despoiled, cattle ranches and farms that the happy days of peace had built up are rapidly being abandoned, and the settlers in terror taking refuge in the settlements, nor do they venture to leave the neighborhood without a troop escort."[27]

For the Comanche, it was a boom time. Flush with horses and mules from their numerous raids, the Comanche Empire could dictate terms to the Spanish, who still desperately needed animals for their campaign on the Gulf Coast. For the Spanish, the dream of a continental empire that had emerged after the Seven Years' War had been dashed. The mirage of a Spanish Empire in the west had transformed into a Comanche Empire, with Spain's border colonies reduced and subordinated to an Indian power. Spain's ambitions for a North American empire had collapsed in the face of the American War and the Comanche Empire, and there were signs that Spain's hold on her southern possessions was under threat as well.

In Central and South America there were further signs of discontent. From James Lawrie, British superintendent of the Mosquito Coast, Governor Dalling of Jamaica had been informed of the local Mosquito Indians' "fixed hereditary hatred for the Spaniards" and that the "the natives of the country were ready to revolt and awaited but for the prospect of success." They would be sure to join in any British expedition against their detested Spanish overlords. Further afield, there were reports that the native people of Peru were deeply dissatisfied with Spanish rule and were nearing open rebellion. New Granada was becoming increasingly restless as well, and even in the north, in New Spain, it was reported that Spain's hold on power was increasingly precarious. With Spain's own empire on the brink of rebellion, Dalling and Germain hoped a British flame in Nicaragua would ignite a continent-spanning revolt, thus visiting on the Spanish Empire the very same plague of revolution that Spain was helping to foment in the British Empire. As a report from Havana printed in an American newspaper declared, the British intent was to do to Spain "only as France and Spain have done towards England, and her possessions in America."[28]

The time was ripe to strike a blow against Spain. In a letter to Secretary of State for North America Lord Germain, Dalling pleaded for permission to act. "Give me but the direction of a force, and that of now great extent," Dalling implored, "and I'll be answerable to give you the domination of Spain in this part of the world." Benjamin Moseley, surgeon-general of Jamaica, concurred with the governor's sentiment, reporting a British desire for "the glory of shaking Spain to her foundation." For many in Jamaica and Britain alike, "the colours of England were, in their imagination, already even on the walls of Lima." With such lofty dreams in mind, Dalling's plan received vigorous support from London.[29]

With official approval, an expeditionary force was gathered in Jamaica consisting of 300–400 regular soldiers from the 60th regiment and the Loyal Irish Corps, 200 volunteers from Jamaica, 60 sailors, and another 70 or so local Irish, African, Indian, and mixed-race volunteers. Overall command of the expedition was given to Colonel John Polson of the 60th regiment, but Horatio Nelson was selected to escort the expedition from Jamaica to the mouth of the San Juan River. The choice made good sense. Nelson was an ambitious, well-regarded junior officer, who had distinguished himself in his vigorous command of Fort Charles during the invasion scare of 1779, catching the eye of Governor Dalling in the process. More importantly, he was one of the select few who had direct experience of the Mosquito Coast. In January 1779, with the prospect of open war with Spain drawing near, he had been sent on several missions to the Mosquito Coast, including one to the British settlements on the Black River in Honduras to help ready their defenses, and to find and transport "King George," the leader of the mixed-race community at Sandy Bay, to Jamaica, in the hope that an anti-Spanish alliance could be formed with King George in the likely event of a Spanish attack on the Mosquito Coast settlements. Nelson's knowledge of the area and good relations with potential allies made him a logical choice to lead the convoy.[30]

Led by Nelson's frigate the *Hinchinbrooke*, on February 3 the convoy set sail from Port Royal en route to the Mosquito Coast. From the beginning, the expedition was plagued by delays and disasters that presaged the eventual fate of the mission. Two soldiers died of illness before they even reached the coast; another was fatally injured when one of the transports ran aground. When they finally landed at Cape Gracias a Dios, the inauspicious start was followed by worse. Their stop on the Mosquito Coast was supposed to be brief, a chance to rendezvous with James Lawrie, who had promised to muster a supplementary force of local British settlers, Mosquito Indians, and Africans. But when they arrived on February 14, Lawrie was nowhere to be found. The soldiers couldn't stay on the ships indefinitely, so after days of waiting, Nelson had them disembarked. The expedition was forced to make camp on a swampy plain for nearly a month while they attempted to recruit local Indian and African communities with gifts and promises of plunder. These local recruits were vital to the success of the expedition, not only adding numbers to the ranks, but also providing crucial knowledge of the interior that none of the British possessed.[31]

After days of waiting, on February 22, Lawrie finally arrived, though with only 300 men, not the thousands he had promised. The delay had caused other problems as well. The soldiers, camped on swampy, malaria-ridded ground, and forced to drink fetid water, were beginning to fall ill in significant numbers, with thirty or more already removed from active duty. On March 7, Colonel Polson gave up hope of recruiting more local volunteers and set sail for the San Juan River. Closer to their destination, Nelson was sent ashore to negotiate with the native people. The British still needed more men with experience of the terrain, and perhaps as important, more boats that could navigate the shallows and cataracts of the San Juan River. Nelson seems to have had the touch with the local Indians, and secured an agreement with them to aid the British expedition. But these further delays meant that the expedition didn't reach the mouth of the San Juan River until March 17, 1780. The expedition had been planned for the winter to avoid the rains and disease that would accompany the warmer weather of spring and summer. Now they risked marching through mangrove forests, malarial swamps, and dense, unknown jungles at the worst possible time of the year. The delays would prove costly.

Leaving his ship behind, Nelson and about fifty of his sailors and marines, had volunteered to lead the convoy upriver in a collection of smaller vessels and local canoes. But traveling up the San Juan River proved difficult. For starters, there were not enough boats to carry all of the guns, ammunition, and supplies, and the river itself seemed to resist British penetration. At that time of year, the river was treacherously shallow. Boats had to be guided through the twisting maze of sandy shoals by expert Indian guides, dragged through shallow spots, and hauled around rapids and falls. Progress was achingly slow, with Nelson's convoy only making about 6 miles a day. The soldiers were of little use. They had continued to sicken since their arrival on the river, and few now had the strength to actively assist. It was the knowledge and the "spirited exertions and perseverance" of the Indians, combined with the efforts of Nelson and his sailors, that slowly pushed and prodded the expedition into the interior.

The British were, according to Thomas Dancer, a surgeon assigned to the expedition, "greatly indebted" to the Indians.[32]

After days of struggle, the expedition reached deeper waters as mangroves and swamps gave way to high banks and thick jungle. On April 9 the party's Indian scouts brought news of the first Spanish outpost on the San Juan River, a "small horse-shoe battery" manned by 12–18 soldiers on the island of St. Bartholomew. The defenses themselves posed little threat to the invaders, but if the more substantial forts further upriver were to be taken before the weather turned ugly, surprise was of the essence. The fort would have to be taken quickly and quietly to prevent the entire region being set on high alert. Polson decided to send Nelson with a small detachment upriver under cover of darkness to attack the fort from the front, while a second party, led by Edward Despard, would circle through the jungle and attack from the rear, ensuring that none of the defenders escaped to bring news of the British advance to the Spanish forces upriver. Polson had already come to rely upon Nelson in most things, but the choice of Despard to lead the second party was inspired as well. Despard had been born in Queen's County Ireland in 1750 into a prominent family with deep military ties. With five older brothers, all of whom had joined the army or navy, Despard's path was seemingly preordained, and he wasted no time in following the family business, joining the army at the age of 16 in 1766. His first posting was to Jamaica, a death sentence for many soldiers, but a world Despard succeeded in making his own. He was a born soldier, well regarded by his superiors and quick to advance through the ranks. Mathematical gifts and a desire to rise further convinced Despard to join the engineers, and it was in this capacity, as "principal engineer," that he had been selected to join the San Juan mission. The Irish engineer and the English sailor would prove to be the most active and daring officers during the San Juan expedition, and it was the healthy regard established in the brutal conditions of the Mosquito Coast that would lead Nelson to testify on behalf of his former comrade when Despard faced charges of treason in 1802.[33]

The ploy worked nearly flawlessly. Despard and his detachment, largely consisting of Mosquito Indians, forged and hacked their way through the jungle and around the fort just in time to intercept the Spanish soldiers fleeing from Nelson's attack. It was Nelson's first experience of hand-to-hand combat. Once

Colonel Polson and the rest of the troops arrive at the island outpost, Nelson and Despard were tasked with reconnoitering the next stage of the route up to Fort San Juan. The scouting party set out under the cover of night, paddling 5 miles from the outpost through the inky darkness of the jungle till at last, at a bend in the river they caught their first sight of the Spanish fort. Even in the black of night, the whitewashed walls of the fort, 14 foot high, 4 foot thick and 65 yards in length, would have shown through the darkness from their perch atop a high promontory on a spur of land jutting out from the south bank of the river. Inside the 50-foot keep, the fort's commander, Don Juan d'Ayssa, with 149 soldiers and 89 assorted followers, swept the river with 20 cannon and 12 swivel guns.[34]

It was a formidable structure, but after such a difficult slog up river and through the dense jungle, with the very land itself seeming to conspire against them (the plagues of mosquitos, poisonous snakes, and prowling jaguars had already thinned the force considerably), when Polson and the main body of soldiers arrived before the fort on April 11, Nelson was one of many who argued for a swift assault on the Spanish position. It soon became clear, however, that the Spanish were prepared. Don Juan d'Ayssa had been warned by a single Spanish soldier who had slipped through Despard's fingers at the island outpost. With surprise no longer on their side, Polson was not willing to risk a direct assault on a well-defended enemy, and so opted for a siege. On April 13, the guns that had been painstakingly hauled from the coast now proved their value. Nelson, with his experience of commanding guns at Kingston, and Despard, in his role as chief engineer, were tasked with placing British guns on a series of hills surrounding the fort. With his first shot, Nelson managed to strike down the Spanish flag fluttering above the keep, but the difficulty of the trip upriver soon began to take its toll on the British besiegers.[35]

The struggle to haul the heavy equipment through twisting shallow waters meant that much of the shot needed to feed the guns had not yet arrived, or had been lost in the murky depths of the San Juan. The men were beginning to drop as well. Few were felled by Spanish bullets, save one foolish soldier who chased a wild hog under the Spanish walls. Instead, it was disease that began to take hold of the British expedition. It was now April. "Incessant rains, alternating with the most extreme heat" laid low British and Indian alike "in great numbers" as they sat and waited in the stifling damp. But conditions inside the fort were even worse. D'Ayssa and his men were under-supplied, and suffering from the same illness that swept through the British camp. After two weeks of siege, the fort had become "worse than any prison," and now the Spanish, cut off from the river and their well, were running out of water. On April 29, D'Ayssa bowed to the inevitable and surrendered his fort. But as his own flag rose above Fort San Juan, Nelson, the man who had done so much to drive the expedition forward, was not there to see it.[36]

From his sickbed back in Jamaica under the able care of Cubah Cornwallis, Nelson wrote to Colonel Polson to congratulate him on the fall of Fort San Juan, assuring his former commander that both he and Governor Dalling had received the news with "the greatest pleasure" and asking that Polson "remember me kindly to the two Despards." Fort San Juan, despite Governor Dalling's joyous response to the news of its capture—"the door to the South Sea is burst open"—was only the first step in the British drive to the Pacific, and though the season was late, and many, like Nelson, had fallen ill, there were reasons to hope that success was still close at hand. A week before the fort fell, reinforcements had arrived from Jamaica. Led by Stephen Kemble, a well-connected New Jersey loyalist commander, brother-in-law of Thomas Gage and former Deputy Adjutant-General of Britain's North American forces, the new arrivals, more than 500 men, sailors, volunteers, and a strong contingent of the Royal American Regiment, had arrived at the mouth of the river in mid-April, and immediately began to ship supplies and soldiers up to the fort. The cautious Polson was relieved of his command, and Despard sent ahead to scout the Spanish defenses on Lake Nicaragua, the key to unlocking Britain's Central American ambitions.[37]

The Spanish forces in Nicaragua, led by Bernardo de Gálvez's uncle, Captain-General Matís de Gálvez, knew they had little chance of relief, little prospect of resupply or reinforcement. To the north and south the Spanish Empire was in throes of revolt. The British, it transpired, had been right to think that the Spanish Empire was ready to explode.

5

⇢ ⇠

REVOLT AND REVOLUTION
IN THE SPANISH EMPIRE

Micaela Bastidas had had enough of her husband's dithering. He had done much to remove the Spanish yoke from around the necks of the Indians of Peru, but the job was not yet finished. He needed encouragement, even chastisement, to bring his attention back to the important work at hand. Everywhere in the region of Cuzco, the native people had risen up in revolt, inspired and united by her husband's leadership to once more challenge an increasingly intrusive and demanding Spanish Empire. This was certainly something to be proud of, but such leadership brought with it responsibilities. If the rebellion was to succeed, if the people were to remain free from Spanish tyranny and avoid the repression and retribution that would surely follow failure, her husband would focus all of his energy and attention on binding the rebels together and keeping the momentum of the conflict safely in the revolution's grasp. Bastidas knew this for a fact, and she at least would not hesitate to use all her power to ensure the revolution did not stall, that her husband would not falter.

And so, in December of 1780 she wrote to her husband, to urge, and even shame him out of his lethargy. "You will kill me with grief," she admonished, "for you go slowly through the villages . . . with great disregard for soldiers who have reason to get bored and who want to go back to their villages." Such disregard, she continued, was unacceptable, adding a threat to her admonishment:

152

I do not have any more patience to face any of this, as I myself am capable of surrendering to the enemy so that they take my life. I see you with very little eagerness in confronting this very serious issue that might take our lives. We are in the middle of enemies and we do not have our lives secured. And it is because of you that the lives of my children are also in danger, and the lives of those who are with us.

His carelessness at such a crucial juncture took her "breath away" when she did not "have any to waste." The stakes were enormous, she reminded him, and although she herself did not "mind losing my life," she hoped her husband would consider the fate of his family, writing "but I do mind losing that of this poor family who needs your help." "You promised that you would honor your word, but from now on I will not believe in your promises, because you have betrayed your world." If he continued to dally now, his honor would be diminished, the men who had flocked to his cause would abandon him, and the initiative would be lost to the Spanish who were likely already gathering their forces in Lima. There was not a moment to spare.[1]

Micaela Bastidas had married José Gabriel Condoraqui four years earlier in May 1776 in Surimana, one of the three communities Condoraqui ruled as *kuraka*, a regional governor-cum-magistrate in the days of the Incan Empire with a similar role in the Spanish Empire that replaced it. The marriage had been a Catholic marriage, performed by Father Lopes de Sosa, a mentor of Condorcanqui, with all the trappings of a Spanish service: a reflection of the couple's position as members of two worlds: as part of the native elite with ties stretching back to the Incas, and as locals coopted into the Spanish imperial machine. The marriage was a good match. Tall and thin, with an aquiline nose, large dark eyes, and hair down to his waist, Condorcanqui possessed the self-assured manners of a Quechua gentleman. According to one observer, "he carried himself with dignity around his superiors, and with formality among the Indians," and was "very well esteemed by all classes of society." Well educated at the Jesuit school of San Francisco de Borja in Cuzco, he had a genteel smattering of Latin, and "spoke the Spanish language perfectly, and Quechua [the indigenous language of Peru] with a special grace." The son of an important indigenous landowner and regional governor, Condorcanqui was also a wealthy man who "lived in luxury." More importantly, despite his elevated position, and perhaps because of his ambiguous status as a Western-educated Indian, an official with a foot in both worlds, Condorcanqui was also a man with a conscience, an advocate for the grievances of his people, and a vocal critic of the multiplying abuses of Spanish rule.[2]

Micaela Bastidas was more than his equal. She had been born in Pampamarca in 1744, the child of a Quechua mother and a father of uncertain heritage. It was suggested by some that her father was of African descent and she herself was referred to as a *Zamba* in some sources, suggesting a contemporary belief that she possessed some African blood. Others believed her father had been a Spanish priest, and both her parents were listed as "Spaniards" on her marriage certificate, but in a time and place when racial identities were more fluid, this was more a marker of status than a reflection of genealogy. Over time, depictions have tended to present a Europeanized Micaela, with lighter skin and European features. But whatever her background, like her husband, Micaela Bastidas was a liminal figure, with a presence in multiple worlds. She was also, like Condorcanqui, a deeply devout Catholic and a fierce, unapologetic advocate for her own rights and the rights of her people. With the coming of the American War and the growing authoritarianism of Spanish colonial government that resulted, Bastidas and her new husband would emerge as the focal point for a new age of Andean resistance.[3]

The Spanish Empire in Peru had never been a pretty affair. Beginning with the violent conquests of Francisco Pizarro, the history of Spanish Peru is shot through with bloodshed, repression, and exploitation. For Spain, the conquests in the Americas had brought great wealth—gold and silver arrived at Cadiz by the boatload—and with it the financial muscle to dominate sixteenth-century Europe. But by the dawning of the eighteenth century, the Habsburgs' American empire was widely believed to be in decline, the wealth that catapulted Spain to preeminence in Europe strangled by inefficiency. Under the Bourbon monarchs, imperial reform was the order of the day, especially after the humbling defeat in the Seven Years' War. From the 1760s, Spain sought to ameliorate what many saw as the backwardness of the Spanish Empire and its concomitant inability to compete globally with Britain by applying Enlightenment principles to imperial governance. Henceforth, imperial policy would be entirely geared toward returning Spain to the ranks of Europe's foremost imperial and military powers.

Central to this reorganization was a reimagining of the very purpose of empire. Pamphlets advocating a new relationship between crown and its colonies flourished. In his highly influential *New System of Economic Government for America*, José del Camillo y Cosíos compared the Spanish Empire to those of France and Britain and found it wanting. José de Gálvez, then still an obscure provincial lawyer, impressed Carlos III with a similar pamphlet, "A Vassal's Discourse and Reflections on the Dependence of Our Spanish Indies," which argued that it was of the utmost importance that power in the empire reside at the center in Madrid, that metropole and periphery were not equal partners in the empire, and that the colonies should not be allowed to become "accustomed to living independently." As had happened in Britain in the years leading up to the American Revolution, many now agreed with Gálvez that the purpose of colonies was first and foremost to enrich the mother country. To achieve this reordering, in 1765 Gálvez was sent to the Indies as Visitor of New Spain to perform an inspection and suggest necessary reforms. After his return in 1771, he was appointed Minister of Indies, from which position he embarked on a complete overhaul of the empire.[4]

To place the empire on a more rational, and more lucrative, economic footing, in 1778 trade was slowly liberalized, with some select Spanish colonial ports now permitted to trade with relative freedom between the empire and Spain. Monopolies on tobacco and other products were extended to ensure regular crown revenue, smuggling—an endemic problem for all European empires—was targeted with new energy, and taxes were extended and tax collection reorganized. The government of the empire was likewise reorganized. Under the Habsburgs, the empire had been divided into separate "kingdoms" governed by a viceroy and possessing considerable autonomy from each other and from Spain. To streamline policy- and decision-making, to ensure the preeminence of the crown and the supremacy of Spanish interests, and to limit Creole power, the kingdoms were divided and replaced by colonies governed by Spanish officials appointed directly by the crown. Finally, the power of the Catholic Church, long a defender of native peoples and critic of imperial policy, was restrained and the Jesuits—seen as a dangerous conduit for the more radical ideas of the Enlightenment—expelled from the New World.[5]

It was hoped that the Bourbon reforms would stop the Spanish rot and reinvigorate the empire, preparing it for renewed competition with Britain. In reality, the reforms mostly served to underline and reinforce long-standing grievances among both Spanish settlers and the subject peoples of the Spanish Empire. As both a landlord and official squeezed by the reforms, and a protector of the native peoples, José Gabriel Condorcanqui was among the most vocal of the critics who emerged to challenge imperial policy. Perhaps the oldest and most deeply loathed of these imperial policies was the *mita* system. Since the late sixteenth century, indigenous communities from across the Andes region had been obligated to provide a quota of men to labor for a year at a time in the infamous mines of Potosí in modern Bolivia. The silver from the mines was the wellspring of Spain's imperial wealth and the font of Spain's geopolitical power, but also the graveyard of the peoples of the Andes. Such service obligations were modeled on earlier Inca practices, but extending them to the brutal work in the mines transformed their social effects, leaving lives and communities devastated. Over the course of centuries, the *mita* obligation had become somewhat lax, but in the 1770s and 1780s was revived in response to the growing imperial need to fund its world war with Britain.[6]

As *kuraka* of territories subject to the *mita*, Condorcanqui and Bastidas had seen the suffering it caused first hand. In 1777, while in Lima seeking official confirmation of his claim to be the direct descendant of the last Inca ruler of Peru, Condorcanqui appealed to the Audiencia for an end to the *mita* system. On behalf of his people and "the imponderable toils that they suffer in the mita of Potosí," he begged Spanish officials to consider the "grave damage" caused by this forced labor. His people, he protested, were forced to travel huge distances to the mines, "uprooting" families and "destroying communities." Many would never return home, "because the harshness and ruggedness of [the] road kills them, annihilates them" or "the strange nature and heavy work of Potosí" takes "away their lives." This was, Condorcanqui argued, "an unbearable toil," made worse by the gradual decline in the population of those subject to the *mita*, meaning that an ever greater burden fell upon those who remained to meet the quotas. In the face of such suffering, he asked that the *mita* requirement be lifted.

The work that they are forced to do, the tasks that they are forced to comply with, and all other abuses that they suffer have been recorded . . . These complaints have been duly submitted . . . because, even though the truth of Indians is not held in esteem, they are, after all, the unfortunate ones and carry the weight and the worst aspects of their humble condition . . . Wickedness [is done in] hiding the wrongs . . . that merit Your Majesty's and Your Excellency's compassion.[7]

Two other, more recent, practices drew Condorcanqui's ire. In the 1750s, as part of the wave of reforms, a system of forced consumerism called the *repartimiento* was formalized. Henceforth, indigenous people would be required to purchase a set quota of European goods regardless of need or desire. Those who refused or could not pay faced forced labor or jail. The idea was to forge a stronger link between indigenous communities and the Spanish market economy both by creating a reliance on European goods and by forcing them to produce marketable trade items to pay for the products they were now obligated to purchase. More recently with the expansion of Spain's role in the American War, a series of new tax policies were introduced. New taxes were levied on goods like wine and sugar, previously exempt native handicrafts and textiles were now to be taxed, and customs duties were raised twice. To ensure the new taxes were rigorously collected, customs houses were set up throughout the Andes. The new taxation, like that faced by British colonists in North America, was part of the logic of imperial reform movements that sought to alter the balance of power between the metropole and the periphery, forcing more and more of the costs of empire onto the colonies while at the same time restricting colonial autonomy. But higher taxes and more efficient collection reflected more immediate needs as well. By 1780, Spain was once more at war with Britain, and if the empire was to be maintained, if Britain was to be defeated, every peso the empire could provide was desperately needed.[8]

Bastidas too had reasons to decry Spanish rule and to push her husband to openly oppose the new reforms. In her earlier years, she had been forced to labor in an *obraje*, the much-despised textile mills where many Indians were conscripted to work. The experience seems to have had an indelible effect on her attitudes toward imperial authorities. A tithe collector complained that, in the presence of the local corregidor (mayor), Bastidas had refused to pay and even threatened to "punch him" if he continued to press her for payment. From the beginning, Micaela Bastidas and José Gabriel Condorcanqui had been equal partners in all their endeavors, sharing both the management of their business interests and their estates, as was common in Andean culture, and their vociferous advocacy for indigenous rights. It is no surprise that the pair would emerge as the center of a growing movement opposing Spanish imperial policy.[9]

In Boston and Philadelphia, American revolutionaries had been angered by similar increase in taxation, and for similar reasons. The money taken out of their pockets was bad enough, but the new tax regime also signaled a shift in imperial policy and an upending of the traditional relationship between colony and crown. In the Andes too, many groaned under the weight of new taxation—and Condorcanqui himself sometimes found it difficult to pay his *repartimiento* obligations—but they also bristled at what they saw as a concerted attack on their traditional autonomy. Creoles were elbowed aside from their former positions as officials and administrators, replaced by peninsular Spaniards, and indigenous peoples saw the bargain they had struck, "a high degree of cultural and political autonomy and the control of communal land, in exchange for subordination and a slate of taxes," threatened by Bourbon policies that sought to transform colonial peoples into Spanish subjects. As in British North America, this attempt to reorder the empire brought outrage, protests, and even some small-scale violence as colonial peoples resisted the coming world.[10]

Spanish officials were not blind to the similarities between their brewing imperial crisis and Britain's sundered empire. News of America's Declaration of Independence was played down and restricted in Spain and her colonies. Efforts were likewise made to restrict access to any Enlightenment texts that might inspire Spaniards to follow the American path to revolution. Among many others, William Robertson's history of Spanish America was banned and burnt in Spain, and in December 1779, José de Gálvez went so far as to instruct to colonial officials to prevent Robertson's work and other books from being imported to or translated in the Americas. Any copies that remained were to be seized and destroyed. As a well-educated member of the colonial elite, it would have been surprising if Condorcanqui was not aware of the more radical currents in European thought, and he was certainly familiar with the independence movement in North America and the conflict between Spain and Britain. Back in 1777, while in Lima to pursue his genealogical claims, Condorcanqui had encountered Creole and mestizo critics of Spanish imperial policy, including a mestizo friend who had direct experience of events and ideas in France and Britain. In the *Lima Gazette*, he was awakened to the inspiring events in North America and in Inca Garcilasco's *Royal Commentaries* found a way to reconcile the spreading revolutionary conflict with his own local, ethnic, and personal history. In a prologue added to this work of Inca history in the early eighteenth century, Condorcanqui found an old Indian prophecy that predicted that the rule of the Inca would be restored with the aid of the British. In the context of increased Spanish exploitation and war between Britain and Spain, the time seemed ripe for the Andes to follow the American example and fulfill the ancient prophecy. The seeds of revolt had thus been planted, both in Condorcanqui's mind and in the minds of the wider populace, combining age-old grievances and recent abuses, Inca revivalism, and eighteenth-century radicalism to make the Andes fertile ground for insurrection.[11]

It had all started smoothly, before the Spanish were aware that anything was amiss. The plot was ingenious. On November 4, 1780, Condorcanqui invited the local Corregidor, Antonio Arriaga, to a dinner to celebrate the feast of St. Charles (the king's patron saint) at his house in Tungasuca. Condorcanqui and Arriaga had had their disagreements in the past, most notably over the *mita*, and as a tax collector Arriaga was a target of considerable complaint, but the Corregidor knew Condorcanqui well and so accepted the invitation without suspicion. When dinner was over, Condorcanqui and a few of his men offered to accompany Arriaga on his return home. After a short ride, Arriaga's erstwhile companions excused themselves, claiming to return to Tungasuca. Once Arriaga was out of sight, however, Condorcanqui and his men sped around and ahead of Arriaga and lay in wait. When Arriaga approached the ambush, Condorcanqui and company sprang from their hiding places, seized the shocked Corregidor and his servants, and, after waiting until the dead of night, hauled them back to Tungasuca where they were shackled and imprisoned in Condorcanqui's house.

With Arriaga in his grasp, Condorcanqui embarked on the next phase of his plan. Arriaga's clerk, who had been captured along with his master, was forced to pen a series of letters that Arriaga was then compelled to sign. The letters, now bearing all the signs of authentic, official commands, were well designed to set the stage for a full-scale rebellion. One ordered Arriaga's treasurer to release 22,000 pesos, ninety muskets, and two boxes of sabers to Condorcanqui, supplies that would be needed in the fight to come. Other letters were sent to local leaders and officials, ordering them to gather their people and converge at Tungasuca. As men arrived at Tungasuca in response to what appeared to be Arriaga's command, Spanish officials were seized and imprisoned, stripping the area of the local leaders who would have been charged with suppressing the revolt. Others, Indians, mestizos, and even some Creoles and Spaniards, many of whom had reasons to resent the Bourbon reforms, were convinced to join in Condorcanqui's anti-colonial cause.[12]

Condorcanqui and Micaela Bastidas' position between worlds did much to help secure supporters for their revolution. "Europeans," Bastidas reminded those who would listen, "treat us like dogs". Condorcanqui used his Inca heritage to appeal to the indigenous and mixed-race people of the Andes, declaring himself to be Tupac Amaru II, heir to the last Inca emperor and "Inca king of Peru, Santa Fe, Quito, Chile, Buenos Aires, and the continents of the seas of the south, highest duke and lord of the Césars and Amazonians." Echoing the grievances of protesters in Boston and Philadelphia, he charged the Kings of Spain with usurping his throne "and the dominion of my people . . . making them vassals with unbearable services, tributes, money, customs, dues," and the administrators of the empire with tyranny, injustice, and greed. The Spanish "trample upon the natives of this kingdom as beasts, and take away the lives of all those who [they] do not wish to rob." Henceforth, Tupac Amaru declared, the tyrannical rule of those who had "pushed to the limit the peace and tranquility of these lands by their ill-treatments and affronts" was at an end. To this end, he published proclamations ending the *mita* system, the *repartimiento*, and slavery, and called on the people of Peru to pledge their loyalty to their new Inca king.[13]

Indigenous peoples would form the backbone of the revolt, but Condorcanqui and Micaela Bastidas also did their best to ensure broad-based support for their movement. In some contexts they continued to insist that the rebellion was against corrupt colonial officials and not against the Spanish as a people or the rule of Carlos III. Likewise, they specifically exempted the Catholic Church from their list of enemies or targets, despite much indigenous anger at Catholic inroads into their religious lives and the many financial abuses of the Church. It was thus a tenuous anti-colonial coalition that gathered at Tungasuca in November 1780, one that reflected the ambiguous, divided background of its leaders and the fractured society that birthed it. Micaela knew that such a movement would be difficult to bind together, and so she urged her husband to take a drastic step, a step that would place the infant revolution beyond the point of no return. A handy symbol of imperial exploitation, Arriaga would have to pay for the sins of the Spanish empire with his life.

As a signal of his impending doom, on November 9, a painting of the Crowning with Thorns was placed in Arriaga's cell. López de Sosa, Condorcanqui's mentor and the priest who had performed their marriage, was sent to take Arriaga's last confession. The Corregidor begged for his life, offering de Sosa's parish his entire estate if he would intervene and save his life. Outside in the courtyard, where the men summoned to Tungasuca by the counterfeit letters had gathered, Condorcanqui told the crowd that he had received instructions from the Audiencia in Lima instructing him to punish Arriaga. This was, of course, untrue, and many must have suspected as much, but it provided a veneer of legitimacy for what was about to happen. The next day, Tupac Amaru, resplendent in a mix of European and indigenous fashion— black velvet coat, knee breeches, silk stockings, gold buckles, and a beaver hat, complemented by an Andean tunic and a gold medallion bearing the Inca sun— led the assembly, now numbering as many as ten thousand Indians, mestizos, and Europeans, in military columns to a nearby hill, where a gallows had been erected. Arriaga was led to the gallows by a procession, including a town crier and three priests, stripped of his staff of office, and forced to exchange his military garb for the clothing of a religious penitent. Before the gallows, a mestizo read a proclamation in both Spanish and Quechua, a symbolic innovation in official ceremonies. The crowd was informed, "Through the king it has been ordered that there no longer be *alcabala* [sales tax], customs houses, or the Potosí *mita* and that Don Antonio Arriaga lose his life because of his destructive behavior." At last, Tupac Amaru himself addressed the onlookers, calling Arriaga "harmful and tyrannical," pledging to abolish Spanish abuses, and promising to usher in a new world in which "Indians and Spaniards" lived together as equals.[14]

In a deathlike silence, Arriaga mounted the gallows where he was compelled "to publically declare that he deserved to die in that way." His African slave was chosen to perform the office of hangman, slipping the noose around his former master's neck. A first attempt failed when the rope snapped, but a second attempt, aided by a new rope and the assistance of several others, opponents and supporters of Arriaga, proved successful. "Not one voice," an observer remembered, "was raised that would disturb the operation." If the men assembled at Tungasuca had doubted Tupac Amaru's seriousness, the execution of the Corregidor dispelled any notion that half-measures would win the day.[15]

Micaela Bastida's role in this most dramatic first bloodletting of the revolution was clear and forceful. Contemporary accounts paint her as an instigator of Arriaga's execution and an active participant in the ceremony surrounding it. It was even said that she "surpassed her husband in spirit and malevolence: she knew all about the execution of Arriaga and despite the weakness of her sex, she carried out that unjust homicide, transporting bullets used by the guards in her shawl." Micaela was perhaps the most important catalyzing force in the early stages of the revolt, helping to create the shift from a local protest against taxes and labor service into a violent anti-colonial insurrection.

News of the execution of Arriaga and the outbreak of rebellion had reached Cuzco, the regional capital, by November 17. A council of war was convened, and against strenuous objections, an army of 800 under Fernando Cabrera was sent forth to crush the uprising. Cabrera pushed his army hard, reaching Sangarará, 5 leagues from Tungasuca, the center of the maelstrom, on November 18. There they entrenched themselves in the local church and prepared for battle. It was a foolish choice. The Spanish army became trapped in the church, unable to escape due to the hail of stones and bullets raining down on their vulnerable position. Inside, their superior firepower was useless. Outside, Tupac Amaru ordered the church's priest to remove the holy sacrament before he burnt it down—and the Spanish army with it. He offered to let any Indians, mestizos, or Creoles in the Spanish force to go free if they renounced their allegiance to Spain. A few weighed their odds and accepted the offer. The rest were burnt alive in the church. Tupac Amaru did not relish the spectacle and seemed genuinely sad to have been forced to such an act. He paid for the bodies to be buried, except for that of Fernando Cabrera, the man who had forced his hand. "Finding

Cabrera's body lying on the ground," one account reported, "he kicked it in the head expressing that . . . due to his thick-headedness he finds himself here."[16]

While her husband was in the field against the Spanish, Micaela Bastidas came into her own as a revolutionary leader. From her headquarters at Tungasuca she emerged as the focal point of the movement. She oversaw the provisioning of the army, directed logistical operations, and ensured discipline among the rebellion's supporters. In her own name she instructed rebel towns in the building of fortifications, secured supplies, recruited reinforcements, and issued orders that rebel troops wear palm crosses in their hats as a rudimentary uniform. As a leader she brooked no dissent and inspired both obedience and fear. She tore official decrees down from church doors and tacked up her own commands. She rallied people to the cause and motivated soldiers with stories of "bad government" and instances of Spanish cruelty. She promised her followers they would pay no taxes other than the traditional tribute owed to Inca kings and held out the hope that they would be able to return to a golden age, "their idolatrous times," before the arrival of the Spanish. Those who resisted the rebellion or refused to join were punished, arrested, and even executed by her order. Letters flew from her pen to a wide range of contacts, organizing the rebellion and bringing its goals to the attention of the wider public. In return, letters poured into Tungasuca, asking her for advice and instructions. It was said that both loyalists and rebels feared her, and that she inspired more loyalty, more obedience, more respect, than Tupac Amaru himself. Her husband was the public symbol of the revolution, but Micaela Bastidas was its heart, its soul, its guts, and its brain.[17]

Bastidas' tactical and organizational insight convinced her that if the revolution were to succeed, Cuzco had to be taken, and communications with and supplies from Lima cut off. She sent letters to her husband urging him to focus his energies on Cuzco, and issued edicts directing her supporters to cut the Apurímac bridge, a vital link between Lima and Cuzco. But, as she feared, it was too late. She had told her husband "many times to go immediately to Cuzco, but you have not paid any attention. This has given them time to prepare themselves, as they have done . . . so you no longer hold the advantage." When Tupac Amaru and his army at last approached Cuzco, at the end of December 1780, it was indeed too late. Without the guns to reduce Cuzco's defenses and capture the city, the rebels were forced to settle for a siege. On January 10, 1781, with fresh Spanish troops approaching, Tupac Amaru was forced to break off the siege and focus his efforts elsewhere.[18]

As the rebel army retreated from Cuzco, fractures in the revolutionary coalition began to appear. Micaela Bastidas and Tupac Amaru had done their best to restrain the violence of their followers, and to couch their rebellion in terms that would appeal to Indians, mestizos, Creoles, and even Europeans. They had been careful not to directly attack the Catholic Church or the Spanish monarchy in action or rhetoric, and had attempted to prevent and condemn attacks on neutral Europeans. As the revolt spread, this restraint became more difficult to enforce, and instances of anti-European violence only served to bolster loyalism. The attempts were further undermined when the Bishop of Cuzco condemned the rebels and excommunicated Micaela Bastidas and Tupac Amaru, for being "rebellious traitors of the King . . . for seditiously working against peace and being usurpers of Royal Rights." This was a worrying development for the highly religious leaders, who had hoped the Church, long the defenders of indigenous peoples against the abuses of the colonial regime, would prove sympathetic. For their followers, many of them committed Catholics, the price of following excommunicated leaders would be excommunication as well.[19]

Bastidas and Tupac Amaru had hoped the old Inca nobility would join the Inca revivalist cause, but they were equally dismissive and critical. They had established themselves at the pinnacle of colonial society, intermarried with Spanish and Creole elites, and accepted positions of authority. They were too invested in the imperial system to welcome Tupac Amaru's rebellion and considered him to be an upstart and a fraud with no real claim to noble or royal Inca heritage. In the wake of the defeat at Cuzco, the fracturing of allegiances within the rebellion caused Tupac Amaru to lash out against all those Spaniards, mestizos, and indigenous elites who refused to join his movement, ordering them to be summarily executed and transforming a broad-based anti-colonial revolution into a race war of Indians against Spaniards.[20]

With his army defeated, and allies melting away, alienated by the new anti-European violence, the end was not long in coming. In the wake of the siege, Spanish forces were bolstered by soldiers sent from Lima and as far away as Cartagena in modern Colombia. Loyalist ranks swelled as first the Creole elite and then mestizos and Indians abandoned what now seemed a doomed cause. The surge became a flood after a series of Spanish victories and an offer of amnesty inspired a mass defection. By late March Tupac Amaru was on the run, Micaela Bastidas and their children now at his side as they fled across the countryside, harried by loyalist forces nipping at their heels. In recent weeks there had been a series of crushing blows as the Spanish closed in around them. They lost two of the rebels' most important commanders and, days later, Tupac Amaru's uncle was captured. They had nowhere left to run, surrounded in a bitter twist of fate by a Spanish army composed almost entirely of native Andeans, the very people the couple had hoped to inspire and lead to freedom. In early April, one last attempt was made to break free from the encircling enemy, but was repulsed.

Still, Amaru and Bastidas vowed to fight on and sought refuge from a trusted ally at Langui. Outwardly Colonel Ventrua Landaeta urged the couple on, pledging to fight beside them with a large number of reinforcements under his command if they would stop running and turn and fight the Spanish. Inwardly, Landaeta, like so many others, had determined that the rebellion was finished. Everywhere around him he saw repression and reprisals as the Spanish chased their quarry through the country. The suffering, Landaeta determined, would only stop when the leaders of the revolt had been captured. So, while the unsuspecting couple paused for lunch in Langui, Landaeta organized a party to arrest them. As Landaeta approached, his intentions now clear, Amaru and Bastidas and their extended family tried to flee, but were seized and imprisoned. Tupac, Micaela, and their children were placed in separate cells, dejected and alone, prevented "from saying good-bye to each other forever, as they would not see one another nor would they be together before eternity, except on their day of execution, to their very great sorrow." In joyous Cuzco, where their fate awaited, the bells tolled for hours.[21]

In Cuzco, Bastidas was interrogated. For Spanish officials, the guilt of her husband was cut and dried. But for the paternalistic Spanish authorities, Bastidas' role in the rebellion was as yet rather murky. In her interrogation, Micaela did her best to fulfill Spanish stereotypes of female weakness. When asked why she was in jail, she answered, "because her husband killed the Corregidor" (Arriaga) and deftly side-stepped follow-up questions about her role in the rebellion. She claimed not to have known beforehand that her husband planned to arrest Arriaga, stated that he had only ever spoken of a desire to abolish the *repartimiento*, taxes, and customs, and insisted that she would have left the rebellion and fled to Cuzco had it not been for her husband's threats of violence and constant supervision. When asked to identify the leaders of the rebellion, she said to ask her husband, she did not know. When confronted with evidence that she had sent myriad orders directing the rebellion, she answered that while she had indeed issued such commands, she had sent them out in complete ignorance of their contents as she could neither read nor write. It was a canny attempt to escape blame for her role in the revolt, but from other sources the Spanish authorities were well aware of her active importance for the movement. She was charged with taking up arms "jointly with her husband," of helping to plan the arrest and execution of Arriaga, of remaining "in charge, giving orders to rally people, even leaving" Tungasuca and riding out on "a horse with her weapons in order to recruit people in the Provinces, to whose pueblos she directed repeated orders with an audacity and boldness that is rare, even authorizing edicts with her signature." This, despite her best efforts to appear the subordinate, submissive wife, was the true Micaela Bastidas, an active, able, inspiring, formidable woman at the very heart of the revolution.[22]

On May 18, 1781, Micaela Bastidas, Tupac Amaru, and their children were finally reunited. It was hardly the venue any of them would have chosen. Chained and shackled, they had been shoved into bags and dragged into Cuzco's central plaza by a team of horses. There, surrounded by soldiers and a throng of spectators noticeably without any Indians, the condemned family gathered one last time at the foot of the gallows. Micaela Bastidas and Tupac Amaru had been sentenced not only to die, but also to watch as their family was mutilated and executed before them. As an eerie silence descended on the square, they watched four of the leaders of the rebellion, including Micaela's brother Antonio and the slave who had been forced to execute Arriaga, hang. Next it was the turn of Tupac's uncle Francisco and the couple's son Hipólito. They were hanged as well but had the added indignity of having their tongues torn out before their bodies were thrown down the stairs of the gallows. Mother then followed son, with Micaela taking Hipólito's place. While her husband watched, as she stood in her son's blood, Micaela Bastidas tongue was cut out and a special garrote wrapped around her neck. As befitted her character, she did not go quickly or quietly. As one eyewitness recalled, "she was put to death through the *garrote* from which she suffered immensely as her neck was long and thin and the spindle could not strangle her, forcing the hangmen to tie ropes around her neck and pull every which way while kicking her in the stomach and breast to finish her." She would have been relieved to be spared the sight of her husband's execution, pulled apart by four horses, beheaded, and quartered while a fierce storm broke out overhead as if in anger at Spanish cruelty. The heads and limbs of Micalea Bastidas and Tupac Amaru were sent across Peru as a symbol of Spanish vengeance and the price of rebellion. What was left of their bodies was burnt, their ashes scattered in the wind, commingling together as they had in their rebellion. "This was the end," a contemporary wrote, "of José Gabriel Tupac Amaru and Micaela Bastidas, whose loftiness and arrogance led them to declare themselves kings of Peru, Chile, Quito, Tucuman and other places . . . with other insanities of this same tone."[23]

The fires of rebellion were not entirely quenched by the blood spilled in Cuzco. Tupac Amaru's cousin Diego had escaped capture and now declared himself heir to the Inca throne. From the highlands of Bolivia, Diego carried out a guerrilla campaign, increasingly targeting Europeans in a more explicitly racialized conflict. In Bolivia, Diego joined forces with Tupac Katari, the leader of an independent revolutionary movement in the region of Lake Titicaca that was inspired by Tupac Amaru's earlier rebellion. With a force of 40,000, Katari laid siege to La Paz, the regional capital. Ten thousand of the cities inhabitants died in the failed attempt to starve La Paz into submission. In November 1781, Katari was betrayed, captured, and executed, but Diego held out until January of 1782, when he at last accepted an offer of amnesty. Sporadic violence would sputter on across 1782, but the rebellion was effectively over, at least in the Andes.[24]

While Tupac Amaru and Micaela Bastidas fled for their lives from the failed siege of Cuzco, in New Granada (modern Colombia), the specter of rebellion was just beginning to emerge. On March 16, 1781, Manuela Beltrán, a grocer from Socorro, ripped down official edicts announcing new taxes on the people of New Granada. Like many, Beltrán was outraged by the series of reforms designed to alter the relationship between Spain and its empire and to ensure funding for Spain's war with Britain. The year before, Gutierrez de Piñeres,

Visitor-General of New Granada, had introduced jarring changes to the administration of the colony. In an effort to increase revenues that closely mirrored reforms elsewhere in the Spanish and British empires, he levied new taxes, cracked down on smuggling and the contraband trade, and reordered vital monopolies on key commodities (brandy and tobacco). At the same time, Creole judges and officials were replaced by Spanish administrators, fundamentally upending the more autonomous relationship that had existed between metropole and periphery. To make matters worse, the cost of the war with Britain necessitated new taxes, and a "voluntary" donation that required every adult male to pay a fee to support the Spanish war effort.[25]

In North America, similar reforms, passed in pursuit of similar ends, had led to protest and revolt, and New Granada followed suit. Manuela Beltran's attack on Spanish edicts sparked riots, which spread throughout the towns of New Granada, eventually reaching into the countryside. Local leaders banded together and created committees to lead an organized protest movement to push for change. A small government force was sent to put down the riots, but it was easily defeated, inspiring further, more aggressive action, including a march on Bogota, the regional capital. There was little that could be done to stop the riots from morphing into full-scale rebellion. Spanish forces were already occupied elsewhere: in Peru, where troops had been sent from New Granada to help confront Tupac Amaru; in the Caribbean, where Spain still struggled with the British in Guatemala and Florida; and in Cartagena where the Viceroy of New Granada was stationed, preparing the coast for the British attack he was certain would come. Indeed, there were only seventy-five professional soldiers available in Bogota to confront an approaching army of 20,000 armed rebels. With the Spanish Empire on the very point of collapse, and with no hope of defeating the rebels, in June 1781, the authorities in New Granada were forced to agree to the rebels' demands, including the abolition of the new taxes and monopolies, the end of tribute taxes paid by Indians, and a virtual "creole monopoly of offices" in New Granada, creating an almost completely autonomous colony. The crisis, at least for now, had been averted.[26]

If Micaela Bastidas, Tupac Amaru II, and their followers had hoped for British aid, and Britain hoped to exploit unrest in the Spanish Empire to divide and conquer, they would all be disappointed in the end. It was reported in

Havana and North America that "three English ships of force have arrived in the south sea, with arms, etc. for the use of the revolted natives," but, in reality, the British expedition had failed to seize the initiative, stalled miles from the Pacific at Fort San Juan. The initial excitement at the arrival of Kemble's reinforcements in April had faded rapidly in the shadow of the conquered Spanish fort. On July 7, Kemble and a force of 250 soldiers embarked upriver toward Lake Nicaragua. By now even the fresh arrivals had spent more than two months in the boiling heat and incessant rain, and it began to show. The illness that forced Nelson's retreat had spread rapidly among the British and their allies. Soon there were not enough healthy soldiers to build shelters, bring up supplies or care for the ill. Soldiers in parties of ten, twenty, even as many as seventy, had to be dispatched to the coast to recuperate, only to be replaced by reinforcements who arrived already ill. By June, Kemble, now incapacitated himself, recorded that "the Officers have been, to a man, almost all sick. The men's tents so bad that they keep no water out. My intention to build huts, but have not the men to do it, and Provisions very scarce, so much so as to alarm me. Relapses certain the moment a soldier does any duty. The Troops so sickly that some corps have not a man fit for duty." The constant rain and "close moist weather" sapped the men of strength, caused boxes held together with glue to fall apart, and brought wave after wave of illness to soldiers without shoes, blankets, or clothing other than the shirt on their backs. The illness returned to the camp so frequently that the surgeon himself was "quite dispirited" and eventually taken ill as well.[27]

British numbers were further depleted when Polson was forced to release most of the volunteers from the British Black River settlements after Spanish raids against the territory necessitated their return. Britain's Mosquito allies began to abandon the cause as well, further depleting Kemble's force. They had been convinced to join the expedition by promises of revenge against the hated Spanish, but also by promises of easy plunder. But when Fort San Juan fell, they had been prevented from looting the fort, and from seizing any of the 200 Spanish prisoners to sell as slaves. This breach of trust, however humane it may have seemed to the British, combined with rampant illness among Mosquito, angered the allies and led them to quit the expedition in large numbers. This was a serious blow to the expedition, not only a depletion of numbers, but a loss of vital local guides and the boats and canoes best suited for travel and transport on the river. Kemble seized some of the Mosquito boats by force, but without the Indians themselves, he had few men capable of piloting them upriver.[28]

Still, Kemble was determined to make it to Lake Nicaragua, even if the force that accompanied him on July 7 was limited to 250 men, 100 of whom were already too weak with illness to do much but enjoy the ride. The final blow came when Kemble learnt that the Spanish on Lake Nicaragua had been warned of the British approach by prisoners from the fort who had escaped from captivity. With his forces decimated and dispirited by illness, his allies evaporated, and the Spanish well prepared, Kemble finally abandoned the dream of the Pacific and returned to fortify Fort San Juan. But conditions for the soldiers at Fort San Juan did not improve. Illness continued to wrack the British expedition, forcing Kemble to send the majority back to the coast to recuperate, leaving Despard and a small contingent to hold the fort. On the coast, the hoped-for recuperation failed to materialize. When Kemble arrived he found an apocalyptic scene. Corpses lay strewn across the sand in every direction,

> the Sick in Miserable, shocking condition, without anyone to attend them, or even to bury the Dead who lay on the beach shocking to behold; the same mortality raging among the poor Soldiers on board ship, where Accumulated filth made all air Putrid; officers dying daily, and so wore down with disorders . . . that they are even as filthy and regardless of where they lay as the Soldiers, never stirring from their Beds for days . . .[29]

With death and decay all around him, when news arrived that the Spanish were likely to attack British settlements on the Black River, Kemble at last ordered Despard to destroy the fort and abandon the position. On January 23, the last of the British expedition sailed back down the San Juan River, leaving the remnants of the fort and hundreds of their dead comrades behind. It had been an unmitigated disaster, with the worst losses of any British campaign in the entire war. It is estimated that the British lost 2,500 men to the climate, combat, and disease, with as few as 130 of the soldiers who joined the expedition living to return to Jamaica, the rest consigned to a shallow grave in the jungle or on the sandy Mosquito shore.[30]

Back in Kingston, the full fury of the British ministry fell down upon the expedition's prime mover. In a letter to Governor Dalling, Lord Germain lamented "exceedingly the dreadful havoc Death has made among the troops . . . especially as from the entire failure of the expedition no public benefit has been derived from the loss of so many brave men." It had been a doomed affair from the start, Germain concluded, a poorly conceived, poorly executed expedition, the "desultory enterprise of adventurers." Nelson had come out of the disaster with his career, if not his health, unscathed. In his official dispatch of April 30, 1780, which was soon printed in London's newspapers, Polson singled out Nelson for special praise, writing, "I want words to express the obligations I owe that gentleman. He was the first on every service whether by night or day. There was scarcely a gun but was pointed by him or Lieutenant Despard." Dalling too commended Nelson's role, urging Lord Germain to bring Nelson's conduct to the attention of the king, and, in a note to Nelson himself, attributing to the young sailor "a great measure" of the expedition's initial success. As ever, Nelson was bluntly forthright in his own assessment of his role, claiming to be "a principal cause of our success."[31]

In June 1784 Horatio Nelson returned to the familiar waters of the Caribbean. Much had changed in the four years since he had been ingloriously forced from the field of battle by illness. The Spanish and French, who had once seemed poised to sweep the British from the Caribbean, had been humbled at the Battle of the Saintes in April 1782, frustrating Franco-Spanish hopes of denting British naval supremacy and ensuring that Britain would retain the dominance of the seas in the years after the war. The crushing British victory ended Spanish hopes for an invasion of Jamaica, and re-set the balance of power between Britain, France, and Spain, ensuring that when peace came in 1783, British concessions in the Caribbean were minimal, and French and Spanish gains almost non-existent. Britain had managed to secure its lucrative West Indian colonies despite Franco-Spanish designs against them. Planned invasions of Jamaica and Barbados came to nothing and smaller islands that had been conquered returned to their former rulers. Britain had emerged from the war with its position in the Caribbean largely unchanged, in some ways even strengthened by the costly failures of its imperial rivals. The French and the Spanish, on the other hand, had ample reason to rue a missed opportunity to shift the balance of power in the region. Though peace now prevailed, it was thus an exceedingly tense Caribbean that Nelson reentered in 1784.

The peace had also transformed Nelson's role. After serving out the war in Canada, where he patrolled the coast in search of American privateers, he was now stationed in the Leeward Islands, at English Harbour in Antigua, commander of the 28-gun frigate *Boreas*, charged with protecting Britain's vital West Indian Trade. The enemy, however, was no longer French men-of-war or American privateers. Instead, Nelson and the *Boreas* were charged with preventing illicit trade between Britain's Caribbean colonies and the newly independent United States. Independence had put America outside of the British Empire, and measures had been taken to ensure that the former colonies felt the sting of their exclusion. In July 1783, the Fox–North government issued Orders in Council declaring that henceforth trade between the British West Indies and the United States would be restricted to British subjects operating British-owned and British-built ships. The policy was designed to protect Britain's trade and punish America's, but it proved deeply unpopular on the ground. Britain's West Indian colonies had long relied on provisions from North America for their survival. The single-minded focus on the production of sugar and other cash crops on these islands meant that they could no longer grow enough food to feed themselves.

Despite the importance of their trade connections with North America, the West Indies had remained steadfastly loyal to Britain throughout the war, even when the disruption of trade brought them to the brink of utter ruin. With provisions scarce and crops ruined by a series of devastating hurricanes, suffering was intense, with as many as 15,000 slaves dying in Jamaica alone. British West Indians had paid dearly for their loyalty and greeted the coming of peace with a sense of relief. They were thus understandably distraught about a post-war trade policy that threatened to sever their much-needed commercial ties with America, the key to their recovery. There were riots against the new policy in St. Kitts in 1784 and 1785, and in Barbados, where several protesters were killed when troops fired on the crowd. In one incident a customs official was even tarred and feathered in what must have seemed to be a worrying homage to the tactics of Patriots further north. As protests spread and petitions flooded in from across the Caribbean, it must have seemed as if history was repeating itself.[32]

Nelson, never one to be overly concerned with the grumbling of merchants, nonetheless took to his new role with his usual unwavering gusto. He began enforcing the letter of the new law almost as soon as hurricane season was over and it was safe to leave English Harbour. In November he boarded a ship bound from Boston to St. Kitts before sailing for Barbados where he ordered several American vessels out of the harbor at Carlisle Bay. Over the next three years he would seize at least ten more American ships for breaching the new Navigation Acts, earning himself a reputation as an unbending rule follower and provoking a lawsuit instigated by a group of merchants from Nevis. This reputation made Nelson the visible personification of a hated policy and thus the target of popular ire. At one point he was forced to remain on ship for three months for fear he would be torn apart by an angry mob if he set foot on shore.[33]

Most of Nelson's colleagues in the Caribbean, however, took a more practical approach. Officially, the British government ignored the pleas of the West Indian merchants and planters for the resumption of free trade with America, but practically speaking, there was little that could be done to stop the trade. With dwindling naval resources and entrenched local opposition, most British officials turned a blind eye to the American vessels that swarmed into British ports in the post-war period. British governors, other naval officers, and even Nelson's superior officer Admiral Hughes largely ignored the illicit commerce. This lassitude incensed a stickler like Nelson, but the rapid resumption of Anglo-American trade was one of the most beneficial outcomes of the peace. Both countries badly needed the trade to recover from the war, and despite French hopes that it would replace Britain as America's principal trade partner, Britain swiftly regained its preeminent position after the war. With the illicit trade booming in the Caribbean and trade relations normalized elsewhere, Britain was well placed to absorb the blows it was dealt during the war.

Nelson's tenure as trade enforcer was largely frustrating. He returned to England in 1787, where he would remain on half pay until war with France broke out once more in 1793. Ironically, Nelson's failure in the Caribbean was Britain's gain. Not for the first time. The failure to capture Nicaragua, like the failure to retain Florida, also ultimately benefited Britain. The expenditure necessary to protect and govern such unproductive colonies from the inevitable Spanish and American attacks would be better spent elsewhere. Both were

Spain's problem now. Nelson would have to wait for another war to become the hero he already imagined himself to be. As for so many others, Nelson's life had been fundamentally altered by the American War, setting him on a course for future success and future glory. For most who lived through the times, the American War would prove less of a boon.

In the fall of 1783, Pedro Pablo Abarca de Bolea, Comte de Aranda, Spanish ambassador to France, informed King Carlos III that the long-wished-for peace with Britain had at last arrived. The treaty ending the war had been signed in Paris on September 3. It should have been a celebratory occasion, the final culmination of a long, but victorious struggle. Spanish arms had seemingly triumphed on every front. In Europe, Britain still clung to Gibraltar, but Menorca had been regained. In North America, José de Gálvez had succeeded in capturing Pensacola, restoring Florida to Spain and driving the British from the Gulf Coast once and for all. In Central America, Matís de Gálvez's forces recaptured Fort San Juan and thwarted British attempts to divide the empire. South America had nearly combusted, but the revolts in Peru and Colombia had been successfully stamped out. To top it all, Britain's humiliating defeat at Yorktown, the turning point of the entire war, had been paid for with Spanish pesos from Havana secured by Francisco Saavedra, a Spanish official who had slipped through British fingers in Jamaica less than a year before.

And yet, Aranda, the man who had directed Spain's successful alliance with France, the keystone of victory, confessed that peace "has left in my soul, I must admit, a painful feeling." For Aranda, the independence of the United States, the issue at the very heart of the conflict, inspired not pride or hope, but "pain and fear." The effort to recover and expand its empire in North America was a chimera. By securing its empire Spain was now set on a collision course with the new United States, with the empire now "exposed to serious dangers at the hands of a new power we have just recognized, in a country in which there is no other in a position to clip its wings." "This federal republic," he warned:

> has been born a pygmy . . . and it needed the support and power of two states
> as powerful as Spain and France to win its independence. The day will come
> in which it grows and turns into a giant, even a frightening colossus, in that
> region. It will then forget the benefits it has received from the two powers,

174

and it will only think of its own expansion. Freedom of conscience, the ability to establish a new population in immense lands, as well as the advantages of a new government, will attract to them farmers and artisans from all nations. And within a few years we will see with real dismay the tyrannical existence of this colossus of which I am speaking. The first step for this power . . . will be to take over Florida, in order to dominate the Gulf of Mexico. After harassing us and our relations with New Spain in this way, it will aspire to conquer this vast empire, which we will not be able to defend against a formidable power established in that very continent and a neighbor of it.[34]

But the danger to Spain's American empire would not come from the new United States alone. Unlike Britain, whose trade-based wealth allowed it to pivot away from territorial empire in North America to other imperial horizons, Spain could not afford to lose her American possessions and hope to compete on the world stage. Without the mineral wealth extracted from the Indies, Spanish power would wither and die. And it had been a near thing. As the future first minister Manuel Godoy would admit, "Nobody is unaware how close we were to losing in the years 1781–2 the whole viceroyalty of Peru and part of la Plata, when the famous Condorcanqui raised the standard of rebellion . . . The swell from this storm was felt . . . in New Granada, and even reached New Spain."[35] For the moment, the crisis was averted, the military presence in the Americas amped up and the program of reform recommenced. The Cassandra cry of men like Saavedra and Aranda was largely, often willfully, ignored as most preferred to bask in the false dawn of a victory that would prove far more disastrous than the much lamented defeat of the Seven Years' War. The expense of military intervention, the aborted armada, the interminable and ultimately unsuccessful siege of Gibraltar, and the defense of the Americas had drained Spanish coffers, ensuring that post-war optimism was gravely misplaced.

Indeed it was the very appearance of Spanish success in the American War that would prove to be the ultimate source of Spanish decline. On the surface, victory over Britain seemed to vindicate Spanish imperial and military policy and signal a new golden age for the resurgent Spanish Empire. As such, the reforms begun in the 1760s and pursued with relentless ferocity under José de

Gálvez in the 1770s were recklessly expanded. Colonial government was further centralized, colonial taxes and revenue more rigorously extracted, and colonial dissent more vigorously suppressed, all for the single-minded purpose of financing an expansion of the military to continue aggressive competition with Britain around the globe. By 1788, nearly a quarter of Spanish expenditure was being spent on the naval arms race with Britain—a figure that would rise to nearly 40 per cent by the 1790s—money that was not invested in the commerce and economic infrastructure that would have allowed Spain to compete with Britain in the long run. But even in the short term, the extraction of imperial revenue in bullion, taxes, and state monopolies, was merely a drop in the ocean of Spanish debt and military expenditure. The American War had drained Spanish coffers, ensuring that more and more colonial revenue was needed to fund continued military expansion. To secure this revenue, colonial administration took on a more centralized authoritarian tone that increasingly geared the entire imperial enterprise toward the extraction of revenue for the benefit of Spain and Spain alone. Such policies alienated colonial populations, who now bore a greater financial burden at the very moment that they were increasingly shut out of colonial office. As a small measure of compensation, Creoles were allowed to join the previously Spanish-dominated colonial military establishment in ever greater numbers, eventually transforming the officer corps with grave consequences for Spanish imperial control.[36]

Still, for all the centralization and focus on revenue extraction at the expense of trade, cost-saving measures were still required to stabilize Spain's precarious post-war financial position. Navy spending, the centerpiece of Spain's military strategy after the seeming success of the American War, could not be reduced, so cuts were made to spending elsewhere. To save money, in 1786, Spain abandoned its traditional policy of rotating colonial garrisons throughout the empire, and replaced it with a policy of fixed garrisons. This saved money spent on transporting troops from Spain around the empire, but when combined with the Creole takeover of the officer corps, the new policy ensured that the colonial military became local, autonomous, Creole institutions with more colonial than metropolitan interests and loyalties. Thus, Spain's war-proven strategy saddled its colonial subjects with a greater financial burden, a more invasive and authoritarian administration, and a lack of political power at the same time that it delivered more military power into colonial hands. It was a recipe for disaster.[37]

In South America, the stage had been set for a new cycle of revolution inspired and influenced by the chaotic years of the American War. As Aranda feared, in the aftermath of the war, Spain's empire would be "exposed to the most terrible disturbances." The violence of Tupac Amaru and Micaela Bastidas' rebellion, which saw 100,000 Indians and as many as 40,000 Creoles and Spanish die, a full tenth of the regional population, had driven a wedge between indigenous peoples and Europeans, hardening once fluid racial boundaries. This had been codified in an official crackdown on indigenous culture. The Inca *Royal Commentaries* that had so inspired Tupac Amaru were outlawed, as was the wearing of Inca dress. Traditional Indian hereditary offices were abolished, restrictions were levied on the use of Quechua, and it was forbidden to depict Inca rulers in plays and paintings.[38]

Spain's natural allies in the Americas, the Creoles, had also been alienated by Spanish policy. They had been incensed by reforms that excluded them from high office in the imperial administration and chafed at measures that restricted their autonomy in the name of greater metropolitan control. Many had initially sided with Tupac Amaru for these very reasons, only abandoning the cause when it became more violently anti-European. As in the British Empire, a new dichotomy had been created that pitted the interests of the center, of Spain, against the needs and desires of the colonies, driving a wedge between Spain and the natural constituency for empire. No longer partners in empire, Creoles and mestizos were thus driven away from metropolitan interests, and toward a more distinct colonial identity, creating among these groups a greater sense of unity in opposition. This emerging colonial identity would be increasingly anti-imperial and pro-independence. The Tupac Amaru Rebellion and the Revolt of the Comuneros were the first flowering of this growing anti-imperialism. In Peru, the revolt had faltered along racial divisions, but the precedent had been set. In Colombia, the weakness of the Spanish Empire was exposed, and the effectiveness of concerted colonial protests, and colonial arms confirmed.

When a financially drained and imperially overstretched Spain collapsed under the strain of further wars in the 1790s, alienated South Americans would rise in a series of revolutions, beginning in Venezuela in 1810 and soon engulfing the entire continent. For the future revolutionaries, like the Venezuelan veteran of the American and French revolutions Francisco de Miranda, the American Revolution, the Anglo-Spanish War, and the South American revolts had all proved instructive. Having fought at Pensacola and Yorktown, Miranda firmly believed that the Anglo-American struggle for independence "was bound to be . . . the infallible preliminary to our own." In both Colombia and Peru the seeds of future revolts had been planted. Many of those who sought to reap the harvest would find their inspiration in the American War and the world it created.[39]

In 1825 Simón Bolívar, liberator of Venezuela, Bolivia, Colombia, Ecuador, and Peru from Spanish rule, received a joyous letter from an old man recently arrived from Spain. "I," the letter read, "in the name of the spirits of my sacred ancestors, congratulate the American Spirit of the Century." The letter, signed "Juan Bautista Tupac Amaru," had been sent by the brother of Tupac Amaru II, who, along with Micaela Bastidas' son Fernando and other relatives, had survived decades of imprisonment and exile in Spain, only returning to Buenos Aires in 1822. For Juan Bautista, the liberation of South America brought all the memories of the last Inca Revolt cascading into his mind and so he wrote to Bolívar both to congratulate him on his achievements and to remind him of where the struggle had truly begun. "If it has been a duty of the friends of the Homeland of the Incas . . . to congratulate the Hero of Colombia and the Liberator of the vast countries of South America," he wrote, "I am obliged by a double motive to manifest my heart filled with the highest jubilation. I have survived to the age of eighty-six, despite great hardship . . . to see consummated the great and always just struggle that will place us in full enjoyment of our rights and liberty. This was the aim of José Gabriel Tupac Amaru, my venerated brother and martyr of the Peruvian Empire, whose blood was the plow which prepared that soil to bring forth the best fruits," which Bolívar had now begun to harvest. The sowing of South American independence had begun with the American War.[40]

6

→→ ←←

EUROPEAN WEAKNESS AND
THE RUSSIAN CONQUEST
OF THE CRIMEA

At almost the same moment in 1781 that Lord Cornwallis was leading his troops out of the Yorktown Peninsula in surrender, 5,000 miles away on the shores of the Black Sea, Sahin Giray, Khan of Crimea, was fleeing the Crimea Peninsula with another group of rebels hot on his heels. Giray had never been a popular ruler. He had succeeded to the throne in 1777 largely due to Russian backing, and only survived a rebellion that same year when Catherine sent Russian troops to crush the uprising against her would-be puppet. But by the early months of 1782, it became clear that the new rebellion was an even more serious affair. By April the contagion had spread to the nobility and the army, forcing Giray and the Russian consul in Kaffa to flee the Crimean capital by boat for the tenuous security of the nearby Russian fortress of Kerch. In the deposed khan's place, the rebels elected his brother Bahadir Giray, a move that was quickly supported and officially recognized by the Ottoman sultan. There were now two khans claiming the crown of Crimea, one backed by the Ottoman Empire and another with Russian support, a divide that aptly reflected the fractious history of the Crimean khanate.

The khanate had its origins in the Mongol Hordes that swept with ruthless violence across the Eurasian steppe in the thirteenth and fourteenth centuries. The Crimean peninsula fell to the Mongols in 1338, becoming part of the Golden Horde. In 1441, Sahin Giray's ancestors succeeded in creating an independent Crimean khanate, ruled by the Giray dynasty for centuries. The steady expansion of the Ottoman Empire in the fifteenth century brought the khanate into Istanbul's sphere of influence, and in 1478 Crimea became a vassal state of the Ottoman sultans. Despite this official subordination, the khanate retained its autonomy, entering into a mutually beneficial relationship with the Ottomans. Crimea would serve as a buffer state between the Ottoman Empire and its enemies in Central Asia, while the khanate would receive protection from its newly aggressive neighbors.[1]

The khanate's relationship with her northern neighbors was much less advantageous. Russia suffered repeated invasions from Crimea, and as late as 1504 Moscow was still forced to pay an annual tribute to the khan. Nearly two hundred years of traumatic incursions and humiliating payments had a profound and lasting effect on the Russian psyche. The khanate became the Russian bogeyman *par excellence*, and when the tide at last began to shift in Russia's favor in the late sixteenth century, the fight against Crimea took on all the patriotic fervor and religious symbolism of a crusade. Russian propaganda painted the Tatars as a cruel, despotic people, the ancient enemy and modern scourge of Moscow. As inheritors of the medieval Kievan Rus, Russia's rulers also claimed the Crimea as part of their rightful patrimony, stolen territory that was theirs by right. As Russia expanded in the seventeenth century, the clashes with Crimea increasingly included the khanate's protector, the Ottoman Empire, initiating a long series of wars between the two expansionist empires. The rebellion against Sahin Giray in 1781 and the election of his brother as rival Khan in 1782 threatened to renew the conflict in Crimea.[2]

One might think that violent unrest on her southern border would be a cause for grave concern for the Russian empress, but Catherine saw opportunity where others might see danger. Catherine had gone to war with the Ottomans in similar circumstance in 1768, seizing a moment in the wake of the Seven Years' War in which war fatigue and French losses left the Ottoman Empire bereft of allies and vulnerable to a Russian land grab. The Russo-Turkish War, which lasted until 1774, had been launched with the aim of gaining a much-needed toehold for the Russian navy on the warm-weather ports of the Black Sea. Kronstadt, St. Petersburg's port and Russia's primary naval base, was choked with ice during the long Russian winter, rendering its fleet ineffectual, "firmly bound in the harbor, dismantled of its rigging, and hung round with icicles." Access to the Black Sea would thus allow Catherine to build and expand the moribund Russian navy, a necessity if Russia hoped to compete militarily and commercially with the great powers of Europe. A Black Sea fleet would also provide a crucial staging ground for further Russian conquests of the Ottoman Empire and perhaps even the glittering capital of Istanbul itself. With the Black Sea a Russian lake, Catherine could realistically imagine the sultan's crown resting on her own brow.[3]

The 1768 war with the Ottomans went well for the Russians, and vast swathes of Turkish territory fell into Catherine's hands. Though still war weary after the cataclysmic Seven Years' War, Britain, France, and Prussia were becoming alarmed by Russian success by the 1770s, fearing that a victorious Russia would destabilize the delicate balance of power established by the Peace of Paris in 1763. Neither Russia nor the Ottomans wished for peace—Catherine still wanted to consolidate her gains, while the sultan still hoped to recover some of his lost territories—but in 1772 Prussia, Austria, and Britain forced a ceasefire and brought the belligerents to the negotiating table. The mediated peace did not entirely satisfy either party, and fighting continued sporadically for nearly two years. Russia gained its bridgehead on the Black Sea when it took control of the port cities of Azov and Kerch and became the recognized guardian of all Christians in the Ottoman Empire (a status that would be used as a pretext for war in the future), but the Ottomans retained most of the territory conquered by the Russians during the war. Crimea, the focal point of the war, was granted its independence from Ottoman control, though its khan came to be increasingly under the Russian thumb, especially after the succession of Sahin Giray in 1777. Russian gains had been important, but due to the meddling of the great powers of Europe, Catherine had been prevented from achieving her true objective of a warm-water port for her navy. With so much at stake, the rebellion of Crimea against Sahin Giray in 1781 offered a tempting opportunity to make up for the unachieved ambitions of the 1768 war.

The key to Russia's plans was the American War and the formation of a League of Armed Neutrality. Catherine and her most trusted minister and former lover, Prince Grigory Potemkin, had been setting the stage for their Crimean drama for years when the rebellion against Sahin Giray provided the long-desired opportunity to act. During the previous Turkish war, Britain had intervened to scupper Catherine's conquest of Crimea, while France had long acted as the Ottoman Empire's European protector. With both distracted by war in the Americas and around the globe, there was little chance that they would have the desire or resources to intervene again. As long as Russia remained threateningly neutral, she might well have a free hand in the east while Europe's great powers were occupied in the west. All that remained was to ensure that the rest of Europe stayed out of Russia's way.

The powers of central and eastern Europe—Prussia, Austria, Sweden, Denmark, and Russia—had been at each other's throats for generations, with intervals of peace seemingly the exception rather than the rule. Indeed, in the first two-thirds of the eighteenth century alone, there had been at least three major wars and many minor skirmishes. Because of these age-old animosities, the eastern powers had largely remained aloof as Britain, France, Spain, and the Netherlands went to war. Even as Europe was being slowly but surely drawn further and further into the conflict, the eastern states—wishing neither to draw the enmity of France or Britain nor to expose themselves to the machinations of their neighbors, did their best to remain neutral. Despite outward posturing, neutrality did not mean disinterest, and as each of the neutral states waited for the opportunity to seize an advantage, the combatants looked on warily for signs of which way the wind might blow. The rumors that began to trickle in to Britain and America from their European agents in 1780, of an alliance between all of the powers of central and eastern Europe, offered tantalizing possibilities and potential dangers for both sides of the conflict. Such an alliance, if it could be brought to throw its support behind one side or the other, would certainly shift the balance of power irrevocably. The very fate of the war, the destiny of the American colonies, might well rest on the nature and interests of this eastern alliance.

In March 1780, Catherine II had formally declared the creation of a League of Armed Neutrality. Comprising the Baltic maritime powers of Russia, Sweden, and Denmark, the league was designed to protect neutral shipping and commerce from the predations of the warring nations. In doing so the league ran directly against British interests. Britain had long considered itself to be the supreme arbiter of the sea, and, especially after the entrance of France into the war in 1778, reserved the right to board and inspect any and all neutral ships for arms or other contraband. Britain's declared "right of search" combined with its declaration of a blockade of the entire French coastline quickly alienated the northern maritime powers whose economies depended on Baltic and North Sea trade.

Catherine's announcement in March 1780 presented the league as a triumph of Russian power and diplomacy. In reality, however, such an alliance was long in the making. The Russian empress may have taken on the mantle of league leadership in 1780, but the driving force behind its creation was the wily French foreign minister Charles Gravier, Comte de Vergennes. As the principal target of British naval depredations both before and after the formal declaration or war, France suffered greatly from the disruption of neutral shipping. Vergennes was quick to recognize that a league of armed neutrality had the potential both to undermine British "tyranny of the seas" and to isolate Britain from the rest of Europe. Indeed, the treaty signed between the United States and France in February 1778 included a number of agreed policies relating to neutral shipping—the free movement of neutral ships and neutral goods, a narrower redefinition of what constituted contraband, and a refusal to recognize the blockade of a port unless naval ships were physically present to prevent entry—that would later appear in nearly identical form in the League of Armed Neutrality.

The first inklings of a concerted effort among neutral powers to influence British, and to a lesser extent American, naval policy began to coalesce in Copenhagen in the summer of 1778. In Stockholm and Copenhagen, as in the rest of Europe, the American War was the leading topic of the day. Newspapers were full of stories of the colonial struggle for independence, and in the salons and coffee-houses there was talk of little else. The poet Carl Michael Bellman remembered his friends "constantly arguing . . . about the English colonies, [George] Washington," and the revolution. Opinions were divided on the merits of the American cause, with some admiring the libertarian ideas of the revolutionaries, or at least the romantic character of their revolt, and others concerned that republican revolt set a dangerous precedent. Sweden's King Gustav III was less ambivalent about the events across the Atlantic. Like many he worried that one day America might become a new Rome and "place Europe under tribute," but more immediately he worried that the spread of such ideas might threaten the fragile stability of his new constitution. In 1778 he confided to Creutz, Sweden's ambassador in Paris, "I cannot admit that it is right to support rebels against their king. The example will only find too many imitators in an age when it is the fashion to overthrow every bulwark of authority." As George Washington later explained: "Considering how recently the King of Sweden has changed the form of the constitution of that Country, it is not much to be wondered at that his fears should get the better of his liberality at anything which might have the semblance of republicanism."[4]

Open support for the American cause was thus limited, but anger at the British for their high-handed control of maritime trade was rife. Few were displeased to see Britain receive its just desserts, and war, especially when it engulfed much of Europe, presented countries like Sweden and Denmark with an opportunity to make inroads in overseas commerce and stake a claim to its lucrative rewards while their traditional competitors were otherwise occupied. After a series of disastrous wars earlier in the century, Gustav III had no desire to commit himself to either side of the conflict, and even when the American conflagration began to ignite the rest of the world, he would keep his own country well out of the fray, joining the League of Armed Neutrality in 1780. Still, formal neutrality did not mean that Sweden had nothing to gain in the conflict. The smaller nations of Scandinavia had been largely squeezed out of expanding international trade by their larger European neighbors. Gustav had a keen sense of history and a strong desire to replicate the international success of his royal forebears in the sixteenth and seventeenth centuries. Like Catherine of Russia, he thus jumped at armed neutrality as a means of enriching his country through trade, and gaining disputed territories from his enemies while no one was looking.

Gustav's aims were to expand Sweden's overseas trade, to gain a foothold in the lucrative West Indies as a base for trade with North America, and to use the money gained to fund a bid to take Norway back from Denmark. In his commercial ambitions, Gustav was largely successful, if only temporarily. Between 1777 and 1783, Sweden's annual exports to the Americans increased in value from a mere 6,107 to 153,005 riksdaler, not counting the value of the growing amount of smuggled goods pouring into Britain and America. Through their French allies, Sweden gained the Caribbean island of St. Bartholomew after the war, which was to serve as the entrepôt for Sweden's newly established West Indies

Company to sell iron to America. In Asia, not normally a Swedish market, the Swedish East India Company recorded annual gains of up to 300 per cent throughout the years of the war. At home, Swedish ports became trade hubs, transit points for the transport of foreign goods at a time when merchants from the combatants feared transporting products on their own ships lest they be seized by the enemy. Overall, the value of Swedish exports rose by nearly 2 million riksdaler during the war, creating a favorable trade balance that was used to support the cultural and artistic flowering of Gustav's reign, as well as his lofty foreign ambitions.[5]

Denmark was similarly well placed to benefit from the war, and Danish West Indies trade, through the island of St. Thomas, and its Indian trade grew exponentially as British trade was disrupted and Dutch and French rivals were displaced. Indeed, the period of the League of Armed Neutrality saw the pinnacle of Scandinavia's maritime trade. Even the tiny and remote Faroe Islands were fundamentally transformed by the American War. Niels Ryberg, a Copenhagen merchant, had established a trading depot at Tórshavn in 1767. During the war Tórshavn became a smuggling hub, bringing contraband, much of it from American vessels shut out of British ports, into Britain and Ireland. Until this moment, the Faroe Islands had been largely cut off from the rest of the world, locked in ancient patterns and rhythms. With the wartime contraband trade, contact with the outside world grew rapidly, spurring a radical change in the nature of life in the islands.[6]

However, as Scandinavian commerce expanded to fill the void left by the belligerent powers, Danish and Swedish ships became the prime target of British searches and seizures. While neither country had a desire to confront Britain directly, they agreed that something must be done to protect their booming commerce. As such, a conference was held at Copenhagen in June, which resulted in the first formal declaration of armed neutrality by Sweden and Denmark. Here too the fingerprints of the French foreign minister were to be found. Vergennes was an enthusiastic supporter of a neutral league, and in an attempt to influence its formation, sent a familiar face to act as his agent, Stephen Sayre. Though the charges never stuck, Sayre had fled London after being accused of treason, offering his services as a sort of freelance mercenary diplomat in France and Prussia before traveling to Copenhagen for the conference of 1778.

According to his own, admittedly self-serving, account, Sayre recognized the importance to American independence of undermining British "tyranny of the seas." He had therefore arranged personal meetings with the kings of Denmark and Sweden, which had done much to convince them to join together to create a neutral league. At the same time, Sayre also claimed to have sent a message to Catherine II urging her to join Russia to the neutral league, thus sowing the first seeds of the 1780 League of Armed Neutrality.[7]

Vergennes' goal in pushing for the creation of a neutral league was to undermine British naval dominance and relieve France from the strain of the British blockade. Catherine's actions, however, would not be dictated by French interests. From Russia's perspective, Britain was not the lone culprit in the attacks on Russian commerce. John Paul Jones's raids on Baltic shipping had included Russian ships among their victims, much to Catherine's displeasure. Spain, who had entered the war against Britain in June 1779 with an eye toward recapturing Gibraltar, attacked neutral ships—Russian vessels among them—heading for the besieged British outpost. In August, an American privateer attacked a convoy of eight Russian ships in the North Sea, capturing three and damaging the rest. This repeated predation of Russian shipping by those on both sides of the conflict drew Catherine's considerable ire, convincing her of the need for a league of neutral states that could use the threat of armed intervention as a means of protecting free commerce on the sea.

But Catherine's desires for a league were not motivated by trade considerations alone. Russia's share of the shipping trade was small compared with other European countries, and while the attacks on Russia vessels were an affront to Catherine's imperial dignity, her commerce suffered less than that of Sweden, Denmark, or the Netherlands. As important as the freedom of the seas, however, was Russia's place among the powers of Europe. The tsars claimed to have inherited the mantle of the Roman emperors and, for Catherine, the league could be used as a tool to increase Russian influence over the balance of power in Europe. The empress hoped to use the league as a means of forcing Britain and France to negotiate peace under Russian mediation, thereby augmenting Russian prestige and freeing Catherine to focus on imperial expansion on her eastern borders.

For the belligerent nations, the announcement of a League of Armed Neutrality was greeted with mixed sentiments. For France, and for Vergennes in particular, the league was welcomed as a means of undermining British sea power and the British blockade that was slowly choking France. France was also open to the idea of Russian-mediated peace negotiations, as long as certain conditions were met. For Britain, the league was a blow, but not a disaster. The combined fleets of all the neutral powers were dwarfed by the British navy, a fact that led Britain to continue to maintain its right to search any and all ships for contraband, a practice that would soon drive the Netherlands into the arms of the league and eventually outright war with Britain. Nonetheless, a huge proportion of Britain's naval supplies, especially wood for masts, were acquired from the Baltic, so some new caution was required. The idea of Russian mediation was in some senses more worrisome, given the fear that such negotiations might allow the rebellious colonies a place at the table, reinforcing their status as an independent power. For the United States, the advent of the league was even more ambiguous. On the one hand, many Americans hoped that the neutral powers would eventually be drawn into the war against Britain, or at the very least isolate Britain from potential allies or trade partners. On the other hand, there were grave concerns that a Russian-mediated peace would result in a separate peace between France, Spain, and Britain, leaving the United States bereft of allies and without a formal recognition of independence. With so much at stake between the contending powers, the creation of the league instantly turned St. Petersburg into a crucial center of diplomacy.

On December 15, 1780, the Congress of the United States acknowledged Russia's newfound importance by resolving to send a minister to reside at Catherine's court. Four days later, Congress officially appointed Francis Dana to the post. Dana had been born in Charlestown, Massachusetts in June 1745. His lineage on both sides was of prosperous puritan stock, well-established families who could trace their ancestors back to the earliest days of the colony. Dana's family had close connections to the colonial establishment, and his grandfather maintained his Tory worldview to the last, but both Francis and his father became conspicuously active in the agitations surrounding the passage of the Stamp Act. Francis was active in a number of Patriot clubs and debating societies, including one with his Harvard classmates John Lovell and Josiah Quincy. As a well-known magistrate, Richard Dana was even more visible, becoming a founding member of the Sons of Liberty and playing a prominent role in the ritual humiliation of the detested commissioner of the offending tax, Andrew Oliver. The whole affair, in which a mob forced Oliver to sign an oath promising not to enforce the Stamp Act, took place in front of Judge Dana's home, with the judge himself presenting Oliver with the oath and signing his own name as a witness. When British troops fired on a crowd of angry protesters in 1770, an event that was quickly christened the Boston Massacre, Richard Dana was once more in the thick of things, taking a very public stand as the committing magistrate in the subsequent trial of Captain Preston for manslaughter. Richard Dana would not live to see the Patriot movement bear fruit, dying in 1772, but his role in the lead-up to the revolution was not forgotten by his peers. Looking back on those days, John Adams would later declare that Richard Dana was one who, "had he not been cut off by death, would have furnished one of the immortal names of the Revolution."[8]

The Danas' principled political opposition gained Francis a wide range of important connections with Whig politicians in America and Britain—including John Adams, Rufus King, and William Ellery of New Hampshire, whose daughter Elizabeth he married in 1773—but they also stymied his still embryonic legal career. Faced with constrained prospects in Boston, Francis volunteered to travel to London as the agent of the Massachusetts Patriots. It was believed that many, if not most, in London were sympathetic to the American cause, especially the famous John Wilkes and his allies. Though he outwardly traveled to visit his brother Rev. Edmund Dana, who had long resided in England, Francis's real mission was to establish contact with Wilkite politicians in the capital with the aim of combining efforts to influence British policies toward the colonies.

London was in a state of nervous, raucous combustibility, a seething hive protest, riot, and disorder. Benjamin Franklin, who had left London just before Dana arrived, described the metropolis as "a scene of lawless riot and confusion, mobs patrolling the streets at midday, some knocking down all who will not shout for 'Wilkes and Liberty' . . . a great black cloud ready to burst in a universal tempest." With so much anger and animosity choking the narrow, twisting streets, Dana felt the city was alive with possibility. Dana and his Massachusetts comrades had long connections with London radicals, and had every reason to believe that Londoners, perhaps the British populace in general, was sympathetic to the American cause that was just then bursting forth in the no longer tranquil fields of Lexington. Dana swiftly made a variety of important contacts, meeting among others the celebrated radical Dr. Richard Price and his fellow future diplomats Arthur and William Lee of Virginia and Stephen Sayre of New York. Much to his disappointment, Dana found that, contrary to American expectations, the tide was turning slowly but irrevocably against the Wilkes faction and the American cause. With little hope of his presence averting all-out war, Dana returned to America in May 1776, bringing with him to Congress news that peace was an increasingly unlikely prospect.[9]

After the frustrating failures of his London mission, the galloping action of the revolution must have been a welcome relief. Dana threw himself fully into the fray, helping to draft the new Massachusetts constitution as a member of the General Court before traveling to the Continental Congress as one of his state's delegates in 1776. In Congress, Dana's bluff honesty, upright character, and radical bona fides meant that he was trusted by all sides of the increasingly factional legislature. He was appointed to the committee that inquired into the military failures that resulted in the loss of Ticonderoga in July of 1777, and to the Committee of Inquiry charged with investigating General Washington's army at Valley Forge. A faction within the army, headed by Horatio Gates and Thomas Conway, and supported by a sympathetic faction within Congress, hoped to remove Washington from his position of command or at least bring the all-powerful general to heel, subordinating him to the appropriate congressional committee. Many in Congress and army were impatient with Washington's cautious Fabian strategy, while others thought his almost mythic status among his soldiers held all the harbingers of a military dictatorship. The Committee of Inquiry then was intended to "rap a demi-God over the knuckles" and bring Washington into line.[10]

Dana's inclusion, indeed his role as principal negotiator, was primarily a result of a misapprehension by the radical faction within Congress. Largely comprised of Virginians and fellow New Englanders, this faction assumed that Dana was sympathetic to their position, "a thorough republican and an able supporter of our great cause," in the words of Samuel Adams. Dana might well have been of their opinion at the outset, but he was never a man to jump to hasty conclusions before seeing the situation for himself. After spending weeks in the miserably cold camp, the committee ultimately vindicated Washington, strengthening his position with Congress and fatally undermining what has come to be known as the Conway Cabal. Despite the committee's findings, Dana remained relatively popular on both sides of the factional divide, though he only narrowly avoided a duel with the ever-hotheaded Alexander Hamilton over a perceived affront in the aftermath of the Conway affair.[11]

At the outset of the revolution, the American diplomatic corps was largely an ad hoc outfit, cobbled together from whoever happened to be at hand in Europe when the war began. This "militia diplomacy" had served its purpose well enough in the early years of the conflict, but by 1778 it was becoming increasingly clear to many in Congress that more formal, more closely managed foreign missions were required to handle the vital and delicate negotiations with Britain and the European powers. To make matters worse, the dearth of formal representatives in Europe also meant that in the early years of the war, much of America's diplomacy, and thus a substantial portion of her foreign policy, was left in the hands of France. For many Americans, there were ample reasons to fear that French interests might not align with America's, and the idea that France might make a separate peace with Britain was always a grave concern. In some corners it was fervently believed that America's representatives in Europe, Benjamin Franklin especially, were part of the problem, dangerously independent and worryingly sympathetic to French interests. To remedy this lack of formal agents, bring American diplomacy more firmly under the thumb of Congress, and blunt undue French influence, Francis Dana and his old friend John Adams were sent to Europe in 1779.

Adams and Dana arrived in Paris in February 1780, weather-beaten and travel worn. The trip had not been an easy one, even by eighteenth-century standards. Sailing east across the storm-tossed seas of the Atlantic winter, Dana's ship had been plagued by leaks, dogged by hostile British ships and the loss of one of its escort ships in a sudden gale. The perilous crossing forced the ship to land at Ferrol on the north-western coast of Spain, necessitating a long, arduous overland journey through the mountains of Galicia and over the Pyrenees before turning north to Paris. If the horrendous sea crossing made the feeling of firm ground beneath their feet a blessed relief, the trip through Spain and France may well have made Dana and Adams long for the creaky confines of their battered ship. In Galicia, their carriage crashed; in the Pyrenees, Dana was struck down by mountain sickness; in France they were buffeted by wind and snow; and everywhere they encountered miserable weather, terrible roads, damp, vermin-filled lodgings and inedible fare. For Dana, it was all a mere foretaste of things to come.

When they finally limped into glittering, glamorous Paris after months of arduous travel, Dana and Adams were granted little time to recover. Negotiations with Britain were ongoing, and there was some hope on both sides that terms of peace could be ironed out. But, from Dana's perspective, the terms offered by Lord North still fell well short of the mark. Dana had been a member of the congressional committee that had rejected North's earlier "Conciliatory Resolution" in July 1775, and he considered the prime minister's new attempt—the ill-fated Carlisle Commission of 1778—with scarcely more favor. While direct negotiations with Britain were dragging on unproductively, American diplomats were busy seeking recognition, treaties, and alliances in all the major European capitals, with one notable exception. American agents were present in Paris, Amsterdam, Madrid, Berlin, and Vienna, but in 1780 the United States still lacked a representative in the capital of one of the great and growing powers of Europe: the Russian Empire.

Mere weeks after Dana arrived in Paris, this diplomatic oversight took on a new importance with the announcement of Catherine the Great's League of Armed Neutrality. Why exactly Francis Dana was chosen for this critical, delicate mission is not entirely clear. When he was named American agent for St. Petersburg in 1780, he had no specific credentials to recommend him for the post. He was not well versed in Russian history, politics or culture, he spoke no Russian, though this was hardly a major hurdle in an age when French was the language of Russian elites and the Russian court. But Dana was no linguist, and even after years spent in Paris, mingling with French officials and attending the court of Louis XVI, his conscious and conscientious efforts to learn the Lingua Franca of European diplomacy had come to naught. But Dana did have some diplomatic experience in Europe, and he could be more easily spared than a John Adams or Benjamin Franklin. Perhaps it was merely the fact he himself had been one of the correspondents who first alerted Congress to the possibility of an alliance of northern and eastern powers that singled Dana out for the mission. Dana also had connections with key members of the Committee for Foreign Affairs, including its chairmen, James Lovell, a fellow son of the Bay State. For Lowell, the choice of Francis Dana made good sense for the sensitive mission to the court of Catherine the Great.

Whatever the rationale, in December of 1780, Francis Dana received his instructions from Congress and began to make preparations for the long journey to St. Petersburg. Dana's mission was to have two primary aims: "to engage her Imperial majesty to favor and support the sovereignty and independence of these United States," and to seek formal admittance of the United States "as party to the convention of neutral powers for maintaining the freedom of commerce." Beyond this his instructions were left intentionally vague. In an age when communications over such great distances could take months, success would depend on the conditions on the ground and a "variety of sources and contingencies." Much therefore rested on Dana's shoulders:

> [T]he greatest room must be left for the exercise of your own penetration and assiduity in gaining proper information, and for your prudence and address in improving it the best advantage. Your zeal for the public interest will lead you to embrace every favorable incident and expedient which may recommend these United States to the friendship of her Imperial majesty and her ministers. Your attachment to the honor and independence of your country will restrain you from every concession unbecoming the dignity of a free people.[12]

On July 7, 1781, after a seemingly interminable delay brought about by French opposition to the Russian mission, Dana finally bid the Netherlands farewell and embarked for the court of Catherine the Great. Traveling in the guise of a private gentleman rather than with the pomp of an official diplomatic mission, Dana's party would have to remain small and inconspicuous. A servant would be needed as no self-respecting gentleman, especially one who wished to make a favorable impression on a foreign court, would have been seen without at least one. And then there were Dana's linguistic deficiencies to consider. He would need a secretary fluent in French to assist with the communications with the Russian court and the various foreign diplomats stationed in St. Petersburg.

His first choice of secretary dropped out at the last minute, and with French-speaking Americans willing to travel to the frozen edge of Europe thin on the ground in Amsterdam, the task fell on the untested shoulders of the young son of John Adams. Only 14 years old when he joined Dana's mission, John Quincy Adams could nonetheless boast considerable experience in Europe—having arrived with his father in 1778—and a facility with languages far surpassing Dana's rudimentary French.

With his little fellowship selected, Dana planned his journey across central Europe. He chose his route through Germany with care, opting for a less common and considerably longer route from Amsterdam through Cologne, Frankfurt, and Leipzig to Berlin in order to avoid having to cross through the Electorate of Hanover. Hanover and Britain had been connected by a common monarch since 1714, when George, the Elector of Hanover, became George I of Great Britain and Ireland. Because of this connection, Hanover had sided with Britain in all of the previous conflicts of the eighteenth century and continued to do so throughout the American War. Hanover was thus enemy territory and if an American agent was discovered traveling across the Electorate, not only would news of his mission to Russia quickly leak to Britain, but "seizure of person and papers" was sure to follow. Circumventing Hanover, Dana traveled through many of the smaller states of the Holy Roman Empire, pausing at the Free Cities of Cologne, a major trading center on the Rhine, and Frankfurt on the River Main, before crossing central Germany to reach Leipzig in the Electorate of Saxony.

While still in the Netherlands, Dana purchased a coach for his embassy and on July 9 set off from Utrecht for Nijmegen on the German border some 50 miles away. The trip south across the Rhine by rope ferry, along the high dykes that kept the River Waal at bay and eventually across the river on a movable bridge of boats, took about ten hours in all, a largely pleasant ride over good roads and flat terrain. From Nijmegen they hugged the banks of the Rhine for 100 miles, through Dusseldorf to Cologne, riding sometimes on one side of the great river and sometimes on the other as it twisted its way through the German plains. Dusseldorf was famed for its art collection, but Dana was not a tourist, and besides, he had had his "Curiosity of that sort" more than sated in London, Paris, and Antwerp. He was no more impressed with Cologne. It was "very ancient" and quite large, but compared to the tidy, rationally planned streets of Boston and Philadelphia also "irregular, and dirty" with decrepit house marring narrow twisting streets. Leaving Cologne behind, they traveled some 70 miles to Bonn, where the staid plains gave way to the romantic mountains and steep, vineyard-clad river valleys of the Rhine, and on to Koblenz. From Koblenz Dana finally took his leave of the Rhine, turning east across the heart of Germany to Frankfurt and Leipzig.[13]

Although his exact route through central Germany is not entirely clear, it is almost certain that Dana would have traversed the territories of Hesse-Kassel, Hesse-Darmstadt, and perhaps Hesse-Hanau, and Ansbach-Bayreuth. As he traveled through these myriad states and principalities of the Holy Roman Empire Dana must have been shocked to realize that, although this was technically a land at peace, a land far away from the fighting in North America, the specter of war still haunted the German lands. As Dana himself well knew, these states, along with Anhalt-Zerbst and Waldeck, were in fact embroiled in the conflict in North America. They were the native lands of the dreaded "Hessians" that plagued the imaginations of Americans everywhere, filling their nightmares with images of brutish and subhuman "Huns."[14]

As early as 1777, American observers in Europe began to notice the ruinous effects the war was having in many German states. From his post in Berlin at the court of Frederick the Great of Prussia, Arthur Lee informed his colleagues on the Committee of Foreign Affairs in Philadelphia:

The consequence of the Prince of Hesse's conduct is beginning to be a lesson to the other German princes, so that it is not probable they will draw any more supplies from them. The country of Hesse is depopulating so fast, from the apprehension of being forced into this service, that the women are obliged to cultivate the lands. At present, therefore, the foreign resources of Great Britain seem to be exhausted.

A few years later, a returning soldier was shocked to discover that women were manning the oars on transport vessels in port cities further north, forced by poverty and a dearth of men to take on traditionally male employment. It seemed as if the lands themselves were being squeezed dry, drained of their men, leaving behind an impoverished land of Amazons in central Europe. The young men, and many not so young, were gone, shipped off in their thousands to America to crush the colonial uprising and fight the wars of George III of Britain.[15]

In 1775, Frederick II, Landgrave of Hesse-Kassel, had agreed to supply Britain with a force of 12,000 troops—augmented by yearly replacements of the dead and wounded—to quell the growing rebellion in America. The negotiations had begun in 1774, when it was still hoped that the deepening crisis in the colonies could be averted, but it was only after the shock of the Battle of Bunker Hill in 1775 that pen was finally put to paper, with similar contracts made with other German princes following quickly. Brunswick would agree to supply some 6,000 men, Waldeck 1,200, Hesse-Hansau 2,500, Ansbach-Bayreuth 2,500, and Anhalt-Zerbst 1,200.

It would have come as no surprise to those familiar with European warfare and diplomacy that George III would turn to Germany for mercenaries to fight his battles. As George was also Elector of Hanover, he would likewise have drawn men and materials from that principality for the fight across the Atlantic. Indeed, Hanover and Britain had long-standing relationships with many of the smaller German states. Since the days of the Reformation and Counter-Reformation many of these states, Hesse-Kassel prominent among them, had been part of a "Protestant System" of alliances with Britain, the Netherlands, and later Prussia, Denmark, and Sweden, which sought to counterbalance the Catholic powers of France and the Habsburgs. These alliances continued through the near constant warfare of the seventeenth and eighteenth centuries, including most recently in the Seven Years' War. Small states like Hesse-Kassel could not hope to survive long without such alliances, nor could they afford to contribute financially, as Britain preferred to do. Instead, they contributed by renting their armies as mercenary forces to their traditional allies, entering into thirty such subsidy treaties between 1702 and 1763.[16]

The *Soldatenhandel*, or mercenary trade, made a considerable impact in the German states. Hesse-Kassel, the most prominent and prolific mercenary state, quickly became proportionately the most militarized state in Europe, with a standing army of 12,000 and an equal number of militiamen out of a total population of only 275,000. Incredibly, 1 out of every 15 citizens was a member of the military in some capacity and a full quarter of all households were represented in the army, a ratio twice that of notoriously militarized Prussia. Standing armies were anathema in Britain, potential tools of monarchical despotism, so when the American rebellion broke out in 1775, Britain looked to states that already possessed armies trained and ready to go. Germany would once more be the human supply depot for British foreign adventures.[17]

For states like Hesse-Kassel, the choice to sell soldiers to the British, familiar though it was, was hardly a free decision. Unlike Germany today, in the eighteenth century German principalities like Hesse-Kassel were deeply poor. Britain itself had witnessed this poverty first-hand earlier in the century, as waves of desperate German peasants, tens of thousands of "poor Palatines," had drifted into the country, many eventually making their way to settlements in America. During the Seven Years' War many of these states found themselves stuck between the opposing forces of France and Prussia, their cities looted and countryside ravaged by the constant combat. Despite official neutrality, Hesse was invaded by the French on three separate occasions during the war and its largest cities conquered and re-conquered again and again. The capital of Kassel changed hands four times and the second city of Marburg was tossed between the belligerents an astounding fifteen times before the fighting finally ceased in 1763. The economy of Hesse-Kassel, like that of many of its neighbors, was almost completely ruined. Fortunately, the worst of the consequences were offset by the subsidy paid by the British for the use of Hesse's army during the war. By 1770, however, the British subsidy had been paid in full, so when a Europe-wide harvest failure hit that same year, the result was famine and financial crisis. The price of grain doubled in 1770, tripled in 1771, and sextupled in 1772. In the capital, mortality rates reached 70 per cent while the principality's 7,500 Jews faced waves of persecution and expulsion from the countryside as peasants and officials alike turned once more to familiar scapegoats. When news of trouble in America reached the continent in 1774 then Frederick II must have greeted the possibility of a new mercenary convention with considerable relief. It was, it seemed, the only way to save his people.[18]

But there was more than money at stake in a potential mercenary contract with Britain. Hesse's size, wealth, and geography placed it in a dicey position. Squeezed between France and Prussia, Hesse found itself too often the battleground between ambitious and bellicose great powers, pressured to take a side in the seemingly endless conflicts that plagued central Europe or pay the price. To maintain its autonomy as a small state in a world of giants Frederick George III, like his ancestors before him, turned to his British kin. George III of Britain was a member of the German House of Hanover and Elector of Hanover, Hesse's neighbor to the north. He was also Frederick George's uncle, strengthening with ties of blood an age-old strategic alliance. A mercenary contract thus served two important purposes for Hesse: it provided much-needed financial relief, and it strengthened a relationship with Britain and Hanover that helped keep the principality free from the grasp of France and Prussia.

This balancing act between solvency and autonomy was not a unique concern among smaller states in eighteenth-century Europe. In his role as head of the War Commission of the Duke of Weimar, the writer Johann Wolfgang von Goethe saw this struggle to maintain both sovereignty and neutrality first-hand. Pressured by Prussia to provide troops for a war with Austria, Goethe found himself, and Weimar, with two choices, neither of them good. He could refuse Prussia's request for troops, at which point Prussia might well seize them anyway, eroding Weimar's sovereignty, or he could acquiesce, and supply Prussia with soldiers, thus voiding Weimar's neutrality and making it a target of Austria in the coming war. Goethe's recommendation of prevarication and the creation of a confederation of small states came to naught, and Weimar was forced to recruit troops for Prussian service, for Goethe, "an unpleasant, hateful, and shameful business." For Hesse and its neighbors, the situation in 1775 was much the same, and many eventually decided that British money and British protection were an unfortunate, even hateful, necessity.[19]

The reaction to the convention of 1775 was decidedly mixed. The Hessian people largely accepted the practice of mercenary alliances, and their armies had fought for the British before, but the American War was something altogether different. In previous wars, they had been asked to fight for the British against their traditional enemies, France foremost among them, nations they feared would one day engulf their tiny principalities and force them to convert to the Roman Church. Fighting as mercenaries in such defensive wars thus made good sense both financially and strategically. Sailing across the sea to put down a rebellion of British subjects, on the contrary, made little sense to

German soldiers and German elites alike. For the intelligentsia of Germany the war was indefensible. Those influenced by the Enlightenment thought just war was only possible when it was a defensive necessity. A war of conquest and repression, especially one against the Enlightenment-inspired American colonists, was almost impossible to support. Kant, Schiller, Herder, and other prominent intellectuals opposed the war, as did the enlightened but often war-hungry Frederick the Great of Prussia, who told Voltaire that the German princes had sold their "subjects to the English as one sells cattle to be dragged to the slaughter." The Comte de Mirabeau went further, urging the German people, and German soldiers in particular, who had been "betrayed . . . oppressed, sold and humiliated" to open their eyes and "quit this country sullied by despotism, cross the ocean, flee to America. Embrace your brothers, defend that noble nation against the arrogant greed of its oppressors!"[20]

Frederick II of Hesse was caught off guard by this outpouring of opposition, especially as the response from the wider population was also decidedly mixed. Although it is unclear whether large numbers accepted the position of the *philosophes* about the justness of the war, many soldiers and their families clearly did their best to avoid participating in it. Scores of soldiers quickly deserted, and potential recruits emigrated to other nearby states to avoid conscription. Families encouraged their sons to desert or hid them before they were supposed to depart. In a desperate attempt to prevent his son from being sent to America, one old man, already bereft of a wife, amputated one of his son's fingers. When the authorities discovered the ruse, father and son alike were arrested. In prison, with all his options seemingly gone, the widower took his own life, an early casualty of someone else's war.[21]

It was not the prospect of warfare itself that frightened so many off, but rather the widespread fear of a perilous Atlantic crossing, rumors of the dangers of the Americas, and uneasiness at the prospect of a long separation from families at a time when every hand was needed to stave off famine and ruin. With few volunteers and plentiful deserters, Frederick and his fellow princes often had to turn to new methods for raising the troops they were now contractually bound to supply. In some areas, individuals who would normally have been exempt from military service due to their vital importance to their families' income were enlisted, as were many who were technically too old or too physically weak to serve. One Hessian salt transporter claimed to have been grabbed in a church and forced into the army, and was only released after a government review of the past nine years of his business records revealed that his impressment would unduly harm the collection of the salt tax. Although impressment was officially illegal, reports were regularly received of Hessian recruiters not only impressing Hessian subjects, especially vagrants and criminals, but also seizing foreign travelers and kidnapping peasants living just across the border. Indeed, Frederick received numerous diplomatic requests for the release of foreign abductees throughout the period.[22]

Still, many Germans were clearly willing to take the risk and fight for the British across the ocean. Although he often had to scrape the bottom of the barrel or resort to dirty tricks, Frederick was in the end able to meet his quota of 12,000 men as well as the 1,000 additional men sent every year between 1776 and 1782 to replace the numbers lost to injury, death, and desertion. For most, the greatest appeal was financial. For the younger sons of impoverished landholders, for young peasants who were surplus to the needs of their families, or for those who just could not make the land pay—the enlistment bonuses and wages were paid at British rates, well in excess of usual German military pay— an army life was worth the risk. For others, who had heard of the bounty of the Americas, the military offered free passage to a new life, and many joined the army with the express plan to settle in America once the colonies had been firmly put back in their place. Whatever the reason, over the next seven years of war, 30,000 soldiers, and countless wives, children, and other dependents who could not survive the long separation, made the journey from central Europe, traveling downriver on the Rhine, the Main, and the Weser to the great ports on the North Sea before crossing the tempestuous Atlantic and landing on the troubled shores of North America. As one soldier later remembered the melancholy departure from Hesse, "when the drums beat all of us had to hurriedly continue our march. However, the good people felt sorry for us, and young and old accompanied us to the edge of the city and bade us farewell with tear-filled-eyes."[23]

After tear-drenched goodbyes and a long and perilous ocean crossing, the German mercenaries landed on American shores to the accompaniment of considerable colonial venom. They knew they were there to put down a rebellion, but they still must have been surprised by the vehemence of American rhetoric, its dehumanizing language and the persistent rumors of Hessian brutality. Before they even arrived, there were reports that as many as 60,000 German mercenaries, many of them specially trained marksmen, were on their way to suppress the revolution. Stories quickly spread of their inhuman, animalistic appearance and their merciless behavior. In the American press they were described as "ugly devils," "orang-outang murdering brutes," "sons of Belial," and compared to other foreign boogey-men, including Lord Dumore's army of freed slaves. They were, it was rumored, to be part of a new 90,000 man strong army of conquest, including all the uncivilized villains of the Patriot imagination, "Hessians, Tories, Negroes, Japanese, Moors, Esquimaux, Persian archers, Laplanders, Feejee Islanders."[24]

Elsewhere, Hessians were accused of digging up graves to expose bodies and indiscriminately plundering the countryside. "If they see anything they want," one newspaper reported, "they seize it, and say, 'Rebel food for Hesse man.' " The *Pennsylvania Evening Post* warned its readers that because they stood up to the tyrannical George III, "we will have our towns burnt, our country desolated, our fathers, brothers, and children butchered ... by Hanoverians, Hessians, Brunswickers, Waldeckers, Canadians, Indians and Negroes." It was "a mercenary army, more venal than a court favorite, more savage than a band of Tatars, more spiritless than the sorry, sooty sons of Afric." A poem titled "To Virginia", published in *Freeman's Journal* in July 1776, encapsulated many American views of German mercenaries as a ravaging horde of foreign oppressors:

> And now, when Britain's mercenary bands
> Bombard our cities, desolate our lands,
> (Our pray'rs unanswer'd, and our tears in vain,)
> While foreign cut-throats crowd th' ensangui'd plain.[25]

Nevertheless, many of those who served opted to remain in America when the war ended. Some hoped eventually to return to Europe, but as officer after officer recorded in the last days of the war, many had no thought of resuming their old lives. Ten privates in New York told an officer that "they have no desire to return to Germany and that they wish to seek their fortune in America." Settling in America had been the ultimate goal of many who signed up to fight for King George. For others, it was the experience of the verdant American landscape that inspired them to remain in the New World after the fighting was over. For men such as Emanuel Hausmann, inured to the poor soil of their native land, America seemed a paradise. In Friedrich von Urff's autograph book he drew a sketch of a Pennsylvania farm, nestled among juniper bushes on the banks of a shimmering river, accompanied by the words, "As beautiful as a rose may be, it still withers on the vine / But a true friend remains true to the end of time!" With this vision of an American life haunting his dreams, Hausmann would remain in America, foregoing old friends for the new vine.[26]

The cost of the American War for the mercenary regiments was steep. The army from Hesse-Kassel, which sent 19,000 men to America over the course of the war, lost 535 men in battle, but a total of nearly 5,000, more than a quarter of those who served, to all causes, primarily disease. An additional 3,000 men deserted or chose to remain behind in America after the war. The casualty rates and rates of desertion for the mercenary contingents from other German states were similarly high.[27]

For such small states, the loss of so many men was a difficult burden to bear. Of the 12 per cent of Hesse-Kassel's able-bodied male population who left for America, nearly half never returned. The American War, for the Hessians, however, was a family affair, and large numbers of wives and children accompanied the soldiers to North America, a fact amply illustrated by the church books of the regimental chaplains, packed full of records of marriages and births among the troops. Many of these wives and children died over the course of the war, or remained with their husbands to settle in America, and a large proportion of the young population of Hesse was lost in the war.[28]

Rural areas were the hardest hit. Peasants made up the bulk of the army, and their absence caused a dramatic labor shortage in many areas. Some farmers attempted to hire foreign laborers to make up the shortage, but government-instituted price ceilings, designed to protect urban areas, prevented them from offsetting increased labor costs. As was usual, the poor suffered the most. Larger farms had been exempted from military service, so the burden fell most heavily on small farmers, who could not do without the labor of the men sent to America. So dire was the predicament that many such families petitioned the government to release their husbands and sons from the army, to no avail. As a result, the numbers of people, especially women, listed on the poor rolls rose dramatically. In Marburg, for instance, 100 soldiers had been sent to America. As a result of this loss, eighty-two new individuals were placed on the poor rolls, including thirty soldiers' wives. When the war ended and British subsidies stopped, many in Germany must have looked around and wondered what it had all been for. As Dana rode through an increasingly empty countryside he must have been astounded that the effects of the war were everywhere to be seen. Even in Germany, thousands of miles from the battle lines of North America, the effects of the war, the deep poverty and the depopulation of the countryside, were manifest.[29]

Dana and young John Quincy Adams arrived in St. Petersburg on August 27, 1781, after a bone-jarring trip from Frankfurt through the impoverished hills and patchwork principalities of central Germany to the university town of Leipzig before heading north to Berlin. Traveling in haste through the night, his carriage had overturned, "broken into pieces" in the "midst of a Forest" on the uneven road. Dana found Berlin much more to his taste than the other German cities he had passed through on his journey. "Berlin is the prettiest City I have anywhere seen," Dana enthused, particularly admiring its wide, well-ordered streets and elegant buildings. But the regimented character of Berlin was also a dark reflection of the character of its ruler and the nature of his rule. Dana, by now no stranger to the tragic effects of the German military state, had no time for the harsh militarism of Prussia or the despotic tendencies of the supposedly "enlightened" Frederick the Great. The king was detested by his subjects, Dana reported, considered to be as "unfeeling a Tyrant as ever existed" and his people "born down by the enormous weight of his Stupendous Military System." His celebrated reforms were no better in Dana's republican eyes, "the arbitrary and capricious regulations of as complete a despot as has ever been sent into the world to curse mankind." The charms of Berlin and his own illness and exhaustion notwithstanding, Dana would have preferred to make for Russia immediately, but the need for a new carriage meant a delay of several days.[30]

The journey from Berlin to St. Petersburg was more than 1,000 miles long, on rough, rudimentary roads, with only the occasional rustic inn to break the dreary slog. Dana was driven by a sense of mission, however, a belief that he had a vital part to play on the world stage at a critical moment in the birth of his country. With friends and family putting their lives on the line back in America, he could brook no delay, afford no physical weakness. From Berlin he journeyed north-east into Poland, stopping at the port city of Danzig with its tree-lined streets and "Dutch stile" buildings before continuing to Konigsberg, home of the great philosopher Immanuel Kant, finally arriving in Russian territory at Riga on August 17. Three days later, Dana and his party began the last leg of their journey, continuing north-east through Estonia to Narva and St. Petersburg. When he finally saw the outskirts of the Russian capital after 50 days of rugged travel, Dana must have been exhausted, but he was also impatient to begin the crucial business of diplomacy. For all his haste, Dana would find no warm welcome in the land of the tsars, no diplomatic reception, none of the desperate urgency that coursed through his own weary body.

St. Petersburg was a new city by European standards, nearly a century younger than Dana's beloved Boston. In 1703 Tsar Peter the Great had ordered the construction of a new city to match his modernizing ambitions, a city that would allow him to escape the stale confines of Moscow. In the years since 1703, Peter's new capital had risen out of the marshes of the River Neva like a Slavic Brigadoon, an Enlightenment city of stone buildings, spacious squares, and scenic canals laid out in a logical grid pattern. By the time of Dana's arrival in 1780, St. Petersburg had a new ruler, but one no less driven to demonstrate her enlightened bona fides in bronze and marble. Catherine had not been born to rule. A princess of Anhalt-Zerbst, she had married into the Russian royal family in 1745 when she wed the future Emperor Peter III. Clever, strong-willed, and utterly ruthless, Catherine was not content with standing in her husband's shadow for long, especially when it appeared that the unstable and much-despised emperor was plotting to remove both Catherine and her son. In July 1762, with the aid of her lover Grigory Orlov, Catherine secured the support of the army and marched on the Winter Palace, outmaneuvering the duplicitous tsar and forcing his resignation. To the nation Catherine presented the coup as a necessary action to preserve Russia from the tsar's mental instability. When Peter III was soon thereafter poisoned and strangled by Orlov and his brothers, Catherine publicly declared the death to have been a "bloody accident," the result of piles and "cholick."[31]

The St. Petersburg Dana encountered in 1780 was in many ways a direct result of Catherine's contentious rise to power. Catherine would always be sensitive about her legitimacy as tsar, a fact that fueled her desire to transform Peter the Great's capital into the magnificent jewel in her own crown. From the early years of her reign, Catherine embarked upon myriad projects of urban improvement, transforming St. Petersburg into a cultural showcase, a model city of the European Enlightenment. Streetlights were added, streets were paved, rivers embanked, and a city of wood slowly transformed into a metropolis clad in stone. It was not merely for show. There was genuine intellectual heft behind Catherine's modernizing endeavors. She corresponded with many of the towering cultural figures of the age and brought celebrated intellectuals, architects, and artists to her city on the Neva. She championed printing and periodicals, painting and sculpture, and sent an army of agents to the capitals of Europe to amass an art collection befitting a world capital.[32]

Despite Catherine's ambitions, St. Petersburg's transformation was not yet complete; it was a city still shaking off its rural roots, still in the act of rising from its provincial slumber. Many streets remained paved only with logs, canals remained squalid with sewage, kitchen gardens still dotted the urban landscape, and 20,000 cows were still kept by city-dwellers. But the city hummed with activity, a welcoming bustling vitality. The weather was deceptively welcoming as well. The Americans arrived in the closing days of summer, a season measured by those who knew the city in weeks rather than months. Winter, "rude . . . unsettled and unfriendly," with temperatures dropping to -40° Celsius, might begin, without warning, as early as November. "You take farewell of Summer at night," one observer warned, "and hail the grim tyrant in the morning."[33]

Dana was ill-prepared for his frigid welcome in Russia, both by Catherine and his fellow diplomats. Count Panin, an advisor to and former favorite of Catherine the Great, was the leader of the pro-Prussian faction in the Russian government and was thought to be sympathetic toward American interests. Charles Oliver de Saint-Georges, Marquis de Vérac, the French minister to the Russian court, was also thought to be a potential ally, though Dana arrived in St. Petersburg already skeptical of French influence in European diplomacy and well aware that Vergennes had done his best to discourage his mission.

Neither, it transpired, would prove particularly useful. Louche and languid, Vérac would do almost nothing to aid Dana's efforts to make contact with the Russian government, while Panin, theoretically an ally, had fallen from favor and could do little to influence events from his rural exile. With few contacts and no friends, Dana would languish in his hotel in months of frustrated, maddening isolation. Vérac and Panin were not, however, entirely to blame for the American mission's frosty reception.

To the travel-worn Dana, the plague that was Stephen Sayre seemed to have preceded him everywhere he went, poisoning the diplomatic well before he could draw from it. After adventures in Copenhagen and Berlin, Sayre had traveled to St. Petersburg in 1780, claiming to be a representative of the United States, though without any actual authorization. His very presence in the Russian capital angered the British and annoyed the tsarina, but that was nothing compared to the damage done to American credibility when Sayre, as interested as ever in conspiracy and intrigue, attempted to implicate the popular British ambassador, James Harris, in a plot to burn the Russian fleet. Harris dismissed Sayre as a spy, "impudent and indiscreet, with better parts than judgment, enterprising in forming a bold project, but unequal to its execution . . . a rebellious adventurer, but without those qualities requisite to obtain even the confidence of his own party." Unsurprisingly given its author, the arson ploy came to nothing, with Harris and the British avoiding the opprobrium that was more appropriately heaped on the Americans.[34]

Dana knew enough of Sayre's character to avoid entangling himself with the rogue would-be diplomat, and seems to have studiously avoided the New Yorker while in St. Petersburg. But Sayre was not alone undermining the American position in Russia. Although he seems to have been unaware of this, Dana had done much to cast himself in a negative light before he even arrived at his post. In May 1780, while Dana was still in Paris, the *Black Prince*, an American privateer owned and outfitted by Robert Morris, had captured and plundered a neutral ship in the English Channel in defiance of the freedom of the seas declared by Catherine's League of Armed Neutrality. It was suggested to Benjamin Franklin, as the United States' senior ambassador in Europe, that the privateers return the captured goods to the rightful owner. Franklin consulted Dana and John Adams about the matter, and the Massachusetts men, despite their support for the League of Armed Neutrality, publicly advised Franklin to refuse all limits on American privateers. Like many Americans, Dana considered the League of Armed Neutrality to be focused on undermining and preventing British naval tyranny. In his mind, American privateers were not the problem the league was designed to address, and should thus be exempt from the strictures of the league. Catherine, however, saw it as yet another example of American piracy. She had been "entirely furious" about American raids against Russian shipping, "the affronts these Americans have placed upon me" in 1778 and the *Black Prince* affair seemed to suggest little had changed. The presence of such an outspoken advocate for American privateers, a seeming hypocrite who championed the neutrality of the seas when it was in his country's interest but undermined its strictures when it was not, was thus hardly likely to receive a warm welcome at her court.[35]

New to the subtle art of European diplomacy, let alone its more boisterous Russian cousin, the young nation and its novice representative proved to be alarmingly ignorant of the nature of statecraft, a naiveté that blunted Dana's effectiveness. Little could be accomplished to influence members of the Russian court without the liberal distribution of cash to the proper parties. Merely gaining an audience with key figures in the Russian government required an outlay of gifts, a requirement that the rather stiff and puritanical Dana balked at and that Congress never properly understood much less approved. Congress had also been blinded by Catherine's enlightened outward presentation. They firmly believed her to be a champion of liberty, progress, and free trade, a keen enemy of a tyrannical Britain and a natural ally of the United States. In assuming Catherine's enlightened bona fides, and taking for granted a close alignment of interests, Congress repeatedly pushed for treaties and agreements with Russia that were never remotely possible. Catherine had her own interests and her own concerns, and while she welcomed the American rebellion for the opportunities it provided her, she had little interest in its ultimate success. Dana eventually came to recognize this fact, but he was never able to convince his government.

If Congress had not been too preoccupied with its own struggles to more closely examine recent events in Russia, they might have been cured of their delusions. In 1774, Yemelyan Pugachev, an obscure Don Cossack landowner, had declared himself to be the deceased Peter III, touching off the most serious rebellion of Catherine's reign. The uprising of Cossacks and peasants was quickly brutally suppressed, but the appeal of Pugachev's promise of an end to serfdom—in a country in which 90 per cent of the population were serfs—and Catherine's refusal to entertain the idea, should have exposed the autocratic nature of Catherine's rule. Furthermore, along with the usual executions and the hanging and quartering of Pugachev, the suppression of the rebellion also saw the beginning of a new stage in the history of Siberian exile. Though criminals and dissidents had been banished to the Arctic steppes of Russia's hinterland since the eighteenth century, Pugachev's rebellion, and Catherine's ferocious reaction to it, began to transform the practice into a formal policy. As for the British in America and Australia, expulsion provided Catherine and her successors with both a handy means of ridding the state of individuals who threatened its stability and of populating and securing the nation's fringes in an age of imperial expansion. By 1781 Catherine had sent 35,000 men into Siberian exile, marking a growing trend in the use of exile to rid the state of criminals and dissidents while securing the imperial frontiers. Lulled by her advocacy for free seas and mediation, and blinded by her improving interests, Congress remained convinced of Catherine's enlightened nature, of her commitment to progress, and her status as a potential champion of liberty. It was a miscalculation that would do much to doom Dana's diplomatic prospects.[36]

Unfortunately for Dana, his British counterpart at Catherine's court showed none of the costly inexperience or misguided scruples that plagued the American diplomatic effort. Though still only 31 years old, Sir James Harris had been "in the midst of Russian barbarity" as Britain's ambassador to St. Petersburg since 1777, and had experience in European diplomacy that stretched back more than a decade. Handsome and socially adept, Harris was a born diplomat, a professional with the deep experience few of America's amateur ministers could match. His presence in St. Petersburg was ample testament to the growing importance of Russia to British interests during the American War. While Dana and Congress balked at the bribery needed to build influence in St. Petersburg, Harris was busy greasing palms to ensure that Russia stayed out of Britain's family quarrel. The British agent had spent considerable time and money building up an information network in the Russian government and creating a pro-British faction in Catherine's court. He worked secretly to undermine the position of the pro-Prussian foreign minister Count Panin and tie himself to the ostensibly pro-British Prince Potemkin. In this he largely succeeded. Prince Grigory Potemkin, Catherine's great favorite and former lover, was persuaded through large monetary inducements to back Britain, and most, perhaps all, of Potemkin's secretaries were in Harris's pocket. Even so, the Russian court remained divided between Potemkin's pro-British faction and a pro-Prussian faction led by another of Catherine's favorites, Count Panin, the man on whom Dana pinned much of his hope for success at the Russian court.[37]

For Harris, who had formally objected to Dana's presence in St. Petersburg, preventing Dana from securing an alliance with Russia was not enough. Harris and the British ministry feared that Catherine's very public desire to serve as mediator between the warring parties might lead to the recognition of American independence, an idea still anathema in Britain. For one so well studied in the art of bribery, the path forward was clear. Harris determined to distract Catherine's attention from neutrality and mediation by means of an audaciously spectacular bribe. Catherine was to be offered a British sugar island in the West Indies or the island of Minorca in the Mediterranean in return for her promise not to push for a negotiated peace. Catherine, however, had her sights set on a greater prize, one that necessitated the continuation of the Franco-British War and the smokescreen of armed neutrality.[38]

In the meantime, Dana remained steadfast in his determination to do what he could to secure a Russian alliance or at least the much hoped-for recognition of his nation's status as an independent state. In December 1781, Dana's stoic resolve was buoyed when the news of the American victory at Yorktown at last reached him on the banks of the Neva. "We receive the great news of the surrender of Lord Cornwallis and his army," enthused a jubilant Dana upon hearing of his country's unexpected triumph in Virginia. "Thus the very first rational plan which has been formed, has been happily crowned with the most ample success." Outwardly at least, Yorktown appeared to inaugurate a new phase in Dana's diplomatic mission. Studiously spurned by both Catherine's court and European diplomats before the pivotal battle, in the immediate aftermath Dana began to feel a thaw in his relations in St. Petersburg. The Prussian minister, who like most European agents had previously ignored Dana's very existence, made contact and even delivered a letter from Frederick the Great himself. The normally self-assured Harris was shaken, sure that he now saw clear signs that Catherine was turning her back on Britain. Back in America, many were convinced that Harris was right, certain that the time was ripe for Catherine to throw the strength of the League of Armed Neutrality into the fight against the British tyrant of the waves, to cow their common enemy and ensure the freedom of trade. And yet the changes that everyone was sure they saw in the disposition of Catherine and her court were merely cosmetic, a surface sheen of cooperation obscuring the machinations of the empress. Dana remained officially shunned, American independence remained unrecognized, and the neutral league exasperatingly neutral.[39]

The League of Armed Neutrality and the persistent offers to negotiate peace between the belligerents were designed to hamstring the British and the French while offering Russia maximum flexibility to pursue its predatory interests on the Black Sea. After all, for an empire the size of Russia, concentrating its military on its south-eastern border would leave its northern and western frontiers vulnerable, and there were age-old enemies besides the Turks to worry about. The League of Armed Neutrality did much to secure Russia's European borders. Sweden and Denmark, who had been waging war with Russia for as long as the Ottomans, joined the league in 1780 with the great central European powers Prussia and Austria joining in 1781. All this promised to lessen the threat of a war on multiple fronts, freeing Catherine to act in the Crimea.

At the same time, in June 1781, Catherine had negotiated a secret alliance with the ever-ambitious and land-hungry Joseph II of Austria. Like Russia, Austria had been engaged in a centuries-long conflict with the Ottoman Empire. The Ottomans had been an object of fear since the days when Suleiman the Magnificent swept through the Balkans, bringing the seemingly irresistible surge of an expansionist empire crashing against the very gates of Vienna itself. The Habsburgs were on the back foot for much of the sixteenth and seventeenth centuries, but by the early decades of the eighteenth, Austria had begun to take the offensive. Huge territorial gains were made in wars with the Ottomans in the years between 1714 and 1739, but humiliating setbacks quickly followed. Belgrade was lost in 1739, and the Seven Years' War, a war that saw Russia make considerable conquests, proved to be largely a disappointment for the over-stretched Austrians. By 1781, Joseph II had learned the lessons of the previous wars. Austria embarked on wide-ranging military reforms and a period of massive military growth. "Vienna has now been transformed into an arsenal," a British resident in the Austrian capital reported. "Every day new regiments arrive . . . Nothing can convey a more striking idea of the greatness of the House of Austria." It was the allure of these new forces that had led a bellicose Joseph into the entirely unsatisfying debacle of the Potato War with Prussia, an abortive war that saw both sides mobilize huge armies but no actual combat.[40]

Despite the inconclusiveness of the Potato War, Joseph II had been pleased by the performance of his newly modernized army—in his eyes it had forced the notoriously bellicose Frederick the Great to stand down—but the negotiating table brought only frustration. He was forced to relinquish his claim to Bavaria—the original source of the conflict—while Frederick was granted his demand of hereditary rights to the Franconian duchies. In a further coup for Prussia, many smaller German states had viewed the emperor as the aggressor, and as the greater danger to the autonomy of the principalities. As a result, Frederick, who had spent most of his life gobbling up territory and increasing his influence over lesser German states, was now able to convincingly portray Prussia as the defender of imperial integrity and the guarantor of German independence in the face of an aggressive, expansionist Austria. When Joseph renewed his attempts to add Bavaria to his domains in 1785, Prussia would draw the principalities even closer with the creation of the *Fürstenbund*, a league of German states dedicated to the protection of the constitutional and territorial integrity of the Holy Roman Empire. Central Europe had long been caught between Prussian and Austrian poles, but the Bavarian war did much to intensify this German dualism, and to swing the balance of power decidedly in a Prussian direction. For Joseph II, the war had done little to quench his thirst for territorial expansion, but it provided a valuable lesson about the need to secure his eastern borders before the seemingly inevitable resumption of hostilities with Prussia. While keeping a wary eye on Frederick II, the Austrian gaze began to turn to the east.

With his territorial ambitions blocked in Germany, and with as much as half of total state expenditure going to fund the military, Joseph began to look elsewhere for a fight. The memory of the loss of Belgrade weighed deeply on the Austria psyche in 1781, and so with revenge in mind, and with Russia's spectacular success in the Seven Years' War as a guide, Joseph settled on the eastern frontier as the key to his ambitions. In furtherance of these ends, Joseph and Catherine entered into secret negotiations known as the "Greek Project." The rulers recognized a common interest in the defeat and dismemberment of the Ottoman Empire and used the negotiations to hash out the division of spoils in the next Ottoman war, a war all were convinced was on the horizon. A secret alliance was thus formed, which stipulated that Catherine would receive Moldavia, Wallachia, and Bessarabia, while Joseph would gain the rest of the Balkans with Belgrade the jewel in the crown.[41]

With Austria on board and her other frontiers suitably secured, Catherine could now afford to mass her troops against Crimea and the Ottomans when the opportunity for war presented itself. The rebellion against the khan in 1781 provided the perfect pretext. In a June 1782 letter to Potemkin, Catherine brought the deteriorating situation in Crimea to the prince's attention. "In Crimea," she wrote, "the Tatars have once again begun to make not insignificant disturbances, which forced the Khan and Veselitsky [the Russian consul in Crimea] to leave Kaffa by water for Kerch . . . It is now necessary to give the Khan the promised defense, to protect our borders and his, our friend's." Signaling that the ongoing Franco-British War would provide cover for Russian actions even after the surrender at Yorktown, the empress concluded the letter with the news of the crushing British naval victory over the French at the Battle of the Saintes near Martinique. The British had not yet been cowed, meaning the war might well continue for the foreseeable future. Potemkin unsurprisingly saw an Ottoman conspiracy behind the uprising in Crimea (a senior Ottoman commander had recently been sent to nearby Taman), and a chance to bring the territory under Russian control for good. "The opportunity to send troops into the Crimea is now at hand, and there is no reason to delay. Your loyal ally and absolute Sovereign of his land requests your aid in suppressing the rebels." Despite the rather flimsy pretext of coming to the aid of an ally, even at this early stage Potemkin hinted that perhaps it would be best to create a permanent Russian presence in Crimea. According to Potemkin, the rebels "intend to kill him [the khan], which they've not yet succeeded in doing, but their intention will remain forever, so even if the Tatars were to submit, how could the Khan live among them without protection?" The stage was being set for a Russian conquest.[42]

Potemkin instinctively realized that Russia would never have as good an opportunity to take Crimea as they had in 1782. In December of that year he sent a long letter to Catherine laying out his reasoning, the favorable timing and the value of the peninsula to Russia's imperial ambitions. "If you do not seize [the Crimea] right now," he warned, "there will come a time when everything that we might now receive for free, we shall obtain for a high price." Cutting across the Russian border, the Crimea was too strategically important to leave in the khan's hands, let alone the Ottomans', who supported the deposed khan's brother. "So now imagine that the Crimea is yours and that wart on our nose is no more," Potemkin continued. "The state of our borders suddenly becomes excellent . . . The allegiance of the inhabitants of the New Russia province [conquered in the previous war and still in the process of being settled by Russian immigrants] will then be beyond doubt. Navigation upon the Black Sea will be unrestricted. Pray take note that otherwise your ships will find it difficult to leave port, and even more difficult to return." Rising to a crescendo of imperialist logic, Potemkin implored Catherine with "infinite zeal" to seize the Crimea as any other European power would do, indeed as other European powers had already done in the Americas, Asia, and Africa. "Believe me, with this acquisition you will achieve immortal glory such that no other Sovereign in Russia has ever had. This glory will pave the way to still another even greater glory: with the Crimea will also come supremacy of the Black Sea. Upon you depends whether the path of the Turks is to be blocked and whether they survive or perish." The tsar's long-held pretensions to the Roman imperial crown could become a reality if only the empress would grasp her chance. Catherine ordered Potemkin to proceed against the Tatar rebels with due haste.[43]

Fighting broke out in the Crimea in 1782, and by early 1783, with Russian troops now massing against the rebels, the true value of the League of Armed Neutrality became apparent. Russian troops would remain on the Swedish border, but the numbers could be reduced, as could those on the border with Prussia. According to Potemkin, there was no need "to keep an eye on the Swedish King" nor was there any need "to arm ourselves against the King of

Prussia." As for other potential European interlopers, on April 8 Catherine received a letter from Joseph II of Austria—who was also greedily eyeing Ottoman territory—promising his support against the Ottomans. With her secret alliance now paying dividends, Catherine announced to the other courts of Europe that she intended to seize the Crimea for Russia. Fearing that such a move would tip the European balance of power east, Prussia and France vociferously objected to the Russian campaign. France had acted as protector of the Ottoman Empire in the past, and Frederick of Prussia attempted to convince them to inter-vene once more. Unfortunately for the Ottomans, the American War provided cover for Russian aggression. Peace negotiations with Britain were still ongoing, and France had been horribly drained by the American War and was in no condi-tion to intercede. Catherine was thus unsurprisingly dismissive of France's bluster, commenting that she had little fear or respect for "the French thunder, or better said, summer lightning." Potemkin concurred, suggesting contemptuously that any action from the European powers would be tame, symbolic rather than serious. "Whatever happens," he confidently predicted, "will be nothing more than an empty gesture." The League of Armed Neutrality, the same entity set up to navigate the choppy waters of European diplomacy during the American Revolution, had been secretly transformed into a vehicle for Russian imperial ambition.[44]

Writing from his post in St. Petersburg, Harris agreed with Catherine and Potemkin's assessment of French impotence, wryly noting that Russia would hardly quiver in fear over "incurring the censure of a nation who writes memoirs and epigrams." But Harris was a man of substance as well as wit, and he astutely observed that Catherine had timed her move for the Crimea perfectly, knowing that she would have a free hand with peace between France, America, and Britain still uncertain. Despite her proclaimed desire to act as mediator and peace-maker, "it is impossible that the Empress can sincerely wish to see peace restored between us and our enemies," Harris reasoned, "since the success of her projects in the East necessarily depends on the House of Bourbon being fully employed with its own concerns." Attempts were made to recruit Britain to the cause of intervention; Britain too was overstretched, still busy fighting in India and elsewhere as the details of the Treaty of Paris were being hammered out. What's more, the failures of the North, Rockingham, and

Shelburne ministries in the war with America had culminated in the meteoric rise to power of William Pitt, who began to inaugurate a more pro-Russian agenda in eastern Europe.[45]

Dana had been treated with condescension and contempt by the more established European diplomats at Catherine's court, but he was no less quick to see the Crimean business for what it was or to grasp its implications for the United States. He had followed developments in the Crimea since early 1782, when news of the secret treaty between Russia and Austria was leaked in the press. By October, when more than 100,000 Russian troops were sent to the Ottoman frontier, Dana was sure that they intended more than merely to restore the deposed khan as they outwardly declared. Dana had been informed that the uprising against the khan had been "effected by the intrigues of the court of St. Petersburg, to raise a pretext for this movement [invasion], and to cover the real object in view [annexation]." Dana understood that the Tatars of the Crimea had been "the constant enemies of Russia from the commencement of the thirteenth century until the last war with the Turks," and thus invasion and conquest was almost an historical inevitability. But he also realized that fear of a new "general conflagration" breaking out while the American War and its effects were still being keenly felt would prevent the powers of Europe from interceding in the east. Likewise, Dana reasoned that a desire to avoid a new war would slow the American peace process, prolong the war, and delay recognition of American independence. "Can it be for the Interests of all the belligerent Powers to close this war," he asked, "with an almost certain prospect before them of being speedily plunged into a new and general one in Europe? . . . my hopes of a Peace are enfeebled." In the end, Dana agreed with his British counterpart, the nations of Europe would not save the Ottomans or the Tatars from the "Tempest which is gathering about them."[46]

Despite his years of loyalty to Russia, Sahin Giray must have seen the writing on the wall. It was evident to all that Catherine had no intention of allowing him to remain on the throne, but the beleaguered khan refused to flee the Crimea, waiting and hoping for a positive response from the Ottomans. The sultan, Abdul Hamid I, was understandably furious over Russian actions. Although Crimean independence had been a condition of peace in 1774, the sultan still considered the khan to be his vassal, and his majority Muslim territory to be under his protection. Worse still, in the years after 1774, Istanbul had seen a steady flow of Tatar refugees trickling into the country, fleeing the tightening grasp of Russian power in the Crimea.

Abdul Hamid found himself in an unenviable position. For all its incessant wars, the first half of the eighteenth century had proved a period of economic growth and prosperity for the Ottomans. By the 1770s, however, the years of plenty had given way to an era of economic contraction. The economic depression was the result of a variety of factors: the mechanization of European cotton mills devastated the vital Turkish cotton industry; Caribbean coffee began to displace Ottoman production in Yemen; and the massive increase in military expenditure implemented by her enemies in Europe forced overspending in an Ottoman economy not yet fully monetized. And the economy was not the only concern. On its eastern border, the Ottomans still had to contend with their Asian rival, Persia, in the age-old contest over Iraq and the profits of the Persian Gulf trade with the British East India Company. By all accounts, the 1780s was not an auspicious time for the sultan. Nonetheless, preparations for war with Russia were begun.[47]

The sultan, however, now found himself thrown to the wolves by his traditional European allies who were too busy with the American War to intervene on the Ottomans' behalf. Instead, they urged the sultan stand down, to accept the Russian seizure of the Crimea as a *fait accompli*. As distasteful as it was, with no allies, the Ottomans were forced to abandon the khan to his fate. The khan's refusal to quit the Crimea was a thorn in Potemkin's side. To ensure the perceived legitimacy of the Russian takeover, Potemkin wished to promulgate signed manifestos in which the Tatars declared their desire to freely become Russian subjects. But the Tatars themselves claimed that they could not publicly express this desire until the khan had departed and abdicated, and Potemkin feared that if the manifestos were published with the khan still present, many Tatars would consider them to be a ruse. The khan needed to go.[48]

Sahin Giray was a puppet, but not a fool. Abandoned first by his people, and then by both his Russian and Ottoman protectors, Giray at last saw the writing on the wall. He fled the Crimea for the lands of the Nogais, a Tatar people settled in Bessarabia and other areas around the Black Sea and on the border between Russia and the Ottoman Empire. Upon arrival among the Nogais,

Giray immediately began to push them into open rebellion against the Russians, which in turn threatened to destabilize the border with the Ottomans, an eventuality not to be taken lightly. As such, Potemkin sent his most trusted general, Alexander Suvorov, the hero of the last Turkish war, to chastise the restive Nogais. Suvorov's methods were brutal—he had been previously sentenced to death for unauthorized actions against the Turks, only to be reprieved by Catherine who believed that "winners cannot be judged"—but the uprising was duly crushed with the slaughter of several thousand. Giray remained at large, but with no base of support, he was quickly brought to terms.[49]

In April 1783, Sahin Giray formally abdicated his throne in favor of Catherine, providing the desired post facto justification for the Russian conquest. Potemkin wasted no time in setting forth his ambitious plans for Russia's new imperial possession. "This is an unspeakably abundant and a most suitable land," he informed the empress from his camp near Karasubazaar in July 1783. For Russia, habitually hamstrung by its icy climate, the weather of the Crimea would prove a considerable advantage. Operating against the natural disadvantages of its geographical position, Russia was falling behind in the international, seaborne trade that had so enriched its European rivals. The Crimea, Potemkin hoped, would provide vital warm-water ports from which to build and launch the navy necessary to join the first rank of European powers.[50]

Potemkin found his ideal site for the new naval base in June 1783 when he inspected the harbor at the Tatar town of Akhtiar on the south-western tip of the Crimean peninsula. Nikola Korsakov, a celebrated Russian engineer, was charged with building new fortifications to protect the harbor of the newly renamed Sevastopol. By the end of the 1780s the new city was already the most important naval base in the entire Russian empire, a status it would retain for at least the next century. With it, Russia could become a major player in the Mediterranean and Atlantic worlds and even threaten to topple the sultan in Istanbul.[51]

The Ottomans remained the greatest threat to Potemkin's design. He believed that with the majority of the territory's residents steadfastly Muslim, the security of the Crimea could only be secured through a thorough Christianization of the Tatar lands. Potemkin believed that the loyalty of Muslim Tatars living so close to the territory of a Muslim power would always be suspect, a constant source of potential danger. For all its attendant advantages, the Crimea would be "better still in every way were we to rid ourselves of the Tatars and send them away . . . for truth, they are not worthy of this land." The policy was not entirely new. Since the days of Peter the Great (1672–1725), Russia's rulers had sought to forge a unified empire out of a hugely diverse swath of conquered territory. Conquest alone, however, would not produce a stable, loyal empire. The creation of a unified imperial culture based on a shared religion and common language was thus consistently pursued in newly won territories as a means of imperial consolidation. Tatars and other Muslims had been replaced by Slavic, Orthodox settlers as early as the sixteenth century, when Muscovy first began its long expansion into south-eastern Europe and Central Asia.[52]

Potemkin's own attempts at social engineering in the Crimea had begun long before the formal annexation of Crimea in 1784. As the Governor of New Russia, he had settled thousands of Orthodox Christians in the peninsula, with 1,200 Greeks settled in Yenikale alone. The influx of Christians quickly led to conflict in the Crimea. Pogroms against Christians resulted in over 30,000 Christian refugees—mostly Armenians—fleeing the violence for the protection of New Russia. The suffering of the exiles was real, with many perishing during the exodus, but the religious conflict in Crimea also worked to Russia's advantage. The religious violence, though in part stoked by Potemkin's Christianization policies, provided one of the key justifications for Russian intervention in Crimea in 1777 and again in 1781. Despite public reassurances, the Christianization of the Crimea would continue apace.[53]

In the aftermath of the annexation, Potemkin abandoned his initial plan to expel the Tatars from the peninsula. He had already followed through on his plans to remove the Nogais from strategically important border areas, forcibly uprooting and resettling perhaps 100,000 or more in less sensitive areas. But for now he decided to leave the Crimea's residents in place. Indeed, in April 1784 an imperial decree guaranteed the Crimean Tatars religious toleration. It had become readily apparent that, in order to secure the stability of the new province, the cooperation of the Muslim elite—the nobility and the religious leaders—would be required. Thus, in return for an oath of loyalty, the Tatar nobility were granted Russian patents of nobility, exemption from taxation (as for Russian nobles), and a confirmation of their property rights. The Muslim imams were granted a status similar to that possessed by Orthodox priests, including some exemptions from taxation, in return for pledges of fealty. This program of securing elite loyalty to the Russian regime was largely successful, especially among senior clerics and the increasingly Russified nobility.

Under the surface, however, the cultural and religious character of the Crimea was undergoing profound and rapid change. Because their status as religious leaders and teachers was formalized, Muslim religious leaders came under greater and increasing government control. Imperial supervision of Islamic religious training tightened, translation and printing of the Qur'an was centralized through a state publishing house in St. Petersburg, and an administrative body created to monitor Crimea's Muslims. At the same time, tens of thousands of Orthodox Christians, including many of the exiles from the religious violence of the 1770s, poured into Crimea, fundamentally changing its religious and ethnic make-up. Even the new name of the province—Taurida, the Greek name for the territory—emphasized its new, Christianized character.

For many among the Tatar peasantry, carrying on in their homeland became untenable. While much had been done to secure the loyalty of Crimea's elite, little attention had been paid to the needs of the common man. Serfdom had been formally abolished, but customary obligations due to landowners—often a ruinous half of their harvest—had been left in place. Under severe economic pressure and facing a changing cultural landscape, thousands of Muslims fled the Crimea for Ottoman territories. In the immediate aftermath of the annexation as many as 30,000 Tatars became refugees, with thousands more following in the decades to come. Potemkin may have abandoned his plan to forcibly remove the Muslims of the Crimea, but through other Russian policies he was able to achieve his vision of a Christianized Crimea nonetheless.[54]

It was the fulfillment of a long Russian crusade, the apotheosis of an imperial ambition modeled on the conquerors and empires of Antiquity.

What Sovereign has ever compiled such a brilliant epoch as you? And this is not merely splendor's luster. There is also great benefit in all this. The lands upon which Alexander and Pompey merely glanced, so to speak, you have bound to the Russian scepter, and Tauric Chersonese—the source of our Christianity, and thus our humanity as well—is now within its daughter's embrace. There is something mystical in that. The Tatar nation was once Russia's tyrant and in more recent times its hundredfold ravager, whose might Tsar Ivan Vasilievich did fell. But it was you who destroyed its root. The new border promises Russia peace, Europe envy and the Ottoman Porte fear. Take up this trophy unstained by blood and order your historians to prepare more paper and ink.[55]

If the historians so commanded to prepare their paper and ink had been honest, they would have acknowledged that the Russian conquest of the Crimea had been a bloody affair, not just on the peninsula itself, but across the Atlantic as well. It was, after all, the bloodshed and turmoil of the American Revolution that had engulfed Europe and provided the cover needed for Catherine to seize her trophy. Nor would the end of the war spell an end to the violence in Crimea. In the years after the Peace of Paris, Russia, Austria, and the Ottomans would once more face off in the east.

Austria had also seen imperial opportunity in its neutrality. Its previous attempts to use its possessions in the Low Countries to break into the world of overseas commerce and colonization had foundered in the face of concerted opposition from Britain, France, and the Dutch Republic. With all of the great commercial powers at each other's throats over America, Empress Maria Theresa and her son and successor Joseph II saw a chance to expand their empire beyond Europe. To this end, in 1776 they dispatched William Bolts from Livorno, the territory of the empress's younger son, Leopold, Grand Duke of Tuscany, with official authorization to open trade from Austria's Adriatic port at Trieste to India and China, as well as to trade in slaves from East Africa to America.

Meanwhile, Francis Dana watched helplessly from his interminable exile in St. Petersburg as Catherine and Potemkin used the cover of his own nation's struggle for independence from an imperial power to subjugate a formerly autonomous people to Russia's imperial will. There was little he could do. He had been frustrated at every turn, shunned by the Russian government, outflanked by his British counterpart, undermined by his French allies, and his advice ignored by his own government. It had become clear that nothing he could do would change his plight. The Russians would not sign a treaty with

America, would not force peace negotiations nor even recognize American independence while they were occupied in the Crimea. The important diplomacy would happen elsewhere, in Paris, in London, and in The Hague. It must have seemed to Dana that he had suffered humiliation and shivered through three Russian winters for nothing. In a despondent state he wrote to Elbridge Gerry, "I am weary of the life I lead here, and shou'd infallibly have quitted this situation . . . had I not entertained some hopes . . . we might have peace."[56]

By January 1783, with peace now finally at hand, he began to request permission to leave his post. He had had his fill of European diplomacy and with the European system more broadly. "I am sick, sick to the heart," he confided to Adams, "of the delicacies and whims of European politicks." In the months after the Peace of Paris, Dana had at last begun the heavy work of negotiation with the Russian ministry, but though American independence was officially recognized in June 1783, he had still failed to secure an audience with the tsarina, and a treaty was still nowhere on the horizon. Resigned to failure and fearful that the Crimean conflict would lead to a new European-wide war, Dana began to develop a new philosophy for American foreign relations, one that would be adopted by many of the men who had spent the war in European diplomacy. In a letter to John Adams he advocated an isolationist policy, an embryonic Monroe Doctrine. "We have a world to ourselves," he told Adams, and that critical separation allowed the United States to "form a system of politics for ourselves," a new balance of power distinct and isolated from the quagmire of Europe. American isolationism, a regular feature of American politics for the next 150 years, was born out of America's first experience on the world stage.[57]

In May 1787, a resplendent Catherine the Great began a triumphal procession through her new-won possessions on the Black Sea. The six-month cruise down the Dnieper River to the Crimea, organized by the ever-present Potemkin, was a lavish spectacle designed to demonstrate and consolidate Russian power in the region. Catherine and her guests—princes, ambassadors, and even her ally Joseph II in disguise—made a stately progress downriver on a series of royal barges. There were even rumors that Potemkin had constructed fake villages along the banks of the Dnieper to create the impression that the depopulated wastelands of the previous war were in fact thriving. The "Potemkin villages" were assembled by and peopled with his own men on the empress's approach and disassembled and reconstructed again further downriver once the imperial party had passed.

The sumptuous statement of intent did not go unnoticed by the Ottomans, who were outraged by the effrontery of the procession. Still smarting from their losses in 1774 and 1783, the Ottomans had reason to fear the ambitions of the Russian empress and the Austrian emperor. Word had reached Istanbul of a so-called Greek Plan devised by Potemkin. Joseph and Catherine had secretly agreed to conquer the Ottoman Empire, partition its territory between them, and establish a new Christian Byzantine Empire with Constantinople as its capital. Catherine's grandiose imperial ambitions were nothing new for a Russia tsar. The Romanovs had long claimed an illustrious pedigree, asserting descent from Roman emperors even as rulers of a relative backwater. As their power grew, however, so too did their genealogical claims. Ivan III had married the niece of the last Byzantine emperor in 1472, and by the sixteenth century the increasing power of Muscovy was burnished by a new claim of descent from the Emperor Augustus. In the seventeenth century the Romanovs' claim to be the rightful heirs of Rome's founding emperor and its last emperor was officially recognized by the Patriarch of Constantinople, the head of the Orthodox Church. Since then, Russia's inexorable expansion had been cloaked in imperial purple, justified as the recovery of its rulers' rightful patrimony as the true heirs of Rome. Before the eighteenth century such pretensions had been little more than empty boasts; the Ottomans remained firmly ensconced in the former capital of the Byzantine Empire. As Catherine chipped away at the borders of a weakened Ottoman Empire, however, the recovery of Constantinople and the crowning of a Russian Roman empress began to seem a real and frightening possibility. When Catherine's second grandson was born in 1779, she used the occasion to make her designs clear. The child, whom Catherine hoped would one day sit on the imperial throne in Istanbul, was named Constantine after the founder of Christian Constantinople and silver coins were minted bearing a depiction of the Hagia Sophia—the iconic Byzantine cathedral the Ottomans had converted into a mosque. The sultan had every reason to be wary.[58]

By 1787 physical signs of Russia's Byzantine ambitions had already appeared. Along with the renaming of Crimean cities, by 1786 the Russians had constructed a new cathedral at Kherson—not so subtly named St. Catherine's—designed to highlight Russia's claims to be the inheritors of the Byzantine Empire. Catherine's Crimean procession seemed to confirm the Ottomans' worst fears, and, with British and French backing, in August 1787 the sultan demanded that Russia evacuate the Crimea. Catherine, however, was not cowed—indeed, she welcomed the renewal of war as a means to put her Greek Plan in motion—and Russia swiftly declared war on the Ottomans in August 1787, with Austria following suit in 1788.

Though they vocally supported the Ottoman Empire in its contest with an emergent Russia, Britain and France were in no condition to offer much more than words of encouragement. Once more, Russia had surveyed the European scene and found that the impact of the American War had left her with a free hand in the east. On paper, France's fight against Britain seemed a smashing success, but beneath the surface lurked the makings of a crisis. The war had been ruinously expensive. When the war began France's minister of finance Jacques Necker was determined to fund France's military without recourse to raising taxes. Instead, he opted to finance almost the entirety of the war effort through loans, mainly from foreign bankers. This was fully in keeping with the latest thinking on government finances, and echoed both British practice and the opinions of the Spanish minister Francisco Saavedra among others. Between 1777 and his downfall in 1781, Necker borrowed 520 million livres to pay for the war. His successor as finance minister, Fleury continued Necker's practice and borrowed a further 250 million livres between 1781 and 1782. By this point, however, France's credit was suspect, and further loans were only successfully secured after raising taxes and borrowing against revenue. Even after the war ended, the new finance minister Calonne was forced to continue borrowing just to ensure interest payments could be met. In total, the American War cost France 1.6 billion livres (not including interest)—more than twice the annual revenue of France—resulting in a gap between revenue and expenditure of 160 million livres per year. In all, 91 per cent of France's war costs were covered by loans, but substantial borrowing came at a cost France was ill suited to bear. Necker and his successors were forced to borrow at high rates of interest, at 4.8–6.5 per cent, almost twice the rate the British were paying. The ruinous interest rates were compounded by rapid repayment schedules, with many loans due within ten years.[59]

Paying down this massive burden of war debt would have been difficult enough if military spending had been drastically cut once peace was made, but, ironically, France's ostensible success in the war had convinced the government that global competition with Britain was not only possible but vital if France were to reap the rewards of victory and recover its place as a world power. Now certain that the policy of naval expansion had been decisive in the war, and with its beleaguered empire still in place but under threat, France committed itself to defense of its imperial territory and continued expansion of its navy. France's naval expenditure had risen fourfold in the years between 1776 and 1783, a trend that continued apace even in peace-time. The most potent symbol of this heedless naval growth was the transfiguration of the harbor of Cherbourg. Fired by the navy's recent success against the British and blinded by the technical wonders of Enlightenment science, 28 million livres was spent between 1784 and 1789 to construct a fanciful system of defense. More than ninety oak cones, measuring 142 feet in diameter and rising 60 feet above the water, were to be partially submerged and chained together as firing platforms. The public was swept away by the impressive feat, and the king even made a personal visit to the site (a rare treat), but despite the great cost, the system was an impractical and expensive disaster.[60]

In many ways, defeat would have proved more beneficial for France than its triumph. Unlike its great rival Britain, which could now demobilize a significant segment of its military, France's geographical position meant that it had to bear the enormous cost of a navy at the same time as it funded an army of 150,000 soldiers or more to defend its land borders. In the eighteenth century, no other European power attempted to be both a continental military power and a global naval power. France was overstretched. It was not just participation in the American Revolution that crippled France, but victory itself.

There had been some hope that access to American markets would help fill French coffers emptied by the war, but almost immediately, indeed before the pen of peace had even been put to paper, there were signs of the United States' rapid reorientation back toward Britain. The degrading wartime experience of American diplomats in Europe had taught men like Francis Dana and his friend John Adams a healthy distrust of European politics in general, and the French in particular. During the war Dana, Adams, and their supporters had grown increasingly wary of the slippery French foreign minister Vergennes, who had done his best to manipulate America's novice diplomatic corps throughout the conflict. For years they had felt that France's commitment to the interests of the United States was only ever skin deep and that France would pursue its own interests to the detriment of America. As the end of the war loomed, Vergennes once more went to work to shape and mold the outcome of the coming peace and urged the Americans to allow France to lead joint negotiations with Britain. The Francophobe, isolationist faction led by Adams and Dana saw the offer for what it was and pushed for a separate American treaty with Britain.

The result was two separate treaties with Britain, one American, one French, and the first sign of a fracture between the erstwhile allies. It also signaled that French hopes of replacing Britain as America's preeminent trading partner would come to naught. Vergennes' hopes of recouping the costs of intervention through expanded trade with the new United States had seemed entirely feasible during the last years of the war. Between 1779 and 1782, French exports to North America had expanded greatly, rising in value to more than 11 million livres per annum. At the same time, the disruption of American shipping meant that French imports of American goods declined, creating a favorable French trade balance with the United States. France's success in the war also meant that it gained or regained potentially lucrative colonial holdings in Tobago, St. Lucia, and the Senegal River. These gains, however, would prove to be only temporary.[61]

In its separate treaty negotiations with the United States, Britain did its best to recapture its place as America's most important trade partner. To this end, it chose as its negotiators Richard Oswald, a Scottish merchant and slave trader with deep American ties and interests from Nova Scotia to Florida, and David Hartley, a vocal critic of Britain's war policy and a friend of Benjamin Franklin. The British also offered the United States generous territorial concessions in Appalachia and the Mississippi basin as a means of winning back economic ties and creating new American markets for British goods. It was clear enough to Vergennes that Britain hoped to use the peace negotiations as the first tool for recovering America's commerce. "The English," he fumed, "buy peace rather than make it."

He was right to be concerned. Before the ink on the treaty had time to dry, problems developed in the trade relationship between France and the United

States. For a start, the countries differed in their interpretation of the Franco-America Treaty of 1778. The French insisted that the treaty stipulated that French commerce receive preferential treatment in American ports. The Americans, committed to free trade, argued that the treaty only guaranteed that all foreign trade was treated equally, an interpretation enshrined in American law when the First Congress passed a law that levied equal customs duties on all foreign vessels. Many in France, Vergennes among them, saw this as a shocking display of ingratitude given France's role in securing American independence, and demanded that France be exempted, but to no avail. France, however, deserved some of the blame for their failure to secure a greater piece of America's trade. France's own monopolistic protections, including duties on American imports, did much to undermine Franco-American commerce. Furthermore, as Lafayette discovered when he investigated France's export trade, many French manufacturers and merchants were slow to change and failed to adapt their products for the American market.

In all likelihood, Britain would have recovered its dominance of transatlantic trade, even if French manufacturers had been quicker to adapt. French exports had increased during the war, but they had never come close to displacing the trade between Britain and America. Throughout the war, American merchants had continued to trade with their British counterparts, ensuring that the value of Britain's American trade remained more than double that of the French, even at the height of the war. After the war, while Americans bought much less from French merchants than they had during the war, Britain's trade, no longer held back by the conflict, surged. British and American merchants were quick to resume the long-established relationships and networks that had existed before the war. British manufacturers and merchants were already familiar with the American market and its demands, and thus were easily able to outmaneuver their French rivals. Britain, wrote the French economic writer Tanguy de la Boissière, had "lost nothing but the sterile right of sovereignty." Its economic dominance remained untouched.[62]

Even France's gains in the West Indies proved ephemeral. France's Caribbean possessions formed the most lucrative part of its imperial economy. Using almost all available land for cash crops—especially sugar and tobacco—made economic sense for the colonists, but it also necessitated the importation of foodstuffs and other supplies that had been crowded out by the sugar mono-culture. Legally, supplying the islands was a French monopoly, but in the post-war period most of this trade was captured by American smugglers, who used the wealth gained by selling supplies to re-export French sugar and coffee, undermining another supposed monopoly. To make matters worse, at the same time that French exports to America declined to about 1.8 million livres annu-ally, French imports from America expanded rapidly to over 20 million livres per year. The wartime trade surplus evaporated, leaving France with a growing deficit and draining the country of much-needed specie. More galling still, America used much of this trade surplus with France to purchase British goods and products, thus impoverishing their former ally while they enriched France's foremost foe. The French consul in Boston, Jean Toscan, spoke for many when he complained bitterly that their former allies "now send their vessels to England taking to their manufacturers the gold and silver France spent in America . . . to help them win their independence."[63]

As the years passed and France's commerce failed to expand to the hoped-for heights, more desperate measures were adopted to shore up French trade. In 1786, France signed a free trade agreement with Britain—the so-called Eden Agreement—in the hope that access to British markets would prove a boon to the French economy. Fatally for France, however, the manufactures churned out by an increasingly industrial Britain were cheaper than their French coun-terparts, which undermined French industry, and angered French manufac-turers, who came to blame the trade agreement for many of their ills. France had hoped that intervening in the American War would enrich France and beggar Britain, but, as was becoming clear in the 1780s, it was the French economy that was crippled by the conflict. In a few short years the French financial crisis would help to push the French people to follow the example of the American Revolution and begin a revolution of their own. The French Revolution would throw Europe into yet more turmoil, but it would also ensure that Russia's resumed assault on the Ottoman Empire would escape French opposition.

The German states, drained and depopulated by the mercenary trade, were also ill equipped to check Russia and Austrian aggression in the east. Sweden and Denmark, Russia's traditional rivals in northern Europe, were likewise too preoccupied by the effects of the American War to offer much in the way of opposition. Scandinavia's wartime economic prosperity proved short-lived, with peace bringing economic stagnation and growing frustration with King Gustav's increasingly authoritarian policies. Some of these critics of rampant absolutism turned to the American Revolution as a source of monarchical critique. Pehr af Lund, for instance, wrote in warning that the fact that "there is one place on earth where a man can be free from his chains . . . [should] frighten despots and hold them in rein." Bengt Linder wrote in praise of the "Brutian Washington," who "snatches a bloody scepter from the tyrant's hand," while Carl Nordenskiöld proclaimed that "the independence of America for all time shall cause wise rulers to govern their subjects under the banner of freedom, for America has taught Nations to know their rights . . ."[64]

Among the officers most deeply influenced by their experience in the American War was a Finnish soldier named Göran Manus Sprengtporten. An officer in the Finnish corps, he had become disillusioned with his lack of personal advancement and by Gustav's absolutism. As a result, he left Scandinavia in 1780 for France, where he joined the French expedition bound for the United States. He returned to Europe in 1782, full of the ideas of the American Revolution and intent on Finnish independence from Sweden. Back in France in 1782, Sprengtporten came into contact with Benjamin Franklin, who helped to cultivate in him a concrete desire to see his Finnish homeland free from Swedish despotism. For Sprengtporten, "North America's independence" gave him hope that "Finland might also be separated from Sweden and become independent." Suffused with the possibility, he began to preach to his fellow Finnish officers, many of whom came to see him as a "true patriot, worthy of treading in the footsteps of Washington." In 1785, he entered into the service of the Netherlands and quickly became involved in the Dutch Patriot Party. He drafted a constitution for the "Republic of the United Provinces of Finland" that combined the aristocratic elements of the Swedish constitution Gustav had replaced in 1772 with aspects of Dutch republicanism and the United States Articles of Confederation. He even approached the Duke of Södermanland about ruling an independent Finland, but the duke wisely declined. There was still insufficient support for his plan in Sweden, so in 1785 he presented his plans for an independent Finland under Russian protection to the Russian minister in the Netherlands and then the Russian minister in Stockholm. Despite these efforts, Sprengtporten's autonomist movement faltered before it ever really got off the ground, as the example of Crimea and Russia's treatment of its Baltic possessions soured many Finns on the prospect of a Russian-controlled Finland. Sprengtporten temporarily abandoned the plan and accepted a military commission in Russia, but his movement would return when Sweden mobilized for an unpopular war with Russia later in the 1780s.[65]

Gustav, who many thought treated statecraft like one of the theatrical performances he so enjoyed, was undeterred by a worsening economy and growing discontent. He still wanted to retake Norway from Denmark and portions of Finland from Russia. At first, he approached Russia about a joint attack on Denmark. It seemed an opportune moment to pounce on an old rival. Like Sweden, Denmark had seen its once buoyant economy crumble in the wake of the American War. Politically, the enlightened government of Bernstorff was ousted in 1780 when it became known that he had made a secret deal with Britain to protect Danish colonies. In his place, the Anglophobic Ove Høegh-Guldberg consolidated his grip on power and set about monopolizing Denmark's overseas trade companies. In Denmark, the reaction to the change in regime was a proliferation of political clubs, but a series of land reforms and legal changes introducing free trade, universal education, and an end to serfdom largely pacified the populace. In Danish-controlled Norway, however, the American Revolution had profound effects, leading to social disorder and near rebellion.

The economic expansion of the war years hit Norway like a bolt of lightning. The opportunities available in seafaring, shipbuilding, and international traded expanded almost inexhaustibly. Traditionally and legally, such industries were the exclusive preserve of Norway's incorporated towns. The unprecedented boom caused by the American War, combined with lean conditions in farming and logging, drew many rural Norwegians into the market and money economy for the first time. When the war ended and trade once more contracted, the towns, jealous of their commercial privileges, pushed to have their monopoly on these trades confirmed. Facing a wider financial crisis, Denmark had little choice but to concede to the towns' demands. In addition, local Norwegian officials, faced with raising revenue in the post-war slump, raised taxes just when the peasantry were beginning to feel the squeeze. As such, many Norwegians, especially in rural areas, were loath to give up the new industries they had forged during the war, especially after a series of poor harvests in 1781, 1782, 1784, and 1785 caused mortality to skyrocket and deaths to exceed births. Starting in 1785, a peasant protest movement began to call for redress.

The protesters were, however, staunch in their loyalty to the crown and thus confident that the king would right the wrongs if only he were made aware of the situation in Norway. In 1786, the leader of the movement, Christian Jensen Lofthuus, traveled to Copenhagen to personally deliver a complaint against local officials and civic authorities to Crown Prince Frederik. Lofthuus had been an improving farmer from Lillesand, but, like many others, he saw the opportunity presented by the American War and diversified into shipbuilding and commercial trade in grain, timber, and other supplies. The pursuit of these new avenues for profit even led him all the way to England. Back in Norway in 1782, he was fined for violating the commercial privileges of the city of Arendal, and the debt that resulted forced him to sell his farm. With other roads blocked to him, Lofthuus became the center of the peasant movement for reform.

After delivering his message to the crown prince, Lofthuus returned to Norway, claiming authority to investigate peasant grievances. He then returned to Copenhagen to present two petitions signed by 532 peasants and rural landowners from thirteen parishes asking for official permission to investigate peasant complaints. By this time the authorities in Norway had had enough and threatened to arrest Lofthuus after his return from Denmark. In response, Lofthuus once more traveled to Copenhagen, this time with an armed guard and representatives from the rural parishes. Fearing a peasant uprising, the authorities attempted to arrest Lofthuus, but he managed to flee. The peasants were furious that their chosen representative had been treated so poorly. They responded by taking up arms and marching on Lillesand where they forced the bailiff to grant Lofthuus and thirty-eight followers a pass to travel to Copenhagen. By November of 1786 more than 800 peasants were in arms. Norway's towns, the source of peasant rage, in turn raised militias to fight the peasants. A merchant from Christiania spoke for many townsmen and officials when he contended, "If the rebellious mob is not punished, it can murder us in our homes and go scot-free. This is a base soul, a rascal in public affairs and a stupid rebel in political life . . . Some call this rude butcher a second Washington, but if I should wish to see him it would be to spit in his face." Sweden was on the brink of civil war.[66]

Lofthuus was not a revolutionary, however, and balked at the prospect of bloodshed. As tensions cooled, Denmark agreed to form a commission to address rural complaints, which recommended actual reforms, but also urged the authorities to arrest "the people's hero." Lofthuus was thus arrested in February of 1787, touching off another peasant uprising. Nearly a thousand peasants rose in arms, seized the offending bailiff, and demanded the release of their leader. Once more, it seemed as if civil war was imminent, but the peasants again backed down when confronted by Danish soldiers called in to quell the disturbances once and for all. Lofthuus and twelve others were sentenced to life in prison, though all but Lofthuus would eventually be released. Lofthuus was no republican, and certainly not a nationalist as some later claimed, but his abortive revolt did set a precedent for united peasant movements and provided inspiration for nationalist independence movements in the nineteenth and twentieth centuries.

The Russians, however, remained distrustful of Sweden's intentions and refused to back a war against Denmark. With Russia uncooperative, Gustav, whom Catherine the Great called "about as reticent as a cannon shot," turned to his second objective and entered talks with the Ottomans and dissident Poles for a joint war on Russia.[67] The Ottomans were already clashing with Russia in the Crimea and could offer little support, so in 1788 Sweden declared war on Russia alone and invaded Russia's Finnish territory. Legally, Gustav needed permission from the Riksdag for an offensive war, but in a neat piece of theater, he had dressed some of his Finnish troops as Russians and had them feign an assault on Swedish territory, allowing him to invade Russian territory in response. Most saw through this charade, and many, like the elder Fersen, believed the war was simply a royal ploy to further undermine noble power. "The preparations for this monstrous war plan were not undertaken against Russia alone," he boomed, "but equally against the Estates of the realm, against the constitution . . . in short, for furtherance of absolutism."[68]

This view of Gustav's war was especially prevalent among the nobility and officer corps of Finland, some of them disciples of Sprengtporten and his autonomist movement. Gustav, they believed, had violated Sweden's social contract and so they took it upon themselves to negotiate peace with Russia on Sweden's behalf. To that end, in 1788, a group of army officers drafted a letter to Catherine of Russia. When Gustav heard of his officers' actions he was apoplectic and demanded an immediate pledge of loyalty. In response, more than a hundred officers stationed at Anjala signed a declaration condemning the war and outlining their plans to negotiate peace with Russia. Some also began to talk of forming an independent government in Finland under Catherine's protection. Catherine was interested in cleaving Finland from Sweden, but she was also occupied with the Ottoman wars and thus overstretched. Her response was thus encouraging but noncommittal.

When Denmark allied with Russia and invaded Sweden it seemed that Gustav had been beaten, and indeed he contemplated abdication. In the end though, the Danish invasion solidified his position in Sweden by winning him the support of the people. Sure of his position in Sweden, Gustav outflanked his rivals by issuing a new constitution that gave concessions to non-noble supporters, ended feudalism, and further undermined the power of the nobility. After defeating the attempted coup and arresting nearly ninety officers, timely monetary aid from Britain, Prussia, and the Turks, and a spectacular naval victory over Russian forces, allowed Gustav to make an advantageous peace with Russia in 1790. But with his position strengthened at the expense of the nobility, a group of disgruntled nobles began to plot his assassination. Among the conspirators was Adolf Ludvig Ribbing, an enthusiastic volunteer in the American War who had brought the ideas of the American Revolution home with him. On March 16, 1792, the noble conspirators struck, killing the king at a masquerade ball. The coup failed, and Gustav was replaced by his son Gustav IV—with his brother Karl serving as regent—but the assassination was a crippling blow for the prospect of Russian containment.

With little to fear from their European rivals, Russia and Austria now had a free hand in the east. When the Russo-Turkish and Austro-Turkish Wars ended in 1792, after four years of violent struggle, Russia had consolidated its gains, and the Ottomans had been confirmed as an empire on the verge of collapse. In the words of one historian, the full annexation of the Crimea, and the loss of further territory on the Black Sea and in the Balkans "signaled that the partition of the Ottoman Empire, like Poland's was imminent." Military defeat initiated a period of steep economic and fiscal decline in Ottoman lands. Over-expenditure on soldiers, ships, artillery, and new border forts bankrupted the empire, leading to a fracturing of political authority as local autonomy grew in the face of central weakness. Mutinies sprang up in the Balkans, Syria, Egypt, and Arabia, threatening to tear the fragile empire to shreds. Russia and Austria waited in the wings, hoping to seize the opportunity of Ottoman weakness to finish their plan to partition the empire among themselves. The prospect of Russian and Austrian empires strengthened by the remains of the Ottoman Empire alarmed the other powers of Europe, leading to decades of fear for the balance of power in Europe. With the conquest of the Crimea, the "sick man of Europe" had been born. From now on the "Eastern Question" would continu-ally plague European politics and diplomacy. Once more, the American Revolution had played an important role.[69]

For Britain, Russia's invasion of the Crimea and its continual focus on its conflict with the Ottoman Empire bore valuable, if unexpected, fruit. The American War and the League of Armed Neutrality had damaged Britain's relationship with Russia and threatened to disrupt British naval and commercial dominance in northern waters. The potential dangers to British trade were so great that Britain initially, if reluctantly, welcomed the prospect of a Russian-negotiated peace with the Netherlands. Britain hoped that such a peace would divide the Dutch from their American, French, and Spanish allies, allowing Britain to make separate and more advantageous peace treaties instead of facing a unified front of avenging powers. Britain's new foreign secretary, Charles James Fox, was intent on both securing the best terms possible and improving relations with Russia. To sweeten the deal, Britain sent word to Russia and the Netherlands that it would be willing to accept the neutral maritime principles of the League of Armed Neutrality if the Dutch would agree to a separate peace brokered by Russia. The Dutch were wary of Russian promises—they had, after all, abandoned the Dutch to their fate when Britain targeted their shipping in the lead-up to the Anglo-Dutch War—and hesitated to betray their French allies, who insisted on a unified front in all peace negoti-ations with Britain. For Russia, however, gaining British acceptance of the league's underlying principles would have been a considerable victory, helping to bolster and protect Russia's maritime trade at the very moment it was attempting to expand its commerce as a means of joining the great powers of Europe.[70]

When rebellion broke out in Crimea, Catherine saw her chance to seize her long-wished-for southern port and abandoned her efforts to act as mediatrix. This was not simply a case of distracted attention, but rather a conscious decision to abandon free trade in the north for an expanded empire in the south. The opportunity to grasp the Crimea was too good to pass up, and Catherine knew full well that she could ill afford to risk British opposition to her Crimean conquests by insisting on the maritime principles of the League of Armed Neutrality. Russia had still hoped to force Britain to accept its maritime principles, but by 1782 Britain had entered into peace negotiations with France. Once peace was made between France and Britain, the likelihood that either country might come to the Ottomans' aid rose exponentially. While still in power, Lord Shelburne had hinted that a joint Anglo-French expedition to protect the Ottomans was actively being considered, but the new regime, with Fox as foreign secretary, agreed to abandon any joint action with the French in return for Russia quietly scrapping its demands for maritime concessions. Britain thus emerged from the American War with its commercial and naval dominance in northern Europe still very much intact, a crucial victory seized from the very jaws of defeat.[71]

In 1787, as Catherine and Joseph were making their tour of the Crimea, an equally extraordinary flotilla was sailing across the Mediterranean bound for Istanbul. The party belonged to the Kingdom of Mysore in southern India, and they had come on behalf of their ruler Tipu Sultan to the court of Abdul Hamid in desperate need of assistance. Since the end of the American War, Mysore had been preparing for a renewal of hostilities with the British Empire. As a fellow Muslim kingdom, Tipu Sultan reasoned, surely the Ottomans would come to their aid as allies against the encroachment of an expansionist Christian Empire. But the American War had cast its long shadow over the Ottoman Empire as well, and Abdul Hamid was in no position to offer help to Mysore. The Ottomans had been drained by the wars with Austria and Russia, and in 1787, with the prospect of yet another war on the horizon, they could not afford to alienate the British. Mysore sent ambassadors to France as well. In 1794, in an attempt to appeal to the new revolutionary republican regime in France, Tipu Sultan, every bit a despot, founded a Jacobin Club in Mysore, planted a symbolic "liberty tree," and gave himself the republican title of "citizen Tipu." But though France would pledge assistance, it was too depleted by the American War to offer more than empty promises. Mysore would have to face the British alone.

7

-->>- -<--

CONFLICT AND CAPTIVITY
IN INDIA

As her ship made its way into the harbor of Calicut (modern Kozhikode) on November 5, 1779, Eliza Fay was worried. It was her first view of India, the destination she had been envisioning for months, but rather than enjoying the turquoise waters and lush forests of the Malabar Coast—a "picturesque beauty equal to any country on earth" in the words of another English traveler—Eliza was plagued by impatience and unease.[1] As for so many British subjects making their way to the major British possessions in Madras and Bengal, Calicut was merely a brief waypoint for Eliza and her husband Anthony; they were not planning to stay for long. Eliza, the daughter of a sailor and Anthony, an aspiring attorney of Irish extraction, had married shortly before departing for India. For the newlyweds, the opportunity for rapid advancement in the emerging legal system of British India was well worth the risks of transcontinental travel and the long months, perhaps years, of separation from family and friends. In the Indian theater of the global American Revolution just then there was a desperate need for men to conquer, defend, and govern the growing British possessions in South Asia. For the British, war with America had led to war with France, and the war with France spread beyond the Atlantic to India, where it burst forth in a vicious imperial struggle with France and its Indian allies. With war in the subcontinent came conquest, and with conquest came the need for administration. With positions in the British bureaucracy of India multiplying rapidly, men like

Anthony Fay arrived in droves to seek their fortunes in the world made by war and revolution.

The British presence on the subcontinent stretched back even before the founding of the East India Company as a monopoly trading company in 1600. In those early years, indeed for more than a century, the East India Company was the junior partner in its relationship with the ruling Mughal Empire, an oft-ignored supplicant clinging to a series of trading posts scattered along the Indian coast. The Company chafed at its subordinate status, but the profits from the monopoly trade with India meant the English were in India to stay. By 1647 the Company had expanded from its initial factory at Surat to a string of twenty-three trading posts across the peninsula. With trade as its impetus, there was no sense that the Company aspired to anything grander than this, a sentiment most forcefully expounded by its first formal ambassador to the Mughal court, Sir Thomas Roe. In the early seventeenth century he had wisely counseled the Company that "it is an error to affect garrisons and land wars in India . . . Let this be received as a rule, that if you will profit, seek it at sea and in quiet trade."[2]

Over the course of the eighteenth century such rules were honored more often in the breach and British territory in India gradually expanded from its bases in Bombay, Madras, and Calcutta as it vied with France, the Netherlands, and a host of emerging Indian powers to fill the power vacuum created by a bankrupt, overstretched, and slowly receding Mughal Empire. Some of these powers, like the nawabs of Bengal, the nizams of Hyderabad, and the nawabs of Awadh had once been Mughal viceroys before gradually gaining their autonomy in the eighteenth century. Others, like the Kingdom of Mysore, had long been independent, while some were aggressively anti-Mughal. The Hindu Maratha Empire had been expanding out from its heartland in the western Deccan since the days of its renowned founder Shivaji's titanic struggle for independence from the Mughals in the late seventeenth century. By the 1770s, the empire had evolved into a confederacy of Hindu states under the nominal leadership of a peshwa. De-centralization did not blunt ambition, and though Maratha expansion had been halted temporarily by Afghan forces at the Battle of Panipat in 1761 and subsequent internal divisions, the 1770s saw the empire re-energized and ready to contest for predominance of India. In 1775, Britain learned the strength of the Marathas first-hand when it intervened in an internal succession dispute, precipitating the first Anglo-Maratha War.

Authority in British India had originally been shared between the three most important posts, Bombay, Madras, and Calcutta, with primacy only moving toward Calcutta as it accumulated territory in Bengal in the first half of the eighteenth century. The Nawab of Bengal launched an attack on British Calcutta in 1756, but a British victory under General Robert Clive at Plassey in 1757, and a subsequent defeat of Bengal, Awadh, and the Mughal Emperor Shah Alam II at Buxar in 1764 confirmed the East India Company as a territorial power. Though no one in 1765 could have imagined that Britain would one day rule over the entire subcontinent, by the time Eliza Fay arrived in 1779, the British were in the midst of a decades long struggle with France, Mysore, Hyderabad, and the Marathas for the remains of the Mughal Empire.

After weeks at sea, the sight of the verdant Malabar Coast should have been inviting, but Anthony was keen to commence his legal career and so the Fays were impatient to move on from Calicut to the capital of British India, Calcutta. As Eliza related in a letter to her sister some months later:

the importance of our speedy arrival in Bengal, which so many circumstances had contributed to prevent, and the apprehension lest our delay should afford time to raise serious obstacles against Mr. Fay's admission to the Court, as an advocate, had long been as so many daggers, piercing my vitals: add to this the heart-breaking thought of what immense tracts lie between me and those *dear* friends, whose society alone can render me completely happy.[3]

The distance between Eliza and her friends back in England was indeed immense, especially by the standards of the eighteenth century. Eliza and her husband had left England on April 11, traveling the well-worn route from Dover to Calais on the French Channel coast, a mere three hours sail in favorable weather. Although France was then at war with Britain, the Fays traveled relatively unmolested and with much pleasure through the French countryside, journeying by carriage from Calais to Paris, stopping at Chantilly and at St. Denis to see the mausoleum of France's medieval monarchs.

Originally the Fays had planned on journeying overland to Marseille before taking ship to Livorno, however, the American War intervened and they were warned that this was a "very uncertain and dangerous method; as between the English and the French scarcely any vessel can pass free." With the sea route closed to them, the Fays decided to purchase two horses and a one-horse chaise and made their way from Paris to Lyons via Chalon-sur-Saône on the south-eastern border of the Kingdom of Savoy. Soon after leaving Paris, a chance storm forced the couple to pause at Fontainebleau, one of the most magnificent royal chateaux, where the famous palace and gardens paled in comparison to the emotional impact made by standing in the very spot where the last war with France had officially ended.[4]

From Savoy they crossed the Alps into Italy, the mountains more sublime than Eliza could ever have imagined. In a vein reminiscent of the Romantics, Eliza rhapsodized:

> having travelled through North Wales, I supposed myself to have acquired a tolerable idea of mountains and their appendages, such as cascades, torrents, and apparently air-hung bridges . . . but the passage of the Alps set at defiance all competition, and even surpassed whatever the utmost sketch of my imagination could have portrayed . . . in short they went so far beyond any idea I had formed of such appearances in nature, that they seemed to communicate new powers of perception to my mind and if I may so express it, to expand my soul, and raise it nearer to its Creator.

The arduous, if sublime, slog through the Alps complete, the Fays journeyed down the Italian peninsula, through Turin and Genoa before finally boarding a ship at Livorno on the Ligurian coast.[5]

Livorno was a rising commercial power on the Italian peninsula. It had been the primary port of Tuscany since the Renaissance, but since the seventeenth century its fortunes had been closely tied to the expansion of British commerce. As British trade expanded in the seventeenth and eighteenth centuries, and British ships began to crowd the Mediterranean, Livorno became a vital link in her commercial chain. The close connection with Britain meant that by the time the Fays arrived in 1779, Livorno was home to many British trading houses and the frequent haunt of British travelers, merchants, artists, and writers, adding a familiar flavor to the Italian city. Unbeknownst to the Fays and their fellow British visitors, however, beneath the bustling commercial cosmopolitanism, there were some secretly working to undermine the British Empire.

The Fay's arrival in Livorno coincided with the return of one of Tuscany's most dynamic native sons, Filippo Mazzei. Born outside Prato, Mazzei had practiced medicine in Italy and the Middle East for several years before relocating to London in 1755, where he set up shop as an Italian language teacher catering to a population still in the throes of an obsession with the Grand Tour and all things Italian. In the British capital, Mazzei forged a close friendship with two like-minded Americans, Benjamin Franklin and Thomas Jefferson, and with their encouragement moved to Virginia in 1773 to set up a silk plantation on land donated by Jefferson. Together, the Italian and the Virginian set up a commercial vineyard, but their relationship transcended shared commercial interests. They regularly conversed and corresponded about political and philosophical ideas, and their discussions helped sharpen both men's commitment to the ideals of liberty. A convinced Patriot, Mazzei returned to Italy in 1779 as a clandestine agent of the state of Virginia, eager to play his part for the American cause. Thus while the Fays arranged passage across the Mediterranean, Mazzei was busy arranging shipments of arms from Livorno to the American rebels. He would continue these activities for the duration of the war and after 1783 would become a champion of republican principles throughout Europe, becoming a fixture of both the Polish and French revolutions. Such was his stature, that after he died in 1816, his family was invited by Jefferson himself to relocate to the new republic.[6]

Livorno had no intention of sacrificing its close commercial ties with Britain on the altar of republican liberty, and while the authorities did little to obstruct Mazzei's gun-running, they offered no official support to America. This was largely the case throughout the fragmented states of Italy, each of which feared any entanglement in the contests between Europe's great powers. Even Venice, which had lost much of its commercial traffic to Livorno, and whose ancient republican government might have made it a natural ally of an emerging republic, rebuffed a joint effort by Jefferson, Franklin, and John Adams to establish commercial and diplomatic relations with the La Serenissima. For Venice there was little to gain and much to lose in allying itself with an infant nation whose ships rarely left the Atlantic for Venice's Mediterranean domain. As Britain and France increasingly dominated the Mediterranean, strict neutrality was seen as the best means of survival for a small, declining commercial state. Besides, despite the outward similarity in form of government, Americans—led by John Adams in his *A Defence of the Constitutions of Government of the United States of America*—had used Venice as an example of how republican institutions could be corrupted by wealth and aristocratic power. Even after formal independence, Venice remained skeptical, interpreting America's early laws and institutions as merely British institutions by another name—"completely like those of England" in the words of Venice's ambassador in London. This was surely a sign that America would soon return to the British fold.[7]

From Livorno, Eliza and Anthony ventured out across a tempestuous Mediterranean, plagued by French privateers and Arab pirates, to Alexandria on the Egyptian coast where they disembarked. Although they admired the lighthouse in the new harbor, Pompey's column and the remnants of Cleopatra's palace, Alexandria failed to impress. "This once magnificent City," Eliza lamented, "built by the most famous of all Conquerors, and adorned with the most exquisite productions of art, is now little more than a heap of Ruins." The trip down the Nile, "that perpetual source of plenty," to Cairo was more to her liking, the dangers of bandits in the night notwithstanding. "As morning broke, I was delighted with the appearance of the country, a more charming scene my eyes never beheld." As their boat meandered its way south, the prospect of ancient Cairo captured the imagination and blurred all sense of temporality, causing in Eliza a potent historical reverie. She confided to her sisters that:

> as I drew near Grand Cairo, and beheld those prodigies of human labour, the Pyramids of Egypt, these sensations were still more strongly awakened, and I could have fancied myself an inhabitant of a world, long passed away: for who can look on buildings, reared . . . above *three thousand years ago*, without seeming to step back as it were, in existence, and live through days, now gone by, and sunk in oblivion "like a tale that is told."[8]

After a short stay in Cairo, the English party, now well-armed, made the treacherous three-day journey across the desert to the Red Sea port of Suez, sleeping "under the canopy of heaven" and dodging "troops of Arabian robbers" along the way. Rather than sailing the roughly 13,000 miles around the entire African continent by way of the Cape of Good Hope—a journey of at least six months—the Fays had elected to travel to Cairo by ship before making their way overland across the Sinai to Suez and thence by sea to India. At Suez the Fays and a small party of English people boarded the *Nathalia*, a Danish ship from Serampore, a Danish trading post just north of Calcutta on the Hooghly River.[9]

Having reached Suez in September 1779, Eliza and Anthony once again boarded ship, sailing from Suez south through the Red Sea before halting once more at Mocha, the Yemeni port famous around the world as a marketplace for coffee. The journey had been smooth, if uneventful, perhaps a welcome relief after the tribulations of that between Cairo and Suez. "Our passage down the Red Sea was pleasant," Eliza wrote, "but afforded no object of interest, save the distant view of Mount Horeb, which again brought the flight of the children of Israel to my mind; and you may be sure, I did not wonder that they sought to quit the land of Egypt, after the various specimens of its *advantages* that I have experienced." Mocha itself was a fairly large walled town with excellent supplies of food and fresh water. The only complaint from the perspective of a northern European was the heat. Such was the scorching heat in the Yemen that the sailors manning the Fays' ship had a proverb, as sailors always did, that there was only a thin sheet of paper between Mocha and Hell.[10]

The longest seaborne leg of the journey, lasting about seven weeks, followed the Fay's departure from Mocha in mid-September 1779. Aboard the *Nathalia* they traveled out into the Gulf of Aden, the body of water pinched between the southern coast of Arabia and the Horn of Africa, and finally into the Arabian Sea and the Indian Ocean proper. Either as a result of good luck or good planning, the passengers sailing in the *Nathalia* were spared the wrath of the Indian Ocean's notorious Monsoon in their journey from Mocha to Calicut. The tranquil seas made other, more mundane reflections possible and Eliza was thus able to survey the motley crew of fellow passengers.

The captain of the ship, Chenu, had only recently, and unofficially risen to the post upon the death of the *Nathalia*'s original commander, Captain Vanderfield, and his first officer during the journey across the desert. Conscious of his new and precarious status, Chenu was overbearing in his insistence on the maintenance of proper forms and appearances. He was, consequently, despised by everyone on board. In addition to Captain Chenu, there were Mr. and Mrs. Tulloh, who never so much as "smiled unless maliciously" and John Hare, a barrister, like Anthony, on his way to practice in the courts of India. Hare was a snob of the highest order, "a little mortal, his body constantly bent in a rhetorical attitude as if addressing the Court," who would not deign to have "a City name on any article" of his attire for fear of being thought the son of the tradesman he in fact was. To this unpleasant cast of characters was added Mr. Manesty, not yet 20, who was going out to India to be a contract writer for the East India Company establishment at Bombay; Mr. Moreau, a musician seeking patronage in an increasingly Europeanized South Asia; and Mr. Fuller, a businessman who, having lost everything, was looking to India as a last chance to fix his ailing fortunes.[11]

In Eliza's words the passengers of the *Nathalia* seem an unusual collection of comic characters, however, in terms of profession, if not in personality, they were standard fare. The British Empire in the eighteenth century was a land of opportunity, a place where fortunes could be made or remade (and just as easily lost), a place where merit might perhaps, for once, outpace birth or connections. With the Revolutionary War and the suspension of America as an outlet for such ambitious or restless individuals, young men and women of all stations, stripes, and professions made the perilous journey from metropole to colony in the hope that fortune would favor them. The men and women aboard the *Nathalia* in 1779 were hardly any different.

On November 4 Eliza finally caught her initial glimpse of the subcontinent. The south-western coast of India had long been a place of cross-cultural contact, a center of trade between Asia and the Middle East, a landing point for Vasco de Gama and Zheng He, and home to a panoply of ethnicities and nationalities: Indians, Arabs, Jews, Portuguese, Chinese, and, more recently, Dutch, French, and British. With India now finally in view, Eliza was feeling optimistic. She wrote, still aboard the ship with the coast slowly approaching, that she was "looking with a longing eye, towards Bengal, from where my next [letter] will be dated. The climate seems likely to agree very well with me, I do not at all mind the heat, nor does it affect my spirits, or my appetite."[12]

Eliza's initial optimism, however, was not to last. As the *Nathalia* came to anchor in the Roads off Calicut there was a worrying sign of the trouble and misery to come. There were no British ships in the harbor, and no flag flew from the British consulate. The fears of what these signs might presage were quickly made manifest. Shortly after entering the harbor, the *Nathalia* was surrounded by foreign vessels that approached "with an air of so much hostility that we became seriously alarmed." Despite the conspicuous absence of guns, ammunition, and fighting men aboard the ship, Captain Chenu felt a show of force was the best course of action, hoping to scare off the threat with pantomime belligerence. The whole scene was made even more ridiculous by Mrs. Tulloh, who, craving some "romantic danger," "insisted on having a chair brought upon the deck, in which she was determined to sit, and see the engagement; observing that, it was the next best thing to escaping from shipwreck." The surrounding vessels must surely have seen through this farcical tableau, the presence of a middle-aged woman in a chair hardly being consistent with a man o'war preparing for battle. Nonetheless, the foreign ships failed to engage, leaving the passengers of the *Nathalia* relieved, if a bit confused.[13]

Confusion quickly turned into apprehension over the next three days as the passengers remained on ship waiting for information about the situation on shore. Men sent from the ship into Calicut to survey the scene returned with troubling news: the British consul had fled the area weeks earlier, taking with him all his belongings. Fearing the worst, the assistance of the Danish consul was sought to help the frightened Britons pass for Danes. From the Danes they learned that there was indeed some sort of conflict brewing between the British and Haidar Ali, the de facto ruler of the Kingdom of Mysore, in which Calicut now lay.

The Malabar Coast had been one of the first flashpoints of globalization. Vasco de Gama, making the first bold venture around the Horn of Africa, had landed in the region—like Fay making landfall at Calicut—almost three hundred years earlier in 1498. He found the region of Malabar—a low, waterlogged plain stretching from the sea to the Western Ghats—teeming with pepper, and in the centuries that followed the Portuguese and Dutch vied with petty local princes to control the lucrative spice trade and the diverse range of merchants who flocked to the area. The British only got involved in southwestern India belatedly, and it was not until the eighteenth century that the

British began to advance, pincer-like, from their bases at Madras on the south-east coast and Bombay, just north of Malabar.

Unbeknownst to Eliza Fay, by the time she arrived on the Malabar Coast, Haidar Ali had had a long and contentious history with the British. The son of a military commander in the service of the Raja of Mysore in southern India, Haidar Ali Khan first rose to prominence in 1749, when he commanded troops during the Second Carnatic War, part of a series of mid-century conflicts for control of the south-eastern coast of India. At their heart, the Carnatic Wars were the result of competition between an expansionist French East India Company based at Pondicherry on the Coromandel Coast and their British rivals based in nearby Madras, which echoed similar imperial rivalries in Europe and North America. The First and Third Carnatic Wars can in many ways be seen as imperial echoes of the War of Austrian Succession and the Seven Years' War respectively. As they jockeyed for position, the French and British made alliances with various local powers, especially the great native powers of south India: the nizams of Hyderabad, the rajas of Mysore, and the peshwas of the Maratha Empire. During the Third Carnatic War (1758–63), Haidar Ali earned a far-reaching reputation as an inspired military commander when he came to the aid of his French allies during the British siege of Pondicherry. Although the French would lose the war and with it much of their power and territory in India, Haidar Ali emerged with a fearsome reputation, an army complete with French artillery and French deserters, and official command of Mysore's armies. By 1761, he had seized the de facto rule of Mysore from its titular ruler Krishnaraja Wodeyar II, and begun the expansion of the kingdom south into Kerala and Malabar, making it a serious regional power.

Conflict between Britain and Haidar Ali's Mysore began in 1767, when the newly installed Nizam of Hyderabad, Nizam Ali Khan (Asaf Jah II), shifted Hyderabad's alliance from the French (his predecessor, whom he deposed in 1762, had been a French puppet) to the British. Both the British and the nizam were alarmed by the growing strength and boldness of Mysore, and worried that Haidar Ali would soon turn his armies north and threaten Britain and Hyderabad's interests in the Carnatic region. Not willing to risk the gains they had made during the Carnatic Wars, the new allies preemptively attacked Mysore, leading to the First Anglo-Mysore War (1767–9).

1. Eyewitness to the shockwaves of the American Revolution, Ignatius Sancho was one of many Britons who felt that the world was spinning out of control. The war brought rampant fears of invasion, revolution, treason, terrorism, and disorder to British shores, precipitating an authoritarian reaction in British politics and criminal justice.

2. Initially a protest against wartime concessions granted to Catholics, the Gordon Riots of 1780 quickly transformed into a week-long assault on symbols of the new penal regime. The burning of Newgate Prison, a well-known symbol of law and order, horrified many Britons and encouraged a growing movement for more stringent legal reform.

3. Britain's precarious position both domestically and internationally provided an opportunity for Ireland's Patriot movement. Originally formed as a means of protecting Ireland from American raids and French invasion, the Irish Volunteers (shown here parading in Dublin) used the threat of force to pressure Britain into imperial concessions, including an independent Irish Parliament.

4. The gains secured by the Irish Patriot movement were short-lived. The American War exposed fault-lines between Protestants and Catholics and reformers and revolutionaries. This would stall further reform and increase sectarian violence, culminating in a failed rebellion in 1798 and union with Britain in 1800, parodied here by James Gillray.

5. Young Captain Horatio Nelson in 1781 with Fort San Juan in the background. The scene of Nelson's first heroics, the British attempt to divide the Spanish Empire by seizing Central America proved a disaster. Spain's efforts to maintain its far-flung possessions, however, would prove costly.

6. As indigenous Andeans chafed at Spanish reforms designed to pay for war with Britain, Inca genealogies became increasingly popular. Tupac Amaru II, who led an uprising against Spain in 1780, consulted a genealogist to solidify his claim as heir to the Inca. His rebellion failed, but it helped sow the seeds of later independence movements.

7. The American War gave cover to Austria and Russia's eastern ambitions and allowed Catherine the Great to seize Crimea as part of a crucial step in her construction of a maritime empire. As this contemporary cartoon suggests, the Ottomans, abandoned by Britain and France, held the contest's worst hand.

8. The view of Calcutta and the Hooghly River that greeted Eliza Fay in 1780. Fay and her husband had unwittingly sailed into trouble when they arrived in South India the year before, where the ferociously anti-British kingdom of Mysore had allied with France and opened the Indian theater of the American War.

9. Dean Mahomet was one of the thousands of Indian sepoys recruited into the army of the British East India Company in the eighteenth century. Like many Indians, Mahomet saw British service as a pathway to success not terribly different from that followed by his ancestors in the service of the Mughals.

10. The loser at Yorktown, after the war Cornwallis became a proponent of British expansion in India as governor-general. With French finances in tatters, Mysore was left alone to face a resurgent East India Company. Cornwallis's 1792 victory over Tipu Sultan confirmed that the American War had tipped the balance of power in India.

11–12. With American ports now closed to the convict trade, in 1788 Britain sent its first fleet of convicts to colonize the recently explored Botany Bay. Bennelong, a kidnapped Eora man, became the most important indigenous informant in the early days of British settlement in Australia. The site of Bennelong's house is now dominated by the Sydney Opera House.

13–14. In desperation, several British commanders offered freedom to American slaves who joined the fight against the colonies. Thousands of enslaved people escaped to British lines during the war, and many fought valiantly against their enslavers. After the war, more than a thousand black loyalists would re-settle in the new colony of Sierra Leone.

15–16. Hoping to loosen the tightly controlled China trade at Canton, after the war Britain sent its first diplomatic mission to China in 1792. George Macartney's ill-fated embassy would mark a sea-change in British attitudes towards China, helping to rationalize an aggressive policy in the nineteenth century.

Haidar Ali once more distinguished himself in battle against the British and the struggle ended in a stalemate, with Britain and Mysore entering into a defensive alliance. According to the terms of the peace, the British were to come to the aid of Mysore in the event of a war with a third power. This was tested in practice in 1764, when the Maratha Empire invaded Mysore, and Britain neglected to fulfill its part of the bargain, earning it the eternal hatred of Haidar Ali and his son and successor Tipu Sultan. Betrayed by the British, Haidar Ali made a new alliance with France.

Arriving in India in November 1779, the passengers of the *Nathalia* likely had little clue that the Malabar Coast was a veritable cauldron of imperial contention. When France declared war on Britain in support of the American colonies in 1778, the conflict had rapidly spread to the Indian subcontinent. The British attacked and captured Pondicherry, the heart of the French presence in India, in October 1778, and quickly began to gobble up French ports and possessions. By 1779 the army of the British East India Company had fixed its sights on the port city of Mahe on the Malabar Coast, a mere 50 miles north of Calicut, where Eliza Fay was shortly to arrive. Mahe, a vital lynchpin in Mysore's arms and munitions trade with the French, was crucial to Haidar Ali's military strength; it was explicitly under his protection and defended by his own troops. When the British captured Mahe they committed a second unforgiveable affront, and open war between Mysore and the British became inevitable. It was into the epicenter of this building maelstrom that the *Nathalia*, a British ship, made landfall in a furiously aggrieved Haidar Ali's territory in November 1779.

As they waited nervously for their ship to set sail for Bengal, Eliza Fay and her shipmates thus found themselves at the mercy of the global struggle that pitted Britain against the rebellious American colonies and their new allies, France and Mysore. After waiting for three days for fear that the unscrupulous Captain Chenu would abandon them if they went ashore, the tension on the ship was heightened by the arrival of a boat full of armed men who boarded the ship under the pretext of preparing the "Danish" ship for an expected attack by the British. Although the Fays were assured that they would be allowed to leave the ship freely with all of their possessions, when Eliza overheard some of the Sepoys discussing new orders to plunder the ship the terrified couple decided to barricade themselves in their cabin.[14]

At two o'clock in the morning the long-feared assault finally commenced. A party of armed men surrounded Fay's cabin and demanded they be allowed to enter. As Fay remembered later:

> I clung round my husband and begged for God's sake that he would not admit them; for what could be expected from such wretches but the most shocking treatment. All this while there was such a noise without, of breaking and tearing, to come at their plunder, as convinced me that should we once lose sight of our little property, *every thing was lost*.[15]

The patience of the assailants quickly ran out. Scimitars were drawn and threats of torture and murder offered as inducements to surrender. In response, Anthony drew his sword and swore "that he would run the first man through the body, who should presume to enter his wife's chamber." Outside, the attackers began to chant, "incessantly calling, 'ao, ao'" or "come, come." With this chilling call ringing in her ears, Eliza began to dress in preparation for abandoning the cabin. Outside the Sepoys continued to chant, threatening her to make haste. With all thought of resistance finally abandoned, the door to the cabin was at last opened and the Fays came face to face with their captor. It must have come as quite a shock to look into the eyes of their enemy only to find an Englishman staring back. Criminal transportation and the revolution had once again marched in lockstep.[16]

The leader of the raiding party that seized the passengers of the *Nathalia* was, to the surprise of all, an Englishman. His name was Captain Ayers, a trusted commander in the forces of Britain's long-time foe, Haidar Ali. Ayers had been born in London and as a boy had been apprenticed to a saddler. Although hardly an idle apprentice, the young Ayers' industry was not focused on saddle-making, but rather on easier forms of employment "more suited to his active genius." Out for some adventure and quick riches, Ayers became a highwayman, targeting and robbing the many coaches that rumbled along the rural roads in and out of London. He boasted that as a highwayman he had "preformed many notable exploits," and that though he occasionally "got inclosed within the hard gripe of the Law" he was always able to escape unscathed. Flamboyant and daring criminals rarely had long careers in the eighteenth century, liable as they were to meet a bullet or the rope, and Ayers was no exception. He was caught and tried, and "the proofs ran so strong against him, that in spite of money and friends (which in his case were *never* wanting) he was *Capitally convicted*."[17]

Some portion of Ayers' luck held, however, and instead of execution the restless apprentice was sentenced to transportation to India as a soldier in the East India Company. In Bengal, Ayers quickly reverted to form and once more plied his trade as a "Gentleman Collector of the Highways." After twice being arrested on suspicion of robbery in Calcutta, Ayers was transferred to Madras in hopes that a new locale would temper his criminal tendencies. The transfer did not, however, have the desired effect. Ayers found army pay to be insufficient to support his lifestyle and so decided to desert from the British forces in favor of those of Haidar Ali, where he saw an opportunity to replace the low-paid drudgery of the British forces with the rich rewards of a turncoat. After stealing two horses and various weapons, the British traitor made his way to the camp of Haidar Ali, where that brilliant and bellicose ruler of Mysore found immediate use for the ruthless Ayers. Assigned to the province of Calicut, Ayers was said to have quelled a rebellion by the inhabitants of the region by massacring those who dared to challenge his authority. As Eliza Fay learned, "the least punishment inflicted by him was cutting off the noses and ears of those miserable wretches, whose hard fate subjected them to his tyranny. In short a volume would not contain half the enormities perpetrated by this disgrace to human nature."[18]

That Eliza Fay and her husband now found themselves at the mercy of such a villain was the direct result of the British practice and policy of criminal transportation, which saw criminals of various stripes shipped out across the sea to populate, labor, and fight in the far corners of the British Empire. Captain Ayers was without doubt one of the most ruthless and influential British deserters, but he was hardly unique. With low pay, harsh discipline, and little loyalty to the country that had banished them, British soldiers, especially those pressed into service, regularly exchanged a British commander for an Indian or French one. Among Haidar Ali's troops stationed in Calicut alone there were at least two further British deserters. Eliza Fay encountered one solicitous turncoat who, on "seeing a country-woman in such distress," offered to find her an umbrella to protect her from the drenching rain that so often soaked the Malabar

Coast. Also among the Mysorean forces at Calicut were a Captain West and a Portuguese officer named Pereira, both of whom had abandoned their countries' armies for service to Haidar Ali. Prisoner though he was, Anthony Fay himself was offered a commission as an officer by Sardar Ali Khan, Haidar Ali's local commander, an offer he steadfastly refused.[19]

As surprising as these scenes might first appear, European mercenaries had been a fixture of the princely courts of India for centuries. When Vasco de Gama landed at Calicut in 1498 following his pioneering voyage around the African continent, he found Italian soldiers were already serving in the armies of the local rajas. Such service was clearly tempting, and when de Gama departed from Malabar he did so without two of his men, who had taken the opportunity to abscond and seek employment in the armies of India. So attractive was defection that by 1565 one Portuguese chronicler claimed as many as 2,000 Europeans were serving as mercenaries in native courts, with the number rising to 5,000 by the dawn of the seventeenth century. As the French and British expanded their interests in India, large numbers of their soldiers followed the Portuguese lead into the princely armies. The British tended to flock to the forces of the Mughal sultans and the Muslim rulers of the Deccan plateau in south-central India, where they joined "Firingi," or foreign, regiments. Indeed, so many French and British soldiers flooded into the imperial capital of Delhi, that a special suburb, "Firingi Pura" or Foreigners Town, had to be built just to accommodate them. These men were required to convert to Islam and undergo circumcision, a heavy price that thousands were nonetheless willing to pay.[20]

Most of the Europeans who deserted to join Indian armies were marginal figures, who saw in the dazzling wealth of Indian courts the chance to make their fortunes. All sorts of European soldiers turned renegade, but gunners and cavalrymen, who possessed skills coveted by Indian rulers, were in the best position to find lucrative employment. The life of a European soldier was often wretched, with meager food, poor living conditions, and dismal wages. For such "scum of the earth," to use the Duke of Wellington's acid phrase, the appeal of service in Indian armies was readily apparent: higher wages, more regular pay, and better living conditions. Beyond mere monetary gain, Indian society also possessed a multitude of attractions for the weary, brutalized soldier. Some were attracted by the ubiquitous practice of concubinage and polygamy among the native elite, while others, used to the endless religious strife back home, found the religious freedom and syncretism offered by Indian society deeply appealing.

Before the more restrictive dictates that began to emerge in the aftermath of the American War, the lines between European and Indian society were more open and fluid, with soldiers and merchants in both Indian and European service assimilating to local customs, local dress, local languages, and local religions. Many took Indian wives or mistresses and fathered mixed-race children, living out their days in subcontinental contentment. Thomas Legge, an eighteenth-century Irish soldier of fortune from Ulster, became so enamored of Indian alchemy and mystic religion that he set himself up as a fakir, choosing to live naked in an abandoned tomb in the Thar desert of Rajasthan.[21]

George Thomas, another Irish soldier, assimilated with a touch more grandeur. Like so many in the late eighteenth century, Thomas did not choose to go to India, but had been taken by a press gang and forced into naval service. He chafed at the rough discipline and restricted opportunities on offer for a poor sailor, so when his ship anchored at Madras in 1781, he went rogue, deserted the navy, and made his way into the service of the wealthy Begum Samru, the ruler of the short-lived principality of Sardhana near Delhi and herself the widow of a mercenary captain from Luxembourg. Thomas was a dynamic and ambitious soldier and eventually created his own kingdom in Haryana, west of Delhi. From his capital at Hansi, Thomas, now styled Jehaz Sahib, minted coins, built a palace, and acquired a harem, until, in 1801, he was driven out of his self-made kingdom by a force led by another European mercenary, Pierre Cuillier-Perron, a French naval deserter who rose to become commander of the forces of Mahadaji Scindia, the Maratha ruler of Gwalior. So fully had the "rajah from Tipperary" assimilated that he dictated his memoirs in Persian, having largely forgotten his native tongue. His bi-racial son, Jan Thomas, would go on to have an illustrious career as an Urdu poet in Mughal Delhi.[22]

Given these temptations, it would have come as no surprise to the British authorities that deported criminals might once more turn to crime. But it must certainly have been a surprise to find, leading the war now waged against them in southern India, an English criminal whom the British themselves had transported to India. By 1779, the military crises spreading across the globe created a heightened need to look everywhere for men, to scour even the prisons for potential recruits, willing or not. As it transpired, it was also a time of fluid loyalties, a time when allegiances could easily be, and often were, cast aside and replaced by new ones. In America and in India, the lines between British and American, British and French, British and Indian, were as yet amorphous and unfixed, and while the colonies sought to win their independence and Britain to hold on to an empire, most individuals sought only to survive and profit.

The victories at Plassey and Buxar had solidified and formalized the British foothold in India, yet war continued to plague the subcontinent throughout the last quarter of the eighteenth century. While Patriots and Redcoats clashed on the streets of Boston and the fields of Lexington and Concord, equally momentous encounters were taking place in South Asia that would help to shape the British Empire just as surely as the events in North America. The victories of Clive and Coote in the 1750s and 1760s had expanded British dominion over large swaths of the old Mughal Empire. The magnificent empire of Babur, Akbar the Great, and Shah Jahan was rapidly becoming a shadow of its former glory, crumbling under its own weight and British rapacity. Trouble, however, now came from dynamic areas of the subcontinent that had long been free from the grasp of Mughal power. Disputes over territory and treaties with the Maratha Empire and the Kingdom of Mysore led to those states creating alliances with the French, and so when war with France broke out in 1778, war in southern India was not long in coming.

With wars erupting with Mysore in 1767 and 1780, in Rohilkhand in 1773, and with the Maratha Confederacy in 1775, and lasting on and off until the early nineteenth century, the East India Company was in desperate need of more soldiers to protect their interests and project their growing authority. Armed conflict with the American colonies, and eventually with France in 1778, however, left British manpower stretched paper-thin and made willing and able volunteers hard to come by. Unlike many other European nations, Britain had no formal system of conscription, as such a practice was deemed contrary to the rights and liberties of the British people. Thus, the first strategy to ensure a steady supply of recruits was through cash incentives.

The most effective measures taken to induce volunteers were the Recruiting Acts of 1778 and 1779. Passed in response to the deepening crisis in North

America and the expected entrance of France into the war, these acts provided cash bonuses to volunteers in addition to regular army pay. The 1778 Act stipulated that volunteers were to receive a bonus of £3, a month's wages for a craftsman of the period. In an attempt to sweeten the deal, the 1779 Recruiting Act upped the cash bonus to £3 and 3 shillings, and added a number of new benefits to veterans. Veterans, who could be discharged after five years if the war had ended, were given exemptions from normal statutory public services such as service on the highways, service as parish officers, and service in the militia. Furthermore, they were given the right to exercise any trade they wished in any place in Britain.[23]

The needs of the British army and the East India Company, however, far exceeded the number of men they were able to recruit through ordinary means. With willing men in short supply, crafty recruiters turned to more desperate measures. Starting in the 1770s, the army and East India Company turned to the courts for a ready, and captive, population of potential soldiers and sailors. With America closed as a dumping ground for convicts and with growing military needs, men convicted of capital offenses and eligible for transportation were offered the chance of serving in India or America instead of a criminal sentence.

The recruits gained in this way must have been of highly variable quality and indifferent commitment as the case of Captain Ayers readily attests. Yet, when faced with the alternatives of death or transportation to Australia, many convicts actively sought out and pleaded for a chance to serve in India. Because many sentences of criminal transportation fail to list a destination, it is difficult to obtain a precise number of men transported as soldiers in East India Company service. Despite the patchy nature of the evidence, it seems as though this forced recruiting was relatively widespread. For instance, on one day in 1782 alone four separate men in four separate cases were sentenced to service with the East India Company army.[24] The practice was common enough by 1775 that a soft-hearted private prosecutor could promise an apologetic defendant that "he would be as easy as he could; he would endeavor to send him for an East India soldier." This method of punishment was thus well known among the general populace by the 1770s at the latest. However, East Indian army recruiting through transportation really began to expand in the 1780s, as the war against the colonies dragged on and the struggles with Mysore and the Marathas picked up steam.[25]

Cash bonuses and pardoned felonies were still not enough to meet the manpower needs of a tiny nation beset by war in the furthest corners of the globe. Britain thus turned to a widely denounced tactic, impressment. In port towns from Portsmouth to Providence, press gangs used intimidation and violence to coerce civilian sailors into joining the ranks of the Royal Navy. Such gangs were accused of a variety of dirty tricks—from rounding up drunks to bodily kidnapping unsuspecting seamen—and their violence was frequently met with resistance and even riots, but the world was at war and the British navy needed men, whatever the means, whatever the price. Contrary to later views of imperial self-confidence, in the late eighteenth century Britons were deeply conscious of their country's small size and limited resources, constantly fretting about whether they had sufficient numbers to administer an ever-growing empire. Chronically short of skilled sailors, the British government turned to what historians have called "the evil necessity," coerced naval service. Gangs of sailors led by a naval officer, and often backed by local muscle, scoured port towns for skilled sailors, using threats and violence to force them into service until death came or peace was reached. This was not a temporary practice, but official imperial policy, and between 1688 and 1815 roughly half of the navy at any one time was made up of impressed sailors. In all, approximately 250,000 men were coerced into naval service over the course of the eighteenth century. With its far-flung theaters, the American War saw a massive expansion of naval impressment, and even the entirely unprecedented extension of the practice of impressment to the army. After 1778, local justices of the peace were given the authority to round up all "able bodied, idle and disorderly persons" for military service.[26]

Although the practice of army impressment was curtailed in 1780, the behavior and tactics of army recruiters remained the subject of much criticism. In contemporary records, East India Company recruiters were frequently referred to as "kidnappers" for their underhanded tactics toward the poor, the homeless, and the drunk. As late as 1789, a man accused of theft claimed as his defense that he had been "trepanned by the East India Company's serjeant" and forced onto a ship. When he became ill on board, the unsympathetic sergeant abandoned him back onshore with no money, forcing him to steal to eat. Many of the poor men who made their way through the courts gave similar accounts of unscrupulous army recruiters. In one such instance in 1795 a constable was attacked by a mob of men who took him for an army recruiter come to kidnap drunk men to serve in India. As the war in America was going badly for the British, there was a desperate need for more and more soldiers. It was reported that some agricultural and industrial laborers were so terrified at the growing prospect of impressment that they intentionally cut off their right thumb and forefinger, hoping that such mutilation would save them from forced military service.[27]

Eliza Fay must have felt something akin to the sense of dread experienced by the hundreds of men pressed or pardoned into service in British India. While she had chosen to go out to India of her own volition, as she stood on the deck of the *Nathalia* in the driving November rain she could not have been at all sure when or if her captivity in Calicut would end. She was now at the mercy of Haidar Ali and his allies, something she had not dreamt was possible only days prior. She could not fathom that "any power on this Continent, however independent, would have dared to treat *English* subjects with such cruelty." In the 1770s it seems that many powers across the world were taking a stand for independence with little regard for the feelings of "English subjects."[28]

Unlike many of the reluctant redcoats, however, Eliza's tribulations were only temporary. She and her husband had been escorted through the churning surf to the beach where they were immediately surrounded by "all the mob of Calicut, who seemed to take pleasure in the beholding the distress of white people, those constant objects of their envy and detestation." Whether the crowd was truly basking in the *Schadenfreude* of the spectacle or merely curious is unclear, but the Fays went unmolested on their way to meet the Governor of Calicut, Sardar Ali Khan, a brother-in-law of Haidar Ali. The governor seemed uninterested in the sodden couple as he smoked his hookah, only stopping to order them to be detained in the now deserted British factory where they spent an uncomfortable evening in the company of lizards, scorpions, and centipedes.

The Fays were shortly thereafter joined in captivity by their fellow English passengers who had been arrested after the blowhard Hare had, in a fit of patriotic feeling toward Ayers, told the turncoat the truth about the prisoners' nationality. The prisoners were next moved from the British factory to the closer confines of the Calicut fort, where they constantly had to contend with standing water, rats, and bats. After a month of waiting in this damp and pestilential prison, all of the English people were given leave to depart Calicut by land. With salvation in sight, the Fays were delivered another cruel blow when they alone were denied the right to leave. And so, on December 5, the Fays bade farewell to the other passengers of the ill-stared *Nathalia* and began to contemplate the desperate nature of their situation.

With hopes of being granted free passage out of Calicut fading by the day, and fears of violence at the hands of their captors growing, Anthony Fay began to take steps to procure their escape. The Fays first sought the assistance of a local man named Isaac, a wealthy Jewish merchant who held many contracts and much sway with Haidar Ali and Sardar Ali Khan. Eliza came to see Isaac as a father figure and sent a loving description of him to her friends in England. "Isaac is a fine venerable old man," Eliza wrote, "about eighty-five with a long white beard; his complexion by no means dark, and his countenance benign yet majestic; I could look at him till I almost fancied that he resembled the Patriarch whose name he bears." Isaac's intercession failed to secure their immediate release, but he was able to secure funds for the Fays from the British Governor of Tellicherry (modern Thalassery), a city recently seized from the French, 40 miles north of Calicut. With the newly acquired money, Anthony approached a Portuguese friar who promised to obtained false papers to aid the Fays' escape. The false pass listed the Fays as two Frenchmen traveling to Mahe, and so with a boatman bribed and with Anthony disguised in sailor's dress and Eliza in a man's nankeen jacket, striped trousers and cap, the couple waited for the signal to depart. For days they waited in ready expectation for their flight from Calicut, but as it transpired the friar was willing to take their money but unwilling to risk actually aiding them in their escape.[29]

A "very melancholy Christmas-day" and New Year passed and the Fays remained confined in Calicut with only the company of Isaac and the much-loathed Captain Ayers. Eliza's fears for their safety were continually heightened by the conduct of Ayres. According to Eliza:

> The visits we receive from Ayers are terrible trials for one who loathes dissimulation as I do. This wretch has once or twice mentioned a cow that annoyed him by entering the little garden, or paddock, in which it appears his house is placed; this morning he entered the factory with his scimitar in

his hand unsheathed and bloody and with an expression of diabolical joy informed me that he had just caught the animal . . . You cannot imagine how *sweetly* the sword did the business; my very heart shuddered with horror . . . I doubt not he would murder me with as much pleasure as he killed the cow[30]

Salvation came at last in February 1780. After the Fays had spent three terrifying months in captivity, Isaac finally succeeded in procuring their release. The merchant had intervened with Sardar Ali Khan and obtained for the couple a pass to travel by one of his own ships to Cochin and freedom. On February 18, Eliza and Anthony Fay began the last leg of their original journey to Bengal and the burgeoning bureaucracy of the ever-expanding British Empire. Isaac surely deserved the touching tribute to him Eliza gave to posterity.

To him we are indebted for the inestimable gift of liberty. No words can I find adequate to the expression of my gratitude. In whatever part of the world and under whatever circumstances my lot may be cast; whether we shall have the happiness to reach in safety the place to which all our hopes and wishes tend, or are doomed to experience again the anxieties and sufferings of captivity; whether I shall pass the remainder of my days in the sunshine of prosperity, or exposed to the chilling blasts of adversity; the name of *Isaac the Jew* will ever be associated with the happiest recollections of my life; and while my heart continues to beat, and warm blood animates my mortal frame, no distance of time or space can efface from my mind, the grateful remembrance of what we owe this most worthy of men.[31]

Eliza could scarcely have realized just how fortunate she was to escape from Malabar in the early months of 1780, just as the war between Britain, France, and Mysore was heating up. Just a few months after the Fays' flight from Calicut, Haidar Ali invaded the Carnatic with a massive force of perhaps 80,000 men. Haidar had designs on Madras, the most important British possession in southern India and a constant thorn in the side of Mysore's expansionist ambitions. In response to the threat posed by the large Mysorean force, Colonel William Ballie was sent from his post at Guntur to join the forces of Sir Hector Munro at Conjeveram, near Madras, to create a strong unified front against

Haidar's invasion. Haidar knew that his odds of success would drop precipitously if the two British forces in the area managed to combine, so he sent Tipu—already a gifted commander and tactician in his own right—to intercept Baillie.

The two forces met at Pollilur on September 10, 1780 with disastrous consequences for the British. Their defeat was near total, the first major setback for British forces since their defeats by the Mughal Emperor Aurangzeb in Child's War in the late seventeenth century. Baillie's force had entered the battle with about 4,000 men. When the fighting ended, there were only about 200 British soldiers and 50 officers, including Colonel Baillie himself, left to take prisoner. The prisoners were marched to the Mysorean capital of Srirangapattam where they would spend the duration of the war with a growing number of other British prisoners of war. Not far from where Baillie and his men were imprisoned, Tipu would commission a massive painting of his triumph at Pollilur depicting British soldiers being cut down by Tipu's triumphant cavalry.

With one British army already in tatters, and Hector Munro hesitant to leave the environs of Madras, Sir Eyre Coote, the hero of the Seven Years' War in India, was sent from Calcutta with reinforcements. Coote had more luck than Baillie, winning victories over Haidar at Porto Novo, Sholinghur, and at Pollilur, but none were decisive. Less than a year later, Madras received the unwelcome news that the American War had expanded ever further: the Dutch Republic had declared war on Britain in aid of America and France. The Dutch bridgehead in India had been in almost terminal decline for decades, but they still held possessions on the Coromandel Coast and the beleaguered British could ill afford to fight yet another enemy in India. Nonetheless, Lord George Macartney, recently arrived from a posting in Grenada and now in command of Madras, welcomed the opportunity to drive both French and Dutch competition off the Coromandel Coast and into the Bengal Sea. In November, the British succeeded in capturing the Dutch Indian capital at Negapatam with the critical aid of the navy.

British gains in Coromandel, however, were quickly threatened by the arrival of the French navy under Admiral Bailli de Suffren in early 1782. The subsequent naval battles between de Suffren and British Vice-Admiral Sir Edward Hughes, and siege of Vandavasi by a combined French-Mysore force, were inconclusive, but with their Madras forces under heavy pressure from the French, Dutch, and Mysore, the British decided it was prudent to open up a second front, thus removing some of Mysore's troops from Coromandel. Troops were therefore sent from British Bombay to Tellicherry on the south-western coast, from where they were to invade Malabar. Haidar responded by sending Tipu with an army to oppose the British and defend Malabar. True to form, Tipu had the Bombay army on the ropes when in December 1782, everything changed.[32]

Haidar Ali had been ill for some time, but still, his death on December 7 came as an inconvenient surprise to a kingdom embroiled in war. Attempts were made to keep the great ruler's death a secret for as long as possible while the succession to the throne was ironed out. Tipu Sultan was the eldest and most powerful of Haidar's sons, but as Haidar's rule had been built on conquest rather than inheritance, there was no guarantee that he would succeed to the throne. Still in the field when he heard the news, Tipu rushed to Chittoor to successfully secure his claim. In Haidar Ali the British had found a deter-mined enemy, but in his son and heir, they would find something much more dangerous: an ambitious, expansionist, forward-thinking ruler with an implac-able hatred of the British and a grim determination to see their influence in India brought to a bloody end.

Britain's territorial gains in India had come slowly, over the course of decades, but Tipu Sultan was fooled by neither the slow place of British impe-rial expansion nor the Brits' protestations that they only had commercial ambi-tions. In a letter to the Nizam of Hyderabad, Tipu had warned his neighbor, "Know you not the customs of the English? Wherever they fix their talons they contrive little by little to work themselves into the whole management of affairs."[33] Certain of the danger posed by the British, Tipu himself fully embraced Mysore's anti-British image. Once on the throne, he did everything he could to encourage his reputation as Britain's unflinching adversary, defi-antly proclaiming that he "would rather live a day as a tiger than a lifetime as a sheep." He commissioned a life-sized automaton of a tiger ravaging a British soldier and paintings depicting his and his father's victories over the British. One observer reported that his capital at Sriringapatam "was ornamented with paintings, such as, elephants whirling Europeans in the air—tigers seizing whole battalions of English Sepoys—five or six English officers supplicating for mercy at the feet of one of his troopers—and companies flying frightened at the charge of ten or twenty of his horse." Everywhere, and in every medium imaginable, Tipu presented Mysore as a vigorous, vengeful predator and the British as cowardly, weak, and ineffectual.[34]

Haidar and Tipu's status as the foremost crusaders against British imperial tyranny in Asia echoed across the globe and captured the imagination of another group of anti-British revolutionaries. Americans quickly recognized a kinship between their own endeavors against British imperialism and those of the rulers of Mysore. As early as 1777, the Irish adventurer Thomas Conway, later famous for his failed cabal that aimed to replace Washington as commander of the American forces, proposed sending American troops to Mysore. The plan was impractical and came to nothing, but Mysore remained on American minds. American troops never reached Tipu's domain, but American ships traded with Mysore and their French allies throughout the war, seeking to undermine the British East India Company's monopoly. Pennsylvania honored Haidar Ali by naming a warship after him in 1781, and Philip Freneau, the great poet of the American Revolution, penned a poem in praise of the ship that also paid tribute to the ship's Indian namesake.

> From an Eastern prince she takes her name,
> Who, smit with freedom's sacred flame
> Usurping Britons brought to shame,
> His country's wrongs avenging.

That a group of would-be republicans should heap such lavish praise upon two monarchs every bit as autocratic and imperially ambitious as the British is perhaps surprising, but the American focus was limited to Haidar and Tipu's heroic victories over the British, rather than their political values. When Tipu Sultan came to the throne, he was hailed or reviled throughout the world, and celebrated in American and France, as one of Britain's most remorseless enemies.[35]

Tipu Sultan was an enemy of British colonization in India, but he was not the anti-imperialist of American imagination. Rather, the Mysore of Haidar Ali and Tipu Sultan was one of the foremost proponents of imperial expansion in eighteenth century India. This was a native, though European-inflected, imperialism that clashed with the competing empires of Britain and France and the Marathas, but it was actively and proudly imperial nonetheless. Tipu's policies, strategies and aims were eerily similar to those of the most imperialist Britons. He used taxes, indemnities, and revenue as a means of controlling petty rulers and landlords, and as an excuse to annex territory. He was merciless to perceived rebels and bandits and sought alliances to defeat his rivals. Tipu's Mysore was one of a number of imperial powers in India in the late eighteenth century seeking to fill the power vacuum left behind by the crumbling Mughal Empire. The coming of the American War intensified this struggle, fatally undermining France and Mysore, while solidifying Britain's grasp on the subcontinent.

Eliza Fay had the bad luck to arrive in India just as the imperial contest was heating up, but she was not the only one to be effected by the American War. The prisons at his capital Sriringapatam, in fact, were full of British captives, including the nearly 300 taken in the aftermath of Pollilur in 1780, a sizable number taken after Tipu's victory at Tanjore in February 1782, and nearly 500 British sailors handed over to Tipu by the French navy in 1782. When peace eventually came in 1784, Mysore would release more than 1,300 British prisoners and as many as 2,000 native Sepoys who had fought for the British. The capture and imprisonment of British soldiers and officers was less a side-benefit of warfare than a conscious tactic for Tipu Sultan. First of all, Tipu was well aware that British prisoners, especially high-status captives or prisoners in great numbers, could be used as a diplomatic chess-piece, adding leverage in negotiations and providing surety for British good behavior in the treatment of Mysorean prisoners. Second, and most importantly, Tipu was well aware that European innovations in drill, tactics, and technology gave their forces a distinct advantage over traditional Indian army units. His father had long known the importance of European advisors, employing at least 210 Europeans in his army by 1767, with the number steadily rising throughout the period. Europeans were especially useful for modern specialized military tasks such as the use of artillery and naval command. In this respect, Haidar Ali selected a European officer named Stannet to lead his fledgling navy. If such benefits were to accrue to Mysore, Tipu would need European advisors familiar with the new practices and technologies, and what better way to gain such knowledge than through prisoners of war. What the example of William Ayers and the other military adventurers of eighteenth-century India taught Tipu Sultan was that, above everything else, the loyalties of European soldiers were precarious at best. He knew from experience that British prisoners could be turned, convinced, and cajoled into joining the Mysore service. He had uses for such turncoats and he treated his captives accordingly.[36]

If Tipu's goal in taking and holding so many British prisoners was designed to drain both British manpower and their technical military advantages, he succeeded very well. In 1784, with peace declared between Britain and Mysore, Tipu agreed to release 1,300 captive British soldiers. Though free to leave the site of their captivity, more than 400 chose to remain in Mysore, most as soldiers or advisors in Tipu's army. Fully 1,700 British men, however, remained in Tipu's prisons after the peace, with a quarter of these eventually joining Mysore's army, many willingly, some by force. For most soldiers of the time, regardless of their country of origin, soldiering was a job not a calling, wage labor rather than a labor of love or loyalty. Conditions, pay, and treatment in the service of a native state were often better than in the British army, and many were more than happy to trade one uniform for another with little hesitation or compunction. The deep divisions between British and Indian, the age of strictly bounded national identities was just beginning in the 1780s.[37]

When Tipu Sultan came to the throne in 1782, he immediately infused his reign with more vigorous Islamic valence, a "colour of religious militancy" in the words of one scholar. Unlike his father, Tipu had been educated in Persian, the language of Muslim rulers throughout India, and was familiar with Islamic theology and Muslim history. He was concerned to project, both to his own Muslim governing class and to his Muslim neighbors, that his rule was divinely ordained, a "God-given government" as reflected in the formal name he gave his government, *sarkar-i Khudadad*. He struck coins with legends that invoked God, the Prophet, and Ali, the first of the Twelve Imams in Shia Islam. The tiger imagery he so famously employed was likewise a direct reference to Ali, whose title also meant tiger (or lion). Religious schools were founded and *qazi* appointed to teach Islam, towns were renamed with Persian names, and the idea of a holy war or *gha͡zwa* was invoked in Tipu's battles against Britain and the Hindu Marathas as a means of inspiring his soldiers and officials. Tipu thus departed from his father's more tolerant practice by employing a belligerent Islam as the "great ideological prop for his power." When Tipu began to expand his territories in the 1780s, this prop was transformed into active persecution of religious minorities.[38]

War with Britain, a Christian power, forced Tipu Sultan to reconsider the loyalties of his Christian and Hindu subjects, leading to persecution and a permanent hardening of religious divisions in south India. When he invaded the territory surrounding Mangalore in 1784, he captured tens of thousands of indigenous Catholics, many of whom were imprisoned, forced to convert, or mutilated. From his own place of captivity, the British sailor James Scurry provided a heart-rending first-hand account of the suffering of the Mangalorean Catholics.

> Their country was invested by Tippu's army, and they were driven men, women and children to the number of 30,000 to Sirangapatam where all who were fit to carry arms were circumcised and forwarded into four battalions. The sufferings of these poor creatures were most excruciating . . . The Chambars or Sandalmakers were then sent for and their noses, ears, and upper lips were cut off. They were then mounted on asses, their faces towards the tail and led through Patan, with a wretch before them proclaiming their crime. One fell from his beast and expired on the spot through loss of blood. Such a mangled and bloody scene excited the compassion of numbers and our hearts were ready to burst at the inhuman sight.[39]

Other accounts confirm Scurry's story, even if the numbers involved sometimes differ considerably, ranging from Scurry's 30,000 to as many as 80,000 in some estimations. In his memoirs Tipu Sultan himself put the number of Christian captives at as many as 60,000 men, women, and children. In typical fashion, he had planned the procedure down to the most minute detail. First, the local diwan was instructed to make a detailed list of every Christian household and every piece of property owned by Christians. Once the Christian population was recorded, soldiers were stationed in every Christian community, with the command that they were to remain vigilant until they received further orders. In order to coordinate the purge, and prevent any Christians from escaping, sealed letters were then sent to each officer with instructions to open and read the letter at a specific time on a specific day, while the Christians were at prayer. It all went off without a hitch. According to Tipu himself, "our orders were every where opened at the same moment; and at the same hour (namely, that of morning prayer) were the whole of the Christians, male and female, without exception of a single individual, to the number of sixty thousand, made prisoners, and dispatched to our Presence . . . and ultimately admitted into the honor of Islamism."[40]

Unsurprisingly, Tipu's account of the Mangalorean captivity is silent on the suffering of the captives, but the stories told by some of the captives in the years after their release seem quite similar to those presented by British captives such as James Scurry. A survivor from Barcoor painted a much grimmer picture of the forced march from Mangalore to Sriringapatam as well. Conditions were brutal, with as many as 20,000 succumbing to illness or starvation before they reached their destination. Others, especially leaders of the Christian community, were said to have been abused by their guards, and some even executed, although on whose orders remains unclear. When they arrived at Tipu's capital, many thousands, especially young men fit for military service, were forcibly converted to Islam, with resisters tortured, their lips, noses, and ears cut off as a warning to others. Many young women were given as wives to Muslim soldiers and officials. Targeting young men and women in such ways served not only to swell the ranks of the Mysorean army, but also to eliminate, quickly and irrevocably, future generations of Christians whose loyalty might be divided or suspect. Once the Christians had been rounded up and removed from Kerala, their churches were destroyed and their lands seized and redistributed to Tipu's loyal followers. It was as if a perceived cancer was being removed from Mysore's territory, eradicated to make it safe for Tipu's purposes and to prevent future British aggression. It was also, in many ways, a deliberate strategy of ethnic cleansing.[41]

Though they had long lived side by side with the largely Muslim ruling class, and made up the majority of Mysore's total population, Hindus were regularly targeted by Tipu as well. The thickly forested mountainous area of Coorg, in modern Karnataka, had been a thorn in Mysore's side since the days of Haidar Ali. The Kodava Hindus who lived in this hostile terrain were fiercely independent and regularly resisted the intrusions of the government of Mysore. With ongoing war against Britain and the Hindu Maratha Empire as part of the American War, this resistance was especially dangerous, and Tipu Sultan became increasingly concerned that the recalcitrant Kodavas might not only undermine his authority in the region, but potentially ally with his enemies, the British and the Marathas. Several attempts had been made to bring Coorg to heel, all without success as the Kodavas merely melted into the jungle hills, engaging in guerrilla warfare. When peace with Britain came in 1784, Tipu used the lull in his war with the East India Company to deal with Coorg once and for all. A force was sent under Runmust Khan, Nawab of Kurnool, which finally succeeded in taking the Kodava capital and capturing the Coorg leadership.

In Tipu's eyes, the Kodava had brought this fate upon themselves with their continuously rebellious behavior. Indeed, such sedition could not be tolerated, and thus, as was now becoming Tipu's regular practice, the conquered people were to be made captives and forcibly converted to Islam. In a letter to Runmust Khan Tipu outlined his policy for defeated rebels.

The exciters of sedition in the Koorg country, not looking to the conse-quences, but agreeably to the nature of children of selfishness and of oppor-tunity-watching rebels, conceiving of vain hopes from the great distance of our victorious army, raised their heads, one and all, in tumult. Immediately on our hearing of this circumstance, we proceeded with the utmost speed, and, at once made prisoners of forty-thousand occasion-seeking and sedition exciting Koorgs, who alarmed at the approach of our victorious army, had slunk into the woods, and concealed themselves in lofty mountains inaccessible even to birds. Then carrying them away from their native country (the native place of sedition) we raised them to the honor of Islam, and incorporated them with our *Ahmedy* corps. As these happy tidings are calculated, at once, to convey a warning to hypocrites, and afford delight to friends, the chiefs of the true believers, the pen of amity has here recited them.[42]

The lesson of the forced removal, captivity, and conversion of the Kodava Hindus was not apparently heeded as carefully as Tipu might have wished. The

Nair Hindus of Malabaar, the people among whom Eliza Fay had been held captive, were also targeted for chastisement through captivity and conversion. A few years after the Fays' stay in Calicut, Tipu crushed a Nair rebellion he feared was inspired by the British. The defeated Hindus were forcibly removed from their homelands and converted to Islam. In letter after letter to his military commanders, Tipu urged them to crush any sedition and convert the populations to Islam. He commanded Buruz Zuman Khan to crucify one rebel leader (and his nephew if he was over 25 years of age) and to convert 200 of his followers, and commended the same officer's forced circumcision and conscription of 135 young Nair captives in a second letter a month later. When the Nair continued to chafe under Mysore's rule, Tipu threatened mass hangings, evoking memories of a previous purge. "Ten years ago," Tipu informed his commander, "from ten to fifteen thousand men were hung from the trees of that district; since which time aforesaid trees have been waiting for more men. You must hang upon trees all such inhabitants of that district, as have taken a lead in these rebellious proceedings." To another officer he gave a blanket command to suppress unrest wherever it cropped up, "to chastise the turbulent wherever they raised the head of revolt; and after making them prisoners, to place those under age in the Ahmedy band [converted regiment], and to hang the remainder."[43]

The exact number of Hindus taken into captivity or forcibly converted to Islam is not entirely clear. Sources put the number of Kodava captives as high as 85,000 and the number of Nair captives at as many as 30,000. In all, more than 100,000 Hindus may have been forcibly removed from their lands, with a large portion of these forced to abandon their religion under extreme duress or even torture. Countless numbers also perished in the fighting and the executions that followed the conquest of new territory or the suppression of dissent within lands controlled by Mysore. As terrible as such practices may seem, this was a deliberate, considered tactic, repeatedly employed by Tipu Sultan during a period of constant warfare and regional chaos.

Tipu's zealous advocacy of a belligerent Islam and concomitant use of religious violence was strategic and tactical rather than merely bigoted or intolerant. He had good reason to be suspicious of the loyalties of the Catholics of Mangalore and the Hindus of Coorg and Malabar. These territories were on the edge of Mysore's expanding domain, and thus were areas of constant contestation between the expansionist ambitions of Britain, the Marathas, and Mysore, changing hands repeatedly in the eighteenth century. In 1768, for instance, Managlore had fallen into British hands, and though it was quickly recovered by Tipu's father Haidar Ali, rumors persisted that the Christians of the area had actively aided the British conquest, sending considerable funds to General Mathews during the campaign. Haidar took a measured approach to the betrayal, imprisoning those suspected of complicity, but refusing to execute anyone or to target the wider Christian community.

When war with Britain broke out in 1780, Mangalore became contentious ground, and the pattern of conquest, re-conquest, and betrayal reared its head. In 1782, when Mangalore fell to the British, rumors swirled that the Christian community, coddled by Tipu's father, had conspired with the enemy against Mysore. Informants reported to Tipu that the Christian community had provided men, money, and supplies to the invading British, and continued to do so during Mysore's subsequent siege of Managlore. As prince, Tipu had advocated a hardline policy toward the Christians of Kerala, and he was convinced that British success in capturing the territory and his own difficulty in retaking it was in large part the result of local Christian treachery. He accused them of "acting as guides and facilitating their [British] communications," and of providing men, money, and material to his enemies.[44]

Although some assistance was certainly provided to the British by local Christians, there is little evidence of widespread, organized collusion. Nevertheless, Tipu had become convinced that his kingdom would never be secure with a potential fifth column of Christians on such a sensitive border with the British. He feared that a British invasion of Kerala would be a constant threat as long as the loyalty of that region could not be guaranteed. Thus, when Mangalore was regained in 1784, Tipu wasted no time in capturing the by now deeply suspect Christians of the area, seizing their lands, and driving them off into captivity in the more secure heart of the Kingdom of Mysore.

Though hardly on the same scale, Tipu's persecution of Hindus likewise reflected fears of treachery and the perceived needs of geopolitical strategy. The Nair and Kodava Hindu communities were located in peripheral areas, or areas only newly conquered by Mysore, making the loyalties of these regions immediately suspect. They were also located on sensitive borders with the Hindu Maratha Empire and the British East India Company. Given that Mysore had been at war with both of these powers for decades, and that the Hindus of Coorg and Malabar had long been restive, it is not in the least bit surprising that Tipu Sultan considered the Nair and Kodavas to be potential sources of sedition or subversion. Indeed, there is some evidence that the Nair uprising had been directly encouraged by the British, lending credence to Tipu's fears of sedition. It must have seemed to Mysore's ruler that his kingdom was riddled with potential fifth columns right on his most sensitive frontiers. By removing such suspect peoples from the borders and converting them to Islam, he thus hoped to remove a potential weak link in his contestation with his enemies in south India. In other areas, especially in the heart of Mysore, Tipu did what he could to cultivate Hindu loyalty. He gave gifts and grants to scores of Hindu temples, especially the Sringeri temple, with whose swami he kept up a respectful correspondence. The gifts were often small, but they were clearly intended to ensure the support of the Hindu majority of Mysore and perhaps to allay any concerns that that community might have had when news of the repression and forced conversions of other Hindu communities reached their ears.[45]

It was equally important for Tipu, given the wider context of the American War in the 1780s, to present himself as a champion of a robust Islam. Indeed, he himself justified his harsh treatment of the Christians of Mangalore as a defense of Islam in the face of a treacherous, expansionist Christianity. In his memoirs, Tipu claims that his "zeal for the faith boiled over" in the face of Christian incursions and proselytizing. He was, he suggested, righting a historical wrong 300 years in the making. The "Portuguese Nazarenes" had established themselves at Goa, and, according to Tipu, as they acquired territory, they "prohibited fasts and prayers among the Mussulman inhabitants . . . finally expelling from thence all who refused to embrace their religion." The Christian plague had spread rapidly, especially among the poor and ignorant, until the time when Tipu conquered Managlore. When he heard of the behavior of the Christians and their priests, he rose to Islam's defense and removed the Christian community. An act of religious barbarity was thus repackaged as an act of religious restoration. Similarly, in his explanation of his treatment of the Hindus of Coorg, he stressed that the forced conversion was meant both as a warning to other rebels, and also, crucially, as a message of his religious bona fides to his co-religionists, to "friends, the chiefs of the true believers."[46]

Repeatedly in the 1780s and 1790s, Tipu Sultan found himself hemmed in, surrounded by enemies. Mysore was almost constantly at war with the British, whose territory pushed in on two sides, and the Hindu Marathas to the north were "infidels" themselves and had been colluding with the British since 1782. Tipu's preferred ally, France, was hamstrung by the peace with Britain in 1784, and was so ruined by the war itself that it could no longer afford to commit so heavily to Mysore's cause. In the face of conflict with these Christian and Hindu powers, Tipu needed to make alliances. He attempted to do so primarily by reaching out to Muslim powers, first to his neighbor and sometime enemy, the Nizam of Hyderabad, and later to the Ottoman Empire. In the instructions Tipu gave to his envoys to the Ottoman sultan he warned of the grave threat the British presented to Muslims in India. The British, Tipu warned, had already seized Bengal, appropriated revenues from the Mughal emperors, converted scores of Muslims, enslaved Muslim women and children, destroyed mosques, tombs, and other holy sites and replaced them with Christian churches. With such depredations too much to bear, Mysore had declared a holy war against the British that Tipu now urged the Ottomans to join. These diplomatic missions ultimately came to naught. The Nizam was already too beholden to the British to turn against them now, and the Ottomans had their hands full with Russia and Austria, who were taking advantage of the American War to target Ottoman possessions in Europe and Central Asia. Nonetheless, in a world in which Muslim allies were being actively sought, presenting oneself as a vigorous proponent of Islam, rather than out for personal or territorial gain, was an appealing strategy.[47]

The image of Tipu as champion of Islam was important not simply in its outward projection, but also in its reception within the kingdom and army of Mysore itself. While Mysore's civilian population was largely Hindu, Tipu's army and administration were largely made up of Muslims. Thus, presenting himself as an Islamic ruler was a strategic step designed, at least in part, to secure the loyalty of his soldiers and officials. This projection of a zealous Islam had to be carefully focused, primarily outside Mysore's borders, to avoid unduly alienating the general Hindu population, but it could be effective if correctly implemented. Rewarding loyal Muslim officers and administrators with confiscated Christian and Hindu property likewise helped to reinforce a sense of common cause between Tipu and the Muslim elites upon whom he relied.

For centuries before Tipu Sultan's reign, India had been a land of stunning cultural, linguistic, and religious diversity. For all the outward differences, the idea that political loyalty might be synonymous with religious identity had never been the accepted truth it was in Europe. With few exceptions, religious conflict between Hindus and Muslims, the subcontinent's two predominant faiths, was minimal and sporadic, the exception rather than the rule. Muslim rulers, like the nizams of Hyderabad, were patrons of Hindu temples and active participants in Hindu festivals. Hindus likewise took part in Muslim holidays and ceremonies with little compunction. In the light of centuries of peaceful syncretism, Tipu Sultan's more hardline actions may seem surprising, but the chaos of the expanding American War caused confessional boundaries to be drawn anew, hardening the line between Hindu, Christian, and Muslim.[48]

There is no reason to doubt Tipu's genuine attachment to his faith, nor does the cynical use of religion for strategic ends preclude a real commitment to religion. Tipu Sultan was merely employing religion in the same manner and in response to the same fears that motivated religious chauvinism and sectarian violence in America and Britain. Just as Americans feared and targeted Native Americans on the frontier, freed slaves in the south, and loyalist and Catholic conspirators everywhere, and just as the British targeted French spies, Irish rebels, and Catholic traitors, Tipu Sultan targeted Kodava Hindus and Mangalorean Christians. Just as the American Revolution had given room and cause for religious and communal violence in the Atlantic world, the Indian theater of the war created the conditions necessary for religious persecution on a shocking scale. The legacy of such violence would endure for generations. The modern states of Kerala and Karnataka would continue to see heightened levels of communal tension and religious violence up to the present day.

Despite the rather self-justifying sanctimonious posturing of the British toward the rule of Tipu Sultan, and their post-war attempts to blacken his name, they were themselves hardly immune from charges of rapacious brutality. Both the British and French press printed regular accounts of British atrocities in India, coalescing around accusations of a massacre and mass rape of innocent Mysorean women at Anantapur in 1783. The reporting of the event was not disinterested (it first appeared in the *Annual Register*, a periodical associated with Edmund Burke and other opponents of the East India Company, and that had also published a glowing tribute upon Haidar Ali's death), but the Anantapur massacre surely reflects the regularity of violence toward prisoners and non-combatants by both sides during the war.

For the common people, the frequency of war could be devastating even when they managed to avoid taking sides. Thus, in addition to the thousands removed into captivity, the Anglo-Mysore War also displaced thousands as they fled the theater of war for the safety of fortified towns and cities. In 1780, the artist William Hodges confronted such a train of refugees at Madras. Hodges was preparing to make a tour of the region, picturesque paintings of oriental scenes then being in fashion, but was:

> interrupted by the great scourge of human nature, the great enemy of the arts, war, which, with horrors perhaps unknown to the civilized regions of Europe, descended like a torrent over the whole face of the country, driving the peaceful husbandmen from his plow, and the manufacturer from his loom . . . I was a melancholy witness to its effects, the multitude coming in from all quarters to Madras as a place of refuge, bearing on their shoulders the small remains of their little property, mothers with infants at their breasts, fathers leading horses burdened with their young families . . . every object was marked by confusion and dismay.

Hodges estimated that 200,000 refugees made their way into Madras in the space of a few days, fleeing in advance of Mysore's invading army. These numbers were too much for Madras to accommodate, so many were resettled further north in the Northern Circars, which had recently become a British possession. It was not their war, indeed, it had begun in a part of the world of which they were probably only dimly aware, but as so often was the case, the peasants and craftsmen of the region found themselves refugees of an imperial struggle.[49]

The war ended almost alarmingly abruptly in the Indian theater. Though negotiations in Paris had been under way for a months, and Preliminaries of Peace

signed at Versailles in February 1783, the vagaries of eighteenth-century communication meant that word only reached Lord Macartney at Madras at the end of
June. For the British, peace could not come too soon. They had failed to strike
when Mysore was in turmoil following the death of Haidar Ali, and in the year
since had been fought to a stalemate by Tipu Sultan and his French allies. When
word of peace arrived, things were looking very bleak indeed. British troops were
under siege by the forces of the Marquis de Bussy at Cuddalore, and Tipu's army
was on the verge of taking another vital British position at Mangalore. They thus
wasted no time in informing the French of the news from Europe, just in case
they had failed to receive the message from Paris—Bussy caustically remarked
that if the British position had been stronger they "would not have hesitated to
conceal from us the news which they had received." Letters were sent to Bussy
and de Suffren, followed by commissioners tasked with negotiating terms. The
French were well aware that their resources were far overstretched, and quickly
came to terms with the British. Peace in India arrived on July 2, 1783.[50]

In March 1784 Tipu Sultan sent a letter to the French Governor of Pondicherry
congratulating him on the news of peace between France and Britain and
stressing that "this information has afforded us much satisfaction." In private,
however, Tipu was fuming over the peace. He had had the British on the ropes,
ready to deliver the decisive blow when his erstwhile ally had agreed to peace. To
Shah Allam, the Mughal emperor in Delhi, he presented an entirely different
perspective on the end of the war with Britain. "This steadfast believer," he
wrote:

> with a view to the support of the firm religion of Mahommed, undertook
> the chastisement of the Nazarene tribe [i.e. the British]; who, unable to
> maintain the war waged against them, solicited peace in the most abject
> manner. This is so notorious a fact, as not to require to be enlarged on. With
> the divine aid and blessing of God, it is now again my steady determination
> to set about the total extirpation and destruction of the enemies of the
> faith.[51]

Although they would have hardly cared to admit it, many among the British
establishment in India and in Britain would have reluctantly agreed with Tipu's

damning assessment of the situation in India. The news of Pollilur, especially coming as it did in the same year as the defeat at Yorktown, and subsequent British defeats in India had, according to Lord North, the prime minister, "engaged the attention of the world . . . and had given rise to so much public clamour and uneasiness." Parliament passed measures calling for an end to any further attempts at territorial conquest. At the same time, public perceptions of the native powers of India, and of Tipu Sultan's Mysore in particular, were changing dramatically as well. The Tiger of Mysore, and the animal that was his namesake, became an object of imperial fear. The Governor of Madras admitted, "The Indians have less terror of our arms." The end of the American Revolution thus brought with it not only the loss of the American colonies, but a new sense that the British Empire in India was overstretched and vulnerable, wounded prey to the emergent predators of Mysore.[52]

While the British faced peace with acrimony and grim relief, Tipu Sultan responded with the righteous anger of a man betrayed. Mysore had made an alliance with the French based on the understanding that a large army and a strong naval contingent would be sent to southern India with the goal of sweeping the British from the region entirely. Instead, Tipu received delays, excuses and undermanned operations. The large army promised by the French did not materialize for months after the conflict began, and when they did finally arrive, the allies quarreled incessantly, with Haidar Ali and Tipu Sultan complaining of French high-handedness, over-cautiousness, and failure to engage the British or follow up victories by attacking weakened British forces. Bussy, in turn, castigated Mysore's leaders as unreliable "brigands and tyrants," and suggested that the French would have been better off making alliances with the Marathas or the Nizam of Hyderabad instead of Mysore. After this catalog of disagreement and disappointments, just when the tide seemed to be turning and the British seemed hemmed in and vulnerable, on the cusp of victory the French had merely melted away at the first word of peace in Europe. Not only had Bussy sent word to the French troops aiding Tipu in the siege of Managlore to abandon their posts, but even French officers serving directly in the Mysore army—Lally and Boudenot in particular—were commanded to withdraw. What was worse, the French had negotiated a peace with Britain without so much as informing Tipu, let alone advocating for Mysore's interests in the final armistice agreement. Tipu attempted to continue the siege of Mangalore on his own, but his French advisors merely stood aloof, and eventually Bussy wrote directly to Tipu pushing him to make peace with the British. The British at Madras were refusing to return French territories seized during the war until Tipu's army left the Carnatic, so there was real pressure to persuade Tipu to come to terms, even if peace was not in Mysore's interest. Bussy himself recognized the betrayal, admitting that the peace would procure "little advantage" for the French and would make it "difficult to preserve the reputation and glory of the nation."[53]

Developments within Mysore itself seemed to confirm the rationality of British defeatism and Mysorean confidence. The second half of the eighteenth century saw the flowering of a veritable military revolution in the lands of Haidar Ali and Tipu Sultan. With vast agricultural resources, the potential for a great power had long been present in Mysore, but the extraction of the revenue needed for modern military investment had been hamstrung by the reliance on local hereditary landholders. Under Haidar Ali and his son, Mysore began the process of centralization by levying taxes directly on the peasantry and collection by salaried government officials (a system later adopted by Sir Thomas Munro in Madras). Tipu saw clearly the importance of a diversified, though state-directed, economy and set about replicating British commercial and industrial practices, founding a monopoly trading company that established factories in Muscat and elsewhere, and encouraging sericulture and the domestic sugar industry. Increased trade and greater central state control over revenue in turn allowed for increased investment in the military and military technology. European instructors were employed, military manuals translated and printed, European-style drilling introduced, and a system of feudal levy of troops was replaced by the *rislas* system that reorganized the Mysorean army into standardized units. Tipu also recognized that European technological superiority was largely responsible for French and British successes in India. With this in mind, he invested in iron production, cannon foundries and gun-making, supplying his army with cutting-edge artillery and flintlock muskets every bit as good as those of his British rivals. Mysore under Haidar Ali and Tipu Sultan was not some backward oriental kingdom, but a centralized, modern, expansionist, imperialist state with significant revenue and a well-trained, well-supplied army of nearly 150,000 men (not to mention a further 180,000 militia men). If the

British thought they could merely step into the gap left by a declining Mughal Empire, they were sorely mistaken. Mysore was the most dynamic power in India, and its ruler had vowed to drive the British into the Bay of Bengal.[54]

On the surface, then, the end of the Second Anglo-Mysore War seemed to signal a new balance of power in southern India. For the British the war had been something of a disaster. The British army suffered its worst losses since the seventeenth century, British troops joined the Mysore army in droves, the cities seized from the French were all returned and a vigorous, modernizing, anti-British Indian state had emerged as a serious rival to British interests. Britain's resources of men and money had been perilously overstretched, and her power in India, as elsewhere, exposed. It seemed clear to most observers that further expansion was not in the interests, let alone the reach of the East India Company, and even retaining the territories it held in 1783 might prove a challenge in the years to come. What they could not know, or at least failed to realize, was that 1783 would represent a nadir of British fortunes and a high-point of Mysore's power and influence. Rather than a harbinger of a new Indian order, the Indian theater of the American War would fundamentally undermine and destabilize native resistance to British encroachment. Had the news of peace failed to reach Madras in June of 1783, had the French not been so slow to act, had Tipu not done so much to destabilize his relationships with other princely states, the American War might have spelt the end of British expansion rather than the calm before the storm, the last missed chance to prevent Britain's conquest of India.

8

⇥ ⇤

THE BIRTH OF BRITISH INDIA

Calcutta, you know is on the Hooghly, a branch of the Ganges, and as you enter Garden-reach which extends about nine miles below the town, the most interesting views that can possibly be imagined greet the eye. The banks of the river are as one may say absolutely studded with elegant mansions . . . surrounded by groves and lawns, which descend to the water's edge and present a constant succession of whatever can delight the eye, or bespeak wealth and elegance.

Eliza Fay's first glimpse of British Calcutta presented to the weary traveler, only recently released from her harrowing captivity in Calicut, a refreshing mix of romantic novelty and the familiar patterns of European civilization, a combination of lush, tropical vegetation and British architecture. As the city unfolded along the Hooghly, with neo-classical mansions lining the shore and the "amazing variety of vessels continually passing on its surface," it reminded her of nothing so much as the Thames transported to Asia. "The general aspect of the country is astonishing," she exclaimed. "I never saw a more vivid green than adorns the surrounding fields." The effect was disorientingly enchanting, "a magnificent and beautiful moving picture; at once exhilarating the heart, and charming the senses: for every object of sight is viewed through a medium that heightens its attraction in this brilliant climate."[1]

But despite this seeming idyll, the Calcutta that Eliza Fay entered in 1780 was no less tense and restive than London. France and Britain were at war in India, and everywhere the preparations for the much-feared French attack were being hurriedly completed. Among the soldiers massing in the forts and cantonments in and around Calcutta for the seemingly imminent French invasion was a young Muslim soldier named Dean Mahomet, a man whose life and career would be shaped by the tangled web of European imperialism in India. Dean Mahomet was born at Patna in the state of Bihar in 1759. His family had arrived in the area generations earlier as part of the Muslim service elite of the expanding Mughal Empire. By the time of Mahomet's birth the Mughal Empire's hold over its expansive realm was ebbing. Like so many empires before and after, the Mughals had over-reached, with rampant spending on the imperial army and court slowly eroding Delhi's control over its more distant provinces. One by one, Mughal regional administrators began to usurp de facto control over their provinces, setting themselves up as hereditary rulers under nominal Mughal suzerainty. When the administrator of Bihar declared himself the hereditary Nawab of Bengal and Bihar, Mahomet's forebears quickly shifted their allegiance to the new power on the ground. It was not the last time their loyalties would change as the reality of local power dynamics shifted.[2]

In April 1758, a year before Dean Mahomet's birth, his father made the fateful decision to join the army of the East India Company during a recruiting drive at Patna. The East India Company army, led by Robert Clive, was then engaged in a massive effort to expand it ranks. Before 1750 the Company's military was tiny, as suited what was still ostensibly a commercial organization. But as the Company gained territory and came into conflict with native states and other expansionist European powers, the need for troops grew. When the Seven Years' War burst forth in 1754, India quickly became a theater of conflict, with France and Britain fighting to seize greater control of south-eastern India and Bengal. The Nawab of Bengal and Bihar, Siraj ud-Daulah, allied himself with the French and the combined threat of French and Bengali arms pushed the British to expand their army. With European troops thin on the ground, Clive tapped the existing mercenary market to fill his ranks, with the Bengal army growing to about 18,000 soldiers by 1760.

The Company had a desperate need for manpower. With Britain already at war with France across the globe, the Company's ruthless expansion in Bengal rapidly destabilized local politics. In 1756 the Nawab of Bengal, furious at illegal encroachment by the British, had captured Calcutta, forcing 146 British prisoners into the infamous "Black Hole of Calcutta," where all but twenty-one died in the choking closeness of a 14-foot-by-18-foot room. The nawab's gambit failed. His army was defeated by Robert Clive's Madras army at the battle of Plassey in 1757, and the nawab himself replaced by Mir Jafar, a more pliant British puppet. With victory at Plassey the East India Company began its transformation from commercial enterprise to territorial power.

In the face of these rising tensions, British success in recruiting Indian soldiers at first seems difficult to explain. Why would so many Indian soldiers opt to join the ranks of an aggressively expanding foreign imperial power? India, however, had long been a diverse, pluralistic society. In Mahomet's native Patna, Hindus and Muslims had long coexisted, and when the British arrived in 1650 to trade for saltpeter, indigo, and opium, they were easily accommodated within a multi-ethnic Mughal state. By the time of Clive's recruitment drive a century later, then, the British were simply one of many local power blocs wrestling for a piece of the crumbling Mughal Empire. Furthermore, the Muslim military and service elite, from which Mahomet's family came, had long been separated from the majority of the local populace by religion, language, and customs, leaving them, perhaps, with more fragile loyalties to the state itself. Perhaps most crucially, families such as Mahomet's relied on military service as their main source of income. As the Mughal Empire faded and the nawab's power declined, professional soldiers naturally began to look to other quarters for employment. The newly ascendant East India Company thus presented a welcome outlet for those Indians left exposed by the collapse of native powers. Thousands accepted the offer, and by 1760 up to 15,000 Indians were serving in the Bengal army, with the number growing exponentially thereafter, to 27,000 in 1767 and 52,000 in 1782. When the thousands of artisans, porters, and camp followers who supported and supplied the army—two or three for every soldier—are included, the number of Indians employed by the Company military expands even further.[3]

Coming from an elite local family, Mahomet's father quickly rose through the native ranks, becoming a subdar, the second highest rank an Indian could achieve, before his early death in 1769 in one of the internecine conflicts that plagued the desperate years of famine. Far from encouraging the Bengali economy, after its victory in 1757 the policies of the East India Company exacerbated, and perhaps did much to cause, widespread famine that killed up to 10 million Bengalis by 1772. "A great dearth overspread the country," starting in 1769, forcing two local rajas to neglect their annual tribute to Shitab Rai, the naib diwani (deputy governor) of Bihar. Mahomet's father was sent "to compel them to pay." With the famine getting worse by the day, resistance was inevitable, and Mahomet's "lamented father" fell at Telarha after having arrested one of the recalcitrant rajas. The painful memory of his father's demise remained with him for the rest of his life.[4]

With his father gone and his elder brother (also a soldier in the Company army) claiming most of his inheritance, Mahomet opted to follow the family trade and seek his fortune with the Bengal army. At the age of 10, the resplendent uniforms and noble bearing of the Company's military men dazzled Mahomet, and he quickly attached himself, informally at first, to a teenage officer fresh from Ireland. As Mahomet remembered, "nothing could exceed my ambition of leading a soldier's life: the notion of carrying arms, and living in a camp, could not be easily removed: my mother's fond entreaties were to no avail." Mahomet was determined to spend as much time in military company as possible and shadowed the European officers wherever they went. "Whenever I perceived their route, I instantly followed them; sometimes to the Raja's palace, where I had free access; and sometimes to a fine tennis court, generally frequented by them in the evenings . . . here among other Gentlemen, I one day, discovered Mr. Baker." The teenage Godfrey Baker—a newly minted cadet in the Third European Regiment of the Bengal Army from Cork, Ireland—was little more than a boy himself, but his attachment to the young Mahomet was real. He would remain supportive of Mahomet for the rest of his life.[5]

Mahomet remained a camp follower, unofficially attached to Captain Baker as he and his unit traveled from post to post in eastern India until a colonial revolt halfway around the world transformed his life. The outbreak of war with France and France's Indian allies Mysore and the Maratha Empire after 1778 provided an opportunity for Mahomet to obtain a more official role in the Company's army. The renewal of the global conflict between France and

Britain could hardly have come at a worse time for the East India Company. To the dismay of the directors in London, the profits of the East India Company were being eaten away by private trading and the seemingly endless expenses incurred in governing a rapidly expanding British territory. The continued conquest of land brought the Company into almost unceasing conflict with Indian states and European rivals. In 1775, while fighting was breaking out in North America, the Company's army, led by Alexander Champion and in concert with the allied kingdom of Awadh, was mopping up after a bloody campaign against the Rohillas, the ethnic Pashtun tribesmen who had come to dominate the hill country of northern Uttar Pradesh. That same year the EIC became entangled in a nasty succession dispute in the Maratha Empire that ultimately resulted in open warfare between the Company and the Marathas.

Mahomet could only watch the victories of his comrades from afar. The British position in India had gone from bad to worse, and while Captain Popham marched on Gwalior, Mahomet and his brigade were summoned to Calcutta to defend against a much graver threat. France had declared war on Britain, and although this declaration was ostensibly in support of the American colonies, Company officials were under no illusion that the subcontinent would escape unscathed. Calcutta became a hive of military activity in 1778 as the Company's headquarters prepared for the near certainty of French invasion. For Mahomet, it would not be the last time that the American War altered his fate.

For the East India Company, already financially pinched by rising costs and falling revenues, the news of war in North America was most unwelcome. As the Company became ever more inextricably linked with the world of Indian politics, the need for men and money to protect its fragile foothold on the subcontinent grew in unison. This need became all the more acute when the war with America began to siphon off British manpower, leaving Governor-General Warren Hastings' administration in Calcutta with a limited range of options for addressing its shortfalls. The desperate shortage of European soldiers in the second half of the eighteenth century, especially when combined with the ever-present threat of France and her Indian allies, created a range of economic opportunities for local people like Dean Mahomet and his family. With these new opportunities, however, came dire consequences for Indian society, the eroding of native states and the expansion of an often predatory British patrimony.

Back in the 1750s and 1760s, when Clive had begun the rapid expansion of the East India Company army, native rulers had quickly realized the effectiveness of European style arms, training, and tactics. In order to keep up with the British and French, many Indian princes began forming their own military units along similar lines. Such armies, however, were ruinously expensive to maintain, and so many rulers were forced to rent East India Company troops for a negotiated fee. This had two disastrous consequences for native states. First, the rented troops were usually commanded by European officers whose primary loyalty was to the Company or Britain rather than their temporary employer, a fact that fatally undermined the autonomy of the rulers, who were thus at the mercy of the goodwill of both the Company and the Company's officers. Second, as the British themselves encountered growing fiscal pressure during the American War, they were liable to raise the rates for their troops. Those who could not or would not pay the increased fees were in danger of being replaced by more pliable rulers or having their lands seized by the British. In 1781, Mahomet witnessed this merciless new economic world first-hand.

When France joined America in its war against Britain in 1778, the coffers of the East India Company were already bone dry. The margins had always been tight, but the constant warfare in India, with the Marathas, Mysore, and the Rohillas, only made matters worse. France's declaration of war thus came at the worst possible time for Hastings and the Company. Fighting with France was sure to erupt on the subcontinent, requiring great sums of money to pay for troops and supplies. In desperation, Hastings turned to his allies, to the many nominally independent states that owed the Company an annual tribute of money or manpower. Hastings focused his fundraising efforts on the young Raja of Benares, Chait Singh, even though he was a British ally and already paid an annual rent of £225,000 to the Company. When Singh succeeded to the throne in 1770, Benares had already been under the suzerainty of the British for five years. The province had been given to the Company by Shuja-ud-Daula, the Nawab of Awadh, in exchange for British protection after his defeat by the British at the Battle of Buxar in 1764 and the subsequent Treaty of Allahabad in 1765. While the overlordship of Benares thus passed from the nawab to the British, the rajas of Benares retained considerable independence and the promise of British protection in return for an annual payment. The arrangement would not outlast the American War.

With fears of French aggression inescapable, and with few attractive options for raising the needed funds, in 1778 Hastings demanded a payment of £50,000 from Chait Singh in addition to the usual annual tribute. According to Hastings' new logic, it is "a right inherent in every government to impose such assessments as it judges expedient for the common service and protection of all its subjects; and we are not precluded from it by any agreement subsisting between the Raja and this government." The echoes of the American Revolution are chilling. The raja knew he was in a weak position and so he paid up under protest. Although it was supposed to be a one-time extraordinary contribution, the demand for an extra £50,000 was repeated in 1779 and 1780. In 1779, Singh had the temerity to ask that the payment be the last such charge, but Hastings responded to his perceived impertinence by demanding the entire sum in one lump payment rather than the usual installments. Singh begged for more time, but Hastings was unsympathetic, informing the raja that a late payment would be regarded as a refusal to pay. EIC soldiers were sent into Singh's territory to force the payment, and the cost of the troops was added to the raja's bill. If this treatment were not enough to engender ill will toward the British, in 1780 Hastings added yet another demand. The raja was told that he was to provide the Company with 2,000 cavalry, despite the fact that Benares' treaty with the British stipulated that there was "no obligation on him" to raise such troops.[6]

Once more, Chait Singh complied with Hastings' ever-growing rapacity. However, the message that the troops had indeed been raised and were ready and waiting to receive their orders failed to reach Hastings (or at least that is what the governor-general later claimed), and so Singh was fined £500,000. As Hastings himself admitted, "I was resolved to draw from his guilt the means of relief to the Company's distress . . . In a word, I had resolved to make him pay largely for his pardon, or to exact a severe vengeance for his past delinquency."[7]

In August 1781, Governor-General Warren Hastings marched from Calcutta with two companies of Sepoys to the ancient city of Benares (modern Varanasi) to chastise Chait Singh. Despite his mission, Hastings' arrival on the Ganges met with no resistance. The abject young raja even wrote a pleading letter to Hastings, begging the governor-general to "pity me, I pray you, in remembrance of the services done by my father, and in consideration of my youth and inexperience . . . It depends on you alone to deprive me, or not, of the country of my ancestors—what necessity is there to deal in this way with me, who am ready to devote my life and property to your service."[8]

Chait Singh's pleas fell on deaf, or at least highly unsympathetic, ears and Hastings quickly ordered his arrest. The raja submitted quietly, "without any appearance of opposition." As news of the arrest spread, however, it "roused the indignation" of the soldiers and subjects of Benares, "who were seen in a large body, crossing the river from Ramnagur to the palace, in which he [Chait Singh] was confined." At one o'clock, the artist and traveler William Hodges, who had accompanied Hastings on his march, heard reports that the raja's palace was surrounded. A note had been received from Lieutenant Staulker, who had been left in charge of the small British force guarding the Chait Singh, that "the people began to be troublesome," and that reinforcements were urgently needed. The British leadership had, it transpired, made a disastrous miscalculation. Because they did not expect any opposition to the raja's arrest, and to allay the raja's fear "of any intention to carry the punishment further than was really proposed," the Sepoys had been instructed not to load their weapons, and were not provided with any ammunition. When the raja's men surrounded the palace, the British detachment was thus in grave peril, defenseless, and at the mercy of a hostile crowd.[9]

When news of a potential revolt reached the rest of the British party, Major Popham, who led the British forces at Benares, rushed to the relief of the beleaguered detachment. He was too late. "His utmost exertions enabled them to arrive only in time to be melancholy spectators of this horrid slaughter, without the power of avenging it." The Sepoys guarding Singh were "mostly massacred by this powerful force which rushed onward, like an irresistible torrent, that sweeps all away before it." With the Company's forces cut down nearly to a man, the newly free raja fled with his army to Latifgarh and eventually to the relative safety of the Maratha stronghold at Gwalior, while the now defenseless governor-general was pursued by the raja's avenging army to Chunar, a proverbially impenetrable fort perched on a rocky escarpment 700 feet above the surrounding countryside. Back at Ramangur, British troops under Captain Mayaffre attempted to fight their way out of the town, but being "hemmed in on very side by the narrow streets and winding alleys of the town" and under "the fire of the enemy from all quarters," Mayafrre and 150 of his men were cut down.[10]

Besieged in the fort at Chunar, Hastings quickly organized an offensive against the rebels. Among those sent to relieve the governor-general and suppress the uprising were Captain Baker and Dean Mahomet. The arrival of fresh troops quickly turned the tide. Company troops under Major Popham scored a critical victory at Sacrut before marching on Pateetah, where the crucial engagement took place. Mahomet, who witnessed the battle, had praise for both sides (perhaps a reflection of his hybrid loyalties and affinities):

> They fought on both sides, with great ardor and intrepidity, till victory perplexed with doubt, waited the arrivals of Lieutenants Fallow [Fallon] and Berrille [Birrell], whose gallant conduct with the united bravery of their countrymen, preponderating in the scale of her unbiased judgment, induced the Goddess to bestow on them her unfading laurels, as the reward for their exertions.

It was, Mahomet lamented, "a dreadful carnage of killed and wounded on each part." The raja's army fled the field in defeat and the mopping up began.[11]

This brief and bloody conflict was just one theater of the wider war sweeping the world in the 1770s and 1780s, tied with unseen tendrils to the battlefields of North America. Chait Singh, whose arrest touched off the fighting, however, was no ally of America, no friend of France. He was in fact a British ally, signatory to a treaty with the East India Company. The Raja of Benares and his subjects were not victims of open war, but a sacrifice to Britain's bottomless need for funds. The economic costs of a world war spared no one.

The repercussions of Chait Singh's rebellion were not limited to Benares alone, instead spreading to undermine the independent foundations of other Indian states. The state of Oudh, the center of a fabulously rich and sophisticated culture emanating from its capital at Lucknow, widely considered to be the most mesmerizingly beautiful city in India, occupied a crucial position between British Bengal and the domains of the Mughals and Marathas. As such, it had long been a key part of Hastings' plans to create a buffer zone between Company possessions and those of their powerful Indian rivals. Indeed, the Nawab of Oudh had been the overlord of the rajas of Benares until 1775, when the new nawab, Asaf-ud-Daula, under pressure from Hastings, agreed to cede sovereignty over the territory to the British. A decade earlier, after defeat by the British at the Battle of Buxar in 1764, Shuja-ud-Daual, the previous Nawab of Oudh, had agreed to a treaty of alliance with the British that stipulated that Oudh would pay a regular fee for the maintenance of troops to support a defensive alliance with the East India Company. Despite the great wealth of Oudh, much of the new nawab's inheritance, in both land and revenue, had already been distributed to officials and retainers as grants or *Jaghires* before he came to the throne. Like many Indian rulers before and since, Asaf-ud-Daula struggled under the weight of his treaty obligations with the British and quickly racked up a massive debt of over £600,000. In order to pay his debts to the British, the nawab was forced to borrow a substantial sum of money from his mother and grandmother, the begums of Oudh, in return for lands worth far more than the loan itself, lands that were in turn seized by the British.[12]

When Chait Singh rebelled in the face of his arrest, Asaf-ud-Daula stood by his British alliance, but the begums were implicated in the rebellion and the lands granted the begums by the nawab were seized by the British as the price of their treachery. Much of Oudh's wealth had passed to the begums when the nawab's father died, contrary to Islamic law, and so, instead of opposing Hastings' seizure of the begums' fortune, Asaf-ud-Daula actually encouraged it. Still, when combined with the already onerous treaty of alliance, granting further revenue to the East India Company only served to undermine the sovereignty of Oudh, and placed it in an even more subordinate position. When Asaf-ud-Daula died in 1797, his adopted son was raised to the throne with British support, only to be deposed by the British a year later and replaced by his brother, Sadaat Ali Khan, who in turn granted the Company fully half of the territory of Oudh.[13]

The rebellion of Benares in 1781 bears a striking resemblance to the revolt of the American colonies in 1775. In both situations, an overstretched British Empire placed increasingly stringent economic demands on its peripheral subjects, pleading the necessity of defending its far-flung possessions against French incursions. In Benares as in America, it was popular resistance that lit the fuse of conflict, a subaltern insurrection against the representatives of empire. But for Benares, the rebellion was short-lived, the raja's army quickly crushed by the superior numbers of the East India Company. Even so, the population of Benares would continue to resist, refusing to pay their customary taxes and attacking collectors of the revenue. Captain Baker and Dean Mahomet were sent with their battalion to put an end to this resistance, and spent months rooting out peasant rebels. Armed only with bows and arrows and home-made long-guns, the locals stood no chance and "the refractory were awed into submission by the terror of our arms." Mahomet did his duty, but he had mixed feelings about his role in the suppression of Benares, writing in a verse lament:

> Alas! Destructive war with ruthless hand,
> Unbinds each fond connection, tender tie,
> And tears from friendship's bosom all that's dear,
> Spreading dire carnage thro' the peopled globe;
> Whilst fearless innocence, and trembling guilt,
> In one wide waste, are suddenly involv'd.
> War wakes the lover's, friend's and orphan's sigh,
> And on empurpled wings bears death along,
> With haggard terror, and with wild dismay,
> And desolation in savage train:
> From slow-consuming time, his lazy scythe,
> With ruffian violence is torn away,
> To sweep, at once, whole Empires to the grave.[14]

And yet, Dean Mahomet was not the only one to have deep misgivings about the actions of Warren Hastings and the East India Company during the years of war. Indeed, there were deep divisions among British authorities in both Calcutta and London over the appropriate role of the East India Company in the affairs of the subcontinent, and it was this divide that was the underlying factor in the fall of Warren Hastings and the authoritarian transformation of British India.[15]

Born to a family of Oxfordshire ministers in 1732, Hastings had arrived in a very different Bengal as a writer for the East India Company in September of 1750. By 1770 Hastings had risen to become a member of the Madras council before being promoted to Governor of Bengal in 1772. By the time of his appointment as governor, the British government had grown weary of the constant mismanagement of British Bengal. In his memorable characterization, Edmund Burke castigated Company rule in Bengal as "animated with all the avarice of age, and all the impetuosity of youth, they roll in one after another; wave upon wave; and there is nothing before the eyes of the natives but an endless, hopeless, prospect of new flights of birds of prey and passage, with appetites continually renewing for a food that is continually wasting." To many eyes, the problem was that what had previously been, at least outwardly, a commercial settlement focused on trade, was by 1770 a British territorial state, but one run by an anti-quated system designed for regulating a solely commercial enterprise. Company officials arrived with pecuniary, mercantile motivations rather than administrative ambitions. Equally vexing was that even in such a rich territory—and all agreed that Bengal had vast potential revenues—the method of revenue extraction was failing to meet the costs of administering such a large territory.[16]

Everyone seemed to agree that the problem with British India was the struc-ture of, and concomitant mismanagement by, the East India Company. What exactly should be done to remedy the situation was, however, a matter of intense debate. Many, like Lord Clive, who had personally done so much to add terri-tory to the Company's patrimony, thought the scope of British possessions in India required "the nation's assistance," being "too extensive for a mercantile company." Others, while conceding the need for reforms, feared that further entanglements in India would drain the resources of Britain, and as the conflict with the American colonies picked up steam, such concerns became more pressing and more vocal. With all of this in mind, Parliament passed the East India Regulating Act in 1773, restructuring the Company's government in India by creating a new executive body, the supreme council, consisting of five members and led by Hastings as the first governor-general. To ensure that justice was properly maintained, a supreme court consisting of royally appointed judges was likewise established.[17]

Hastings had taken up the mantle of governorship with a keen sense of the immense potential of Bengal to provide revenue for Britain and a steely deter-mination to make the province pay. When he was appointed governor-general, Hastings realized that Bengal—with its 20 million inhabitants, revenue equal to fully a quarter of Britain's, and exports valued at upwards of £1 million—was a potential gold mine. He had instructions to help the region's economy recover from the 1770 famine and to take a more direct role in the collection of tax revenue. Prior to his arrival, taxes had been collected through quotas levied on local hereditary landholders known as *zamindars*. The quota each zamindar was obligated to pay was supposed to be based on the value of cultivation of peasant lands in his possession. Hastings thought these customary tax obligations were inefficient and considered zamindars to be hereditary government officials, tax collectors, rather than landholders with long-held rights and obligations. He thus opened tax collection to the highest bidder, thinking this tax-farming system would maximize revenues.[18]

Though he reformed the revenue system and pushed for greater supervision of tax collection, Hastings sought to do so in a way that maintained Indian officials and Indian forms of administration and government. He had little faith in the ability or probity of European officials, and by 1781, he had replaced most British "collectors" with Indian supervisors of tax collection. Overall, Hastings was concerned to implement what he saw as needed reforms, but in ways that would not disrupt Indian tradition nor alienate Britain's new Indian subjects. In the words of one historian,

> He believed that Bengal must be governed in ways to which its people were presumed to be accustomed. Indian methods of government and Indian law must be preserved. The British should aim "to rule this people with ease and moderation according to their own ideas, manners, and prejudices" (Gleig, 1.404). He considered that Hinduism and Hindu and Islamic law were in certain respects admirable in themselves as well as being suited to the needs of the population who had come under British rule. He encouraged British officials to learn languages, make studies, and translate texts. While he believed that there could be no limitations on the company's sovereignty and that no Indian authority could be allowed to compete with it, he felt that the exercise of the powers of government under British direction should for the most part be left in Indian hands. He had no high opinion of the capacity or the disinterestedness of the great bulk of the company's British servants.[19]

With tax income from land thus becoming such a vital component of the Company's revenue, Hastings was convinced that concentrating solely on commercial activities was counterproductive. Yet, with resources already stretched near to breaking point, he was adamant that further territorial acquisitions were undesirable and even dangerous. He proposed to follow a middle path between further conquest and pure commercialism; he would seek alliances with neighboring native states with an eye to creating a "ring fence" of allies to protect British Bengal, but at the same time resolved not to be drawn into Indian affairs. It would be "a general system . . . to extend the influence of the British nation to every part of India not too remote from their possessions, without enlarging the circle of their defence or involving them in hazardous or indefinite engagements and to accept the allegiance of such of our neighbours as shall sue to be enlisted among the friends and allies of the King of Great Britain." Hastings therefore created buffer zones around British interests—Arcot, the Carnatic, and eventually Hyderabad, around Madras, Oudh and Benares around Bengal—by entering into alliances with pliant native powers, stationing British troops in these territories, and billing their rulers for the cost of maintaining these defenses. In this way, the rich territory of Bengal could be mined for its wealth, without danger to British possessions or the costs of further warfare.[20]

Deposing Chait Singh was thus the logical result of a policy that sought Indian alliances that would pay their own way. Not only had Benares refused to pay the fees Hastings felt he urgently required in the context of war, and that he felt Benares could readily afford, but the state had gone so far as to rebel, threatening the fragile buffer zone around Bengal. Such behavior could not be tolerated from allies, and an example had to be made. What is more, Hastings could convince himself that a policy of billing allies for troops and seizing their lands when they failed or refused to pay, was consistent with his desire to retain Indian forms of government and administration. When Mir Jafar had been forced to accept financial and military obligations upon his accession as Nawab of Bengal in 1757, and when Chait Singh was made to do the same in 1775, British leaders were hardly reinventing the wheel. Such obligations had long been a part of the Mughal Empire's fragile federation, and would continue to be pursued by other native rulers. For instance, the cause of the war between the Marathas and Mysore, which did so much to drive a wedge between the two foremost Indian states and to undermine Tipu Sultan's ability to defeat the

British, was largely a matter of a disagreement between Tipu and the Marathas over Mysore's right to extract tribute and military obligations from a zamindar on the borderlands between the two powers.

Indeed, Hastings' governorship can be seen as both the apogee of the Orientalist approach to Company rule, and part of a wider trend in governance among post-Mughal states more broadly. Within India, and indeed beyond, indigenous *and* European imperial states were moving along a similar trajectory, emphasizing centralization, the displacement of local aristocracies, the development of a substantial tax base, and the organization of the state for the purposes of war. The strategies employed in developing these fiscal-military states, and the ideologies employed to legitimate them, were remarkably similar. For example, both Haidar Ali of Mysore and Warren Hastings attempted to secure their landed revenue base by removing hereditary rights from local elites, and in both cases this was justified through appeals to Mughal precedent, which considered local landholders to be zamindars, with no permanent right to the revenue from their lands. Thus in Mysore and Bengal, revenue reforms designed to support a centralizing fiscal-military regime were based on existing forms of governance and couched in terms of continuity with the Mughal past.[21]

For Hastings, relying on Mughal precedent made sense. He genuinely admired Indian history and culture, and firmly believed that indigenous forms of administration were best suited for governing India. What is more, he understood that if a tiny number of British officials were to rule a large Indian population, the manner of British governance had to be made acceptable to the people. He thus made attempts to cultivate both Hindu and Muslim support by presenting his regime as "neo-Brahmanical and neo-Mughal." To this end, Hastings sponsored the codification and translation of Hindu and Muslim legal codes as a means of restoring indigenous forms of justice, and supported efforts by scholars such as William Jones to translate and publish Indian works of history, literature, and religion that stressed the inherent similarity and compatibility of Hinduism and Islam and their commonalities with Western culture and religion. Though such measures were certainly useful instrumentally as a means of shoring up support for British rule, Hastings, William Jones and others of this circle also hoped to present Indian culture and history to Europe in a positive light as a way of undermining the wrong-headed prejudice they felt was undermining efficacious relations between the two. As one historian has suggested, for Hastings, "Knowledge of Asian languages was not simply a tool for ruling in Asia; it created awareness of rich cultures of which British people were ignorant and inclined to be contemptuous. Such awareness would be, he was later to write, the means of a 'reconciliation' of 'the people of England to the natives of Hindostan'."[22]

Others strongly disagreed with Hastings' reforms and tactics, and were not convinced that a trading company was designed to rule such a large and populous territory. At the same time, many in Britain hoped to prevent the machinations of the Company from drawing the British state too deeply into Indian affairs, with its attendant costs. Instead, they advocated for a policy in which the EIC would concentrate on commerce, keeping itself free from the costly and byzantine entanglements of the subcontinent. Philip Francis, Hastings' most vociferous opponent in India, "argued that the overriding policy should be peace, that Britain should not seek territorial extensions, nor make entangling alliances with Indian princes . . . that the company ought to be confined purely to trade and have no part in the government of India: 'a trading company is unqualified for sovereignty.'" Hastings' Orientalist regime was becoming increasingly interventionist, consistently drawing the British into the affairs of their neighbors. It was on these grounds that Francis had attacked Hastings' conduct in the Rohilla War shortly after his arrival in Calcutta, and it was on these grounds that he had opposed the expansion of the Maratha War, leading to the duel with the governor-general. The "rebellion" of Chait Singh was merely another instance of Hastings' expansionist ambitions, and, in Francis's eyes, another example of the dangers of unnecessary entanglements in India affairs.[23]

It seemed clear to many that Hastings had only proceeded against the Raja of Benares after the departure of his most virulent critic. Philip Francis had left for London in November 1780, leaving Hastings with a free hand for the first time since 1774. In a letter to a friend in England, Hastings crowed about his new, unchallenged position. "Mr. Francis has announced his intention to leave us. His departure may be considered as the close of one complete period of my political life and the beginning of a new one . . . I shall have no competitor to oppose my designs, to encourage disobedience to my authority, to excite and foment popular odium against me. In a word, I shall have power, and I will employ it." And employ it he did, in Benares, Gwalior, Malabar, and the Carnatic, but all the while, back in London, his enemies had been busy sharpening their knives.[24]

With the British defeat at Yorktown in 1781, and the dawning realization that Britain's interests in America were drawing to an ignominious end, attention in London began to shift toward Indian affairs. Two select committees were organized by Parliament to investigate the failures of the East India Company and its officials. Hastings' revenue reforms had been largely a failure. Replacing the zamindars with tax-farmers had succeeded in alienating almost everyone without significantly increasing revenues. The landholding class resented being denied their traditional role, the exactions were considered unduly harsh by the peasant cultivators of Bengal, while quotas remained unmet due to overbidding and overestimation of the value of land. With revenue stagnating, Hastings was forced to turn to unpopular indirect taxes on goods such as salt and opium. By 1784, the economy of Bengal was still not placed on a proper footing, while costs continued to skyrocket and rural resentment grew apace. Likewise, despite a strong desire to remain separate from internal Indian politics and warfare, Hastings' vaunted ring fence had only served to draw the Company into the very wars it was designed to prevent, with the Company forced to fight against the Marathas, Benares, and Mysore, all while tangling with its traditional French foe. Peace with the Marathas had come in 1782 and with Mysore and France in 1784—but at a cost. Men, money, and prestige had all been sacrificed, seemingly to no avail. Britain's enemies in India faced peace with confidence while the Company could only lick its wounds.

The loss of the American colonies also provided an object lesson of the dangers of the expansion of overseas landed empires. Indeed, while the war was still raging, in the somber panic after the defeat of British forces at Saratoga, Secretary of the Treasury John Robinson argued that, despite the "absurdity" of Company rule in India, the rebellion of the American colonies aptly demonstrated the danger of the British state assuming direct control of far-flung imperial possessions. The American rebellion was rapidly draining British coffers and British manpower, as had the costs of defending the colonies during the Seven Years' War, costs that had done so much to cause the revolt in the first place. Replacing Company rule with direct government control would only serve to create the very same conditions that were at that very moment threatening to beggar the nation. Direct rule would simply set the stage for further colonial unrest. Charles James Fox concurred (with the nature of the problem if not the proper solution), asking Lord North, then prime minister, whether he was content with losing the American colonies alone, or if he "wished to ruin the company's possessions in India" as well.[25]

At the same time, the fact that the American War had spread so quickly and violently to the subcontinent was ample testimony of the failures of Hastings' strategy to keep the Company unencumbered with Indian warfare. In the perspective of many in London and Calcutta, Company rule had led to war with European and Indian powers and would surely continue to do so, but direct government administration would simply lead to a second colonial revolution in British India. If not for the American Revolution, then, the British government might well have embarked on a total reform of Indian administration, removing Company sovereignty for once and for all, and replacing it with direct state rule. Instead, a middle path was attempted.[26]

In 1781 Cornwallis surrendered at Yorktown, making the loss of America all but certain and creating new pressure to finally solve Britain's India problem. With the smell of defeat in the air, Lord North's ministry rapidly unraveled. America might be beyond hope, but the war was still dragging on, and the loss of India on top of America was still a terrifying possibility. So, with all of the costs and consequences of the American Revolution stingingly in mind, attention turned more fully to India. A number of reform proposals were put forth, all designed to alter the East India Company and its Indian possessions in such a way as to prevent a second imperial revolution from further splintering the British world. Two parliamentary committees were formed: a Select Committee led by Edmund Burke, which delved once more into the alleged corruption and abuse of Company officials; and a Secret Committee led by Henry Dundas and John Robinson ostensibly tasked with investigating the causes of the wars with Mysore. Both committees made clear the urgent need for drastic reform, and when William Pitt the Younger came to power as prime minister in December 1783, he introduced a compromise reform bill based on those presented by Fox and Dundas.

Pitt's India Act of 1784 sought to address the major flaws that persisted in Company administration of its Indian possessions. First, in order to eliminate the dangerous independence of the Company and prevent further corruption and abuse, the Act created a "Board of Control" located in London that would oversee Company affairs in all their forms, civil, military, and financial. Unlike the Company's Board of Directors, the new Board of Control would replace stock-holding directors with members of the ruling government ministry, with the Secretary of State presiding as president of the new body. In view of fractious infighting between members of the supreme council in Calcutta, the number of its members was cut from five to three, and the power of the governor-general to act independently, especially in times of war, was greatly increased. The independence of the governors of Bombay and Madras, a freedom that had in large part caused the wars with the Marathas and Mysore, was to be eliminated as well. The new, more powerful governor-general, however, was henceforth to receive his appointment directly from the crown. The aim of these reforms was clear. The East India Company was still to govern in India, but it was to do so as an arm or agency of the British state.[27]

It was not enough merely to reform the Company, however. As governor-general, Hastings was clearly in the crosshairs. For his perceived failures to reform revenue collection and avoid costly wars, Hastings would certainly be recalled from his post, but this was not enough for some. Hastings had made enemies in Calcutta and these foes had returned to England to combine with such enemies of the Company and its governor-general as Edmund Burke, Richard Brinsley Sheridan, and Charles James Fox. For Burke and his allies, Company rule in India was nothing less than a stain on Britain's national character, and India a country despoiled and exploited by rapacious, corrupt, and violent Company officials. Hastings was held to be responsible for this state of affairs, as well as for the costly expansion of warfare in India at the very moment when British resources were needed elsewhere. They were convinced the Hastings' policies in India had been not merely incompetent or misguided, but criminal, and they set about advocating for impeachment.

Five main charges were leveled against Hastings and presented to the House of Commons in 1787. Hastings was charged with pursuing a war with the Rohillas for personal gain, with forcing the Raja of Benares to make military contributions beyond those stipulated by treaty, with exploiting the begums of Oudh, with personally accepting gifts beyond the limits allowed for Company officials, and with favoring friends with advantageous contracts. The Rohilla charge was dismissed by the House of Commons, but the others were accepted, and the trial of Warren Hastings began in the House of Lords in 1788.

In February 1788, Edmund Burke addressed the members of the House of Lords assembled in Westminster Hall with the full force of his considerable rhetorical power, castigating Hastings and imploring the Lords to right a historical wrong.

> I impeach . . . Warren Hastings, in the name of our Holy Religion, which he has disgraced, – I impeach him in the name of the English Constitution, which he has violated and broken, – I impeach him in the name of Indian Millions, who he has sacrificed to injustice, – I impeach him in the name, and by the best rights of human nature, which he has stabbed to the heart. And I conjure this High and Sacred Court to let not these pleadings be heard in vain![28]

The trial, opened by Burke's thunderous condemnation, was a spectacle of histrionic oratory, vicious invective, and a stubborn refusal to conciliate or bend. Day after day, year after year, for nearly seven years, Burke and Sheridan and Fox lashed Hastings with evidence of his perfidious incompetence while crowds of curious onlookers crowded the galleries to witness what was surely to be the trial of the century. Through it all, Hastings remained utterly steadfast in his conviction that he was not only innocent of the charges arrayed against him, but that he deserved the grateful admiration of the government and the nation for his role in India. He was certain that he acted honorably—telling the assemblage, "My Lords, I do most solemnly declare that I acted to the best of my judgment, paying due regard on the one hand to the laws of justice, and on the other to the interest of my employer"—but also that he had saved India for the Company and country.

> To the Commons of England, in whose name I am arraigned for desolating the provinces of their dominion in India, I dare to reply, that they are . . . the most flourishing of all the state in India. It was I who made them so. The valor of others acquired—I enlarged and gave shape and consistency to—the

dominion which you hold there. I preserved it . . . I gave all; and you have rewarded me with confiscation, disgrace, and a life of impeachment.

Throughout the tiresome ordeal, he never wavered in his belief that, in the end, the trial, for all its drama, would prove him right. As he told a friend back in India, "you may rest assured that the worst shall affect me no more than the spray of the wave, or the Beating of the Tempest, can injure the Plumage of an Albatross in the wide Ocean."[29]

When the verdict was read in 1795, after years of public humiliation, Hastings was vindicated. The American War had ushered in a "new climate of opinion of a more assertive nationalism" that, in the years since the trial commenced, had been solidified by the horrors of the French Revolution. The result was a shift in attitudes toward empire. No longer was Hastings seen as the personification of the shame and tragedy of empire, but as the defender and savior of a crucial aspect of British greatness. The conservative, authoritarian turn, which had done so much to squelch British liberties at home, now gave a new shine to empire. Indeed, at his trial Hastings had done his best to paint himself as the defender of British interests in an age of imperial contestation, arguing that rather than think of his own fortune or prospects, he had been "too intent upon the means to be employed for preserving India to Great Britain, from the hour in which I was informed that France meant to strain every nerve to dispute that empire with us." Hastings was convinced of the merits of his behavior, and in the climate of nationalism and imperial expansion, he succeeded in convincing the public and, crucially, the House of Lords. He was found not guilty of all charges.[30]

While Hastings sweated in the dock in London, his replacement as governor-general, Lord Cornwallis, made his way to Calcutta. Charles Cornwallis, 2nd Earl Cornwallis, might seem a curious choice to spearhead the new, reformed government of British India. He was, after all, the commander whose surrender at Yorktown in 1781 did so much to change the tide of the American Revolution in the favor of the rebellious colonies. Paroled by the triumphant Americans, he had shamefacedly returned to England in the company of Benedict Arnold in 1782, but despite widespread critique, Cornwallis crucially retained the confidence of the king and many of his ministers. In 1786, after serving as an ambassador to the court of Frederick the Great in Prussia, and a series of protracted negotiations about the nature of the post, Cornwallis was appointed governor-general and commander-in-chief of British forces in India. He arrived in Calcutta in February of 1786, with a mandate to reorder, reform, and remake Britain's growing possessions in India.

The change engendered by the transition from Hastings to Cornwallis was momentous. Pitt's India Act had given the new governor-general more absolute, centralized powers in India, and Cornwallis was not shy in using them to correct the abuses he perceived in Hastings' system. As we have seen, Hastings had sought to organize British rule along lines similar to indigenous modes of governance, focusing on continuities with the now faded Mughal system in direct parallel with the other successor states that emerged over the eighteenth century. His concentration on greater centralization and the creation of a fiscal-military state based on revenue extraction through a reformed tax-farming system echoed Mughal policy and reforms instituted by Mysore, the Marathas, and other expansionist native states. His use of alliances and a system of clientage resting on military obligations and fees to expand British influence and increase military power was likewise consistent with indigenous political and fiscal practices. In the realm of law and justice, Hastings had encouraged the continued use of various strands of local Hindu and Muslim law, and even clashed with Chief Justice Impey over the expansion of the jurisdiction of English-inflected courts.

To many, perhaps most in Britain, Cornwallis among them, Hastings' Orientalist regime had proved an abject failure. When Cornwallis arrived in India in 1786, the East India Company was mired in a post-war economic crisis. The revenue of the Company was still failing to meet its costs, corruption and incompetence seemed to invade every corner and crevice of Company administration, and Britain's enemies in India seemed to be worryingly in the ascendant, poised to strike at vulnerable, mismanaged Company territories. The American War had been costly for the East India Company, requiring a massive outlay of capital to defend its interests at the very moment when global warfare disrupted the overseas commerce that was the foundation of its wealth. The British government and Company officials in London placed most of the blame for the poor state of the Company's finances squarely on the shoulders of Warren Hastings, and the corrupt, venal incompetence of his administration in India. Edmund Burke and other critics believed that empire imparted a moral responsibility to govern for the benefit of both Indians and Britain. Hastings' actions and tactics during the war, they argued, had breached this compact between governors and governed, alienating the Indian population in the same way British colonial officials in America had alienated the colonial population in the lead-up to the American Revolution. If British India were to avoid a similar revolutionary fate, the Company administration would have to be reformed, corruption eliminated, abuses weeded out. Though he had failed as a military commander, Cornwallis was well-suited to spearhead the reform of British India. Honest, upright, and rigidly moral, Cornwallis shared Burke's commitment to the overhaul of colonial government. To ensure the support of the Indian population, Cornwallis's reformed government would target corruption and abuses, but would also seek to establish a loyal class of Indian property owners with fixed interests in the country by transforming the institutional basis of British colonial rule.[31]

There were other lessons to be taken from the American Revolution as well. In the years since settlement in colonial America, British settlers had slowly established a Creole political class with its own divergent American interests. As Americans came to identify more with the interests of the colonies than with the wider interests of Britain and the British Empire, conflict and revolution were almost inevitable. Cornwallis, who had seen the disastrous consequences of American separatism first-hand, feared that British India was well on its way to repeating the mistakes of British America. To prevent the growth of a distinct British political class in India, Cornwallis passed measures intended to divide British officials from India and Indians. Outside of Calcutta, Company officials were forbidden to purchase property. To prevent the intermarriage common in eighteenth-century India—and the local ties it inevitably created—Cornwallis passed laws barring Indian women from Company society, and limiting the employment options for mixed-race children in both the military and civil service. By 1790, native Indians were forbidden from holding offices worth more than £500 per year, and Sepoys were excluded from the ranks of commissioned officers. By 1791, it was decided that "no person, the son of a Native Indian shall . . . be appointed by this Court to Employment in the Civil,

Military or Marine Service of the Company." Eventually, in 1795, all Company officials were required to have proof of two European parents to be eligible for office.[32]

The effects of this attempt to avoid the mistakes that had doomed British America were drastic and long-lasting. From the 1780s, once-fluid ethnic boundaries became more and more rigid as the divide between British and Indians grew to become an impenetrable barrier. As the means of rule changed and British rulers and Indian subjects diverged, British India ceased to be merely one of a number of Mughal successor states modeled on Mughal precedents and emerged for the first time as a foreign imperial occupation with laws and institutions based not on indigenous forms and practices, but on explicitly European models. The American War, in many ways, signaled the birth of the "British Empire" in India.

Cornwallis thus gradually began to overhaul Hastings' system, replacing a hybridized indigenous Indian continuity with a Europeanized colonial state. Before Cornwallis arrived, Company officials had been allowed, at least tacitly, to combine their official responsibilities as Company agent with private trading for personal enrichment. This allowed the Company to pay its employees very little, but also encouraged corruption and inattention, and beggared both the Company and communities as wealth was siphoned into private hands. The private fortunes that could be made were immense, and back in Britain, these wealthy "nabobs" were viewed with a combination of fear and disgust. With money plundered from the Orient, it was believed, the nabobs could indulge their dubious tastes, and use their capital to purchase power and influence in a Britain where both were readily for sale. Hastings himself had acquired a massive fortune from his time in India, and this ill-gotten wealth was one of the targets of his impeachment.

To ensure that all income from trade was flowing into the Company's coffers, and to prevent corruption among its officials, Cornwallis banned private trading, compensating Company officials with higher wages to offset the loss. Cornwallis himself led the way, encouraging conscientious officials through the example of his own scrupulous and principled behavior, studiously refusing the customary gifts of Indian diplomacy. Though his refusal to play by the traditional rules of indigenous statecraft annoyed native rulers, it largely seems to have worked as a means of rooting out graft. Though corruption and incompetence still plagued Company rule, the sort of open fraud that angered Indians and disgusted Britons was becoming the exception rather than the rule. The replacement of rapacious officials with upright administrators did much to secure the trust of the governed, or at least to begin the process of eroding decades of mistrust, but it had more sinister consequences as well. For the young men who came out to govern British India, the ability to make a life-changing sum of money relatively quickly was one of the foremost induce-ments to leave behind their native shores for a dangerous career in Asia. With private trading and the acceptance of large gifts now off limits, these ambitious Company officials had to find new ways of making their India experience pay off. For many, political or military preferment replaced money-making as the primary mode of social advancement.

The best way to ensure that one's time in India helped one ascend the ladder of office, then, was to win a successful campaign against foreign powers or to secure a favorable treaty with an Indian ally. Careful management of existing peace and prosperity would hardly make people back in Britain stand up and take notice, but adding to British patrimony or prestige could secure favor and honors, whatever the anti-imperial rhetoric might suggest. The result was that despite near constant and unanimous repudiation of further territorial conquest by government and Company officials in Britain, a succession of senior officials in India actively pursued conflict and conquest in the years following the American War. When the Marquis of Wellesley, the older brother of the more famous Duke of Wellington, arrived as governor-general in 1798, for instance, he did so with a keen desire to secure the political advancement he had so far conspicuously failed to secure in Britain. Thus, despite instructions not to engage in war with other Indian powers, and his own later claim that he arrived with no such ambition, he quickly seized on a convenient pretext to invade Mysore. Cut off from the spoils of private trade, officials now had to turn to the spoils of war and politics.

In his reformist search for Company fiscal stability, Cornwallis also remade the revenue system instituted under his predecessor. Hastings' use of tax-farmers, though in line with developments in other Indian states, had proved highly unsuccessful, both in raising more revenue for the Company and in winning the hearts and minds of the Company's subjects. The use of tax-farmers not only failed to stimulate local economic growth, but also led to greater financial burdens being passed on to the peasantry, who occasionally rose up in opposition. The zamindars, denied their hereditary rights to their lands, were likewise alienated by Hastings' system. Cornwallis's solution to this problem was to create what was afterwards known as the Permanent Settlement, which granted the zamindars hereditary rights to their former lands in perpetuity in return for a fixed annual sum. This system would remain the basis of the British land-revenue system in India until the mid-nineteenth century.

The result was a drastic transformation, an authoritarian revolution, in the nature of British governance in India. Where once local rulers had possessed considerable autonomy and room to negotiate, from the 1780s, India became more thickly, more intensely governed. As late as the 1770s, only one-fifth of the East India Company's 430 civil officers had resided outside of the three capitals of Calcutta, Bombay, and Madras. By the end of the century, fully one-half of the Company's 600 officials were spread throughout the countryside, operating as tax collectors, diplomats, and judges. And while the Permanent Settlement did ensure regular income for the East India Company, it also set a permanent ceiling on the revenue the Company could extract from its lands, limiting the financial benefits of established territories and necessitating the conquest of new territory to augment the dwindling returns. For the Indian landowners, the new settlement also eliminated the previous, more flexible system that had allowed tax rates to be adjusted to reflect local conditions and temporary crises. The zamindars were no less likely to squeeze peasant cultivators for greater and greater sums than before, and in addition the peasantry now had to face a new entrenched class opposed to further reform. A new social rift was opening with the Permanent Settlement, one that "inaugurated a clear break with the past." In the end, both landlords and the peasantry, who bore the brunt of the new financial requirements, were dissatisfied with the new revenue system.[33]

Under Hastings, the judicial system had proceeded largely along Indian lines, with local law stressed, and many native inhabitants occupying places in the legal system. To many British officials and observers, the result was a confused mess. The tangle of various strands of Hindu and Muslim law, and the reliance on Indian interpreters to parse the many legal sources used, made it difficult for British magistrates and officials to be sure that the law was fairly and consistently enforced. Under Cornwallis, with the help of such officials as Sir William Jones, a polymath magistrate and a brilliant, pioneering linguist, Hindu and Muslim law were codified and translated, allowing British magistrates and advocates to take greater control of the legal process. Along these same lines, native Indians were removed from senior judicial and administrative positions and replaced by Europeans. In Cornwallis's opinion, Indians were inferior, and could not be trusted to be honest or competent. "As on account of their colour & extraction," Cornwallis reasoned, "they are considered in this country as inferior to Europeans, I am of opinion that those of them who possess the best abilities could not command that authority and respect which is necessary in the due discharge of the duty of an officer." From 1791, therefore, Cornwallis mandated that "no person, the son of a Native Indian, shall henceforward be appointed by this Court to Employment in the Civil, Military, or Marine Service of the Company." As such, central and local judicial powers were removed from the hands of Indians, and judicial power granted to Company revenue collectors and a new system of circuit courts.[34]

The effects of this new authoritarian "Cornwallis Code" were drastic. For the first time, official British policy enshrined race or ethnicity as a primary consideration in the appointment of administrative officials. The codification of Hindu and Muslim law, though done with real care and intellectual rigor by William Jones and his colleagues, could not help but alter and interpret Indian law in British ways. The result was what one historian has called an "unreal guide to current usage in evolving legal traditions" and a hybrid Anglo-Indian law that would largely remain in force until the present day. The Anglicizing of Indian law, however, did allow some abuses, which had been overlooked or excused because they were thought to be legitimate under Indian law, to be addressed and reformed. Of greatest import was new legislation, Cornwallis' "Proclamation against the Slave Trade," designed to outlaw child slavery and the slave trade, which had been previously allowed as consistent with native law.[35]

On the whole, the reforms instituted by Cornwallis reflected the conservative, authoritarian reaction that swept the British world as a result of the American War. In the face of dwindling coffers, the revenue of the Company and of British India were to be placed on more sound footing by weeding out corruption, eliminating private trading, and reforming the land-revenue system. In the face of global competition with European powers and the threat of regional rebellions on the model of America, the administration of India was remade, emphasizing the centralization of power in the hands of Calcutta, ensuring government oversight from Britain, and replacing native officials with European administrators. As centralization and Europeanization replaced a more diffuse, syncretic system, squeezing out native peoples and practices, British India began to move ineluctably from a loose trading federation to an authoritarian administrative unit of the British crown. According to one veteran of colonial administration:

> The fundamental point necessary to be established and which ought to precede all others is the supremacy of Government; or in other words that no persons excepting its delegates should be permitted to exercise any act of authority, which properly and exclusively belongs to the controlling power; the zamindars should of course be compelled either immediately or gradually to disband the bodies of armed followers which they retain that the sword may exclusively be held by the company.[36]

The American Revolution had spurred Britain to rethink the nature and aims of imperial governance, ensuring that a rebellion in one corner of the world would not bring the entire system to its knees. For Hastings, the goals of Company rule were to create a system that maintained British control, but did so in a way that was consistent with Indian history and amenable to Indian sensibilities, "to rule this people with ease and moderation according to their own ideas, manners, and prejudices." Power was to reside ultimately in British hands, but the exercise of governance was left to the Indian people, on whose behalf the government was assumed to operate. For Cornwallis, the Company's Indian possessions were first and foremost a resource to be used by and for the British. As such, the priorities of his administration were, in the opening words to a draft of Cornwallis's Permanent Settlement, "to ensure its political safety, and to render the possession of the country as advantageous as possible to the East India Company and the British nation." With such goals in mind, Indians, who Cornwallis maintained were incompetent, untrustworthy, and irredeemably corrupt, could not be trusted with positions in the administration. In the years after the war, an Orientalist regime had been replaced by a colonial regime and the tools of this brave new world would be information, bureaucracy, and violence.[37]

Though the peace of 1784 was viewed differently by the various combatants, almost everyone realized that the cessation of hostilities brought on by the end of the American War was a pause in, rather than an ending of the imperial scramble for southern India. The new *casus belli* was Tipu Sultan's invasion of the Kingdom of Travancore, a British ally on the very south-west tip of the Indian peninsula. Tipu had long coveted the territory of Travancore, and had attempted to seize it by force in the previous fighting. Aware of the predatory designs of their powerful neighbor, Travancore had built a series of forts along the border with Mysore and even purchased two forts from the Dutch East India Company. Tipu was alarmed by this aggressive posturing and angered by the fact that some of the newly built and newly acquired forts were located in territories that were client states of Mysore. In 1789, Tipu responded with an invasion of Mysore, which alarmed both the Tavancore and the British, to whom the Raja of Travancore appealed for military aid. Company officials had long known that Travancore was a likely place for the renewal of hostilities with Mysore, and had gone so far as to warn Tipu Sultan that an attack on their ally would be considered a declaration of war against the East India Company as well.

Tipu was well aware of this British threat, and had used the intervening years of peace to strengthen his army and to seek allies among the other regional powers. In an attempt to break up the alliance between the Marathas, Hyderabad, and the Company that had so vexed his expansionist agenda, in 1790 Tipu made an agreement with Peshwa of Pune, nominal leader of the Maratha Confederacy, for Mysore to pay an annual tribute of 1.2 million rupees to the Marathas. In return, the Marathas were supposed to abandon their alliance with the British, or at least remain neutral in the coming war. Given the almost constant fighting between the Marathas and Mysore in the second half of the eighteenth century, and the very recent warfare over local land rights on their borders, it is perhaps unsurprising that the peshwa declined the offer and instead joined the British attack on Mysore in 1791.[38]

Desperate for allies, Tipu had also reached out to the Ottomans and the French for assistance against the British. What Tipu needed above all was ships. He was well aware that Britain's naval advantage had played an outsized role in the previous war, and was likely to do so again. He would have surely agreed with his father's comment, "I can defeat them on land, but I cannot swallow the sea." Tipu had attempted to build up Mysore's navy, with an eye toward creating a trading company to rival the British and to reduce his tactical disadvantage at sea. He made some strides, but the technological deficit was too difficult to overcome in so short a time. With this in mind, Tipu sent ambassadors to the Ottoman sultan in 1785 and to France in 1787. Both countries had been drained of men and money by the costly combat of the American War, the Ottomans in their war with Russia and Austria and the French by their global contest with the British. Neither was in any position to send troops or funds to aid Mysore, nor were they willing to risk antagonizing the British by directly supporting Tipu Sultan. The French officially recognized Tipu's status as monarch of Mysore, but would not even go so far as to allow his ambassadors to arrive on a Msyorean ship, instead insisting that they travel up the Seine to Paris in a smaller group aboard a smaller French vessel.[39]

The weight of France's debt was already beginning to tell in the 1780s. Far from emerging from the war with its global position strengthened and secured, ready to challenge the British for world supremacy, France's financial quagmire meant that in reality it was forced to withdraw from foreign commitments. Already, France had found itself unable to intervene in the vital contest for the fate of its neighbor and erstwhile ally, the United Provinces of the Netherlands. When Tipu Sultan's pleas for help arrived in 1787, France was thus deep in the midst of the financial crisis that had followed close on the heels of the ruinously expensive American War, teetering on the brink of revolution and in no position to help their erstwhile Indian ally. When the Third Anglo-Mysore War began in 1790, France would remain strictly neutral, once more undermining Tipu's prospects at the very moment where French aid might have proved decisive.

The newly independent United States, which had valorized Haidar Ali and the Tiger of Mysore as brothers in the anti-imperial struggle, abandoned their subcontinental allies as well. In the years since the Peace of Paris, America had been concerned to avoid foreign conflicts, to remain neutral, and to secure and restore the lucrative trade with Britain. As such, American merchants in India avoided their old French and Mysorean trading partners, opting instead to trade with the British. Full intervention in the Anglo-Mysore War was never a serious option, but America put profit before former allies, helping to fill British coffers and denying the French much-needed revenue from trade. Calcutta and Madras quickly became the favored centers for American trade with diplomatic relations following apace. While American consulates were set up in Calcutta in 1792 and Madras in 1794, Mysore, which had been one of the first states to recognize American independence, received no formal ties of trade or diplomacy.

Meanwhile, Cornwallis had arrived in India with designs for defeating Mysore already developing. The previous war with Mysore had been viewed by most in Britain as a loss, eroding British power and prestige in India. Cornwallis had himself been plagued by responsibility for British defeat in America after his capitulation at Yorktown in 1781 and was in desperate need of victory and redemption. As a result, from the moment of his appointment as governor-general, he was searching for a pretext for another war with Mysore. He began shoring up allies almost immediately, granting the Nizam of Hyderabad a detachment of British troops, and agreeing to share any territories taken from Mysore should war come once more. Realizing that Travancore might well be the flashpoint for the next conflict, Cornwallis almost ensured that war would come by guaranteeing Travancore British protection with full knowledge that the raja was doing his level best to provoke Tipu Sultan.[40]

Rather alarmingly, the Third Anglo-Msyore War that burst forth in 1790 did not begin more auspiciously than the previous war had ended. Tipu once more drove into the Carnatic, threatening Madras and putting Cornwallis on the back foot. It was at this moment, however, that the Company's success in securing and maintaining native alliances paid off. Tipu had alienated the Marathas and the nizam, and his other erstwhile ally—the bankrupt French— hoped only to survive the fighting unnoticed and unscathed. With memories of Tipu's belligerent imperial drive, and promises of a dispersal of rich Mysorean territory, the Marathas invaded the heartlands of Msyore, relieving Cornwallis to march on Bangalore and Sriringapatam. By February 1792, Tipu's capital was under siege, and though the British ultimately failed to take the city, Mysore was forced to sue for peace and accept a debilitating settlement.

In the end, Tipu lost 67 forts, 801 guns from his beloved artillery units, and fully half of his entire kingdom, annexed by the East India Company. For their timely intervention, the Marathas and Hyderabad also gained huge swaths of Mysore's territory. The cost to Tipu and his future power was immense. He had lost Mysore's foremost food-growing region (Dindigul) and its primary outlets to the western coast, on which Tipu had depended as the entry point for French aid from Mauritius. The loss of half his lands also meant a huge loss of tax revenue, and when combined with a massive indemnity placed on Mysore (estimated to have been three times Tipu's annual gross revenue), the fiscal-military state Tipu and his father had done so much to construct was fatally undermined. The British victory in 1792 could rightly be said to have "paved the way for British supremacy throughout India," and to have fundamentally undermined one of the last native states with the economic and military power to challenge Company rule. The Third Anglo-Mysore War had proved decisive, ending for good Mysore's challenge to British hegemony, but by freeing up British resources to fight in India and by bankrupting the French, thus depriving Tipu of his greatest ally, it was the American Revolution that had been the real turning point in the imperial scramble for India.[41]

Hyderabad and the Maratha Confederacy might well have congratulated themselves on choosing the right side and participating in the humbling of their most intractable foe. But the wars initiated by the wider American War had consequences for these native powers as well. For the Marathas, however, while peace with the British brought short-term advantages—the defeat of Mysore and expansion of Confederacy territory into Tipu's former domains—it was a strategic blunder in the long term, a crucial opportunity lost. The early 1780s represented, in the words of one historian, the "most favourable opportunity for the Marathas to destroy the EIC." If, instead of making peace with Hastings, the Marathas had joined with Mysore and France, the British might well have been driven out of India altogether. British resources were already stretched perilously thin by the American War, and by the 1780s Haidar Ali was holding down the forces of both Madras and Bombay, with the two presidencies only hanging on by dint of the greater resources of Bengal. At this juncture, Maratha intervention, especially an attack on Calcutta, would likely have doomed Madras and Bombay, leaving the Company with a rather precarious foothold, reduced resources, and a concerted enemy alliance. British prospects in India would have been bleak indeed.[42]

The clashes between Britain, the Marathas, Hyderabad, Mysore, and France that convulsed India in the late eighteenth century, had been the result of both long-term trends and the immediate geopolitical context of the wider American Revolution. Since the beginning of Mughal decline in the late seventeenth and early eighteenth centuries, a number of dynamic regional successor states had been developing and expanding, aided by local economic growth and administrative reorganization. As these states developed and grew, they pursued similar strategies of centralization, revenue extraction, and military growth, spurred on by competition with each other. Though they all developed organically over a long period of time, there was no binary opposition between the European and Indian successor states that emerged, and little difference in the methods and policies they employed. Thus, by the mid-eighteenth century, the East India Company was merely one of a number of centralizing, modernizing, expansionist, imperialist states that emerged.

With states like Bengal, Oudh, Mysore, Hyderabad, the Maratha Empire, and the French and British East India companies all expanding, searching for greater revenue, greater control over land and trade, and greater military power, warfare was always likely. Fighting had regularly occurred in India in the decades before the American Revolution, and would continue for decades after, but although the Anglo-French, Anglo-Mysore, and Anglo-Maratha wars of these years were not the final confrontation between these European and Indian imperial powers, they were decisive in shifting the balance of power toward the British. When the wars broke out in the 1780s, there was every reason to believe that the British might be driven out of many of its Indian strongholds, or at least contained and restrained; there was every reason to believe that Mysore or the Marathas might emerge as the foremost power in the subcontinent, or at least secure a lasting detente with their European neighbors; and there was every reason to fear that the French might well become the only European power in India worth the name. When peace came in 1784, despite

Tipu Sultan's confidence and Britain's fears of decline, the balance of power had irreparably shifted.

Unbeknownst to Tipu, the American War had ruined his French allies, who abandoned him when war resumed, leaving him without the material and naval support he so desperately needed. But Tipu had undermined his own position as well. His fractious relationship with his neighbors—the Marathas, Hyderabad, Travencore—exacerbated by his consistently expansionist agenda and his heavy-handed treatment of religious minorities, deprived him of crucial local allies and ensured that when Msyore went to war with Britain in the 1790s, it would do so as an isolated, besieged power. By turning the wars of the late eighteenth century into a confessional struggle, Tipu alienated potential allies instead of creating a pan-Indian alliance against the British. For most of the inhabitants of the Indian subcontinent, India was a geographical expression, not a focus of common identity or national cohesion. The British were not seen as imperial oppressors of some nascent united India, but rather as simply one in a long line of overlords that had ruled parts of the subcontinent for centuries. Indeed, before the reforms of the late eighteenth century, the British had consciously modeled their rule on indigenous precedents, adopting native law, finance, and administration. Their armies, courts, and civil service employed scores of Indians and, until the nineteenth century, interference with native religion was intentionally minimal.

It should come as no surprise that many people in the Hindu majority of India thus saw little practical difference between the British ruling class and the Persianate ruling classes that had held sway in Bengal or Benares, or still ruled in Mysore, or Hyderabad. Like the British, these overlords spoke a different language, practiced a minority religion, often married among themselves, and maintained communications and cultural ties outside of India. Moreover, like the British, they ruled in a largely similar manner, focusing on extraction of land revenue for the building of armies. Given their rather minuscule numbers in India, the British could only succeed with some degree of consent from the people they ruled. This they generally secured, not because they offered some better alternative to the rule of native states, but because they offered basically the same thing. For most Indians, there was little distinction to be made between British and native rulers in the eighteenth century. All were rapacious to some degree, all were centralizing and expansionist, all attempted to placate their people by ruling along long-standing indigenous lines. Tipu failed and the British succeeded in the wars of the period not because of British exceptionalism, but because of the very unexceptional nature of British rule in India. The American War, however, would prove to be a turning point, the moment when the balance of power shifted toward Britain for good, and the moment when British rule began to diverge sharply from the established norms of the subcontinent. The American War thus transformed British India from an indigenous state to a European imperial possession.

For thousands of Hindus and Mangalorean Christians held by Tipu Sultan, the trials of captivity would not end with the peace of Paris in 1783. As many as 12,000 Kodava Hindus had taken advantage of the Third Anglo-Mysore War to escape in 1792, but for many other prisoners it would take the fall of Tipu Sultan and his fortress capital of Sriringapatam to secure their freedom. In 1799, the Marquess Wellesley, the new governor-general, seized upon a flimsy pretext to put an end to the tedious machinations of Tipu Sultan once and for all. An army was sent to Mysore, led by George Harris, David Baird, and the governor-general's brother, the future Duke of Wellington, and in May 1799, Tipu's capital fell after fierce fighting. When the smoke cleared, the Tiger of Mysore's broken body was found among the dead. With his long-wished-for demise, the men and women held in captivity for more than a decade were finally released. Of the up to 80,000 Christians taken prisoner in the 1780s, only between 10,000 and 25,000 remained to be freed. According to Francis Buchanan, sent to survey these newly acquired territories, as many as 15,000 were returned to Mangalore and 10,000 emigrated to Malabar, where the first British collector in the region, Thomas Munro, helped to restore some of the lands taken from them so many years before. Those Kodava and Nair Hindus who had not previously escaped, were freed as well, though many had converted to Islam and could not, or did not, wish to return to their former religion. For these targeted religious groups, the price of the war that began in America had been not only long years of captivity, but also the decimation of their peoples and their way of life. They would continue on as best they could, but the price of the war had been steep.[43]

For Eliza Fay, the experience of Calicut and the specter of William Ayers would continue to haunt her through the subsequent years. Even after reaching the safety of Calcutta, she kept abreast of news from Malabar, giving aid to West, one of Ayers' abused subordinates when he fled to Bengal, and recording with rancorous relief in February 1781 that:

Sudder Khan [sic] and Ayers our chief enemies have both closed their career of wickedness. The former died of wounds received before Tellicherry; and the latter having repeatedly advanced close to the lines of that place, holding the most contemptuous language and indecent gestures towards the Officers; setting everyone at defiance and daring them to fire at him, (I suppose in a state of intoxication, miserable wretch!) was at length picked off . . . Too honourable a death for such a monster of iniquity. My hope was, that he would have been taken prisoner, and afterwards recognized and shot as a deserter.[44]

Though she had lived through the wars and escaped the clutches of such a traitorous villain as Ayers, she could never fully return to the hopeful days of her outward journey. Her marriage had failed, leaving her alone in Calcutta while Anthony returned to Britain to join the chorus baying for Hastings' blood. Undaunted, she attempted to make a go of it on her own, but in 1782 returned to Britain. After an extended and difficult passage home, Eliza finally reached British waters in February of 1783. It had been four years since she had first left for India and three years since she found herself in the clutches if William Ayers. It must have been with a sense of dreadful irony then that so close to home, Eliza found herself once more in captivity when her ship was "taken for an American" vessel and "we forlorn creatures set down at once as prisoners." The peace treaty between Britain and her former colonies had been signed, but this crucial information had yet to reach every ship in the Channel fleet. The mistake was quickly rectified, but the trauma of the event was more difficult to shake. Eliza Fay had arrived in India an unwitting prisoner of the war that had come to engulf the globe, and perhaps it was only fitting that she returned to Britain once more as a prisoner of the war now ended.[45]

The year 1782 would also prove to be a fateful one for Dean Mahomet. Early in the year Captain Baker and his men had been sent to Benares to arrest three men charged with the murder of a prominent Brahmin. It should have been a relatively straightforward task, but in the days and weeks following the arrival of Baker and his troops, Calcutta began to receive reports and complaints that rather than arresting the suspected murderers, Baker was instead extorting money from the entire village. Baker was later cleared of the charges, but given the tensions in the region after the deposing of Chait Singh and the metropolitan criticisms of Hastings' corruption and mismanagement, such accusations were not taken lightly. Baker was thus recalled to Calcutta in disgrace. Humiliated by this stain of corruption and by the very public vote of no confidence in his command, Baker promptly resigned his commission and made plans to leave India and return to Ireland.[46]

Dean Mahomet decided to join him, desiring to see the world and for fear of being left without his friend and patron. The friendship between Baker and Mahomet was real and deep, but it also seems likely that Mahomet was becoming disillusioned with the violence that permeated India in these years and his role in it, and increasingly unsure of how he fitted into the world of his birth. Mahomet had risen as far as it was possible for an Indian to rise in the British army. Nonetheless, he resigned his commission and in January 1784 embarked on the *Fortitude* for England. The voyage was uneventful, with nothing to report other than "several kinds of the finny inhabitants of the liquid element" and a storm between Madras and the Cape. At St. Helena, where they stopped briefly to resupply, they met Warren Hastings' wife Marion, sent to England ahead of the under-fire, soon to resign governor-general, and the remains of Sir Eyrie Coote, military hero of so many of the Company's wars in India. The presence at St. Helena of Warren Hastings' beloved wife and the body of one of the great generals of Indian conquest presaged the end of an era—a retreat from the free-wheeling, swashbuckling days of eighteenth-century conquest, but also a retreat from the ideals of a British India concerned with understanding and preserving indigenous forms of governance. Dean Mahomet had played his role in this era and its eclipse, but when he arrived at Dartmouth in September 1784 or Cork a few months later, his was not a homecoming or a retreat but a new beginning. He arrived in Britain not as part of an imperial retreat, but instead as part of an advance of the empire into the heart of Britain itself. No longer was the British Empire to be something that happened beyond the familiar realms of domestic British consciousness. The empire was becoming central to British lives and British imaginations, a fact brought forcefully and spectacularly to the fore by the trial of Warren Hastings and the reforms that followed, but likewise a fact more modestly embodied by Dean Mahomet.[47]

Mahomet was 25 when he arrived at Cork at the end of 1784. It was an almost entirely alien world, but the patronage of Godfrey Baker and his family eased his entrance into Irish society. With Baker's support Mahomet began studying English language and literature, which fortuitously brought him into contact with Jane Daly, a fellow student and the teenage daughter of a Protestant gentry family. The pair eloped in 1786, but the rather hurried marriage seems to have been largely accepted in Cork. Godfrey Baker died that same year, after which the young couple lived on the estate of Godfrey's brother William, recently returned from his own service with the Bengal army. Mahomet seems to have been employed by William Baker in some capacity, as an estate manager rather than a servant, and maintained his own home, as was reported by Abu Talib Khan, a fellow member of India's Muslim service elite who visited William Baker in 1799. The relationship with the Bakers must have soured, however, for in 1807, after twenty-three years in Cork, Mahomet moved his growing family to London.[48]

In London he worked in the vapor baths of the fabulously wealthy Scottish nabob Basil Cochrane, where he later claimed to have introduced "shampooing" or therapeutic massage to Britain. After two years with Cochrane, Mahomet struck out on his own and opened the Hindoostanee Coffee House on the corner of George Street and Charles Street, near glitzy Portman Square. Catering to British gentlemen who had lived or worked in India, the Hindoostanee Coffee House served Indian cuisine in rooms decorated to appeal to the nostalgia of its Orientalist clientele. Mahomet's restaurant was well received, but it never quite gained a stable customer base, leading to Mahomet's bankruptcy in 1812. In search of a fresh start, in 1814 Mahomet and his family relocated to the burgeoning seaside resort of Brighton. Under the patronage of George IV, who had recently completed the renovation of his Brighton Pavilion in faux oriental splendor, the once sleepy port had become a fashionable destination for wealthy holiday-makers and elites searching for trendy medical cures. With his exotic background and experience with medicinal baths,

Mahomet was well placed to take advantage of Brighton's boom, and established himself as "shampooing surgeon" to the smart set. Between 1816 and 1841 he became the successful proprietor of a series of bath-houses known for their Indian décor and eastern cures. As his business flourished he emerged as a popular fixture of Brighton society, rising to become royal shampooing surgeon to both George IV and William IV and appearing regularly at Brighton Pavilion in the garb of an Indian prince, a costume of his own design, before his death in 1851.[49]

As the life and career of Dean Mahomet so vividly attests, the costs and benefits of the American Revolution for those living in the Indian subcontinent were much more ambiguous. Imperial warfare in Asia both lifted individuals out of poverty and brought rulers and villagers alike to their knees. Like Mahomet, tens of thousands found opportunity in the armies that plagued the country, while others found only suffering and ruin in their wake. On the one hand, the British conquest of India that gathered steam in the late eighteenth century could not have been accomplished without the active support and service of thousands, perhaps millions, of Indian people, many of whom directly benefited in the process. On the other hand, millions suffered, losing their lives, lands, and livelihoods as a result. This ambiguity is perhaps fitting. There was no single Indian perspective, no one Indian culture nor one Indian experience. As such, there was no real sense of us versus them, Indian versus European. Loyalty to native dynasties, who often differed from their people in religion, culture, and language had always been tenuous and conditional. Europeans had been on the scene since before the arrival of the Mughals and had been serious players in Indian politics for nearly two centuries by the 1770s, merely one power among a multitude. If they could see the future of centralized oppressive exploitation they might indeed have felt differently, but in the context of the late eighteenth century, the nature of the struggle between the British, French, Mughal, and Maratha Empires, and the Kingdom of Mysore depended almost entirely on personal circumstances and experience.

For Mahomet too, the consequences of the war were ambiguous. The East India Company army provided him with an opportunity to rise through the ranks to a position of command and opened a path to a successful life as an author and businessman in Ireland and England. But at the same time, his long association with the British alienated him from his family and his country, making him a stranger in his own land. His migration to Europe was thus both the pursuit of a path previously closed to Indians, but also a reaction to the reality that he now stood apart, not really British, and yet not entirely Indian either. For the only Indian in Cork and Brighton, his experience of the imperial civil war must have been bittersweet.

9

---->>- -<-<----

CONVICT EMPIRE

On April 16, 1794, Westminster Hall was packed nearly to bursting. A curious multitude had gathered day after day since February 1788 to witness one of the most celebrated trials of the age, the impeachment of Warren Hastings, eighteenth-century Britain's foremost empire builder and the one-time Governor-General of India. The trial was a celebrity affair, a public spectacle of self-righteous oration and politically motivated accusation that filled London's many newspapers and occupied the gossip of coffee-houses and drawing rooms across the nation. The onlookers who crowded into every corner of the hall were well rewarded for their trouble. For 148 days they were transfixed by the thunderous rhetoric of Edmund Burke—who led the prosecution—and the caustic quips of Richard Brinsley Sheridan, Charles James Fox, and Philip Francis as they condemned Hastings for corruption, malfeasance, and judicial murder.

As Warren Hastings gazed out from the center of this tempest on the sea of faces, two men would have stood out among the throng. Crammed in with the lords and ladies, with the Grub Street hacks and the gawking plebs, with the elect and the dregs of London society, were two men of conspicuous difference, two representatives of a country and a culture as far removed from the British metropolis as it was possible to be: Bennelong and Yemmerrawannie, Australian Aborigines of the Eora people. What the visitors thought of the trial, whether they heard a personally familiar story in the accounts of British imperial violence and corruption in India, is unrecorded. How they came to witness the trial of Warren Hastings, however, was a direct result of the violent civil war that had so shaken the British world in the 1770s and 1780s. The loss of the American colonies had forced the British to search for new outlets to relieve their overcrowded prisons, setting in motion a chain of events that would lead to the settling of a new continent, the journey of the two native leaders, and ultimately to the decimation of an indigenous population.

It must have seemed unnaturally cold to Bennelong as he shivered in his English clothes aboard the HMS *Reliance*. It was January after all, and in this strange part of the globe the chill could seep deep into the bones, infecting body and soul. He had been in this foreign, frozen land for too long, and now on the brink of returning home to the sunnier climes of his previous life, Bennelong found himself stuck on a ship anchored in Plymouth Sound, still awaiting instructions, provisions, and favorable winds before it could haul anchor and sail for the Pacific. Only eight months earlier, Bennelong had stood in the churchyard of St. John the Baptist in Eltham, Kent and watched as his young companion Yemmerrawannie was lowered into the hard English ground, the chalky foreign soil heaped upon his remains. The English weather had never agreed with Yemmerrawannie, and for months after their arrival he had suffered and weakened, despite, or perhaps because of, the best attempts of English medicine. Now he was gone, buried as a Christian among the local dead of Eltham, an inscribed stone monument marking the spot where one of the first two Australians to visit Europe was laid to rest. In the month that followed Yemmerrawannie's demise, Bennelong had returned to the Kentish graveyard, perhaps to mourn or to perform the death rites that in this remote island he alone knew.

Perhaps his friends and relatives had been right after all when they marked his departure from Australia with their "united distress . . . and dismal lamentations." He was now all alone in England, and if he were impatient to embark for home before, now the need to be back among his people hit him with a combination of desperation and weary despondency. Accompanying him on the *Reliance* as it lay frustratingly anchored at Plymouth was the new governor of the British colony of New South Wales, Captain John Hunter, who was quick to grasp Bennelong's depressed condition and readiness to depart what for him must have become a land of sadness. In a letter to the Admiralty from Plymouth, Hunter made manifest his concern for the homesick Eora man:

> The surviving native man, Benelong is with me, but I think in a precarious state of health. He has for the last twelve months been flattered with the hope of seeing again his native country—a happiness which he has fondly look'd forward to, but so long a disappointment has much broken his spirit, and the coldness of the weather here has so frequently laid him up that I am apprehensive his lungs are affected—that was the cause of the other's death. I do all I can to keep him up, but still am doubtful of his living.[1]

Bennelong and Yemmerrawannie had arrived in England nearly two years earlier in the more pleasant weather of May 1793. The voyage—from Port Jackson across the Indian Ocean, around the Cape of Good Hope, across the Atlantic to Rio de Janeiro and north through the Atlantic to the British Isles—had been relatively uneventful, as transoceanic voyages go, the monotony only broken by the appearance of a French privateer, which fired three guns at the *Atlantic* as it passed into the English Channel. Everything, however, changed when they disembarked at Falmouth on May 20 and were greeted by the impossibly unfamiliar sights of England.

The British, for their part, were curious about, if condescendingly dismissive of, the new arrivals. One newspaper, the *London Packet*, reported that "Governor Phillip has brought home two natives of New Holland, a man and a boy," but was quick to add a disparaging critique of the visitors. Before the Eora men even had a chance to make a good impression, the *London Packet* told its readers that the pair were "totally incapable of civilization" and "form a lower order of the human race." Perhaps the world-weary scribblers and Grub Street hacks thought that they had seen it all before. After all, the steady spread of Britain's empire around the globe had brought with it a steady stream of captives, ambassadors, merchants, and tourists from parts beyond the seas. In the years following the settling of North America a veritable parade of Native Americans had regularly provided the gawking crowds of London with a taste of exotic worlds beyond their shores. The famous Powhatan princess Pocahontas had traveled to England in 1616, sadly presaging the future fate of Yemmerrawannie. After being presented to King James I and attending a Ben Jonson masque, she succumbed to an undiagnosed illness and was buried at Gravesend in 1617. The young Australian would not be the first transoceanic traveler to breathe their last far from home in the capital of their colonizers.

The scurrilous screed of the London press at Bennelong and Yemmerrawannie's arrival was an opening salvo in an ongoing attempt to justify the colonization of an already inhabited land. By labeling the indigenous people of Britain's new imperial target "incapable of civilization," such writers were merely reiterating the very same pretext that had been used since the seventeenth century to justify taking land from an already established society. In the eyes of imperial apologists, such peoples did not use or improve the land as Europeans would, and thus had no right to it. The new arrivals were compared to Africans as well, who, as descendants of Ham were, according to the Book of Genesis, destined to be "a servant of servants to his brothers." In this view, irredeemably uncivilized and inherently subordinate, Bennelong and Yemmerrawannie's people would have to give way to British colonization. British settlement and exploitation of Australia could proceed with a clear conscience.[2]

We cannot be sure if Bennelong and Yemmerrawannie were aware of these unflattering characterizations, or if they sensed beneath their hosts' generous veneer the canny logic of empire, but outwardly at least they seemed to embrace their role as tourists. From Falmouth, the pair made their way to London, where they were given lodgings, board, a servant, and a washerwoman to clean the new clothes ordered for them by Arthur Phillip, the former Governor of New South Wales who had accompanied them to England. Phillip hoped to introduce the visitors to King George III and so had them dressed identically in green coats with blue and buff striped waistcoats, slate-colored breeches and silk stockings. Whether their European kit stripped them of their previous identity or accentuated their exoticness in British eyes, dressing them identically robbed them of their individuality, making them into empty cyphers for a new British spot on the map rather than presenting them as distinct humans.

The audience with the king never materialized, but the newly Europeanized tourists were kept busy. In July 1793, they moved to more fashionable lodgings in Grosvenor Square in the glamorous West End, where books were bought and reading and writing teachers acquired to see if the pair were truly "incapable of civilization." Phillip had told Sir Joseph Banks, president of the Royal Society and the resident naturalist on Captain Cook's first Australian expedition, that much information could be gleaned from the men once they were taught English. They were taken by coach and carriage to see the sights of London—the Tower, St. Paul's—and attended performances at Sadler's Wells and Covent Garden theaters. In an odd or malicious twist, they were also taken to Parkinson's Museum, which housed an entire room dedicated to a display of items brought to England from the Pacific by Captain Cook. If they were less inclined to view the two Pacific "chieftains' " heads with the comfortable curiosity of the genteel London crowds, we should not be surprised.[3]

Beneath the surface of this busy itinerary, however, things were becoming bleak. As the weather turned inclement and intemperate in September, Yemmerrawannie fell ill. He and Bennelong, periodically ill himself, were moved to the house of Edward Kent in Eltham, then 7 miles outside of London, to distance themselves from the fetid air and pestilential damp of the metropolis. For the next seven months, the two were moved back and forth between London and Eltham, continuing their tour while remedies were sought to cure the ailing Eora youth. Despite the ministrations of a Dr. Blane and his regimen of bleeding, emetics, diuretics, and even Dr. Fothergill's famous pills, Yemmerrawannie continued to languish. Almost exactly one year after arriving in England, he eventually succumbed to a pulmonary illness, or perhaps pneumonia, in May 1794, aged about 19.[4]

We only know the outline of Bennelong and Yemmerrawannie's itinerary, but if in their trips around the capital they happened to find themselves in Woolwich they would have encountered a new fixture blighting the bank of the Thames. Anchored there were the infamous prison hulks, teeming with convicts forced to labor on the improvement of the Thames. Before 1775, these convicts would have been destined for penal servitude in America, but now they were held in the pestilential dank of the rotting ships. If Bennelong and Yemmerrawannie did indeed gaze upon the overcrowded hulks during their London sojourn, they might not yet have realized the profound effect these vessels had wrought on their native shores. For just as the trial of Warren Hastings was about to commence, a fleet of ships was landing its first cargo of convicts on the shores of Australia. The same events that had led the Governor-General of India to the dock had also set in motion the founding of a new penal colony in the South Pacific. The story of the founding of British Australia and the story of how two Australian Aborigines came to witness the trial of Warren Hastings in London are both, at their base, stories of the unforeseen impact of the American Revolution.

By 1785 the penal problems caused by the revolution was only becoming worse. Britain still retained imperial possessions in the Americas in the aftermath of the American Revolution, but criminal transportation across the Atlantic had ground to a halt. In defense of a client charged with returning from transportation, the celebrated attorney William Garrow made the de facto embargo on transportation clear. He informed the court that "your Lordships know, that you no longer have the power to transport to America, or at least you no longer exercise it."[5] Indeed, the law had been altered to reflect the new geopolitical reality, though the language of the bill did its best to ignore the growing rebellion in the colonies. Instead of recognizing the practical state of affairs in the colonies, the bill stated that "the transportation of convicts to his Majesty's colonies and plantations in America . . . is found to be attended with various inconveniences, particularly by depriving this kingdom of many subjects whose labour might be useful to the community, and who, by proper care and correction, might be reclaimed from their evil course." Hard labor was to replace transportation, and, at least officially, no further felons would be sent to America.[6]

Transportation to the Americas might have all but ended, but the bloody legal code remained in need of more merciful options for those convicted of minor felonies. With one safety valve closed forever, new destinations were sought for Britain's unwanted criminal population. At first, British authorities thought that perhaps they could turn their new problem to their advantage. Troops were always in demand in the various theaters of war around the empire, and so some convicts were offered pardons if they agreed to enlist in the British army. The felons aboard the *Tayloe*, loaded and ready to depart for America when news of passage of the Criminal Law Act of 1776 reached them, were given the option of joining up. Despite attempts to substitute hard labor and imprisonment for transportation—a move some progressive reformers, following the arguments of the influential judicial reformers Cesare Beccaria and Jonas Hanway, had long advocated as a means of instilling "labor discipline" among the criminal classes—Britain did not possess the infrastructure needed for such a monumental shift in carceral policy. William Eden, a criminal justice reformer, gave voice to the penal crisis caused by the American Revolution, stating that "the fact is, our prisons are full, and we have no way at present to dispose of the convicts."[7]

A variety of solutions to manage the surfeit of convicts were attempted, including, most infamously, the use of prison hulks. The idea was to use men who had been sentenced to transportation to dredge the River Thames, improving the carrying capacity of London's increasingly crowded port. The act authorizing this plan did not specify where these forced laborers were to be housed, but the prisons were too full to cope with any more residents. Duncan Campbell, a former convict transporter who had won the contract to dredge the Thames, thus decided to house the felons in two ships refitted for the purpose. Conditions on the hulks, as the prison ships were known, were dreadful, and overcrowding and poor diet and sanitation led to astonishing death tolls (more than a quarter of the convict population in a twenty-month period), escapes and mutinies.[8]

The hulks and their soul-crushing conditions captured the imaginations of contemporaries and posterity alike, most famously in Charles Dickens' *Great Expectations*, but they could never hope to accommodate even a small fraction of the men and women convicted in British courts each year. Although the ships were packed to the gunwales with convicts, with transportation to America at an end there were far too many convicts for the hulks to house. As Campbell, in his capacity as superintendent of the convicts at Woolwich, informed the Court of King's Bench in 1785, there were as many as 800 convicts housed in the hulks and many more who had been sentenced to transportation with no prospect of being sent abroad. The jails throughout the country were full of convicts awaiting discharge onto the hulks, but there was neither space nor work at Woolwich for them. Lord Mansfield, the long-serving chief justice, received the information with great alarm and recommended Campbell's report to the attorney-general and other government ministers.[9]

By 1781, the crisis was so great that judges once more began to sentence criminals to transportation. One ship delivered convicts to the African coast, but conditions at the chosen landing site were so poor that the captain proclaimed the felons free men who could make their way as they saw fit. In 1783, a second transport ship, the *Swift*, left London bound for Nova Scotia, although its actual, secret destination was Maryland, long a favored landing point for British convicts. However, before the *Swift* had managed to leave British waters, the convicts—fearing their true destination was Africa—rose up and escaped to the coast of Kent, where most were eventually recaptured and successfully transported to Baltimore. Shortly after, a second ship bound for Maryland was turned away, putting a definitive end to the second period of convict transportation to America.[10]

With other outlets proving to be a distinct failure, a solution finally was found in the form of a remote, hardly explored new continent: Australia. Australia, or New South Wales as it was then known, was certainly on the minds and lips of many in the late eighteenth century. The famous Captain Cook, whose voyages, discoveries, and tragic death had so captivated a war-weary nation, had charted the eastern coast of Australia in 1770. On April 23 of that year, Cook and his party made their first landfall on mainland Australia on a sandy peninsula in a shallow bay originally christened "Stingray Harbour." The name was quickly changed to Botany Bay after Joseph Banks and Daniel Solander, two pioneering naturalists traveling with the expedition, had great success in their botanical collecting at the bay.

To British officials, the location seemed perfect for a penal colony. It was far enough away to be considered a harsh punishment and thus a real criminal deterrent; its distance was also sufficient to prevent any of the felons from returning to Britain. Settling convicts halfway around the world in New South Wales also had strategic geopolitical benefits. In an era of intense competition between imperial powers, planting Britons, whatever their origins, in the South Pacific would help solidify British territorial claims and potentially open up new markets for British trade. Willing settlers would be hard to find, given the plethora of more well-known and well-established colonial outlets for those looking for opportunities not available in Britain. Forced-settlers were thus a perfect solution both to the problem of overcrowded jails and imperial ambition.

In December 1785, Orders in Council were made for the creation of a penal colony at Botany Bay, and by early 1787 the first convicts from the London courts had been sentenced to transportation to Botany Bay. This rather dubious distinction went to twenty-nine men and four women sentenced at the January 10 session of the Old Bailey. As the official summary reads:

> The following prisoners who were capitally convicted at former Sessions received his Majesty's pardon, on condition of being transported for the following terms, to the Eastern coast of New South Wales, or some one or other of the islands adjacent, (viz.) Charles King, Thomas Thompson, Benjamin Rogers, Hugh M'Donald, Joseph Dyer, George Charlwood, Thomas Colebrook, John Langford, Sarah Parry, Thomas Harris, Hannah Mullens, James May, Edward Paild, John Delove, Henry Asser, Daniel Chambers, John Turwood, Thomas Freeman, and John Crawford, for life. George Dunstan, Thomas Scrivenor, John Bateman, Abraham Boyce, John Mears, George Shepherd, John Lockey, Mary Smith, Henry Palmer, Joseph Burdett, James Evans, William Knight, Joseph Butler and Margaret Dawson for the term of seven years.[11]

On January 19, 1788, Arthur Bowes Smyth, one of the surgeons assigned to accompany the First Fleet, stood on the deck of the *Lady Penrhyn* staring out at the endless expanse of the Pacific Ocean, desperately searching for a dark speck on the horizon, listening for the excited shouts of the crew that would mean their long journey was finally at an end. Two hundred and fifty long, weary days earlier, on May 13, 1787, they had left Portsmouth, entered the English Channel, and sailed by way of Tenerife, Rio de Janeiro and the Cape of Good Hope to the Great Southern Ocean, riding the uninterrupted winds of the "roaring forties" to the South Pacific. Eleven ships under the command of Commodore Arthur Phillip had been selected to comprise the now famous "First Fleet" that was to establish a penal colony at Botany Bay. More than 750 convicts—548 men, 188 women, and 17 children—were bundled onto six transport ships, partially separated by sex. Two Royal Navy vessels, the *Sirius* and the *Supply*, provided an armed escort and three store ships conveyed much-needed supplies—food, seeds, tools, agricultural equipment—to help establish the colony and bridge the gap until it became self-sufficient. Smyth had risen at five o'clock that morning in hopes of catching a first glimpse of his new home, but his optimism had been quickly dashed. There was nothing but ceaseless blue as far as the eye could see. They had been expecting to see land for days, and Smyth had confided to his diary the night before, "A gentle breeze—Expect to see Land this Evening . . . No land seen at 8 o'clock for wh. reason the fleet were order'd to lye to all night."[12]

The journey from England had been relatively smooth, but it had been ten weeks since they had left the Cape of Good Hope, ten long weeks without even the hint of land, "the longest period of any we had been at Sea without touching at any Port." At seven o'clock, after eight months at sea, Smyth, the crew and the 101 female convicts of the *Lady Penrhyn* caught their first tantalizing glimpse of New South Wales. The feeling of sighting solid earth after so long a time was indescribable. "The joy everyone felt upon so long wish'd for an Event," Smyth wrote, "can be better conceiv'd than expressed, particularly as it was the termination of the Voyage to those who were to settle at Botany Bay." The next day the *Lady Penrhyn* sailed into Botany Bay, spying through an eyeglass "7 of the Natives, running among the trees."[13]

The leader of this unlikely flotilla, the expedition's commander, and the colony's first governor was Arthur Phillip. Phillip had risen from inauspicious circumstances to his position of command. Born in Cheapside, London, the future governor's father was a modest language teacher and former sailor born in Frankfurt and his mother the widow of a sailor. When his father died a year after his birth in 1739, Phillip's life chances seemed dim; however when he was given a place at the Greenwich Hospital School, a charitable foundation meant to help the children of impoverished sailors, his luck changed. He began his nautical career as a sailor aboard a whaling ship before enlisting in the Royal Navy in 1754. He saw action at the Battle of Minorca and the Battle of Havana during the Seven Years' War, distinguishing himself enough during the conflict to receive promotion to lieutenant. With Britain at peace, in 1774 Phillip enlisted as a captain in the Portuguese navy, fighting off South America during the Spanish–Portuguese War. France's entrance into the American War in 1778 led to Phillip being recalled to his position in the British navy.

The choice of Phillip as leader of the expedition to settle New South Wales was not without merit. He had previous experience of leading convict trans-ports, having commanded a Portuguese fleet shipping convict laborers to South

America during the Spanish–Portuguese War. His knowledge of South America was also seen as a boon by British authorities. One of the benefits of a colony in the South Pacific was its perceived usefulness as a base and staging ground for attacks on the Spanish colonies of the Pacific coast of South America. During the Revolutionary War, Phillip had been charged with planning and leading a mission to raze the Spanish colonies of Chile, Peru, and Mexico before crossing the Pacific to attack the Philippines. This plan was scuppered when peace with Spain was reached in 1783, but Phillip's knowledge of Spain's Pacific strength made him an appealing choice to lead the expedition to Botany Bay.

Phillip quickly endeared himself to the crew of the *Sirius*, the flagship of the First Fleet, as well. After leaving English waters in May en route to Tenerife, one of the ship's officers had begun flogging some of the sailors for a petty infraction. The sailors complained to Captain Hunter that "if this was the usage they ware to have, it would be better to jump overboard at once than to be murdered in a foreign land." The captain informed Governor Phillip of the dispute, who quickly let his officers know that the usual harsh naval discipline would not be tolerated on this journey. Phillip "ordered every officer on board the ship to appear in the cabin . . . and told them all if he knew any officer to strike a man on board, he would break him immediately." In normal circumstances, such physical punishments might be overlooked, or even encouraged, but, as the governor realized, the sailors were all that stood between the officers and civilians and hundreds of angry convicts. As he explained to his officers,

> Those men are all we have to depend upon, and if we abuse those men that we have to trust to, the convicts will rise and massacre us all. Those men are our support. We have a long and severe station to go through in settling this collona [colony], at least we cannot expect to return in less than five years. This ship and her crew is to protect and support the country, and if they are ill treated by their own officers, what support can you expect of them? They will all be dead before the voyage is half out, and who is to bring us back again?[14]

The governor's sobering predictions of prisoner uprisings had the intended effect, and for most of the remaining journey landfall held as much danger as life at sea. The fleet spent six weeks in Brazil gathering supplies and refreshing the convicts. Whenever sailors went ashore, they were forced to be accompanied by a uniformed soldier in order to prevent their being pressed into service by another navy or another vessel. Between Rio and the Cape of Good Hope, where the fleet arrived for another six-week sojourn in October, the much-feared convict uprising first materialized. The prisoners on the *Alexander*, one of the convict transports, began plotting to "rise and take the ship," but the ringleaders were discovered and captured before their plan could fully develop. The would-be Spartacuses were brought onboard the *Sirius*, where they were severely flogged before being returned to their ship in chains. Phillip's warning had not been an idle threat.[15]

The sailors of the First Fleet were, as befitted the age of sail, a motley crew, hailing from every corner of Britain as well as from farther afield. Jacob Nagle, a sailor aboard the *Sirius*, had a particularly varied though hardly unusual background. He had been born to a family of German and English Quakers in Reading, Pennsylvania in 1762. In 1777, at the age of 15, he followed his father into the Continental Army and saw action at the Battle of the Brandywine under General Washington. His term of service ended while the army was camped at Valley Forge, but Nagle was a restless lad and, inspired by the stories of the sailors who gathered at his father's tavern on Water Street in Philadelphia, Nagle joined the crew of a series of privateers starting in 1780. In 1781 he was captured by the British while serving on the *Trojan* and sent to the Caribbean island of St. Christopher as a prisoner of war. St. Christopher fell to the French later that same year, but Nagle's freedom was short-lived. While in French Martinique waiting for a ship bound for America, Nagle was arrested by the French for aiding an escaped French prisoner from Pennsylvania. Nagle was freed once more in 1782, this time as part of a prisoner exchange after the British victory at the Battle of the Saintes, but instead of being released was pressed into service in the British navy.[16]

Nagle served in the British navy until the war officially ended in 1783, at which point his ship returned to England where he and the other sailors were to be discharged. He left the naval life behind at Plymouth and traveled with some fellow demobbed sailors to London in search of back pay and passage back home to Philadelphia. Finding a ship that would take him back to America proved more difficult than Nagle anticipated, perhaps owing to a lack of the necessary funds. With transport home not forthcoming, Nagle rejoined the British navy, participating in the third and final relief of Gibraltar in 1783. At first glance, the fact that Nagle would once more willingly join the very navy that had forced him to serve against his own country is surprising, but for common soldiers and seamen, service on multiple, even opposing sides was hardly unusual. Military service was a profession as much as it ever was a cause. By 1787, Nagle had become accustomed to life at sea and so inured to a peripatetic existence of travel and adventure that he jumped at the chance of a voyage to the newest spot on the globe. The youth who had walked in the shadows of Independence Hall in the heady summer of 1776, when America declared its independence from Britain, who had fought with George Washington against the British Empire, now found himself en route to the Pacific as a member of a new project of British imperial expansion.[17]

Nagle was not the only American to find himself sailing with the First Fleet. Among the crew of the *Sirius* alone there were five other American sailors, two of whom were Pennsylvanians like Nagle himself. The other three, John Rowley, James Proctor, and John Harris, came from Virginia, Massachusetts, and New York respectively. Perhaps somewhat awkwardly, the six Americans were serving on the *Sirius* under the command of Captain David Collins, a Scotsman who had seen action in the British army at Bunker Hill. Indeed, many of the officers of the First Fleet had previously served in the British army or navy during the war.

There were less willing travelers of American origin as well. Fourteen of the transportees came from North America, and at least eight of the prisoners had begun the war as slaves in the American colonies. Referred to as "a negro" in the court records, John Martin was most likely a former slave who had used the revolution as an opportunity to make his bid for freedom. After escaping a life of servitude in America, Martin had made his way to London, where he took employment as a sailor. Martin's newfound freedom was not to last, and in 1782 he was arrested and convicted of stealing clothing. He was imprisoned at Newgate and sentenced to transportation to Africa. A bout of typhus saved Martin from the disastrous attempt to settle convicts on the African coast, and he remained imprisoned at Newgate from 1782 until he was added to the convicts on the First Fleet. With him aboard the *Alexander* transport ship were Janel Gordon, Caesar, and John Randall, who had escaped slavery in Connecticut and joined the British army. After the war, Randall had been discharged from the army at Manchester where he was arrested for theft and sentenced to transportation.[18]

The whole affair thus had an American flavor. The war with America was itself the primary catalyst for the creation of a new penal colony in the Pacific, and one of the earliest proponents of the colonization of New South Wales was himself an American. Mario Matra, a New Yorker of Italian descent, had traveled with Captain Cook on his famous voyage to Botany Bay in 1770 (Matra in fact claimed to have been the first European to set foot in the area). Matra remained loyal to Britain during the revolution, fleeing like so many of his countrymen to London. His experience as a loyalist refugee neglected by the British authorities, and his observation of the suffering of his fellow Americans in exile, led him to propose a new settlement in New South Wales "to atone for the loss of the American colonies." While his plan to settle American loyalist refugees in Australia would be scrapped in favor of a penal colony, his proposal was instrumental in raising the possibility of planting a marginal population, unwanted in Britain, in New South Wales.[19]

For Americans and British alike, the leg of the journey between the Cape and Botany Bay was, despite its relatively uncharted nature, perhaps the most pleasant, with fair weather and good winds allowing for rapid progress. Despite a freak gale off the Australian coast, the fleet reached Botany Bay on January 21, 1788, a little over eight months after departing from England. In a letter home to his brother, George Worgan, a surgeon assigned to the *Sirius*, painted a dazzling portrait of Botany Bay as it appeared to the eyes of the first British arrivals. "This Part of the Coast," Worgan explained,

is moderately high and regular, forming small Ridges, Plains, easy ascents and descents. It is pretty generally clothed with Trees and Herbage Inland; the Shore is rocky and bold, forming many bluff Heads, and overhanging Precipices. On approaching the Land which forms Botany Bay (but I shall speak more particularly to that which forms Port Jackson) It suggests to the Imagination Ideas of luxuriant Vegetation and rural Scenery, consisting of gentle risings & Depressions, beautifully clothed with variety of Verdures of Evergreens, forming dense Thickets, & lofty Trees appearing above these again, and now & then a pleasant chequered Glade opens to your View. Here, a romantic rocky, craggy Precipice over which, a little purling stream makes a Cascade There, a soft vivid-green, shady Lawn attracts your Eye. The Whole, (in a Word) exhibits a Variety of Romantic Views, all thrown together into sweet Confusion by the careless hand of Nature.[20]

Arthur Smyth was not fooled by the paradisiacal prospect of Botany Bay and quickly realized that settlement would be arduous to say the least. Aptly presaging the problems the settlers would face, Smyth lamented that:

upon first sight one wd. be induced to think this a most fertile spot, as there are great Nos. of very large & lofty trees, reachg. almost to the water's edge, & every vacant spot between the trees appears to be cover'd wt. verdure: but upon a nearer inspection, the grass is found long & coarse, the trees very large & in general hollow & the wood itself fit for no purposes of buildg or anything but the fire — The Soil to a great depth is nothing but a black sand wh. when exposed to the intense heat of the Sun by removing the surrounding trees, is not fit for the vegitation of anything, even the grass itself then dying away, wh. in the shade appears green & flourishing; add to this that every part of the growth is in a manner cover'd wt. black & red Ants of a most enormous size.

Time would shortly prove Smyth's disenchanted assessment correct.[21]

In the days after their arrival in Botany Bay, Governor Phillip began exploring the area for a more suitable place to settle. To the north of Botany Bay, a more promising site was found at Port Jackson, where Phillip described finding "the finest harbour in the world, in which a thousand sail of the line may ride in the most perfect security." It was decided that this natural harbor would be a much more felicitous place to build the new colony, and thus, six days after making their initial landfall at Botany Bay, the troops and convicts were landed at Port Jackson, and the hard work of building the colony began in earnest. According to Jacob Nagle:

The troops landed and pitched their tents, and convicts to clear away the ground. The governor had a frame canvas house brought from England and that was set up on the east side of the run of fresh water at the head of the cove, and the Lieutenant Governor, Major Ross, officers and troops encamped on the west side of the run of water. In the center, the men and women were incamped on the west side, but the women by themselves, and sentries placed through all the camp, likewise a guard on the Governors side . . . The convicts ware amediately employed in cutting down timber and clearing to build log houses for the officers and soldiers on the west side, and fencing in ground, and the women employed carrying stones away into the corners of the fences.[22]

Around 150,000 men, women, and children would be forcibly resettled in New South Wales over the course of the next fifty years. As in so many colonial contexts, as European settlement expanded conflicts with indigenous peoples intensified, for despite what many in Britain may have thought, Australia was not an empty land. The area around Botany Bay was inhabited by a fair number of indigenous Australians—the Wangal, Cadigal, and Cammeraygal clans of the Eora people, numbering between 1,500 and 4,000—and thus contact between the British and indigenous inhabitants occurred as soon as landfall was made. Cook had spent time in the area a mere eighteen years before, and it is thus likely that strange men landing on their shore were not entirely unfamiliar or unexpected by the Eora. Still, those on both sides of the first encounters were wary as well as curious. We have no written accounts of these early meetings from the Eora perspective, but the British accounts describe the Eora with a typical combination of superior racist condescension and genuine humanity, a mix of wondrous admiration and disgust.

George Worgan's description of the Eora is more sympathetic than most, and while he certainly viewed them as crude, and wretched, savages, his account also contains notes of sympathy, admiration, and understanding. From our vantage point, we tend to assume a uniform European chauvinism toward non-Europeans, but there was never a singular attitude toward indigenous peoples. In practice, Western accounts of native peoples ran the gamut between simple revulsion and empathetic romanticism, between Hobbes' nasty brute and Rousseau's "noble savage." Worgan's account embodies these contradictions beautifully, and is worth quoting at length.[23]

They are of a moderate Height, few reaching up to 6 Feet, rather slight than Robust their Complexion is of a reddish, Blackish Soot Colour, filthy & dirty to Disgust; Men Women and Children go entirely naked, scorning a Veil as big as a Fig-leaf . . . The Generallity of them, Men & Women, have Scars in different parts of their Body, which in some, seem to have been cut in particular Lines by way of ornament . . . Many of the Women, Old & Young, Married & Unmarried have had the two first joints of the little Finger of the left Hand cut off, this Custom being apparently, practised indiscriminately, We do not know what to conjecture of it. Almost all the Men have had one of the Fore-teeth extracted, but from being so universal we are equally at a Loss as to ye Motive of this Custom, they will sometimes thrust their Fingers into your Mouth to see if you have parted with this Tooth, the Governor happens to want this Tooth, at which they appear somewhat pleased & surprised . . . They are wonderfully expert at the art of Mimickry, both in their Actions and in repeating many of our Phrases, they will say—"Good Bye" after us, very distinctly, The Sailors teach them to swear. They laugh when they see us laugh, and they appear to be of a peaceable Disposition, and have a Generosity about them, in offering You a share of their Food. If you meet with any of them, they will readily offer You Fish, Fire, & Water . . . In a Word, to sum up the Qualities Personal & Mental, (those at least we have been able to discern) They appear to be an Active, Volatile, Unoffending, Happy, Merry, Funny, Laughing Good-natured, Nasty Dirty, Race of human Creatures as ever lived in a State of Savageness.[24]

For their part, the Eora were skeptical of the newly arrived strangers, and they certainly had cause to be so. Within weeks of the arrival of the First Fleet, Bennelong and his people were well aware of the dangers posed by the invaders. As had become standard practice for British explorers and settlers, Arthur Phillip had been charged with opening a dialogue with the local inhabitants—invaluable sources of information about the terrain, its peoples, and its flora and fauna. George III had instructed Phillip to "endeavor by every means possible to open an intercourse with the natives, and to conciliate their affections." Governor Phillip would come to take the royal command to use *every means* quite literally.

At first Phillip attempted to obey the crown's mandate to "conciliate" the "affections" of the locals. According to Nagle, who as one of Governor Phillip's boat crew usually accompanied him on his explorations:

> Whatever excursions we went on with the Governor, he endeavored to naturalize them, and giving them clothing and trinkets, and would not purmit them to be mislisted by any means, though he may run many risks of his life by them. When we would be shooting . . . and came across a school of fish, and the natives see us, they would come down with spear in hand and take what fish they thought fit until we could get them into the boat and push off. The Governor would not allow us arms to defend ourselves, for fear we would kill them in our own defence.[25]

Phillip's attempt to prevent the various misunderstandings likely to occur between two such alien cultures from turning deadly seems like sound policy, especially in the light of the many tragedies that plagued relations between British colonists and Native Americans in the early years of North American settlement. Unfortunately for the indigenous peoples of Australia, Phillip did not learn all of the lessons from the North American precedent. After a year of trying to establish firm connections with little to show for it, Phillip became frustrated at the paucity of sustained contact and dialogue with the Eora. He knew that if the fledgling settlement were to survive in such a foreign land, learning from the native inhabitants would be vital. So, Phillip employed a tried and tested strategy for securing indigenous informants: he simply kidnapped them. British explorers and settlers had been capturing native peoples for information since the early days of North American settlement. The pilgrims who landed at Plymouth in what would become Massachusetts were helped in the early years by Tisquantum, better known as Squanto, an English-speaking Patuxet man who had learned the language after being kidnapped by an English adventurer years earlier in 1614. With such well-known precedents firmly in mind, and with little willing cooperation among the Eora, on December 31, 1788, Phillip ordered Lieutenant Ball to take two boats and with Lieutenant George Johnston and a party of his marines "to seize and carry off some of the natives."[26]

The lieutenants and their men proceeded to Manly Cove, north-east of the British settlement, where they spotted a group of Eora standing on the beach. The cove had been named for "the manly undaunted behaviour of a party of natives seen there," so the British used their best subterfuge to lure in the unsuspecting locals, enticing them into conversation "with our courteous behavior and a few presents." Once the Eora's guard was down, the trap was sprung. "A proper opportunity being presented," an eyewitness later recounted, "our people rushed in among them, and seized two men: the rest fled." The Eora had been surprised by the British gambit, but they were not cowed. As the two men struggled with their British captors, the rest of the Eora regrouped and attacked the British in a desperate attempt to free their kinsmen. In the pitched battle that ensued, one of the captives managed to escape, but the second, a man named Arabanoo, was thrown into one of the boats and tied fast. The British were used to the local peoples retreating in the face of British guns, but now the Eora renewed their attack, driven on by "the most piercing and lamentable cries of distress" emanating from the distraught Arabanoo. The British quickly cast off amidst a cascade of projectiles. "The boats put off without delay; and an attack from the shore instantly commenced: they threw spears, stones, firebrands, and whatever else presented itself, at the boats; nor did they retreat, agreeable to their former custom, until many musquets were fired over them."[27]

Arabanoo was taken back to Port Jackson and placed in fetters. A convict was assigned to sleep with him and shadow his movements, and although he was well fed, his spirits remained low. One British observer noted that "sullenness and dejection strongly marked his countenance on the following morning; to amuse him, he was taken around the camp, and to the observatory: casting his eyes to the opposite shore from the point where he stood, and seeing the smoke of fire lighted by his countrymen, he looked earnestly at it, and sighing deeply two or three times, uttered the word 'gweeun' (fire)."

The British did their best to cheer their captive, playing him music and showing him pictures of birds, including some he recognized, and people, including the Duchess of Cumberland. They also made efforts to placate the Eora in the days and weeks after his capture, though the methods were heart-rendingly cruel. "To convince his countrymen that he had received no injury from us, the governor took him in a boat down the harbour, that they might see and converse with him: when the boat arrived, and lay at a little distance from the beach, several Indians who had retired at her approach" returned after seeing Arabanoo. The Eora captive "was greatly affected, and shed tears. At length they began to converse. Our ignorance of the language prevented us from knowing much of what passed; it was, however, easily understood that his friends asked him why he did not jump overboard, and rejoin them. He only sighed, and pointed to the fetter on his leg, by which he was bound." On another occasion, while sailing aboard the *Supply* with Governor Phillip, Arabanoo dove from the ship to make his escape. He was a strong swimmer but unused to swimming in European clothes and was quickly recaptured.[28]

Kidnapping and captivity were not the only wrongs perpetrated by the new arrivals. While the British command was content with their new informant, others among the settlers were restive. In March of 1789, a group of sixteen convicts hatched a plan to raid a nearby Eora settlement, hoping to seize their fishing equipment. One day while working at the brick kiln, the felons crept out of the British camp armed with clubs and tools and made their way to Botany Bay. If the convicts hoped to surprise their intended prey they were gravely mistaken, and as they arrived near the bay:

A body of Indians, who had probably seen them set out, and had penetrated their intention from experience, suddenly fell upon them. Our heroes were immediately routed, and separately endeavoured to effect their escape by any means which were left. In their flight one was killed, and seven were wounded, for the most part very severely: those who had the good fortune to outstrip their comrades and arrive in camp, first gave the alarm; and a detachment of marines, under an officer, was ordered to march to their relief. The officer arrived too late to repel the Indians; but he brought in the body of the man that was killed, and put an end to the pursuit.

Governor Phillip was incensed. The convicts had left the kiln without permission, and their actions threatened to upend the fragile peace with the

Eora. The felons claimed to have been attacked by the Eora without cause, but the truth eventually emerged and the guilty men were "severely flogged." Arabanoo was present at the flogging, perhaps to witness that the rigors of British justice applied to those who attacked his people. If the flogging was an attempt to win the approval of a representative of the Eora, however, it did not have its desired effect. As one onlooker recorded, "Arabanoo was present at the infliction of the punishment; and was made to comprehend the cause and the necessity of it; but he displayed on the occasion symptoms of disgust and terror only." For Arabanoo and the Eora, the British brought to Australian shores not justice or civilization but only violence and death.[29]

Arabanoo's assessment of the British interlopers had its merits, and it must have seemed that they were often as violent and cruel to each other as they were to the Eora. In the second year of settlement, a group of eight soldiers, perhaps tiring of a hard life so far from home and seeking to drown their miseries in a bottle, hatched a plan to steal a large quantity of liquor from the settlement's storehouse. They had a duplicate key made by a convict blacksmith, and when one of the conspirators took his turn as sentry, robbed the storehouse of booze and other provisions. The key, however, broke off in the storehouse door, alerting the storekeeper to the theft. Fearing discovery, one of the soldiers turned king's evidence and informed the governor of the entire affair. In addition to the theft, he admitted that the conspirators, drunk on stolen spirits, had beaten to death one of their mates who had threatened to turn them in. Rather than feeling remorse, the soldiers had proceeded to their fallen comrade's grave with a keg of stolen liquor, "sat in the grave, and stuck a bayonet in to the grave, and renewed their oath not to discover." The soldiers were duly tried, condemned, and hanged, despite pleas of mercy from other soldiers, who asked the governor to spare some of the conspirators. Governor Phillip replied that "if he saved one he must forgive all, and that was out of his power, to do justice to his country."

The soldiers were not the only colonists to feel the full weight of eighteenth-century justice. In November 1789, as the American sailor Jacob Nagle looked on in disgust, Ann Davis, a female convict, was hanged for stealing some laundry. She was led to the gallows by two women, because "she was so much intoxicated in liquor that she could not stand without holding her up."

For Nagle, "it was a dreadful to see going to eternity out of this world in such a senseless, shocking manner." The convicts had been shown mercy, it was thought, in being spared the gallows in Britain in exchange for transportation to Australia. As such, any further criminal behavior would not be tolerated.[30]

Keeping control of the large convict population was a constant concern for the leaders of the colony, and the rough justice meted out to those who transgressed was intended to provide a edifying example for the rest of the convicts. The difficulties of discipline were exacerbated by the ever-present lure of the frontier. Sentries were placed throughout the camp and fences erected, but these posed little hindrance for the convict determined to take his chances in the bush. Subsistence outside of the confines of the camp might be difficult, but a number of convicts were willing to stake their lives for the freedom provided by the vast Australian interior.

One of the most difficult convict runaways in the first years of settlement was John Caesar, a man of African descent, and given the classical bent of his name, likely one of the handful of former slaves transported with the First Fleet. His troubles began in April 1789 when he was charged with theft. Caesar was a very large, powerful man and widely considered to be the most formidable laborer in the entire settlement. With rations purposely meager so as to make them stretch until the colony could be resupplied, the hard-working Caesar stole food to support his outsized frame and exhausting labor. In early May, Caesar escaped from confinement and fled to the bush, taking with him a pilfered musket and ammunition. Even with a firearm, surviving in the wilds beyond the settlement was clearly arduous, and at the end of May he was spotted stealing supplies from a party of convict brick-makers. After a month of tenuous freedom, the fugitive was recaptured in June. With multiple thefts and an escape marring his ledger, Caesar realized he was likely to hang, but he seemed little affected by the possibility. Captain David Collins described him as "so indifferent about meeting death that he declared while in confinement, that if he should be hanged, he would create a laugh before he was turned off, by playing off some trick upon the executioner." Caesar was prevented from such a ghoulish performance, however, as questions about his mental capacity and his indifference to death led Governor Phillip to conclude that his execution would not produce the wished for didactic example for the other prisoners. As

Collins relayed, "Holding up" John Caesar "as an example was not expected to have the proper or intended effect." As a result, Caesar's sentence was commuted and he was instead sent to Garden Island.[31]

Governor Phillip had not, as it transpired, heard the last of John Caesar. In December 1789 he escaped from his Garden Island exile, once more taking with him a gun and ammunition. Those tasked with his recapture were not at all sanguine, admitting that "it was dangerous to strive to retake him, being both ignorant and very powerful and strong." If he hoped for a more permanent existence in the bush, he was once more disappointed, and finding scraping a long-term existence on his own increasingly onerous, he surrendered himself a month later in January. He was clapped in "double irons" to prevent yet another escape, and "tried for his life and condem'd." The governor tried his best to persuade Caesar of the seriousness of his predicament and the likely consequences of his continued thefts and escapes. You can almost hear a sense of gentle pleading in Governor Phillip's conversation with the condemned man, a vain attempt to convince John Caesar of the finality of death and the remorseless judgment of the world to come. He asked Caesar "what he thought would become of him when he had to die," but the prisoner only laughed, "and seemed to rejoice, saying he would go to his own country and see his friends." Perhaps Caesar's perceived simplicity is belied by this heart-rending retort. For a man who likely spent much of his life as a slave, either stolen from his homeland or raised in the brutal world of Atlantic slavery, a man who gained a modicum of freedom in Britain, yet another foreign land, only to be arrested and sent around the world to a new colonial captivity, for such a man the distant call of home, of family and of friends, must have made the prospect of earthly death laughably quaint.[32]

Governor Phillip once more commuted Caesar's sentence, sending him this time to the more remote Norfolk Island, but such a determined runaway could not be contained for long. In 1793 he was returned to Port Jackson, but continued his pattern of flight and surrender until 1796, when a price of five gallons of liquor was finally put on his head. That year, after eight years of persistent resistance to his captivity, John Caesar was shot and killed in the bush by an Eora man seeking the reward. It was reported that Caesar escaped so often in part because he wished to establish himself "in the society of the natives, with a wish to adopt their customs and to live with them: but he was always repulsed by them; and compelled to return to us from hunger and wretchedness." That an indigenous Australian would come to kill an escaped British convict of African descent for a prize set by colonial authorities is one of the many horribly surreal conjunctures of the expanding world in the late eighteenth century.[33]

The Europeans brought other, more insidious, perils in their train as well. Tragically, as so often happened when formerly isolated groups of people met, contact was followed by epidemic. A mere year after the arrival of the British, smallpox, the scourge of Native Americans, broke out among the Eora. By April 1789 British foraging parties began to encounter the bodies of Eora floating in the coves and inlets of Sydney Harbor. It was clear that something was dreadfully wrong, and some of the surgeons and medical men of the colony acquired some of the corpses for examination. What they found was truly alarming: "On inspection, it appeared that all the parties had died a natural death: pustules, similar to those occasioned by the small pox, were thickly spread on the bodies; but how a disease, to which our former observations had led us to suppose them strangers, could at once have introduced itself, and have spread so widely, seemed inexplicable." British observers found it hard to conceive how smallpox could have reached such distant shores. No European had shown symptoms or signs of the disease in the seventeen months since they left the Cape of Good Hope. Some theorized that smallpox had been spread by the French, or by Captain Cook, or even across the continent from western Australia via earlier contacts made by William Dampier. Whatever the original source of the virus, by May 1789 the Eora were dying.[34]

When Arabanoo heard a family of his people living in a nearby cove had been struck with the new illness, he sped to the scene with Governor Phillip and one of the colony's surgeons. They arrived to a devastating scene.

Here they found an old man stretched before a few lighted sticks, and a boy of 9 or 10 years old pouring water on his head, from a shell which he held in his hand: near them lay a female child dead, and a little farther off, its unfortunate mother: the body of the woman shewed that famine, superadded to disease, had occasioned her death: eruptions covered the poor boy from head to foot; and the old man was so reduced, that he was with difficulty got into the boat.

The old man and the boy were put in a boat to transport them back to the colony hospital, but Arabanoo refused to leave until he had seen to the burial of the dead. With his own hands he dug a grave in the sandy soil, lining it with grass. With gentle care he placed the body of the girl into the simple grave and covered the tiny corpse with more grass before burying her with sand until a mound rose over her.[35]

Despite Arabanoo's tender ministrations, the old Eora man died mere hours after arriving in Port Jackson. His deathbed scene was a heart-rending sight. According to a witness:

> he bore the pangs of dissolution with patient composure; and though he was sensible to the last moment, expired almost without a groan. Nanbaree [the Eora boy] appeared quite unmoved at the event; and surveyed the corpse of his father without emotion, simply exclaiming, "boee" (dead). This surprised us; as the tenderness and anxiety of the old man about the boy had been very moving. Although barely able to raise his head, while so much strength was left to him, he kept looking into his child's cradle; he patted him gently on the bosom; and, with dying eyes, seemed to recommend him to our humanity and protection.

Arabanoo once more saw to the burial. Remarkably, Nanbaree recovered, and was adopted into the family of Mr. White, the colony's surgeon-general.[36]

As the days passed, the outbreak only became worse. Two Eora youths, a brother and sister, arrived in the British settlement in great distress, both afflicted with smallpox. Once more Arabanoo and the surgeons did what they could, but the young boy quickly weakened and died. In silence his sister lay down beside his body, remaining by his side until the cold of night forced her to retreat. As his people died around him, Arabanoo, who had done so much to aid his sick brethren, himself fell ill. The British surgeons did their best to see him through the ordeal, but after six days of illness, Arabanoo died, a victim of his "humanity and affectionate concern towards his sick compatriots," but also of an illness unknown before the arrival of the British.[37]

With no immunity to the disease the mortality rate was staggering. So too were the dislocating effects. When the disease first began to break out in April

1789, the Eora had no previous reference for understanding the causes of their suffering, nor how to combat it. Nothing in their traditional repertoire seemed to have an ameliorating effect, and, as more and more of their people were laid low by the terrifying, disfiguring pestilence, many simply fled, leaving scores of the sick "laying Dead on the Beaches and in the Caverns of Rocks, forsaken by the rest as soon as the Disease is discovered on them. They were generally found with the remains of a Small Fire on each Side of them and some Water left within their Reach." But flight did not save them and the disease merely spread more rapidly as the infected population scattered. Death, and flight from it, left behind broken communities in which hunting, fishing, and gathering—the keys to survival among the Eora—were severely disrupted by the loss of the adult population. This was only exacerbated by the fact that smallpox was most virulent among those under 5 years of age and those above 14. More than half of the adult population would have succumbed, with many more absent as they attempted to escape the disease. Pregnant women and children under 5 died at an even higher rate, meaning that almost an entire new generation of Eora were wiped out in an instant. In the aftermath of the outbreak, local communities were greatly reduced, but also newly imbalanced. More Eora between the ages of 5 and 14 survived than any other group. Young children and adults would have been scarce on the ground, leaving communities struggling to survive in both the present and the future. By the time the worst of it had passed, perhaps as many as 70 per cent of the local population were dead. It had been barely more than a year since the arrival of the British at Botany Bay.[38]

As had happened in North America two centuries earlier, the outbreak of virulent disease among the indigenous peoples of Australia quickly undermined effective local resistance to British incursions and provided both space and justification for subsequent British settlement. Because the effects of the disease were seen to be a positive boon for British interests, in both North American and Australian contexts it has been suggested that the release of smallpox was an intentional act and early instance of biological warfare rather than merely a tragic but accidental result of contact between previously isolated human populations. There is no direct evidence of a concerted plan to release smallpox among Native Americans or Australian Aborigines, but the circumstantial evidence in the Australian case is at least suggestive.[39]

Bennelong's fate was inextricably tied to that of Arabanoo. He certainly would have heard about the capture of Arabanoo, and may even have been present at the mêlée on the beach or seen the melancholy man himself on one of his many excursions under British guard. Perhaps he heard stories of Arabanoo's selfless care for his sick countrymen and of his untimely demise in reluctant captivity. Bennelong had himself suffered from the smallpox at this time, but unlike other ill Eora, had not sought aid in the British settlement. Whatever he knew of Arabanoo's life and death, when the captive died in May 1789, the course of Bennelong's life changed forever. Despite his unhappiness and his attempts to escape, Arabanoo had proved highly useful to Governor Phillip. He had begun to provide the British with accounts of the "customs and manners" of the local peoples, as well as the indigenous names for plants, animals, rivers and bays, the starting point for translation. His death, however, disrupted this new flow of information, and Phillip quickly ordered his men to capture another Eora. "By his death, the scheme which had invited his capture was utterly defeated," a British settler observed. "Of five natives who had been brought among us, three had perished from a cause which, though unavoidable, it was impossible to explain to a people, who would condescend to enter into no intercourse with us. The same suspicious dread of our approach, and the same scenes of vengeance acted on unfortunate stragglers, continued to prevail."[40]

By November 1789, Governor Phillip had decided that new captives must be acquired if the British were to gain any information about the resources of the country. A party led by Lieutenant Bradley was duly dispatched and returned with two young Eora men, Bennelong and Colbee. Bradley reported that the two were captured without firing a shot, but this seems unlikely given the resistance encountered when Arabanoo was taken. Jacob Nagle, who was likely present as well and perhaps had less reason to mask the violence of the abduction, presents a different story. Nagle recalls that he was in one of three boats sent "down the harbor . . . to take some of the heads of the natives to naturalize them." They landed at a likely spot in Manly Bay, and were approached by a group of friendly Eora. The two targets were pointed out to the men and when a signal was given, "the boats' crews seized them and carried them into the boats in an instant." Far from acquiescing to the kidnapping, the Eora fought back, "the spears begin to fly, the officers and sum marines firing upon them, but losing their chiefs they were very resolute, but retreating in the bushes, they hove their spears at random." Under a hail of spears, and with a heavy covering fire, the three boats just managed to escape, returning to Port Jackson where the captives were greeted by a pair of friendly faces. They were welcomed by Abaroo and Nanbaree, two Eora previously captured by the British who seemed to have had some previous acquaintance with the new arrivals, calling them by name.[41]

When he was captured, Bennelong was about 26 years of age, a tall, stout young man with a brave, defiant character not altered by his imprisonment. Bennelong's battle experience was visibly marked on his body. His head was covered in the scars of battle, and an arm, leg and thumb bore the marks of spear wounds. Bennelong's intelligence and resourcefulness served him well during his years in captivity. He quickly became accustomed to British ways, learning the language and manners of his captors rapidly, regaling his captors with song and dance, and tales of his conquests in love and war. Unlike previous Eora prisoners, Bennelong freely provided information about the customs and economy of his people and developed a relationship of mutual respect and friendship with Governor Phillip. Outwardly at least, Bennelong played the role the British hoped for, the happy informant. His true feelings about his situation, however, were much more complex, as would be revealed in 1790.[42]

The necessity of native information became more starkly apparent to the British in that year. Although they had been living in Australia for nearly two years, the settlement was still not completely self-sufficient. Like the Plymouth colony in North America, the Port Jackson colony depended on supplies from Britain and other colonies to survive. In 1790, the supply ship failed to appear as scheduled and famine and despair began to creep into the British camp. As the prospect of starvation began to stalk the land, prisoners and soldiers alike began to steal from the gardens and storehouses that provided the only tangible means of subsistence. In such trying times, the full weight of British law was once more applied. According to Watkin Tench:

> Because, as every man could possess, by his utmost exertions, but a bare sufficiency to preserve life, he who deprived his neighbour of that little, drove him to desperation. No new laws for the punishment of theft were

enacted; but persons of all descriptions were publicly warned, that the severest penalties, which the existing law in its greatest latitude would authorise, should be inflicted on offenders. The following sentence . . . on a convict detected in a garden stealing potatoes, will illustrate the subject. He was ordered to receive three hundred lashes immediately, to be chained for six months to two other criminals, who were thus fettered for former offences, and to have his allowance of flour stopped for six months . . . Such was the melancholy length to which we were compelled to stretch our penal system.[43]

This acute lack of provisions, and the brutal eventualities it precipitated, only made the importance of local knowledge all the more stark. If the settlement was to have any chance of long-term success it would have to learn how to grow, hunt and gather its own resources. If they were to make a stab at true self-sufficiency, the colony needed information about native resources from men like Bennelong. At the same time, however, they attempted to prevent Bennelong from learning of their dire circumstances, fearing that if news of their weakened state reached the local Eora, they might seize the opportunity to be rid of the British once and for all.

When Bennelong escaped in May of 1790, these fears seemed to have been realized. At two o'clock in the morning on May 3, Bennelong feigned illness, sending his watcher out of their house to seek aid. With no one watching, he crept out of the house, jumped over a fence and made his break for freedom. Months later, contact was made with Bennelong once more, with near fatal consequences. On September 7, a party from Port Jackson heading for Broken Bay spotted roughly 200 Eora gathered around the carcass of a whale at Manly Cove, roasting its meat over dozens of fires. A beached whale was a great boon to the Eora, and on such occasions a festive atmosphere often prevailed, but as the British approached the Eora were clearly on their guard. When they spotted the British party making ready to land, they scrambled to collect their spears to confront the looming threat. The British party were alarmed by the hostile response to their approach, but when they spotted a familiar face among the crowd, they relaxed a little. With two new scars marring his face and a scraggly beard hiding his features, Bennelong was difficult to recognize at first, but the reunion of former captive and captors eased tensions enough for the British to enter into conversation with the Eora. They enquired after the governor, and asked for hatchets—better for breaking apart the fibrous whale carcass than the shell blades they traditionally employed—but were disappointed when they were given knives, shirts and handkerchiefs instead. Despite the outward amiability of the encounter, the Eora remained wary and their women and children stood well apart, refusing to come nearer even at the offer of rewards.

Despite the somewhat strained meeting, the British party decided to continue on to Broken Bay as originally intended, while a few of the sailors returned to Port Jackson to acquaint the governor of the encounter with Bennelong and the large party of Eora. In their boat they also carried a large hunk of whale meat, a gift from Bennelong to the governor. When Governor Phillip heard that Bennelong had been found, he immediately gathered a crew and set out for Manly Cove. Butchering and consuming a whale is a laborious task, even for 200 hungry people, so when Governor Phillip arrived at Manly Cove, Bennelong and company were still on the beach. The governor and three men proceeded onshore, and although Bennelong at first seemed a bit aloof, he quickly transformed into the affable person the British had come to know and admire. He accepted a glass of wine, offering a toast to the king before downing it, asked after British friends in Port Jackson, performed his familiar mocking impression of the settlement's French cook, and inquired about a woman he had kissed, giving a surprised lieutenant a kiss in re-enactment of the amorous event.

The convivial calm was broken, however, when the governor's party attempted to make their way inland from the beach. They were quickly surrounded on all sides by the Eora and though no violence was offered, were forced to retreat back to their original position on the beach. Back on the beach, peace once more prevailed, but after another half hour of conversation, the tension was ratcheted back up by the appearance of an Eora warrior with spear in hand. The spearman approached the party, eventually coming to a stop about 20 yards from the four Europeans. In an attempt to put the newcomer at ease, the governor slowly approached him, holding out his hand in a sign of friendship and throwing down the dirk he kept at his belt. The governor's amiable gestures did not have the desired effect, and as he came nearer, the Eora man became more tense, and readied his spear for action.

Whether because he did not wish to appear weak in front of the assembled Eora or because he thought it the best way of diffusing the situation, Governor Phillip continued his steady advance. It would be a costly error in judgment. As Watkin Tench later related:

> To retreat, his excellency now thought would be more dangerous than to advance. He therefore cried out to the man, Weeeree, Weeree, (bad; you are doing wrong) displaying at the same time, every token of amity and confidence. The words had, however, hardly gone forth, when the Indian, stepping back with one foot, aimed his lance with such force and dexterity, that striking the governor's right shoulder, just above the collar-bone, the point glancing downward, came out at his back, having made a wound of many inches long. The man was observed to keep his eye steadily fixed on the lance until it struck its object, when he directly dashed into the woods and was seen no more.[44]

The scene now descended into chaos. Bennelong disappeared into the hinterland while a cascade of spears showered the British. The men left in the boats attempted to reach their besieged comrades, but only one of their muskets would fire. Meanwhile a grievously wounded Governor Phillip struggled to make his way to safety. According to Tench:

> A situation more distressing than that of the governor, during the time that this lasted, cannot readily be conceived: the pole of the spear, not less than ten feet in length, sticking out before him, and impeding his flight, the butt frequently striking the ground, and lacerating the wound. In vain did Mr. Waterhouse try to break it; and the barb, which appeared on the other side, forbade extraction, until that could be performed. At length it was broken, and his excellency reached the boat.[45]

The governor was quickly transported back to Port Jackson. Although many thought he would surely die, the spearhead was successfully removed and the bleeding stopped.[46]

The governor was quickly on the mend, but it was clear to all that relations with the Eora had soured. Some have since suggested that the attack on

Governor Phillip was a deliberate plan, hatched by Bennelong as a means of seeking revenge or evening the score for his kidnapping. There is little evidence of Bennelong's thinking in this period, so it is impossible to know whether the attack had been planned, but whatever its immediate cause, the mêlée at Manly Cove was the beginning of a period of heightened tensions, even hostility, between the British and the Eora. The Eora stopped all contact with the British and at least one other European party was ambushed. Jacob Nagle and a group of sailors were attacked while pushing away from shore a short time later. The boat's coxswain was speared through the right arm, and Nagle himself saw a spear strike the side of the mast next to which he was standing. The governor's earlier attempts to ensure peace by limiting the use of firearms was reversed and soldiers and sailors now went armed when they left the relative safety of the settlement.[47]

When contact with the Eora sporadically resumed, the British learned that the governor's attacker was a man from Broken Bay. With renewed contact also came clues about the possible reasons for the attack and the hardening of relations. Two Eora men from Rose Hill asked after the governor's health and were please when informed that he was on the mend, but also "expressed great dissatisfaction at the number of white men who had settled in their former territories." By 1790, the Eora living closest to the British settlement were likely resigned to their continued presence. With the arrival of a second fleet carrying nearly a thousand more convicts in June of 1790, and the gradual expansion of the British presence, however, new groups of Eora, previously somewhat insulated from the European influx, were likely awakening to the seriousness of the threat. The fact that Phillip's attacker came from Broken Bay, an area initially more removed from the British but now being invaded, is unsurprising. It certainly seems a more likely cause of the attack than Bennelong's desire to balance the scales, especially given Bennelong's actions in the coming months.[48]

In September, after a period of heightened tension between Eora and European, a fire was spotted on the north shore of Sydney Harbor. A party sent out from the British settlement to investigate found Bennelong and several of his countrymen gathered on the beach. Despite the previous bloodshed, the meeting was civil and a dinner was arranged between the two parties later in the day. While they may have been bemused by his escape and the attack on

Governor Phillip, the British remained keenly aware of the crucial utility of indigenous informants. As such, they made a considerable effort to patch things over with their former captive, hoping to gradually convince him to return, at least on occasion, to Port Jackson. Toward this end, gifts were given, food and wine provided, and Bennelong given a shave, an act that for Bennelong had the added benefit of deeply impressing his countrymen. It is clear, even from British accounts, that Bennelong was using the British as much as they were using him. He was aware that the British needed the knowledge and information he could provide, and he leveraged this need for his own ends. Not only did Bennelong receive handsome gifts from the British, but on a number of occasions he used his knowledge of British goods and customs, and a lack of fear in the face of British practices such as shaving, to improve his standing in his own community.[49]

For their part, the British quickly recognized Bennelong's understandable wariness about returning to the settlement, and attempted to use his wife, Barangaroo, as a conduit for improved relations. She was given a petticoat to wear, but was quickly "laughed . . . out of it" by the combined ridicule of Bennelong and the British. Her hair was combed and cut, and her timid behavior during this attempt to impose European standards of feminine beauty was enough for one observer to suggest that she brought to mind the "civilized women" they had left behind. Watkin Tench recorded his surprise:

> that amidst a horde of roaming savages, in the desert wastes of New South Wales, might be found as much feminine innocence, softness, and modesty (allowing for inevitable difference of education), as the most finished system could bestow, or the most polished circle produce. So little fitted are we to judge of human nature at once! And yet on such grounds have countries been described, and nations characterized. Hence have arisen those speculative and laborious compositions on the advantages and superiority of a state of nature.[50]

The British may have viewed her through a misogynistic lens of female simplicity, but Barangaroo was no fool. Not only did she fail to encourage Bennelong to return to the British settlement, she vociferously opposed it, and even went so far as to attempt to persuade Boorong, another Eora captive, to return to her people. Fearing the loss of yet another Eora interpreter, the British requested that Bennelong find a husband for Boorong, hoping to both placate Boorong and tie Bennelong more closely to the British settlement. A likely candidate was found in the guise of a 16-year-old Eora youth named Yemmerrawannie, Bennelong's future companion on his European voyage, but Boorong was not at all interested. Though rejected as a potential suitor, Yemmerrawannie, with his youthful energy and adventurous spirit, soon became a regular fixture in British–Eora relations.

One British gambit to smooth over relations with Bennelong and the Eora had failed, but another was quickly tried. Since the first days of contact, the Eora had regularly complained about, and sometimes responded violently to, the new arrivals' penchant for stealing their boats and fishing equipment. Bennelong's previous affiliation with the British had both increased his authority among his own people and made him the most obvious candidate to request the return of stolen goods. Knowing they could easily derail the sensitive process of building a harmonious relationship with the local peoples, Governor Phillip had always attempted to prevent such thefts and tried to return stolen property when it came to his attention. Later, when a convict was charged with stealing fishing tackle from an Eora man, the governor immediately ordered a severe flogging in the presence of as many Eora as could be convinced to attend. Many Eora men and women gathered for the punishment, and the reasons for the procedure were explained to them, but their reaction was anything but accepting of European penal practice. As Watkin Tench observed,

If the behaviour of those now collected be found to correspond with it, it is, I think, fair to conclude that these people are not of a sanguinary and implacable temper. Quick indeed of resentment, but not unforgiving of injury. There was not one of them that did not testify strong abhorrence of the punishment and equal sympathy with the sufferer. The women were particularly affected; Daringa shed tears, and Barangaroo, kindling into anger, snatched a stick and menaced the executioner. The conduct of these women, on this occasion, was exactly descriptive of their characters. The former was ever meek and feminine, the latter fierce and unsubmissive.[51]

In October 1790, an arrangement was made to fulfill Bennelong's request that the stolen property be returned, which seems to have precipitated a general relaxation of tensions. The full and final reconciliation between the two camps, however, seems to have been almost wholly on Bennelong's terms. Once he had succeeded in getting the British to return his people's stolen property, he made a calculated inquiry after the governor's health. From all his actions, it is clear that Bennelong's regard for Phillip was genuine and his desire to see him well not manufactured, but it seems probable that he was also asking about the governor as a means of signaling that he was once more willing to visit the British settlement. In mid-October, he did just that, traveling to Port Jackson with several companions, but only after a British hostage was left under the watchful eye of one of his countrymen.

Over the next several months Bennelong made regular appearances among the British. He was regularly bestowed with gifts, and Governor Phillip even had a brick house, 12 foot square, built for his personal use at what is now known as Bennelong Point in Port Jackson—today the site of the Sydney Opera House. Bennelong's return to his position as intermediary between Eora and British helped to ensure good relations with the native peoples of the immediate area. Further afield, however, the violence engendered by British encroachment continued to rage.

The solicitousness with which the British approached Bennelong was in other interactions with the local peoples nowhere to be found. Like the recurrent theft of Eora property, much of this brutish treatment ran counter to Governor Phillip's express orders and his own instructions from Britain. Nonetheless, the behavior of some settlers was enough to repeatedly undermine efforts to prevent open hostilities between the invaders and the invaded. The situation took a conspicuously dark turn when a convict was killed in December of 1790. McEntire—a convict who doubled as the governor's gamekeeper—and a small group of settlers had traveled out beyond the north arm of Botany Bay to hunt kangaroos. The strange creatures were best tackled at night, so the hunting party hunkered down for the evening in a hut made of boughs. Around 1 a.m., the hunters were awoken by a rustling in the brush. Assuming the sound was made by their would-be prey, McEntire and the rest crept out of the hut with guns primed and ready.

To their surprise, in the place of kangaroos, they found five Eora men stalking into their camp, spears in hand. McEntire, recognizing a few of the Eora, laid down his gun and approached the men, speaking to them in their own language. After being spotted, the Eora began a slow retreat, followed by McEntire who continued his attempts at calming conversation. In a flash, everything went wrong. Seemingly out of nowhere, one of the Eora, a man named Pimelwi, leapt up onto a fallen tree and drove his spear deep into the side of the advancing McEntire. With the spear lodged between two ribs, a fading McEntire was taken back to the settlement. Despite deeming the patient beyond hope, the surgeons sought the medical advice of a number of Eora who happened to be visiting the settlement. Even if it was too late to save the game-keeper, the surgeons hoped to learn from the local men how best to treat the wounds made by native spears. With their backward-facing barbs, these spears were difficult and dangerous to remove, and the Eora's unanimous medical opinion was that removing one as deeply lodged as the one in McEntire's side would spell a quick and certain death. At first the surgeons complied with the advice they had received, but two days later they made a rather clumsy attempt at the operation. As the Eora had foreseen, the spear was removed, but the barbs broke off inside the patient, who expired a short time later.[52]

Perhaps because he had grown attached to his gamekeeper, or because the killing was just the latest in a series of attacks on British settlers, Governor Phillip was apoplectic when he learned of McEntire's demise. To his mind, he had done his best to ensure that the clash of civilizations between British and Australian was as peaceful and harmonious as possible. Learning his lesson from the hair-triggered violence of the settlement of North America, Phillip had visibly punished those who stole from the local peoples, and even limited the use of guns outside of the settlement as a means of preventing the understandable tension of early encounters from devolving into shooting. He had given gifts, forged friendships, and upheld justice, and still, by the end of 1790 he could count seventeen separate instances when Eora had killed or wounded his men. While he wished to maintain the peace, Phillip believed that this would be impossible if the Eora believed they could attack the settlers with impunity, and so he ordered a party of upwards of fifty men to proceed to the place of the attack on McEntire to capture the guilty men. An order was issued to this effect stating:

Several tribes of the natives still continuing to throw spears at any man they meet unarmed, by which several have been killed, or dangerously wounded, the governor, in order to deter the natives from such practices in future, has ordered out a party to search for the man who wounded the convict McEntire, in so dangerous a manner on Friday last, though no offence was offered on his part, in order to make a signal example of that tribe. At the same time, the governor strictly forbids, under penalty of the severest punishment, any soldier or other person, not expressly ordered out for that purpose, ever to fire on any native except in his own defence; or to molest him in any shape, or to bring away any spears, or other articles which they may find belonging to those people. The natives will be made severe examples of whenever any man is wounded by them; but this will be done in a manner which may satisfy them that it is a punishment inflicted on them for their own bad conduct, and of which they cannot be made sensible if they are not treated with kindness while they continue peaceable and quiet.

The governor was aware that the Eora were not an undifferentiated mass but divided into tribes or clans, each with its own territory and with its own political relationships with other tribes. Warfare was as endemic among the Eora as it was among Europeans, and as in North America, the coming of the British had done much to destabilize the delicate balance between the local clans. This balance, as Phillip surmised, was central to indigenous politics, observing that "although they did not fear death individually, yet that the relative weight and importance of the different tribes appeared to be the highest object of their estimation, as each tribe deemed its strength and security to consist wholly in its powers, aggregately considered." Phillip identified the Bidjigal clan, whose territory lay to the north of Botany Bay where McEntire had been assaulted, as the prime agents in the attacks on British settlers. What the governor might not have fully realized, however, was that by forging a close relationship with the clans of Port Jackson he had upset the local balance of power, inviting a hostile response from clans threatened by any alliance between the newcomers and their age-old rivals. The authorities in Britain, and Phillip himself, had been concerned to learn from the mistakes of North America, and had taken steps to ensure that the violence that consumed Atlantic colonies was not repeated in the Pacific. And yet, once more, British settlement had led to devastating disease, casual violence, and factional fighting. Violence was simply a necessary condition of imperialism and the British, as ever, agents of disruption and death.

The instructions given to the British party sent to chastise the Bidjigal, led by Watkin Tench, project a mixture of justice and terror. On the one hand, Governor Phillip wanted "to strike a decisive blow, in order, at once to convince them of our superiority and to infuse an universal terror, which might operate to prevent farther mischief." To that end, he ordered Tench to capture two Bidjigal men and put ten to death on the spot. They were instructed to cut the heads off the executed men and bring them back as grisly proof of British power. On the other hand, Tench was to ensure that no women or children were harmed, no huts burnt, and nothing but weapons taken or destroyed. He was also to proceed in the open and not use treachery or promises of a friendly meeting as a means of getting close to the targets. In all their behavior it was to be clear to all observers that this was a judicial mission, designed to punish the guilty, and by no means an act of war. Phillip hoped to demonstrate the fate of those who attacked the British, while not undermining future relations with the local peoples. This was hardly likely to be the message received by the Eora, but it does reflect Phillip's attempts to maintain a firm line between the methods of Australian settlement and those used in North America.[53]

As it transpired, the avenging party was a conspicuous failure, in every sense of the word. News of McEntire's death and the governor's intended retaliation spread quickly through the area, and when Tench's cumbersomely large raiding party approached the nearby Eora simply melted into the bush, leaving the British to slog between one empty village and another with nothing to show for it. After two humiliating attempts to punish the Bidjigal, the cause of justice was abandoned. In the end, Governor Phillip's righteous rage came to naught. Even among the British many pointed the blame for McEntire's death squarely at the dead man himself. The convict cum-gamekeeper, as everyone knew, had a black reputation among the Eora. Bennelong openly despised the man, and he was not alone in his hatred. Tench himself records that the aversion toward McEntire was so universal as to lead many of the settlers to believe the rumors that the gamekeeper regularly shot at and injured Eora he encountered on his hunting trips. So widespread was this belief that on his deathbed he was questioned about it. The dying man admitted to once shooting an Eora man, but claimed it was in self-defense. Despite his strident deathbed denials, most remained convinced that he was killed not in cold blood but in retaliation for his own previous barbarity. McEntire had been reassured when he recognized his soon-to-be assailants, but the fact that they knew him and his previous atrocities likely sealed his fate.

On September 7, 1795, HMS *Reliance* finally landed at Port Jackson. Bennelong had been away from home for nearly three years. He had seen the wonders of London and the gentle beauty of the English countryside, but he had also lost his companion and experienced the unrelenting cold of an English winter and the illness it brought in train. He had been dressed in fine clothes, fed fine food, entertained and fêted by London society, he had seen the best that Britain had to offer, the best of European culture, of Western modernity. He found it wanting. He had been impatient to return to his homeland, but not just for familiar sights and familiar faces. After nearly three years living as the British did, Bennelong was eager to throw off the guise of Europeanization and return to his people. According to one observer, he "laid aside, all the ornaments and improvements he had reaped from his travels, and returned as if with increased relish, to all his former loathsome and savage habits. His clothes were thrown away as burthensome restraints on the freedom of his limbs, and he became again as compleat a New Hollander, as if he had never left his native wilds." He still visited the British settlement from time to time, but less often than he had in the time of Governor Phillip. "Upon his return to the Colony," it was recorded, "he fell off spontaneously into his early habits, and in spite of every thing that could be done to him in the order of civilization, he took to the bush, and only occasionally visited Government House." The British could still not quite grasp that their culture was part and parcel of the coercion of imperialism. It was their fatal blind spot, even among those with the best of intentions.[54]

In the years after 1795 Bennelong rose to a position of considerable authority among his people. He became head of a clan of around one hundred people living along the Parranatta River, becoming a prominent figure among the Eora of the area and a fixture in the ritual duels and warfare that determined status and power among and between clans. He died on January 2, 1813, in a house he had built in the orchard of the brewer James Squire, and was buried with one of his wives at Kissing Point. His death was well marked by European settlers, though with more venom than regard, in language that demonstrates a hardening of attitudes toward the native people of Australia and a new separation of European and Aboriginal society.

Bennelong died on Sunday morning last at Kissing Point. Of this veteran champion of the native tribe little favourable can be said. His voyage to and benevolent treatment in Great Britain produced no change whatever in his manners and inclinations, which were naturally barbarous and ferocious.

The principal officers of Government had for many years endeavoured, by the kindest of usage, to wean him from his original habits and draw him into a relish for civilised life; but every effort was in vain exerted and for the last few years he has been but little noticed. His propensity for drunkenness was inordinate; and when in that state he was insolent, menacing and overbearing. In fact, he was a thorough savage, not to be warped from the form and character that nature gave him by all the efforts that mankind could use.[55]

Since his death Bennelong has often been held up as an example of a man between two worlds, a man who, through contact with Europeans, could never again be fully accepted in his own society nor ever attain equal membership in European society. His likely cause of death, succumbing to a combination of wounds from traditional payback battles and the effects of alcohol introduced by the British, seems to reflect the negative consequences for the man who tried to live in both worlds. But this picture is not the whole reality. Bennelong seems a man caught between two clashing civilizations because he was adept at operating in both, taking what he needed from each and rejecting the rest. He used his connections with the British to gain goods, protection, and power among his own people. Bennelong stands out in Australian history not because he simply represents the costs of British settlement, but because he lived in a brief time in which an Eora man could successfully play both sides and live in two worlds, a moment when attitudes and animosities were not yet fixed, when the balance of power was yet to swing so drastically in British favor. By the time of his death in 1813 things had changed. British settlement was expanding rapidly, pushing the Eora off their lands. Missionaries and schools were targeting Eora culture— after his death Bennelong's own son would attend one such school—and Europeans were becoming increasingly intolerant of indigenous civilization. Bennelong's people had faced invasion, epidemic disease, and violence. A few, like Bennelong, thrived in these times, but for most this was an era of suffering and of dislocation.

As in so many other areas, the loss of the American colonies in the west forced Britain to turn to the east. Britain still needed an outlet for its restless young men, and with America closed to British armies and British felons alike, new safety valves were needed. In the years after the Irish Rebellion of 1798, Irish revolutionaries and political prisoners would join the ordinary criminals in New South Wales as the penal colony became the favored outlet for Britain's internal and imperial enemies. When traditional weavers and farm laborers destroyed new industrial machinery in the early nineteenth century, they too were exiled to Australia, once more allowing Britain to export its unrest while avoiding making martyrs in the name of order. With fewer interests across the Atlantic, British soldiers, sailors, and even surgeons were funneled into the Indian and Pacific Oceans, the growing arenas of imperial conflict. With the loss of its primary penal colony in America, Britain had been forced to innovate, pushing criminals into prisons, penitentiaries, and eventually to Oceania. The forced movement of soldiers, sailors, and convicts to the east helped to transform the world. By disrupting and displacing the long-standing judicial practices of the British Empire, the American Revolution had fundamentally altered the lives of tens of thousands, sending countless poor and downtrodden Europeans across the globe against their will. In turn, these forced migrants collided with existing populations and civilizations in Asia and Oceania, the first destabilizing waves of European conquest. Thus the inter-ethnic tensions and the resulting depopulation of native peoples far away in the South Pacific had their roots in the American Revolution. Without the American colonists' successful struggle for independence, the peoples of eastern Australia—the Wangal, Cadigal, and the Commeraygal—might well have remained free from European encroachment, and European diseases, for a while longer. Instead, over 150,000 convicts were transported to what would become Australia between 1788 and 1840, bringing with them the British Empire and the disease, violence, and cultural annihilation that followed in its wake.[56]

10

⇥ ⇤

EXILES OF REVOLUTION

That John Randall found himself a forced settler in the South Pacific was merely the last in a calamitous series of indignities wrought by the American Revolution. He had been condemned to his present fate in the penal colony of New South Wales because he stole, but he stole because of events beyond his control. In the course of a decade he had been torn from one temporary home after another until he found himself in England bereft of hope. John Randall had been born into slavery in Connecticut in 1764, likely the property of Captain John Randall of Stonington. He was still just a teenager in 1777 when British raids along the Connecticut coast provided him with the opportunity to cast off his shackles and join the enemy of his American captors. He was too young to join the British army as a soldier, but his skills with the flute and tambour won him a place as a drummer with the 63rd Regiment of Foot and a chance to win his freedom. Without a home, when the war ended Randall followed his regiment back to England, where he was demobilized in Manchester in 1783.

In post-war England, packed with demobbed soldiers and loyalist refugees in the tens of thousands, jobs were scarce and relief spread thin. He did his best to make do in a foreign country without friends or family, but with five regiments demobilized in Manchester alone, there was little prospect of legitimate employment. After two years of desperately struggling just to survive, in 1785 John Randall, like many others who found themselves in such dire straits,

356

turned to crime. In April 1785, he and a partner, another black man, possibly a former slave like himself, were convicted of stealing a watch. When Randall was arrested, the jails of Manchester were already packed with the thieves and beggars that had proliferated in the post-war city. Unable to cope with the flood of felons, local officials instead sentenced them to transportation to Africa. From Manchester, Randall and his partner were thus dispatched to London, where they were shackled below deck on the prison hulk *Ceres* to await transportation to Africa. After several years of waiting in the fetid hulk on the Thames, when it became clear to London officials that transportation to Africa was not feasible, John Randall found himself a penal pioneer aboard the First Fleet, bound for Britain's new penal colony in the South Pacific. He had been a pawn in the larger game of imperial competition, subject to whims of others and the tides of history. In this he was not alone.[1]

John Randall was only one of many former slaves who found themselves unwanted refugees of the American War set adrift in a country they had never known. Sitting in the cramped quarters of the *Ceres*, Randall might well have seen many men with faces like his own in the bustling crowds of the capital. As many as a thousand former slaves had limped into London and the other ports of England in the years after the war. They had done their part for king and country, volunteering to fight against rebellious colonies and their former masters in exchange for the promise of freedom. For many the decision was an easy one. By the time the war began, Britain had become a symbol of freedom, a beacon of hope for many enslaved Americans. When the British at last bowed to the inevitable and capitulated in 1783, however, the former slaves had little choice but to follow their defeated allies into exile in Canada, the Caribbean, or Britain.

Everywhere they went on their weary exodus, the refugees faced prejudice, hostility, poverty, and often violence. Many must have wondered what exactly their sacrifice had won them, whether British promises were more self-interested bluster than substance, whether they would ever find a place within the empire they had fought to save. But these men and women who had so daringly fought their way out of bondage had become tireless advocates for their own freedoms, never resting until the new world they had envisioned was firmly in their grasp. From slavery in America, to uncertainty and exploitation in the Caribbean, Nova Scotia, Britain, and finally Africa, the journeys of the black refugees of the American Revolution would fundamentally reshape the British Empire, take the first hesitant steps in the European scramble for empire in Africa, and pave the way for the eventual abolition of the slave trade that had smuggled generations of their people to American captivity.[2]

Boston King was somewhat unusual in Britain's black community. Unlike the established black British who had arrived as slaves or servants since the sixteenth century, or the "Black Poor" who had come more recently with the defeated British army, he had arrived in 1794 directly from Africa itself. He did not come to England as slave or servant or refugee, but rather as an enthusiastic agent of British imperialism. In England, he hoped to acquire the education and religious training he thought was necessary to continue his most cherished ambition, to bring Christianity and European civilization to his African kin. But though he came to Britain from Africa, he had not been born there. Like so many around the British Empire, Boston King's story had been shaped by the American Revolution.

As far as he knew, Boston King had been born into slavery around 1760 on the plantation of Richard Waring, about 28 miles outside of Charles Town, as Charleston was then known. His father had been "stolen away from Africa" as a child and survived the notorious Middle Passage before being sold into slavery in South Carolina. Through skill and determination, King's parents had achieved relatively privileged positions within the circumscribed world of the plantation. His father acted as plantation overseer for years, and his mother, who had learned from local Native Americans how to use local plants and herbs to make medicine, cared for the sick and injured. At the age of 6, King himself had been assigned to work as a servant in his master's house. At 9, he was charged with looking after the plantation's cattle, and eventually traveled across America caring for his master's race-horses. Though he was spared the rigors of the brutal labor in the fields, King's life was far from easy, and any minor slip could result in brutal punishment. Once, when he misplaced one of the groom's boots, he was forbidden to wear shoes all winter.[3]

As war was breaking out in the north, King found himself in Charleston apprenticed to a carpenter. His master was a brutal man, and King was frequently and savagely beaten for lost or misplaced tools and other minor infractions, leaving him unable to move for weeks on end. As word of events further north began to trickle down to South Carolina, the routine horrors of life in Charleston must have ensured that King was among the more enthusiastic listeners. News spread fast, even in the mostly illiterate world of the slave communities. In the dim light of slave cabins after the day's back-breaking labor was done, on the streets of Charleston where skilled enslaved artisans were trained and then rented out by their masters, a palpable, if cautious, sense of hope was building as rumors swirled of a war between the American colonies and the British.

Since he was a boy, King had heard whites throughout the colonies adopt the language of bondage and slavery in their deepening conflict with the British government. The Stamp Act of 1765 and the Townshend Act of 1767, passed in the wake of the Seven Years' War as a means of recouping imperial expenses for a war fought on the colonists' behalf, created an immediate backlash in America. Colonists up and down the Atlantic seaboard fumed about increases in taxation levied without their consent. In the crisis that followed, white Americans repeatedly bemoaned their "Wretched and miserable State of Slavery," warning that Britain was preparing to "enslave her own children," and, in the words of George Washington, sought to "make us as tame, and abject Slaves, as the Blacks we rule over with such arbitrary sway." In South Carolina, Boston King may well have heard such hypocritical histrionics first-hand. In 1769, the *South Carolina Gazette* had joined the chorus declaiming against the Stamp Act, telling its readers that "whatever we may think of ourselves, we are as real SLAVES as those we are permitted to command." When the hated Act was at last repealed, among the revelers who crowded around joyous bonfires on Charleston's streets were white sailors wearing blackface to mark their status as Britain's political slaves.[4]

If King did hear such words he must have marveled at the gall it took to equate a lack of political representation with his own bruised and bloodied life as an actual slave. Such rhetoric, however, was not simply rank hypocrisy. For men who knew the cruel reality first-hand, who had themselves wielded yoke and chain and whip, the cries of political enslavement were the most potent means in their linguistic repertoire of expressing their anger and frustration. The discourse of enslavement thus served as clever Patriot propaganda, aimed not at British officials, who saw the ludicrous hyperbole for what it was, but at the colonists themselves, most of whom remained ambivalent about the coming conflict with Britain. Slavery was the worst fate such people could possibly imagine. Unlike most Britons, they had seen the horrors of slavery up close. In their eyes, if the slumbering colonial populace was to be awakened to the dangers of British imperial policy, such chilling metaphors had to be employed. The American Revolution was thus a project of fear as much as it was a project of hopeful idealism. Dire predictions of slavery and enslavement were joined by warnings of savage Indian raids, Hessian brutality, and British reprisals to terrify the broad, uncommitted middle into joining the Patriot cause. The rhetoric of slavery was not a matter of white Americans ignoring their own role as slave-holders but of using their lived reality to give weight to their warnings and gravity to their threats.

For slaves like King, however, the rhetoric of bondage that accompanied the Stamp Act crisis was joined by language and ideas altogether more inspiring. Alongside the shouts about British enslavement came talk of natural rights, of universal freedom, and of the brotherhood of man. Some of the men who joined this new, enlightened chorus even began to raise questions about the morality of African slavery itself. Such ideas thrilled many Americans, but none more so than those actually in fetters. Enslaved Americans absorbed and adapted such ideas and began to employ them in their own calls for freedom and independence. In Charleston, King might have seen the results first-hand. As early as 1765, black Carolinians seized upon the example of the Stamp Act protests to advocate for their own natural rights. For day after day, they marched through the streets of the city "crying out 'Liberty' " until the authorities became so nervous that they put a stop to the protests.[5]

When fighting broke out in Massachusetts in 1775, enslaved Americans saw in the emerging conflict a ray of hope. Given the rhetoric of the rebellious colonists, there was reason to believe that an American victory would see attacks on political slavery expanded to include slavery more broadly and reify ideas of natural rights and universal freedom. In such circumstances, they thought, emancipation surely could not be far behind. But while some held out hope that the colonies would take their enlightened ideals to their logical abolitionist conclusion, most looked to the British as the source of liberty. Over the previous decade, while white colonists were busy transforming Britain into a symbol of tyranny and political enslavement, unfree Americans were beginning to see Britain as the font of freedom. In 1772, Britain's chief justice, Lord Mansfield, had found in favor of James Somerset, an American slave brought to England by his master. While in England, Somerset had escaped, only to be recaptured. Somerset's owner wanted to sell him to another master in the West Indies, but the case was seized by abolitionists and became an early *cause célèbre*. Mansfield attempted to issue a narrow ruling setting Somerset free, but in declaring that slavery had no basis in English common law, his decision was popularly believed to have ended slavery in Britain. Slave-owning Americans saw the decision as a betrayal, yet another signal of Britain's tyrannous intent, and began to consider separation from Britain. Enslaved Americans, unsurprisingly, saw the case as a sign that if their longed-for emancipation were to come, it would come in Britain or through British means.

Back in Charleston, Boston King was at the center of the unfolding drama between colonies and king. However, if he were among those who held out hope that white Americans would live up to their lofty rhetoric, he was violently disabused of that notion in the summer of 1775. That August, a large crowd gathered in his city to witness the execution of Thomas Jeremiah for instigating a slave rebellion. Thomas Jeremiah was one of the fewer than 500 free men of color in the entire colony, and certainly the most successful. As a harbor pilot and fisherman he had amassed a considerable fortune that made him quite possible the wealthiest person of African descent in all of British North America. In June of 1775, however, Jeremiah was accused of attempting to supply guns to local slaves as part of a wider plot to revolt against colonial rule. Informants testified that Jeremiah was telling every slave who would listen that "a great war . . . was coming to help the poor Negroes" and that in order to aid the British he wanted to get guns "placed in the hands of Negroes to fight against the inhabitants of the province."[6]

For white South Carolinians, these stories of British allied slave insurrections confirmed their worst fears. South Carolina had the largest proportion of slaves in America, with as many as 107,000 slaves far outnumbering the white population of roughly 71,000. With this imbalance came a deep and abiding terror of slave rebellion. That nightmare had come true only thirty-five years earlier in

1739 when as many as 100 slaves from the Stono River area had marched for Spanish Florida under a banner reading "Liberty!" razing plantations along the way. In 1766 a supposed slave plot was again discovered in the midst of the Stamp Act crisis. When war broke out with Britain in 1775, it was thus dread rather than hope that percolated down to the slave-holding south with the news from Massachusetts. Throughout America, but especially in the southern colonies, many Patriots fully believed that the British administration was devising a "black plan" to foment slave rebellions as a means of suppressing American dissent. When Sir William Campbell arrived in Charleston to take up the post of Royal Governor in June 1775, he was dogged by accusations that he had been sent to organize slave insurrections. Talk in the town had it that he had brought with him 14,000 guns to arm slaves, that slaves and servants had been intentionally "deluded by some villainous persons into the notion of being all set free," and that "His Majesty's ministers and other servants instigated their slaves to rebel against their masters and cut their throats." "Massacres and Insurrections," one official remembered, "were words in the mouth of every child."[7]

The evidence against Jeremiah was flimsy at best, and the accusations almost certainly invented, but such was the mindset of slave-holding whites that he was nonetheless sacrificed to appease the mob. As a free man and a slave owner himself, Jeremiah was hardly likely to encourage, let alone lead, a slave rebellion. In reality, however, in a time of such heightened tensions, it was likely Jeremiah's very success as a free man that singled him out as the embodiment of white insecurities. Henry Laurens, who was among his chief prosecutors, considered Jeremiah "a forward fellow, puffed up by prosperity, ruined by Luxury and debauchery and grown to an amazing pitch of vanity and ambition." In the context of the opening stages of the revolution, a black man who threatened to upend the racial hierarchy was a convenient target. But the Jeremiah affair was not merely about easing the slumber of worried whites, it was also about manufacturing fear as a means of gaining converts to the colonial cause, stoking age-old anxieties about the racial unbalance to secure support. According to a local British official, Patriots needed "to have recourse to the instigated insurrection among their slaves, effectually to gain the point proposed." The Patriot General Committee of South Carolina itself admitted that "the dread of instigated Insurrections at home" was enough "to drive an oppressed People to the use of Arms." Fear of slave revolts was real, especially in a time of war, but these fears were intentionally ratcheted up to vilify the British and gain adherents.[8]

It is thus unsurprising that Jeremiah's trial was a sham. Despite his free status, Jeremiah was nonetheless tried in a slave court under the Negro Act of 1740, which meant that he was considered guilty until proven innocent. Sir William Campbell, South Carolina's embattled British governor, attempted to intervene, only to have the Council of Safety declare that if he did not desist they would hang Jeremiah from the post at the governor's mansion. There would be no reprieve. In August 1775, Thomas Jeremiah was hanged, his body then burnt in what would become a common ritual of lynching. It was a joint warning: to slaves not to imagine that the British could bring them freedom; to the British not to contemplate fomenting insurrection; and to Americans that it was time to choose a side. Writing to England, a despondent Campbell confessed that "my blood runs cold when I read on what grounds they doomed a fellow creature to death . . . the man was murdered." "They have now dipt their hands in Blood," he concluded with foreboding. "God almighty knows where it will end."[9]

As slave and free man across South Carolina contemplated the fate of those who reached too high, and wondered about the possibility of emancipation in the coming war, the Royal Governor of Virginia, Lord Dunmore, played right into hands of slave dreams and Patriot propaganda. On November 14, 1775, the beleaguered Dunmore responded to growing colonial intransigence by declaring martial law and announcing that any slave or indentured servant who joined his forces against the rebels would be granted their freedom. Dunmore had contemplated the idea of raising a slave army as early as 1772, and had threatened to do so as recently as the spring of 1775. Indeed, escaped slaves had been flocking to his army at Norfolk to offer their services before the official proclamation was ever made, convincing the governor of the viability of the plan and undermining colonial conceptions of natural slave servility. Dunmore's official proclamation paid immediate dividends. Word of the offer of freedom spread rapidly, and from across the southern colonies slaves rushed to seize their chance at liberty.

Dunmore's pledge became the talk of all Americans, free and unfree. White Americans were sure that the proclamation would encourage disobedience in slaves and servants, set off insurrections everywhere, and upend the racial order. In Philadelphia, the supposed heartland of liberty, a white woman reported that a black man refused to show her proper deference by giving her the right of way on a narrow street, compounding the insult by informing her that if she stayed "till Lord Dunmore and his black regiment come . . . we will see who is to take the wall." Another white Philadelphian complained, "Hell itself could not have vomited anything more black than his [Dunmore's] design of emancipating our slaves . . . the flame runs like wild fire through the slaves." Robert Carter gathered his slaves at his Virginia plantation and tried to convince them that Dunmore's Proclamation was a British ploy to sell them into slavery in the West Indies. He was sure that none of his bondsmen would flee to Dunmore, but was swiftly proved wrong when they organized a well-planned breakout with fellow slaves from neighboring plantations. Outraged at Dunmore's Proclamation, Thomas Jefferson went so far as to add complaints about the British "exciting those very people [slaves] to rise in arms," and purchase their liberty by murdering Americans.[10]

When the news of Dunmore's Proclamation flowed through the sophisticated slave communication networks down to South Carolina, many enslaved Carolinians jumped at the chance to secure their freedom. The proclamation had been purposefully limited—he was himself a major slave-holder after all—but to enslaved Americans, already primed to believe that Britain was the font of liberty, his declaration seemed to be a more universal offer of freedom in exchange for service to the crown. Beginning as early as December 1775, a trickle, then a flood, of African Americans began to slip away to Sullivan Island in the middle of Charleston harbor, where British ships were anchored. Sullivan Island was a fitting place for these former slaves to cast off their shackles. Since 1707, the sandy, windswept island had been the unloading point and place of quarantine for thousands of men, women, and children who had survived the horrors of the Middle Passage before they were sent to the slave auctions in Charleston. Many of the hundreds now drawn to the protection of the British ships must have taken their first chain-bound steps on American soil on the sands of Sullivan Island.

Boston King, though he was now resident in Charleston and, as an apprentice, in possession of some freedom of movement, was not among the hundreds of slaves who packed onto Sullivan's Island in hope of British favor. There was considerable risk involved in running to the British. Many slave owners, like Robert Carter mentioned above, warned their slaves that the British offer was false, and that promises of freedom merely cloaked a ploy to sell American slaves to the notorious sugar plantations of the Caribbean. For those not fooled by this sort of claim, colonial slave-holders increased patrols and sentinels to catch runaways and force them back into bondage. Those caught fleeing to the British, or captured after enlisting in the British army, saw punishments that could be brutal in the extreme. Recaptured slaves were sold to the West Indies, condemned to work in lead mines, and even executed. One former slave who served as a guide for the British was captured and beheaded, his head left on a post as a gruesome warning to other slaves and runaways. The conditions for slaves in British camps were little better, with provisions scarce and disease rampant. When Dunmore abandoned Norfolk, he left as many as 500 dead refugees behind him, many putrefying in the sun "without a shovelful of earth upon them," as the *Virginia Gazette* reported. With such serious disincentives, flight was not a decision to be made lightly, and there is considerable evidence that those who did choose to escape did so after careful planning, or when British lines were near enough to make the chances of success more certain. But despite the risks, thousands of enslaved Americans were only to ready to take their chance for freedom.[11]

In January 1776, before he could make up his mind to make a break for freedom and join the British forces gathered at Charleston, Sir William Campbell and his soldiers were driven out of Charleston harbor. Since early in 1775 persistent rumors had spread that Campbell was plotting to foment a massive slave rebellion to resolve the dispute with the colony. It was said that 14,000 guns had been smuggled into Charleston to arm South Carolina's avenging slaves, and many saw the rapidly expanding refugee settlement on Sullivan's Island as the tip of an insurrectionary iceberg. By the fall of 1775, more than 500 former slaves were living on Sullivan's Island under British protection. As the year progressed, Charleston's Committee of Public Safety heard testimony of refugees joining night raids on neighboring plantations and skulking about Charleston's streets encouraging other slaves to escape and join them on Sullivan's Island. The existence of British-protected fugitive slaves in

Charleston's midst was thus seized upon as a pretext for an assault on Sullivan's Island: better to drive off the British instigators and retake their human property before their nefarious plot could unfold. Campbell took some of the refugees with him when he fled, but others were recaptured.[12]

Considering the sad plight of the slaves who had sheltered under British guns on Sullivan Island, Boston King may well have been relieved that he had not joined them. The absence of the British, however, cut off the most viable path to freedom that had perhaps ever existed for South Carolina's slaves. For King and many others, it must have seemed as if their chance for liberty had sailed away with the British fleet. There would be another chance, however. After the disastrous defeat at Saratoga, in March of 1778 the British army, despairing of ever breaking the deadlock that had developed in the north, altered its strategy. Sir Henry Clinton, now in command of British forces, was ordered to turn his sights on the southern colonies, where it was hoped that loyalists and slaves would flock to the British banner and tip the balance of the war in their favor. The first targets were Savannah and Charleston, both vital engines of the colonial economy.

In December 1778 Savannah fell to British forces after a sharp but one-sided battle. Just 100 miles away in Charleston, Patriots, loyalists, and slaves all waited in nervous anticipation for the siege they were sure was on the horizon. But if he hoped that the coming fight would secure his freedom, Boston King was again disappointed. Like many white residents of Charleston, King's master looked at the prospect of a British invasion with apprehension and fled the city, taking King with him. When Clinton's army began its siege of Charleston on April 1, 1780, Boston King, by now a trained carpenter, was nearly 40 miles outside the city building a house for a Mr. Waters. The city fell to the British six weeks later on May 12, to the cautious rejoicing of Charleston's enslaved population. Stuck in the countryside, it must have seemed to King that he had once more missed his chance.

Shortly after the conquest of Charleston, however, King was given permission to visit his parents, who lived some 12 miles from Mr. Waters' house. He borrowed a horse from Waters to make the journey, but one of Waters' white servants commandeered it, leaving King in a tenuous bind. He knew he would be held responsible for the absence of the horse, and fully "expected the severest punishment" from its owner, a man who "knew not how to show mercy." He chose instead to take the chance to flee. Four years earlier, when faced with similar violence, King had opted not to escape to the British on nearby Sullivan's Island, even though many other slaves had already done so. The British had since returned to South Carolina, but they were now miles away, seemingly beyond reach. Nonetheless, much had changed in the years since King last contemplated flight.

Back then, in 1776, Lord Dunmore, the man who made the proclamation that offered freedom to those who joined the British, was leagues away in Virginia, and the stories about the refugee camps that filtered down to South Carolina painted a bleak picture of the conditions and fate of those who had answered Dunmore's call. In 1776, British officials in South Carolina had made no such promises, and conditions on Sullivan's Island were hardly better than those that prevailed in Virginia. But now, in 1780, Charleston was governed by Sir Henry Clinton who, in preparation for his southern offensive, had issued his own proclamation at Philipsburg in June of 1779 offering freedom to any slave who deserted to the British. After the fall of Savannah, black refugees had joined the British in droves, setting a potent precedent for South Carolina's bondsmen.

In the years since 1776, the stories and articles that detailed the tragedy of the refugees had also been supplanted by tales altogether more heroic. Instead of cowering behind British lines, easy prey for disease and reprisals, by 1780 former slaves had joined regiments like Dunmore's Ethiopian Regiment, the Black Pioneers, and Watts' Blacks to take the fight to their former captors. The Black Pioneers had served with courage and distinction in New York, Pennsylvania, and Rhode Island, and even joined the fight against Francis Marion's guerrillas in the Carolina Low Country. In New Jersey, a former slave named Colonel Tye had cast off his shackles, joined the British, and blazed a path across the colony, ambushing Patriot militias and raiding plantations. For a young man like Boston King, after a lifetime of bondage, such tales of black action, of former slaves fighting back, must have been exhilarating. They certainly made the prospect of joining the British even more appealing. And now, these very black heroes were among the British conquerors of Savannah and Charleston. Facing a choice between the whip of enslavement and the clenched fist of the fight for freedom, Boston King was one of many enslaved South Carolinians to "go to Charles-Town and throw myself into the hand of the British." He was "grieved" to leave behind his friends and family still in slavery, but the British welcomed him warmly, and after twenty years a slave, for the first time Boston King "began to feel the happiness of liberty, of which I knew nothing before."[13]

Nothing could have prepared Boston King for the sight of New York. When he arrived in December 1782 the city was already packed to the gills with loyalists and refugees. The city had been a British stronghold since September 1776, and a refuge for loyalists and escaped slaves since the days of Dunmore's Proclamation. Others had arrived more recently, thousands limping into the city with the defeated British forces just evacuated from Yorktown, Savannah, and Charleston. There were now more than 3,000 black refugees crowded into the city, most packed into tents and makeshift shelters in the fire-blackened ruins between Broadway and the Hudson River that had been set alight by Patriot terrorists shortly after the city's capture by the British in 1776. Prior to the war, most escapees were predominantly male, but New York's refugee camp housed an unprecedented mix of men, women, and children, whole families who had risked everything in the dash for freedom.

King's path to New York had been equally harrowing. Almost as soon as he arrived in Charleston a free man, King was laid low by the smallpox that ravaged the crowded quarters of the city, especially among the refugees. The British command feared that illness would spread to the army, so sick refugees were hauled a mile or more away from the British camp where they were largely left without adequate food or water to recover or die on their own. King was lucky enough to receive aid from a fellow volunteer, and rejoined the army at Camden, where Lord Cornwallis, in command of British forces in the south after Clinton returned to New York, was camped following the Battle of Camden. King, like most refugees, did not join an infantry unit, but instead served as a laborer, messenger, guide, and servant to a British officer by the name of Captain Grey. The work often involved foraging for supplies in hostile territory and delivering communications across a confused, faction-ridden landscape. Twice, he faced the very real prospect of capture, re-enslavement, or execution, once by Patriot forces while delivering a message for the commanding officer at Nelson's Ferry, and once when the deserting captain of a loyalist militia unit attempted to re-enslave him. King encountered the loyalist captain while alone catching fish for Captain Grey. The loyalist asked him "how will you like me to be your master?" Not about to surrender his newly won liberty so easily, King responded with "sharp words" about his status as a free man. But the captain responded with words of bone-chilling familiarity, calmly warning King that "if you do not behave well, I will put you in irons, and given you a dozen stripes every morning." King was able to escape back to the British army, but for the refugees who joined the British side, the threat of capture and re-enslavement was constant.[14]

King's luck continued to hold. While he dodged Patriot pickets and loyalist renegades, the majority of Cornwallis's army, now trailing the plague-stricken corpses of thousands of ill soldiers and refugees in its wake, made its way to Virginia, where they were trapped at Yorktown. Those refugees well enough to work were employed digging ditches and raising earthworks for the coming siege. But the British were surrounded, low on supplies, and riddled with disease. As days of bombardment passed without relief, soldiers and refugees sickened and died in droves, until Cornwallis was left with only 3,500 active men to face the besieging Franco-American force of 16,000. With no other option left, on October 19, 1781 Cornwallis at last surrendered. Of the nearly 5,000 former slaves who had followed Cornwallis to Yorktown, only a few managed to escape with life and liberty intact. As many as 3,000 had already succumbed to the typhoid and smallpox that raged in the camp, and the American forces set sentinels to capture many of those who attempted to slip away after the surrender. Some managed to flee to the French, and some succeeded in boarding British ships bound for New York, but as many as half of the surviving refugees were captured and re-enslaved by the Americans. Their gamble for freedom had failed.

Boston King escaped the horrors of Yorktown, but he too was forced to contemplate the prospect of re-enslavement. King was in Charleston when Cornwallis capitulated, and it soon became clear that the city would be evacuated and turned over to the Americans. Slave owners and their agents swarmed into Charleston from across the south, looking to cajole, or even steal, their former slaves back to their plantations. As General Leslie, the British commander of Charleston, negotiated their retreat, South Carolina's governor, John

Mathews, gave an official imprimatur to these attempts and demanded that all runaway slaves be left behind when the British quit the city. So desperate were the Americans to re-enslave the refugees that the governor even threatened to default on South Carolina's debt to British merchants if their former slaves were not returned. Given the amount owed by South Carolina's merchants, this was a serious threat, but for General Leslie the promise made to the refugees was a point of honor that could not be breached. "Those who have voluntarily come in under the faith of our protection," he reasoned, "cannot in justice be abandoned to the merciless resentment of their former masters." And so in December 1782, Boston King was among the 8,000 former and current slaves who boarded British ships for exile in New York, Florida, or the Caribbean.[15]

King was one of the fortunate few—perhaps 500 in total—to be sent to New York from Charleston. Most of the south's black refugees, almost all still the property of loyalists, had been transported to east Florida and eventually to Jamaica and the Bahamas, where they faced conditions of unspeakable harshness on the sugar plantations of the British Caribbean. The population of the Bahamas increased by 7,000 in the three years after the war, with most of the newcomers arriving as the property of white loyalists. Despite the disruption of the slave trade from Africa, Jamaica's enslaved population also grew rapidly, with the addition of perhaps as many as 80,000 slaves by 1785. Established planters and white loyalist refugees alike were eager to make up for lost time and lost profits, and the Caribbean sugar industry rapidly began to recover from the lean years of the war. There were some attempts to protect black loyalists with claims to free status—as Governor of the Bahamas since 1787, Lord Dunmore established a "Negro Court" to adjudicate such claims—but by and large most black refugees in the Caribbean were doomed to re-enslavement.[16]

King must have been apprehensive as he stepped out onto the bustling streets of New York for the first time. The prospects were far from certain for the thousands who crammed into New York City after 1782. The British defeat at Yorktown was the beginning of the end of the war, but only the beginning. For month after month, while British and American officials hashed out the terms for peace, loyalists and refugees cooled their heels in New York, agonizing over their post-war fate. At least King could console himself with the fact that, unlike most former slaves, he at least had a trade. Surely skilled carpenters would be in high demand to help rebuild the war-ravaged city. Unfortunately for King, however, he had been forced to leave his tools behind when he fled to the British. It must have been a tremendous blow for King to relinquish his hard-won status as an independent tradesman and enter into domestic service. Even this indignity proved insufficient. With so many refugees, even menial work was scarce and wages so low that King, like many others, was not able "to keep myself in clothes." A second employer promised better wages, but failed to pay at all, forcing King to find odd jobs throughout wherever he could just to survive the harsh winter.[17]

King's struggles were not unusual. As loyalists and refugees flocked to the British held city, its pre-war population of 5,000 swelled to as many as 35,000 by 1783. The press of people, most without money or employment, led to an explosion of poverty and racial tensions. To make ends meet, one entrepreneurial refugee from Virginia, Judea Moore, rented a basement kitchen. But with competition for space fierce, she was soon outbid for the property by a white man named John Harrison. Her landlord was willing to let her stay, but Harrison was determined to drive her out. Moore went to the mayor seeking redress from his harassment, but his acid reply was that "it was a pity that all we black folk who came from Virginia was not sent home to our master's."[18]

Nonetheless, the New York refugee community did its best to carry on. Many found solace in the new social relationships that developed in the new free community of African Americans. The war had forced thousands of former slaves into exile in unfamiliar places, but the shared trauma and common experiences bound the new communities together in novel ways. In this emerging community, Boston King found a wife. Her name was Violet, formerly enslaved in Wilmington, North Carolina, and twelve years his senior. In the context of a time both desperate and hopeful, a partner would have proved a great solace and a constant reminder of the possibility for a brighter future of freedom.

With a wife, and the likelihood of a family on the way, King continued to search for more stable employment. Though he had little experience of the sea, he joined the crew of a pilot boat guiding ships through the confusion of channels and islands into New York harbor. If the job paid better, it was certainly more dangerous. Shortly after joining the crew, King's boat found itself swept out to sea, adrift for eight days with supplies meant only for five. They were lucky enough to encounter an American whale boat, which gave the bedraggled crew food and water and transported them back to land at New Brunswick, New Jersey. New Jersey, however, was American territory, outside British lines, and to King's horror, he quickly found himself enslaved once more. He was well fed and generally well-treated—he was even allowed to go to school at night to learn to read—so much so that he marveled at the treatment of slaves in the north, but as he remembered, "all these enjoyments could not satisfy me without liberty . . . I could not find the least desire to content myself in slavery." Boston King had had a taste of freedom, and was determined not to remain in bondage.

Between enslavement in New Jersey and freedom and family in New York, however, stood mighty obstacles. He would have to cross two rivers, both a mile or more in width while avoiding the guards posted to prevent runaways from escaping. In New Brunswick there was an all too visible reminder of the price of failure, a friend from New York, who had also been captured and re-enslaved, now fasted in stocks day and night after a failed flight attempt. Still, King was undeterred, and so, one night at one o'clock he made his way to a shallow river crossing at Amboy. Finding the usual guards not present, King waded across the Raritain River and traveled for four hours before hiding at daybreak. At nightfall the next day, he bush-wacked his way through the marshes that enveloped the coast, before finding an abandoned boat and rowing across the Arthur Kill to Staten Island and safety.

While King was negotiating his way through the rivers and swamps of New Jersey back to freedom, British and American officials in Paris had begun to hammer out a preliminary peace agreement. It was a complicated process, but for New York's refugees, the most consequential component of the treaty was Article VII. Article VII had been inserted at the eleventh hour through the last-minute intervention of Henry Laurens. Representing America's substantial slave-owning lobby, Laurens demanded that the British return all confiscated American property, especially the thousands of former slaves now huddled in Manhattan. Several British commanders had made promises to these refugees, but rather than stand by his country's commitment, the British representative Richard Oswald accepted Laurens' proposal without protest. Oswald was a canny advocate for British trade interests, but he was no advocate for the enslaved. He had made much of his fortunes from his ownership of a slave factory on the coast of Sierra Leone, from whence he shipped thousands of slaves to ports across the Americas. In South Carolina, one of the primary destinations for Oswald's slaves, his partner and factor was none other than Henry Laurens. If that was not enough, Oswald had already discussed with Laurens his plans to establish a plantation in South Carolina once peace arrived. Oswald and Laurens both stood to gain from the return of America's freed slaves.

News of the faithless betrayal hit New York's refugee community like a bolt of lightning. "This dreadful rumor," King recalled:

> filled us all with inexpressible anguish and terror, especially when we saw our old masters coming from Virginia, North-Carolina, and other parts, and seizing upon their slaves in the streets of New-York, or even dragging them out of their beds. Many of the slaves had very cruel masters, so that the thoughts of returning home with them embittered life to us. For some days we lost our appetite for food, and sleep departed from our eyes.

Among the many slave-holders champing at the bit to recover their human property was George Washington, now camped at Newburgh outside the city. As he negotiated the surrender of the city with the British commander Sir Guy Carleton, he sent letters to agents in the city instructing them to find and kidnap his former slaves, men like Harry Washington, who had escaped Mt. Vernon and joined the Black Pioneers in the siege at Charleston before retreating to New York. He wanted to prevent, he wrote to his agent Daniel Parker, the British "carrying off any Negroes or other property of the inhabitants of the United States." And Washington was not alone. One Hessian officer recorded that "almost five thousand persons have come to this city to take possession again of their former property." Former slaves were seized, bound, and bundled into waiting boats by former masters and their agents. Some were spared this awful fate by the intervention of British authorities, who arrested kidnappers like those who ambushed Frank Griffin and were on the point of forcing him on a ship when Colonel Cuff, a former slave in Ward's Blacks, arrived to arrest Griffin's tormentors.[19]

Carleton and Washington met in person at Tappan on May 6, 1783 to discuss the British evacuation of New York, where Washington reminded his counterpart of his obligation to obey Article VII of the Paris treaty. Carleton, to his immense credit, stoically refused. He considered Article VII to be "a disgrace," an indelible stain on British honor. The article, he somewhat disingenuously informed Washington, was meant to apply only to slaves who reached British lines after the initial ceasefire in 1782. The refugees who had escaped before that time would be "permitted to go wherever they please . . . to Nova Scotia or elsewhere as they desire." To do otherwise "would be a disagreeable violation of public faith." Washington was shocked and furious, but there was little he could do without risking the tenuous peace.[20]

Even before his meeting with Washington, Carleton had determined that he would do whatever he could to secure the safety and liberty of the former slaves who had sacrificed so much on behalf of the British. He had already begun shipping refugees out of the city on British ships bound for Nova Scotia earlier in the year. After his conference at Tappan, Carleton made his renewed commitment to the refugees more official, announcing that all refugees that had been in British lines for more than a year, or could prove their status as free men, would be granted permission to settle elsewhere within the British Empire when his forces evacuated the city. To placate the Americans, Carleton set up a commission to review the cases of the refugees who came forward for their certificates, including Washington's agent, and allowed American officials to inspect private ships leaving New York for stowaway slaves. However, few of the refugees had any documentary evidence of their status, and the commission, led by Samuel Birch, readily believed most of the oral accounts presented by the refugees, even though many claims of free status were clearly invented. Much to Washington's chagrin, few were denied their "Birch certificates," as they became known. In all, 3,000 former slaves, 1,336 men, 914 women, and 750 children were enrolled in the "Book of Negroes" that recorded the details of all those granted leave to depart New York as free people.[21]

Boston King and his wife Violet were both granted certificates, and on July 31, 1783 they sailed out of New York harbor with 407 other refugees aboard *L'Abondance* bound for a new life in Nova Scotia. In all, as many as 100,000 American slaves—out of a pre-war total of 500,000—ended up in British lines when the war ended. Perhaps 9,000 were lucky enough to cast off their shackles and enter the British Empire in freedom. Many more, in the tens of thousands, left American shores still enslaved to the more than 60,000 white loyalist refugees who resettled in the British Empire. For Boston King and many of the 9,000 new freemen, leaving New York was merely the first stage in a life-long quest for liberty.[22]

Nova Scotia serves as a healthy reminder that the thirteen colonies that became the United States were not the only British possessions in North America, merely the only ones that rebelled. While thirteen colonies in North America asserted their independence, Britain's colonies in Canada and the Caribbean remained loyal. Loyalty, however, came at a price. St. John, in what is now New Brunswick, was raided by privateers from Maine as early as 1775. In 1777, American militia forces under John Allan briefly occupied St. John as part of a wider expedition against British Canada. By the end of the war, most of the ports of Nova Scotia and New Brunswick had been raided, with Annapolis Royal attacked in 1781, and Lunenburg sacked and plundered by American privateers led by Noah Stoddard in July 1782. Even the remote reaches of northern Canada felt the sting of the American War. In 1782, a French naval expedition under the Comte de la Pérouse launched a series of raids on the trading posts of the British Hudson Bay Company. The seizure of more than 12,000 furs, and the valuable expedition diary of the area's governor, Samuel Hearne, cost the Company so dearly that it failed to pay a dividend to its investors for almost five years.[23]

King and his family arrived in Nova Scotia in August 1783, settling at Birchtown with as many as 1,500 other refugees. Another 1,200 former slaves opted for nearby Shelburne, with smaller communities of refugees scattered across the colony. They had suffered much to reach the rocky shores of Canada and the promise of freedom. As a reward for their sacrifice and an encouragement to settle—some British administrators hoped Nova Scotia would soon rival Boston and New York as a North American entrepôt—each head of household had been promised a plot of land. For men and women accustomed to laboring on the land of others, ownership of land was the very source of independence and the bedrock of their future as a free people. As ship after ship arrived with new refugee settlers, they wasted little time transforming their plots into homes and farms. King vividly remembered the esprit de corps that suffused the newly free settlers upon their arrival; "we exerted all our strength," he later recalled. Most of the settlers came from the balmy southern colonies—more than half from Maryland, Virginia, and the Carolinas alone—and they had no conception of the chilling vagaries of winter so far north, but as 1783, the year of their liberty, came to an end, Boston King and his fellow refugees were sure that their long exodus was over at last and that their new lives were sure to be better.[24]

Nova Scotia was not the promised land. Of the roughly 3,000 former slaves who managed to secure passage there, only 500 or so actually received the grants of land promised by the British to every American refugee, black or white. Each head of household had been offered 100 acres of land with an additional 50 acres for each family member, but with a cascade of 30,000 newly arrived loyalists, refugees, and former soldiers all asserting claims, the pressure on land was immense, and the process of distribution slow and complicated. The British administration was committed to keeping its pledge to compensate all who had suffered and sacrificed during the war, including former slaves. To this end, Lord North authorized the distribution of more than half of Nova Scotia's arable land, almost 14 million acres. Assessing the thousands of claims, surveying the land, and dividing it into plots, however, was a mammoth task, and priority was given to those "such as have suffered most" in the war. Suffering was measured by the amount of property lost, so large landowning loyalists were usually the first to receive their grants, and former slaves, recently property themselves, often the last to be considered. Furthermore, potential grantees were required to officially petition the local government before they were assigned their plots, which proved advantageous to well-connected, literate white loyalists, and often problematic for friendless, often illiterate black refugees. Refugees banded together as communities to petition for their grants of land, but as a small minority within the larger loyalist diaspora they were often overlooked.[25]

The process of distribution was slow, even for white loyalists, especially after the costs of the American War forced the British authorities to economize and drastically reduce the number of paid surveyors. For black refugees, the process was glacial. Even those who did receive their allotted land had been shortchanged. They were granted smaller plots than white loyalists and were often segregated from white communities, on more marginal, more remote, and less productive land. Even at Shelburne and Birchtown, both of which had been largely built through the labors of the Black Pioneers before the major influx of loyalists and refugees, fewer black claimants received land, having waited on average three years longer when they did receive it, and their land averaged half the acreage of grants to white people. Most were forced to make do with small "town plots" of less than an acre. To make matters worse, the crops they were familiar with from their former lives in the southern colonies did not grow as well in the frozen, rocky soil of Nova Scotia. In 1787, famine ripped through the refugee communities. Even the lucky few who had secured their land grants found survival challenging. They clung to their independence in whatever way they could, desperate to retain their new autonomy. "Many of the poor people," King lamented, "were compelled to sell their best gowns for five pounds of flour, in order to support life. When they had parted with all their clothes, even to their blankets, several of them fell down dead in the streets, thro' hunger. Some killed and ate their dogs and cats; and poverty and distress prevailed on every side."[26]

In the end, even their independence was stripped from them. Supplies were few and dear, and, as the refugees struggled to scrape out a living, many were forced to abandon the dream of becoming independent cultivators and return to service in the homes and on the farms of their more prosperous white neighbors. As one concerned British observer reported, many former slaves had been "reduced . . . to such a state of indigence, that they have been obliged to sell their property, their clothing, even their very beds," eventually becoming "obliged to live upon white-men's property which the Govr has been liberal in distributing—and for cultivating it they receive half the produce so that they are in short in a state of Slavery."[27]

Boston King had land and a skilled trade, but even he was forced to abandon his hard-won property in Birchtown for a peripatetic life searching for employment. He finally settled at Shelwin, where he found work building boats for the salmon fishery. Others, King remembered, were not so lucky and had been obliged by their "wretched circumstances" to "sell themselves to the merchants" as indentured servants "for two or three; and others for five or six years."

Indentured servants could be bought and sold during their terms of service, often leading to the separation of families. Fully one-third of refugees had arrived as family groups, and many others married upon arrival, but the economic realities of Nova Scotia meant that familiar patterns of employment reemerged. Once more, many black servants and laborers were forced to live away from their spouses and families and with their employers, while others were forced to sell their children into indentured service. The trauma of returning to a life almost akin to slavery—as indentured servants, sharecroppers, farm laborers, and domestic servants living apart from their families—must have been almost too much to bear.[28]

The parallels with their former lives in the slave-holding south did not end there. Slavery was legal in Lower Canada until 1793, and many white loyalists brought their slaves with them into exile, increasing the enslaved population of Nova Scotia from about 100 to nearly 1,500 and providing the refugees a constant reminder of their former lives and precarious present condition. When Shelburne, facing decline from its post-war peak as the fourth-largest settlement in North America, opened up free trade with the United States, many refugees faced the grim prospect that their former masters would come to kidnap them back into slavery. So great was the concern that in 1789 Nova Scotia's legislative assembly was forced to pass an ordinance to prevent the smuggling of free refugees "out of the Province, by force and Stratagem, for the scandalous purpose of making property of them." There was also the very real, and fully legal, prospect that those who had managed to escape New York without a "Birch certificate," though free for ten years or more, would be legally reclaimed as the property of loyalist or American slave-holders. In one such case, four refugees, all of whom had fought for Britain during the war, were claimed by a North Carolina loyalist and only narrowly managed to avoid re-enslavement. Another refugee, Mary Postell, was claimed by a loyalist named Jesse Gray who sought to re-enslave her despite her possession of a Birch certificate. When two other refugees testified on her behalf, their house was burnt and one of their children killed.[29]

If this were not enough, while free black settlers paid taxes, served in militias and on work crews, they were shut out of the full privileges of citizenship. They were denied trial by jury and the right to vote, pushed into segregated communities, banned from holding dances or other social gatherings, and paid a quarter of the wages of white workers. Their lower wages in turn angered poor whites who decried the competition represented by the arrival of the refugees. Violence, long the tool of racial oppression, was not long in coming. In the courts, justice was segregated. White offenses were punished with fines, while black refugees faced whipping and other physical punishment for the same infractions.

Within a year of their arrival, the refugees became the explicit target of white rage. In Shelburne in July 1784, a group of former British soldiers who had settled in Nova Scotia after the war, leveled twenty or more refugee homes in an attempt to drive out their economic rivals. Benjamin Marston, an eyewitness of the events, recorded that "the disbanded soldiers have risen against the Free negroes to drive them out of the Town, because they labor cheaper than they . . . The soldiers forced the free negroes to quit the town—pulled down about 20 of their houses." The riot, the first race riot in Canadian history, lasted for ten days, eventually spreading to nearby Birchtown where Boston King watched as a mob of white laborers and artisans set fire to black people's dwellings as part of a growing protest against black refugees. The disturbances would continue to rage for a month or more.[30]

In the face of such conditions, King, like many other refugees, turned to religion. He already had some experience of Christianity from his days in America and may well have heard the famous slave preacher and fellow refugee George Liele when he was at Charleston, but it was in Nova Scotia that King found himself compelled to take up a religious calling. For all that it was the religion of their persecutors and enslavers, Christianity proved a great comfort to many African Americans, slave and free alike. There was a persistent belief among slaves that conversion or baptism imparted freedom from slavery and protection from re-enslavement. It was not true, but it was a comforting misapprehension nonetheless. Regardless, the message of Christianity—at its heart a religion of the poor and downtrodden—with its tales of a chosen people freed from captivity in a foreign land, and its promise that present suffering would pave the way for blessed relief in the hereafter, was deeply appealing to slaves and former slaves, providing solace, hope, and direction.

In Nova Scotia, King found an abundance of ministers, black and white, ready to teach and preach to the refugee community. He heard the impassioned sermons of Moses Wilkinson, a "Blind and lame" former slave who had escaped bondage in Nansemond county, Virginia, and David George, who was born a slave in Sussex county, Virginia, and converted to Christianity after hearing George Liele preach to slaves in a cornfield. When the war broke out, George fled his brutal master only to be re-enslaved by Creek Indians before escaping once more for British-occupied Savannah. After the war, he remained a close correspondent of George Liele, who had been evacuated to Jamaica, but like King, George had fled Charleston for Nova Scotia, where he made his way to Shelburne to preach, as he said, to "my own color." King also met Freeborn Garretson, a missionary and former slave owner from Maryland who had freed his slaves when he embraced Methodism, and William Black, a Methodist missionary from Yorkshire.[31]

King too saw the appeal of evangelicalism and opted to join the Methodists. By 1791, he had even begun to preach the gospel and was sent by William Black to minister to the small black Methodist community at Preston. But even the refugee embrace of Christianity ran afoul of white Nova Scotians. David George and other refugee preachers were repeatedly threatened, attacked, and beaten, driven from town to town by white neighbors still fearful of black gatherings of any kind and jealous of the popularity of black preachers among the white community. In 1790, seven years after they had arrived in Nova Scotia entranced by a spirit of optimism, a report delivered in Britain's Parliament described the refugee community in Nova Scotia as "unimproved and destitute." Within the refugee community itself, many had become disillusioned with their lives in Canada. Freedom in Nova Scotia, it seemed, was little different than slavery in America.[32]

11

AFRICA, ABOLITION, AND EMPIRE

On October 12, 1791 Boston King received a call from an unlikely visitor. He was a stranger to Preston, indeed a stranger to Nova Scotia, a white man in his mid-twenties, but it was no salesman or missionary who knocked at King's door. King would have known something of the man, or at least guessed at the reason for his presence in Halifax's black suburb. For the past few weeks the talk among the hundred or so refugee families in Preston had been fixed upon this man and what he had traveled across the Atlantic to offer the beleaguered community. Accounts of his mission had been published in local newspapers before he even landed at Halifax, but now he had come personally to Preston, going door to door in the black community to explain his purpose more fully. His name was John Clarkson, a former British naval officer who had served in the Caribbean until he resigned his commission when the pursuit of such a violent trade began to clash with his pacifist religious scruples. His time in the West Indies had a profound effect on his worldview, the first-hand encounter with the brutality of Caribbean slavery transforming him into a committed abolitionist. He had come to Preston in 1791 as part of this new commitment, to offer the refugees of Nova Scotia the opportunity to take part in a radical new British colonial project on the coast of Africa.

As the representative of the newly formed Sierra Leone Company, Clarkson was authorized to offer Nova Scotia's black refugees the opportunity to join in a new effort to form a colony on the coast of West Africa near the mouth of the

Sierra Leone River. If prospective settlers could provide testimonials of their good, sober character, they would be transported to across the Atlantic free of charge and given "not less than" 20 acres of land for each head of household and an additional 10 acres for every family member, along with sufficient supplies to see the colonists through the lean early years. The refugees had heard such promises before, but the Sierra Leone Company hoped to succeed where the authorities of Nova Scotia had failed. To that end, Clarkson promised equal distribution of land, equal distribution of provisions, equal commercial rights, and equal taxes and duties between black and white settlers. With an eye toward the Nova Scotians' renewed fear of re-enslavement and to alleviate their concerns about settling in the heart of slave-trading country, the Company also gave "full assurance of personal protection from Slavery," and explicitly vowed not "to deal or traffic in the buying or selling of slaves," or to "have, hold, appropriate, or employ any person or persons in a state of slavery."[1]

This assurance was central to the mission of the proposed colony. Concerned as they were about the plight of the American War's black refugees, the Sierra Leone Company had a greater purpose in mind beyond the alleviation of the suffering of Nova Scotia's Black Poor. Their larger aim was use the settlement of former slaves on the African coast as a means of undermining the slave trade and burnishing the movement for its abolition. The Company was just the latest in a growing wave of anti-slavery institutions and societies created in the wake of the American War. The war had caused a profound transformation of British attitudes toward slavery and the slave trade. Critiques of the slave trade had existed from the moment Britain became involved in it, growing steadily as Britain's role in the trade expanded over the eighteenth century. Men such as James Oglethorpe, and groups such as the Bray Associates pressed the British government to abandon the trade, but though many were convinced of its immorality, the profits made from slavery were too great to seriously consider banning the trade. If anything, the years before the outbreak of the American War saw an expansion rather than a contraction of the volume of human beings sold into bondage in the Atlantic world. There were certainly growing numbers of committed abolitionists before the war, but their cause seemed rather hopeless in the face of the British Empire's economic interests—that is until the American Revolution intervened.

Before the American War, abolition was not merely unpromising and unlikely; one could hardly even speak of a coherent abolition movement. There were certainly individuals ready to publicly condemn slavery and the role it played in propping up Britain's expanding empire. Though no radical, Ignatius Sancho could still decry "the unchristian and most diabolical usage of my brother Negroes, the illegality, the horrid wretchedness of the traffic, the cruel carnage and depopulation of the human species," as well as the "contempt of those very wretches who roll in affluence from our labours." Such criticism was not unique, but the many isolated instances of anti-slavery rhetoric failed to gain much traction with the wider public. To create a movement, it was necessary both to unify public opinion against slavery and to transform this "moral opinion" into concerted "moral action." The American Revolution provided the main impetus for both. Perhaps the most important single event in the early history of the abolitionism, the event more than any other that galvanized the movement and transformed public opinion was a legal case over marine insurance.[2]

On November 11, 1781, the crew of the British slave ship the *Zong* gathered pensively on deck under a blistering Caribbean sun to discuss their options. They were running desperately low on water, with perhaps only enough remaining to quench the thirst of the sun-beaten crew and the sweltering, heat-choked men and women cramped and shackled in the cargo hold for another four days. Jamaica, their destination, still lay 120 miles to the east, a journey of at least ten days, perhaps two weeks, against the prevailing winds and strong currents of the Caribbean Sea. It was clear to the crew, now reduced to eleven men and bereft of their captain after a long disease-ridden crossing, that they did not have enough water to make it to Jamaica as things stood. There were simply too many thirsty mouths to quench, for in addition to the eleven crew and their stricken comrades, the *Zong* carried 380 slaves, men, women, and children, for sale in Jamaica. In peacetime, the crew would have had available a wide range of options for refuge and resupply, but now, with the American War raging, all of the nearby islands were off limits as enemy territory.

The *Zong* had originally been a Dutch ship christened the *Zorgue*, but she had been captured by a British privateer and renamed when Britain declared hostilities against the Dutch in 1780, in retaliation for persistent Dutch efforts to aid the rebellious American colonies. When the *Zorgue* was seized by the *Alert* in December 1781, it was already carrying a cargo of 244 slaves. As contraband captured during war, the *Alert*'s captain sold the ship and its human cargo on to a representative of the Gregson syndicate, a slave-trading firm based out of Liverpool. Like most British slavers, the Gregson syndicate had seen its commerce disrupted and profits decimated by the American War, especially after France and Spain joined the war. Dodging hostile ships was too dangerous and potentially ruinous for most traders, leading to a 60 per cent decline in the volume of slaves shipped across the Atlantic during the years of the conflict. It had certainly been a lean couple of years for the Gregson syndicate, as they had been prevented from sending a single cargo across the Atlantic for more than three years. The *Zorgue*, however, provided a tempting opportunity to break this dry spell, by taking advantage of a captured ship already funded, stocked, and outfitted by its Dutch owners. So in March 1781, the syndicate decided to risk a run across the Atlantic to British Jamaica, purchasing more slaves to raise the number to 442 and cobbling together a makeshift skeleton crew led by a former ship's surgeon and first-time captain named Luke Collingwood.[3]

Collingwood and his crew opted for an unusually long, southerly route across the Atlantic, hoping that this less trafficked passage would allow them to avoid the swarms of French, Spanish, Dutch, and American ships prowling the sea-lanes for British prizes. On November 27, after seventy-one days at sea, and already low on water, the crew of the *Zong* spotted land on the horizon. The decision to take the longer southern route had been a calculated risk, but now the crew made a fatal error. With navigation imprecise, and both the captain and first mate unavailable, the crew mistook the coast of Jamaica for French St. Domingue. Since entering the war in 1778, the French had adopted a highly aggressive posture in the Caribbean, attacking a capturing British ships and islands in quick succession. Already on high alert because of the dangers posed by the war, the crew of the *Zong* now feared that they had sailed into the very mouth of the beast, and so hurriedly decided to skirt south and west around what they thought was St. Domingue to reach Jamaica. By the time they realized their error they had sailed 120 miles past their destination without the supplies to make it back.

And so on November 29 the crew gathered to debate their options. Someone suggested that the only viable recourse if anyone was to survive was that "Part of the Slaves should be destroyed to save the rest and the remainder put to short allowance" of water. Some of the crew later claimed to have been appalled by the suggestion, but if any of them raised their voice in protest, they were soon persuaded, for the crew voted unanimously to murder a portion of the slaves in order to save themselves and the rest of their human cargo. They wasted little time in going about their grim task. At 8 p.m. on the night of the vote, the crew selected fifty-four women and children liable to fetch lower prices in Jamaica and forced them one by one "through the Cabin windows" and into the jet black abyss. Two days after the first mass killing, a second culling was made. Once more, the crew were deliberate in their selection of victims, choosing forty-two ill and weak men and saving the more valuable, healthy men. The marked men, still "handcuffed and in Irons" to make their murder more manageable, were dispatched in batches, cast over the side of the ship to sink beneath the waves. Over the next few days a further thirty-eight Africans were sacrificed in the name of profit. The slaves still crammed into the hold were well aware of their comrades watery demise, and at least ten of them opted to deny the crew the satisfaction of their lives by seizing their own fate and jumping overboard to their deaths. By the time the *Zong* limped into Jamaica on December 22, only 208 of the original 442 enslaved Africans remained, many having died of disease, exposure, and starvation, but as many as 150 deliberately murdered by the desperate crew.[4]

As gruesome as it was, the story might well have ended with the delivery of 208 slaves in Jamaica. After all, the Middle Passage had always been a deadly affair, with hugely high rates of mortality, brutal punishment, and frequent suicide. The fate of the *Zong*'s unwilling passengers might have been just one in a long litany of all too familiar horrors. However, the Gregson syndicate was not willing to let matters stand. Like all overseas traders, especially those dealing in slaves, the syndicate had taken out an insurance policy on the *Zong* and its cargo. In their eyes, they had lost more than half of their valuable property, and so pursued a claim against their insurers. Claiming slaves lost at sea to shipwreck, disease, or starvation was a well-established practice among slave traders, but few if any had had the gall to make a claim on slaves deliberately killed en route. The insurers, with more of an eye to their own profit margin than to the dictates of humanity, balked at paying out the claim, and thus the disputing parties went to court to settle the matter.

The affair might have remained a closely guarded secret, if not for the efforts of Olaudah Equiano. Equiano, or Gustavus Vassa as he was known throughout his life, came from the Igbo people of what is now Nigeria, but spent most of his life as a slave in South Carolina and the Caribbean before purchasing his own freedom in 1767 and relocating to England. Here he became an influential figure in the black community and a pioneering abolitionist, helping to found the Sons of Africa, an abolitionist society of former slaves and other black Britons. Equiano had heard about the *Zong* trial, and the massacre of at least 130 slaves, in March 1783. Outraged, and sensing an opportunity to shine a more public light on the brutality of the slave trade, Equiano brought the case to the attention of Granville Sharp, a clerk in the Ordnance Office, and one of England's foremost advocates for abolition. Through Sharp's network of reforming and abolitionist contacts the *Zong* affair rapidly became the talk of the town, reported in detail in London's voluminous news press.

The trial became headline news, a call to arms, the subject of stories and pamphlets denouncing the gross inequities of the slave trade. Like no other event in British history, the trial and its testimony brought the Middle Passage vividly to life in all its inhumanity, and catalyzed a mass movement demanding change. In J.M.W. Turner's achingly evocative *The Slave Ship*, based on the *Zong* affair, the shackled, outstretched arms of Africans desperately claw at the heavens as they sink into a blazing, almost blood-red sea. Such potent images charged the minds of Britons with the violence and depravity of the slave trade. Most chillingly, the *Zong* tragedy demonstrated, for perhaps the first time in such a public way, that violence was not merely an unfortunate byproduct of slavery, but intrinsic to its very logic. Violence begat profit, and profit begat violence in an endless cycle. There could be, the *Zong* affair illustrated, no slavery without violence. The only way to end this cycle of violence was to end the trade in slaves. As its most prominent historian has argued, the *Zong* affair "helped spark a seismic shift in public mood," which in turn transformed the abolition movement into public *cause célèbre*, based not on economic or political calculations but on moral imperatives.[5]

The *Zong* incident, with its horrendous callousness and its avaricious post-script, thus captured the imagination of a British public in many ways inured to the suffering of slaves and the moralizing of abolitionists. In part this was a result of the sheer calculated enormity of the killings and the manner in which mass murder was intertwined with a greedy financial calculus. However, the outrage that the *Zong* case engendered, and the impact it had on the abolition movement, would likely have been much more muted if not for the American Revolution. In the early days of the dispute with the American colonies, Britons had been recep-tive to American criticisms of the British Empire. They might not have approved of their subsequent rebellion, but their charges that the British Empire was based on immoral premises, that it operated in favor of elites and to the detriment of the greater public, rang as true in London as in Boston or Philadelphia. Even oppo-nents of the American rebellion began to see that the direction and function of the empire needed to be reconsidered and reformed. Many began to see a link between slavery and a corrupt political system, between the act of denying the liberty of slaves, and the trampling of the liberties of British subjects. The American War, and its discourse of imperial critique, provided room to debate and reimagine the British Empire on a new moral foundation of free labor and free trade.

Many of the reformers, especially those who were, like Granville Sharp, most sympathetic to the American cause, came to believe that the American War was divine retribution for the sins of the British Empire. In their minds, no sin was greater than the slave trade, and its evil was most hauntingly symbol-ized by the *Zong* tragedy. For Sharp, it was "proof of the extreme depravity which the Slave Trade introduces amongst those that become inured to it." If Britain did not rid itself of the sin of slavery it would infect everyone and everything. In the wake of the war and the *Zong* affair, the arguments of aboli-tionists began to take on a new moral tone. A British Empire built on slavery only served to enrich a few wealthy merchants while sullying the rest of the population with the collective taint of the slave trade. Slavery corroded the morals of the entire nation. The disastrous defeat in the American War only confirmed this moral truth, that the sins of the empire must be expiated if Britain were to avoid further chastisement.[6]

By the time the *Zong* affair was becoming headline news, other potent symbols of the immorality of empire were beginning to appear on British soil.

When the war ended in 1783, the cash-strapped British were forced to demobilize tens of thousands of soldiers and sailors. Among this horde of newly unemployed military men were hundreds of the former slaves who had escaped bondage to join the British armed forces. Many of these refugees made their way to London, already home to an African community perhaps 10,000 strong, where their numbers were augmented by the arrival of black refugees who had escaped bondage during the war but who had not joined the British army. In all, as many as a thousand former slaves now joined the heaving mass of the capital, most settling in the poorer areas, especially in the chronically impoverished East End and the maritime districts such as Stepney, Wapping, Shadwell, and Deptford. For these former slaves now cast into the swirling chaos of post-war London, the prospects were slim indeed. The city, already a cramped and crowded warren of glittering wealth and desperate poverty, stinking with the fetid effluvia of three-quarters of a million people, was now teeming with demobbed soldiers and sailors, and American loyalists, all looking for employment and relief.

Like Boston King, Samuel Burke had been evacuated from Charleston in 1782. Born into slavery in South Carolina, Burke had been taken to Ireland in 1774, and then to the Bahamas in 1776 as a servant of Monfort Browne, the colony's new governor. When Browne was transferred to New York during the American War, Burke accompanied his master and became a recruiting agent for Browne's loyalist regiment. Like many black loyalists, he had taken part in Sir Henry Clinton's southern campaign and was present at the British capture of Charleston in 1780, but was grievously wounded at the battle of Hanging Rock. When the British abandoned Charleston in the wake of the Yorktown debacle, Burke, as a wounded veteran, was discharged and sent to London rather than joining King and other refugees in New York and Nova Scotia. Burke's ship, however, was captured by French forces, and he spent the last months of the war in prison in France before at last making his way to London, where he hoped to find relief and compensation for his losses and his sacrifice.

Upon arrival in the capital, Burke and his wife found lodging in a cramped boarding house in Goodmans Fields with at least twelve other refugees. Burke found transient work as a paper flower seller, roaming London's twisting streets desperately hawking counterfeit blooms for a scant penny a day. This was hardly enough money to survive, especially with a chronically ill wife, so Burke and five of his fellow tenants submitted a joint petition to the recently established Loyalist Claims Commission in hopes of finding succor. The commission had been established to hear and adjudicate claims made by loyalists, and provide compensation for property lost or confiscated as a result of their service to the British Empire during the war. Burke and his fellow petitioners could not write and did not know the proper forms, so they turned to one of their former officers, Colonel Edmund Fanning, who composed the petition on their behalf. In the petition they informed the commission that the war had left them "unemployed, unprotected and homeless objects of poverty, want and wretchedness," and yet despite their condition and their service, they had as yet received no "reward, recompense, or emolument."[7]

The Commissioners, however, were suspicious—not necessarily out of racial animus, but because the sheer mass of fraudulent petitions from both black and white refugees prompted them to require extensive documentation and testimonials to prove lost property. Few of London's "Black Poor" had access to such evidence and as many as a third of black people's petitions sent to the Loyalist Claims Commission were denied. Most of Burke's joint petitioners were denied, but Burke had the good fortune to possess testimonials from Monfort Browne and succeeded in securing compensation of £20. This only proved a stop-gap for Samuel Burke, and, like most refugees, his situation rapidly deteriorated as consistent employment and government support failed to materialize. Within two months of his windfall, Samuel Burke was once more in dire straits, his money spent and his wife dead.

He was not alone in his suffering. For poor Britons, relief was available, but only through a system in which one was only eligible for relief in the parish of their birth. As most refugees had been born in Africa or in America, they were thus shut out of the traditional poor relief system, and were forced to look to other sources to ensure their survival. Some refugees found work as domestics or street-sellers. Many begged on the streets or sought refuge in the notorious workhouses—during the harsh winter of 1784, three former slaves died in the workhouse at Wapping alone. Rather than starve, others, like Joseph Scott, turned to crime. Scott had been a slave in the West Indies before joining the British navy in the early years of the war. He served loyally for seven years aboard the *Antigua*, the *Favorite*, and the *Cornwall* until he lost both his feet and the use of his hands in a naval engagement. Discharged in England bereft of friends, family, and options, Scott was confined to a hospital and reliant on what charity he could find. Eventually, he forged documents in an attempt to secure the back wages of another sailor, leading to his arrest, conviction, and execution in September 1783. Joseph Scott's case may seem remarkable on its face—surely his level of need was unique—but so common was the sight of maimed refugees that a witness who identified Scott at trial had to be asked a second time if he was sure he had the right man. After all, as the deponent was reminded, "there are more black men without legs in the city of London."[8]

If official sources of relief were not forthcoming, the plight of the "Black Poor" did not go unnoticed. Many Britons agreed that the public suffering of men who had sacrificed everything for the British Empire was a national disgrace. *The Times* thought that their "appearance in such numbers" had for too long "disgraced our streets." Indeed, their visible suffering helped to transform attitudes toward black Britons and even toward abolition. As with the *Zong* affair, the immediacy of the suffering of London's refugee community and the context of the American War roused the sympathy and indignation of many Britons who had previously been able to turn a blind eye to Britain's deep complicity in the slave trade. Britain may have offered freedom to America's slaves for strategic reasons, a necessary measure taken under trying circumstances. However, offering freedom to enslaved people willing to serve the British Empire set an important precedent, by redefining citizenship, even Britishness, as something based on service and loyalty rather than race. The offers made to America's slaves transformed bondsmen into Britons, into individuals to whom the British government, and by extension the British people, owed a debt of gratitude and a responsibility to protect them and relieve their suffering. By bringing the plight of former slaves to Londoners' doors, by demonstrating their fragile humanity, by remaking perceptions of Africans, and reconfiguring the relationship between the state and its formerly enslaved subjects, the Black Poor helped contribute to the rapid rise in the popularity of abolitionism.[9]

But sympathy is not the same thing as action, and moral outrage still had to coalesce into moral action if Britain was to be purged of the evils of the slave trade. American and British critiques of empire and imperial policy in the 1760s and 1770s, however, had forced Britons to reconsider the purpose, structure, and moral basis of the British Empire and its institutions. As such, the crisis of imperial authority that surrounded the American Revolution made "slavery matter politically in ways it had never mattered before." Already disgusted by the horrors of slavery, the American War now gave Britons room to reimagine their empire on a new moral footing, as an empire free from the sin of slavery. The tools and tactics for transforming popular outrage into a political move- ment were also to be found in the history of the American War. The emerging abolitionist movement took its strategic cues from the networks, petitioning campaigns, and boycotts of the Wilkites in the 1760s, the American Patriots in the 1760s and 1770s, and the Association movement in the 1780s. In the past the wealthy and influential West Indian planter lobby had ensured that there was little serious consideration of anti-slavery policies. However, though the war left the British Caribbean and its slave economy intact, it fatally undermined the image and power of the West Indian lobby, giving new space for critics of Britain's imperial policy. By the war's end in 1783, a true abolition movement had at last been born.[10]

As the abolition movement gathered greater moral force, the British public, conditioned by the war to reimagine the role of the empire, were increasingly drawn to the cause. The result was a massive growth in abolitionist societies and a cascade of petitions calling for an end to the slave trade that had mired Britain in immorality and defeat. In June 1783, a group of Quaker abolitionists unsuccessfully petitioned Parliament to end the slave trade, the first of many such petitions in a growing movement. Crucially, at the same time the spirit of abolitionism also began to invade the upper echelons of British society. What had been a movement largely limited to Quakers and other religious non- conformists, began to be adopted by the Anglican clerical establishment who began to espouse the moral imperative of the arguments against slavery. That same year, the influential Bishop of Chester Beilby Porteus preached against slavery, denouncing the Anglican Church's role in propping up the system and its ownership of slave plantations in the West Indies. Porteus's sermon marked a turning point in Anglican attitudes toward slavery, and he would remain an influential proponent of the moral cause of abolitionism, both from the pulpit as Bishop of London and in the House of Lords. The American War and the *Zong* affair had helped to turn a fringe cause into the cause of the righteous.

Central to this transformation was a well-designed publicity campaign that sought to force Britons to confront their role in the horrendous suffering of the enslaved. Led by the Society for Effecting the Abolition of the Slave Trade, which had been founded in 1787, abolitionists crisscrossed the country gathering information about the slave trade, publishing accounts of its horrors, and convening public lectures, all designed to humanize Africans and publicize the oft ignored abuses of the system. Thomas Clarkson, a founding member and driving force behind the Society, traveled some 35,000 miles around Britain researching the slave trade and promoting abolition. He interviewed some 20,000 sailors and ships' surgeons about their experiences of the slave trade, acquired the gruesome tools of the trade—branding irons, shackles, thumbscrews—for public display, and bought samples of African manufactures as evidence of the sophistication and common humanity of African civilization. Clarkson and his colleagues hoped that publishing first-hand accounts of slavery and confronting the populace with images of slave ships and their instruments of torture would shock the British public into action. To this end, they also printed pamphlets advocating abolition and featuring the life stories of former slaves. Perhaps the most important of these publications was *The Interesting Narrative of the Life of Olaudah Equiano*, which proved enormously popular, going through eight editions within eight years of its publication in 1789. Equiano's account, one of the first to detail African society, the Middle Passage, and slavery from the perspective of a former slave, presented the fate of a living, breathing, feeling human being to devastating effect.[11]

In 1787, abolitionists peppered Parliament with 100 petitions demanding the end of the slave trade. In 1792, the annual number of petitions had grown five-fold, by which point over 1.5 million British men and women—one out of every eight Britons—had signed an anti-slavery petition. In addition to the flood of petitions, some anti-slavery advocates adopted more active means of rousing the conscience of the nation and shaming the public into action. Boycotts of sugar and other products that relied on slave labor were advanced. The anti-slavery climate was so charged that some even turned to more forceful measures. In April 1793, John Hatton, a notoriously quarrelsome former colonial official and slave-holder from New Jersey woke to find that a "ridiculous, ludicrous, scandalous monstrous . . . Effigy" had been erected outside his door. Hatton, a loyalist during the war who had suffered similar treatment at the hands of vengeful Patriots, had relocated to London, but his knack for inciting a mob had not been dissipated by distance or time. But instead of being targeted for loyalty to the crown, in 1793 John Hatton was being attacked for his perceived opposition to Britain's new moral crusade. Over the space of two weeks, his neighbor John Tye twice attracted crowds in Hatton's garden with effigies of Hatton in chains, and shouts that he would sell the likeness of the "damned Scoundrel" for 200 guineas. It is tempting to hope that John Tye was a relative of Colonel Tye come to continue his vengeance on New Jersey's slave-holders; the iconography of the shaming ritual certainly suggests that Hatton's role in the slave system was the source of his trouble and that London crowds that had once smashed windows in support of "Wilkes and Liberty" were now willing to torment neighbors for their support of slavery. This is not to say that all Britons had at last seen the light—many, especially those with interests in the empire, defended slavery just as vigorously as abolitonists now opposed it—but the moral tide was at least beginning to turn.[12]

Abolitionists, who explicitly connected the plight of the post-revolution Black Poor and the evils of the slave trade, used this growing public sympathy to advocate on behalf of London's refugees. Granville Sharp met regularly with refugees and provided what money he could, but by the beginning of 1786, it was clear that government channels had failed the refugees, that individual charity was insufficient, and that something more—on a larger scale—had to be done to alleviate their suffering. To that end, on January 6, 1786, a "Committee of Gentlemen," most of them Quakers and Anglican evangelicals, and all opponents of the slave trade, created "the Committee for the Relief of the Black Poor." The committee was chaired by Jonas Hanway—one of the great advocates for prison reform—and included Granville Sharp, Thomas Clarkson, and the bankers Samuel Hoare and Henry Thornton as members. In their advertisement, the committee declared their intention to raise money for black refugees now in "extreme distress" who had "served in the late war." The committee's call for donations quickly saw results—luminaries such as William

Wilberforce and Prime Minister William Pitt donated—and within a few months £890 was raised for clothing, food, and medical care.[13]

The donations raised by the Committee for the Relief of the Black Poor were a vital life-line for London's beleaguered refugee community, but they were not a long-term solution and did not address the underlying causes of their poverty. What refugees needed was land of their own. Land, however, was not forthcoming in England or, so it seemed, in Nova Scotia. The solution came from an unlikely source. In 1786, Henry Smeathman, a naturalist who had spent four years in West Africa chasing after insects and scouting possible sites for penal colonies, published a pamphlet touting the potential benefits for Britain and the Black Poor of a new settlement in Sierra Leone. After the American War, many in Britain had begun to look for new markets for British commerce and new venues for Britain's undented imperial ambitions. Attempts had already been made to settle British convicts on the African coast, and though these proved disastrous, there was still considerable interest in gaining British footholds in Africa. Granville Sharp had been considering just such a plan since as early as 1783, but he lacked the expert knowledge of Africa to convince others of its viability. Sharp and his colleagues were intrigued by Smeathman's proposal, especially when its viability was confirmed by a former slave who was a native of the region, and published a recruitment advertisement offering land, free transportation, three months' provisions, and farming equipment to any refugee who joined the colony. The British government saw the potential benefits of a British colony in Africa, and approved the plan. The offer was clearly appealing: 600 refugees initially responded to the ad, and nearly 500 made their way to Plymouth to board ships sailing to Africa. In an ominous augury of things to come, fifty would die before they even left the harbor.[14]

In December 1786, 411 passengers—including 60 white women recruited as wives for the settlers—boarded three ships bound for Sierra Leone. Escorted by Captain Thomas Thompson of the British navy, the refugees at last reached what they hoped would prove their promised land on May 9, 1787. Thompson, who had been given temporary command of the colony, arranged a meeting with the local chief, known as "King Tom" to the British, and secured an agreement to purchase a tract of land along the Sierra Leone River for £59 in trade goods. The British, who had been trading in the area since 1562 and had eight trading posts in the vicinity, were not strangers to King Tom, though his decision to sell them land outright was unprecedented. African polities had long allowed Europeans to occupy their lands as tenants, but they had never before ceded territory in perpetuity. King Tom may not have fully understood the document he and Thompson signed, and the conflicting claims to the land would prove a source of continual friction between the colony and the local peoples for the foreseeable future.[15]

The colony was intended to be self-regulating, with minimal British intervention after Thompson's initial escort and diplomacy. As such, the settlers were to govern themselves democratically, and they selected Richard Weaver to be their commander and elected a range of officials and officers to run the colony and administer justice. For Granville Sharp and his colleagues, this had been a key aspect of the colony, providing proof against pro-slavery claims that Africans did not have the capacity for self-rule. For the refugees too, the prospect of political power was vitally important to their transatlantic search for freedom. In this spirit they named their new colony the "Province of Freedom," and their first settlement Granville Town, after the man who had done so much to secure their independence.

Such optimism was short-lived. After years of poverty and penury in London, many of the settlers arrived in Africa already ill. The sickness was further compounded by the timing of their arrival in Sierra Leone. Shortly after landing, the rainy season began, making planting impossible, construction difficult, and disease rampant. By the time Captain Thompson returned to Britain in September 1787, only 268 settlers remained. By the following April, the numbers had been further reduced to 130. Dozens had succumbed to disease—malaria, typhoid, dysentery—during the rainy season. Others, in despair, had abandoned the colony, forced in a cruel twist of fate to take refuge or employment with nearby slave traders, like those stationed on Bance Island. In addition, King Tom and other local chiefs, who had never granted permission for a permanent settlement, launched retaliatory raids on the already vulnerable settlement. Within months of their arrival, King Tom began to kidnap settlers and sell them into slavery as compensation for the unpaid tribute he felt was due. In December 1789, King Jimmy, a local Temne chief who likewise expected tribute for the colonists' use of a watering hole in his territory, attacked Granville Town and razed the village to the ground in retaliation. The settlers, aided by local slave traders also at loggerheads with the local chiefs, fought back, but came out the worse. By 1790, the colony was almost completely abandoned, its remaining settlers having fled to nearby trading posts and slaving stations.

To be sure, the failure of the first Sierra Leone settlement was troubling, but Granville Sharp and his colleagues were not about to give up on a cause near and dear to their hearts. Sharp, however, had already spent more of his own money than he could afford trying to prop up the ailing settlement. It had become clear that a fresh infusion of cash and energy was needed if the project was to be salvaged, and so, on February 17, 1790, a group of twenty-two men, including Sharp, Wilberforce, Clarkson, and Thornton, convened a first meeting of a new company, and petitioned Parliament for permission to incorporate. Eventually 500 proprietors would purchase shares at £20 a piece and appoint a twelve-man board of directors with Thornton as the chair. Sharp hoped the new company, soon officially christened the Sierra Leone Company, would continue his original mission, focusing on providing a free homeland, access to land, and self-determination for refugees of the American War. Most of the new members, however, had been recruited from the Committee for the Abolition of the African Slave Trade, and thus saw Sierra Leone primarily as a potential tool in the fight against African slavery. Indeed, newspaper announcements detailing the formation of the Company explicitly reported that it had been created "for the purpose of undermining the Slave Trade."[16]

The best way both to save the colony and achieve their higher aims, the directors concluded, was to adjust the economic basis of the settlement. Instead of a refuge of former slaves scratching out a meager existence from the African soil, they conceived of the new Sierra Leone Colony as an engine of free trade on the African coast, helping to create lucrative African markets and producers that the directors hoped would supplant and eventually eliminate the slave trade. If trade in local commodities, products, and handicrafts could be invigorated, and free trade between Britain and Africa expanded, Africans, so the directors believed, would see the benefits of legitimate trade and voluntarily cease selling slaves. At the same time, British merchants, like their African counterparts, would find this new trade more profitable, or at least more palatable, than buying and selling their fellow man, and willingly embrace free trade over the slave trade.

From the first days of the abolitionist movement, advocates of emancipation had hoped to substitute a free trade in African commodities and manufactures for the trade in human beings. Thomas Clarkson had even purchased a range of such goods in the hope of convincing the public to support just such an exchange. In many ways, the American War provided the space necessary to contemplate such a drastic shift in the nature of the British Empire. Since the seventeenth century, British political economists and politicians had debated the merits of an empire based on conquest of land versus an empire based on free trade. The debate had formed an important part of the ideological conflict on both sides of the Atlantic in the lead-up to the American War and continued to be central to British attempts to recoup their losses when the war was over. After the war, with a large swath of the slave-based Atlantic economy now carved off, many in Britain saw the loss of the American colonies as an opportunity to remake the empire on the basis of free trade. This was all the more possible, all the more appealing, given Britain's simultaneous gains in India. In the years after the war, campaigns were begun to replace slave-based economies with free trade economies, and to substitute commodities produced with slave labor—American and West Indies cotton and sugar—with commodities produced with free labor—Indian and Asian cotton and sugar. An imperial reorientation from slave labor to free labor would, its advocates believed, allow Britain to distance itself from the taint of the slave trade without undermining its prosperity, ushering in a moral transformation without economic sacrifice. In the years after the American War, as Britain remade its empire along more authoritarian, centralized lines, Britain's imperial resources thus began to shift toward new markets and expanding interests in India, China, and perhaps, the abolitionists hoped, even Africa. An African market could help replace the loss of America, providing needed foodstuffs for Britain's Caribbean colonies and potential buyers for British textiles and manufactured goods.[17]

With Africa brought more firmly into the European market economy, advocates believed, there would be other benefits as well. Once Africans became familiar with all that Europe had to offer, commerce would bring with it "civilization," and Christianity, a fundamental part of European civilization in the minds of the evangelical directors, trailing in its wake. "Commerce," Ignatius Sancho had argued a decade earlier, "attended with strict honesty, and with Religion for its companion, would be a blessing to every shore it touched," especially in Africa, where the British pursuit of slaves and "money, money, money" had destroyed the blessings of Providence. Thomas Clarkson, the indefatigable abolitionist, evangelical, and member of the board of directors, concurred and summed up the mission of the Sierra Leone Company thus: "the Abolition of the Slave-Trade, the Civilization of Africa, and the Introduction of the Gospel there." Others, including Thornton, echoed the sentiment, sure that abolition, civilization, and evangelization would all naturally and necessarily follow the introduction of commerce.[18]

The directors were idealists, not fools, and they fully understood that all their lofty goals depended on the profit motive. They knew well enough that no merchant, British or African, would voluntarily abandon the slave trade or adopt a new legitimate trade unless the exchange proved profitable. Thus, despite their lofty rhetoric of equality, to ensure that the new colony succeeded where the first settlement had failed, the directors concluded that the government of Sierra Leone could not be left in the hands of the settlers themselves. "A respectable establishment" of white British administrators, educators, officials, and commercial agents would therefore replace the hard-won democratic self-government of the "Province of Freedom." As its charter of incorporation, issued by Parliament in May 1791, stated, the land that had been purchased for the settlers would now be owned by the Company. Trade with Britain and with the rest of Africa would now be controlled by the Company as well. To ensure its efficient management, "all matters, civil, military, political and commercial," would be entrusted to a superintendent and an advisory council of Europeans appointed by, and responsible to, the directors in London. Sharp abhorred this loss of self-determination, but feared the settlement would collapse without the new investors and bitterly bowed to the inevitable. "The Community of settlers," he lamented, "are no longer the proprietors of the whole district as before . . . so that they can no longer enjoy the privileges of granting land by the free vote of their own Common Council, as before, nor the benefits of their own Agrarian Law, nor the choice of their own governor and

other officers, nor any other circumstances of *perfect freedom* . . . all these privileges are now submitted to the appointment and control of the Company." "I
could not prevent this humiliating change," he continued, "the settlement must
have remained desolate if I had not thus far submitted to the opinions of the
associated subscribers."[19]

All the new regulations and administrators in the world could not succeed
without more settlers. Most of the original colonists had died or been driven
out by hunger or violence. The few who remained were too few, too scattered,
to carry on the thriving trade that the directors envisioned. Over a hundred
white settlers, officials, soldiers, and craftsmen were selected to form the administrative and moral backbone of the colony, but many of the directors still
hoped the settlement could serve as a place of refuge for former slaves. The
more practically minded among them also thought that the work of civilization
and Christianization would proceed more smoothly if it were directed by
Africans. What they needed, then, was a population of black Christians willing
to settle in Africa. As if directed by fate, at the very moment when the Sierra
Leone Company was searching for new settlers, Thomas Peters arrived in
London from Nova Scotia.

Peters had been born in Nigeria, sold into slavery in Louisiana, and then
sold on to North Carolina, where he escaped in 1776 to join the Black Pioneers
in their fight against the Americans. A natural leader, Peters rose to the rank of
sergeant, a high honor at a time when the ranks of commissioned officers were
closed off to former slaves, and maintained his influential role within the
refugee community after their evacuation to Nova Scotia. Like many Black
Pioneers and their families, he settled at Digby, where he became a spokesman
for the refugees and worked hard to ensure his neighbors were adequately
clothed and fed. Throughout his forced tour of North America, Peters retained
an indomitable spirit of independence, a stubborn streak that fed a lifelong
quest for freedom and justice. When the promised grants of land failed to materialize, Peters, never one to shy away from action, took up the cause and
peppered the colonial administrators with a steady stream of petitions. Three
times, land was promised, even surveyed and parceled out, but each time the
land slipped through the refugees' desperate grasp, reassigned to other purposes
or for other people. Peters had little quit about him, and reasoned that if the

authorities in Canada would not see his people settled, he would take their grievances to London, the heart of the empire, and ensure that they were heard.

He arrived in London at the end of 1790, clutching a petition on behalf of 202 refugee families in Nova Scotia and New Brunswick. He hoped, as the petition read, "to procure for himself and his Fellow Sufferers some Establishment where they may obtain a competent Settlement for themselves and be enabled by their industries to become useful Subjects to his Majesty." His plan was to present his petition to William Grenville, the Secretary of State, but had no idea how to manage the feat. Resourceful as ever, Peters made contact with Sir Henry Clinton, his former commanding officer. Clinton felt responsible for the plight of the refugees—it was in part his promises to them that were now going unfulfilled—and put Peters in contact with two of the men, Granville Sharp and John Clarkson, most likely to help. Sharp, Clarkson, and their abolitionist colleagues were moved by the accounts Peters brought detailing the ill-treatment of the refugees in Canada and helped Peters sharpen his petition. In conversation, Peters and the abolitionists arrived at a neat solution to all their problems: the star-crossed refugees of Nova Scotia would become settlers in Sierra Leone.[20]

For Sharp and the Sierra Leone Company, the Nova Scotia refugees would provide just the infusion of westernized Christians of African descent they needed to jump-start their ambitious new colony. For Peters, after nearly a decade of frustration and failure in Canada, the prospect of a homeland back in Africa seemed, in the words of one supporter, "likely to afford him and persons of a like description, an Asylum much better suited to their constitutions, than Nova Scotia and New Brunswick." To reflect this willingness to settle wherever the longed-for land was offered, a clause was inserted in the petition stating that "some part . . . of the said Black people [of Nova Scotia], are earnestly desirous of obtaining their due allotment of land and remaining in America, but others are willing to go wherever the wisdom of the Government may think proper to provide for them as free subjects of the British Empire."[21]

The government, led by Secretary of State Henry Dundas, was willing to back the plan and even provide the transportation for the new settlers. However, after the disaster of the 1787 colony, which many blamed on the deficient character of the settlers from London, the Company wanted an agent on the ground to assess the prospective colonists and the viability of the scheme. They found him in John Clarkson, already a committed member of the abolition movement, working with the most prominent anti-slavery advocates in Britain. Fired by Peters' pleas for aid, Clarkson offered to sail to Nova Scotia on behalf of the Sierra Leone Company to assess the condition of Canada's former slaves and recruit settlers for the new colony in Africa.

Though he agreed to serve as the Company's agent, he resolved not to solicit or cajole any refugee to accept the Company's offer. He was personally unsure of the proposed colony's prospects for success, and from the information he had gleaned about the 1787 settlement, he knew that disease, exposure, starvation, and hostile locals were all likely to take their toll. So rather than urge anyone to join the new colony, he decided to merely present the information— the Company's offer, the potential risks, everything he knew about the proposed settlement—as neutrally as possible and let the refugees decide for themselves. He did so because he recognized the equal humanity of the refugees, "for I considered them as men, having the same feelings as myself and therefore I did not dare sport with their destiny."[22]

Clarkson left Gravesend aboard the aptly named *Ark* on August 19, 1791 and arrived at Halifax on October 7. After meeting with Governor Parr and ensuring the publication of the Company's offer, Clarkson made his first recruiting stop at Preston on October 12, where he "called at the huts of several of the inhabitants and stated to them the offer of the Sierra Leone Company," adding that "their situation seemed extremely bad . . ." As a minister and leader of the Preston refugee community, Boston King was likely one of the first in Nova Scotia to receive a visit from John Clarkson. If so, Clarkson was fortunate in his choice, for Boston King had experienced fully the deferred dream represented by Nova Scotia and had already been contemplating the benefits of a British presence in Africa. According to King's memoir, as early as 1787 he had begun to think about, and pray for, his "poor brethren in Africa." Although thus far they had escaped slavery, King pitied them for not having been "brought up in a Christian land, where the Gospel is preached . . . what a wretched condition then must those poor creatures be in, who never heard the Name of GOD or of CHRIST." When John Clarkson appeared on his doorstep four years later, King saw in his offer to settle Sierra Leone a chance to bring the Word of

God, and the civilization of Britain to "the poor benighted inhabitants of that country which gave birth to my forefathers." In many ways, King was an ideal settler. He was of good character, likely had some sway among his congregation, and his goals of "civilizing" and proselytizing the people of Africa were in line with the aims of the Sierra Leone Company. Within a week, perhaps with King's endorsement, Clarkson received 79 applications from Preston and Halifax to join the proposed settlement, with the number rising to 220 within a month of his first visit. Boston King and his family were among them.[23]

Energized by his success at Preston and Halifax, Clarkson traveled to Shelburne and Birchtown, the two largest refugee communities, where he entrusted the recruitment of settlers to David George and Moses Wilkinson as influential religious leaders. The result was overwhelming. Whole congregations signed up en masse, eager to recreate in Africa the communities they had first established in Nova Scotia. The numbers grew to such an extent that Clarkson began to fear that there would not be space to transport and settle so many, and called off further recruitment trips to St. John, Annapolis, and Digby, the very community that had sent Thomas Peters to London in the first place. Peters, who was in constant communication with Clarkson, was not a man to be deterred, however, and visited refugee communities himself, especially fellow veterans of the Black Pioneers, managing to recruit a further 400 settlers.

As ever, trouble and complication dogged the refugees. From the beginning the Governor of Nova Scotia had been dead set against Clarkson's mission, sure that eagerness to join the Sierra Leone settlement would be seen as proof of his failures as an administrator. Many members of Nova Scotia's white community were equally opposed to allowing the refugees to leave. Free they might have been, but white Canadians still viewed the refugees through the lens of slavery. They considered the former slaves only in terms of cheap labor, and were loath to let them leave without a fight. Some refused to give refugees testimonials, hoping to scupper their chances of being accepted by Clarkson, while others spread tales of the nefarious designs of the Company, of re-enslavement, and of high mortality of the transatlantic journey and of life in Africa. Accounts of the deadly failure of the 1787 settlement were published in local papers, and read aloud to refugees "in every part of the town."[24]

Few were discouraged, however, and Clarkson considered it his moral duty to risk all to aid the refugees. "These poor unfortunate men," he explained, "have ever since Europe called herself enlightened experienced the greatest treachery, oppression, murder and everything that is base, and I cannot name an instance where a body of them collected together have ever had the promises made them performed in a conscientious way." He was soon overwhelmed with inquiries and applications. So desperate were some to secure a better life for their families that they confronted the prospect of permanent separation from loved ones. As he recorded:

A most affecting scene occurred this afternoon occasioned by a Black *slave* who came to me in order to resign his wife and family who were free. With tears streaming down his cheeks he said, that though this separation would be as death to himself, yet he had come to a resolution resigning them up for ever, convinced as he was, that such a measure would ultimately tend to render their situation more comfortably and happy. He said he was regardless of himself or the cruelties he might hereafter experience for though sunk to the most abject state of wretchedness he could at all times cheer himself that his wife and children were happy.[25]

Another refugee, a man who could remember his earlier life in Africa before he had been enslaved, told Clarkson in halting English that he now worked "like a slave" and as a result could not do worse "in any part of the world." When Clarkson warned him of the hardships and danger he was likely to face if he joined the settlement he replied, "if me die, me die, had rather die in me own country than in this cold place."

In January 1792, all 1,190 settlers had at last been gathered together at Halifax. On January 16 they departed Canada as a group on fifteen vessels, altered by Clarkson's orders so that they would in no way call to mind the dreadful conditions of the Middle Passage. Boston King and the Preston refugees, who Clarkson called "better than any people in the labouring line of life in England: I would match them for strong sense, quick apprehension, clear reasoning, gratitude, affection for their wives & children, and friendship and good-will towards their neighbours," traveled together. King and his companions had been disappointed by their years in Nova Scotia, but as they continued their seemingly endless wandering in the British Empire, they did so not as a defeated, subjugated people, but as men and women convinced of their equality, sure that if only the constraints of prejudice could be removed, their community would grow and prosper. These refugees of American slavery and American rebellion had imbibed not the language of bondage and inferiority favored by slavery's apologists, but instead drank from the same Enlightenment well as their erstwhile masters, internalizing and coopting ideas of universal equality and natural rights. Generations of enslavement had not created a Stockholm syndrome of internalized inferiority but a vast reservoir of strength and an iron-willed commitment to struggle and fight until freedom and prosperity became a reality. Despite the failures of Canada, they continued to believe that, as British subjects, protected by British justice and the rights of British citizenship, the best opportunity to achieve their dream lay within the secure embrace of the British Empire. They were, in this way, committed imperialists engaged in a colonizing, civilizing mission.

As the convoy neared the coast in March 1792, Boston King caught his first glimpse of Africa. The mountains that gave the region its Portuguese name were the first to appear, rising "gradually from the sea to a stupendous height, richly wooded and beautifully ornamented by the hand of nature, with a variety of delightful prospects." As the mountains crept closer, crowding out the horizon, the Sierra Leone River at last came into view. Ten miles wide at its mouth before narrowing rapidly, the river was speckled with verdant islands, most of them uninhabited apart from Bance Island, 15 miles upriver, which housed a British slave factory. As he sailed upriver, the scenery speeding by, King saw flashes of color from the "variety of beautifully plumed birds" and the clusters of orange trees "overloaded with fruit," among the greens and browns of steel-straight palms of "gigantic height." There were other signs of life visible through the trees, glimpses of African villages that appeared and vanished as the ship moved upstream. For those who had spent their youth in Africa, "the perfumes of fragrant aromatic plants" wafting on the sultry breeze must have smelled of home, triggering long-forgotten memories in the deep recesses of their minds. Some 10 miles from the sea, huddled on a deep bay on the south bank of the river, King's ship at last reached the few dozen huts of Granville Town, rebuilt by the settlers under the direction of Alexander Falconbridge, a former slave ship surgeon and informant of Thomas Clarkson, who had been sent to Sierra Leone the year before to re-gather and reconstruct the settlement. This bedraggled settlement of mud and thatch and wood clinging to the river was to be King's new home.[26]

It had been a rocky, storm-tossed voyage. A few days out from Halifax the fleet had run into a "dreadful storm." For sixteen days, King recalled, the ships were buffeted by screaming winds and roaring seas, the fleet driven apart and dispersed. In the squall one of King's fellow passengers was swept overboard to his death, leaving a wife and four children behind. For King, the raging storms outside his berth seemed to mirror the sickness that had taken hold within. His wife was now "exceeding ill," and as the days passed and the weather at last released the convoy from its grip, he became increasingly sure she would not live to see the African shore. For weeks she held on to life by a thread as King obsessed over the dreadful prospect of having "to bury her in the sea." So it was with double relief that King greeted the sight of land on March 6.[27]

By the time King arrived, several of the ships that had been separated by the storm were already anchored 6 miles upriver from the site of Granville Town. They had arrived two weeks earlier on February 26. A few days later, they left the ships and waded through the turquoise-blue waters to stand on the soil of their ancestors. Thomas Peters, who spent his early years 1,500 miles to the south and east in what is now Nigeria, and who had now crossed the Atlantic four times in his journey into slavery and back again, was overjoyed. He had done as much as anyone to bring his people to these shores, and in a euphoric mix of elation and relief he broke into song, providing a stirring soundtrack to what was a most momentous occasion. As Peters, George, and the other preachers led their flocks into this promised land, they lifted their voices to the heavens, singing "the day of Jubilee is come; return ye ransomed sinners home."

They were greeted on shore by the remnants of the "Province of Freedom," forty or so men and women in a dejected state, some "decrepid with disease," and "so disguised with filth and dirt" that they were hardly recognizable. There was also a contingent of local Temne people, a wary welcoming party come to meet the new arrivals. All of the refugees must have been overcome by the scene, their exodus, at least it seemed, was over. A few of their number had greater cause to greet the landing with nervous anticipation and search the crowds gathered on the sands for familiar longed-for faces. Three men at least had been born in the region, and one of these was a son of Sierra Leone itself. He had passed the time under sail across the Atlantic regaling his fellow passengers with stories of his once and future home. As luck, or destiny, or chance would have it, the fleet anchored "nearly on the spot from whence he had been carried off," the very stretch of beach where he had been caught and sold to an American slave ship lying in the river. He had been a boy then, fifteen years ago, but he still remembered the way to his native village a couple of miles away. The trauma of his enslavement and his long years away convinced him not to risk the journey, and so he remained among the refugees constructing their camp, christened "Freetown" on one of the banks of the Sierra Leone River.[28]

King joined the camp in early March, but the sight of the new settlement and its novel setting held little interest for him. His wife had made it to their new home, but she was now so sick she had "lost her senses"; within weeks of landing she had become delirious, speaking of visions of God before she at last "expired in a rapture of love." Violet King was among the first to perish in their new homeland, but she was far from the last. Boston King himself soon fell ill and within months the sickness was "a universal complaint." Like their predecessors in 1787, the Nova Scotia refugees arrived just before the rains began. Temporary huts were erected where sick and sodden refugees shivered in the rain, but there had been no time to build the more permanent houses and storerooms that would protect the colonists and their provisions from the ever-present damp. The lack of fresh provisions and the exposure to the weather exacerbated illnesses brought from Nova Scotia. While still in Halifax, disease had raged among the fleet, leaving sixty-five dead before the convoy ever reached its destination. Weak and ill, the settlers were vulnerable to the unfamiliar tropical diseases that followed with the rains. Within the first few weeks, forty of the refugees had died. Settlers, King recalled, "died so fast that it was difficult to procure a burial for them."[29]

King was lucky to survive the sickness of the first rainy season and, like many who spent their first months huddled in their shacks, greeted the end of the rains with restless gratitude. They threw themselves with an almost religious fervor into herculean labors required to build their colony. King worked for the Company, helping to clear land and build a chapel, heavy but rewarding work for a believer. As Freetown began to rise around him, King began to think of his own reasons for journeying for Nova Scotia and found his mind "drawn out to pity the native inhabitants."[30]

While the settlers set about constructing their new Eden, in the local villages there was great interest in the commotion on the beach. A group from one such village decided to go and see for themselves the new settlement springing up upon the shore. With them went an elderly woman, worn with age and care. Her husband had died some years back, her son disappeared without a trace and "given up for lost." As they approached the sea of tents that made up the settlement, and watched the newcomers at their work, the old woman became agitated. There was among the strangers a profile not so strange. At every glimpse of this young man her excitement climbed as suspicion turned into certainty. She knew this man, she told her friends, though it had been fifteen years since last she saw his face. At last she ran to him, embraced him, pressed him close. "She proved to be his own mother."[31]

It was not precisely a homecoming for the many, like Boston King, who had been born into slavery on the opposite side of the ocean. Africa was the place of their ancestors, a fabled place, a place of stories told by firelight by those who knew it from their youth, a place of history, and now of the future, but it was not a home. For men like King there had never been a home, not a true one, a place of comfort and belonging. There had been family, that much was true, but family had not been rooted in a place, a landscape richly laden with custom, with history, with meaning. Instead there had been the stolen existence of the slave, a pilfered, shifted life, moved place to place, master to master, bought and sold on a whim. In such a world there was no lodestar, no compass rose to guide one back to home; there was no home, no deep and holding roots. The American War had brought freedom with it, but the tenuous life of constant motion continued nonetheless; freedom brought still more weary wanderings in its train. But freedom also kindled hope, a restless search for independence and a home, until at last they reached this forlorn terminus on the banks of the Sierra Leone. For King and most of his companions, there was little chance they would ever find a true homeland. But that was beside the point. The long restless years that led to Sierra Leone were as much about posterity as they ever were about the present. In Africa, they hoped, even believed, they might have found a place where they could rebuild a stolen world, "our children free and happy."[32]

The Africans who watched the armada unload its threadbare cargo on their coasts had reason to welcome the immigrants with a wary eye to the future. As their raids on Granville Town had forcefully demonstrated, the local chiefs had no intention of ceding their lands to another batch of interlopers, whatever their skin color or shared ethnicity. They had long ago become accustomed to the ever-present impermanence of European merchants and their trading posts, but settlers were another matter entirely. And yet, at least some of the local rulers would have welcomed the ambitious aims of the new arrivals. Most would have embraced an expanded trade with the British. Many would have likewise welcomed an effort to undermine the slave trade. Over the years, some coastal rulers had made a tidy profit selling neighbors, rivals, and conquered captives to the slavers at Bance Island. The costs of this enrichment, however, were becoming difficult to bear.

The entire region, stretching from Sierra Leone north to Senegambia, and south to the Gulf of Guinea, had been ravaged by the slave trade. One local ruler openly encouraged the Sierra Leone Colony, "in order," as he said, "that there might be a stop put to the horrid depredations that are often committed in this country by all countries that come here to trade." The vile trade left few untouched, and even this powerful man had seen three of his relatives captured from his own territory and sold to the West Indies. "I know not how to get them back," he told the colonists. Reports from the north told much the same story of kidnapping, raids, and wars, all for "the sole purpose of procuring slaves." Conditions inland were hardly better; the interior was plagued by incessant wars instigated by the unquenchable need for slaves. These accounts were confirmed by another local informant, the mixed-race "mistress of a large town in the Mandingo country." Her English name was "Mrs. B. Heard" and she had spent time in England in her youth. For her, the slave trade was a source of "constant terror," never knowing "when she lay down at night, whether she might be assassinated before the morning." By drying up the demand for slaves, the American War had been a blessing. In those years, Heard explained, "there had been no wars in the interior country," for "the wars do not happen when there is no demand for slaves." But the respite had been only temporary and with peace in Paris came the return of slaving wars in Africa.[33]

To ensure their continued supply of slaves, Europeans openly encouraged warfare between African states. One informant who visited Freetown from the headwaters of the Sierra Leone River reported that Europeans often encouraged quarrels and fomented wars, even arming both sides with arms and ammunition. The man himself was in the midst of a five-year war prompted by a British slaver. The slaving wars could become a vicious, inescapable cycle, as the informant outlined. He was forced to "waylay and sell strangers" in order to buy the arms and ammunition his people required to protect themselves from enslavement by their neighbors. He acknowledged that the trade in slaves was "a bad thing," but he could not abandon his part in it without leaving his community vulnerable. War begat slavery, and slavery begat war ad infinitum.[34]

Further south, the Company's agents found further evidence of this post-war renewal, scores of villages "depopulated," their former residents enslaved or fled. A mixed-race slaver, educated in Liverpool, had laid waste to the entire region with his raids. His method was to lend goods to local chiefs and village headmen, and when they could not pay, arm 200 men or more, led by white deserters from European ships, and seize slaves as compensation. This was common practice among European slavers as well, who used unpaid debts as leverage to press coastal peoples into raiding their neighbors for human stock to meet their leaders' debts. In one such case, a local chief approached the colony for relief. His daughter had been seized by his creditor, and sold to a slave ship anchored off Freetown. The governor attempted to intervene and redeem the girl, but the captain of the vessel refused unless another slave could be found to take her place. In another example of the cycle of enslavement, the father thus went "off in quest of a slave," to capture some other poor soul as a substitute for his child. There was considerable opposition to slavery within African society, but after centuries of involvement in the trade, the slavers had become enmeshed in the economy and politics of the region. Together with local rulers who were themselves "deeply engaged in the slave trade," some slavers formed confederacies that ensured their raids would go unchecked. The effects were grim. The African interior was beset by near constant warfare, which destabilized and depopulated whole regions, disrupting societies and economies, and preventing capital accumulation. On the coasts, some African polities accumulated wealth and power from their role in the slave trade, but they too remained in a precarious position, increasingly reliant on European trade to survive. Africans everywhere bemoaned the terrible impact of the slave trade, but few could see a way out of the vicious cycle.[35]

As part of their larger quest to disrupt and end the slave trade, the agents of the Sierra Leone Company sought out and recorded the accounts and grievances of the local people. These stories were part of a wider campaign by abolitionists to gather information about African civilization and the impact of the slave trade. Mostly confined to coastal trading posts, Britain knew remarkably little about Africa in the eighteenth century. To address this issue, a number of wealthy Britons, led by Captain Cook's former botanist Sir Joseph Banks, founded the Association for Promoting the Discovery of the Interior Parts of Africa in 1788. The Africa Association as it was known, had genuine scientific interests in the exploration of West Africa, and funded a series of expeditions led by men such as Daniel Houghton and Mungo Park, charged with locating the fabled city of Timbuktu and finding the source of the River Niger. The exploits of such doughty explorers captured the imagination of the British public, turning them into heroes of empire and Africa into a new stage for British endeavor. But knowledge was not the only reason for their wanderings. The membership and interests of the Africa Association closely overlapped with other contemporary groups such as the Society for the Abolition of the Slave Trade, and thus one of the Africa Association's goals was to acquire evidence of the sophistication of African civilizations as a counterweight to the dangerously dismissive stereotypes of slavery's defenders. Claims of innate African backwardness and barbarity had long been used to rationalize their enslavement, but first-hand evidence that such claims were convenient lies would go a long way to transforming the hearts and minds of the British public.

The information about the deleterious effects of the slave trade collected by the Company's officials served an allied purpose: to demonstrate that the admirable cultures the explorers documented were being destroyed by slavery. In letters and official Company accounts designed for public consumption, the British people heard of stinking slave ships filled with despondent, dispirited, suicidal slaves "filled with fears either of a horrid death or a cruel servitude; and without the most distant prospect of ever beholding the face of one of those friends or relatives from whom they were forcibly torn. Their cup is full of pure, unmingled sorrow, the bitterness of which is unalloyed by almost a single ray of hope." They heard of brutal slave factors, "inhuman monsters" so corrupted by their violent trade that they murdered their white servants, drowned unsellable slaves, and eventually met their own gruesome end, murdered by their captives, "an end worthy of such a life." Stories such as these flipped familiar scripts on their heads, humanized slaves and de-humanized their captors, helping to form the building blocks, the very ammunition, of the abolitionists' case against the slave trade. During the parliamentary debate over the abolition bill of 1799, two former governors, Dawes and Macaulay, even offered expert testimony in support of the bill.[36]

Other accounts sent from Sierra Leone for British consumption helped to undermine long-held myths about the nature of the slave trade. For instance, in May 1796, Zachary Macaulay, Sierra Leone's governor from 1794, intervened on behalf of four slaves purchased by an American slave trader anchored just off Freetown. The victims were local, and included a 30-year-old man sold by a local chief, a 14-year-old girl captured by a second native chief on her way to visit a relative and sold for a cask of rum, and a girl named Maria who had attended the colony school run by Mary Perth, herself a former slave. Macaulay was appalled that this brazen human trafficking had taken place beneath his nose, and insisted that the American captain release his captives. The captain complied, and the almost-slaves were reunited with their relatives. Macaulay's description of the scene is clearly intended to be didactic. The emotional reunion between the young victims and their families, he informs the reader, "was truly affecting," a real life echo of the famous abolitionist slogan "Am I not a man and a brother?" "Shame on those," he concludes, "who would strip these poor creatures of the feelings of humanity and of the claims of brother-hood." But the account also serves to undermine the frequent justification of slavery apologists that the Africans purchased by European traders had been born slaves or were enslaved as punishment for crimes or unpaid debts. "I think this incident strongly marks the nature of the trade," Macaulay argues. "No crime alleged, no plea of being born in slavery, no debt exists in any of the cases. But how is it possible to reason calmly on a business of such frightful enormity passing immediately before one's eyes! May God stay this dreadful scourge which has given it birth!"[37]

The leadership of the colony did its best to make good its claim to be an instrument of anti-slavery. In addition to their contributions to the publicity campaign in Britain, the governors encouraged European slavers and African chiefs to abandon the slave trade. Macaulay, unyielding and upright, engaged in heated, often rancorous debates with local slave traders about the morality of their professions. When Mr. Tilley, an agent posted to the slave factory at Bance Island visited the colony, Macaulay organized a performance of African children, many rescued from slavery, to demonstrate to the slaver "what might be expected from the hundreds he yearly consigns to that state [i.e. slavery]." Most of the men involved in the trade continued to rationalize their involvement, usually hiding behind pleas of their own poverty. "Would you have me starve?" one defensive slaver asked Macaulay. "I do no more than others, and rich men too have done. If they are satisfied that they do right, so may I. I am a poor man, and only strive to make a living." An American slave ship captain responded more flippantly to the governor's moralizing harangue, quipping that "religion is no doubt a very fine invention . . . But, sir, I am no Methodist, I have no intention of being righteous overmuch." Macaulay did manage to convince some undecided visitors. He took a Captain Ball on a visit to Bance Island and Ball was so horrified by "the view of human wretchedness" that he later responded to one of the factors' toasts with the cry, "Come, let us drink the speedy termination of a still more enormous evil, the Slave Trade." When the factor opened his mouth to object, Ball interrupted him. "What can any man of common feeling allege on its behalf," he interjected, turning to Macaulay, "It is indeed a cursed trade. I pray God that your friends' [the abolitionists] labours to abolish it may at length meet the success they deserve."[38]

The Company and its agents understood that if the slave trade were to be undermined, they could not ignore the central role played by local African rulers. The colony's neighbors had an ambivalent attitude toward slavery. Most of the chiefs were involved in capturing and selling slaves to some degree, as part of power struggles with their rivals, and out of a desire, increasingly a need, for European goods and manufactures. Many rulers realized the precariousness of their situation. They needed European goods as gifts and symbols of status to bind their followers to them, and guns and ammunition to defend their people from their enemies. However, the easiest way to secure these manufactures was to sell what the European traders wanted most, Africans themselves. Thus, many African rulers responded to the Company's urgings that they abandon the slave trade with a sort of jaded resignation. When Macaulay visited Addow, paramount king of the Sherbo people living to the south of the Sierra Leone, to ask if he would allow Company merchants and missionaries to reside in his territory, the king admitted that he sometimes engaged in the slave trade, but nonetheless seemed to "rejoice in the prospect of its abolition." Years before, his own village had been raided by a slaver named James Cleveland, and "many of his people carried away into slavery." He had seen both sides of the trade, as trafficker and victim, and though he could not give up the trade unilaterally, he still hoped it would be brought to an end. Others felt the same. Signor Domingo, a Sherbo chief, told Macaulay he wished to embrace Christianity and abandon the slave trade. "What more have I to do with the Slave Trade? It is time I should leave it off, and settle my account with God. I am old; I ought to think only of heaven."[39]

The colony's settlers and officials did not limit their interventions to words alone. In June of 1793, Macaulay intervened to secure the release of seventeen "black mariners" who had been captured with a French naval vessel and sold to Bance Island by a British captain as prizes of war. Macaulay raged at the hypocrisy of selling black sailors while treating white sailors as prisoners of war. "Why were the French seamen not put up to auction?" he wondered caustically. "Is black and white to be permitted by Government to constitute the line that will separate the captive in war from the slave? These men were not only free, but some of them the sons of Chiefs." The Sierra Leone Colony also became a beacon of freedom for slaves in the region. Runaways flocked to the settlements, convinced that their presence on colony soil would guarantee their freedom. Settlers regularly hid fugitive slaves within the colony, though on a few occasions runaways were re-sold by settlers themselves.[40]

Macaulay was often called upon to shield fugitives from recapture, but the issue of harboring escaped slaves placed the colony's officials in a delicate position. On the one hand, the slave trade was still legal under British law and, as such, actively interfering with the human cargo of British merchants could well bring lawsuits against the Company it could ill afford. "The very Act which incorporated the Sierra Leone Company," one governor reminded the settlers, "had directly and explicitly prohibited them from injuring the rights of any British subject trading to Africa." Likewise, alienating the nearby British slave factories at Bance Island and the Îles de Los would cut off vital sources of aid. In its early years, the colony was forced to beg the factors at Bance Island for needed supplies of rice and other supplies. The slave traders, as suppliers of highly desired European manufactures, also had considerable influence with the local African chiefs, who would not appreciate the disruption of their trade. Surrounded by potentially hostile chiefdoms, and after 1793 under constant threat of French attack, good relations with the slave factories also provided much-needed military aid. Though the relationship was often tense, colony officials cultivated a mutually beneficial relationship with Bance Island, exchanging visits as well as supplies and information.[41]

The settlers did not always appreciate this attempt to balance morality and practicality. On one occasion in June 1794, Macaulay fired a dockworker for assaulting a slave trader who had antagonized the former slaves with taunts of "what manner he would use them if he had them in the West Indies." The governor's seeming breach of faith caused a riot as outraged settlers attacked his office and threatened to destroy his home. The turmoil was eventually quelled by the threat of a cannon and the promise to return to Nova Scotia any settlers dissatisfied with Sierra Leone. The settlers' anger was more than understandable given their experiences, but Macaulay's actions were informed by a wider strategy. The Company and its agents were first and foremost playing to a British audience. They knew that public pressure was the only way to secure parliamentary action, and that parliamentary action was the only way to end the slave trade. Seizing slaves from local traders or allowing settlers to assault them not only would not work—the problem was far too big to address in this ad hoc way—but it might well alienate the British population, convince them that the abolitionists and former slaves were thugs and extremists, thereby eroding the broad support necessary to effect change. It was a pragmatic strategy, if not always an appealing one in the moment. It must have been deeply frustrating for many of the settlers to see slavers operating on their borders with impunity and even hosted in Freetown, but men like Macaulay, Clarkson, Sharp, and

Thornton sought to outlaw the trade entirely, not merely disrupt or inconvenience the few individual slave traders who interacted with the colony.

Still, the colony's officials took their mission to undermine the slave trade seriously, and were loath to hand back fugitives whose only crime, in the words of Zachary Macaulay, was "an attempt to regain their liberty, or rather to avoid being forced into slavery." Macaulay thus adopted a clever stratagem born of the necessity of both appeasing local slave traders and advancing the moral basis for the colony. In a display of masterly inactivity, the governor responded to demands for the return of fugitive slaves by reiterating his commitment not to entice, encourage, or physically prevent the recapture of slavers' legal property, while refusing to do anything at all to effect their recovery. He could not legally confiscate their slaves, but nor would he be compelled to aid in their return. Behind this mask of indifference, Macaulay frequently took further steps to obstruct the recapture of fugitive slaves. What this meant in practice was that slaves who fled to the colony, often aided and hidden by settlers, were protected from re-enslavement.[42]

The region's slave traders were quick to recognize the threat posed by the new colony, and did their best to undermine it. They had long and deep commercial relationships with the local peoples, and used this influence to set the chiefs against Sierra Leone. Signor Domingo, the reluctant African slave trader, warned Macaulay that though outwardly cordial and welcoming, the slavers of Bance Island had from the beginning "endeavored to convince the natives of our sinister designs, and had instigated them to oppose our landing by promises of a supply of arms and ammunition." Later, when European goods became scarce and prices skyrocketed during the interminable war with France, slave traders did their best to convince the African chiefs that the colony and its abolitionism were to blame, while at the same time surreptitiously aiding French attacks on the colony.[43]

In November 1792, Boston King, along with twenty-seven of the foremost settlers, signed his name to a petition to Governor Clarkson. The petitioners raised issues that would become perennial sources of disagreement between the settlers and the Company—low wages and expensive provisions—and suggested reasonable remedies "by which there will be no grumbling." This was not the first petition composed by the settlers, nor the first supported by Boston

King. King and his comrades had learned well the lessons of the American Revolution—the rhetoric of liberty and the power of collective action—and put them to use for the benefit of the colony from the moment they landed. As the colony's first year progressed, the letters and petitions became more urgent, shifting from careful requests made by individual leaders, to self-confident articulations of rights signed by large swaths of the settler population. The November 1792 petition seems to have been a turning point in this process, and many of those who signed their names would go on to become leaders of the opposition to Company policy. Boston King, however, would take another path, as evidenced by his support for a more conciliatory message to Governor Clarkson a week later, wishing him a safe journey back to England. King was one of the few leaders to sign both letters, demonstrating his precarious position as both a leader of the more "ranglesome" Methodist faction and a loyal supporter of the Company's greater mission. While many of his fellow settlers became disillusioned with the Company, King would never waver in his commitment.[44]

The refugees had quite reasonably expected that their new colony would be self-governing, a republic of and for former slaves, but their hopes for independence and self-determination began to wither almost as soon as they arrived. John Clarkson had been tasked with gathering recruits from Canada and seeing them safely established in their new home, but who would lead the new colony and how it would be governed had not been established when the fleet left Halifax in January 1792. Thomas Peters, in so many ways the driving force behind the whole endeavor, was not alone in expecting that he himself would be given the command. When the convoy arrived at Sierra Leone, however, they found a letter from the directors waiting. The directors had decided to name John Clarkson governor, much to Peters' chagrin, with a council of eight Europeans as advisors. Though the refugees would be represented by elected representatives, many were outraged that the colony's highest posts had not been given to any of their number. Peters attempted to drum up support for his appointment as governor, visiting church services and prayer meetings to urge his comrades to throw their weight behind him, and even succeeded in compiling a petition to the directors in London signed by 100 settlers. But Clarkson was not unpopular among the settlers, and was able to outmaneuver Peters and secure the support of the majority of the colony.

Peters died suddenly in June of 1792, but Clarkson's problems with the settlers continued. That same month, he received a petition from Henry Beverhout on behalf of his Methodist congregation, demanding a change in the structure of Sierra Leone's government. The settlers were "all willing to be governed by the laws of England," the petition stated, but would not consent to be ruled by Clarkson or any other government without having "aney of our own Culler in it." The petitioners reminded Clarkson of the promises he had made in Nova Scotia that all who came to Sierra Leone "wold be free . . . and all should be equal." Clarkson could do nothing to alter the rule of governor and council, but he did see the merits of the petitioners' broader argument and appointed black constables and instituted trial by settler juries.[45]

For the moment, the issue of the colony's administration had been settled, but the settlers had other grievances and did not hesitate to make their voices heard. In the first months after their arrival, the settlers sent a steady stream of petitions to the governor requesting the distribution of the promised grants of land. The work of surveying, clearing, and disbursing the plots was repeatedly delayed; by the rains, by the inefficiencies of the administration, and by the difficulty of processing so many claims. For the settlers, there must have been an eerie sense of *déjà vu* as the land that offered independence was once again withheld. Without land, the colonists were dependent on the Company for provisions, a grating dependence in its own right, but after the first couple of months the Company compounded the problem by insisting that supplies be bought rather than granted gratis. To pay for supplies, the settlers would work for the Company, clearing land and constructing houses, storerooms, and schools. Land, supplies, and wages would become the subject of numerous complaints and petitions in the first decade of the colony. As a preacher and a leader of a "company" within the colony, Boston King signed several of these petitions.[46]

Clarkson did not remain in his post for very long, and in December 1792, he returned to London, leaving the governorship in the hands of William Dawes, one of the two councilors sent out by the directors to replace the unworkable eight-man council. Like many of the settlers, Dawes had seen action during the American War. As a marine officer he had fought against the French fleet at the crucial Battle of the Chesapeake in 1781, where he was wounded. After the war,

Dawes volunteered to join the marine regiment accompanying the First Fleet to New South Wales. There he played a vital role in the construction of the settlement, using his skills as an engineer to help construct batteries and plot the first streets, and lots of what would become Sydney. A keen scientist, he helped construct an observatory, joined exploratory expeditions into the Australian interior, and became something of an authority on the languages of the local Eora peoples. He likely would have remained in New South Wales if not for a series of disputes with Governor Arthur Phillip, especially over the treatment of Aborigines. This breach convinced Dawes to return home to England in 1791, where he met William Wilberforce and became a member of his evangelical reforming group the Clapham Sect. Wilberforce thought highly of Dawes, and in August 1792 sent the former marine to Sierra Leone to join Zachary Macaulay on the new advisory council. When Clarkson left shortly thereafter, Dawes succeeded him as governor.

Though committed to the mission of the colony, Dawes was less sympathetic to the plight of the colonists, less willing to address their grievances. Fully convinced of his own unwavering rectitude, Dawes' overbearing rigidity made him immediately unpopular, especially with the colony's Methodist faction. Most of the settlers still had not received their land, still worked for meager wages, still paid too much for provisions. What land had been distributed by Clarkson was taken back by Dawes, who required the settlers to move to new plots he himself had allocated. Many settlers came to see Dawes as a tyrant, the personification of the Company's self-interest and broken promises. To them, the colony seemed to be designed to enrich the Company at the settlers' expense.

As a result, in October 1793 they sent two representatives, Cato Perkins and Isaac Anderson, to London with a list of grievances. The petition Perkins and Anderson presented to the directors detailed how the failure to distribute land, along with low wages and high prices, had made the settlers feel that though the Company had made promises "better than we ever had before from White People," they were now "so oppressed that we are forced to trouble your Honrs so that your Eyes as well as ours may open." Echoes of the American Revolution can be heard in the language the settlers employed time and again in their dispute with the Company. The 1793 petition spoke of "the Privileges of

Freemen," explained that the former slaves had "feelings the same as other Human Beings," and "would wish to do every thing we can to make our Children free and happy." A petition to the directors in 1795 detailed how the settlers had been "empressed upon with Tyranny," but remained fixedly determined to "enjoy the privileges of Freedom." Elsewhere, settler petitions spoke of the "oppression that King Pharoh where with oppressed the Egyptians" and claimed "we now find our Selves truly Opress." The petitioners used the rhetoric of tyranny and enslavement for many of the same reasons as their former masters had in their dispute with Britain. But they were also savvy enough to understand that such language could be used to play on the sympathies of men they knew to be inimical toward slavery and hopeful that the colony's success would undermine it.⁴⁷

The directors knew that all of Britain was watching their African experiment, weighing its results, and applying the lessons learned to the growing debate over slavery and abolition. News that the American refugees were angry and rebellious and that the colony of freed slaves was mired in chaos and failing to thrive threatened to sway public opinion against further experiments in emancipation. If their test case failed, the directors knew, it would prove a serious setback to the nascent anti-slavery movement in Britain. So in their response to the Sierra Leone petitioners, and in their published report to the Company's shareholders, the directors did their best to mitigate the potential fallout. To the petitioners they replied with a condescending, paternalistic dismissal of the settlers' grievances. The petition was "hasty" and based on "facts founded on mistake and misinformation." The high prices complained of by the settlers had been caused by the war with France, and their "low wages" were still twice as high as those paid to native African workers. Other failures were blamed on poor lands, and a lack of industry among the colonists. "The unreasonableness of many settlers in estimating their own merits, and their very inadequate sense" of their obligations, combined with their "false and absurd notions . . . concerning their rights as freeman," had undermined the success of the colony. As such, the directors urged the settlers "as freemen and Christians, to discourage all unreasonable discontent," and "to pay respect and obedience to government." After all, it was "on their obedience to governed," that, "their happiness, their liberty, and perhaps their very lives, depend."⁴⁸

And yet, the directors continued with an eye toward their British audience, the money and the headaches were "the price paid for the civilization that is now begun in Africa: it has been sacrificed to that cause, which the Sierra Leone Company have considered as their own, the cause of Christianity and Freedom and Civilization among the race of Africans." The experiment, they insisted, was worth it. The blame for the fractiousness of the settlers should be laid at the feet of the institution of slavery, not at the former slaves. "Great allowance," had to be made for the "various sufferings which some of them have undergone, and the very unequal measure of justice which they have formerly received, and are now habituated to expect, at the hands of whites." As such, any deficiencies among the settlers were not the result of "any original fault in their moral character more than in any other men, nor any natural inferiority in their understanding," but to the "system of servitude" and "all the enormities attending it."[49]

The greatest fear among the directors was that the failures of the colony would be used to argue against further emancipation. To forestall arguments that the troubled colony proved that Africans in general, and former slaves in particular, were not capable of civilization, or of being governed except by force, the directors reminded the public "how extremely unfavorable the circumstances through which they [the settlers] have passed into a state of freedom" had been. Future slaves "who might be emancipated on a prudent principle of discrimination; to whom liberty having been first held out in prospect, in order to prepare them for it, might be granted after a certain period of service, as the professed reward of industry and merit; or might perhaps be communicated by degrees . . . privilege after privilege being added," would surely do better. If carefully, thoughtfully, intentionally, and gradually emancipated, the results, they promised, would prove more salubrious. Far from being evidence of the impossibility of emancipation, the Sierra Leone Colony instead proved its viability, if it was carefully managed.[50]

By the time the directors had compiled their public defense of the colony, Governor Dawes had had enough, and returned to England in March of 1794. With him came Boston King, seeking further education. While still in Nova Scotia, King had been plagued by thoughts of the sad plight of his African kinsmen who had not heard the Word of God. He had, at least in part, joined the Sierra Leone Colony with the express intent of bringing the gospel to the people of Africa. It had not been idle talk. Within months of his arrival, after the rains ended and his illness receded, King began preaching to native Africans whenever he could. He asked to be given employment at the Company plantation at Bullom Shore so that he would have more regular contact with the local people, and even succeeded in gaining permission to move to an African town so that he could instruct the native children in reading and religion. But his early efforts were often stymied by his inability to speak African languages and by a lack of local interest in his school. This initial failure of his mission had convinced King of the necessity of traveling to England in pursuit of the further education he was sure would help him to reach the native Africans.

Unlike the Black Poor who had flooded into London after the war, King arrived in England with a broad network of connections. His role as a Methodist preacher meant that when he sailed up the Thames in June 1794, he was greeted by a Mrs. Paul, a Methodist acquaintance from America who ushered him into the capital's Methodist community. From London he traveled to Bristol, where he met with Thomas Coke, a close associate of Methodism's founder, John Wesley, a committed opponent of slavery, and a tireless traveler and missionary. Under Coke's auspices, King entered Kingswood, the Methodist School outside Bristol founded by Wesley himself in 1748. Kingswood represented the pinnacle of Boston King's desires, and he worked hard "to acquire all the knowledge I possibly could, in order to be useful in that sphere which the blessed hand of Providence may conduct me into."[51]

King arrived back in Sierra Leone in September 1796 to succeed James Jones as schoolmaster of Granville Town. When he had left two years earlier, the colony had been beset with anger and frustration, but he arrived in a colony on the precipice of revolution. The Company had spent huge sums getting the colony up and running, but as yet the hoped-for commercial development had failed to balance the ledger. The directors viewed the colony as an act of charity, but they were also certain that its success in the long run depended on its profitability. To make up the shortfalls of the first hard years, the Company thus instituted a new requirement—all settlers would be henceforth required to pay a fee of one shilling per acre on receipt of their land. Not only was this yet another expense for people who could ill afford to pay it, but it also signaled precisely what many of the settlers already feared. They were not to be the owners of their lands or the governors of their new home. The land, it was now clear, was owned by the Company, and the settlers were merely renters. "If the Lands is not ours without paying a shilling per acre," they reasoned in a letter to the governor, "the Lands will never be ours, no not at all." If the Company owned the land, as they were now informed, the Company was free to "take it if they think proper in so doing." Bitter experience and the rhetoric of the American Revolution had taught the settlers that independence was only possible with access to land, but now that access was restricted. If they could not own their land, they could not be truly free.[52]

As his fellow settlers protested quit-rents and adopted the motto "liberty or death," Boston King remained aloof. King's years in England had solidified his belief in the benefits of British civilization. While still in Sierra Leone in 1793, he had lectured native Africans who had rejected his offers of education on the value of European society. "It is a good thing that God has made the White People," King told them, "and that he has inclined their hearts to bring us into this country, to teach you his ways, and tell you that he gave his Son to die for you." His kind treatment in England reinforced this view, and as he reported, he "found a more cordial love to the White People than I had ever experienced before. In the former part of my life I had suffered greatly from the cruelty and injustice of the Whites, which induced me to look upon them . . . as our enemies." He was now, however, "fully convinced, that many of the White People, instead of being the enemies and oppressors of us poor Blacks, are our friends, and deliverers from slavery, as far as their ability and circumstances will admit." King was thus staunchly loyal to the colonial administration, and, as his letters back to England show, remained so even as his co-religionists took the lead in the deepening dispute between the settlers and the Company.[53]

When Governor Macaulay, fed up with the constant quarreling, quit his post in April 1799, the settlers saw their chance to act on their own behalf. As they had stated in vain in petition after petition, they had done their part in the American War, had even "received a Proclamation from government for our good behavior in the last war," but now, after a trail of broken promises leading from New York to Nova Scotia to Sierra Leone, they found themselves "oppressed," "shut out from government," and "not used here as free men." So in September 1799, before a new governor could arrive, they convened a meeting of settlers, elected their own officials, and resolved that they themselves were "the Propriatives of the Colenney, and no forenners shall com in as a right of making Lawes . . . nor shall they have a vote with ought their concent." It was a bold declaration of independence. The former slaves, they declared, would rule themselves.

Into this maelstrom of open rebellion came 23-year-old Thomas Ludham, the Company's newly appointed governor. He brought with him a compromise. The Company had heard their just grievances and was prepared to abolish quit-rent, but the government formed by the settlers would have to be disbanded, and the officials they had elected dismissed. For many of the settlers, however, Ludham's offer was too little, too late. Their faith in the goodwill of the Company and its agents had been completely eroded, and they were now certain that they could not "get justice from the White people." In September 1800, 150 families, perhaps half the families in Freetown, thus gathered in the chapel of Cato Perkins and "resolved to persist in their appointment of judges to make and execute laws themselves." Together they drew up a "Paper of Laws," a quasi-constitution, and officially seceded from the Sierra Leone Colony. Isaac Anderson, a former slave originally from Angola, was elected governor of the breakaway colony, which now announced that "all that come from Nova Scotia, shall be under this law or quit the place."[54]

While Anderson and his followers barricaded the bridge between Freetown and Granville Town, Ludham gathered the remaining loyal settlers, the colony's white employees and forty African sailors at Thornton Hill, and prepared for a fight. The rebels might well have been able to win the looming battle, or force a more advantageous peace, but before their stab at independence was even a month old, fate intervened. On September 28, Zachary Macaulay's brother, Alexander, arrived at Freetown with 47 British soldiers and 550 Maroons from Jamaica. The Maroons were escaped slaves and their descendants who had formed free communities in the mountainous interior of Jamaica. The Maroons were a constant source of concern for the island's British authorities, especially after the example of the American Revolution, leading to two wars between the Maroons and the British. The second war was a particularly bloody affair, charged with British fears that the radical ideologies of the

American, French, and Haitian Revolutions had infected Jamaica's Maroons. The war ended in a negotiated peace, but despite promises to let the Maroons re-settle in Jamaica, the British deported nearly six hundred to Sierra Leone.[55]

Like the Nova Scotia settlers, the Maroons had been promised land in Sierra Leone. The rebellion, Ludham informed them, threatened to deprive them of their rightful land. The Maroons thus promised to support the governor and crush the rebellion in return for their land. Ludham now had the upper hand, and demanded an unconditional surrender. Most of the separatists saw writing on the wall, and the rebellion quickly fizzled out. In the aftermath, fifty-five rebels were tried for treason. Two, Isaac Anderson and Frank Patrick, were executed as the leaders and instigators of the revolt. Thirty-three others, including Harry Washington, had their property confiscated and were banished to Bullom Shore. At almost the same time, a Royal Charter arrived transforming the colony from the private enterprise of the Sierra Leone Company into a crown colony, nixing any possibility that the settlers would be allowed to govern themselves. The Sierra Leone experiment was at an end.

By the time the rebellion was at last suppressed, King was 100 miles south living among the Sherbo people. The settler rebellion had placed Boston King in a difficult position. The ringleaders of the secession movement were, after all, Methodists like King. What's more, Isaac Anderson, the leader of the movement, and Cato Perkins, who acted as intermediary between the rebels and the governor, had both been residents of Charleston in the years before the American War set them all free. King likely knew these men well, and certainly sympathized with their grievances, but his energy remained fixed on what he saw as a greater calling, his efforts to teach and convert Africa. The fate of the souls of the Africans had never left his mind, and so he had joined the growing flood of missionaries streaming out from Sierra Leone to Christianize and civilize the continent. In this, Boston King had placed himself at the forefront of British imperialism in Africa, the true legacy of Sierra Leone.

In his eagerness to convert his African kinsmen, Boston King was, like Macaulay and the British missionaries, a conscious agent of British imperialism. Indeed, the whole colonial endeavor was an exercise of imperial expansion. Schooled in the ideas and language of the American Revolution, the refugees of the American War were relentless in their quest for independence, unceasing champions of liberty and self-determination. But they were also, especially committed evangelicals like Boston King, tools of European imperialism. Some were unwitting imperialists, but many like King himself, were fully cognizant of their role in bringing European culture, religion, and civilization to their "benighted" relatives.

Abolitionism and the Sierra Leone Colony, like the India Act, helped Britain reimagine its empire on a new moral basis and recover its imperial pride and imperial unity after the disorienting loss of America. In the years after the American War, familiar criticisms of an immoral empire were replaced by a more supportive public sentiment as the empire was portrayed as a force for good around the world. Thus it was a high-minded imperialism that the Sierra Leone Company sought to enact, constructed on an admirable platform of sympathy and moralism. Company and colonists alike sought not to rule the world, but remake it in their own image, fully believing that the benefits of European civilization were real and that extending them to all and sundry was a genuine kindness. That empire should be brought back to Africa by its former sons and daughters should not surprise, for though their time among the "civilized" Europeans had been an almost unending string of suffering, the refugees who settled Sierra Leone had, in their own way, embraced the "civilization" of their erstwhile oppressors. Stripped of their African identity by enslavement, most had cobbled together new identities, not quite African, not sufficiently British, a people of two worlds and none. As men and women of such hybridity their sense of kinship with Africans merged with a firm belief in the benefits of a British civilization, that had at last, belatedly, self-interestedly set them free. Such men, men like Boston King, were the perfect agents of the new British imperialism.

And so it was in 1802 that Boston King, a slave from South Carolina who had never set foot on African soil, came to die a British Christian missionary among the Sherbo people. The Sierra Leone Colony might have failed to meet the expectations of its settlers, and even of its supporters in Britain, but in other ways it was remarkably influential. It served as a bridgehead for Britain's empire in Africa, with merchants, missionaries, and explorers fanning out across the region, the tentacles of imperialism worming their way into the interior of the "Dark Continent" as never before. With this came a sea-change in attitudes and conceptions. The colony helped to transform views of Africa from an opaque mystery into a place where British people lived and labored, a place where merchants and missionaries plied their trades, a place where British interests lay. To smooth the way for British civilization, African children, especially the children of the elite, were educated in British schools within the colony, inculcating British culture and values in the next generation. Some African children, like King Tom's son, were even brought to Britain for education and indoctrination. As part of this effort, Zachary Macaulay brought dozens of African children with him when he returned to England in 1799. Sierra Leone thus began to make Africa visible to the British public and legible to British government in new ways. It was no coincidence that the same abolitionist impulses that created Sierra Leone also fueled the African Association, which combined its efforts to provide a positive view of the continent with information gathering that would further British interests in Africa. In many ways, the abolitionist movement and the settling of Sierra Leone touched off the first era of African exploration that would pave the way for British imperialism. Going forward, merchants, missionaries, and explorers would be the point of the imperial spear, paving the way for eventual British encroachment.

Even in its express purpose to undermine the slave trade, the Sierra Leone Colony proved remarkably effective, if not in the way its creators expected. If it failed to mount an argument in favor of emancipation and resettlement, it also furnished the campaign to abolish the slave trade with mountains of evidence about the nature of the trade, and Britons' role in it, direct from the source of the problem. Most previous accounts of slavery had focused on America, the West Indies, or the Middle Passage, but now there came accounts from Africa itself: first-hand accounts of African suffering, of British and American brutality, of the corrupted and corrupting nature of the slave trade itself. When Wilberforce and his allies at last achieved the abolition of the slave trade in 1807, Sierra Leone became a center for British efforts to end the trade. The colony became a base for the West African Squadron—the British naval force charged with capturing and arresting slave traders—and the site of a British Admiralty court charged with prosecuting captured slavers, at once both a site for freedom and of imperialism. As a focal point for the fight against the slave trade, Sierra Leone became a clearing-house and processing point for the 81,745 slaves seized from slave ships, more than anywhere else in the British Empire. When Samuel Samo, the first slave trader to be charged under the Slave Trade Felony Act of 1811, was tried at Sierra Leone in 1811, John Macaulay Wilson, one of the African children Zachary Macaulay had brought to England in 1799, was among the jurors to decide his fate.

12

→→ ←←

OPIUM AND EMPIRE

On November 6, 1792, eleven years after François Henri de la Motte's naval espionage resulted in the Battle of Porto Praya, mere months after Boston King passed by the Cape Verde islands on his way to a new life in the fledgling colony of Sierra Leone, a similarly unusual collection of ships rode at anchor among the gentle swells of Praya Bay. One was an American whaling vessel from Nantucket, pausing at Cape Verde on its way south to the whaling grounds of the South Pacific. On four ships the new Tricolor, emblem of the revolutionary French Republic, snapped in the breeze. Outfitted in Dunkirk, and manned by a combination of French and British sailors, the French ships posed as whaling vessels as well, but their cargo of clothes and other such articles belied their outward posturing: in reality, they were smugglers engaged in the contraband trade with the Spanish colonies of South America. On the three remaining ships in the harbor of Praya Bay, the men who had gathered on deck to gaze at the rugged mountains of Saint Iago, the largest of the Cape Verde Islands, bristled with indignation. These were British vessels, and though the imperial civil war with their American cousins was not yet a decade in the past, and though they were at times alarmed by the growing frequency of their encounters with American ships as the United States began to stretch out into the wider world of international trade, their ire was directed elsewhere. France and Britain were once more rushing headlong into war, but in November 1792 open hostilities were still months away. So while many among the British contingent looked with a mixture of horror and disdain on the Tricolors, symbols of chaos, disorder, and violence, it was only one of the French ships, the ship christened with the suitably revolutionary name of *La Liberté*, that raised the hackles of the British.

Many among the British ships recognized *La Liberté*, or at least the ship she had once been. Under the French flag and the new name lay the *Resolution*, the immortal ship of Britain's greatest naval hero, Captain Cook. The transformation of the *Resolution* from a symbol of British imperial ambition to a smuggling ship of the detested French Republic was enough to drive some to despair. "I am not ashamed to confess," John Barrow wrote from his vantage point aboard the *Hindostan* Indiaman:

> that my feelings were considerably hurt in witnessing this degradation of an object so intimately connected with that great man . . . Few, I believe, will envy that man's feelings, who can see without emotion the house in which he was born, and in which he spent his happiest years, either wholly demolished or degraded to some unworthy purpose. The *Resolution* was the house of the immortal Cook and, out of respect to his memory, I would have laid her up in a dock, till she had wasted away plank by plank.[1]

John Barrow could perhaps be forgiven his rather melodramatic response to his encounter with the Republicanized *Resolution*. For unbeknownst to the French and American ships sharing the harbor of Porto Praya, Barrow and his companions were, like Cook before them, bound for the Pacific on a mission of grave imperial importance. The *Hindostan*, HMS *Lion*, and the brig *Jackal* had been tasked with a momentous charge, carrying the first official embassy from the King of Great Britain to the Emperor of China. In the world created by the American Revolution, Britain was forced to look east for the imperial prosperity so disrupted by her colonies' rebellion. India was to become the jewel in the British imperial crown, but, as seemed increasingly clear, the viability of British India would depend on Britain's ability to maintain and expand its burgeoning trade with China. It was in service of this increasingly vital trade that John Barrow and his companions found themselves in the islands of Cape Verde contemplating the glorious history and still tenuous future of Britain's empire.

Britain had been trading with China since 1635. The Portuguese had arrived on the shores of the Middle Kingdom even earlier in 1513, so early that they had been awarded their own island, known as Macao, at the mouth of the Pearl River from which to conduct their trade. As its Middle Kingdom moniker implied, China considered itself to be the middle or center of the world, and with such a worldview came a superior and disdainful attitude toward other nations and their trade. Diplomatic relations were always conducted with the clear understanding that all other nations were suppliants, that they had little to offer the Celestial Kingdom, and that any goods China deigned to sell to them were favors and blessings rather than the byproducts of equal exchanges of mutual benefit. This was not mere jingoism. Much had changed since the days when the treasure ships of Zheng He sailed the seas in search of exotic goods and imperial tribute. Under the Qing dynasty (1644–1912), China had little interest in affairs beyond its own expanding borders, and both Chinese migrants in Southeast Asia and European traders in Macao were viewed with indifference at best and suspicion at worst. Merchants, of whatever nation, were not to be trusted. By their very nature they were transgressors of borders, transforming secure frontiers into security risks. As such, coastal populations were closely monitored and European trade with China was rigorously controlled.

Despite official Qing distrust, Britain's trade with China grew and flourished to become the centerpiece of the East India Company's trading empire by the middle of the eighteenth century. In Britain and America, China, and its exotic products, became the darling of the *beau monde*. The pinnacle of fashion, *chinoiserie*, real and counterfeit, proliferated in the drawing rooms of the elite, while everyone, from artisans to the aristocracy, sipped and guzzled gallons of tea, the Chinese brew that was fast elbowing coffee aside as Briton's beverage of choice. And it was not only China's trade goods that were admired. There was a veritable craze for all things Chinese, and the nation itself, cast in an admiring light by missionaries and French *philosophes*, became a byword for stability, rational government, and moral rectitude. China was all the rage, and there was every reason to believe that Britain's trade with the Middle Kingdom would continue to grow and flourish.[2]

Beginning in the 1760s, however, everything seemed to change. Whereas once Britain had been allowed to trade at multiple ports, now the Qianlong Emperor decreed that all European trade would be restricted to the port of

Canton on China's south-eastern coast. But the restrictions did not stop there. Henceforth, European merchants would not be allowed to reside on Chinese soil. They were to have no contact with the Chinese population, were forbidden to learn the Chinese language, and were only allowed to enter Canton itself to conduct business during the brief trading season between October and March. Further, British merchants were required to wait at Macao until the season's ships arrived, and only then were they allowed to move to their factories in Canton and commence business. Once in Canton, all trade was to be conducted with a small, closed cartel of Chinese merchants known as the Hong. The Hong, nominally ten in number and supervised by an official called the Hoppo, were a monopoly guild licensed by the state and granted sole right to trade with Europeans. The only legal point of contact for Western merchants, and the sole conduit for European complaints and grievances, the Hong were able to dictate prices, levy tariffs, and control the flow of trade.[3]

With higher prices and new tariffs passed on to British and American consumers, the incentive to smuggle tea grew exponentially across the eighteenth century, as we have seen. Indeed, some nations' entire China trade was geared around smuggling tea into British territories. To undercut the price of smuggled tea and prop up a flailing East India Company, Britain passed the Tea Act of 1773, which for the first time allowed the Company to ship tea directly to North America rather than being required to auction off its imported tea in London first. The Tea Act also refunded part or all of British import duties on EIC tea, passing on the burden of tariffs established with the Townshend Acts to American consumers and threatening to ruin American tea merchants who had bought wholesale tea at the London auctions.

When, in response, rebellious colonials cast the products of China into the harbors of Boston, New York, and Annapolis, the war that followed turned a building crisis into a full-blown disaster. With many of its most lucrative trade routes cut off and its coffers drained to pay for war around the world, the East India Company teetered on the brink of financial collapse. By the time peace came in 1783, the EIC and the China trade had been crippled by a ruinous shortage of credit and specie. The most pressing concern, the anxiety that kept government officials and company directors awake at night with nightmares of financial ruin, was Britain's enormous and growing trade deficit with China.

The source of the problem was a fundamental imbalance between the desires of European and Chinese markets. Europeans wanted almost everything China had to offer; China wanted almost nothing Europeans brought to trade for its tea, silk, and porcelain. To meet the demand of their countrymen, British merchants were thus forced to buy tea with silver, quickly draining Britain of its specie. In the 1760s Britain exchanged about 3 million Taels of silver for Chinese goods (1 Tael equaling 40 grams). By the 1780s, however, this trade imbalance had ballooned to an unsustainable 16 million Taels, or roughly 1.4 million pounds of silver.[4]

British hopes for righting this damaging trade imbalance and saving the East India Company from ruin lay with the one product that was in high demand in China; a product that could be grown in Britain's expanded territories in India; a product that might refill Company coffers and pay for the administration of the territorial empire it was constructing in the subcontinent: opium. Opium, which had been consumed by Asian elites for centuries, was produced by making incisions in the poppy plants that grew naturally in India. From these incisions, a sticky sap emerged, which was scraped off, boiled into a thick paste, and rolled into balls for transport. The East India Company had a monopoly on the growth and sale of Indian opium, which it used to sell licenses to private merchants known as "Company Traders," who bought opium from India and transported it to China where it was sold for silver. This silver was then deposited with East Indian Company officials in Canton in exchange for letters of credit. The Company officials then used the silver to purchase the tea, silk, porcelain, and other goods it sold back in Britain. In the years after the American Revolution began, this new "triangle trade" helped to replace the war-disrupted Atlantic triangle trade. Between 1773 and 1790, annual exports of opium from British India to China quadrupled to 600,000 pounds or more, with grave consequences for both British pushers and Chinese consumers.[5]

Still, Britain could not hope to make up the ground lost during the war, or to reinvigorate the flagging East India Company given the strict Chinese controls put into place in the 1760s. If the Commutation Act was to succeed in undermining smuggling and raising revenue, stable prices for tea sold in Britain were a necessity. To ensure prices remained stable in Britain, the prices and tariffs for tea purchased in Canton also needed to remain stable. This could only be ensured with formalized relations with China. Likewise, if a growing triangular trade between India, China, and Britain was to revive British and East India Company fortunes, it was vital that the Canton trade be normalized. With this firmly in mind, what Britain desired, what the flotilla that limped into Cape Verde in November 1792 was tasked with securing, was a permanent diplomatic presence at the Chinese capital of Beijing, the end of the hated Canton system, the opening of other Chinese ports to British trade, and the reduction of tariffs on British trade. If these could be achieved, and opium substituted for British silver, Britain might yet conquer the world on the back of her trade.

The *Hindostan*, *Lion*, and *Jackal* had left Spithead six weeks before, on September 26, 1792. The ships had been specially chosen and were among the best the British navy had to offer. The *Hindostan* was reputed to be the largest and fastest East Indiaman the East India Company had to offer, while the *Lion* represented the cutting-edge of late eighteenth-century naval warfare. The men who boarded these emblems of British power and technological ingenuity were no less carefully chosen, likewise selected to provide a combination of outward prestige and practical competence. The squadron would be led by Sir Erasmus Gower, a naval officer who had served with distinction in the Indian Ocean theater of the American War. The diplomatic mission was placed in the similarly capable and experienced hands of Lord George Macartney. Both men had long imperial experience to recommend them, and both had been fundamentally shaped by their roles in the wars of the American Revolution.

George Macartney was born in County Antrim in northern Ireland in 1737 and educated at Trinity College in Dublin before moving to London to fulfill his deep ambition for a conspicuous life of public service. In London he became friends with Edmund Burke, Samuel Johnson (becoming a member of his Club), Lord Holland (elder brother of the influential Whig politician Charles James Fox), and Lord Sandwich. With such august connections, Macartney was well placed to succeed in public life, and in 1764, at the age of 27, he was appointed to his first diplomatic post as envoy to the court of Catherine the Great of Russia. In the direct aftermath of the Seven Years' War, young Macartney was tasked with securing an alliance with Russia against France. A natural diplomat with a cool charm and instinctual ability to ingratiate himself with those in power, he succeeded in securing the commercial treaty which gave

British merchants an elevated place in the Russia trade and made the US envoy Francis Dana's attempts to secure a similar treaty with Russia increasingly difficult. However, Macartney failed to achieve the hoped-for military alliance with Catherine, who insisted as a condition of any such treaty that Britain agree to aid Russia against the Ottoman Empire, setting the stage for later Russian aggression against the Turks.

Macartney's mixed success at St. Petersburg was not held against him, and in 1769 he was appointed Chief Secretary of Ireland and in 1775 Governor of the British Caribbean possessions of Grenada, the Grenadines, and Tobago. He arrived in the West Indies as the war with America was commencing, and quickly came under fire himself in 1779 when forced to surrender the islands to French forces under Comte d'Estaing. After a short stint in Paris as a prisoner of war, Macartney, now raised to the peerage, was reassigned to India where he was appointed Governor of Madras. In moving to the subcontinent, Macartney did not escape the increasingly global conflict, and arrived at Madras in 1781 just as it was being threatened by the forces of Haidar Ali. Never entirely trustful of military men, as Governor of Madras, Macartney clashed with Sir Eyre Coote and General Stuart, the commanders of British troops in the war against Mysore. After removing Stuart as commander and sending him to Britain under arrest, Macartney shifted gears, opting for diplomacy where arms had failed. In 1784, he succeeded in negotiating the Treaty of Mangalore with Tipu Sultan. Though he achieved a temporary peace with Mysore, repeated disputes with Governor-General Warren Hastings led Macartney to resign his post in 1785 and return to Britain in 1786. General Stuart, humiliated by his removal, was waiting in London and quickly issued a challenge to Macartney. Macartney accepted and the two men met near the Tyburn turnpike to settle their dispute. Macartney was wounded in the arm, but after a brief period of recuperation in Ireland eagerly accepted the offer to lead a mission to China in 1791.[6]

Lord Macartney was an obvious choice to lead the China embassy. By 1792 he had much to recommend him. He had served ably in several important and difficult diplomatic posts and had repeatedly achieved tangible results. As an Indian official who had left his post in excellent financial shape, with no inkling of any irregularities or improprieties—a rare feat—he provided a stark contrast with public men like Warren Hastings who was just then being publicly skewered for his governance of British India. In his youth he had leveraged good looks and debonair charm into favor at the court of Catherine the Great; now it was hoped that his long diplomatic experience, his familiarity with despots, would help the British make vital inroads at the court of the Qianlong Emperor.

For a task of such obvious import, Lord Macartney would require a large and committed staff. The embassy would come to include ninety-five members, but choosing his second in command, his primary assistant and advisor, the man who would take over the embassy if he should die, was the most crucial personnel decision he had to make. There was no man Lord Macartney trusted more than his old friend George Staunton, who readily agreed to join the mission. A fellow Irishman, Staunton had trained as a physician before immigrating to Grenada in 1762, where he made enough money as a doctor to set himself up as a prominent landholder. When Macartney had arrived in Grenada as governor in 1776, Staunton was one of the leading citizens of the island, and the two literary-minded Irishmen became fast friends. Staunton lost everything when the French took Grenada in 1779, and so when Macartney was chosen as Governor of Madras in 1780, Staunton was only too happy to accept the position as his secretary. In both Grenada and India, Staunton had proved himself very capable, and constantly useful—it was Staunton who had negotiated the treaty with Tipu Sultan—and so when Macartney was appointed ambassador to China there was never any question who he would choose as his right-hand man.[7]

After Staunton, the embassy was staffed with a wide range of men with a variety of occupations responsible for the multifaceted tasks of the China mission. Since almost no Europeans knew enough of the Chinese language to serve as interpreters, Staunton was forced to turn to the Chinese College at Naples to find men who spoke the language. There he agreed to give two newly ordained Chinese priests, Jacobus Li and Paolo Cho, passage back home to China in return for their services as interpreters. Knowing that permission to travel within China was a rarity, two painters, William Alexander and Thomas Hickey, were employed to provide pictorial documentation of China. Also included were a surgeon, a physician, an experimental scientist, a metallurgist, a watchmaker, an instrument maker, a gardener, five German musicians and a fifty-man military escort led by Lt-Colonel George Benson.

To assemble and arrange the vast quantity of gifts at the imperial court, John Barrow was chosen as comptroller of the embassy. Barrow had been born to a poor family in northern Lancashire in 1764, but a fascination with, and aptitude for mathematics, science, and navigation helped him to rise to the position of mathematics teacher at a school in Greenwich. By chance he met George Staunton when the former Grenada planter was looking for a tutor for his young son. It was Staunton's patronage that secured Barrow the position in the embassy, a position that would be the making of him.[8]

The journey did not begin auspiciously. The flotilla had departed Spithead with a "fair fresh breeze," but as so often happened in the English Channel, the breeze rapidly deteriorated into a gale, forcing the fleet into Torbay, where they spent a monotonous two days waiting out the weather. When favorable winds returned, the party sailed south from Torbay along the French coast and across the Bay of Biscay to Cape Finisterre at the north-western tip of the Iberian Peninsula. At Cape Finisterre the waters calmed and the ships turned south-west to the cloud-enveloped island of Madeira in the Azores chain. The Azores were a common waypoint for European ships bound for both the Americas and Asia, well positioned to attract the growing current of commerce connecting the globe. For many in Britain, Portuguese possession of the islands was an ideal situation. Portugal had long been a British ally, the only European country to join, albeit briefly, with Britain in the American Wars. But Portuguese control had other benefits as well. The islands provided a crucial place of rest and resupply for British ships, without the need for costly British investments in infrastructure or defense. Controlled by a minor maritime power, the Azores would also be unlikely to serve as a base for attacking or disrupting British commerce with Asia. The lesson of America was being painfully learned. Possession of land cost money and men; possession of the seas made money.[9]

From Madeira, the fleet sailed for the Canary Islands, a comfortable journey of four days, though the much celebrated peak of Tenerife came into view almost a full day before their arrival. The harbor at Santa Cruz was full of the ghosts of previous conflicts—Admiral Nelson had lost his arm here in 1797— and suffused with the tensions of a world about to descend once more into war. The Spanish governors did their best to keep the peace, but one rather testy French frigate nearly touched off a battle when, assuming that the incoming

British squadron was a sign that war between Britain and France had at last commenced, fired its guns "pour l'honneur de la Grande Nation." The British were characteristically appalled by this "true spirit of Gallic liberty" but Erasmus Gower's restraint prevented further hostilities. For Barrow, this was yet more evidence of French hypocrisy and the hollowness of the charges of maritime tyranny lobbed at the British by France, America, and the League of Armed Neutrality during the American War. The French, Barrow complained, were the "loudest in complaining of the tyranny of the English in exercising the sovereignty of the seas; but, were the exercise of that sovereignty placed, unluckily for the world, in the hands of the French, their conduct on the continent is a sufficient test to evince with what degree of moderation they would hold the dominion of the ocean." It was to reinforce and retain the dominion of the ocean, and of trade, that Barrow and his companions had come to Tenerife.[10]

The presence of naturalists and artists in the embassy gave the China mission the flavor of an anthropological expedition. This was hardly an accident. Knowledge of the produce and products of a territory provided information about its extractive potential, while details of a territory's peoples helped create a sense of the potential for trade and commerce. Thus, at every opportunity, Barrow and some of his comrades ventured forth in search of information about zoology, botany, geology, agriculture, and society of the country. At Tenerife, they made just such a tour, climbing its formidable peak—the locals "bestowed" on them "very liberally the epithet of *mad Englishmen*"—where they were caught in violent storms and temperatures below freezing.[11]

In Cape Verde, the British were struck by the heat, the poverty of the place, but above all by the degree of African control in this erstwhile Portuguese colony. The governor on the main island of St. Iago was Portuguese, and the commander of the garrison a huge Scotsman who had served in the American army during the war, but otherwise, the clergy, judges, customs officials, civil administrators, merchants, soldiers, and even the governors of the other islands, were all African, a fact that could not help but remind the expedition of the new colony of former slaves just then being established on the nearby coast of Sierra Leone.[12]

The fleet did not tarry long in Cape Verde, weighing anchor on October 7 and heading south-west, skirting the southern borders of the famous Sargasso

Sea on their way across the equator, and the Atlantic. Three weeks after leaving Cape Verde, the passengers got their first view of South America when Cape Frio was sighted on the horizon. The next day, October 30, the embassy fleet passed the stony sentinel of Sugarloaf and entered the awe-inspiring harbor of Rio de Janeiro, the capital of Portuguese Brazil. The sight was truly enchanting. An ecstatic John Barrow was swept away as the scene slowly unfolded before his eyes.

> Having cleared this channel, one of the most magnificent scenes in nature bursts upon the enraptured eye. Let anyone imagine to himself an immense sheet of water running back into the heart of a beautiful country, to a distance of about thirty miles, where it is bounded by a skreen of lofty mountains, always majestic, whether their rugged and shapeless summits are tinged with azure and purple, or buried beneath the clouds—Let him imagine this sheet of water gradually expand, from the narrow portal through which it communicates with the sea . . . to be everywhere studded with immeasurable little islands, scattered over its surface in every diversity of shape, and exhibiting every variety of tint that an exuberant and incessant vegetation is capable of affording . . . Let him figure to himself this beautiful sheet of water . . . to be encompassed on every side by hills of moderate height, rising in gradual succession above each other, all profusely clad in lively green, and crowned with groups of the noblest trees, while their shores are indented with numberless inlets, shooting their arms across the most delightful valleys, to meet the murmuring rills, and bear their waters into the vast and common reservoir of all.[13]

The town itself was charming enough, but beside the jaw-dropping magnificence of its natural setting, the best Barrow could say about it was that while it did little to improve upon God's creation, at least the settlement did not "disfigure" it. But what struck Barrow most of all were the plantations and the slaves who worked them.

The Portuguese of Brazil congratulated themselves for treating their slaves better than other European nations (a rationalizing practice common to all European nations), but Barrow was suspicious of such self-justifying cant, and given the rotten nature of the entire system, not sure it really mattered. "Where the whole system is bad," he wrote, "the degrees of atrocity may perhaps be the less discernible." Despite Portuguese claims of gentle treatment, "whole cargoes of these ill-fated people [slaves] were annually transported from their native country and their connections, cut off from every hope of returning, and doomed to toil for the remainder of their days in the foreign fields of South America." Likewise, the fact that the staggering mortality rates on American plantations meant that new shipments of slaves were constantly required just to maintain their numbers put the lie to the contention that Africans were better off as slaves. "It is vain to tell us that the condition of the African negro is meliorated in the colonies, when a constant importation is required to keep up their numbers. But even admitting that their situation was improved by a passage across the Atlantic, by what rule of right do we assume ourselves the power of compelling people to be happy contrary to their wishes?"[14]

The "horrid calamity" of "perfidy and brutality" that was Atlantic slavery could not continue for long. Soon enough, Barrow believed, the slaves would take matters into their own hands. They had done so in Haiti the year before, breaking the "chains of Gallic tyranny" in the "glorious struggle for liberty." It had been a violent revolution, but for Barrow, one in which, unlike the "French subversion," the violence had been justified or at least understandable. And that necessary violence was sure to come to the British West Indies before too long. "The secret spell, that caused the negro to tremble at the presence of the white man, is in a great degree dissolved; the supposed superiority, by which a hundred of the former were kept in awe and submission by one of the latter, is no longer acknowledged; the mind has broken its fetters with those of the body, and freedom of thought has produced energy of action." But in this danger, there was also opportunity, the opportunity to reform and re-envision the nature of the British Empire, to gain financially, and save their souls in the process.[15]

For Barrow, and many like him in Britain, the whole project of Atlantic imperialism had been a costly error, economically and morally. The plantation-based economies of North America and the West Indies cost money to govern and protect, proving over the years to be a constant drain on Britain's finances. The costs of maintaining this Atlantic empire had led directly to the disastrous war with America, and the immorality of an empire built on slavery, as Granville

Sharp had observed, had contributed to Britain's humiliating defeat. Just as abolitionists sought to cleanse the British Empire of the sin of slavery, men like John Barrow hoped to create a new, moral empire out of the ruins of the old. The products of the Atlantic colonies most valued by Britain, sugar, cotton, etc., Barrow realized, were "originally transplanted from the East, where the labour of slaves is not required, nor any extraordinary waste of Europeans occasioned." There was thus no need to create colonies of plantations in the Americas when the same commodities could be had through trade with Asia, all without the burdens, both financial and moral, engendered by Atlantic empires. All that was needed to correct this error then was to re-concentrate Britain's resources in the east, to create an empire of free trade and free labor in Asia. With such an empire, "India and China may eventually prove the great sheet anchors of our commercial prosperity."[16]

This was the reason why the China mission was so vitally important. In the wake of Britain's American debacle, it was nothing less than a mission to save Britain's soul. The expansion of British trade in Asia provided the possibility of resetting the terms and conditions of British imperialism. In the place of territorial Atlantic empires built on the backs of slaves, a new empire of free trade and free labor could be constructed in the east. Without territorial possessions to weigh them down with costs, this new empire would be an economic boon to Britain. Without economies reliant on the labor of slaves, they believed, this new empire would be a moral empire of mutual, if unequal benefit. In this sense, the loss of the American colonies had been fortuitous rather than disastrous. Without the weight of North American obligations, Britain could at last reimagine its empire as one of trade and morality rather than of exploitation and sin. That it sought to do so on the back of an expanded opium trade seems not to have troubled them overmuch.

Reinvigorated by a renewed sense of mission, the embassy departed Rio de Janeiro on December 17, striking out east across the south Atlantic. Rather than making the usual stops at the Cape of Good Hope and southern India, the embassy fleet had opted to take advantage of the uninterrupted winds of the "great southern ocean," voyaging across the southern Indian Ocean before turning north-east at Amsterdam Island and heading for Indonesia. The embassy arrived at the Sunda Strait, the heavily trafficked passageway between the islands of Sumatra and Java, on February 26 after an open ocean journey of twenty-four days. The passage through the strait itself, on seas "as smooth as the Serpentine . . . in Hyde Park," weaving between a "crowd of little islands" too numerous for even the "indefatigable Dutch" to name, through the "constantly prowling" shoals of sharks, past tropical shores choked with vegetation, "one mass of soft and luxuriant green," took three full days. About halfway through the passage they paused to resupply at Anjerie, a considerable village with a small Dutch outpost on the Java shore. The choice of stopping place was fortuitous, if sobering, for within the bamboo palisade of the Dutch fort, under a simple wooden grave maker lay the remains of Colonel Charles Cathcart. The homage paid to their fallen countryman and his corner of a foreign field was pregnant with meaning for the embassy. Only five years earlier Cathcart himself had been selected to lead a mission to the Emperor of China only to die en route. After following in his footsteps across the ocean, they now gazed down at his final resting place, recording his grave marker before the wood deteriorated in the tropical heat, marking his life and his death before they were consigned forever to foreign oblivion. Surely, they hoped, someone would do the same for them if the worst were to happen.[17]

Once through the Sunda Strait, the squadron veered east along the northern coast of Java to Batavia (modern Jakarta), the capital of Dutch Indonesia and one of the most important trade centers of Asia. What immediately struck the crew upon entering the harbor of Batavia was the vast number of vessels dotting the bay. Dutch Indiamen were to be expected, as were the Javanese canoes and Malay proas, but it seemed as if all the world was represented at Batavia. There were massive Chinese junks, "whose singular forms seemed to bespeak an antiquity as remote as that of Noah's ark," French ships "carrying into the Eastern world, in addition to the natural products of their country, the monstrous doctrines of the Rights of Man," and a plethora of British vessels from Bengal, Bombay, and across the empire. Only a few years earlier the presence of British ships in Dutch Indonesia would have portended war, but much had changed during the American War.[18]

When the Dutch were drawn into war with Britain in 1780, they took part in the name of free trade, hoping to prevent British ships from obstructing Dutch commerce. They hoped too that victory over their most inveterate trade rival would undermine British dominance of maritime trade and provide a jump-start for their own flagging East Indian Company (Vereenigde Oostindische Compagnie—VOC). But though Britain was forced to sue for peace in 1783, the Dutch had hardly been victorious: Britain had captured important Dutch imperial possessions in India, Sri Lanka, and Indonesia, and might even have taken the Cape Colony had not François Henri de la Motte's well-timed treachery prevented it. As part of the peace settlement, the British had agreed to return the territories it conquered, but Britain had forced the Dutch to agree to crucial trade concessions. Henceforth, Britain was to have free navigation and free trade in Dutch Indonesia. Britain's entrance with new force into the trade from Indonesia to China (a second source of opium), combined with increased competition from the newly viable British outpost at Penang on the Malaysian peninsula, rapidly ate into the margins of the VOC, helping push it further down the path to decline and preventing Dutch commerce from helping the mother country recover from the expenses incurred during the American War.[19]

The British decision not to attempt to conquer and occupy Indonesia was a conscious one, part of a political theory of empire that emphasized trade and naval power over costly territorial possessions. This was a sentiment that John Barrow could fully support, especially after the American Revolution, his experience in Brazil, and his consideration of Dutch Batavia. The city of approximately 150,000 was "neat and handsome" with straight streets laid out at right angles, each with a canal in the middle. Separate from the city on the north side of the bay was a citadel containing the Dutch government headquarters, a chapel, and the public offices of the colonial administration. The countryside surrounding the city was flat and so thickly covered with trees that only the cupola of the great church was visible from the bay. But though the city had a pleasant appearance, its location proved a major hazard for its European residents. The low, swampy terrain was a breeding ground for tropical diseases, and staggeringly high mortality rates cut an unending swath through the Dutch inhabitants. Barrow blamed the choice of Batavia for the colonial capital on "the predilection of the Dutch for a low swampy situation" such as they knew back home. Whatever the reason for the choice, the effects of the terrain and climate were monstrous. The Dutch authorities estimated that three-fifths of those who came out to Batavia died within a year. Those who survived their first year would still have a 10 per cent chance of perishing thereafter. The mortality for the Dutch army and navy was worse still, with the military hospital recording as many as 78,000 deaths in 62 years. Overall, it was believed that perhaps 4,000 Batavians succumbed each year. "Never," Barrow disgustedly concluded, "were national prejudices and national taste so injudiciously misapplied, as in the attempt to assimilate those of Holland to the climate and the soil of Batavia."[20]

What this meant, for Barrow and those of his line of thinking, was that territorial possessions in such far-flung, inhospitable locales were not worth the expense in money or men. Commerce was the key to wealth and power; land brought only costs. Barrow hoped that the example of Dutch Batavia would help remind Britain of this eternal truth:

> It is to be hoped, that this consideration will always operate with the British government as sufficient reason for not attempting to wrest it [Indonesia] out of the hands of the Dutch. For as the shipping may at any time be taken out of the bay by a superior naval force, their possession of the town and garrison cannot be of material injury to the interests of Great Britain, provided we have a strong and active squadron in the Indian seas.[21]

Despite the pestilential reputation of Batavia, the embassy remained in the capital of the Dutch East Indies for several weeks, mixing with crowds of people from every corner of Asia. There were Arabs, Armenians, and Persian merchants, "always grave and intent on business," traders from every port in India, local Javanese with their studied indifference to the press of humanity, Malays with their reputation for ferocity, and everywhere slaves, from Mozambique, Madagascar, Malabar, and every nation of the east. Here too, for the first time, were Chinese merchants and migrants, some in "long satin gowns and plaited tails reaching almost to their knees," others dressed in "large umbrella hats, short jackets, and long wide trowsers," traders and artisans of every stripe, but above all famed as gardeners. The Chinese community of Batavia, first established in the early fifteenth century, made a favorable impression on the men of the embassy. Compared to the Dutch, Barrow found the Chinese industrious, charitable, and sober, far and away the most admirable community in Batavia. If this was what they could expect from the people of China, their mission would surely succeed.[22]

443

The fleet finally quit the steamy, swampy coast of Java on March 17, 1793. They had all enjoyed the gracious hospitality of the aged Dutch governor and the members of his council, joining in with the fireworks, fairs, and feasting of the Prince of Orange's birthday, but they had stayed too long. Thus far, the embassy and its crew had been spectacularly lucky not to lose a single man to the rigors of the journey or the danger and disease of their various ports of call. But now they left Indonesia short a man, stabbed in the back by a group of Malays while washing his linens in a stream. Others were laid low with typhus and dysentery acquired during their extended stay. There was nothing to do but minister to the sick as best they could and press on to China.[23]

The fleet next made landfall on May 24, at Turon Bay (modern Da Nang), on the coast of what is now Vietnam. The area was uncharted as far as the British were concerned, so the ships had to make their way blindly up the coast and into the sheltered harbor of the bay. Typhus and dysentery had spread rapidly among the crew, and fresh supplies were desperately needed, but a Portuguese merchant vessel informed the fleet that the entire area was convulsed by civil war. Vietnam was theoretically ruled by the Lê Dynasty (who were in turn nominally subordinate to the emperors of China), but since the seventeenth century real power had been in the hands of two warring dynasties—the Trinh at Hanoi and the Nguyen at Hué. In 1770, heavy taxes in Nguyen lands, used to fund wars against Siam, led to a peasant uprising against the Nguyen led by three brothers from the village of Tây Son. The Tây Son rebellion spread like wildfire, engulfing southern Vietnam, and tempting the Trinh into intervening to ensure the destruction of their hated Nguyen rivals. By 1776 Trinh forces had capture Hué and the Tây Son rebels had driven the last remaining Nguyen, Nguyen Anh, out of Saigon and into exile.[24]

Portuguese, Spanish, and French merchants and missionaries had been plying their respective trades in Southeast Asia since the seventeenth century, but thus far the British had shown only sporadic interest in the region. This, Barrow felt, was a grave mistake. The French had seen in the Tây Son revolt an opportunity to outflank the British by aiding the Nguyen dynasty of Annam against their rivals, sending Jean-Baptiste Chevalier from the French factory at Chandernagar in Bengal to Da Nang in 1777. War with Britain in both India and the Atlantic scuppered the plans temporarily, but with peace in 1783 and the re-formation of the Compagnie des Indes in 1785, the need for a recovery of French imperial interest in Asia was once more at the top of the geopolitical agenda. In 1787 attempts to secure French influence in Vietnam were renewed. Under the influence of Pierre Pigneau de Behaine, a French priest and leader of the Séminaires des Missions Étrangères, Nguyen Anh, nephew of the ruler of southern Vietnam, was sent to France for protection and to negotiate a military alliance with Louis XVI. The treaty signed at Versailles promised French military support and a substantial loan in return for granting the French the port and territory of Da Nang, the right to place French consulates along the coast, and, crucially, the right to demand Vietnamese troops and ships in the event that France went to war in India. The treaty collapsed with the French Revolution, but the danger such a move posed to British interests was clear.

The French, who had lost many of their Indian possessions during the American War, desperately needed new territories and new trading partners if they were to recover and once more compete with the British on equal footing. Even though the outbreak of the French Revolution once more disrupted their plans in Southeast Asia, there was no question that France would once more turn to Vietnam as the centerpiece for a new imperial strategy. A permanent presence in Da Nang would provide France a veritable Vietnamese Gibraltar, providing a stable base from which they could disrupt British trade with China and mount attacks on British India. The local ruler, even in the midst of a civil war, was able to build and arm 1,200 ships. When combined with the fleet the French had planned to build in Southeast Asia, France would have at its disposal a naval force capable of destroying British trade and "overawing our territorial possessions in the East." But it was not too late to prevent this. As Barrow reported, the king showed signs of favor to the British, treating them to feasts and declaring all his ports open to British shipping without tariff. Now was the time to seize the initiative, to extend "the paws of the British Lion" and "grasp every point which may add to the security of what British valour and the industrious and adventurous spirit of the British nation have acquired and annexed to her original dominions." This did not mean grabbing more territory. Barrow recognized that Britain already possessed "as many colonies as we can well maintain, and as much territory as is rendered useful to the state," yet the danger a French presence in Southeast Asia presented to British commerce necessitated the acquisition of "places of convenience and accommodation for our shipping." Lord Macartney, whose journal reveals a much greater preoccupation with military strategic matters, was fully in agreement.[25]

As Macartney may well have realized, his old enemy Warren Hastings, when Governor-General of India, had attempted to establish just such a British foothold in Vietnam. British merchants had made fitful efforts to add Vietnam to its burgeoning trade networks since the early seventeenth century, and the East India Company had even briefly established a factory in the north of the country, but it was the recognition of French inroads in Vietnam and the danger they posed to British commercial interests that spurred renewed interest in the 1770s. Like the French, Hastings realized that the civil war in Vietnam provided an opportunity to secure both land and trade agreements in return for British aid and intervention in the conflict. When two Nguyen officials fortuitously fell into Hastings' hands in 1777, rescued by British country merchants trading at Da Nang, the moment seemed opportune for British intervention. The two dignitaries were thus returned to Vietnam with a British escort, but the mission was a disaster from the start, with one of the Nguyen dying en route and the other refusing to risk his life by going to shore. Eventually the British party came under fire from a rebel faction and were forced to beat a hasty retreat. A second attempt at intervention was mooted, but with war with France breaking out in India in 1778, it was impossible for Hastings to spare any further British troops for Vietnam.[26]

After the war, a British base in Southeast Asia became even more crucial, especially with renewed French interest in Vietnam, but the initiative had by then been seized by an audaciously enterprising country trader named Francis Light. While the East India Company held a monopoly on trade between the East Indies and Britain, the "country trade" between Asian territories was officially open to independent merchants like Francis Light, who oftentimes paved the way for later, larger-scale British commercial and imperial expansion. After establishing himself in trade in the region of the Malacaa Straits, Light had recognized the immense potential of a British outpost in Malaysia. Britain needed a base in Southeast Asia to check French and Dutch expansion and as a waypoint for British vessels trading between India and China. He had petitioned Warren Hastings for a Company outpost on the Malay Peninsula as early as 1771, and in 1786 accepted the Sultan of Kedah's offer of the Island of

Penang. Sultan Abdullah Mukarram Shah had come under pressure from his expansionist neighbors to the north, Siam and Burma, and thinking Light was an official representative of the British East India Company, offered the island in return for British aid against his neighbors. Unfortunately for the sultan, Light had no such authority, and when he requested the promised British aid, he was informed that none would be forthcoming. In 1791 the sultan attempted to recover Penang—which Light had since renamed Prince of Wales Island—but was defeated by Company forces. Penang, Britain's first settlement in Southeast Asia, was to prove a wise investment, undermining Dutch trade and touching off centuries of British colonization in the region.

In all the excitement, Vietnam had been neglected by the British, and subsequent history would prove Barrow and Macartney's fears about Vietnam correct. Though official French support for Nguyen Anh would evaporate during the French Revolution, Pigneau de Behaine would continue to press for French intervention in Vietnam, eventually cobbling together a private force of mercenaries, adventurers, and speculators who helped modernize the Nguyen army and fortifications. With French (and Chinese) backing, by 1802 Nguyen Anh succeeded in subduing his Tây Son rivals and unifying Veitnam as the first Nguyen Emperor Gia Long. French frustration at the lack of practical benefits, or even recognition, granted to them for their aid in the civil war would form a major part of the pretext for their eventual conquest of Vietnam in 1858.[27]

Barrow and Macartney both recognized that any threat to British commerce had to be met swiftly and forcefully. France, the perpetual enemy, had a larger population and more abundant resources. If it hoped to compete, to retain its rank in the "scale of nations," Britain had to rely on foreign trade. Everything depended on commerce, "from Tyburn turnpike or from Hyde Park Corner to Whitechapel almost every house is a shop or warehouse . . . stored with articles of foreign growth. Any check, therefore, to our commercial prosperity, and to the preponderancy which we now enjoy in foreign trade, could not fail to be attended with the most injurious consequences to the country at large." The most vital area for British commerce was the China trade. India received more attention, but in many ways it cost as much or more than it produced. The growing China trade, however, was already "the grand prop of the East India Company's credit, and the only branch of their trade from which perhaps they may strictly be said to derive a real profit." It was to expand this vital trade that the embassy had traveled so far.[28]

In the afternoon of June 19, 1793, three days after leaving Turon Bay, the fleet's travel-worn eyes of the embassy and the fleet's crew had their first sight of China on the northern horizon. The next day they anchored off the coast of Portuguese-controlled Macau, allowing a party led by Staunton to consult with the British merchant community. He received news that the emperor had been informed of the embassy and had responded with "great satisfaction," going so far as to send commands to the ports of China to grant whatever assistance the British fleet might require. Most crucially, the embassy had been granted permission to proceed directly to Beijing, the Qing capital, rather than being obligated to enter China at Canton, the only port through which foreign trade and foreign contact were generally permitted. Not only would this drastically cut the travel time to the imperial court, but it would also allow the embassy to circumvent the obstructions of the Canton trading community, which was jealous of its monopoly over European trade and thus antagonistic toward the free trade agenda of the Macartney mission.[29]

With their goal now seemingly close at hand and the approbation of the emperor secured, the fleet hurried on through the Strait of Formosa, though "dark, heavy, rainy, moist, and stormy" weather entirely obscured the island of Taiwan from view, and into the Yellow Sea. The ban on foreign trade outside of Canton meant that the Yellow Sea was almost entirely unknown to Europeans. With its shallow seas, myriad islands, treacherous currents, and unpredictable weather, the Yellow Sea could prove perilous even for those well-accustomed to its dangers. For the unfamiliar British fleet, navigating the Yellow Sea, threading through the hundreds of coastal islands and the dozens of boats that issued forth from "creek and cove" to see the strange Western ships, it was akin to sailing blind. At Zhoushan near Ningbo and Shanghai, local pilots were taken on board to help guide them to Tianjin, the port of Beijing. The local officials were obviously well-informed about the embassy, and in a pattern that would be repeated at every stop along their journey, the Mandarins of the area made an official visit to Lord Macartney.[30]

By July 20, the fleet was approaching the Bohai Strait, the entrance to the Bohai Sea, Bohai Bay, and the mouth of the White River. From here the sea was too shallow—"the road is bad and dangerous" Macartney recorded—with unequal, rapidly shifting depths making the *Lion* a dangerous liability. The embassy transferred to the brigs and the *Hindostan* and sailed to the mouth of the White River, the gateway to Tianjin and Beijing, arriving on July 25. Here they met with two important Chinese officials, men who would be constant companions throughout their stay in China and real advocates for the embassy. Wang Wen-Hsiung, a soldier of Han Chinese origins who had risen steadily through the ranks after showing conspicuous bravery in campaigns in Burma and elsewhere, was the military commander at Tungchow. He was to share responsibility for the embassy with a civilian administrator, Ch'iao Jen-Chieh, an able bureaucrat from Shansi who had just been promoted from District Magistrate to Tao-t'ai of Tientsin in 1790, in which position he had distinguished himself in famine-relief efforts following the great floods of 1792. The two men were relatively senior administrators, though not the sort of officials with any real say in imperial decision-making. Nonetheless, they would prove cordial and supportive hosts throughout the embassy's stay.[31]

It took almost three full days to transfer the presents and baggage of the embassy into 30–40 flat-bottomed junks for the next stage of the journey up the Yellow River to Tianjin. On August 5, with the unloading complete, the embassy left the British fleet behind and sailed upriver accompanied by a cacophony of gongs and drums. By this point, the fleet's crew had been decimated by disease, and rather than wait for the embassy's return, sailed south for Zhoushan, where it was hoped much-needed medicine and fresh supplies could be acquired. As the *Hindostan* disappeared over the horizon, the embassy realized, for the first time, that they were all alone in a foreign land, far from assistance, at the mercy of their reluctant hosts. And though they had been treated impeccably by their Chinese hosts thus far, with none of the stiff, condescending formalism they had been taught to expect, there were inauspicious signs as well. As the motley fleet sailed upriver the British passengers noticed that each of the junks was outfitted with yellow flags decorated with broad black Chinese characters. When the curious Britons asked what the symbols denoted, they were taken aback by the reply. The flags, they were told, labeled each ship as part of the British embassy, "bringing tribute to the Emperor of China." Already, it seemed, there was a fatal misunderstanding.[32]

The scene that confronted the British visitors as they sailed up the Yellow River into the heart of China dispelled their worries, at least for the time being. They were immediately struck by China's abundance. High-prowed boats in "inconceivable" numbers flitted across the placid river, as wide here "as the Thames at Gravesend," with neat, thatched roofed houses processing along the low banks, on boat and bank alike a multitude of people, men, women, and children, "weather-beaten, but not ill-featured," and everywhere the signs of industry, of prosperity, of life. Macartney, not usually one to be stirred to flights of poetic fancy, was so moved by this first immersion in Chinese culture that his normally laconic, business-like diary entries give way to pointed exclamations from Shakespeare.

> "Oh wonder!
> How many goodly creatures are there here!
> How beauteous mankind is! Oh, brave new world
> That has such people in it!"[33]

After six days and 80 miles of pleasantly disorienting travel upriver, the embassy finally reached Tianjin. Up to this point the travelers had nothing but praise for China and its people. They had been enthusiastically received at every port of call by generous locals who betrayed nothing of the cold, formal reserve and distrust of outsiders that previous European accounts had led them to expect. The country seemed to be stable, wealthy, and thriving, a perfect partner for Britain's commercial ambitions. The officials sent to accompany the embassy to Beijing, Wang Wen-hsiung and Ch'iao Jen-Chieh (Wang and Chou, as the British called them), seemed forthright, friendly, and even encouraging. Even the yellow flags that marked the embassy as a mission of tribute could be chalked up to the idiosyncrasies of Asian diplomacy. But beginning with their arrival at Tianjin, the tone of their reception began to shift subtly.[34]

The embassy was greeted in sublime fashion by an impressive martial display. Troops lined the riverbank for a full mile, accompanied by "flags, standards and pennants, and by the clangor of various instruments of war-like music." On shore, the aged local viceroy, whom they had met a few days earlier, and a legate of the emperor were waiting to greet them. Cheng-jui, a Manchu of the Plain White Banner and Salt Administrator of Tientsin, was known to be opinionated, touchy, vain, and stubborn, and Macartney came away from their meeting convinced that the legate opposed the embassy, and was "perverse and unfriendly . . . toward all our concerns." His cold, suspicious disposition was a marked contrast to that of the viceroy or the much-liked Wang Wen-hsiung and Ch'iao Jen-Chieh. Macartney believed that this disparity was in part a result of a cultural difference between the civilized, urbane Han Chinese and the crude, war-like Manchus, and though this armchair ethnography reveals more about British prejudices than reality, the divisions between Manchu and Han were real enough.[35]

Qing China was an empire of conquest. Originally members of the Jurchen Aisin Gioro clan, in the early seventeenth century, the Qing had managed to unify the Jurchen clans into a new group called the Manchus and drive the Ming Chinese out of Manchuria. In 1644, the Qing Emperor Hong Taiji exploited a massive peasant revolt in China to intervene in Ming affairs, eventually defeating both rebels and Ming alike. The conquest of China by the Qing outsiders, which lasted until the reign of Kangxi in the late seventeenth century, led to ethnic divisions between the favored minority of Manchus, and the majority Han Chinese. The Han Chinese filled many roles in the imperial administration, rising to high office in the bureaucracy, however, many of the most important positions in the army and at court were the preserve of the Manchu elite, a fact that caused much resentment and division.

It was also at Tianjin that one of the thorniest issues facing the embassy first manifested itself. Qing court ritual was complex, and there was concern among the officials that the British might undermine their own dignity, or that of the emperor, with their ignorance of its finer points. Out of sensitivity to the feelings of the embassy, they chose a round-about way of informing the British of the ceremonies they would be required to perform at their imperial audience. On the pretext of examining and admiring the ambassador's clothing, and contrasting it with their own, an official suggested that the hose, garters, and tight-fitting garments of European attire had one serious drawback when compared to the loose, flowing robes of Chinese officials: it was too close-fitting to allow for the kneeling and prostrating that the ambassador would soon need to execute in the imperial presence. An old diplomatic hand, Macartney quickly grasped the point of the not-so-subtle discussion of comparative couture. To the official's dismay, however, the ambassador replied that he could not in good conscience offer greater obsequies to a foreign ruler than he gave to his own sovereign. Instead, he offered a compromise. Either he would kneel and kiss the hand of the emperor as he did George III, or he would perform the Chinese bowing ritual on the condition that a Qing official of equal rank prostrate himself in identical fashion before a portrait of the British monarch. They had reached an impasse for the moment, but both sides were as yet sure that a compromise could be found.

The embassy proceeded with their escort to Tongzhou, arriving on August 16. At Tongzhou they left the Yellow River behind and proceeded to Beijing overland. The 6 miles between the river and the Qing capital were so choked with crowds of curious Chinese, hoping to catch a glimpse of the foreign embassy, that a troop of soldiers brandishing whips was required to clear a path through the throng. Originally the party was housed in quarters outside the city, ostensibly for their comfort but really to make it easier to control their movements and prevent too much mixing with the Chinese population. Both Barrow and Macartney thought the accommodations inadequate, and at the ambassador's request, the embassy was relocated to new quarters within the city.[36]

In Beijing, the British began for the first time to feel that they were being closely watched. The surveillance was constant: Servants and officials were constantly present, their access to the rest of the city tightly restricted, and their mail intercepted and read. Even the disease-ravaged crew of the *Lion* recuperating in Zhoushan were strictly quarantined, and not simply for reasons of public health. Once more they received a visit from Cheng-jui, as unpleasant as always, but this time accompanied by nine European clerics: French, Italian, Portuguese, and Spanish missionaries living in the Chinese capital where they combined their religious vocation with diplomatic, scientific, and technological service to the emperor. The British were not entirely pleased to see other Europeans. Back in Tianjin, Macartney had received a letter from a French missionary named Joseph de Grammont who offered the embassy any aid he could provide. However, Grammont also offered a warning that the Portuguese contingent, and Joseph-Bernard d'Almeida in particular, could not be trusted. Almeida had risen to a position of some influence within the administration of the Qianlong Emperor, and he and his Portuguese brethren were jealous of their influence and quick to undermine other Europeans who might pose a threat to their position. With potential Portuguese treachery in mind, Macartney asked to be allowed to choose which of the missionaries would serve as the official translator for the upcoming imperial audience, a request that was thankfully granted.[37]

The now-familiar issue of the ritual prostration also resurfaced, this time discussed with a more senior Qing official, one of the emperor's Grand Secretaries. With neither side willing to give an inch, it was decided that Macartney would submit his compromise proposals in writing, which he did in a letter translated and transcribed by the younger George Staunton, who had managed to learn the language well enough on the journey from England to impress the Chinese officials.

On September 2, with the weather beginning to turn cool, the embassy set out on the last leg of its journey. They still had over 130 miles to travel before their audience with the Qianlong Emperor, and they needed to cover that ground quickly if they were to arrive in time for the emperor's birthday. Though Beijing was the imperial capital, the emperor was at that moment residing at Jehol (modern Chengde), the summer capital of the Qing in Hebei Province, north-east of Beijing. This last stage would take them through mountainous, romantic countryside, and finally beyond the Great Wall that had once marked the northern border of China. After seven days, they arrived 2 miles outside of Jehol, where preparations for their official entrance were made. Dressed in parade uniforms and especially designed costumes, and organized in a neat procession with mandarins, soldiers, musicians, servants, and embassy officials all leading Lord Macartney's chariot, the first British embassy to a Chinese ruler marched into the summer capital under the watchful eyes of the Qianlong Emperor.

13

➤➤ ◄◄

THE DAWN OF THE CENTURY
OF HUMILIATION

As he watched the strange contingent parade into Jehol, it must have seemed to the Qianlong Emperor as if ominous storm clouds were appearing on the horizon. Though he had long ago ceded most aspects of the day-to-day administration to his Grand Council, and especially to his great favorite Heshen, outwardly he was still the very picture of vigor:

> [A]bout five feet ten inches in height, and of a slender but elegant form; his complexion is comparatively fair, though his eyes are dark; his nose is rather aquiline, and the whole of his countenance presents a perfect regularity of feature, which, by no means, announce the great age he is said to have attained; his person is attractive, and his deportment accompanied by an affability, which, without lessening the dignity of the prince, evinces the amiable character of the man.[1]

He still enjoyed an active life. In his younger days he had been a devotee of the bow, and though his routine was now a bit more sedate, it was still full. He generally rose at 3 a.m. for private worship at one of the shrines in the palace and then read dispatches from officials and administrators until breakfast at 7. After a brief relaxation in the palace gardens—he was very proud of his extensive, well maintained grounds—he spent much of the day in business with his chief secretaries and other advisors. At 3 p.m. they broke for dinner, after which he attended the theater or other entertainment before retiring to read before bed at 7 p.m. But just days shy of his 82nd birthday, the emperor was beginning to feel his age. It must have seemed ages ago that he had ascended to the imperial throne at the age of 25. The fourth son of the Emperor Yongzheng, but the favorite son of both father and grandfather, Hongli, as he was then known, had been groomed to rule. He had been included in key rituals and allowed to participate in discussions of military affairs. Still, to avoid the factional strife that so often accompanied the transition between rulers, his father had written the name of his chosen successor on a piece of paper sealed inside a box kept above the throne in the Qianging Palace. When his father died suddenly in 1735, the box was unsealed and the name of Yongzheng's designated successor revealed to the assembled members of the imperial family and the senior officials of the empire. Hongli chose, rather fittingly if ambitiously, as his era name Qianlong, or "lasting eminence". But even then he had known that he had enormous shoes to fill.[2]

His father and grandfather had set an impossibly high bar. His grandfather, Kangxi, came to the throne at the age of 7 in 1661, the fourth emperor of the Qing Dynasty but only the second to rule China. Over his sixty-one-year reign—the longest in Chinese history—he finally put an end to the years of chaos and instability that characterized the period following the collapse of the Ming Dynasty and the rise of the Qing. Under Kangxi, Qing rule was consolidated internally and externally, the frontier was stabilized, and an era of peace, prosperity, and stability was ushered in to replace the uncertainty and civil wars of the preceding era. It was a golden age, a highpoint of Qing rule and a model for subsequent rulers. When the Kangxi Emperor's long reign came to an end in 1722, he was succeeded by his son, the Yongzheng Emperor, then in his mid-fifties. The Kangxi reign had been one of stabilization, allowing the Qianlong Emperor's father to turn his attention toward much-needed internal reforms. The government was reorganized, corruption and waste were rooted out of the administration, and authority was centralized in the hands of the emperor and his newly invented "Grand Council," which took on the consultative and administrative powers of a privy council.

Though he would never dare to compare his reign to those of his glorious predecessors, Qianlong had much to be proud of in his fifty-seven years as emperor. Hoping to live up to the example of his illustrious predecessors, he had

worked hard to be a conscientious ruler, meeting regularly with his senior officials, reading documents, issuing official edicts, traveling extensively throughout
his empire, and even taking a personal role in the planning of his many military
campaigns, of which he was extremely proud. His most cherished accomplish-
ment had been to expand and secure his northern and western borders against
the predations of the hostile nomads of the Mongolia Steppe. The Zunghar
people of Mongolia had long served as a rival source of authority for the
Manchus, and since the dawn of the Qing era had posed a constant threat to the
integrity of China's northern and western borders. Between 1755 and 1759, in a
series of three violent but victorious campaigns, Qing armies had succeeded in
conquering the Zunghar and incorporated their territories into the new province
of Xinjiang (meaning "New Territories"), which doubled the size of the empire.

With the Zunghar pacified and the northern border with Russia secured
through a treaty, Qianlong turned to other sources of danger on China's
southern frontier. Campaigns were launched against the rebellious tribal people
of Jinchuan in north-west Chengdu and western Sichuan provinces in the 1740s
and 1770s, against Burma in the 1760s, and against Tibet in the 1750s. The territories conquered in these wars were too sensitive to be trusted to civilian officials, or to Han Chinese, and so were administered by Manchu military governors
with large garrisons. Closed to Chinese migration and settlement, they were
maintained as strategic frontier buffer zones, a means of securing the stability of
the empire from the perpetual danger of outside attack or incursion.[3]

Culturally, Qianlong had attempted to follow the example of his father and
grandfather as well. He had always had a keen interest in art and literature,
especially calligraphy and poetry, and during his reign had done much to
expand the imperial art collection, even going so far as to employ Western
artists and architects. He was perhaps most proud of the great work he commissioned, the so-called "Four Treasures," an encyclopedic compilation of all the
most important literary and historical works of Chinese history. Eventually
running to an astounding 36,000 volumes, the Four Treasures represented both
the cultural clout of the Qianlong reign and also an act of filial piety, a recognition of the great works of Chinese history.

And yet for all his accomplishments, the weight of maintaining the empire
built by his grandfather and his father, the most important act of filial piety, was

exhausting. Despite the very real achievements of his reign, his attempts to expand and solidify the borders, to make a homogenous, unified whole out of a fractured empire, it was all still so fragile and impermanent. Soon he would officially step down as emperor so as not to reign longer than his revered grandfather's sixty-one years, one final act of respect for the achievement of his ancestors, but there was yet so much to be done, so many dangers to be faced, so many obstacles to be surmounted, and he was not entirely sure his heirs were equal to the task.

But for now, he had to focus his attention on the problem in his very midst, the embassy from the King of Great Britain. Though he feigned a superior disinterest in the world outside his empire, he knew enough of Europeans, and of the British in particular, to understand the threat they posed. From the time Qianlong came to the throne, the British had been persistent in their continuous demands for an alteration of their commercial and diplomatic relationship with China, constantly trying to outmaneuver or undermine the customary restrictions placed on foreign traders. But matters began to become even more strained in 1741, when a British ship under Commodore George Anson had attempted to take shelter in Canton harbor after his ship was damaged in a storm. Anson had been sent to Pacific to raid Spanish shipping during the War of Jenkins' Ear. Anson assumed that Canton abided by the same international laws as European nations, and thus that in entering Canton his ship would be openly welcomed by a neutral power. He was, however, gravely mistaken. He was forbidden to make repairs to his ship and denied an audience with local officials (who studiously ignored his very existence and would only sell him supplies at exorbitant prices).

Anson shouted his perceived ill-treatment from the rafters when he returned to Europe, which encouraged the growth of negative stereotypes about the Chinese as well as awareness that further diplomacy was needed. To this end, the East India Company sent James Flint, a country trader familiar with both the Canton trade and the Chinese language, to the Qing capital to present the rapidly accumulating grievances of the British. Despite restrictions on foreign travel beyond Canton, Flint managed to reach Tianjin and forward his petition on to Peking. The emperor at first agreed to investigate the British complaints but then had Flint arrested for breaking the restrictions on foreigners sailing to ports beyond Canton, for circumventing the usual procedure for submitting petitions, and for illegally learning Chinese. Flint would spend three years in a Chinese prison.

British aggressiveness was not the sole reason for suspicion about their present embassy. Chinese merchants and migrants, like their European counterparts, had also gone forth into the wider world in search of profits, spreading across the South Pacific and the Indian Ocean. The emperor had certainly heard enough from these expatriates to be wary of Europeans and the slippery slope from trade to conquest. From Chinese settlers in the Philippines, Taiwan, and Batavia he would have heard of the terrible suffering of the Chinese at the hands of the Spanish and Dutch. In 1740, more than 12,000 Chinese residents of Batavia—men, women, and children—were massacred when the Dutch governor, angered by their refusal to pay an extortionate fee leveled upon them, accused the Chinese community of plotting to overthrow Dutch rule. Barrow, who was horrified by Dutch treatment of the industrious Chinese of Batavia, called the massacre "one of the most inhuman and apparently causeless transactions that ever disgraced a civilized people," a sentiment with which the emperor would have surely agreed (though perhaps less so with the characterization of the Dutch as "civilized").[4]

British disgust notwithstanding, there was little reason for the emperor to suppose that they would behave any differently than their fellow Europeans. Indeed, British India might well have presented a timely warning. They had, after all, arrived in the great empire of the Mughals just as they had in China, as suppliants, merely seeking permission to trade. But by the time Macartney's mission arrived at Jehol, the toehold of trade had been rapidly transformed into a territorial empire, with native rulers transformed into suppliants or toppled altogether. As yet there had been no evidence of British designs on Qing territory, but rumors had begun to trickle in from the frontier between China and British India of British intervention in the internal affairs of the emperor's domains.

It was well known that Warren Hastings had sent an emissary from Bengal to Bhutan and to the Panchen Lama at Lhasa in Tibet in both 1774 and 1782 as a means of opening up trade with Tibet, but also in an effort to establish a new trade route into China that would circumvent the Canton system. Sending emissaries to a rival source of religious authority in such a sensitive and restive border zone was bad enough, but even more recently there were reports that the British had sent military aid from Bengal to Ghurka invaders and Tibetan rebels. Chinese officials questioned Lord Macartney closely about this on multiple occasions during his visit, and though he vociferously denied any British involvement, many among the emperor's party, especially the celebrated General Fu-k'-ang-an who had personally led the fight against the Tibetan insurgents, were convinced that the British posed a threat to the integrity of China's borders.[5]

That the British would resort to arms to defend their interests there was little doubt. In 1784 the *Lady Hughes*, a British ship plying the country trade, had fired a salute upon entering Canton harbor, as was customary among Western ships. Unfortunately, the salute went awry and two unsuspecting Chinese were killed by the errant shot. Under Chinese law a violent death, even an accident, necessitated the death of the man responsible, unless clemency was granted. The local authorities thus demanded that the captain of the *Lady Hughes* hand over the man responsible. The captain was understandably at a loss to identify exactly which gunner had fired the fatal shot, and so refused to hand over anyone. In response, the Chinese seized the ship's supercargo as collateral and, in a move that suggested that they believed all Westerners in some way culpable for the actions of the British, ceased all trade in Canton. Alarmed at this turn of events, the Westerners—British, French, Dutch, Danish, and even Americans—banded together and sent their ships fully armed to protect their factories and warehouses. The Chinese were not intimidated by this show of force, however, and continued to demand the culprit be handed over. With their livelihood at stake, the Europeans gradually abandoned the British (the Americans, led by Samuel Shaw, were oddly the last to remain in support), who were forced to hand over the man most likely to be responsible. Despite British pleas for mercy, the poor gunner was strangled to death in January 1785.[6]

With this in mind, the emperor made sure that the British embassy was under constant surveillance, their movements shadowed and restricted, their mail opened and read, and their contact with Chinese civilians limited. The embassy's interest in fortifications, including the Great Wall, was noted with considerable unease, and the ambassador's rather too casual display of British artillery firepower greeted with discomfort, alarm, and suspicion. These were a dangerous people, but they were also an important source of silver, and so they would be placated with the singular honor of an audience with the emperor.[7]

The official audience on September 14 went as smoothly as could be expected, despite the mutual misunderstandings. The emperor was clad in a "loose robe of yellow silk, a cap of black velvet with a red ball on the top, and adorned with a peacock's feather . . . [he wore] silk boots embroidered with gold, and a sash of blue girded his waist." The British ambassador, resplendent in his scarlet robes and plumed hat, refused to perform the appropriate rituals of submission. This was perhaps a sign of British arrogance, a confirmation of the emperor's concerns about their intransigent ambition, but for all that was made of this breach of protocol by his officials, and by European observers, it merely offered a handy public justification for what had already been decided long before the embassy reached Jehol. Despite the outward stability of his long reign, the Qianlong Emperor was keenly aware of the fragility of his realm.[8]

The massive Qing Empire had been built by conquest, but empires so built are apt to overextension and vulnerability on their borders. The Qianlong Emperor had spent much of his reign stabilizing his frontiers, but still his domain was no exception to the dangers of expansion. Beginning in the 1760s, the Qing Empire faced a series of crises that threatened to bring down the façade of stability. The Qing had always considered Southeast Asia to be within their sphere of influence, and repeatedly intervened in the affairs of these supposedly tributary nations, with disastrous results. Between 1765 and 1769 China launched four invasions of Burma, losing men and money to no real effect. The lesson clearly not learned, in 1788 China attempted to intervene in the civil war then raging in Vietnam. The Chinese army succeeded in taking Hanoi and proclaimed the restoration of the Lê Dynasty, but mere months later were driven out of Vietnam by an Nguyen army at a huge cost. These attempts to tamp down fires that had broken out in the crucial border zones, were only made worse when Gurkhas from Nepal invaded Tibet in 1790 (perhaps aided by the British). Qing armies successfully drove the Gurkhas back almost to the border with India, but again the costs were enormous. If this were not enough, the Russians, fresh from their seizure of the Crimea, had begun to test the borders with China, causing real concerns that Russia too had designs on China's frontiers.[9]

The insecurity of China's borders might have been easier to bear if internal stability reigned, but there were major problems developing within China as well. Perhaps a result of his ancestor's golden age, the population of China had risen rapidly across the eighteenth century after years of decline in the troubled years of the mid-seventeenth century. Recovery quickly turned into runaway growth, and by the time of Macartney's arrival, the population of China had more than doubled. This demographic expansion had dire consequences for the internal stability of the empire. Pressure on land grew as more people clamored for property, leading to smaller landholdings, landlessness, and migration, all of which increased poverty and undermined government control of the population. As more and more land was brought under cultivation, and new imported crops were adopted (corn and potatoes especially), the countryside was deforested, the soil began to erode, rivers silted, and floods, always a scourge of a civilization so closely tied to great rivers, became more frequent and deadly. Like their rural countrymen, China's elites were also gradually alienated. As the population grew, there were not enough positions in the bureaucracy to meet the demand of an elite who relied on such positions for their livelihood. Elite joblessness, combined with growing corruption and frustrations over the favoritism shown Manchus at the expense of the majority Han population, led to elites becoming divorced from the administration they normally helped maintain.[10]

Internal dissatisfaction turned rapidly to civil strife. An outbreak of sorcery accusations roiled the countryside in 1768, leading to fear and executions as people looked for scapegoats to explain their struggles in a changing world. In 1774, in Shandong Province, the White Lotus Rebellion saw anti-tax rebels, members of a secret religious society with ancient roots, rise up and take three cities, then besiege the strategically important city of Linqing before being violently suppressed. In the 1780s another rebellion burst forth in Taiwan when the anti-Manchu Heaven and Earth Society captured several cities and proclaimed a new dynasty. Beginning in 1784, two major fundamentalist Muslim revolts began in Gansu, with the tribal Miao people of the south-west also rising up.

The rebellions were successfully suppressed, but the anxiety and hopelessness of the age had other detrimental effects. Unemployed and disillusioned, many, starting with the elite, took to smoking opium. As demand increased, the British began to flood the market with Indian opium, leading to declining prices and mass consumption of the drug, thus began one of the great drug epidemics in modern history, with the number of addicts rising to perhaps a million or more. And if it were bad enough that opium was flooding into a vulnerable country, it was also becoming apparent that tea, China's cash crop that had for decades brought huge quantities of silver to buoy the Chinese economy, was now instead being purchased with China's own silver, the proceeds of Britain's opium sales. With the people becoming enslaved by opium's deadly allure, and the trade balance beginning to shift in Britain's favor, it would have been natural to wonder exactly what benefit China received from its trade with Britain. Even the Hong merchants increasingly found themselves in debt to the British. With his borders threatened, his people restless, and his trade undermined, the Qianlong Emperor was hardly being intransigent when he refused Britain's demands and sent her embassy packing. The outsiders could very well destabilize an empire that seemed balanced on a knife's edge. This was not an immobile empire, but a fragile, fractured, anxious empire.

With this in mind, the Qianlong Emperor sent a letter of response to King George III of Britain:

You, O King, live beyond the confines of many seas, nevertheless, impelled by your humble desire to partake of the benefits of our civilisation, you have dispatched a mission respectfully bearing your memorial. Your Envoy has crossed the seas and paid his respects at my Court on the anniversary of my birthday. To show your devotion, you have also sent offerings of your country's produce . . .

Surveying the wide world, I have but one aim in view, namely, to maintain a perfect governance and to fulfil the duties of the State: strange and costly objects do not interest me . . . Our dynasty's majestic virtue has penetrated unto every country under Heaven, and Kings of all nations have offered their costly tribute by land and sea. As your Ambassador can see for himself, we possess all things. I set no value on objects strange or ingenious, and have no use for your country's manufactures . . . It behoves you, O King, to respect my sentiments and to display even greater devotion and loyalty in future, so that, by perpetual submission to our Throne, you may secure peace and prosperity for your country hereafter . . .

Your England is not the only nation trading at Canton. If other nations, following your bad example, wrongfully importune my ear with further impossible requests, how will it be possible for me to treat them with easy indulgence? Nevertheless, I do not forget the lonely remoteness of your island, cut off from the world by intervening wastes of sea, nor do I over-look your excusable ignorance of the usages of our Celestial Empire.

Unaware of the internal issues confronting the Qianlong Emperor, Europeans took the letter's dismissive, condescending tone and its repeated mentions of breached diplomatic norms at face value. They thus ascribed the failure of Macartney's mission to his refusal to prostrate himself before the emperor and on a more general Chinese inflexibility and backwardness. Still smarting from his very public humiliation, when Macartney returned to Britain he joined this critical chorus and placed the blame for his failure squarely on the Chinese. He famously compared the Qing Empire to an aged, faltering ship, quipping:

The Empire of China is an old, crazy, first-rate Man of War, which a fortu-nate succession of able and vigilant officers have contrived to keep afloat for these hundred and fifty years past, and to overawe their neighbours merely by her bulk and appearance. But whenever an insufficient man happens to have the command on deck, adieu to the discipline and safety of the ship. She may, perhaps, not sink outright; she may drift some time as a wreck, and will then be dashed to pieces on the shore; but she can never be rebuilt on the old bottom.[11]

Macartney and the members of his embassy had more direct experience of China than anyone else in Britain, and thus their assessment of China and its rulers held real weight. As such their reports and views went a long way toward convincing the people and nations of Europe, who had once held China up as a model of stable, successful imperial governance, that China could not be reasoned with diplomatically, that the best policy was to circumvent any and all restrictions on trade wherever possible, and that force was more likely to succeed where diplomacy had failed. Just as the American War had helped transform British attitudes toward the Mughal Empire from admiration to disdain, the debacle of the Macartney embassy began a sea-change in British attitudes toward China. This shift in perception would in turn help Britain justify an increasingly belligerent policy toward China. Barrow's hoped-for empire of morality and free trade was not to be, replaced by imperial expansion built on a foundation of force-fed opium. For China, the embassy would mark the beginning of what came to be known as "the century of humiliation."

John Barrow had been left behind in Beijing to arrange and assemble the embassy's gifts to the emperor. Though he regretted missing the trip to Jehol, preparing the presents was no simple task. Complex scientific and astronomical instruments, with delicate, precise mechanisms and fragile materials, had to be constructed in the emperor's palace, requiring expertise and close supervision. This work filled most of Barrow's hours, with little time for sightseeing, but even in Beijing, in the midst of his labors, troubling news about the embassy began to reach his ears. On October 19, two days after the emperor's birthday— honored in Beijing by ritual prostrations before the empty throne—Barrow found himself locked out of the audience hall in the imperial palace. Everyone seemed in a sullen mood; no one would speak to him. Finally, he was informed by a friendly missionary that all was lost. Lord Macartney had refused to perform the kow-tow ritual.

Barrow's informant reported that none of the officials at Jehol considered the affair a serious matter and that a compromise had been reached that served the interests of both parties well enough, but in Beijing the officers and admin-istrators were "mortified, perplex[ed], and alarmed." They feared that the scandal would "tarnish the luster of his [the emperor's] reign, being nothing short of breaking through an ancient custom, and adopting one of a barbarous nation in its place." By accepting the compromise, the emperor, the physical manifestation of the empire, had allowed himself to be dictated to by a foreign power, demeaning the nation and undermining its fervently held belief in its unchallenged status as the center of the world. For Barrow and the British in Beijing, the change in mood was night and day. The princes and officials who had previously flocked to see the foreigners and their gadgets now stayed away, the friendly eunuch who had guided them through the palace now called them all "proud, headstrong Englishmen," and the fabulous meals that had weighed down their tables with the sheer multitude of dishes were now replaced by simple fare. And so it was with mixed feelings that Barrow learned that the embassy was to return to Beijing on September 26.[12]

On September 30, the reunited embassy trudged a few miles back up the road to Jehol to participate in the ceremonial welcoming of the emperor, returning to Beijing for the winter. The road was lined on both sides with painted lanterns and crowds of officials and onlookers, a trumpet blast and music announcing the emperor's arrival. For Barrow, the return of the emperor to Beijing meant an official review of the presents he had so lovingly assembled. For Lord Macartney, it meant, or so he hoped, the beginning of the real work of negotiation now that the formalities had been rather painfully dispensed with. However, though the gifts met with official approval, Macartney's attempts at diplomacy were repeatedly stonewalled.

Macartney knew from experience that diplomacy was a slow process, and he was fully prepared to take the long view of things, to reside at Beijing for months or even years until the details of a treaty could be hashed out. The early setbacks were certainly frustrating, but he believed that his proposals were in the best interests of both empires, and that eventually an understanding would be reached. Britain desperately needed to expand its China trade if it were to recover from the American War. It rapidly became clear, however, that the Chinese reticence was not a negotiating tactic. Only a few short days after they had returned to Beijing, Macartney was informed that the embassy was to leave the capital in short order. Embassies to China had never been permanent, as in the European model, a few weeks usually being the standard timeframe allowed. With the harsh winter weather of Beijing fast approaching, the emperor had set their departure date for October 7. For all the Chinese insistence on concern for custom and for the health of the British party, Macartney was at last convinced that the prospects for fruitful negotiations were at an end. There was little left to do but limp home.

With the British fleet still recuperating at Zouzhan, the embassy could not merely retrace their steps to Tianjin and the Bohai Sea. Instead, they would travel south along the Grand Canal, the inland system of interlinked canals and rivers which formed one of the great trade, travel, and communication routes of China—before heading east to rendezvous with Gower and the fleet. This was a rare experience. Few outsiders had been granted permission to travel across inland China, but the novelty of the trip could not entirely displace the sense that their trip south was an inglorious retreat.

The trip south along the White River would be made in a flotilla of thirty broad, flat-bottomed boats, and in the company of their Chinese champions Wang and Chou. At first, the scenery that flitted past as they floated away from Tianjin held little that captured British imaginations. Broad plains stretched on indefinitely, only broken by the occasional clump of trees, immiserated village, or sandy tumuli. From the city of Tianjin, where the flotilla entered the Grand Canal beneath a resplendent octagonal pagoda, the countryside became more densely populated, more prosperous. From the entrance of the canal they traveled 200 miles south and east through island-studded lakes and seemingly endless swamps before entering into a well-cultivated area of rolling hills "crowded with temples and villages and towns and cities." The Grand Canal seemed to swell to match the population, reaching its greatest width of nearly 1,000 foot and lined with stone. As they approached Hangzhou, the canal's path cut through a veritable forest of mulberry trees, a visual reminder of China's silk production, before reaching the city itself. The terrain now became almost sublime, with a vast crystal-watered lake surrounded by tree-clothed, temple topped mountains, stretching out to the horizon. On the lake, a countless multitude of gaily colored and gilded barges crisscrossed its cerulean surface.[13]

In Hangzhou the newly appointed Viceroy of Canton joined the party, having been directed to escort the British to their point of departure. The Viceroy was a friendly, gracious man, full of encouragement, but impossible to nail down on matters of British–Chinese trade relations, about which he was distressingly well-informed. With the Viceroy in tow, the embassy left the canal and turned east to Zhoushan. At Zhoushan the party learned that Erasmus Gower, unsure of their arrival and informed that war had been declared with France, had taken the fleet south to Canton where he hoped to be of more use to the British war effort. The only option left to the embassy was to continue their inland journey south to Canton, where they hoped to catch the fleet. The journey up the Yangtze to Poyang Lake then south and west on series of ever narrowing rivers was more difficult than the earlier legs. Their path now cut through mountains, with the fast-moving rivers squeezed into narrow canyons and plagued with strong currents, boulders and cataracts. They were forced to portage around these obstacles and between rivers until they reached the "steep and lofty" mountain pass at Meiling that marked the entrance to the Beijang River that would take them to Canton.[14]

On December 18, about 30 miles from Canton, the embassy was greeted by the East India Company's Canton commissioners Harry Browne, Eyles Irwin, and William Jackson, who had been given special and unusual permission to leave the confines of the European settlement in Canton. From the commissioners they learned that Britain and France were now at war, and that Gower and the *Lion* thankfully remained at anchor at Canton. With the commissioners came the Hong merchants, whose monopoly on British trade Macartney and his embassy had done their best to disrupt. The next day they set out on state barges for Canton itself, where they made an official entrance and were received by the Viceroy, Treasurer and the administration of Canton.

From their quarters on an island across the river from the English factory, the members of the embassy could see the signs of commerce everywhere. In the harbor there were fourteen British ships, representing the full reach of Britain's Asia trade. There were five Indiamen, fully loaded and about to sail for England, five ships newly arrived from Manila, three ships from the Coromandel Coast, and another from Bombay. One of the Indiamen, the *Bellona*, had recently arrived from the prison colony at Botany Bay, where it had delivered a cargo of supplies and seventeen female convicts. It was now purchasing a cargo of tea at Canton, a means of offsetting the cost of shipping convicts from England to Australia. But if the view of the harbor, with its physical manifestation of Britain's global reach, warmed the cockles of the hearts of those with mercantile inclinations, it was not without its sour notes. For alongside the British Indiamen were four smaller ships, each flying the stars and stripes, colors that until recently had been the flags of rebellion.[15]

For Americans, tea, and the free trade it represented, was at very the core of their violent split from the British Empire. Taxing tea without colonial input was bad enough, but it was being shut out of the expanding world of international commerce that really rankled. Trade had always been the lifeblood of American prosperity, and it was feared that British control of America's trade would drain away the essence of her vitality, stunting her growth artificially in an attempt to ensure the continued prosperity of the British East India Company. In this sense, for many Americans free trade was not merely about money, but about freedom, about the future ability of the colonies to develop and prosper independently. The Tea Act of 1773 was thus, as one broadside put it, a plot to subject the colonies to the fate of India, to conquest and extraction. "The East India Company," the broadside warned, "if once they get a footing in this (once) happy country, will leave no stone unturned to become your masters . . . They have a designing, depraved, and despotic ministry to assist and support them. They themselves are well versed in TYRANNY, PLUNDER, OPPRESSION and BLOODSHED." British tea represented Britain's monopoly over international trade and thus Britain's ability to subjugate America.[16]

Britain's American colonies had thus embarked on their war of independence in part because of the restrictions the mother country placed on American international trade, and in response to the tariffs placed on British imports such as tea. With independence, many such restrictions disappeared, allowing American merchants to engage in avenues of trade that had previously been closed off. But international trade was not simply a possibility in the post-war years, it was also an imperative, a necessity if the American experiment was to survive and compete with the nations of Europe. America had long been reliant on trade, but with independence came the loss of access to British markets in the Caribbean and elsewhere. With many port cities suffering from the disruption of trade during the war, and the loss of crucial markets after, there was a clear need to find new outlets for American commerce, new partners in foreign trade. China, one of the few rich trading centers not controlled or monopolized by hostile European powers, presented the perfect solution, in some eyes the last or only option for a young nation in search of free trade. With an ailing port of Boston firmly in mind, John Adams contended that only "one branch of commerce is left us, for which we owe no gratitude to the European powers. Thank God the intrigues of a Christian court do not influence the wise decrees of the eastern world. Our pretensions there are equal: nor is it in their [Europe's] power to prevent us sharing the most profitable trade, whenever we have the ability and spirit to build and fit out proper ships for the purpose."[17]

As it transpired, at the very moment that Adams was calling his nation to greater action in their trade with China, a mission, America's first trading venture with the Middle Kingdom, was already well on its way to the increasingly important trading hub at Canton. The initial idea for expanding American trade into the Pacific had originated with John Ledyard, an explorer from Connecticut who had joined Captain Cook's third and final expedition in 1780.

His experience of America's Pacific coast convinced him that the bountiful furs of the Pacific north-west could be used as a valuable commodity in the Chinese market. After he returned to America, Ledyard convinced Robert Morris, the British-born merchant who had helped finance the revolution, and a group of prominent investors to outfit a ship for the China trade. The ship they selected, a three-masted, 360-ton vessel, was fittingly christened the *Empress of China* and its hold crammed with items it was hoped would appeal to Chinese consumers: a box of beaver skins, 12 casks of spirits, 20,000 Mexican silver dollars, and 30 tons of Appalachian ginseng.[18]

As it sailed out of New York harbor in February 1784, it was clear to many that its departure betokened the start of a brave new world of American commerce. Philip Freneau, later called the poet of the American Revolution, marked the auspicious occasion with a poem glorifying a new American Empire built on defiance of Britain's monopoly of trade:

> With clearance from Bellona won
> She spreads her wings to meet the Sun,
> Those golden regions to explore
> Where George forbade to sail before.
> Thus, grown to strength, the bird of Jove,
> Impatient, quits his native grove,
> With eyes of fire, and lightning's force
> Through the blue æther holds his course.
> No foreign tars are here allowed
> To mingle with her chosen crowd,
> Who, when returned, might, boasting, say
> They shewed our native oak the way.
>
> . . .
>
> To countries placed in burning climes
> And islands of remotest times
> She now her eager course explores,
> And soon shall greet Chinesian shores.
> From thence their fragrant teas to bring
> Without the leave of Britain's king;

And Porcelain ware, enchased in gold,
The product of that finer mould.
Thus commerce to our world conveys
All that the varying taste can please;
For us, the Indian looms are free,
And Java strips her spicy tree.
Great pile proceed!—and o'er the brine
May every prosperous gale be thine,
'Till freighted deep with Asia's stores,
You reach again your native shores.[19]

To lead this vital trade mission, the American investors had been no less careful in selecting its leader than the British would be when they chose Lord Macartney as the head of their Chinese embassy. At the head of a crew of forty-two men aboard the *Empress of China* was Major Samuel Shaw, a man with sterling credentials. Shaw had been born a merchant's son in Boston in 1754, and thus even as a child had a front seat to the growing conflict between Bostonians and Britain over free trade. With such a background, Shaw was unsurprisingly precocious in his revolutionary sentiments. It was later reported that when still a young man, Shaw had challenged a British officer quartered in his father's house to a duel after the soldier made disparaging remarks about Americans. With such a fiery devotion to his country, when war broke out in 1775 Shaw was eager to enlist, joining George Washington's army at Cambridge, eventually rising to the rank of Major of the Brigade in the army.

Shaw was quick to recognize the global dimensions of the war with Britain. Instead of a "babyish quarrel with your daughter," the British were now faced with France, Spain, and America. The Seven Years' War had ended in triumph, with Britain's "arms victorious in every corner of the globe—your fleets triumphant on the ocean" and with her "then colonies contributing cheerfully in supporting your credit and independence, in which their own welfare seemed so closely interwoven." This was a war between empires, but also a war about the future of empire, and, for many Americans, the growing belief that the British Empire no longer served their interests was one of the causes of the war. The ramifications of this imperial war would shape the globe in the years to come.[20]

Thus, when rumors that peace was finally in the offing reached Shaw in 1783, he could not help but ruminate on the potential dangers of peace to an ill-prepared nation that had cast off the British Empire but was not yet sure of exactly how to expand its own. For Shaw and many Americans, the United States had arrived at a crucial juncture. They were finally independent from the British Empire, but if the American Empire was to rise to take its rightful place on the world stage, it needed a system of government adequate to the task, and a network of trade to match or supersede that lost with independence. "Is America prepared for the reception of the long-wished-for blessing [of independence]?" he asked a friend back in Massachusetts, "What system has she adequate to the government and prosperity of her rising empire?" In a letter written from West Point shortly before the Treaty of Paris was signed he continued, "America is now become an empire, and the eyes of the world are fastened upon her. If ever the spirit of wisdom was necessary to direct a nation, it is most peculiarly so at this instant. We have a character to establish among the great powers of the earth, who will . . . form their opinion of us from the manner in which we set out."[21]

For Shaw, who found himself without a career and deeply in debt when peace came, the solution to his own problems were part of the very same solution for his country's post-war economic woes: trade. And so, when Shaw—with glowing testimonials from George Washington and Henry Knox—was approached by Robert Morris and his fellow investors, he leapt at the chance to make a new start in the world of international trade. Like many commercially minded Americans, Shaw realized not only that there were great fortunes to be made from the Canton tea trade, but also that if American vessels did not step in to supply America's growing thirst for tea, that role would quickly be recaptured by the British. "The inhabitants of America must have tea," Shaw recognized, "the consumption of which will necessarily increase with the increasing population of our country." And, he continued, if they were going to drink tea, "they ought to employ the means most proper for procuring it on the best terms."[22]

However, if the United States was to take its rightful place in the China trade, it was crucial that her merchants identify commodities desired in the Chinese market. For a cash-poor new nation, draining America's already inadequate supply of specie to pay for China's silk and tea was an even less viable option than it was for the British. Shaw and his investors thought that the abundant produce of the expanding American empire, especially furs and ginseng, would find a ready market in China. This, Shaw believed, would prevent the United States from falling into the predicament that had threatened to undermine her balance of trade. He reasoned, "While, therefore the nations of Europe are . . . obliged to purchase this commodity for ready money, it must be pleasing to an American to know that his country can have it on easier terms; and that the otherwise useless produce of her mountains and forests . . . will supply her with this elegant luxury."[23]

After a journey of six months, the *Empress of China* finally arrived at Canton in August 1784. The Americans' reception by the European factors already present was friendly and encouraging (though the Portuguese governor at Macao was unaware of the outcome of the American Revolution). The British were a bit standoffish and more than a little cold toward their erstwhile countrymen, bitter not simply at the outcome of the war but at the close relationship that quickly developed between the new arrivals and their former allies. The French helped secure a factory for the Americans and, even more crucially, secured the necessary introductions with the Chinese authorities. The response of the Chinese to the new arrivals was even less encouraging. "Our being the first American ship that ever visited China," Shaw wrote, "it was some time before the Chinese could fully comprehend the difference between Englishmen and us. They styled us the *New People*." However, when Shaw produced a map and showed the Chinese officials the extent of the American continent, they were quick to grasp the potential benefits of a relationship with such a vast new market for China's produce.[24]

The *Empress of China* returned to New York in triumph, arriving in May 1785 to a 13-gun salute, one for every American state. News of the arrival, and advertisements for her exotic goods—25,000 lbs of tea, plus a quantity of porcelain and cloth—littered the country's growing periodical press, and the profits, $30,000, were enough to spur imitators in abundance. Shaw sent a letter to Congress giving details of his momentous mission, and received their thanks in return. Shaw's journey had created a sensation, but beneath the surface of adulation, the venture had made little money for its leader, certainly not enough to secure Shaw's future. Over the next eight years Shaw made three further trips to Canton, now as official American consul, and he was hardly alone. In the fifteen years following his first mission, over 200 American ships would follow in the *Empress of China*'s wake, making the volume of America–China trade second only to the Britain–China trade. But, after the Commutation Act of 1784, the number of British ships was expanding as well, as Shaw was careful to note. This greater competition in turn led to a spike in the price of tea of 25 per cent or more. At the same time, the ginseng market that Shaw was sure would secure America's trade advantage was collapsing as American imports over-saturated the market. From $30 per pound on Shaw's first trip, the price rapidly fell to $4 per pound and by 1790, 25 cents per pound. Faced with the real possibility of a growing trade imbalance, Shaw and his fellow American merchants scrambled to find new products to sell on the Chinese market.[25]

Like their British counterparts, American merchants quickly discovered that there was also an almost unquenchable demand for opium. When Shaw first arrived in Canton, the opium trade from India to China was in the midst of a period of massive, unprecedented expansion as the British sought new products to stabilize their trade balance with Celestial Empire. With no access to the poppy fields of British India, American merchants intent upon following the British lead into the lucrative opium trade were forced to look elsewhere for supplies. Fortunately, a ready supply of opium was found in another area of expanded American trade, the Mediterranean. By the early decades of the nineteenth century American merchants were purchasing more than three-quarters of Turkey's entire annual opium crop of 150,000 lbs, worth as much as $1 million in China. There were, however, drastic, unforeseen consequences of America's growing commercial presence in the Mediterranean.[26]

Prior to the American Revolution, ships from Britain's colonies had been able to sail the Mediterranean without peril, sheltered from the ravages of the notorious Barbary corsairs by the might of the British navy. During the course of the war, American ships generally remained free from Barbary predations as well, in part because the Barbary States were unaware that the American colonies had declared independence from Britain, and in part because America's treaty of alliance with the French provided them with French naval protection. The Treaty of Amity and Commerce signed between France and America in 1778 had charged France with securing "the immunity of the ships, citizens, and goods of the United States, against any attack, violence or depredation of . . .

the States of Barbary." With peace declared, and with formal independence from Britain a reality rather than a claim, American ships lost the shelter of the British Empire. At the same time, the end of the war meant that the French, their coffers emptied and always sensitive to new incursions into their jealously guarded Mediterranean trade, walked away from their obligations to ensure the safety of American ships, reasoning that there was "no advantage to us in procuring for them a tranquil navigation of the Mediterranean." When Spain made peace with the Barbary States in 1785, all previous protections were lost, and for the first time, American ships became fair game.[27]

Most Americans had no conception of this ripple effect of the American Revolution, of the new dangers of Mediterranean trade. American ships had fallen prey to the Barbary corsairs soon after English settlement began—the first recorded capture of an American ship came in 1625, and in 1678 alone fourteen American vessels had been seized—but in the intervening century American shipping had felt little and thought less about this North African scourge. Indeed, Americans had every reason to believe that a new relationship with the Barbary States was close on the horizon. After all, Morocco had been the first nation to formally recognize American independence. In April 1778, Sidi Muhammad, Sultan of Morocco, had contacted Benjamin Franklin through a French intermediary and requested a trade agreement with the United States. Short on allies, Congress responded warmly in 1780, but during the chaos of the war, failed to follow up on the initial contact to formalize the relationship.

In the wake of the revolution, attempts were made to renew contact through American merchants at the Spanish port of Alicante, but inexperience, delays, and indecision slowed the process to such a degree that Sidi Muhammad decided to jolt the infant nation awake. In 1784, he decided that perhaps the United States needed an incentive to speed up the treaty process. His corsairs at the Atlantic port of Sale were thus tasked with capturing an American ship that could be used as leverage to jump-start the faltering negotiations. By October they had their ship, capturing the *Betsy* and its crew off Cape St. Vincent as it returned to America from Cadiz.[28]

As if the capture of the *Betsy* and her crew was not bad enough, the British, still stinging from their defeat, wasted no time in informing the other Barbary States of the implications of their former colonies' independence. Charles

Logie, the newly arrived British consul at Algiers, had informed the Dey of Algiers of the war between Britain and the United States, and declared that American shipping was no longer under British protection, that such vessels "were good prizes and wished them success in their attempts to capture those who refused allegiance" to Great Britain. Shortly after receiving Britain's blessing, the cruisers of Algiers were sent out on the hunt, capturing the *Maria*, and five days later the *Dauphin* of Philadelphia.[29]

In all, twenty-one American sailors were taken on this first Algerian raid on American shipping. They were brought back to Algiers as hostages, destined to serve as slaves until they were ransomed. Many would remain in slavery for a decade or more, joined by dozens more American captives. Others would be buried there. But at the time, none realized the magnitude of the events they were now swept up in; all were sure that redemption would come soon. As one of the American captives, James Leadner Cathcart, an 18-year-old sailor who had emigrated from Ireland to the American colonies at the age of 8, later explained, in a diatribe full of understandable bitterness, that the captives had "placed the greatest confidence in the generosity" of their country. "I thought it impossible that a nation just emerged from slavery herself would abandon the men who had fought for her independence to an ignominious captivity in Barbary . . . and I hesitate not to assert that no class of men suffered in any degree so much by the consequences attending the American Revolution as those who were captured by the Algerines in 1785."[30]

As early as 1786, it was clear to some in America that something had to be done to redeem the captives and ensure peace with the Barbary States. The former colonies emerged from their struggle with Britain independent, but hardly united and on the brink of financial disaster. The war had taken a heavy toll on American shipping, and as a still largely coastal nation dependent on overseas commerce, the United States desperately needed a rapid recovery of its mercantile trade if it were to avoid bankruptcy and financial disaster. However, with independence came the loss of the well-worn trade networks of the British Empire and the previously vital links to the West Indies. With other avenues of commerce cut off or temporarily disrupted, the Mediterranean, still a free trade zone open to the shipping of all nations, seemed to provide a crucial outlet for American merchants and a source of commodities that could be sold on to consumers in the equally crucial Chinese market. It was thus with a mix of hope and desperation that ships like the *Maria* and the *Dauphin* packed their holds with timber, tobacco, sugar, and rum and sailed for the ports of the Mediterranean.

Almost overnight, American ships became a frequent sight in the Mediterranean. By the beginning of the 1780s, as much as one-fifth of American exports, carried by as many as a hundred ships, were bound for the Middle Sea. To Europeans with long experience in the trade, the sea and its ports seemed to be choked with a plague of Americans, haggling for capers, raisins, figs, and, above all, Turkish opium. As one British merchant complained, "there is hardly a petty harbor . . . but you will find a Yankee . . . driving a hard bargain with the natives."[31]

The growing ubiquity of American merchants, however, placed a bright target on their backs. After the revolution ended, the Barbary States wasted little time introducing the Americans to the costs of doing business in the Mediterranean. Back home, Americans were outraged by the news of the capture of their ships, but their rage was entirely impotent and the outcry came to nothing. The Barbary States respected two things, and two things only, gold and guns, and in the years after the revolution, America had neither. During the war, the States had been able to cobble together some semblance of a navy, but it was disbanded when the fighting ended. The Articles of Confederation, the document that governed the hardly united States, made anathema the very existence of a national navy during times of peace, for fear that such a force might become a tool of federal tyranny. Even if the States had wanted to create a navy, the Articles made it nearly impossible to raise the required funds by placing barriers in the way of national taxation. For many Americans, the creation of a navy was perceived to be a dangerous, and overly expensive project. With no navy, and no real prospect of one on the horizon, American ships were sitting ducks for the Barbary pirates.

As the trade linking the United States to the Mediterranean and China expanded, and the importance of these networks to the American economy grew, so too did the realization that piracy threatened to upend this fragile, interwoven system of commerce, and indeed threatened the entire economy of a country just setting out on the path to prosperity. The Barbary corsairs thus not only imperiled the vital Mediterranean trade but, by cutting off supplies of Turkish opium, they also undermined the China trade. It was becoming increasingly evident that North African piracy posed a threat to two of the emerging tent-poles of American commerce at the very moment when these were needed most. According to one outspoken advocate of free trade, "our commerce is on the point of being annihilated, and, unless an armament is fitted out, we may very soon expect the Algerines on the coast of America."[32]

By 1797, treaties had been signed with all four of the Barbary States, and the surviving American captives released. But without the threat of military force, the terms had been ruinous. Peace had cost about $1.25 million and, going forward, as much as 20 per cent of U.S. government revenue would go toward tribute payments to Algiers, Morocco, Tripoli, and Tunis. The situation was unsustainable. To make matters worse, the United States had fundamentally misunderstood the role of peace treaties for the Barbary States. Their economies relied heavily on the proceeds of piracy and on the bribes and tributes paid by European nations to secure peace. This meant that if the Barbary States were to remain solvent, they needed an endless series of wars and treaties. It did them little good to remain at peace with any given nation for very long, and sooner or later they always broke their treaties to ensure further bribes and tributes. Thus, while the United States considered the matter closed by 1797, the Barbary States were merely biding their time, waiting for another cycle of piracy, war, and treaty. In the end it would take force and two further wars—with Tripoli between 1801 and 1805, and with Algiers in 1815—to finally break the cycle and free American ships from Barbary predation for good. In the meantime, Britain had seized the commercial initiative in both the Mediterranean and China.[33]

By March 1794, Samuel Shaw was more than ready to leave China. The trading season at Canton was over, and after four globe-spanning voyages in ten years, the appeal of hearth and home beckoned with a rising strength impossible to ignore. He had been ill for months, but the prospect of seeing his young family buoyed his spirits and made him eager to depart. With war still raging between Britain and revolutionary France, and pirates always a possibility, it was agreed that, for safety's sake, the American vessel would convoy with a British squadron just returned from an embassy to the Qianlong Emperor. They had come to terms with their British brethren in the years since the revolution, once more becoming trading partners as well as rivals, and besides, any friend was valuable on the perilous seas. Shaw spent most of the journey in his cabin, his feverish eyes staring at a miniature of his wife Hannah, whom he had married in 1792 on a brief visit home. He hoped to see her in the flesh soon, but ten weeks out from Canton, as they approached the Cape of Good Hope, he took a turn for the worse. The ship's surgeon, James Dodge, did all he could, but was not above seeking the opinions of Dr. Macrea from the *Hindostan* and Dr. Gillion, Lord Macartney's own surgeon, from the *Lion*. But there was little to be done. Shaw himself seemed to realize this, and taking one final look at the portrait at the foot of his berth, he sighed aloud and said, "God's will be done." Shortly after, he slipped away, dying on May 30, 1794.[34]

His friend Thomas Randall, who had accompanied him on all his voyages, sent a letter to Hannah, informing her of her husband's death and eulogizing his character. But the panegyrics were not reserved for friends. Obituaries appeared in many newspapers singing his praises, with one christening him "an ornament of his country." They could already sense the momentous role Samuel Shaw had played in the history of their young nation, but if they had been able to glimpse the future, the praise might have reached an even higher pitch. In the years after Shaw's first voyage on the *Empress of China*, America's trade with China boomed, filling the pockets of many men who would go on to form important mercantile and commercial dynasties: including Jacob Astor and Warren Delano, progenitors of the Astor and Delano-Roosevelt fortunes. But the country as a whole was enriched as well. The expansion of the China trade led to a boom in shipbuilding and all the attendant industries needed to float a merchant fleet and process its commerce. In the search for commodities to trade for Chinese tea, America began to explore its continent's Pacific coast in search of furs, speeding up the settlement of the American West. American ships also began to traverse the Mediterranean in greater numbers to purchase Turkish opium for the Chinese market, thus playing an important role in the two wars with the piratical Barbary States that did so much to bind together a fractured country and announce her arrival among the powers of the earth. The need for America's merchants to purchase their own tea had started America down the path of empire.

As the American consul lay dying in his cabin, his British counterpart could not help dwelling on the failures of his own mission. He too had come to China with great need and high hopes for the future of his country's trade with the Celestial Kingdom. After the American War the British economy, and the East India Company that was such a central part of it, had been in a shambles, but the stubborn refusal of the Qianlong Emperor to see British reason, to realize the new world that was dawning, had scuppered his lofty ambitions. Now, as he returned home in defeat, all he could do was imagine the consequences of China's intransigence. The Chinese had made opaque promises of "greater indulgence and favor," but none of their concrete aims. "If the Court of Pekin[g] is not really sincere," Macartney wondered, "can they possibly expect to feed us long with promises? Can they be ignorant that a couple of English frigates would be an overmatch for the whole naval force of their empire, that in half a summer they could totally destroy all the navigation of their coasts and reduce the inhabitants of the maritime provinces . . . to absolute famine?" If China were to "interdict us their commerce," Macartney imagined, the China trade could as easily be captured and forced open with a few ships and a small force from British India. There would be consequences of course, but "the breaking-up of the power of China" would in the end, benefit Britain, who would "rise superior over every competitor" on the back of her "riches and the genius and spirit of her people."[35]

It was a prescient thought, but the growing opium trade was already having a profound effect. The proceeds from the China trade, the wealth created from the trade in tea and opium, flowed into the coffers of the East India Company just at the moment when they were most desperately needed to fund the expansion and administration of British India, a new empire built on a new triangle trade. And this narcotics trade was encouraged by the views created by the accounts of Macartney's mission, presenting a stereotype of an inflexible, backward kingdom that turned British hearts and minds against the Chinese, helped to justify a distasteful trade, and made it easier to feed a growing addiction and ignore the repeated pleas of China's rulers to stop the trade. But if this rationalization helped to enrich one empire, it would drive another to its knees. As the opium flooded into China in the nineteenth century, it became cheaper and more widely available, creating an epidemic with disastrous consequences for millions.

Though in 1794 he still hoped for a diplomatic solution, Macartney would get his war with China. By 1839, the social and physical corrosion of British and American opium had become too much to bear. The Daoguang Emperor once more refused to legalize opium, and instead seized over 2.5 million pounds of opium and closed Canton to foreign trade. The British responded by invading to reopen trade by force, touching off the first of two Opium Wars that would fatally undermine Chinese sovereignty, to say nothing of Chinese public health.

But all this was in the future. For now, Lord Macartney was still connected to the corridors of power; the failure of the China mission was merely one isolated failure in a decorated imperial career. In 1796, he would be appointed British Governor of the Cape Colony, captured from the Dutch in 1795, fourteen years after the first mission to take it had been intercepted by Admiral de Suffren at Porto Praya. John Barrow would follow Macartney to Africa as the new governor's private secretary, exploring deep into the interior of southern Africa on a mission to reconcile the Dutch Boer settlers with the native Africans, before returning to Britain to take up a fruitful career as Secretary of the Admiralty. From this post he would sponsor and encourage numerous scientific expeditions to the Arctic including those of John Ross, William Perry, and John Franklin. Barrow, Alaska and the Barrow Strait are named for him. It was China that was the making of him. Once more the effects of the American Revolution had rippled out from the Atlantic, aiding the expansion of the British Empire, and undermining its imperial rivals.

NOTES

INTRODUCTION: THE WORLD THE AMERICAN REVOLUTION MADE

1. *The Times*, March 27, 1811.
2. "Aborigines Want Remains Returned," *Canberra Times*, January 30, 1988.
3. *Morning Post*, May 29, 1794; "Aborigines Want Remains Returned," *Canberra Times*, January 30, 1988; "A Campaign to Bring Home Australia's First 'Ambassador,' " *Canberra Times*, February 9, 1991.
4. Gary Nash, *The Unknown American Revolution: The Unruly Birth of Democracy and the Struggle to Create America* (New York, 2006); Carol Berkin, *Revolutionary Mothers: Women in the Struggle for American Independence* (New York, 2005); Holger Hoock, *Scars of Independence: America's Violent Birth* (New York, 2017); Alan Taylor, *American Revolutions: A Continental History, 1750–1804* (New York, 2016).
5. Justin du Rivage, *Revolution against Empire: Taxes, Politics, and the Origins of American Independence* (New Haven, 2017); Nick Bunker, *Empire on the Edge: How Britain came to Fight in America* (New York, 2014); P.J. Marshall, *The Making and Unmaking of Empires: Britain, India, and America 1750–1783* (Oxford, 2007); R.R. Palmer, *The Age of Democratic Revolutions* (Princeton, 1964); Lester Langley, *The Americas in the Age of Revolution: 1750–1850* (New Haven, 1996); Jonathan Israel, *Expanding the Blaze: How the American Revolution Ignited the World* (Princeton, 2017); Janet Polasky, *Revolution without Borders: The Call to Liberty in the Atlantic World* (New Haven, 2015).
6. C.A. Bayly and Maya Jasanoff each illuminated some of the important consequences of the American War for the British Empire. Bayly has suggested that the post-war period saw a shift toward a more closely controlled, centrally governed empire, while Jasanoff has suggested that the experience of the loyalist diaspora after the war demonstrates the legacy of a "Spirit of 1783," which encouraged expansion, liberal humanitarianism, and growth of a hierarchical centralization within the British Empire. Both accounts are surely correct, though neither considers the full scope of the British imperial world, nor how exactly this reorientation of the empire functioned in practice. C.A. Bayly, *Imperial Meridians: The British Empire and the World, 1780–1830* (London, 1989); Maya Jasanoff, *Liberty's Exiles: American Loyalists in the Revolutionary World* (New York, 2011).

1 THE REVOLUTION COMES TO BRITAIN

1. Ignatius Sancho, *The Letters of the Late Ignatius Sancho, An African* (London, 1784), 269–70.

2. Ignatius Sancho, *Letters of the Late Ignatius Sancho, An African* (Cambridge, 2013), vol. 2, 174; Tim Hitchcock and Robert Shoemaker, *London Lives: Poverty, Crime, and the Making of the Modern City* (Cambridge, 2016), 349; Peter Linebaugh, *The London Hanged: Crime and Civil Society in the Eighteenth Century* (London, 2006), 336.

3. Sancho, *Letters*, vol. 2, 176–7; Hitchcock and Shoemaker, *London Lives*, 340, 349; Frances Burney, *The Diary and Letters of Madame D'Arblay* (London, 1843), vol. 1, 400–8.

4. Old Bailey Sessions Papers (OBSP), t17840915-146; Hitchcock and Shoemaker, *London Lives*, 353–5.

5. Richard Platt, *Smuggling in the British Isles: A History* (Stroud, 2011), 129–31.

6. Frank McLynn, *Crime and Punishment in Eighteenth-century England* (Oxford, 1991), 178–9.

7. Ibid., 172–92.

8. Platt, *Smuggling*, 48–9.

9. McLynn, *Crime and Punishment*, 179.

10. Ibid., 194.

11. Platt, *Smuggling*, 54–5.

12. McLynn, *Crime and Punishment*, 172.

13. Ibid., 184–95.

14. Ibid., 179, 195.

15. J.M. Beattie, *Policing and Punishment in London, 1660–1750: Urban Crime and the Limits of Terror* (Oxford, 2001), 424–32; Hitchcock and Shoemaker, *London Lives*, 363.

16. Douglas Hay, "War, Dearth and Theft in the Eighteenth Century: The Records of the English Court," *Past and Present* 95 (May 1982): 125–42.

17. OBSP, t17830604-56.

18. OBSP, t17821204-7.

19. J.M. Beattie, *Crime and the Courts in England, 1660–1800* (Princeton, 1986).

20. Douglas Hay, "Property, Authority and the Criminal Law," in Douglas Hay et al., *Albion's Fatal Tree: Crime and Society in Eighteenth-century England* (London, 1975).

21. Roger Ekirch, *Bound for America: The Transportation of British Convicts to the Colonies, 1718–1775* (New York, 1987); Hitchcock and Shoemaker, *London Lives*, 322–3.

22. *Maryland Gazette*, November 2, 1775.

23. Ibid., April 10, 17, 24, 1751.

24. James Boswell, *The Life of Samuel Johnson LL.D* (London, 1823), vol. 3, 316; Benjamin Franklin as quoted in Emma Christopher, *A Merciless Place: The Lost Story of Britain's Convict Disaster in Africa* (Oxford, 2011), 33; Paul Ford, ed., *The Writings of Thomas Jefferson*, ed. Paul Ford (New York, 1894), vol. 4, 158–9.

25. *The Parliamentary Register, or the History of the Proceedings and Debates of the House of Commons*, vol. IV (London, 1776), 106.

26. *Maryland Gazette*, July 13, 1775.

27. Emily Jones Salmon, "Convict Labor during the Colonial Period," *Encyclopedia Virginia* (Virginia Humanities and Library of Virginia, 2011, online).

28. Charles Davenant, *An Essay on the probable Methods of making a People Gainers in the Balance of Trade* (London, 1699), 50.

29. Hitchcock and Shoemaker, *London Lives*, 355.

30. Adam J. Hirsch, *The Rise of the Penitentiary: Prisons and Punishment in Early America* (New Haven, 1992), 14–18.

31. Cesare Beccaria, *Of Crimes and Punishments* (London, 1778).

32. John Howard, *The State of the Prisons* (Warrington, 1777).

33. Ibid.

34. William Smith, *The State of the Gaols in London, Westminster and the Borough of Southwark* (London, 1776), 35–6, 76.

35. As quoted in, Hitchcock and Shoemaker, *London Lives*, 328–9.

36. *London Magazine*, vol. 46 (1777), 264; *Town and Country Magazine*, July 1779, 338.

37. *Westminster Magazine*, September 1778, 455.

38. Hitchcock and Shoemaker, *London Lives*, 334–7.

39. Jonas Hanway, *Solitude in Imprisonment* (London, 1776), 4.

40. *The Universal Magazine*, April 1782, 208.
41. Penitentiary Act of 1779, 19 George III, c. 74.

2 TREASON, TERROR, AND REACTION

1. Henry Clinton, "Manifesto and Proclamation to the Members of Congress," May 1778. Gilder Lehrman Institute of American History, GLC01032.
2. Horace Walpole, *Journal of the Reign of King George the Third* (London, 1859), vol. 2, 253–4, 277, 282, 284, 301, 303.
3. Sancho, *Letters*, vol. 2, 76–7. As quoted in Ian Haywood and John Seed, eds., *The Gordon Riots: Politics and Insurrection in Late Eighteenth-century Britain* (Cambridge, 2014), 2.
4. Haywood and Seed, *The Gordon Riots*, 2.
5. Robert Shoemaker, *The London Mob: Violence and Disorder in Eighteenth-century England* (London, 2007), 120–44; John Stevenson, *Popular Disturbances in England, 1700–1832* (Abingdon, 1992), 81–4.
6. Arthur Cash, *John Wilkes: Scandalous Father of Civil Liberty* (New Haven, 2006), 231–3; *Rivington's Gazetteer*, July 6, 1775.
7. Sancho, *Letters*, vol. 2, 88.
8. Ibid., 149–55.
9. *The Letters of Horace Walpole*, ed. Peter Cunningham (London, 1891), vol. VI, 423; vol. VII, 86.
10. Sancho, *Letters*, vol. 2, 169, 191; Linda Colley, *Britons: Forging the Nation, 1707–1837* (New Haven, 2014), 138–44.
11. *London Public Advertiser*, October 25, 1775; *London Public Advertiser*, October 26, 1775, November 30, 1775; *Pennsylvania Gazette*, January 31, 1776; *Virginia Gazette*, February 10, 1776; *Maryland Gazette*, February 8, 1776; *The Pennsylvania Packet*, January 29, 1776; Horace Walpole, *Journal of the Reign of King George the Third*, vol. I, 508–9; Julie Flavell, *When London Was Capital of America* (New Haven, 2010), 115–62.
12. As with all criminal confessions, John Aitken's account of his life should be taken with a grain of salt. For one, he seems to have been prone to exaggeration and even outright falsehoods. In addition, by 1777, the confessions or last speeches of condemned criminals had become a familiar literary genre, with their own didactic conventions of the wages of sin and the repentant sinner. In such works, the gravity of the crimes only served to heighten the ultimate repentance before the gallows. *The Life of James Aitken Commonly Called John the Painter* (London, 1777).
13. *Maryland Gazette*, July 17, 1777.
14. *The Life of James Aitken*, 17–19.
15. Jessica Warner, *John the Painter: Terrorist of the American Revolution* (London, 2004), 92–6.
16. *Public Advertiser*, March 11, 1777.
17. Cited in William Doyle, *The Oxford History of the French Revolution*, 2nd edn (Oxford, 2003), 63–6; Peter McPhee, *Liberty or Death: The French Revolution* (New Haven, 2017), 37; Simon Schama, *Citizens: A Chronicle of the French Revolution* (New York, 1990), 25.
18. Doyle, *French Revolution*, 66; Laura Auricchio, *The Marquis: Lafayette Reconsidered* (New York, 2014), 28.
19. Doyle, *French Revolution*, 66.
20. Auricchio, *The Marquis*, 29.
21. Ibid., 32–3.
22. Warner, *John the Painter*, 111–15.
23. Thomas Schaeper, *Edward Bancroft: Scientist, Author, Spy* (New Haven, 2012).
24. Ibid.
25. *Maryland Gazette*, July 17, 1777 (reprinted from the *London Evening Post*).
26. Warner, *John the Painter*, 167–75.
27. *Waterford Chronicle*, March 18, 1777; *Public Advertiser*, March 11, 1777; *Maryland Gazette*, June 19, 1777.
28. *Public Advertiser*, March 13, 1777.
29. *Waterford Chronicle*, March 18, 1777. The account of Aitken's passport followed directly a story about the French government's solemn promise not to join the war on either side. The juxtaposition is telling.

30. Ibid.; *Public Advertiser*, March 13, 1777.
31. James Sharpe, "John the Painter: The First Modern Terrorist," *Journal of Forensic Psychiatry and Psychology* 18(2) (2007): 278–81.
32. *London Public Advertiser*, March 8, 1777; *Waterford Chronicle*, March 18, 1777.
33. OBSP, o17770219-1; Paul Halliday, *Habeas Corpus: From England to Empire* (Cambridge, MA, 2010), 249–53.
34. Michael Franklin, *Orientalist Jones: Sir William Jones, Poet, Lawyer, and Linguist, 1746–1794* (Oxford, 2011), 137–8; Halliday, *Habeas Corpus*, 252.
35. Walpole, *Journal of the Reign of King George the Third*, vol. 2, 342–3, 350.
36. T.M. Devine, *Scotland's Empire: The Origins of the Global Diaspora* (London, 2012), 70–3; 171–7.
37. Walpole, *Journal of the Reign of King George the Third*, vol. 2, 297, 303, 337–8; Michael Fry, *A Higher World: Scotland, 1707–1815* (Edinburgh, 2014), 136, 283.
38. Haywood and Seed, *Gordon Riots*, 3.
39. Ibid.
40. Centre for Buckinghamshire Studies, County Hall, Aylesbury, UK, D/LE/F3/33.
41. Haywood and Seed, *Gordon Riots*, 6; Centre for Buckinghamshire Studies, D/LE/F3/33.
42. Sancho, *Letters*, vol. 2, 169–72.
43. Linebaugh, *The London Hanged*, 334–41.
44. Ibid.
45. Ibid., 7–8.
46. Sancho, *Letters*, vol. 2, 179–81.
47. William Hickey, *Memoirs of William Hickey*, ed. Albert Spencer (London, 1919), vol. II, 72, 78, 265; James Harris, *A Series of Letters of the First Earl of Malmesbury* (London, 1870), vol. 1, 462–5.
48. Hickey, *Memoirs*, vol. II, 265.
49. Ibid.; Sancho, *Letters*, vol. 2, 181–9;
50. Linebaugh, *The London Hanged*, 343–54; Nicholas Rogers, "The Gordon Riots and the Politics of War," in Haywood and Seed, *The Gordon Riots*, 21–3.
51. Ibid., 347; Walpole, *Journal of the Reign of King George the Third*, vol. 2, 362.
52. OBSP, t17810711-1.
53. Ibid.
54. Ibid.
55. Ibid.
56. Ibid; Madame d'Auberade, *The Authentic Memoirs of Francis Henry de la Motte* (London, 1784).
57. *Hampshire Chronicle*, August 31, 1782.
58. The official punishment for male traitors since 1351, hanging, drawing, and quartering was officially replaced by hanging and posthumous beheading in 1814. Edward Despard was the last man sentenced to the full punishment when he was charged with treason in 1803, but he was spared the complete ritual and was instead hanged and beheaded. Although his name has been largely forgotten by history, consigned to his fate as one of many who met his end at Tyburn, the trial and execution of François Henri de la Motte long resonated in the minds of Englishmen, first as the arch-fiend and bogeyman, and later as a potent symbol of a brutal and archaic judicial regime. When he wanted to conjure up a trial scene for *A Tale of Two Cities* pervaded by a sense of the inescapable grotesquerie and horror of eighteenth-century justice, Charles Dickens turned to the trial of François Henri de la Motte for a model. Dickens' great contemporary rival, William Makepeace Thackeray, went even further, creating a fictionalized account of the tormented and dolorous life of de la Motte and his partner turned condemner, Henry Lutterloh. Neither work attempts to rehabilitate the spy's image—even fifty years and more after the events a French traitor won little sympathy in Britain—but his legend was reworked to provide a sanguinary lesson on the brutality of English justice and the costs of revolution. Charles Dickens, *Tale of Two Cities*; William Makepeace Thackeray, *Denis Duval*.
59. David Lemmings, *Law and Government in England During the Long Eighteenth Century* (Basingstoke, 2011), 89–92.
60. Ibid., 93.

61. *The Letters of Horace Walople*, vol. VII, 403.
62. Ibid., 112–13; Drew Gray, *Crime, Policing and Punishment in England, 1660–1914* (London, 2016); Stanley Palmer, *Police and Protest in England and Ireland, 1780–1850* (Cambridge, 1988), 73.

3 REVOLUTION, REACTION, AND SECTARIANISM IN IRELAND

1. As quoted in Stephen Brumwell, *Turncoat: Benedicta Arnold and the Crisis of American Liberty* (New Haven, 2018), 217, 220.
2. Sancho, *Letters*, vol. 2, 91–2.
3. Jonah Barrington, *Sketches from his Own Time* (London, 1830), vol. 1, 86–7.
4. *Middlesex Journal*, February 23, 1776. Gay's play, written in 1728, presented a trenchant opposition Whig critique of the ministry of Sir Robert Walpole, so it seems likely that the reference to rebellious Americans in the epilogue was added to calm the concerns of government supporters who may have seen the performance as a veiled attack on the ministry of 1776.
5. Henry Grattan, *Memoirs of the Life and Times of Henry Grattan* (London, 1839), 267–70; Jonah Barrington, *The Rise and Fall of the Irish Nation* (Dublin, 1868); 43; Thomas Bartlett, "Ireland, Empire, and Union, 1690–1801," in Kevin Kenny ed., *Ireland and the British Empire* (Oxford, 2004).
6. Barrington, *Rise and Fall of the Irish Nation*, 43.
7. Grattan, *Memoirs*, 174, 208–9, 268.
8. Thomas Malone, *The Life and Death of Lord Edward Fitzgerald* (London, 1832), 9, 12, 16–17.
9. Barrington, *Rise and Fall of the Irish Nation*, 44.
10. Grattan, *Memoirs*, 342, 347–8.
11. Ibid., 348–9.
12. Barrington, *Sketches from his Own Time*, vol. 1, 86–7.
13. Barrington, *Rise and Fall of the Irish Nation*, 73–4.
14. Grattan, *Memoirs*, 286, 317, 336.
15. Barrington, *Rise and Fall of the Irish Nation*, 77–8.
16. Ibid., 81–2.
17. Ibid., 91.
18. Ibid., 115–20.
19. Ibid., 114, 128, 133.
20. Henry Grattan, *Speeches of the Late Right Honourable Henry Grattan, in the Irish Parliament in 1780 and 1782* (London, 1821), vol. 1, 19.
21. Barrington, *Rise and Fall of the Irish Nation*, 180–3.
22. Grattan, *Speeches*, vol. 1, 4, 10, 18.
23. Christopher Wyvill, *The Secession from Parliament Vindicated* (York, 1799), 8.
24. Paul Langford, *A Polite and Commercial People: England 1727–1783* (Oxford, 1994), 347–9; Frank O'Gorman, *The Long Eighteenth Century* (New York, 1997), 227–31.
25. Christopher Wyvill, *Political Papers* (London, 1794), vol. 3, 47, 70, 76, 115–16, 167.
26. Wyvill, *Political Papers*, vol. 3, 53; Walpole, *Journal*, vol. II, 359–61, 371–8, 384–90.
27. Barrington, *Rise and Fall of the Irish Nation*, 32–3.
28. Ibid., 44–5.
29. Grattan, *Speeches*, vol. 1, 144, 158–9.
30. Ibid., 133–4.
31. Ibid., 133.
32. Ibid., 101–2.
33. Ibid.
34. Thomas Bartlett, *Ireland: A History* (Cambridge, 2010), 178–9.
35. Warden Flood, *Memoirs of Henry Flood* (Dublin, 1844), 144–7.
36. Grattan, *Speeches*, vol. 1, 98–102.
37. Flood, *Memoirs of Henry Flood*, 191, 235–9.
38. Ibid., 176.
39. Ibid., 148, 261.

40. Grattan, *Speeches*, vol. 1, 291–5.
41. Ibid., vol. 2, 2–6.
42. Jonathan Bardon, *A History of Ulster* (Belfast, 1993), 223–5.
43. As quoted in ibid., 226.
44. Malone, *Life and Death of Lord Edward Fitzgerald*, 173.
45. Ibid., 275.
46. Ibid., 28
47. Barrington, *Sketches from his Own Time*, vol. 1, 270–3.
48. Ibid.
49. Ibid., 274–5.
50. Ibid., 276–7.
51. Franklin and Mary Wickwire, *Cornwallis: The Imperial Years* (Chapel Hill, 1980), 243.
52. Linda Colley, *Britons*, 145–52; Eliga Gould, *The Persistence of Empire: British Political Culture in the Age of the American Revolution* (Chapel Hill, 2002).

4 HORATIO NELSON AND THE IMPERIAL STRUGGLE IN SPANISH AMERICA

1. Anon., *The Trial of Edward Marcus Despard for High Treason* (London, 1803), 174–5, 186, 208–9.
2. Peter Linebaugh and Marcus Rediker, *The Many-headed Hydra: The Hidden History of the Revolutionary Atlantic* (London, 2013), 272–81.
3. John Sugden, *Nelson: A Dream of Glory* (London, 2004), 153–72; Benjamin Mosely, *A Treatise on Tropical Diseases* (London, 1789); Thomas Dancer, *A Brief History of the Late Expedition Against Fort San Juan* (London, 1781).
4. Roger Knight, *The Pursuit of Victory: The Life and Achievements of Horatio Nelson* (New York, 2005), 59. In 1792 HMS *Lion* would be the ship that carried Lord Maratney on his famous diplomatic mission to China.
5. Nicholas Harris, ed., *The Dispatches and Letters of Vice Admiral Lord Viscount Nelson*, ed. Nicholas Harris Nicolas (London, 1845), 48.
6. Ibid.
7. Horatio Nelson, *Sketch of my Life*, in *The Dispatches and Letters of Vice Admiral Lord Viscount Nelson*, ed. Nicholas Nicolas, 3; Knight, *Pursuit of Victory*, 28–33.
8. Nelson, *Sketch of My Life*, 1–4.
9. Ibid., 5.
10. Nelson to Captain Maurice Suckling, April 19, 1778, in *Nelson: The New Letters*, ed. Colin White (Woodbridge, 2005), 131–2.
11. Thomas Chavez, *Spain and the Independence of the United States* (Albuquerque, 2002), 23–8.
12. Ibid., 29–32.
13. Ibid., 31.
14. Sam Willis, *The Struggle for Sea Power: A Naval History of the American Revolution* (London, 2016), 252.
15. Ibid., 255–6.
16. Ibid., 255; *Dispatches and Letters of Vice Admiral Lord Viscount Nelson*, 25–26, 34.
17. Nelson, *Sketch of My Life*, 5–7; Knight, *Pursuit of Victory*, 602–3, 663.
18. Sugden, *Nelson: A Dream of Glory*, 143–5; Nelson, *Sketch of My Life*, 6–7.
19. *Dispatches and Letters of Vice Admiral Lord Viscount Nelson*, 31–2.
20. *The Journal of Don Francisco Saavedra de Sangronis*, ed. Francisco Morales Padrón (Gainesville, 1989), xxvii.
21. Ibid., 3–7.
22. Roy Adkins and Lesley Adkins, *Gibraltar: The Greatest Siege in British History* (New York, 2018).
23. Chavez, *Spain and the Independence of the United States*, 170–7; David Narrett, *Adventurism and Empire: The Struggle for Mastery of the Louisiana–Florida Borderland* (Chapel Hill, 2015), 91–109; Kathleen DuVal, *Independence Lost: Lives on the Edge of the American Revolution* (New York, 2015), 135–87; Larrie Ferreiro, *Brothers at Arms: The American Revolution and the Men of France and Spain who Saved It* (New York, 2016), 161–3.

24. Claudio Saunt, *West of Revolution* (New York, 2014), 34–91; Carlos Herrera, *Juan Bautista de Anza: The King's Governor in New Mexico* (Norman, 2015), 60–73.

25. Pekka Hämäläinen, *The Comanche Empire* (New Haven, 2008), 1–3, 68–75.

26. Ibid., 76–7.

27. Ibid., 75–80, 90–9.

28. Moseley, *On Tropical Diseases*, 76–8, 88; *Hartford Courant*, March 30, 1784, 3.

29. Moseley, *On Tropical Diseases*, 77.

30. Sugden, *Nelson: A Dream of Glory*, 136–9.

31. Dancer, *A Brief History*.

32. Ibid., 11.

33. Ibid., 12–13; Anon., *Memoirs of Colonel E.M. Despard* (London, 1803), 3–5: Linebaugh and Rediker, *The Many-headed Hydra*, 248–87.

34. Dancer, *A Brief History*, 14–16; Sugden, *Nelson: A Dream of Glory*, 164–5.

35. Stephen Kemble, *The Kemble Papers* (New York, 1884), vol. 2, 4.

36. Dancer, *A Brief History*, 18–19.

37. *Dispatches and Letters of Vice Admiral Lord Viscount Nelson*, 35; *Kemble Papers* vol. 2, 12–17.

5 REVOLT AND REVOLUTION IN THE SPANISH EMPIRE

1. *The Tupac Amaru and Catarista Rebellions*, ed. Ward Stavig and Ellen Schmidt (Cambridge, 2008), 109–10.

2. Ibid., 3, 9, 11.

3. Ibid.; Charles Walker, *The Tupac Amaru Rebellion* (Cambridge, 2016), 20–2.

4. Allan Kuethe and Kenneth Andrien, *The Spanish Atlantic World in the Eighteenth Century* (Cambridge, 2014), 290–5.

5. Ibid., 231–71; Mark Burkholder, "Spain's America: From Kingdoms to Colonies," *Colonial Latin America Review* 25(2) (2016): 125–53.

6. Walker, *The Tupac Amaru Rebellion*, 5.

7. *The Tupac Amaru and Catarista Rebellions*, 21–2.

8. Ibid., 43–4; Walker, *The Tupac Amaru Rebellion*, 5.

9. Walker, *The Tupac Amaru Rebellion*, 21–2.

10. Ibid., 5–6.

11. *Journal of Don Francisco Saavedra*, xxi–xxii; *The Tupac Amaru and Catarista Rebellions*, 41–2; J.H. Elliott, *Empires of the Atlantic World: Britain and Spain in America* (New Haven, 2007), 251, 357–8.

12. *The Tupac Amaru and Catarista Rebellions*, 61–3.

13. Ibid., 67–71; Bastidas as quoted in Walker, *The Tupac Amaru Rebellion*, 56.

14. *The Tupac Amaru and Catarista Rebellions*, 63, 87; Walker, *The Tupac Amaru Rebellion*, 3–4.

15. Walker, *The Tupac Amaru Rebellion*, 3–4.

16. *The Tupac Amaru and Catarista Rebellions*, 77–9.

17. Ibid., 76–7, 110–13; Walker, *The Tupac Amaru Rebellion*, 43, 55–6, 135.

18. *The Tupac Amaru and Catarista Rebellions*, 110.

19. *The Tupac Amaru and Catarista Rebellions*, 74; Elliott, *Empires of the Atlantic World*, 359–60.

20. Elliott, *Empires of the Atlantic World*, 359–60.

21. *The Tupac Amaru and Catarista Rebellions*, 119–21.

22. Ibid., 93, 122–7.

23. Ibid., 139–40.

24. Sergio Serulnikov, *Revolution in the Andes: The Age of Tupac Amaru* (Durham, NC, 2013), 107–33; Nicholas Robins, *Genocide and Millennialism in Upper Peru: The Great Rebellion of 1780–1782* (Westport, CT, 2002).

25. Elliott, *Empires of the Atlantic World*, 361–2; John Phelan, *The People and the King: The Comunero Revolution in Colombia, 1781* (Madison, WI, 1978).

26. Elliott, *Empires of the Atlantic World*, 362.

27. *Hartford Courant*, March 30, 1784, 3; *Kemble Papers*, vol. 2, 13–15.

28. *Kemble Papers*, vol. 2, 7.

29. Ibid., 36.

30. Ibid., 31–57; Mosely, *On Tropical Diseases*, 88–90; Sugden, *Nelson: Dream of Glory*, 173.
31. Sugden, *Nelson: Dream of Glory*, 173; Nelson, *Sketch of My Life*, 7–8, note 5.
32. Andrew Jackson O'Shaughnessy, *An Empire Divided: The American Revolution and the British Caribbean* (Philadelphia, 2000), 239–41.
33. Ibid.; Knight, *The Pursuit of Victory*, 565–9.
34. Conde de Aranda, *On the Independence of the Colonies* (1783) in Jon Cowans, ed., *Early Modern Spain: A Documentary History* (Philadelphia, 2003), 234–7.
35. As quoted in Elliott, *Empires of the Atlantic World*, 367.
36. Kuethe and Andrien, *The Spanish Atlantic World*, 271–335.
37. Ibid.
38. Aranda, *On the Independence of the Colonies*.
39. Ibid., 368.
40. *The Tupac Amaru and Catarista Rebellions*, 166–7.

6 EUROPEAN WEAKNESS AND THE RUSSIAN CONQUEST OF THE CRIMEA

1. Neil Kent, *Crimea: A History* (London, 2017), 22–30.
2. Ibid.; Serii Plokhy, *Lost Kingdom: The Quest for Empire and the Making of the Russian Nation* (New York, 2017), 3–5.
3. As quoted in Jonathan Miles, *St. Petersburg: Three Centuries of Murderous Desire* (London, 2017), 127.
4. H. Arnold Barton, *Scandinavia in the Revolutionary Era* (Minneapolis, 1986), 107–8, 121.
5. Ibid., 114–15.
6. Ibid., 114–17.
7. W.P. Cresson, *Francis Dana: A Puritan Diplomat at the Court of Catherine the Great* (New York, 1930), 105–6; Isabel de Madariaga, *Britain, Russia, and the Armed Neutrality of 1780* (New Haven, 1962). The authenticity of Sayre's account is undermined by the fact that his claims were made years later in an attempt to receive financial compensation from the U.S. government for services to diplomacy. Whatever his actual role, he was certainly present in Copenhagen in 1778, almost certainly in the service of Vergennes as his role was not recognized or encouraged by American diplomats in Europe.
8. Cresson, *Francis Dana*, 14–20.
9. Ibid., 24–5.
10. Ibid., 39–41.
11. Ibid., 53–5.
12. *Revolutionary Diplomatic Correspondence of the United States* (*RDCUS*) (Washington, DC, 1888, online), vol. 4, December 19, 1780, 201–3.
13. Cresson, *Francis Dana*, 159–63.
14. *RDCUS*, vol. 4, Francis Dana to the President of Congress, July 28, 1781, 610–11.
15. Ibid., vol. 2, Arthur Lee to the Committee on Foreign Affairs, June 11, 1777, 335; Bruce Burgoyne, ed., *Enemy Views: The American Revolutionary War as Recorded by the Hessian Participants* (Westminster, MD, 1996), 548.
16. Charles Ingrao, *The Hessian Mercenary State: Ideas, Institutions and Reform under Frederick II, 1760–1785* (Cambridge, 1987), 122–37.
17. Ibid., 132.
18. Ibid., 57–95.
19. Rudiger Safranski, *Goethe: Life as a Work of Art* (New York, 2017), 212–15. Goethe's *Iphigenia in Tharsis*, written in the same period as the negotiations with Prussia, is at some level a meditation on the intersection of sovereignty and purity or peace. Unlike its Greek namesake, Goethe's *Iphigenia* focuses on the titular character's attempts to secure her release from a barbarian king whom she serves as priestess, without having to sacrifice the man she comes to find is her brother. This attempt to secure freedom or autonomy without necessitating bloodshed mirrors Weimar's position in 1778–9, when Weimar hoped to maintain its independence from Prussia while still remaining neutral in the coming war.
20. Ibid., 1, 139.
21. Ingrao, *The Hessian Mercenary State*, 142.

22. Ibid., 144, 151.
23. Burgoyne, ed., *Enemy Views*, 8.
24. *Constitutional Gazette,* April 20, 1776; *Pennsylvania Evening Post*, September 14, 1776, March 8, 1777; *Freeman's Journal*, November 12, 1776, February 18, 1777, March 22, 1777.
25. *Pennsylvania Evening Post*, June 1, 1776; *Freeman's Journal*, July 27, October 29, 1776, April 12, 1777.
26. Burgoyne, ed., *Enemy Views*, 527–8, 530–1, 587–8.
27. Ingrao, *The Hessian Military State*, 157–8.
28. Burgoyne, ed., *Enemy Views*, 549.
29. Ingrao, *The Hessian Military State*, 145–50.
30. *RDCUS*, vol. 4, Dana to the President of Congress, July 28, 1781, 610–11.
31. Isabel de Madariaga, *Catherine the Great* (New Haven, 2002), 1–24; Miles, *St. Petersburg*, 133–4.
32. Miles, *St. Petersburg*, 130–6, 139–40.
33. Ibid., 126–7, 130, 140.
34. Cresson, *Francis Dana*, 179; Madariaga, *Britain, Russia, and the Armed Neutrality*.
35. Cresson, *Francis Dana*, 108.
36. Miles, *St. Petersburg*, 171–3; Daniel Beer, *The House of the Dead: Siberian Exile Under the Tsars* (New York, 2016), 21–7.
37. *A Series of Letters of the First Earl of Malmesbury* (London, 1870), 351–483; Madariaga, *Britain, Russia, and the Armed Neutrality*, 3–4, 20, 202–9.
38. Madariaga, *Britain, Russia, and the Armed Neutrality*, 241.
39. *RDCUS*, vol. 5, Dana to Livingston, March 5, 1782, 223–4.
40. William Wraxall as quoted in Richard Bassett, *For God and Kaiser: The Imperial Austria Army* (London, 2015), 175; Virginia H. Aksan, *Ottoman Wars 1700–1870: An Empire Besieged* (New York, 2013), 137.
41. Bassett, *For God and Kaiser*, 176; Aksan, *Ottoman Wars*, 137–8.
42. *Love and Conquest: Personal Correspondence of Catherine the Great and Prince Grigory Potemkin*, ed. Douglas Smith (DeKalb, 2004), 256, 257.
43. Ibid., 259.
44. Ibid., 260, 262, 262, 263, 266.
45. *Diaries and Correspondence of the Earl of Malmesbury* (London, 1844), 1–29; Cresson, *Francis Dana*, 274–5.
46. *RDCUS*, vol. 4, March 30, 1782; October 14, 1782; January 15, 1783; February 10, 1783; May 30, 1783; July 8, 1783. Cresson, *Francis Dana*, 273–4.
47. Suraiya Faroqhi, *Subjects of the Sultan* (London, 2005), 225–8; Abbas Amanat, *Iran: A Modern History* (New Haven, 2017), 153–62.
48. *Love and Conquest*, 266, 267, 268, 274.
49. Ibid., 286.
50. Ibid., 280.
51. Kent, *Crimea*, 54–5.
52. *Love and Conquest*, 280; Plokhy, *Lost Kingdom*, 48–50.
53. Kent, *Crimea*, 52–3.
54. Ibid., 53–5.
55. *Love and Conquest*, 282.
56. Cresson, *Francis Dana*, 265.
57. Ibid., 281, 288, 298–318.
58. Plokhy, *Lost Kingdom*, 11–15; Kent, *Crimea*, 55; Paul Robert Magocsi, *The Blessed Land: Crimea and the Crimean Tatars* (Toronto, 2014), 55–6.
59. Doyle, *French Revolution*, 67–8; McPhee, *Liberty or Death*; Schama, *Citizens*.
60. Doyle, *French Revolution*, 32; Schama, *Citizens*, 55–60.
61. Peter Hill, *French Perceptions of the Early American Republic, 1783–1793* (Philadelphia, 1988), 45.
62. Ibid., 22, 173–4.
63. Ibid., 45–7, 172–4.
64. Barton, *Scandinavia*, 123.

65. Ibid., 135–8.
66. Ibid., 153.
67. Franklin D. Scott, *Sweden: The Nation's History* (Carbondale, 1988), 270–5.
68. Barton, *Scandinavia*, 157.
69. Ali Yaycioglu, *Partners of the Empire: The Crisis of the Ottoman Order in the Age of Revolutions* (Stanford, 2016), 37–8.
70. Madariaga, *Britain, Russia, and the Armed Neutrality*, 387–412, 447–58.
71. Ibid.

7 CONFLICT AND CAPTIVITY IN INDIA

1. William Hodges, *Travels in India during the years 1780, 1781, 1782 and 1783* (London, 1783).
2. As quoted in John Keay, *India: A History* (London, 2010), 370.
3. Eliza Fay, *Original Letters from India*, ed. E.M. Forster (New York, 2010), 110.
4. Ibid., 31–47. Despite her "great pleasure" as an "Englishwoman" in seeing the council chamber where the peace was signed, Fay was mistaken about which treaty was signed at Fontainebleau. The Treaty of Fontainebleau, which was signed a year before the Treaty of Paris officially ended hostilities in 1763, was a secret arrangement between France and Spain to cede Louisiana to the Spanish. Fay's patriotic sentiment, however, seems entirely genuine.
5. Ibid., 51–7.
6. Philip Mazzei, *Philip Mazzei, Virginia's Agent in Europe: The Story of his Mission as Related in His own Dispatches and other Documents*, ed. Howard Arraro (New York, 1935), 4–15.
7. Thomas Madden, *Venice: A New History* (New York, 2012), 354–63.
8. Fay, *Original Letters from India*, 76–7.
9. Ibid., 83–7.
10. Ibid., 101.
11. Ibid., 105–7.
12. Ibid., 109–11.
13. Ibid., 111–12.
14. The tension on board the *Nathalia* had become so intense that Captain Chenu and Hare had twice agreed to duel, only for the matter to be settled peacefully by the timely intervention of other passengers. Other duels between Englishmen were also reported at the Danish factory in Calicut.
15. Fay, *Original Letters from India*, 117.
16. Ibid., 118.
17. Ibid., 115.
18. Ibid., 116.
19. Ibid., 120, 122, 142, 144.
20. William Dalrymple, *White Mughals: Love and Betrayal in Eighteenth-century India* (London, 2002), 14–16, 24–25; Shelford Bidwell, *Swords for Hire: European Mercenaries in Eighteenth Century India* (London, 1971).
21. Dalrymple, *White Mughals*, 32–3.
22. George Thomas, *Military Memoirs of George Thomas* (London, 1805).
23. 18 George III, c. 53; 19 George III, c. 10.
24. OBSP, t17820109-23, 34, 51, 1.
25. Ibid., t1775101804.
26. Denver Brunsman, *The Evil Necessity: British Naval Impressment in the Eighteenth Century Atlantic World* (Charlottesville, 2013), 2–8; 18 George III, c. 53.
27. OBSP, t17890422-13, t17950916-50. See also: t17870523-98; t17720219-58; t17720219-1; t17790113-6; t177910216-2.
28. Fay, *Original Letters from India*, 120.
29. Ibid., 149.
30. Ibid., 144.
31. Ibid., 152.
32. The decision to target Vandavasi was full of meaning for the French, who, under the ill-fated Thomas Lally, had lost the city to Sir Eyre Coote and the British in 1760. Lally would later be

executed in Paris as a scapegoat for the failures of the French in India during the Seven Years' War.

33. As quoted in, William Dalrymple, "An Essay in Imperial Villain-Making," *Guardian*, May 23, 2005.

34. James Scurry, *The Captivity, Suffering and Escape of James Scurry* (London, 1824), 108.

35. Philip Freneau, "Barney's Invitation," in *The Poems of Philip Freneau: Poet of the American Revolution* (State College, PA, 1902); Jonathan Eacott, *Selling Empire: India in the Making of Britain and America, 1600–1800* (Chapel Hill, 2016), 317.

36. Linda Colley, *Captives: Britain, Empire and the World, 1600–1850* (London, 2002), 276–282; Irfan Habib, "Introduction: An Essay on Haidar Ali and Tipu Sultan," in Irfan Habib, ed., *Confronting Colonialism: Resistance and Modernisation under Haidar Ali and Tipu Sultan* (London, 2002), xxii.

37. Colley, *Captives*, 288.

38. Habib, "Introduction: An Essay on Haidar Ali and Tipu Sultan," xx–xxxi.

39. Scurry, *Captivity*, 103–5.

40. *The Letters of Tipoo Sultan to Various Public Functionaries*, ed. William Fitzpatrick (London, 1811), 59.

41. Kranti K. Farias, *The Christian Impact in South Kanara* (Mumbai, 1999), 74.

42. *Letters of Tipoo Sultan*, 228.

43. Ibid., 242, 256, 381, 390, 433, 438.

44. Habib, *Confronting Colonialism*, 135.

45. Ibid.

46. *Letters of Tipoo Sultan*, 57–9, 229.

47. Habib, "Introduction: An Essay on Haidar Ali and Tipu Sultan," xxv.

48. Dalrymple, *White Mughal*, 84–8. The major exception to the general religious tolerance, if not harmony, was the reign of the Mughal Emperor Aurangzeb (r. 1658–1707), whose persecution of non-Muslims is notorious to this day. Even so, Aurangzeb's religious violence was largely directed toward the physical symbols of religion, Hindu temples for instance, rather than the believers themselves.

49. Hodges, *Travels in India*, 5–7.

50. As quoted in Mohibbul Hasan, "The French in the Second Anglo-Mysore War," in Habib, ed., *Confronting Colonialism*, 43.

51. *Letters of Tipoo Sultan*, 13, 91.

52. Colley, *Captives*, 262, 271.

53. Ibid., 43–5.

54. Kaushik Roy, *War, Culture and Society in Early Modern South Asia, 1740–1849* (Abingdon, 2011), 70–87; Habib, "Introduction: An Essay on Haidar Ali and Tipu Sultan."

8 THE BIRTH OF BRITISH INDIA

1. Fay, *Letters from India*, 171–2.

2. Michael Fisher, ed., *The Travels of Dean Mahomet* (Berkeley, 1997), 15–17, 35–7.

3. Ibid., 13.

4. Ibid., 36.

5. Ibid., 38–42.

6. H.H. Dodwell, *The Cambridge History of the British Empire* (Cambridge, 1929), 295–8.

7. Warren Hastings, *A Narrative of the Insurrection that Happened in the Zamindary of Benares* (Calcutta, 1782), 27.

8. Fisher, ed., *Travels of Dean Mahomet*, 120.

9. Hodges, *Travels in India*, 49–50.

10. Ibid., 50–1; Fisher, ed., *Travels of Dean Mahomet*, 115–17.

11. Fisher, ed., *Travels of Dean Mahomet*, 117.

12. Nicholas Dirks, *The Scandal of Empire: India and the Creation of Imperial Britain* (Cambridge, 2008), 19–20, 100–19.

13. Ibid.

14. Fisher, ed., *Travels of Dean Mahomet*, 121–3.

15. Hodges, *Travels in India*, 49.
16. John Keay, *The Honourable Company: A History of the English East India Company* (London, 1993), 366.
17. Ibid., 362; P.J. Marshall, "Hastings, Warren (1732–1818)," *Oxford Dictionary of National Biography* (Oxford, 2004; online edn, Oct. 2008).
18. Ibid.
19. Ibid.
20. Ibid.
21. Seema Alavi, ed., *The Eighteenth Century in India* (Oxford, 2008), 11–12, 20–1; Habib, *Confronting Colonialism*, xxi.
22. Marshall, "Hastings, Warren (1732–1818)"; Michael Franklin, *Orientalist Jones*, 212–15, 351. As we have seen previously, Hastings' genuine attempts to understand and textualize Indian religion, law, and culture had the unintended effect of helping to harden the lines between Hindu and Muslim, undermining the very syncretism he so admired and so ardently wished to cultivate.
23. John Cannon, "Francis, Sir Philip (1740–1818)," *Oxford Dictionary of National Biography* (Oxford, 2004).
24. Henry Elmsley Busteed, *Echoes from Old Calcutta* (Calcutta, 1882), 171.
25. Franklin, *Orientalist Jones*, 163.
26. Keay, *The Honourable Company*, 362–4.
27. 24 George III, c. 25.
28. Dirks, *Scandal of Empire*, 105.
29. Ibid., 87, 117; Marshall, "Hastings, Warren (1732–1818)."
30. Dirks, *Scandal of Empire*, 121.
31. Jon Wilson, *India Conquered: Britain's Raj and the Chaos of Empire* (London, 2016), 121–34; P.J. Marshall, *The Making and Unmaking of Empires* (New York, 2005), 207–2, 355–70.
32. Alexander Baillie, *Call of Empire: From Highlands to Hindostan* (Montreal, 2017), 86–7; Halliday, *Habeas Corpus*, 288–90.
33. Ibid.; Alavi, *The Eighteenth Century in India*, 24.
34. Wickwire and Wickwire, *Cornwallis*, 89.
35. Marshall, "Hastings, Warren (1732–1818)"; Franklin, *Orientalist Jones*, 299–308.
36. Centre for Buckinghamshire Studies, D-MH/H (India)/A/E6. Lord Hobart (Earl of Buckinghamshire) had begun the American War as Lord Lieutenant of Ireland, was Governor of Madras from 1793 to 1798, and later held the post of Secretary of State for War and the Colonies and President of the Board of Control.
37. Marshall, "Hastings, Warren (1732–1818)"; Franklin, *Orientalist Jones*, 309–10. When he received a copy of the draft of Cornwallis's Permanent Settlement, William Jones crossed out the first sentence and wrote instead, "Surely the principal object of every Government is the happiness of the governed," a sentiment with which Hastings would have agreed and that nicely sums up the difference in approach between Hastings and Cornwallis.
38. Roy, *War, Culture and Society*, 87–9.
39. C.A. Bayly, *Indian Society and the Making of the British Empire* (Cambridge, 1988), 97; Roy, *War, Culture and Society*, 87–9; Habib, *Confronting Colonialism*, xxx–xxxi, xxxvii, 35; Colley, *Captives*, 274, 296; Keay, *India*, 397–9.
40. Habib, *Confronting Colonialism*, xxxvii; Keay, *India*, 399–400.
41. Keay, *India*, 400–1; Habib, *Confronting Colonialism*, xxxii, xxxvii.
42. Roy, *War, Culture and Society*, 129–30.
43. Francis Buchanan, *A Journey from Madras through the Countries of Mysore, Canara and Malabar* (London, 1807); Kranti Farias, *The Christian Impact in South Kanara* (Mumbai, 1999), 84–6.
44. Fay, *Letters from India*, 187–92.
45. Ibid., 214–23.
46. Fisher, ed., *Travels of Dean Mahomet*, 26–7.
47. Ibid., 124–35.
48. Ibid., 135–44.
49. Ibid., 145–78.

9 CONVICT EMPIRE

1. Jack Brook, "The Forlorn Hope: Bennelong and Yemmerrawannie go to England," *Australian Aboriginal Studies* 2001 (spring): 36–47.
2. Ibid.
3. Ibid.
4. Ibid.
5. OBSP, t17850914-181.
6. 16 George III, c. 43. See also Marilyn Baseler, *Asylum for Mankind: America 1607–1800* (Ithaca, 1998), 125–6.
7. As quoted in, Hitchcock and Shoemaker, *London Lives*, 334.
8. Ibid., 334–40.
9. *The Scots Magazine*, December 1785, 614.
10. A. Roger Ekirch, "Great Britain's Secret Convict Trade to America, 1783–1784," *American Historical Review* 89(5) (December 1984): 1285–91. The ship tried to land its felons at Honduras as well but was similarly rebuffed.
11. OBSP, o17870110-1;o17870110-2.
12. Paul Fidlon and R.J. Ryan, eds, *The Journal of Arthur Bowes-Smyth: Surgeon, Lady Penrhyn, 1787–1789* (Sydney, 1979), 43.
13. Ibid.
14. *The Nagle Journal: A Diary of the Life of Jacob Nagle, Sailor, from the Year 1775 to 1841*, ed. John Dann (New York, 1988), 85–6.
15. Ibid., 87–91.
16. Ibid., 5–15.
17. Ibid., 46–67.
18. OBSP, t17820703-5; Hitchcock and Shoemaker, *London Lives*, 355; *The Nagle Journal*, 84; Tom Keneally, *The Commonwealth of Thieves: The Story of the Founding of Australia* (London, 2006), 65.
19. Keneally, *Commonwealth of Thieves*, 19.
20. George Worgan, *Journal of a First Fleet Surgeon* (Sydney, 1978), 5.
21. Fidlon and Ryan, eds, *The Journal of Arthur Bowes-Smyth*, 53.
22. *The Nagle Journal*, 95.
23. Although it has become widely associated with him, Rousseau never used the term "noble savage." The term was coined in 1672 by John Dryden in his play *The Conquest of Granada*, but the idea of primitive men free from the trivial concerns and vices of modern life was ubiquitous in the early modern period, running through the works of Alexander Pope, Tobias Smollett, and Benjamin Franklin to name just a few.
24. Worgan, *Journal of a First Fleet Surgeon*, 8–13.
25. *The Nagle Journal*, 99.
26. Watkin Tench, *A Complete Account of the Settlement at Port Jackson* (London, 1793), 9.
27. Ibid., 9–10.
28. Ibid., 10–12.
29. Ibid.
30. *The Nagle Journal*, 109–10.
31. Ibid., 111, 360.
32. *The Nagle Journal*, 111.
33. Ibid., 111, 360; Tench, *Complete Account*, 33.
34. Tench, *Complete Account*, 33.
35. Ibid., 19.
36. Ibid., 20.
37. Ibid., 23.
38. Craig Mear, "The Origin of the Smallpox Outbreak at Sydney in 1789," *Journal of the Royal Australian Historical Society* 94(1) (June 2008): 1–22.
39. Ibid.; Christopher Warren, "Could First Fleet Smallpox Infect Aborigines?" *Aboriginal History* 31 (2007): 152–64.

40. Tench, *Complete Account*, 24.
41. *The Nagle Journal*, 104.
42. Ibid.
43. Tench, *Complete Account*, 43.
44. Ibid., 59.
45. Ibid.
46. *The Nagle Journal*, 104.
47. Ibid., 104–5.
48. Tench, *Complete Account*, 61.
49. Ibid.
50. Ibid., 63. It is clear from his later accounts that Tench's statement is meant to foreshadow future, less flattering descriptions of Barangaroo's character, and thus his suggestion that we ought not to judge a person or civilization on their first appearance takes on a less positive aspect.
51. Ibid., 65.
52. Ibid., 111.
53. Ibid., 59.
54. Kate Vincent Smith, "Bennelong Among His People," *Aboriginal History* 33 (2009): 19–22.
55. *Sydney Gazette and New South Wales Advertiser*, January 9, 1813.
56. George Rudé, *Protest and Punishment: The Story of the Social and Political Protestors Transported to Australia* (Oxford, 1979); Jack Brook, "The Forlorn Hope: Bennelong and Yammerrawannie Go to England," *Australian Aboriginal Studies* 1 (2001): 36–47.

10 EXILES OF REVOLUTION

1. *Manchester Mercury*, April 19, 1785; Cassandra Pybus, *Epic Journeys of Freedom: Runaway Slaves of the American Revolution and their Global Quest for Liberty* (Boston, 2007), 29, 69, 95.
2. For the most complete account of the Black loyalist diaspora see: Schama, *Rough Crossings*.
3. Boston King, "Memoirs of the Life of Boston King," in *Unchained Voices: An Anthology of Black Authors in the English-Speaking World of the 18th Century*, ed. Vincent Carretta (Lexington, 2004), 351–2; Schama, *Rough Crossings*, 106–10.
4. Douglas Egerton, *Death or Liberty: African Americans and the American Revolution* (New York, 2011), 47–9.
5. Ibid., 50.
6. William Ryan, *The World of Thomas Jeremiah: Charleston on the Eve of the American Revolution* (New York, 2012), 51.
7. Ibid., 40–9.
8. Ibid., 40, 50, 157.
9. Ibid., 68, 161–9.
10. Ryan, *Thomas Jeremiah*, 18; Egerton, *Death or Liberty*, 70–2; Pybus, *Epic Journeys*, 9.
11. Egerton, *Death or Liberty*, 86; Pybus, *Epic Journeys*, 17–19.
12. Ryan, *Thomas Jeremiah*, 11–24.
13. King, *Memoirs*, 352–3.
14. Ibid., 353–5.
15. Pybus, *Epic Journeys*, 59.
16. Egerton, *Death or Liberty*, 200–2; James Corbett David, *Dunmore's New World* (Charlottesville, 2013).
17. King, *Memoirs*, 355.
18. Ruma Chopra, *Choosing Sides: Loyalists in Revolutionary America* (New York, 2013), 167.
19. King, *Memoirs*, 356; John Fitzpatrick, ed., *The Writings of George Washington from the Original Manuscript Sources* (Washington, DC, 1938), vol. 26, 364–5; Pybus, *Epic Journeys*, 63.
20. Fitzpatrick, *The Writings of George Washington*, vol. 26, 402–6.
21. Graham Russell Hodges, *The Black Loyalist Directory* (New York, 1996).
22. Jasanoff, *Liberty's Exiles*, 6.
23. John Dunmore, *Where Fate Beckons: The Life of Jean-François de la Pérouse* (Fairbanks, 2007),

155–7.

24. King, *Memoirs*, 356.
25. James Walker, *The Black Loyalists: The Search for the Promised Land in Nova Scotia and Sierra Leone* (Toronto, 1993), 18–20; Jasanoff, *Liberty's Exiles*, 147–209; Schama, *Rough Crossings*, 221–55.
26. King, *Memoirs*, 360.
27. John Clarkson, *Mission to America*, 66–7, in New York Historical Society Digital Collections, nyhs_jc_v-01_00a.jpg..
28. Ibid.
29. Walker, *Black Loyalists*, 50–1.
30. Ibid., 48–9.
31. David George, *An Account of the Life of David George* (London, 1793); George Liele, *An Account of several Baptist Churches* (London, 1793).
32. Liele, *An Account of several Baptist Churches*; George, *Life of Mr. David George*; King, *Memoirs*, 357–363; Egerton, *Death or Liberty*, 208.

11 AFRICA, ABOLITION, AND EMPIRE

1. Clarkson, *Mission to America*, 15–17.
2. Sancho, *Letters*, vol. 1, 39, 158–9.
3. James Walvin, *The Zong* (New Haven, 2011), 67–70.
4. Ibid., 92–9.
5. Ibid., 211–12.
6. Ibid., 159.
7. National Archive, AO 13/79/774; AO 12/99/357.
8. *London Lives*, t17830910-31; Jasanoff, *Liberty's Exiles*, 113–45.
9. *The Times*, November 14, 1786.
10. Christopher Leslie Brown, *Moral Capital* (Chapel Hill, 2006), 26–7; Kenneth Morgan, *Slavery and the British Empire* (Oxford, 2008), 157; Richard Huzzey, *Freedom Burning: Anti-Slavery and Empire in Victorian Britain* (Ithaca, 2012); Andrew Jackson O'Shaughnessy, *An Empire Divided: The American Revolution and the British Caribbean* (Philadelphia, 2000), 240.
11. James Walvin, *England, Slaves, and Freedom, 1776–1838* (London, 1986), 106–8, 123–43; Adam Hochschild, *Bury the Chains* (New York, 2005), 154–5.
12. Morgan, *Slavery and the British Empire*, 157; London Lives Database, LMSMPS508910013.
13. *Public Advertiser*, January 6, 1786; Walker, *Black Loyalists*, 96.
14. Walker, *Black Loyalists*, 97–8.
15. Ibid., 99; Simon Schama, *Rough Crossings*, 321–97; Jasanoff, *Liberty's Exiles*, 279–309.
16. *The Times*, October 27, 1791.
17. Ulbe Bosma, *The Sugar Plantation in India and Indonesia* (Cambridge, 2013), 44–52.
18. Sancho, *Letters*, vol. 1, 189.
19. Walker, *Black Loyalists*, 103–4.
20. Clarkson, *Mission to America*, 5–10.
21. Ibid.
22. Ibid., 1, 8–10, 26.
23. King, *Memoirs*, 359, 363; Clarkson, *Mission to America*, 30–3; Walker, *Black Loyalists*, 117.
24. Clarkson, *Mission to America*, 35.
25. Ibid.
26. Anna Maria Falconbridge, *Two Voyages to Sierra Leone During the Years 1791–2–3* (London, 1794), 18–19, 42, 49, 51, 74–5.
27. King, *Memoirs*, 364.
28. Falconbridge, *Two Voyages*, 64.
29. King, *Memoirs*, 364.
30. Ibid.

31. Anon., *An Account of the Colony of Sierra Leone* (London, 1795), 107–8.
32. *Our Children Free and Happy: Letters from Black Settlers in Africa in the 1790s*, ed. Christopher Fyfe (Edinburgh, 1991), 37.
33. Anon., *An Account of the Colony of Sierra Leone*, 96–7, 103–4.
34. Ibid., 105–6.
35. Ibid., 99–100, 112–13.
36. Zachary Macaulay, *Life and Letters of Zachary Macaulay* (London, 1900), 87–9, 176, 212, 215.
37. Ibid., 133–4.
38. Ibid., 127, 140, 165, 188–9.
39. Ibid., 29, 34.
40. Ibid., 26–7.
41. Ibid., 43.
42. Ibid., 47.
43. Ibid., 29, 214.
44. Fyfe, *Our Children*, 29, 30–2; Jasanoff, *Liberty's Exiles*, 11–12; 279–309.
45. Fyfe, *Our Children*, 25–7.
46. Ibid., 29–32.
47. Ibid., 35–7, 43, 48, 51.
48. Anon., *An Account of the Colony of Sierra Leone*, 29–32, 81.
49. Ibid., 85–7.
50. Ibid., 88–9.
51. King, *Memoir*, 365–6.
52. Fyfe, *Our Children*, 56–7.
53. King, *Memoir*, 365–6; Fyfe, *Our Children*, 54–6.
54. Fyfe, *Our Children*, 63–4.
55. Ruma Chopra, *Almost Home: Maroons between Slavery and Freedom in Jamaica, Nova Scotia, and Sierra Leone* (New Haven, 2018).

12 OPIUM AND EMPIRE

1. John Barrow, *A Voyage to Cochinchina, in the Years 1792 and 1793* (London, 1806), 63–4.
2. Jonathan Spence, *In Search of Modern China* (New York, 1990), 132–4; Jürgen Osterhammel, *Unfabling the East: The Enlightenment Encounter with Asia* (Princeton, 2018), 1–33; Stephen Platt, *Imperial Twilight: The Opium War and the End of China's Last Golden Age* (New York, 2018), xxv–xxvi.
3. Spence, *In Search*, 120–1.
4. H.V. Bowen, *The Business of Empire* (Cambridge, 2006), 239–49; Stephen Conway, *The British Isles and the American War of Independence* (Oxford, 2000), 63–4; Spence, *In Search*, 129.
5. Spence, *In Search*, 130–1; Hunt Janin, *The India–China Opium Trade in the Nineteenth Century* (London, 1999), 31–40.
6. Helen Robbins, *Our First Ambassador to China: An Account of the Life and Correspondence of George, Earl of Macartney* (New York, 1908), 13–17.
7. John Barrow, *Narrative of the Public Life of Lord Macartney* (London, 1807), vol. 1, 230–1, 342–3; George Staunton, *An Authentic Account of an Embassy from the King of Great Britain to the Emperor of China* (London, 1797).
8. John Barrow, *An Auto-Biographical Memoir of Sir John Barrow* (London, 1843), 1–43.
9. Barrow, *A Voyage to Cochinchina*, 2.
10. Ibid., 28.
11. Ibid., 41–5.
12. Ibid., 66.
13. Ibid., 75–6.
14. Ibid., 110–15.
15. Ibid., 116–18.
16. Ibid., 118–19.
17. Ibid., 158–64.

18. Ibid., 169.
19. Friedrich Edler, *The Dutch Republic and the American Revolution* (Baltimore, 1911), 238–46. Samuel Shaw, *The Journals of Major Samuel Shaw* (Boston, 1847) 260–1, 290.
20. Barrow, *A Voyage to Cochinchina*, 169–79.
21. Ibid., 174.
22. Ibid., 203.
23. Aeneas Anderson, *A Narrative of the British Embassy to China* (London, 1795), 43–4.
24. Ben Kiernan, *Việt Nam: A History from Earliest Times to the Present* (Oxford, 2017), 221–80; Spence, *In Search*, 111.
25. Spence, *In Search*, 336–7; Lord Macartney, *An Embassy to China*, ed. J.L. Cranmer-Byng (London, 2004), 3–4.
26. Keay, *The Honourable Company*, 425–9.
27. Kiernan, *Việt Nam*, 256–95.
28. Macartney, *An Embassy to China*, 5.
29. Ibid., 4–5; John Barrow, *Travels in China* (London, 1805), 22.
30. Macartney, *An Embassy to China*, 6–7; Barrow, *Travels in China*, 36–9.
31. Macartney, *An Embassy to China*, 12, 266 n. 3; Barrow, *Travels in China*, 47.
32. Macartney, *An Embassy to China*, 14–31; Barrow, *Travels in China*, 45–46.
33. Ibid., 15–16. The line is from Shakespeare's *The Tempest*.
34. Macartney, *An Embassy to China*, 20; Barrow, *Travels in China*, 47–51. Even the practice of foot-binding, which so fascinated and repelled European visitors, was excused by an interesting exercise in moral relativism. Barrow thought the practice appalling, but suggested that rather than hold it against the Chinese, one should remember that the practice of circumcision prevalent in Europe would be sure to shock the hypothetical Chinese traveller.
35. Ibid., 268, n. 6.
36. Macartney, *An Embassy to China*, 23–35.
37. Ibid., 37–50.

13 THE DAWN OF THE CENTURY OF HUMILIATION

1. Anderson, *A Narrative*, 262.
2. Mark Elliott, *Emperor Qianlong: Son of Heaven, Man of the World* (London, 2009), 1–25.
3. Ibid., 25–33, 68–106; Peter Perdue, *China Marches West: The Qing Conquest of Central Eurasia* (Cambridge, 2010), 256–92, 409–57; Spence, *In Search*, 97–8.
4. Barrow, *A Voyage to Cochinchina*, 216–21; Joanna Waley-Cohen, *The Sextants of Beijing: Global Currents in Chinese History* (New York, 2000), 93, 97.
5. George Bogle had been sent to Tibet in 1774, and Samuel Turner in 1782. Kate Teltscher, *The High Road to China: George Bogle, the Panchen Lama and the First British Expedition to Tibet* (London, 2006); Macartney, *An Embassy to China*, 30, 46, 275 n. 24.
6. Shaw, *Journals*, 186–95; Waley-Cohen, *Sextants*, 100–1; Spence, *In Search*, 127.
7. Macartney, *An Embassy to China*, 33, 58.
8. Anderson, *A Narrative*, 262. Macartney, *An Embassy to China*, 65–73. Staunton chose to wear his Oxford gown, making the meeting perhaps the most august assembly ever graced by academic robes.
9. Spence, *In Search*, 110–12. Platt, *Imperial Twilight*, 49–70.
10. Ibid., 93–5, 114.
11. Macartney, *An Embassy to China*, 165. Though he was in agreement with the general sentiment of Chinese stubbornness, Barrow was clear that the failure to kow tow had nothing to do with the failure of the mission. As he mentioned, a subsequent Dutch embassy to Peking agreed to perform all of the required rituals and was still treated even worse than the British had been. Barrow, *Travels in China*, 1–16.
12. Barrow, *Travels in China*, 79–80.
13. Ibid., 330–53.
14. Ibid., 358–68.
15. Macartney, *An Embassy to China*, 154–60.

16. Eric Jay Dolin, *When America First Met China* (New York, 2012), 69–70.
17. As quoted in Dolin, *When America First Met China*, 89; John Pomfret, *The Beautiful Country and the Middle Kingdom: America and China, 1776 to the Present* (New York, 2016), 10–11.
18. Pomfret, *The Beautiful Country*, 10.
19. Fred Lewis Pattee, *The Poems of Philip Freneau: Poet of the American Revolution* (Princeton, 1902), vol. 2, 261–2.
20. Shaw, *Journals*, 69.
21. Ibid., 100, 105.
22. Ibid., 231, 305.
23. Ibid., 231.
24. Ibid., 166, 181, 183.
25. Ibid., 228–9; Pomfret, *Beautiful Country*, 10–11, 18–19.
26. Pomfret, *Beautiful Country*, 19–20.
27. Michael B. Oren, *Power, Faith, and Fantasy: America in the Middle East, 1776 to the Present* (New York, 2011), 21.
28. Frank Lambert, *The Barbary Wars* (New York, 2005), 50–2.
29. James Cathcart, *The Captives* (La Porte, 1899), 3–6.
30. Ibid., 27–8.
31. Oren, *Power, Faith, and Fantasy*, 18.
32. Ibid., 35.
33. Lambert, *Barbary Wars*, 92–3.
34. Shaw, *Journals*, 123–7.
35. Macartney, *An Embassy to China*, 165.

SELECT BIBLIOGRAPHY

Adkins, Roy and Adkins, Lesley, *Gibraltar: The Greatest Siege in British History* (New York, 2018)

Adleman, Jeremy, *Sovereignty and Revolution in the Iberian Atlantic* (Princeton, 2009)

Aksan, Virginia H., *Ottoman Wars 1700–1870: An Empire Besieged* (New York, 2013)

Alavi, Seema, ed., *The Eighteenth Century in India* (Oxford, 2008)

Amanat, Abbas, *Iran: A Modern History* (New Haven, 2017)

Anderson, Aeneas, *A Narrative of the British Embassy to China* (London, 1795)

Anon., *An Account of the Colony of Sierra Leone* (London, 1795)

Anon., *Memoirs of Colonel E.M. Despard* (London, 1803)

Anon., *The Trial of Edward Marcus Despard for High Treason* (London, 1803)

Aranda, Conde de, *On the Independence of the Colonies* (1783), in Jon Cowans, ed., *Early Modern Spain: A Documentary History* (Philadelphia, 2003)

Armitage, David and Braddick, Michael, eds, *The British Atlantic World, 1500–1800* (Basingstoke, 2002)

Armitage, David and Subrahmanyam, Sanjay, *The Age of Revolution in Global Context, c. 1760–1840* (Basingstoke, 2010)

Atwood, Rodney, *The Hessians: Mercenaries from Hessen-Kassel in the American Revolution* (Cambridge, 2002)

d'Auberade, Madame, *The Authentic Memoirs of Francis Henry de la Motte* (London, 1784)

Auricchio, Laura, *The Marquis: Lafayette Reconsidered* (New York, 2014)

Baillie, Alexander, *Call of Empire: From Highlands to Hindostan* (Montreal, 2017)

Bardon, Jonathan, *A History of Ulster* (Belfast, 1993)

Barrington, Jonah, *The Rise and Fall of the Irish Nation* (Dublin, 1868)

—— *Sketches from his Own Time* (London, 1830), vol. 1

Barrow, John, *An Auto-Biographical Memoir of Sir John Barrow* (London, 1843)

—— *Narrative of the Public Life of Lord Macartney* (London, 1807), vol. 1

—— *Travels in China* (London, 1805)

—— *A Voyage to Cochinchina, in the Years 1792 and 1793* (London, 1806)

Bartlett, Thomas, *Ireland: A History* (Cambridge, 2010)

—— "Ireland, Empire, and Union, 1690–1801," in Kevin Kenny, ed., *Ireland and the British Empire* (Oxford, 2004)

—— *The Rise and Fall of the Irish Nation: The Catholic Question in Ireland, 1690–1830* (Savage, Maryland, 1992)

Barton, H. Arnold, *Scandinavia in the Revolutionary Era* (Minneapolis, 1986)

Baseler, Marilyn, *Asylum for Mankind: America 1607–1800* (Ithaca, 1998)

Bassett, Richard, *For God and Kaiser: The Imperial Austria Army* (London, 2015)

Bayly, C.A., *Imperial Meridians: The British Empire and the World, 1780–1830* (London, 1989)

—— *Indian Society and the Making of the British Empire* (Cambridge, 1988)

—— *The Making of the Modern World, 1780–1914* (Oxford, 2004)

Beattie, J.M., *Crime and the Courts in England, 1660–1800* (Princeton, 1986)

—— *Policing and Punishment in London, 1660–1750: Urban Crime and the Limits of Terror* (Oxford, 2001)

Beccaria, Cesare, *Of Crimes and Punishments* (London, 1778)

Beer, Daniel, *The House of the Dead: Siberian Exile Under the Tsars* (New York, 2016)

Berkin, Carol, *Revolutionary Mothers: Women in the Struggle for American Independence* (New York, 2005)

Bernstein, Jeremy, *Dawning of the Raj: The Life and Trials of Warren Hastings* (Chicago, 2000)

Bickham, Troy, *Making Headlines: The American Revolution as Seen through the British Press* (DeKalb, 2009)

Bidwell, Shelford, *Swords for Hire: European Mercenaries in Eighteenth Century India* (London, 1971)

Black, Jeremy, *British Foreign Policy in the Age of Revolution, 1783–1793* (Cambridge, 1994)

Blanning, Tim, *The Pursuit of Glory: The Five Revolutions that Made Modern Europe* (London, 2007)

Bolkhovitinov, Nikolai, *Russia and the American Revolution* (Tallahassee, 1976)

Bosma, Ulbe, *The Sugar Plantation in India and Indonesia* (Cambridge, 2013)

Boswell, James, *The Life of Samuel Johnson LL.D* (London, 1823), vol. 3

Bourke, Richard, *Empire and Revolution: The Political Life of Edmund Burke* (Princeton, 2015)

Bowen, H.V., *The Business of Empire* (Cambridge, 2006)

—— *Revenue and Reform: The Indian Problem in British Politics, 1757–1773* (Cambridge, 2009)

Brendon, Piers, *The Decline and Fall of the British Empire, 1781–1997* (New York, 2008)

Brewer, John, *The Sinews of Power: War, Money and the English State, 1688–1783* (Cambridge, MA, 1988)

Brittlebank, Kate, *Tipu Sultan's Search for Legitimacy: Islam and Kingship in a Hindu Domain* (Oxford, 1998)

Brook, Jack, "The Forlorn Hope: Bennelong and Yemmerrawannie go to England," *Australian Aboriginal Studies* (March 2001)

Brown, Christopher Leslie, *Moral Capital: Foundations of British Abolitionism* (Chapel Hill, 2006)

Brumwell, Stephen, *Turncoat: Benedict Arnold and the Crisis of American Liberty* (New Haven, 2018)

Brunsman, Denver, *The Evil Necessity: British Naval Impressment in the Eighteenth Century Atlantic World* (Charlottesville, 2013)

Buchanan, Francis, *A Journey from Madras through the Countries of Mysore, Canara and Malabar* (London, 1807)

Bunker, Nick, *Empire on the Edge: How Britain came to Fight in America* (New York, 2014)

Burgoyne, Bruce, ed., *Enemy Views: The American Revolutionary War as Recorded by the Hessian Participants* (Westminster, MD, 1996)

Burk, Kathleen, *The Lion and the Eagle: The Interaction of the British and American Empires 1783–1972* (London, 2019)

Burkholder, Mark, "Spain's America: From Kingdoms to Colonies," *Colonial Latin America Review* 25(2) (2016): 125–53

Burney, Frances, *The Diary and Letters of Madame D'Arblay* (London, 1843)

—— *The Early Diaries of Frances Burney, 1768–1778* (London, 1889)

Busteed, Henry Elmsley, *Echoes from Old Calcutta* (Calcutta, 1882)

Cain, P.J. and Hopkins, A.G., *British Imperialism, 1688–2000* (Harlow, 2002)

Cannon, John, "Francis, Sir Philip (1740–1818)," *Oxford Dictionary of National Biography* (Oxford, 2004)

Carretta, Vincent, *Equiano, the African: Biography of a Self-made Man* (New York, 2005)

Cash, Arthur, *John Wilkes: Scandalous Father of Civil Liberty* (New Haven, 2006)

Cathcart, James, *The Captives* (La Porte, 1899)

Chavez, Thomas, *Spain and the Independence of the United States* (Albuquerque, 2002)

Chopra, Ruma, *Almost Home: Maroons between Slavery and Freedom in Jamaica, Nova Scotia, and Sierra Leone* (New Haven, 2018)

—— *Choosing Sides: Loyalists in Revolutionary America* (New York, 2013)

Christopher, Emma, *A Merciless Place: The Lost Story of Britain's Convict Disaster in Africa* (Oxford, 2011)

Clark, Christopher, *Iron Kingdom: The Rise and Downfall of Prussia, 1600–1947* (London, 2007)

Clark, J.C.D., *The Language of Liberty, 1660–1832: Political Discourse and Social Dynamics in the Anglo-American World* (Cambridge, 1994)

Colley, Linda, *Britons: Forging the Nation, 1707–1837* (New Haven, 2014)

—— *Captives: Britain, Empire and the World, 1600–1850* (London, 2002)

—— *The Ordeal of Elizabeth Marsh: A Woman in World History* (New York, 2007)

Conway, Stephen, *The British Isles and the American War of Independence* (Oxford, 2000)

Craven, Elizabeth, *A Journey through the Crimea to Constantinople* (London, 1809)

Cresson, W.P., *Francis Dana: A Purtian Diplomat at the Court of Catherine the Great* (New York, 1930)

Crews, Robert, *For Prophet and Tsar: Islam and Empire in Russia and Central Asia* (Cambridge, MA, 2006)

Cunningham, Peter, ed., *The Letters of Horace Walpole* (London, 1891), vols VI, VII

Curtin, Philip, *The Image of Africa: British Ideas and Action, 1780–1850* (Madison, 1964), vol. 1

Dalrymple, William, *White Mughals: Love and Betrayal in Eighteenth-century India* (London, 2002)

Dancer, Thomas, *A Brief History of the Late Expedition against Fort San Juan* (London, 1781)

Dann, John, ed., *The Nagle Journal: A Diary of the Life of Jacob Nagle, Sailor, from the Year 1775 to 1841* (New York, 1988)

Darwin, John, *After Tamerlane: A Global History of Empire since 1405* (London, 2008)

Davenant, Charles, *An Essay on the Probable Methods of Making a People Gainers in the Balance of Trade* (London, 1699)

David, James Corbett, *Dunmore's New World* (Charlottesville, 2013)

Davis, David Brion, *The Problem of Slavery in the Age of Revolution, 1770–1823* (Oxford, 1999)

Devine, T.M., *Scotland's Empire: The Origins of the Global Diaspora* (London, 2012)

Dirks, Nicholas, *The Scandal of Empire: India and the Creation of Imperial Britain* (Cambridge, 2008)

Dodwell, H.H., *The Cambridge History of the British Empire* (Cambridge, 1929)

Dolin, Eric Jay, *When America First Met China* (New York, 2012)

Doyle, William, *The Oxford History of the French Revolution*, 2nd edn (Oxford, 2003)

Drescher, Seymour, *Abolition: A History of Slavery and Anti-Slavery* (Cambridge, 2009)

Dunmore, John, *Where Fate Beckons: The Life of Jean-François de la Pérouse* (Fairbanks, 2007)

du Rivage, Justin, *Revolution against Empire: Taxes, Politics, and the Origins of American Independence* (New Haven, 2017)

DuVal, Kathleen, *Independence Lost: Lives on the Edge of the American Revolution* (New York, 2015)

Dym, Jordana and Belaubre, Christopher, *Politics, Economy, and Society in Bourbon Central America, 1759–1821* (Boulder, 2007)

Dziennik, Matthew, *The Fatal Land: War, Empire, and the Highland Soldier in British America* (New Haven, 2015)

Eacott, Jonathan, *Selling Empire: India in the Making of Britain and America, 1600–1800* (Chapel Hill, 2016)

Edler, Friedrich, *The Dutch Republic and the American Revolution* (Baltimore, 1911)

Egerton, Douglas, *Death or Liberty: African Americans and the American Revolution* (New York, 2011)

Ekirch, A. Roger, *Bound for America: The Transportation of British Convicts to the Colonies, 1718–1775* (New York, 1987)

—— "Great Britain's Secret Convict Trade to America, 1783–1784," *American Historical Review* 89(5) (December 1984): 1285–91

Elliot, J.H., *Empires of the Atlantic World: Britain and Spain in America* (New Haven, 2007)

Elliott, Mark, *Emperor Qianlong: Son of Heaven, Man of the World* (London, 2009)

—— *The Manchu Way: The Eight Banners and Ethnic Identity in Late Imperial China* (Palo Alto, 2001)

Falconbridge, Anna Maria, *Two Voyages to Sierra Leone During the Years 1791–2–3* (London, 1794)

Farias, Kranti K., *The Christian Impact in South Kanara* (Mumbai, 1999)

Faroqhi, Suraiya, *Subjects of the Sultan: Culture and Daily Life in the Ottoman Empire* (London, 2005)

Fay, Eliza, *Original Letters from India*, ed. E.M. Forster (New York, 2010)

Ferriro, Larrie, *Brothers at Arms: The American Revolution and the Men of France and Spain who Saved it* (New York, 2016)

Fidlon, Paul and Ryan, R.J., eds, *The Journal of Arthur Bowes-Smyth: Surgeon, Lady Penrhyn 1787–1789* (Sydney, 1979)

Fisher, Michael, ed., *The Travels of Dean Mahomet* (Berkeley, 1997)

Fitzpatrick, John, ed., *The Writings of George Washington from the Original Manuscript Sources* (Washington, DC, 1938), vol. 26

Fitzpatrick, William, ed., *The Letters of Tipoo Sultan to Various Public Functionaries* (London, 1811)

Flavell, Julie, *When London Was Capital of America* (New Haven, 2010)

Flood, Warden, *Memoirs of Henry Flood* (Dublin, 1844)

Ford, Paul, ed., *The Writings of Thomas Jefferson* (New York, 1894), vol. 4

Franklin, Michael, *Orientalist Jones: Sir William Jones, Poet, Lawyer, and Linguist, 1746–1794* (Oxford, 2011)

Freneau, Philip, *The Poems of Philip Freneau: Poet of the American Revolution* (State College, PA, 1902)

Fry, Michael, *A Higher World: Scotland, 1707–1815* (Edinburgh, 2014)

Fyfe, Christopher, ed., *Our Children Free and Happy: Letters from Black Settlers in Africa in the 1790s* (Edinburgh, 1991)

George, David, *An Account of the Life of David George* (London, 1793)

Grattan, Henry, *Memoirs of the Life and Times of Henry Grattan* (London, 1839)

—— *Speeches of the Late Right Honourable Henry Grattan, in the Irish Parliament in 1780 and 1782* (London, 1821)

Gray, Drew, *Crime, Policing and Punishment in England, 1660–1914* (London, 2016)

Greene, Jack, *Evaluating Empire and Confronting Colonialism in Eighteenth-century Britain* (Cambridge, 2013)

Griffin, Patrick, *The Townshend Moment: The Making of Empire and Revolution in Ireland* (New Haven, 2017)

Gould, Eliga, *The Persistence of Empire: British Political Culture in the Age of the American Revolution* (Chapel Hill, 2002)

Habib, Irfan, *Confronting Colonialism: Resistance and Modernisation under Haidar Ali and Tipu Sultan* (London, 2002)

Hall, Catherine, *Macaulay and Son: Architects of Imperial Britain* (New Haven, 2012)

Halliday, Paul, *Habeas Corpus: From England to Empire* (Cambridge, MA, 2010)

Hämäläinen, Pekka, *The Comanche Empire* (New Haven, 2008)

Hamnett, Brian, *The End of Iberian Rule on the American Continent 1770–1830* (Cambridge, 2017)

Hanway, Jonas, *Solitude in Imprisonment* (London, 1776)

Harris, James, *Diaries and Correspondence of the Earl of Malmesbury* (London, 1844)

—— *A Series of Letters of the First Earl of Malmesbury* (London, 1870), vol. 1

Harris, Nicholas, ed., *The Dispatches and Letters of Vice Admiral Lord Viscount Nelson* (London, 1845)

Hasan, Mohibbul, "The French in the Second Anglo-Mysore War," in Irfan Habib, ed., *Confronting Colonialism: Resistance and Modernisation under Haidar Ali and Tipu Sultan* (London, 2002)

Hastings, Warren, *A Narrative of the Insurrection that Happened in the Zamindary of Benares* (Calcutta, 1782)

Hay, Douglas, "Property, Authority and the Criminal Law," in Douglas Hay et al., *Albion's Fatal Tree: Crime and Society in Eighteenth-century England* (London, 1975)

Hay, Douglas, "War, Dearth and Theft in the Eighteenth Century: The Records of the English Court," *Past and Present* 95 (May 1982), 125–42

Haywood, Ian and Seed, John, eds, *The Gordon Riots: Politics and Insurrection in Late Eighteenth-century Britain* (Cambridge, 2014)

Herrera, Carlos, *Juan Bautista de Anza: The King's Governor in New Mexico* (Norman, 2015)

Hevia, James, *Cherishing Men from Afar: Qing Guest Ritual and the Macartney Embassy of 1793* (Durham, 1995)

Hickey, William, *Memoirs of William Hickey*, ed. Albert Spencer (London, 1919), vol. II

Hill, Peter, *French Perceptions of the Early American Republic, 1783–1793* (Philadelphia, 1988)

Hirsch, Adam J., *The Rise of the Penitentiary: Prisons and Punishment in Early America* (New Haven, 1992)

Hitchcock, Tim and Shoemaker, Robert, *London Lives: Poverty, Crime, and the Making of the Modern City* (Cambridge, 2016)

Hochschild, Adam, *Bury the Chains* (New York, 2005)

Hodges, Graham Russell, *The Black Loyalist Directory* (New York, 1996)

Hodges, William, *Travels in India during the years 1780, 1781, 1782 and 1783* (London, 1783)

Hoock, Holger, *Scars of Independence: America's Violent Birth* (New York, 2017)

Hopkins, A.G., *American Empire: A Global History* (Princeton, 2018)

Howard, John, *The State of the Prisons* (Warrington, 1777)

Huzzey, Richard, *Freedom Burning: Anti-Slavery and Empire in Victorian Britain* (Ithaca, 2012)

Ingrao, Charles, *The Hessian Mercenary State: Ideas, Institutions and Reform under Frederick II, 1760–1785* (Cambridge, 1987)

Israel, Jonathan, *The Dutch Republic: Its Rise, Greatness, and Fall 1477–1806* (Oxford, 1998)

—— *Expanding the Blaze: How the American Revolution Ignited the World* (Princeton, 2017)

Janin, Hunt, *The India–China Opium Trade in the Nineteenth Century* (London, 1999)

Jasanoff, Maya, *Liberty's Exiles: American Loyalists in the Revolutionary World* (New York, 2011)

Keay, John, *China: A History* (New York, 2009)

—— *The Honorable Company: A History of the English East India Company* (London, 1993)

—— *India: A History* (London, 2010)

Kemble, Stephen, *The Kemble Papers* (New York, 1884), vol. 2

Keneally, Tom, *The Commonwealth of Thieves: The Story of the Founding of Australia* (London, 2006)

Kent, Neil, *Crimea: A History* (London, 2017)

Kiernan, Ben, *Viêt Nam: A History from Earliest Times to the Present* (Oxford, 2017)

King, Boston, "Memoirs of the Life of Boston King," in *Unchained Voices: An Anthology of Black Authors in the English-Speaking World of the 18th Century*, ed. Vincent Carretta (Lexington, 2004)

Knight, Roger, *The Pursuit of Victory: The Life and Achievements of Horatio Nelson* (New York, 2005)

Kuethe, Allan and Andrien, Kenneth, *The Spanish Atlantic World in the Eighteenth Century* (Cambridge, 2014)

Lambert, Andrew, *Seapower States: Maritime Culture, Continental Empires and the Conflict That Made the Modern World* (New Haven, 2018)

Lambert, Frank, *The Barbary Wars* (New York, 2005)

Langford, Paul, *A Polite and Commercial People: England 1727–1783* (Oxford, 1994)

Langley, Lester, *The Americas in the Age of Revolution: 1750–1850* (New Haven, 1996)

Lemmings, David, *Law and Government in England During the Long Eighteenth Century* (Basingstoke, 2011)

Levine, Philippa, *The British Empire: Sunrise to Sunset* (Harlow, 2013)

Liele, George, *An Account of several Baptist Churches* (London, 1793)

Lieven, Dominic, *Empire: The Russian Empire and Its Rivals* (New Haven, 2000)

Linebaugh, Peter, *The London Hanged: Crime and Civil Society in the Eighteenth Century* (London, 2006)

Linebaugh, Peter and Rediker, Marcus, *The Many-headed Hydra: The Hidden History of the Revolutionary Atlantic* (London, 2013)

Lloyd, T.O., *The British Empire, 1558–1995* (Oxford, 2008)

Lockhart, James and Swartz, Stuart, *Early Latin America: A History of Colonial Spanish America and Brazil* (Cambridge, 1983)

Macartney, George, *An Embassy to China*, ed. J.L. Cranmer-Byng (London, 2004)

Macaulay, Zachary, *Life and Letters of Zachary Macaulay* (London, 1900)

Madariaga, Isabel de, *Britain, Russia, and the Armed Neutrality of 1780* (New Haven, 1962)

—— *Catherine the Great* (New Haven, 2002)

—— *Russia in the Age of Catherine the Great* (New Haven, 1981)

Madden, Thomas, *Venice: A New History* (New York, 2012)

Magocsi, Paul Robert, *The Blessed Land: Crimea and the Crimean Tatars* (Toronto, 2014)

Major, Andrea, *Slavery, Abolitionism and Empire in India, 1772–1843* (Liverpool, 2012)

Malone, Thomas, *The Life and Death of Lord Edward Fitzgerald* (London, 1832)

Marques, Leonardo, *The United State and the Transatlantic Slave Trade to the Americas, 1776–1867* (New Haven, 2016)

Marshall, P.J., "Hastings, Warren (1732–1818)," *Oxford Dictionary of National Biography* (Oxford University Press, 2004; online edn, Oct. 2008)

—— *The Making and Unmaking of Empires: Britain, India, and America 1750–1783* (Oxford, 2007)

—— ed., *The Oxford History of the British Empire*, vol. II: *The Eighteenth Century* (Oxford, 1998)

—— *Remaking the British Atlantic: The United States and the British Empire after American Independence* (Oxford, 2012)

Mazzei, Philip, *Philip Mazzei, Virginia's Agent in Europe: The Story of his Mission as Related in His own Dispatches and other Documents*, ed. Howard Arraro (New York, 1935)

McLynn, Frank, *Crime and Punishment in Eighteenth-century England* (Oxford, 1991)

McPhee, Peter, *Liberty or Death: The French Revolution* (New Haven, 2017)

Mear, Craig, "The Origin of the Smallpox Outbreak at Sydney in 1789," *Journal of the Royal Australian Historical Society* 94(1) (June 2008), 1–22

Metcalf, Thomas, *Ideologies of the Raj* (Cambridge, 1997)

Miles, Jonathan, *St. Petersburg: Three Centuries of Murderous Desire* (London, 2017)

Miller, Kerby, *Emigrants and Exiles: Ireland and the Irish Exodus to North America* (Oxford, 1985)

Morely, Vincent, *Irish Opinion and the American Revolution, 1760–1783* (Cambridge, 2007)

Morgan, Kenneth, *Slavery and the British Empire* (Oxford, 2008)

Mosely, Benjamin, *A Treatise on Tropical Diseases* (London, 1789)

Narrett, David, *Adventurism and Empire: The Struggle for Mastery of the Louisiana–Florida Borderland* (Chapel Hill, 2015)

Nash, Gary, *The Unknown American Revolution: The Unruly Birth of Democracy and the Struggle to Create America* (New York, 2006)

Nechtman, Tillman, *Nabobs: Empire and Identity in Eighteenth-century Britain* (Cambridge, 2013)

O'Gorman, Frank, *The Long Eighteenth Century* (New York, 1997)

Oldfield, J.R., *Transatlantic Abolitionism in the Age of Revolutions* (Cambridge, 2015)

O'Neil, Daniel, *Edmund Burke and the Conservative Logic of Empire* (Oakland, 2016)

O'Neill, Kelly, *Claiming Crimea: A History of Catherine the Great's Southern Empire* (New Haven, 2017)

Oren, Michael B., *Power, Faith, and Fantasy: America in the Middle East, 1776 to the Present* (New York, 2011)

O'Shaughnessy, Andrew Jackson, *An Empire Divided: The American Revolution and the British Caribbean* (Philadelphia, 2000)

—— *The Men Who Lost America: British Leadership, the American Revolution, and the Fate of Empire* (New Haven, 2013)

Osterhammel, Jürgen, *Unfabling the East: The Enlightenment Encounter with Asia* (Princeton, 2018)

Padrón, Francisco Morales, ed., *The Journal of Don Francisco Saavedra de Sangronis* (Gainesville, 1989)

Pagden, Anthony, *Lords of All the World: Ideologies of Empire in Spain, Britain, and France c. 1500–1800* (New Haven, 1995)

Palmer, R.R., *The Age of Democratic Revolutions* (Princeton, 1964)

Palmer, Stanley, *Police and Protest in England and Ireland, 1780–1850* (Cambridge, 1988)

Paquette, Gabriel, *Enlightenment, Government, and Reform in Spain and its Empire 1759–1808* (Basingstoke, 2008)

Pattee, Fred Lewis, *The Poems of Philip Freneau: Poet of the American Revolution* (Princeton, 1902), vol. 2

Peers, Douglas and Gooptu, Nandini, *India and the British Empire* (Oxford, 2016)

Perdue, Peter, *China Marches West: The Qing Conquest of Central Eurasia* (Cambridge, 2010)

Peterson, Derek, ed., *Abolitionism and Imperialism in the Britain, Africa, and the Atlantic* (Athens, Ohio, 2010)

Phelan, John, *The People and the King: The Comunero Revolution in Colombia, 1781* (Madison, WI, 1978)

Phillips, Kevin, *The Cousins' Wars: Religion, Politics, and the Triumph of Anglo-America* (New York, 1999)

Platt, Richard, *Smuggling in the British Isles: A History* (Stroud, 2011)

Platt, Stephen, *Imperial Twilight: The Opium War and the End of China's Last Golden Age* (New York, 2018)

Plokhy, Serii, *Lost Kingdom: The Quest for Empire and the Making of the Russian Nation* (New York, 2017)

Polasky, Janet, *Revolution without Borders: The Call to Liberty in the Atlantic World* (New Haven, 2015)

Pomfret, John, *The Beautiful Country and the Middle Kingdom: America and China, 1776 to the Present* (New York, 2016)

Poser, Norman, *Lord Mansfield: Justice in the Age of Reason* (Montreal, 2013)

Pybus, Cassandra, *Epic Journeys of Freedom: Runaway Slaves of the American Revolution and their Global Quest for Liberty* (Boston, 2007)

Rapport, Mike, *Rebel Cities: Paris, London and New York in the Age of Revolution* (London, 2017)

Rieber, Alfred, *The Struggle for the Eurasian Borderlands: From the Rise of Early Modern Empires to the End of the First World War* (Cambridge, 2014)

Robbins, Helen, *Our First Ambassador to China: An Account of the Life and Correspondence of George, Earl of Macartney* (New York, 1908)

Robins, Nicholas, *Genocide and Millennialism in Upper Peru: The Great Rebellion of 1780–1782* (Westport, CT, 2002)

Rothschild, Emma, *The Inner Life of Empires: An Eighteenth-century History* (Princeton, 2011)

Rowe, William and Brook, Timothy, *China's Last Empire: The Great Qing* (Cambridge, MA, 2012)

Roy, Kaushik, *War, Culture and Society in Early Modern South Asia, 1740–1849* (Abingdon, 2011)

Rudé, George, *Protest and Punishment: The Story of the Social and Political Protestors Transported to Australia* (Oxford, 1979)

Ryan, William, *The World of Thomas Jeremiah: Charleston on the Eve of the American Revolution* (New York, 2012)

Safranski, Rudiger, *Goethe: Life as a Work of Art* (New York, 2017)

Salmon, Emily Jones, "Convict Labor during the Colonial Period," *Encyclopedia Virginia* (Virginia Humanities and Library of Virginia, 2011, online)

Sancho, Ignatius, *Letters of the Late Ignatius Sancho, An African* (Cambridge, 2013), 2 vols

—— *The Letters of the Late Ignatius Sancho, An African* (London, 1784)

Saunt, Claudio, *West of Revolution* (New York, 2014)

Scanlan, Padraic, *Freedom's Debtors: British Anti-Slavery in Sierra Leone in the Age of Revolutions* (New Haven, 2017)

Schaeper, Thomas, *Edward Bancroft: Scientist, Author, Spy* (New Haven, 2012)

Schama, Simon, *Citizens: A Chronicle of the French Revolution* (New York, 1990)

—— *Patriots and Liberators: Revolution in the Netherlands 1780–1813* (New York, 1977)

—— *Rough Crossings: Britain, the Slaves and the American Revolution* (New York, 2006)

Scott, Franklin D., *Sweden: The Nation's History* (Carbondale, 1988)

Scurry, James, *The Captivity, Suffering and Escape of James Scurry* (London, 1824)

Serulnikov, Sergio, *Revolution in the Andes: The Age of Tupac Amaru* (Durham, NC, 2013)

Sharpe, James, "John the Painter: The First Modern Terrorist," *Journal of Forensic Psychiatry and Psychology* 18(2) (2007): 278–81

Shaw, Samuel, *The Journals of Major Samuel Shaw* (Boston, 1847)

Shoemaker, Robert, *The London Mob: Violence and Disorder in Eighteenth-century England* (London, 2007)

Simms, Brendan, *Three Victories and a Defeat: The Rise and Fall of the First British Empire* (New York, 2008)

Sinha, Manisha, *The Slave's Cause: A History of Abolition* (New Haven, 2016)

Smith, Douglas, ed., *Love and Conquest: Personal Correspondence of Catherine the Great and Prince Grigory Potemkin* (DeKalb, 2004)

Smith, Kate Vincent, "Bennelong Among His People," *Aboriginal History* 33 (2009), 7–30

Smith, William, *The State of the Gaols in London, Westminster and the Borough of Southwark* (London, 1776)

Spence, Jonathan, *The Chan's Great Continent: China in Western Minds* (New York, 1998)

—— *In Search of Modern China* (New York, 1990)

Staunton, George, *An Authentic Account of an Embassy from the King of Great Britain to the Emperor of China* (London, 1797)

Stavig, Ward and Schmidt, Ellen, eds, *The Tupac Amaru and Catarista Rebellions* (Cambridge, 2008)

Staving, Ward, *The World of Túpac Amaru: Conflict, Community, and Identity in Colonial Peru* (Lincoln, 1990)

Stevenson, John, *Popular Disturbances in England, 1700–1832* (Abingdon, 1992)

Sugden, John, *Nelson: A Dream of Glory* (London, 2004)

Taylor, Alan, *American Revolutions: A Continental History, 1750–1804* (New York, 2016)

Teltscher, Kate, *The High Road to China: George Bogle, the Panchen Lama and the First British Expedition to Tibet* (London, 2006)

Tench, Watkin, *A Complete Account of the Settlement at Port Jackson* (London, 1793)

Thomas, George, *Military Memoirs of George Thomas* (London, 1805)

Travers, Robert, *Ideology and Empire in Eighteenth-century India: The British in Bengal* (Cambridge, 2007)

Van Alstyne, Richard, *Empire and Independence: The International History of the American Revolution* (New York, 1965)

Waley-Cohen, Joanna, *The Sextants of Beijing: Global Currents in Chinese History* (New York, 2000)

Walker, Charles, *The Tupac Amaru Rebellion* (Cambridge, 2016)

Walker, James, *The Black Loyalists: The Search for the Promised Land in Nova Scotia and Sierra Leone* (Toronto, 1993)

Walpole, Horace, *Journal of the Reign of King George the Third* (London, 1859), 2 vols

Walvin, James, *England, Slaves, and Freedom, 1776–1838* (London, 1986)

—— *The Zong* (New Haven, 2011)

Warren, Christopher, "Could First Fleet Smallpox Infect Aborigines?" *Aboriginal History* 31 (2007), 152–64

Warner, Jessica, *John the Painter: Terrorist of the American Revolution* (London, 2004)

Welsh, Frank, *The Four Nations: A History of the United Kingdom* (New Haven, 2003)

Wharton, Francis, ed., *Revolutionary Diplomatic Correspondence of the Untied States* (Washington, DC, 1889), 6 vols

White, Colin, ed., *Nelson: The New Letters* (Woodbridge, 2005)

Wickwire, Franklin and Wickwire, Mary, *Cornwallis: The Imperial Years* (Chapel Hill, 1980)

Willis, Sam, *The Struggle for Sea Power: A Naval History of the American Revolution* (London, 2016)

Wilson, Jon, *The Domination of Strangers: Modern Governance in Eastern India, 1780–1835* (Basingstoke, 2010)

—— *India Conquered: Britain's Raj and the Chaos of Empire* (London, 2016)

Wilson, Kathleen, *The Sense of the People: Politics, Culture and Imperialism in England, 1715–1785* (Cambridge, 1998)

Woodforde, James, *The Diary of a Country Parson* (Norwich, 1999)

Worgan, George, *Journal of a First Fleet Surgeon* (Sydney, 1978)

Wyvill, Christopher, *Political Papers* (London, 1794), vol. 3

—— *The Secession from Parliament Vindicated* (York, 1799)

Yaycioglu, Ali, *Partners of the Empire: The Crisis of the Ottoman Order in the Age of Revolutions* (Stanford, 2016)

INDEX